International Handbook on Information Systems

Series Editors
Peter Bernus, Jacek Błażewicz, Günter Schmidt, Michael Shaw

T0134749

Titles in the Series

M. Shaw, R. Blanning, T. Strader and A. Whinston (Eds.)
Handbook on Electronic Commerce
ISBN 3-540-65822-X

J. Błażewicz, K. Ecker, B. Plateau and D. Trystram (Eds.)
Handbook on Parallel and Distributed Processing
ISBN 3-540-66441-6

H.H. Adelsberger, B. Collis and J.M. Pawlowski (Eds.)
Handbook on Information Technologies for Education and Training
ISBN 3-540-67803-4

C.W. Holsapple (Ed.)
Handbook on Knowledge Management 1
Knowledge Matters
ISBN 3-540-43527-1
Handbook on Knowledge Management 2
Knowledge Matters
ISBN 3-540-43527-1

J. Błażewicz, W. Kubiak, T. Morzy and M. Rusinkiewicz (Eds.)
Handbook on Data Management in Information Systems
ISBN 3-540-43893-9

S. Staab and R. Studer (Eds.)
Handbook on Ontologies
ISBN 3-540-40834-7

S.O. Kimbrough and D.J. Wu (Eds.)
Formal Modelling in Electronic Commerce
ISBN 3-540-21431-3

P. Bernus, K. Mertins and G. Schmidt (Eds.)
Handbook on Architectures of Information Systems
ISBN 3-540-25472-2 (Second Edition)

Stefan Kirn
Otthein Herzog
Peter Lockemann
Otto Spaniol
Editors

Multiagent Engineering

Theory and Applications in Enterprises

With 135 Figures and 24 Tables

 Springer

Professor Dr. Stefan Kirn
Universität Hohenheim
Wirtschaftsinformatik II (510 O)
Schwerzstraße 35
70599 Stuttgart
Germany
kirn@uni-hohenheim.de

Professor Dr. Otthein Herzog
Universität Bremen
Technologie-Zentrum Informatik
Am Fallturm 1
28359 Bremen
Germany
herzog@tzi.de

Professor Dr. Peter Lockemann
Universität Karlsruhe (TH)
Institut für Programmstrukturen
und Datenorganisation (IPD)
Am Fasanengarten 5
76131 Karlsruhe
Germany
lockemann@ipd.uka.de

Professor Dr. Otto Spaniol
RWTH Aachen
Lehrstuhl für Informatik 4
Ahornstraße 55
52074 Aachen
Germany
spaniol@informatik.rwth-aachen.de

ISBN 978-3-642-06848-5   e-ISBN 978-3-540-32062-3

Cataloging-in-Publication Data

Springer is a part of Springer Science+Business Media

springeronline.com

© Springer Berlin · Heidelberg 2010
Printed in Germany

Hardcover-Design: Erich Kirchner, Heidelberg

Preface

1 Multiagent Engineering: A New Software Construction Paradigm

Multiagent systems have a long academic tradition. They have their roots in distributed problem solving in Artificial Intelligence (AI) from where they emerged in the mid-eighties as a distinctive discipline. Research in multiagent systems owes much to the work of Rosenschein on rationality and autonomy of intelligent agents, the European MAAMAW workshop series, and last but not least the famous readings of Bond & Gasser (1988) and Jacques Ferber´s book on multiagent systems (1991). It gained further by a public discussion via the Distributed AI mailing list in summer 1991, when the pioneers of the field compared in much detail the concepts of distributed problem solvers to multiagent systems. Within only five years, a new exciting field of research had been established.

Now, 15 years later, the field has matured to a degree that allows the results of academic research to be passed on to practical use and commercial exploitation. This potential coincides with a need for much larger flexibility of our IT infrastructure in light of its highly distributed character and extreme complexity, but also the global character of the business processes and the large number of business partners due to outsourcing and specialization. Many experts claim that multiagent systems are the right software technology for the needed IT infrastructure at the right time.

The appeal has much to do with the broad perspectives of multiagent systems research.

1. The *sociological perspective* considers agents as members of a collection of agents (groups) of a more or less formally established agent organization, or of an agent society. In that perspective, agents have acquaintances, exhibit social behaviors, and establish social relationships. Important themes are collective action, joint intentions, and group behaviors.
2. The *AI perspective* is concerned with intelligent behavior on the individual and on the collective level. It studies strategies for collective problem solving, and is particularly interested in cooperative planning algorithms, negotiation protocols, distributed representations of knowledge, and collective forms of temporal and spatial reasoning. All these are re-

quired in physically distributed systems, where the nodes exhibit to a substantial degree locally autonomous behavior.

3. The *economic perspective* claims that bounded rationality, limited physical resources, and incomplete knowledge require agents to behave "economically rational." That is, the agents need goals and objectives, they need appropriate decision-making rules, they may display strategic behaviors, and they must be capable of coping both with intra-agent (e.g., role) conflicts, and with inter-agent conflicts. Important contributions come from game theory and decision theory.

4. Finally, the *application perspective* developed, often experimentally, applications in a wide range of fields. Examples can be found in mechanical engineering, robotics, production planning and control, in business, the natural sciences (e.g., simulation of ant colonies, of fish populations, etc.), and in the social sciences.

Once we start to exploit the field of multiagent systems in the practical world we pass from research to engineering. This book – *Multiagent Engineering: Theory and Applications in Enterprises* – intends to support the passage by focusing on the technology of multiagent systems as a powerful, productive tool in the hands of software engineers satisfying extremely complex, dynamic new applications in enterprises.

This book, thus, concentrates on a fifth, the *engineering perspective*. After introducing the basic concepts of agent technology it gives an overview of two powerful multiagent systems in promising application scenarios, production logistics and health care. It then turns to the technical details of multiagent technology all the way from (early) requirements engineering to system testing. The evaluation section summarizes the main results and presents new and interesting insights from a legal perspective, which, of course, is highly relevant if enterprises decide to employ multiagent technology in order to improve their competitiveness through extremely adaptive new enterprise information systems architectures.

2   Who Should Read This Book, and Why?

Why would we claim that multiagent systems satisfy extremely complex, dynamic new applications in enterprises? The thinking goes that the various aforementioned perspectives in their combination make multiagent technology – and by extension the software systems relying on them – extremely flexible. Then when would we need flexibility? Certainly when the applications and their environments are highly dynamic, i.e. change on short notice and in many and often unforeseen ways. Multiagent systems should be capable of quickly adapting the behavior of the local subsystems (agents) as well as of the overall (multiagent) system, of exchanging cooperation protocols, of integrating new agents or withdrawing older agents.

To turn promise into reality is foremost an engineering task. Engineering must take place on two levels: The individual agent as the basic entity and the multiagent system as the collaborative effort of several agents governed by an intelligent interplay between these two levels. And since agent technology goes beyond traditional object-oriented or component-oriented software, it raises new challenges for the software engineer.

First of all, then, the book has been written for *software engineers*. They will find answers to questions such as: What are the relevant new features of this new tool, compared with other recent software technologies like object orientation and component technology? Which software development challenges can and should be addressed by it? How shall the software development process be organized? What are the concrete benefits and are they really worth the risks coming with each new technology? What are the "hidden costs" of the technology that need to be considered?

The last two questions are not merely technical. Rather, they express concerns of *business managers* as well. They must ultimately decide how well multiagent technology can contribute to their business objectives, whether their IT systems must indeed cope with rapidly changing production technologies, enterprise processes, supply chains, business models, markets, and customer demands, and whether multiagent technology seems to be a solution superior to today's enterprise software.

The book is thus a unique source of knowledge about multiagent engineering, starting from its basics and then considering all phases in the software lifecycle from early requirements engineering through system design and implementation to testing and illustrating these in the framework of two applications with a high degree of dynamics.

3 A Reader's Guide

The book has to keep in mind that it addresses a diverse readership ranging from business managers to software engineers and that even software engineers are a heterogeneous group exhibiting different levels of knowledge in software technology, artificial intelligence, and multiagent systems.

The book starts with a management summary that gives a brief overview of the most important issues and their solutions. As the title suggests, the chapter intends to put the business manager in a position to decide whether the investment in agent technology is worth the desired benefits and which issues deserve closer inspection by the IT specialists in the enterprise. Part I addresses both the business manager and the software engineer new to agent technology. It gives a concise introduction to multiagent technology and lays the foundation for the remainder of the book. In particular, its last chapter presents operational definitions for the different types of flexibility of multiagent systems. Parts II and III, Agent.Enterprise and Agent.Hospital respectively, have been written for readers primarily interested in the application of multiagent technology in important business domains. They illustrate to the software engineer how one builds large multiagent systems and at the same time demonstrate to the business manager the benefits of agent technology or, to some degree, how difficult it sometimes can be to be absolutely sure when one technology is superior to another one. Each part starts with an overview and is followed by further chapters that give more details on the design, implementation, and evaluation of the multiagent system. Since both systems take a fairly strict supply chain/logistics perspective, their designs can easily be compared. It is thus recommended that readers primarily interested in manufacturing information systems focus on Part II, but they may also gain useful insights from Part III and vice versa for readers interested in new approaches to health care information systems. Part IV concerns itself with the methodical underpinning for engineering multiagent systems software. Its readers should primarily be software architects, software designers, and software engineers. This part should be understood even without knowing the details in Parts II and III. On the other hand, after having gone through Part IV it may well be worth the reader's effort to go through Parts II and III as illustrative examples for applying the methods, protocols, architectures, and tools introduced in Part IV. Finally, Part V evaluates multiagent technology and thus presents interesting new insights from different evaluation perspectives. The reader of this part should be familiar with the basics of multiagent technology as gained from Part I and Chapters II.1 and III.1.

4 Acknowledgements

This book as a whole as well as the individual chapters could not have been written without the personal engagement and help of numerous colleagues who supported us in many different ways.

The beginning of this project dates back to September/October of 1998 when five colleagues started to initiate a new research program in business applications of agent technology. In this early phase, Matthias Jarke/

Aachen, Hermann Krallmann/Berlin, Peter Mertens/Nürnberg, Alexander Schill/Dresden and Stefan Zelewski/Essen, among many others, shared our vision and invested much of their personal time into the definition of a research program in multiagent systems for business applications. Once accepted for funding by the Deutsche Forschungsgemeinschaft (German Research Foundation), this program received further substantial support from seven colleagues serving as reviewers for the full six-year duration of the program: Andreas Drexl/Kiel, Matthias Jarke/Aachen, Peter Mertens/Nürnberg, Claus Rollinger/Osnabrück, Elmar Sinz/Bamberg, Kurt Sundermeyer/Berlin, and Rolf Wigand/Syracuse, N.Y. and Little Rock, AR. We also express our gratitude to Michael Schuster from the Deutsche Forschungsgemeinschaft who was always available to provide any necessary organizational and administrative support.

When we started to write this book many friends and colleagues spent their time and made a personal commitment to make this book as valuable as possible to its readers. Our thanks go to A. Battino, T. Bürkle, A. Eichinger, F. Freiling, C. Heine, R. Hill, D. Kossmann, H. Langer, A. Lattner, J. M. Leimeister, P. Levi, P. Liedtke, V. Mascardi, K. Maximini, A. Moreno, H. J. Müller, J. P. Müller, M. Petsch, R. Röhrig, M. Rovatsos, H. Stormer, A. Unruh, H. Wache, and T. Wagner. It was a privilege to share their experiences, to receive their professional feedback on earlier versions of the various chapters, and on the book as a whole.

Last, but not least, we express our thanks to those who made it possible to produce this handbook: Werner Müller from Springer/Heidelberg supported the vision of this project from its very beginning. Günter Schmidt/Saarbrücken, editor in chief of the Springer Series "Handbooks in Information Systems" agreed to publish it in this series.

Finally, Marc Thomas Bauer and Martin Hafner, both affiliated with Universität Hohenheim deserve our special thanks. They did an excellent job in transforming about three dozen electronic manuscripts into one coherent, complete paper version of this book. They managed very successfully a complex "agent-based" organization of autonomous authors, they provided very carefully the formal layout of this book, they met all deadlines with high reliability, and they made it very easy especially for all the editors of this handbook to bring this exciting project – of course itself a multiagent engineering project – to a fruitful end.

As always, however, the full responsibility for structure and content, for any shortcomings and in particular for any remaining mistakes within this book remains with the authors and in particular with the editors.

Stefan Kirn   Otthein Herzog   Peter Lockemann   Otto Spaniol
Hohenheim   Bremen   Karlsruhe   Aachen

Table of Contents

Management Summary

Peter C. Lockemann
Universität Karlsruhe (TH), Institut für Programmstrukturen und
Datenorganisation, lockemann@ipd.uka.de

Stefan Kirn
Universität Hohenheim, Wirtschaftsinformatik II
kirn@uni-hohenheim.de

Otthein Herzog
Universität Bremen, Technologie-Zentrum Informatik
herzog@tzi.de

1 Agent Technology

Originally agent technology was a social systems technology, with roots in distributed artificial intelligence. Social organizations are known to be able to tolerate many unexpected situations and, given enough time, to adapt to even dramatic changes in their environment. They do so by division of competences and a balance between individual and collective intelligence. These are the properties that made agents attractive to software engineering. Thus, today's agent technology is also a software systems technology geared to deal with information systems that are highly distributed, with the components only loosely connected.

In a nutshell, then, agent technology is a marriage between software engineering and social engineering. Agent technology is the basis of an IT infrastructure that flexibly follows the changes in a business rather than slowing or inhibiting them, particularly if the application environment is highly dynamic.

Such a technology does not come cheaply and as a latecomer to the business world it carries not only its own promises but also its own risks. To the engineer, though, risks constitute the challenges that are to be overcome in order to realize the promises. This book takes the attitude of the engineer. After introducing the basic concepts underlying agent technology it gives an overview of two promising application scenarios, one in production logistics and the second in health care. It then turns to the technical challenges before closing with further issues that have a bearing on the application of the technology. In the remainder we summarize the main results and insights of the various sections.

2 What Agents Are and What They Are Good for

Flexibility of an IT infrastructure that can cope with the dynamics of business processes is a vague concept. Vendors of enterprise software will argue with good reason that their systems have been designed with just that in mind. But there is a limit: When the changes in the processes become too drastic or too numerous, part of the software will have to change as well.

The book claims that with agent software the limit can be pushed further afar. But how does agent software achieve its flexibility? It does so on two levels: the individual agent as the basic entity, and the multiagent system as the collaborative effort of several agents.

The individual agent can be characterized by eight properties altogether. The first four are essential for any piece of software to qualify as an agent.

1. A software agent is a computer system that is situated in some environment. As such, agents do not dissolve once a task has been finished, rather the interaction with the environment is an ongoing, non-terminating one.
2. A software agent offers a useful service. Its behavior can only be observed by its external actions, its internal processes remain encapsulated. Thus, an agent has all the traits of a conventional component or object software.
3. A software agent is capable of autonomous action in its environment in order to meet its design objectives, i.e. to provide its service. The agent's functionality does not directly depend on the properties or states of other entities within the system the agent is part of it has the sole control over the activation of its service.
4. The autonomy of a software agent is guided by its own goals, with goal deliberation and means-end assessment as parts of the overall decision process of practical reasoning. Hence, the non-deterministic, seemingly chaotic latitude an agent has is tempered by the agent's own goals.

Properties 3 and 4 set software agents apart from object-oriented or component-oriented software. In essence, goals are what makes agent tick. These goals are imposed from outside, for example by the enterprise served by the IT infrastructure. An agent is authorized by some other entity, called its principal, to take actions on its behalf. The agent acts as the principal's representative.

However, the four properties do not yet relate to flexibility. Indeed, the need for flexibility arises when the environment appears non-deterministic as well. We refer to a software agent that is capable of operating in a non-deterministic environment as an intelligent software agent, and describe it by several additional properties.

1. An intelligent software agent is reactive, that is, it continuously perceives its environment and responds in a timely manner to changes that occur.
2. An intelligent software agent achieves an effective balance between goal-directed and reactive behavior. That is, timely response must be seen in the light of autonomy: The environment cannot dictate to the agent when and how to react.
3. An intelligent software agent may be proactive, that is, take the initiative in pursuance of its goals.
4. An intelligent software agent may have to possess social ability, that is, it is capable of interacting with other agents to provide its service.

Agents are just stepping stones on the way to complex, flexible services. Multiagent systems (MAS) are defined as consisting of heterogeneous agents that are generally self-motivated and act to fulfill internal goals, but may also share tasks with others. There is no global or centralized control mechanism. Agents have to reason to co-ordinate their actions, plans, and knowledge. Agents, in these systems, can cope with situations in a flexible way involving inconsistent knowledge about the environment (world, other agents), partial domain representation, and changing, overlapping plans resulting from the need to interact with other agents. The properties of MAS appear to be almost infinite regarding the number of agents, their flexibility, their abilities, the ways of interaction, the initial state of the system, etc.

One may say that agents must coalesce into a social organization to leverage their full potential. This is the reason why even a technical view of multiagent systems has an organizational perspective and makes use of social models. Central to these models is the interaction and the protocol that it follows, such as negotiations, auctions, blackboards.

Clearly then, agent software is complex software. The system-level behavior often cannot be predicted analytically from the description of individual agents. Hence, one would like to have a kind of operational criterion that tells when to turn to agent technology. Suppose we define technical flexibility as the set of options that are available to the software system to react to demands from the environment. We claim that agent software should be considered whenever the range of observed environmental situations (the problem space) and the range of options to respond to them (the solution space) is so large as to elude enumeration by conventional means.

3 Application I: Agent.Enterprise

One of the areas where flexibility is essential to survival in a highly competitive world is manufacturing logistics. The manufacturing domain, once entirely restricted to intra-organizational processes, today is dominated by complex networks of actors across enterprise boundaries. Mass customization, short development cycles, concentration on core competencies, and increasing customer orientation pose additional challenges. Production technology, already well versed in centralized production planning, has added strategies, methods and tools to modify a production plan on short notice. Consequently, manufacturing logistics offer an ideal environment to study whether agent technology can beat the already proven approaches when it comes to even higher flexibility at the same or even lesser cost.

To pursue the study both from a technological and organizational perspective we developed a scenario and platform called Agent.Enterprise. Agent.Enterprise integrates intra-organizational value chains, specifically the underlying production planning and control, into inter-organizational supply chains. Flexibility is needed both within the individual enterprise and across the enterprises. Hence, a multiagent approach should apply to both. More specifically, if intra-organizational value chains are supported by multiagent systems, the inter-organizational supply chains resulting from interacting local value chains result in a combination of MAS into what could be called a multi-multiagent system (MMAS).

Manufacturing is a wide field. We select five issues, each with its own specific scenario, and study MAS support on both the information logistics and the material transformation level.

In a flexible production environment the separation and sequencing of process planning, production control and scheduling can no longer be maintained. Rather they should be interleaved so that a fast response is possible to sudden customer requirements and trouble situations, such as broken tools, machine breakdowns, or missing devices, in a manufacturing environment. We demonstrate with around 2,000 experiments that a multi-agent system with a three-layer architecture, capability management, and most importantly, internal and external conflict management can indeed add considerable flexibility over and above traditional approaches.

Centralized planning assumes that nothing can go wrong. But things can go wrong, surprises may occur, high-priority orders must be processed, and machines may break down. Deviations from the norm are usually taken care of in the job shop. The job shop should thus be an ideal target for agent technology. We introduce a priority-based decision algorithm for Job-Shop scheduling for the solution of a mixed-model sequencing problem in a multiagent system. By benchmarking the solution in more than 1,000 simulation runs and comparing the results to a centralized solution of the same problem based on an optimal OR algorithm for the undisturbed case it was possible to demonstrate the superiority of the multiagent system solution in the case of production disruptions and close to equal performance when everything runs normal. Indeed, guidelines for the successful application of multiagent systems in production planning and control can be developed.

One of the most complex manufacturing domains is semiconductor wafer fabrication and, hence, should be an ideal candidate for a multiagent solution. We examined whether a hierarchically organized multiagent system for production control in semiconductor wafer fabrication facilities would yield significant benefits. Among the three-layer hierarchy the top layer takes care of the decisions concerning top priority due dates of the lots. The middle layer manages the detailed lot schedules by start and end dates of the lots where an agent is assigned to each work area. The base layer assigns lots to machines based on the middle-layer schedules. In a 50-day simulation using three simulation models the agent-based system produced the same solution quality as a centralized load-balancing heuristic. The result is particularly significant because it assumed that no machines break down. One would expect the agent approach to be superior if breakdowns occur.

While the first three scenarios deal with the individual enterprise a fourth study examines how software agents can reduce the negative effects of disruptive events across inter-organizational supply chains. An event management system based on software agents monitors the supply chain and identifies potential disruptive events in order to improve the robustness against time delays and defective events. Extensive simulations demonstrate that it is possible to achieve reductions in cost and cycle times in multi-level supply chains using agent technology.

In a final setting we demonstrate how to plan, on an inter-organizational level, a multi-multiagent system so that one gains the full benefits of decentralized supply chains. The required global planning function is based on a decentralized negotiation protocol for cooperative economic scheduling. Cooperation can only function if the participants trust each other. Therefore, the individual nodes in the net maintain trust accounts to protect themselves against exploitation while allowing the local solution to temporarily deviate from the optimum and still proceed towards a globally optimal solution. It can be shown that the global welfare could be increased by a search strategy similar to altruistic Simulated Annealing without adverse effects on the global solution quality.

Agent.Enterprise integrates the five aforementioned scenarios. It was implemented as a network of multiagent systems, Agent.Enterprise Net-Demo, across several universities. Agent.Enterprise does indeed indicate the potential of a decentralized, multiagent system-based solution for flexible supply chain management.

4 Application II: Agent.Hospital

Health care services seem a most natural application of multiagent systems. Where else are events less predictable and the needs for flexibility more pronounced? Hence, health care services look like an ideal scenario to demonstrate the merits of agent technology.

But what exactly would be gained by employing agents? To study the issue we model the services by orienting them along the individual patient. As he or she receives one treatment after another, what evolves could be called a *healthcare supply chain*. No two chains are completely alike because each relates directly to the patient's individual disease(s) or injury(ies), and his or her personal situation. A chain may commence with an emergency service called to a car accident, or a practitioner being visited by a new patient. In serious cases, it may involve one or more hospitals and even external experts providing specialized competences for diagnosis, surgery, and other forms of patient treatment.

The problem is compounded and the need for flexibility multiplied because a large, say, 1,000 bed hospital may have to manage 1,000 different supply chains at the same time. Each of these 1,000 supply chains occupies a possibly large number of persons each with his or her individual contexts, which often display highly dynamic behaviors. Each supply chain competes for typically short resources (e.g., emergency services in a town, doctors and surgery rooms at a hospital), at the same time interacting with other supply chains through synergistic, antagonistic, causal and temporal relationships, etc. The high degree of autonomy of the most important actors – patients, and doctors – increases the overall complexity further, often making it impossible to establish any centralized form of supply chain planning, monitoring, and control.

To design, implement and apply the supply chain model, we developed Agent.Hospital, an open platform that integrates as its 'members' multiagent systems that were developed independently and that provide services for diagnostic, therapeutic, managerial and administrative processes in health care institutions, respectively. It provides platform services (e.g., directory services), architectural patterns (e.g., gateway implementations), and tools (e.g., ontology management) with the explicit objective of integrating already existing multiagent systems that may belong to different enterprises (their 'owners'). Particular attention has being paid to preserving the technical and organizational autonomy of new Agent.Hospital members. I.e., the integration into Agent.Hospital does not (at least not substantially) affect the internal definitions, structures, and behaviors of the respective multiagent system nor does it affect the availability, production, and delivery of any of its services to its local owner institution.

Once technically integrated, cooperation between the members of Agent.Hospital may emerge. The cooperation is supported through existing agent communication languages, specific interaction protocols for controlling agent collaboration and maintaining up-to-date global knowledge and an ontology repository including reasoning capabilities for the semantically correct use of formally represented knowledge.

In health care, humans care for humans. Thus, at the center of the MAS are *artificial software agents as representatives of their human principals*. In case of centralized operating theatres in large hospitals, human principals – e.g., surgeons, anesthetists, and operating room nurses affiliated with different organizational units – independently delegate scheduling tasks to their agents. Based upon formal models of the preferences, and constraints of their principals, the agents then cooperate on developing an appropriate solution for a set of interacting scheduling problems. The result is a cooperative solution, which simultaneously optimizes 'social welfare' and the use of medical and organizational resources.

Coordination requires effective information logistics, in our case *agent-based information logistics*. This involves the management of information flows, information storage, information access, information use (including information interpretation), and information manipulation. Typically, immediate treatment starts with an almost empty array of information which fills continuously over time by examinations conducted and decisions taken by organizationally and geographically distributed departments. Information logistics is the basis for, among others *agent-based patient scheduling*. It focuses on the efficient allocation of scarce resources in hospitals to the treatments and examinations of different patients. Particular attention has been paid to the most important reasons for coordination complexity in hospitals: stochastic patient arrivals; stochastic durations of patient examinations and treatments; many doctors and nurses involved due to medical specialization as well as work shifts of hospital employees; patient transportation depending on the type of disease or injury, patient constitution, status, and treatment; complications and emergencies; etc. The challenge is to coordinate a high number of parallel logistical activities in such a way that all necessary conditions are appropriately satisfied and all medical, technical, financial, and administrative constraints are adequately considered. In particular we choose shift scheduling, appointment scheduling, and surgery team scheduling as relevant examples and include a detailed introduction into the SeSAM hospital simulation toolkit and a comprehensive discussion of the obtained simulation results.

Diagnosis and therapy require documentation at all stages of a patient's treatment. For this we suggest the approach of *active, medical documents* as a special solution to information logistics in agent-based systems. We propose an agent-based architecture of medical documents in order to draw on the benefits of inherent distribution, local autonomy, dynamic contexts, etc.

In health care, many of the agents have humans as their principals and humans tend to move around. This raises additional questions. How can all the mobile 'resources', e.g., patients, hospital staff, etc. be kept informed about decisions and other types of information relevant to them which emerge from processes at other geographical locations? How can relevant information from local sources be integrated into the global picture and, of course, how can this information continuously being kept up to date? And how can the human movements and activities be controlled and monitored in order to implement new scheduling decisions within acceptable time spans? The technical answer is a solution based *on mobile devices and their connection to software agents*, with each agent representing a particular human principal within a health care supply chain.

The section on Agent.Hospital attempts to demonstrate the great benefits that agent technology offers to scenarios where complexity, physically distributed autonomy, and dynamics scale up extensively.

5 Agent Engineering

As defined in Section 2, multiagent systems (MAS) are distributed, dynamic and open software systems that consist of heterogeneous components that are generally self-motivated and act both to fulfill internal goals and share tasks with others. Because there is no centralized control mechanism, agents have to reason to co-ordinate their actions, plans, and knowledge.

Consequently, traditional or modern software engineering methods and techniques, while important, do not suffice. Rather, agent-oriented software engineering (AOSE) should combine them with knowledge engineering techniques. Software engineering can contribute process models such as the Rational Unified Process with its emphasis on feedback, model-driven architectures, or rapid prototyping and agile development approaches such as Extreme Programming. Knowledge engineering can add Knowledge Analysis and Design Support (KADS) that integrates knowledge, relations between components, and a model-building process that includes organizational, application, task, expertise, cooperation, conceptual, and design models.

A number of AOSE methodologies have emerged in recent years. All tend to be strong on certain aspects and weak on others. To choose among them it seems useful to establish some kind of benchmark against which to judge them. To this end we discuss seven process steps that should somehow become part of any AOSE method: requirements engineering, interaction design, architectural design, semantics specification, dependability specification, tool and platform selection, and validation.

Requirements engineering should reflect the peculiarities of agent technology. In a nutshell, one must account for the desired flexibility, with the agent properties of proactivity, sociability, autonomy and reactivity forming the building blocks. Information about goals is required to implement proactive or reactive behavior. The capability to communicate, coordinate and cooperate with other agents in an organizational setting determines a social context. The aspect most resistant to capture by present-day requirements engineering is the notion of autonomy. Hence, the modern tendency is to start from goals as the fundamental concept. Such a process is referred to as Goal-Oriented Requirements Engineering (GORE). Goals are the core concept in terms of modeling the stakeholders' interests and concerns, organizational goals, reasons for the later system to exist or hints on the alternatives for the subsequent development decisions.

A requirements specification must be turned into a working software system. The first objective is to isolate the various issues that determine the usefulness to the environment and localize them within specific software parts. By employing a particular architectural pattern a particular structural organization schema for software systems can be expressed. Agent software patterns are needed for both the *architectural design* of the individual agent and the *interaction design* of the multiagent system. For the individual agent this book recommends a layered architecture that assigns the agent properties to five levels of abstraction altogether. The interaction design is governed by the notion of conversation between agents as a specialized form of asynchronous message exchange. Message software is known to follow a layers pattern referred to as a protocol stack, with the lowest layer representing the physical transport and the remainder realized as part of the agents themselves. Merging the layered architecture of the individual agent and the layered protocol stack is then a relatively straightforward affair. The approach can be kept general enough to result in a reference architecture that covers all agents no matter what their service is and where only certain details must still be filled in for a concrete agent.

The reference architecture still leaves open the general philosophy governing agent behavior. To lend precision to the behavior and interaction, these should be formalized in a framework of *semantics*. Such a formal specification should pursue three objectives: external use, e.g., a logical language to specify the agent's behavior; internal use to implement the agent's reasoning processes; and interaction among the agents. The book introduces a number of formalisms together with a characterization of what to expect from them. Starting from an abstract view on the foundations of semantics defined as meaning and reference, communication aspects and foundation of logics are discussed, followed by a description of interaction and reasoning in a dynamic context via temporal logic, situation calculus, non-monotonic reasoning, belief revision and uncertainty inference due to incompleteness and incorrectness in the domain model. They may be applied as part of the most popular formalization of rational agency, the belief-desire-intention (BDI) model. As a logical basis for interaction among agents, ontologies are introduced and the integration of heterogeneous ontologies is discussed.

An environment should be able to justifiably place reliance on the services of a multiagent system, i.e. the system should appear dependable. It is well known that *dependability* should be designed right into a system rather than added as an afterthought. Particularly due to the high degree of distribution and the autonomy of agents, multiagent systems pose numerous and often novel challenges but also offer new opportunities to deal with dependability. Thereby, a distinction should be made between unintentional and intentional failures. Processing of unintentional failures should follow a dependability model. We introduce a model for endogenous disturbances that distinguishes between internal faults that have causes internal to the agent and external faults that may be due either to infrastructure failures or to peer failures, along with various dependability techniques such as transactional approaches, belief management, or trust and reputation. This model can be related to the reference architecture for agents such that for each layer one can identify the faults originating from it, determine which faults can be taken care of within the layer and which ones are to be passed upwards to the next higher layer where the principle repeats itself.

A technology becomes widely accepted only if it can economically be developed and deployed. The maturity of a technology is reflected in its engineering *frameworks and tools*, runtime *platforms*, and the industrial *standards* that underlie them. And indeed, several exist for multiagent systems. Moreover, it is possible to associate them with the layers of the reference architecture so that one obtains good indications on what kind of platform addresses which agent issues. On the lower layers middleware platforms provide a solid basis for developing open, interoperable agent systems, as they primarily tackle interoperability, agent management and communication means. Best suited to the middle layers are reasoning platforms that employ an internal reasoning architecture for systematically deducing an agent's actions from some internal world knowledge. On the uppermost layer social platforms address the organizational architecture and its cooperation and coordination mechanisms. Standards that apply to the middleware platforms in particular are provided by the specifications of the Foundation for Intelligent Physical Agents (FIPA). They address in detail all building blocks required for an abstract agent platform architecture. Standards like RDF and OWL capture the semantics of symbolic representations for ontology descriptions.

Agent software is no different from other software systems when it comes to assuring the quality of the product: *Verification and validation* are essential aspects in the development life cycle. Verifying agent software is particularly difficult due to the combination of complex semantics, goals, non-determinism, concurrency, and distribution. We should admit that to this day verification and validation remain a challenge to the agent system community. There is as yet no standard for verification and assessing of agent technologies available for ensuring adequate quality of a system. Fortunately, a mix of methods from software engineering, knowledge engineering and artificial intelligence and their more or less artful combination seem to work reasonably well. They can be organized into five approaches (in order of increasing strength of proof but also computational complexity): testing, run-time monitoring, static analysis, model checking, and theorem proving. Still, they require expertise and best-practice know-how on the part of the individual developers to design, execute, and evaluate complex evaluation procedures.

6 Evaluation

At the end of the day we have to answer the question of what the real benefits and risks of agent technology are and how these can be evaluated with reliable results. This is a particularly difficult question since a direct comparison of a multiagent-based solution against any other conventionally designed enterprise software system is often impossible, or at least extremely expensive and time-consuming. At the same time, however, this problem is by itself an important innovation barrier preventing enterprises from reinventing their technologies as a basis of future competitiveness.

The last section of this book thus tackles the evaluation question from three independent perspectives: benchmarking, simulation systems, and legal concerns.

Before developers and users may utilize a new technology such as multiagent systems, several questions need to be answered. Under what circumstances, for example, might the use of a multiagent system be appropriate or superior to that of other systems? The *evaluation and benchmarking* of the two (multi-)multiagent systems Agent.Hospital and Agent.Enterprise – their system objects, system components, and system functionalities – against typical real world requirements demonstrates that the agent approach is indeed appropriate and of practical relevance.

While Agent.Hospital and Agent.Enterprise are the result of intensive collaboration between scientists and potential users, a large-scale transfer of the results to the real world would have been too risky. Hence, one could view both as multiagent-based *simulation systems*. Seen from this viewpoint the two scenarios provide an interesting opportunity to evaluate multiagent-based simulation technology against other types of simulation technologies, and to study, based upon these two complex systems, in full detail the particular promises of agent technology for the design and performance of simulation systems.

Agent-based simulation or multiagent simulation applies the concept of multiagent systems to simulation. The corresponding model consists of simulated agents and a simulated environment. Simulated agents may represent concrete individuals or abstract active entities of an original system. The agents act and interact with their environment according to their behavior and emergent phenomena, and dynamic interdependencies of agents can be examined. The evaluation clearly demonstrates that the most important strengths of agent technology, i.e. goal-driven behavior, local awareness and autonomy, social abilities, intelligent interplay of active vs. reactive behaviors, and high flexibility, also significantly enhance the capabilities of complex, distributed simulation systems for highly dynamic applications.

If intelligent agents are substituted for human decision makers, who then is to be held legally responsible for the results? Apparently, the study of multiagent systems remains incomplete unless we also consider the *legal issues* related to software agents (and collections of them) if these comprise an enterprise software system or are part of it. The discussion of these issues reveals a need to control the agents' autonomy by legal regulations, either by interpreting existing laws or by suggesting new regulations. Legal issues constitute an interesting new perspective: While they introduce hardly any new challenges to software design, maintenance, or control, they can no longer be ignored if multiagent systems are to be useful.

Part I

What Agents Are and What They Are Good For

1 Agents

Peter C. Lockemann

Universität Karlsruhe (TH), Institut für Programmstrukturen und
Datenorganisation, lockemann@ipd.uka.de

Abstract. Agents are many things to many people. This is not a sound basis for
engineering software agents or multiagent systems. Since this book deals with engineering such systems, the first thing to do is to agree on the notion of software
agent that is to be used throughout the book. The approach will be in terms of the
qualitative properties that are deemed essential or at least important.

1.1 Introduction

Flexibility – the capability to adapt quickly to a changing environment – is
one of the foremost challenges to today's business processes. In the introductory Part I we claim that the technology of software agents is one of
those software technologies that hold particular promise for an IT infrastructure that enhances rather than inhibits the rapid response of business
processes to newly arising requirements.

Where could these requirements come from? Basically from a worldwide competition where market share is not only determined by cost considerations but as much or even more by novel product and service ideas,
functions and qualities that serve the actual or just perceived needs of a
large customer base better than those of the competitors, or by the supply
of products and services at a shorter time than the competition, or by better
differentiation between the needs and wishes of individual customers, or
by more agility in utilizing new technologies and more intelligent service
and production processes than those at competing companies.

But agent technology is not an easy and cheap technology. And it competes with other software technologies and organizational structures that
offer a good measure of flexibility. Hence, a second claim of this book is
that agents are superior to other technologies and organizations when the
environmental situations are highly complex. As a working definition, we
call a situation complex if there is no practical way to enumerate both the
potential problem space and the potential solution space.

Nor is agent technology a new technology. Even though, it is not yet widely employed in practice. Therefore, a first step in this book should be to introduce the concept of software agent in some detail and argue why systems of software agents (multiagent systems) have the potential for adding the necessary flexibility to business processes that operate in a complex world.

1.2 Metaphoric Notion of Agent

To use a colloquial term for a technical artifact is dangerous because it may lead to misleading associations and conclusions. On the other hand, if one explicitly employs the term as a metaphor it makes it easier for those that ultimately decide on the investment into a certain technology to take an educated decision.

In fact, in the standard dictionaries one finds three clearly distinctive definitions of "agent":

1. a person who does something or instigates some activity;
2. one who acts for or in the place of another and by the other's authority;
3. something that produces or is capable of producing an effect.

The third definition seems to have the least relevance for us, if we interpret "agent" as a kind of catalyst, as in "cleansing agent". The first definition often has a very narrow interpretation along spy novels like "secret agent" or "agent provocateur".

Hence, the second definition seems to be the most natural, particularly if its combined with the first. Take the travel agent, the insurance agent, the real-estate agent, whom we charge to act on our behalf, and whom we expect to do something for us. We shall use the term "agent" in that sense as a metaphor: An agent is an entity capable of action, and it takes its actions on behalf of another entity.

Why would we turn to an agent? Because it offers a range of potential actions that we deem useful to our present purpose. Or in modern terminology, because *the agent offers a useful service*, where a service is a set of obligations – functions and associated qualities – the agent is willing to undergo. Obviously, obligations can only be met if *the agent restricts itself to a certain domain*. The travel agent offers a range of travel functions, like seat reservations, hotel reservations, tour bookings, travel insurance (which it may in turn secure from another agent, an insurance agent), or simply travel information. Some may be specialized further to, e.g., business travel, leisure travel, vacations, adventure trips, or airline travel, or South East Asian vacations.

How do we get the agent to work for us? Usually by *asking the agent to perform a certain task*, i.e., by requesting one of its functions. Typical of services, the asking customer has less interest in how the agent proceeds to dispose of its obligation but more so in the final result. Nor has the agent an interest to reveal in all its details the process by which it produces the result. Therefore: *An agent's behavior is solely judged by the quality of its results.*

In other words, we give *the agent a certain degree of latitude in performing a task*. How much latitude it needs, and how well it will use it will depend on the *agent's own goals*. Such goals may be customer satisfaction, but also earning a reasonable return. Some of its goals may be in conflict, so it has to choose among them or at least to rank them.

How wide the *latitude* is *has something to do with the complexity of the situation* the task has to support. Take as one extreme that you know exactly which train to take and where to change trains, but you do not want to go through the hassle of finding the best fare, to order the tickets and make seat reservations. That does not leave that much latitude on the part of the agent, and does not require that much expertise. On the other hand, suppose that as a European you have heard about the great experience of skiing in the Rockies and you want to spend a week there, have at least 200 kilometers of runs, and pay no more than 5.000 Euros. In this case the agent has to leaf through several catalogues, develop a number of alternatives, compare them and finally choose one, or even go back to the principal for the final choice.

Along with the latitude goes a responsibility to use it wisely. Suppose that the customer last time was dissatisfied with the choice of hotel. The agent should keep that in mind when acting again for that customer: *An agent should be able to learn from past experiences in order to improve on future solutions.*

One may argue that by entrusting the agent with a task and by the agent obliging itself to the task customer and agent enter into a contract. It is only fair then to give the agent the *liberty to decline the task or pose conditions, or to break off its work, perhaps incurring some penalty, or to decide when to start or complete work.*

So far agents became active only on a customer's demand. Should agents take initiatives as well? Take the travel agent who now knows of the principal's love for skiing in the Rockies. Since his own goal is a good return on his business he may decide on his own to contact the principal to remind him of attractive offers. From a principal's perspective an agent may spring to life *on its own initiative to further its own goals.*

Agents and customers may sometimes pursue goals that are in conflict. Such conflicts may arise in particular if an agent serves several customers. Take a real-estate agent. It must satisfy the prospective buyer's needs. But it does not review the entire market, rather it has a group of sellers who put up their property on his block, so they are its customers, too. And it earns a commission from the sale whose size depends on the sales price. This looks like the real-estate agent is in a constant conflict-of-interest situation whose resolution is not entirely transparent to the customers involved. Or take an insurance agent who is expected to find the best bargain for his customer given his needs. It may be a neutral agent arranging policies with many insurance companies, or instead the agent may work for one par-ticular company in which case the best bargain is limited to the offerings of the company. Thus: *Pursuance of goals may lead an agent into con-flicts. Its clients should become aware of the agent's policy for resolving these conflicts of interest.*

Does the metaphor of agent as used above satisfy our original need for flexibility in a complex world? From a purely social viewpoint it does not seem that demanding. If we had to implement all the traits by software, we would exceed present-day capabilities. So after all, it seems a useful meta-phor for our further discussion.

1.3 Software Agents

1.3.1 From Metaphor to Software

The previous section developed a real-world metaphor for the notion of "agent". Our goal is a technical artifact as part of an IT infrastructure for business. To indicate its technical foundation we refer to it as "software agent". More precisely, a program deserves to be called a *software agent* only if it *exhibits a behavior that has many traits of that of our metaphoric human agent*. But we would certainly accept further opportunities that go beyond human performance.

Now, software agents are not a new concept but have long been known from a field called Distributed Artificial Intelligence (DAI). Unfortunately, the range of definitions is very broad, often reflecting phenomena impor-tant to an application domain rather than neutral criteria that could guide both their technical construction and the decision on their applicability. Take [Nwan1996] with his phenomenological typology of agents. In fact, there are complaints that software "agent" is one of the most overused words that masks the fact that there is a heterogeneous body of research and development being carried out under this banner. An indication of the situation is the inflation of adjectives to the word "agent". Take search agents, report agents, presentation agents, navigation agents, management agents, help agents, smart agents, user agents, collaborative agents, interface agents, mobile agents, information agents, hybrid agents, reactive agents, to name a few.

Nonetheless, if one strips all these definitions of their application aspects and human-looking traits there remains a solid body of properties for which technical solutions can be developed. We base the discussion on the properties as introduced by [Wool2002] and relate them to the metaphoric agent characteristics of Section 1.2.

1.3.2 Minimal Properties of Agents

Our characterization of agent started off with the observation that *the agent offers a useful service*, provided *the agent restricts itself to a certain domain*. Consequently, there must be some environment that defines the domain, and that makes use of the service.

There is a DAI counterpart to that characterization, the simple software model Figure 1 taken from [Wool2002].

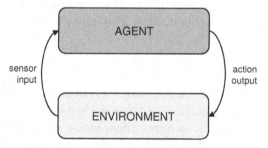

Figure 1. Simple model of an agent in its environment

Everything outside the agent is called its environment. The agent is said to sense its environment and to act on its environment. Like its real-world counterparts, agents do not dissolve once a task has been finished, rather the interaction is an ongoing, non-terminating one. This gives rise to a first property of software agents:

Property 1

A software agent is a computer system that is situated in some environment.

Not only should the agent offer a useful service, *its behavior is solely judged by the quality of its results*. To reflect this characterization, we formulate a second property of software agents, one that could also be derived from Figure 1:

Property 2

A software agent offers a useful service. Its behavior can only be observed by its external actions, its internal processes remain encapsulated.

The two properties do not by themselves as yet justify the term "agent". Classical machine control software meet Property 1, and objects in object-oriented software, components in component software or a Web Service satisfy Property 2. There must be something else that sets agents apart from other pieces of software. Take the characterization of real-world agents that they have *a certain degree of latitude in performing a task*, where the degree of latitude depends on the *agent's own goals*, and where the latitude includes the *liberty to decline the task or pose conditions, or to break off its work, perhaps incurring some penalty, or to decide when to start or complete work*.

In DAI all these characteristics translate into the single notion of autonomy: The agent's functionality does not directly depend on the properties or states of other entities within the system the agent is part of, it has the sole control over the activation of its service and may refuse to provide it, or ask for compensation [Sheh2001]. This gives rise to the central property:

Property 3

A software agent is capable of autonomous action in its environment in order to meet its design objectives, i.e., to provide its service.

The key problem facing an agent, then, is that of deciding which of its potential actions it should perform and when, in order to best satisfy its objectives. A decision process where the key factor is the agent's own goals is referred to as practical reasoning. There are two aspects of practical reasoning, goal deliberation and means-end assessment. Often the agent may pursue several goals some of which may be in conflict, so during goal deliberation the agent may have to give priority to one. And once a goal has been chosen, there may still be several means how to achieve the goal, so the agent has to assess them before choosing among them.

Property 4

As a corollary to Property 3, the autonomy of a software agent is guided by its own goals, with goal deliberation and means-end assessment as parts of the overall decision process of practical reasoning.

Properties 3 through 4 set software agents apart from object-oriented or component-oriented software. Even though in object-oriented software each object may run in a separate thread and may thus exhibit some traits of autonomy, it is the lack of own goals that makes the inferior to software agents [LuAI2004].

1.3.3 Intelligent Agents

From an outsider's standpoint, due to practical reasoning software agents exhibit unpredictable, or non-deterministic behavior. One may benignly call such a behavior flexible, but so far we did not relate it to the need for flexibility.

Following Wooldridge we claim that the need for flexibility arises when the environment appears non-deterministic as well. All too often an agent cannot observe its entire environment, and hence explain all the observations by its own actions or those of known players. Hence, the agent does not have complete control over the environment, it can just influence it. Just take a group of travel agents who try to make airline reservations, perhaps on the same flight. Agents that are capable of dealing with such environments seem to be a special breed:

Definition

An intelligent software agent is a software agent capable of operating in a non-deterministic environment.

According to Wooldridge such environments are either inaccessible, i.e., the agent cannot obtain complete, up-to-date information, and/or uncertain, i.e., the agent's action has no single guaranteed effect, and/or dynamic, i.e., there are changes in ways beyond the agent's control, and/or continuous, i.e., there are uncountable many states. Wooldridge stresses the fact that the real challenge to the agent are the changes taking place while the agent is executing a task. This gives rise to a first property of intelligent agents:

Property 5

An intelligent software agent is reactive, that is, it continuously perceives its environment, and responds in a timely fashion to changes that occur.

Reactivity is a passive trait: The agent remains in a receptive state, and responds once it recognizes changes of certain kinds. For example, a client *asking the agent to perform a certain task* is such a change. Continuous observation goes beyond responding to a request, though, and is the direct result of the need for dealing with a non-deterministic environment [Pnue1986]. Timely response must be seen in light of autonomy: The environment cannot dictate to the agent when and how to react. As a consequence, Wooldridge extends Property 4:

Property 6

An intelligent software agent achieves an effective balance between goal-directed and reactive behavior.

At any particular time the goal-directed or the reactive behavior will be subordinate to the other. The normal modus will be the reactive behavior, with the agent responding to some event in the environment in a goal-directed fashion. On the other hand, if the goals dominate the behavior the agent must become active, take *its own initiative* to affect changes in the environment in order *to further its own goals*.

Property 7

An intelligent software agent may be proactive, that is, take the initiative in pursuance of its goals.

In the real world, agents may become clients of other agents, for example when they cannot solve a given problem on their own but must delegate part of the problem solution to other agents. In the world of software agents this property cannot taken for granted. Rather we must explicitly state whether agents should be able to interact with one another. Wooldridge refers to this capability as social ability. Social ability may also be a way to overcome or resolve *conflicts in the pursuance of goals*.

Property 8

An intelligent software agent may have to possess social ability, that is, it is capable of interacting with other agents to provide its service.

Goal deliberation and plan selection may be affected by past experiences of an agent. Or as we noted, a real-world agent *should be able to learn from past experiences in order to improve on future solutions*.

Property 9

An intelligent software agent may be able to learn.

For this book we are interested in intelligent software agents that at least satisfy Properties 1 to 6 and 8.

1.3.4 Agent Authorization

What has been missing from our discussion so far is the metaphoric characteristic that an agent takes its actions on behalf of another entity. Such an entity is called the agent's principal. In the real world, the principal must have authorized the agent for the desired actions (in a legal or contractual sense). The principal may be a single person, a homogeneous group of persons, or a legal entity, to name a few.

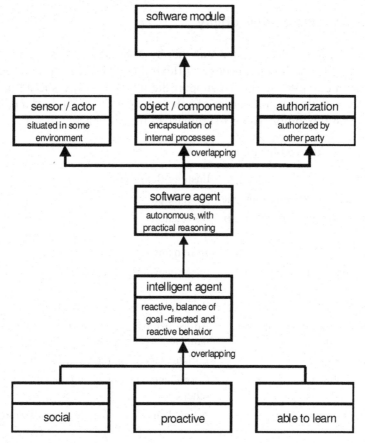

Figure 2. Hierarchy of agent properties

In a metaphoric sense the agent acts as the principal's representative. As such its actions must be guided by the principal's goals. Consequently what we termed in Property 4 the agent's own goals are in fact those of its principal. It makes little sense to assign an agent to more than one principal because this would instill in it different, perhaps conflicting goals. On the other hand, the same principal may be responsible for more than one agent. Translated into the software world we will have to name a principal for each software agent, be it a real person or another agent.

An agent serves clients. There may be a single client (perhaps identical to the principal), or many clients, and this even simultaneously and when their interests are in conflict. It is the principal's responsibility to supply its agent with the policy for resolving conflicts of interest.

See Figure 2 for a summary for the discussions in Section 1.3.

1.3.5 Properties and Flexibility

Our hypothesis for this chapter was that systems of software agents have the potential for adding the necessary flexibility to business processes that operate in a complex world. To support the hypothesis, we should be able to demonstrate that the properties of software agents have indeed a positive influence on flexibility. Table 1 summarizes the influence.

Table 1. Properties and flexibility

Property	Ensuing flexibility
1. Situated in some environment	No relation
2. Service-orientation and encapsulation	No relation
3. Autonomy	Take many factors into account
4. Goal-based practical reasoning	Large decision space
5. Reactivity	Respond to environmental changes
6. Balance between goal-direction & reactivity	Adjust behavior to the environmental dynamics
7. Proactivity	Initiate changes in the environment
8. Social ability	Coordinate adjustment of behavior with others
9. Learning capability	Adjust behavior to the environmental trends

1.4 Agents or Not?

1.4.1 Testing the Waters

While the properties in Section 1.3 seem to give some precision to what we mean by the term of agent, by offering a number of criteria to judge them, one should admit that they still are rather qualitative in nature. Suppose that we wish to take the properties and develop a software architecture such that with each property we associate specific methods, algorithms and data structures. Or suppose that we place an agent in an environment and wish to decide which properties the agent should include to operate in this environment. Or even, do we need an agent at all or would an ordinary object or component do the job? Ultimately, then, we need to be able to make the properties operational. In a nutshell, this is what this book tries to achieve.

To get a feeling how easy or hard this promises to be we take a short look at a few popular pieces of software that go under the term of agent. This sounds like an academic exercise. But since agent technology is a complex technology we should not fool ourselves into calling a needed piece of software an agent if a simple software approach would do. Hence, the yardstick should be whether the environment is large, complex and dynamic, or if many goals have to be observed, i.e., whether, the need of practical reasoning seems large.

1.4.2 Thermostat

Hardly a book on agents that does not use the example of the thermostat. Thermostats have a sensor for detecting room temperatures, the sensor is directly embedded within the environment (the room) and produces two outputs, either temperature is o.k. or temperature is too low. The actions available to the thermostat are to turn the heat on or off.

The term agent is a misnomer, though. The environment is deterministic because it is just the room temperature that is observed, no matter what factors affect the temperature like open doors or windows. No flexibility is needed, and indeed everyone could quickly write down a simple algorithm for it! (Ignore the fact that the thermostat is a piece of hardware. For all we know it may as well be a piece of software residing on a chip.)

1.4.3 Auction Agents

Everyone knows it, the ebay agent. It is a piece of software, and it provides a service. It is created for a customer when he or she bids for a particular article. Hence, it is tied to a specific combination of bidder and article. The two constitute its environment.

We claim that the ebay agent does not deserve to be called an agent. From the agent's viewpoint the environment is deterministic because even though other bids for the article arise from actions outside it is sufficient for it to observe the bids on the article. Nor is the ebay agent autonomous. Its actions are entirely predictable, and that is what we as bidders expect from it. It is given an upper limit for the bid, and it is supposed to submit the currently highest bid as long as it stays within the limit. It does not pursue any own goals, so everyone could quickly write down a simple algorithm!

1.4.4 Webrobots

Search engines for the Web consist of three major components, a Webrobot system to generate and update an information base to describe the content of (parts of) the Web, an information retrieval system for building a searchable data structures from the documents discovered by the Webrobot system, and a query processor for querying the Web via the data structures built by the information retrieval system [Gloe2003]. The term Webrobot seems to suggest that the collection of Web data involves some sort of machine intelligence, and indeed it is suggested in [Klus1999] that Webrobots fall into the class of (non-cooperative) information agents.

From an environmental viewpoint one could see a need for agents. The environment appears non-deterministic due to its size, continuous growth and fluctuations. The authors of Google while they still were Ph.D. students describe some of their experiences with their robot (more precisely, the crawlers) [BrPa1998]. It seems that when they started running their crawlers across half a million servers they ran into all kinds of unexpected situations, and they conclude "because of the immense variation in web pages and servers, it is virtually impossible to test a crawler without running it on a large part of the Internet".

Not surprisingly, then, Webrobots are highly complex software systems with four major components. The gatherer visits the Web sites worldwide – in fact, though, it stays put at a central site and downloads the Web pages. For performance reasons several gatherers work in parallel. Gatherers receive their orders from a loader which supplies them in the form of

URL lists. The loader is the strategic component, because it has to take decisions which Web sites to visit, and – more important – when to revisit them (to "crawl" them in the narrow sense) to discover changes and to maintain an information base that is as fresh as possible or meaningful or economical. The basis for the strategies is a URL database which characterizes all Web sites – in a way this database is a description of the observable parts of the environment – and it contains all the information that enters into the strategic decisions. The checker decides whether a document should be passed on to the information retrieval system, i.e., it acts as a filter.

Do Webrobots meet the important properties? Are they autonomous? Do they pursue conflicting goals like high performance, up-to-date information, large Web covering, economy, avoidance of malicious sites, gain of sponsorships, and so on, where we leave it to the Webrobot how to resolve conflicts? Do they have some learning capability? The providers will not tell. If we knew we would know more about how complex an environment should be before one would have to resort to agent technology.

1.4.5 Interface Agents

The metaphor underlying interface agents is that of a personal assistant who is collaborating with the user in the same work environment. These agents emphasize autonomy and learning in order to perform tasks for their owners. An agent tracks the actions taken by the user in the interface, i.e., "watches over the shoulder of its user", learns new shortcuts, and suggests or chooses better ways of doing the task. As [Nwan1996] points out, interface agents learn by observing and imitating the user, through receiving positive and negative feedback from the user, by receiving explicit instructions from the user, or by learning from peers like asking other agents for advice.

Particularly daunting environments are huge information spaces, like the worldwide network of scientific libraries and publishers, and perhaps also highly unstable, like the Web. The best known interface agents are information agents that support users in their information retrieval tasks in such spaces. [Lieb1999] distinguishes between agents for information reconnaissance, remembrance agents, agents for common interests, and matchmaking agents. Reconnaissance agents try to continuously bring new Web pages to the user's attention by following links from new pages that seem pertinent to the user's interests. These interests may have gathered from questionnaires filled out by the user, but even better, by automatic inference from the user's actions or reactions. Such agents, then, are reactive, proactive and capable of learning. Remembrance agents differ in that they take the user's current interests rather than their general interests into account and search for and present information pertinent to the user's current context. Again, these agents are reactive, proactive and capable of learning. Agents for common interests explore an information space on behalf of small groups, by finding what interests they have in common. Finally, matchmaking agents help a user find others who have similar interests from a large, anonymous group, for example to pool their experiences for the information search (collaborative filtering).

Do these agents pursue their own goals? In RETSINA [Syca1999] the user provides the agent (a combination of an interface agent, a task agent and an information agent, with the decision making concentrated in the task agent) with a description of his overall goals. In addition the agent acquires and models user preferences to guide the performance of a task once it has been initiated. In particular, the task agent interprets the task specification and extracts the solutions to the problem, forms a plan to reach the associated goals, identifies the subgoals, and initiates plan execution.

Interface agents clearly are full-blown intelligent agents. They pursue their own goals, but these goals have been imposed their users (the principals). Or the other way round, the agent makes the user's goals his own.

1.4.6 Shopbots

Superficially, shopbots appear similar to interface agents in that they also search an information space based on the user's interests. In fact, though, there are significant differences. Their environment is much more limited, generally a list of participating vendors with their advertised offers, usually through a catalogue. The user enters a specific purchase request, frequently a particular kind of article with a number of desired or mandatory features [GuMM1999], and the shopbot searches the list for the appropriate vendors. The shopbot may but need not include learning capabilities, for example by learning and implicitly using known preferences of the user.

Some shopbots enable consumers to narrow down the products that best meet their needs by guiding them through a large product feature space, using filtering techniques by allowing shoppers to specify constraints on the product's features and then to solve a constraint satisfaction problem. Other shopbots recommend products by automated collaborative filtering that compares a shopper's product ratings with those of other shoppers and identifies the shopper's nearest neighbors (recommender system). Other shopbots again may do price comparisons as the first criterion of choice, but are known to depend heavily on the willingness of vendors to participate and to have weaknesses when a price tells only half the story (e.g., ignores added value through services).

Do shopbots have to be agents? It depends on circumstances. If the environment is fairly stable with a known community of vendors, i.e., deterministic, and the shopper's goals are straightforward, algorithmic solutions that leave no latitude may suffice. If the shopbot has to reconcile the conflicting goals of the shopper and of vendors and perhaps other shoppers, practical reasoning may be needed.

1.5 Conclusions

The chapter has shown that there is a good deal of agreement among the community on when a piece of software deserves to be called a software agent. The characterization is in terms of qualitative properties rather than any precise formal notation. Hence, there will always be borderline cases where it is more a matter of taste whether to call a software module just sophisticated or an intelligent agent.

For the engineer the issue is less one of academic discussion but more so of whether the solution to his problem must exhibit a flexibility that can only be attained with the fairly demanding agent technology.

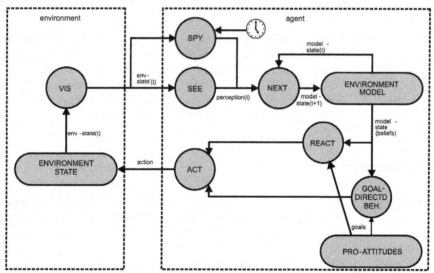

Figure 3. Dataflow model of an agent

How agents achieve this flexibility is shown in the data flow diagram of Figure 3. It refines Figure 1 by adding Properties 1 through 9. On the left, the environment is presented by a state as the origin of a continuous flow of state information. Function VIS filters out the stimuli that can be perceived by the agent. On the right the agent continuously observes the environment through the function SEE. Function NEXT combines the perception with the state of the environmental (mental) model that the agent currently holds, and produces a modified model.

Properties 3 to 7 are reflected by the lower half on the right. Property 3 is reflected by a model state that is not directly associated with the change at a specific time t (therefore often called a belief), and Property 4 by the goals that affect all routes to the action. Function REACT reflects the reactive behavior and is influenced both by the beliefs and the goals (Property 5). A second path via function GOAL-DIRECTED BEHAVIOR accounts for practical reasoning and leads to function ACT as well. The two inputs to ACT mirror Property 6. Property 7 is simulated via function SPY that perceives the environment only if woken up (indicated by the clock). The further behavior follows one of the other properties.

On this level of abstraction, Property 8 is implied in the environmental state, and Property 9 can be suitably incorporated in the environment model and function NEXT.

Further Reading

[Ferb1999]   Ferber, J.: Multi-agent Systems - An Introduction to Distributed Artificial Intelligence. Addison-Wesley, Boston, 1999.
[Weis1999]   Weiss, G. (Ed.): Multiagent Systems – A Modern Approach to Distributed Artificial Intelligence. MIT Press, Cambridge, 1999.
[Wool2002]   Wooldridge, M. J.: An Introduction to Multiagent Systems. John Wiley & Sons, New York, 2002.

References

[BrPa1998]   Brin, S.; Page, L.: The Anatomy of a Large-Scale Hypertextual Web Search Engine. In: Proceedings of the 7th International Conference on the World Wide Web. Elsevier Science, Amsterdam, 1998, pp. 107-117.
[Gloe2003]   Glöggler, M.: Suchmaschinen im Internet. Xpert.press series, Springer Verlag, Heidelberg, 2003.
[GuMM1999]   Guttman, R.; Moukas, A.; Maes, P.: Agents as Mediators in Electronic Commerce. In: Klusch, M. (Ed.): Intelligent Information Agents – Agent-Based Information Discovery and Manage-

ment on the Internet. Springer Verlag, Heidelberg, 1999, pp. 131-152.

[Klus1999] Klusch, M. (Ed.): Intelligent Information Agents – Agent-Based Information Discovery and Management on the Internet. Springer Verlag, Heidelberg, 1999.

[Lieb1999] Lieberman, H.: Personal Assistants for the Web: An MIT Perspective. In: Klusch, M. (Ed.): Intelligent Information Agents – Agent-Based Information Discovery and Management on the Internet. Springer Verlag, Heidelberg, 1999, pp. 279-292.

[LuAI2004] Luck, M.; Ashri, R.; d'Inverno, M.: Agent-Based Software Development. Artech House, Boston, 2004.

[Nwan1996] Nwana, H. S.: Software Agents: An Overview. Knowledge Engineering Review 11(1996)3, pp. 205-244.

[Pnue1986] Pnueli, A.: Specification and Development of Reactive Systems. In: Proceedings of the 10th IFIP International World Computer Congress – Information Processing 86, 1986, pp. 845-858.

[Sheh2001] Shehory, O.: Software Architecture Attributes of Multi-Agent Systems. In: Ciancarii, P.; Wooldridge, M. J. (Eds.): AOSE 2000. Springer Verlag, LNCS series vol. 1957, Heidelberg, 2001, pp. 77-90.

[Syca1999] Sycara, K.: In-Context Information Management through Adaptive Collaboration of Intelligent Agents. In: Klusch, M. (Ed.): Intelligent Information Agents – Agent-Based Information Discovery and Management on the Internet. Springer Verlag, Heidelberg, 1999, pp. 78-99.

[Weis1999] Weiss, G. (Ed.): Multiagent Systems – A Modern Approach to Distributed Artificial Intelligence. MIT Press, Cambridge, 1999.

[Wool2002] Wooldridge, M. J.: An Introduction to Multiagent Systems. John Wiley & Sons, New York, 2002.

2 From Agents to Multiagent Systems

Ingo J. Timm, Thorsten Scholz, Otthein Herzog

Universität Bremen, Technologie-Zentrum Informatik
{i.timm | scholz | herzog}@tzi.de

Karl-Heinz Krempels, Otto Spaniol

RWTH Aachen, Lehrstuhl für Informatik IV
{krempels | spaniol}@informatik.rwth-aachen.de

Abstract. In the previous chapter agents and their properties have been introduced. In real-world business applications, it is assumed that the benefit of agent technology is reached by dynamic interaction of autonomous agents. This interaction and co-operation forms a multiagent system ("MAS"). The organization of agents within such systems is strongly related to organization theory. The specific flexibility of MAS arises from the ability to follow predefined structures or evolve structures from dynamic interaction. In this chapter, fundamental concepts and properties of MAS are introduced with special focus on interaction and communication, roles, and structures.

2.1 Introduction

In the previous chapter intelligent agents have been introduced as autonomous, flexible problem solving entities which operate in a specific environment. Agents meeting in the environment may interact and co-operate, and thus form a multiagent system ("MAS"). Since there is a strong analogy between real organizations and MAS this chapter will discuss MAS in detail with the focus on the organizational perspective. First, an overview of the evolution of MAS is provided, followed by the identification of key properties of MAS. The key properties 'communication', 'interaction', 'structures', and 'roles' are each detailed out in separate sections.

2.2 The Evolution of Multiagent Systems

The descriptive definition of the illusive animal *agent* given in the previous chapter leads to the assumption that many different branches of science influenced its evolution, and also the kind of possible flexibility for a given application area. Academic and industrial researchers with very different goals have investigated agents, agent systems, and their capabilities. Nevertheless, the consolidation efforts made by standardization organizations passed the point of inflexion in the development of agents and agent systems, allowing the agent technology's graduation and its deployment within real industrial environments.

Today it is nearly impossible to determine which sector first focused on agents. However, in this section we try to sketch the development process of agents and agent systems, and their evolution to multiagent systems without any pretence of a correct chronological order of contributions, but of their influence on the development process.

The first agent property refers to the agent environment that enables an agent to exist. That is, the agent environment must provide a kind of elementary "energy" for the hosted agents. In an agent environment we can think of an agent as a consumer of computational power, network bandwidth, memory, and also higher-level resources like services, similar to an operating system process or thread. In a more abstract way, an agent should be seen as an entity in its environment consuming existing services like "life energy". How the environment can offer services, and how an agent is able to search, select and use offered services is investigated under the aspect of agent systems infrastructures. Furthermore, under this aspect the following topics are also considered:

- low level communication: agent to agent, agent to platform, and platform to platform, offered as blackboard or message passing service,
- service directories: service descriptions, service registration, service discovery, and also quality of service,
- reliability: mechanisms to recover crashed agents with using transaction logs and data backups, or hot or cold stand-by approaches,
- mobility: migration of an agent from one agent platform to another one, based on the assumption that it is cheaper to move computation to the place where the data is provided than moving the data.

Agent systems of the first generation were developed with the objective to analyze one or more topics of the infrastructure aspects and first appeared around 1985. They suffered from being closed systems due to the lack of standardized communication and interaction interfaces, resulting from their ad-hoc design process (e.g., Voyager, Aglets, Grashopper, EMIKA). Their developers usually were research teams in the area of communication networks, distributed systems, and network management. The investigation of these agent systems and their behavior also covers the properties 2 and 3. The provision of a useful service by an agent may vary from a simple communication service, like a message delivery service for other agents, agent systems, and users, or a more complex service, like planning, scheduling, or co-ordination. A service can be offered by an agent depending on its availability as a continuously available service, or as a service made available on demand. Furthermore, a service can be pre-defined, or be composed at demand time from a collection of other services that also can be predefined or composed.

In Artificial Intelligence the investigation of knowledge management, planning, scheduling, automated learning, and reasoning led to many new combined approaches with target applications in robotics, support decision systems, and expert systems. Many of these approaches were adapted to agent systems with the aim to build intelligent agents, able to act and react autonomously in their environment. The outcome of this process, and the efforts made by the standardization organizations MASIF and FIPA, led to a new generation of agent development frameworks (e.g., JADE, FIPA-OS, SeSAm, Zeus, etc.). The improved software engineering process and the implemented standardized communication layer of the second generation of agent systems have removed the "closed systems characteristic" of the first generation of agent systems. The powerful technical capabilities of these systems, e.g. their simple syntactic and semantic adaptivity, the standardized communication layer, and the broad range of existing interfaces to already deployed industrial systems enabled them to be deployed as middleware for semantic integration of distributed heterogeneous systems, e.g. databases, knowledge bases, data mining tools, monitoring applications. In the second generation of agent systems the focus moved from one to multiagent communication, interaction and problem solving. Because of their semantically very flexible ontology-based communication and reasoning, multiagent systems ("MAS") are able to act as semantic routers between connected applications and interfaces, enabling developers to integrate existing systems within a shorter time. Furthermore, this high flexibility of MAS enables developers to accelerate the development process of new applications, and finally to achieve a faster time to market.

2.3 Properties of Multiagent Systems

In [BoGa1988] MAS are defined as consisting of heterogeneous agents that are generally self-motivated and act to fulfill internal goals, but may also share tasks with others. There is no global or centralized control mechanism. Agents have to reason to co-ordinate their actions, plans, and knowledge. Agents, in these systems, can cope with situations in a flexible way involving inconsistent knowledge about the environment (world, other agents), partial domain representation, and changing, overlapping plans resulting from the need to interact with other agents. The properties of MAS appear to be almost infinite regarding the number of agents, their flexibility, their abilities, the ways of interaction, the initial state of the system, etc.

From the very beginning emergent behavior has been one of the most important criteria for MAS. It can be described by three aspects: The first aspect is focused on emergent properties as a large-scale effect of locally interacting agents: *"Emergent properties are often surprising because it can be hard to anticipate the full consequences of even simple forms of interaction"* [Axel1997]. In [Ferb1999] the focus lies on emergent organization: *"Even societies considered as being complex such as colonies of bees or ants, should not necessarily be considered as individuals in their own right if we wish to understand their organization and the regulation and evolution phenomena prevailing there. In terms of multiagent systems, this means that an organization can emerge from the juxtaposition of individual actions, without its being necessary to define a specific objective (an element from the assembly O) which represent such an outcome"*. The third aspect links emergence with the transition from reactive agents to deliberative ones. Doing so *"the idea that intelligent behavior emerges from the interaction of various simpler behaviors"* [Wool1999] emerges from this theoretical basis.

A closer look at all three aspects suggests that communication is the main source for achieving global structures by local interaction, dynamic organization by simple (communication) rules, and intelligent behavior of the MAS as a whole.

Despite the diversity of MAS properties it is possible to describe the organizational structures within MAS [Ferb1999]. In [HiFU1994], an organization is defined as the entirety of measures to accomplish aims and goals. It is socially structured based on the division of labor, and organizes the activities of people which are part of the system as well as the deployment of resources and the processing of information. [KiKu1992] identify five properties of organizations which can be adapted to describe properties of MAS: a set of goals, perpetuity, members, formal structure, and activities of members. Goals are inherently part of, and reason for, MAS. The design of MAS is geared towards meeting a set of specified goals which are pursued for a given period of time, allowing for flexible system behavior. Agents within the system pursue their own goals depending on their roles and are organized in some structures. Depending on their roles and goals, agents solve problems and interact, communicate, and co-operate.

In the following, the operational behavior will be detailed by analyzing interaction and communication within MAS. Furthermore, organizational structures will be examined with respect to roles and structures. Fundamental concepts will be also discussed in the context of an exemplary scenario: enterprises are using MAS for the management and implementation of supply chains.

2.4 Interaction and Communication

The implementation of an operational behavior within MAS requires the interaction between agents, e.g., in order to share information, coordinate actions, flexibly resolve conflicts, and optimize the organizational processes. [Ferb1999] identifies a set of assumptions fundamental for the interaction and communication within MAS: the presence of agents capable of acting and/or communicating, constructs which can serve as a meeting point for agents, and dynamic elements allowing for local and temporary relationships between agents.

2.4.1 Blackboard Communication

All these assumptions require the agents to be able to communicate. The most general approach for communication is interaction via the environment where an action of an agent causes an effect which is perceivable and interpretable by other agents (see Figure 1).

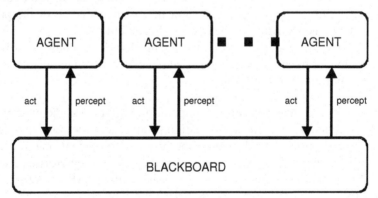

Figure 1. The blackboard architecture

A special kind of interaction was described by [Newe1962] with the blackboard metaphor:

"Metaphorically we can think of a set of workers, all looking at the same blackboard: each is able to read everything that is on it, and to judge when he has something worthwhile to add to it. This conception is just that of Selfridges Pandemoneums' a set of demons, each independently looking at the total situation and shrieking in proportion to what they see that fits their nature."

With 'blackboard technology' the effects of the actions of an agent are recognizable by all other agents in the environment. It is characterized by [Cork1991]:

- *Independence of expertise*: problem solving agents do not depend on the expertise of other agents – they can proceed once they find required information on the blackboard. They can contribute independently from other agents.
- *Diversity in problem-solving techniques*: the internal knowledge representation and inference mechanisms of each agent contributing to the blackboard may differ.
- *Flexible representation of blackboard information*: there is no restriction to what kind of information is placed on the blackboard.
- *Common interaction language*: a common representation of information placed on the blackboard is required in order to allow the agents to interpret the information.
- *Positioning metrics*: in order to allow for an efficient retrieval of information, the context of each piece of information is used for structuring.
- *Event-based activation*: interaction between agents is not direct but is triggered by events on the blackboard (e.g., new/changed information).
- *Need for control*: a control component that is independent of the problem solving agents manages the course of problem solving.
- *Incremental solution generation*: no agent alone is capable of solving the problem at hand – the solution is achieved by incrementally building on contributions of other agents.

With respect to the scenario of co-operating enterprises, the enterprises use a shared memory for the co-ordination of their activities, e.g., a custom order is placed on the blackboard by the original equipment manufacturer (OEM). Following a priority scheduling mechanism the enterprises are sequentially producing partial orders, or assemble them. The co-ordination between the participating enterprises is carried out by writing results on the blackboard to make them accessible for any other participants.

Recent research focuses on distributed blackboards with more sophisticated formalization, management, and access mechanisms [OmZa1999]. This may become more important especially in the field of eTeaching and eLearning. Nevertheless, flexibility of communication is restricted by the need for a blackboard.

2.4.2 Message Passing

Communication based on varying access rights influenced by the information provider for accessing information within the system is called directed communication. Directed communication in MAS is performed by message passing, where a message is sent from one agent to another, and the environment is used only as a means of transportation (see Figure 2). In message passing in MAS, messages are sent from a sender agent to a receiver agent. The messages are based on the speech act theory [Aust1962], and are encoded in an agent communication language. A series of messages produces a dialog and often follows predefined structured protocols.

Figure 2. Message passing

The speech act theory is based on the observation that certain classes of natural language utterances are capable of changing the state of the world. A speech act has three different aspects [Wool2002]: the elocutionary act, which is the act of making an utterance; the illocutionary act, which is the action performed in saying something; the perlocution, which is the effect the act has on the state of the world. Additionally, performative verbs like *request* or *inform* denote different types of speech acts. The work of [Sear1969] extended the speech act theory by adding a classification of possible types of speech acts. It consists of five key classes: representative acts, committing the speaker to the truth of an expressed proposition (e.g., "A new order has been released."); directive acts, expressing the attempt of the speaker to get the audience to do something (e.g., "Company A has to produce part C."); commissive acts, committing the speaker to a course of action (e.g., "We are going to produce part C."); expressive acts, expressing a psychological state (e.g., "Thank you for delivery."); declarative acts, effecting a change in an institutional state of affairs (e.g., "Company A is the default supplier for part C.").

With the help of the speech act theory agents become capable of not only planning how to autonomously achieve their goals, but additionally of planning their interaction with other entities like agents or other software systems in the environment. Thus, agents obtain a high degree of flexibility in interaction. In the early times of distributed AI research, [CoPe1979] characterized the semantics of speech acts with the plan representation language STRIPS [FiNi1971]. Pre- and post-conditions of speech acts represented in a multimodal logic enable a smooth integration into formally defined agents as well as the use of standard planning algorithms.

2.5 Roles in Multiagent Systems

Communication – as introduced in the last section – is a very flexible way of coordinating agents. However, there could be a huge overhead for enabling co-ordination between agents leading to a high communication complexity, e.g., if the relationship between agents has to be negotiated. In the context of real-world applications – like the supply chain scenario – it is crucial to provide an efficient approach for scalability, i.e., if the amount of agents increases linearly the communication complexity should not increase exponentially. The solution for a reduction of complexity is the introduction of organizational structures in MAS. Following the organization theory, there are two major measures: roles and structures. In this section roles in MAS will be discussed with respect to organizational theory, as well as some specific requirements.

In an organizational model roles are among the key components as they allow for the abstraction from individuals which eventually will adopt the role. In addition to roles there are positions within organizations which are occupied by individuals. In the organizational context there are three dimensions of roles: position-specific (e.g., the CEO of an enterprise), task-specific (e.g., seller or supplier), and individual-specific (e.g., person B of company A) [Scot1967]. A position is always in correlation with a social or organizational role [RoSt1981] [Kah+1964] [JaCL1951]. While an individual usually occupies only one position, it can hold different roles which may vary in the course of interaction. Since a position in an organization is more persistent than an individual which occupies it, individuals may change the position within the organization while holding the same roles. In an organizational context, [GrMM1958] and [Dahr1968] define roles as consisting of:

- generalized expectations of the interaction partner (behavior, appearance, properties, character),
- allocation to defined functional areas and hierarchical levels, leading to expectations for the role (the role achieves sanction powers),
- definition of goals, action programme, and communication channels,

- range of authority, in which a role can define mandatory expectations for other roles, e.g., defining a superior.

The role models used in MAS are motivated by approaches from organization theory and social science. Thus, the underlying understanding of roles is similar to the definition introduced above. With respect to applications, it is useful to restrict the concept of roles in such a way that it is representing cognitive states on the basis of knowledge permissions or responsibilities [Lind2001]. This reduction appears to be too restrictive with respect to expressiveness, and not restrictive enough with respect to communicational efficiency. However, such concepts could be used for implementations of views on internal representations of even huge world models, which allows for efficient inferences. Recent approaches towards the design of open MAS are explicitly modeling social models, including roles, which are not limited to cognitive states [DaDD2003] [Pets2002].

Obviously, the concept of positions and roles leads to potential conflicts of interest, especially if an agent holds multiple roles. [KiKu1992] distinguish between inter- and intra-role conflicts. Intra-role conflicts are caused by a specific role and internalizations of external conflicting expectations, e.g., by contradicting instructions from different superiors. Agents that hold multiple roles have to deal with potential inter-role conflicts, i.e., a current action which is consistent with role A and in conflict with role B. The management of such conflicts is crucial to realize robust behavior in MAS, and has been discussed, for example, in [Timm2004] [DaTo2004]. Additionally, ambiguity of roles can cause problems, if role specifications are not communicated efficiently, or if specifications are vague. In contrast to role conflicts, which have to be handled dynamically at run-time, role ambiguity is a problem which should be solved partly at design time (vagueness); the communication problem, however, has to be dealt with dynamically.

The main difference between MAS and real world organizations is that individuals (humans) in real organizations can always act autonomously, i.e., overcome role restrictions. Reliability in an organization is ensured by rewarding role conformant behavior and sanctioning misdemeanor [Scot1967]. Transforming the role paradigm to MAS leads to the question whether agents should be allowed to overcome role restrictions. In a computational system there is the possibility to explicitly exclude misdemeanor. However, this would limit benefits of MAS significantly: disjunctive (non-conflicting) roles, restricted autonomy of agents, and limited openness of MAS may lead to a loss of flexibility and may prevent emergent effects. In analogy to real organizations a computational system has to include mechanisms ensuring reliable behavior if individuals are allowed to break restrictions. These mechanisms are in the focus of current research on trust in MAS [FaCa2004] [DaRJ2004].

Summarizing, roles are a means for enabling more flexible system behavior, i.e., they allow for the exchange of individuals adopting a role without changing the configuration of the system, as well as for an adaptive, context-dependent behavior of agents.

2.6 Structures in Multiagent Systems

The concept of roles focuses on different views on individuals, and realizes an abstraction of individual abilities, goals and behaviors. Due to external expectations on roles, communication efforts are reduced significantly. However, if a set of individuals is required, communication efforts can increase considerably due to coordination activities, e.g., managing inter-role conflicts. Thus, in large scale systems it is necessary to develop institutionalized co-ordination through reusable structures, providing for flexible system behavior. In organizations there are concepts for individuals joining with respect to task classes, tasks, and capabilities.

Organizational structures can be viewed as abstract sets of individuals, i.e., they are represented externally by a subset of individuals and have a hidden internal structure, e.g., an enterprise participating in a supply chain may be represented by its buying department. For an implementation of these structures it is important to decide on internal and external functions which have to be performed, e.g., problem representation, solution presentation, directory structure, and structure management. These functions can be realized by the concept of roles introduced above. There is a general distinction between internal (e.g., directory) and external (e.g., representation) roles. Role assignment depends on the system design and is discussed later. Additionally, roles within a structure can be subdivided into operational and management functions. Mandatory properties for structures include organization (control) of managerial and operative processes. The control of processes follows four approaches: centralized, decentralized, hierarchic, and democratic [ThJa2001]. In context of the supply chain scenario, the OEM would control the complete chain, i.e., it would not only control 1st tiers, but also 2nd, 3rd, etc. tiers directly. Hierarchical structures are a specialization of centralized structures, where the OEM controls 1st tiers, 1st tiers control 2nd tiers, etc. These structures are used for most supply chains. In a decentralized as well as in a democratic approach there is no leading entity, and the network is managed dynamically by the interaction of participating enterprises. Thus, the supply chain is an emergent effect of these interactions. The approaches differ in available com-munication channels: in democratic networks communication is not lim-ited, i.e., each enterprise is able to communicate with others, while in de-centralized approaches the network is organized in a peer-to-peer manner. Obviously, democratic approaches are providing the highest flexibility, al-though decision-processes as well as their underlying communication ef-forts can increase dramatically. In real organizations hierarchical structures are showing a good balance between flexibility and coordination efficiency [KiKu1992].

These four types of structure management result in specific communi-cation channels with significantly varying effects on communication and co-ordination efficiency as well as flexibility. [HiFU1994] introduce four approaches to intra-organizational communication: star (centralized, Fig-ure 3a), ring (decentralized, Figure 3b), chain (hierarchy, Figure 3c), and network (democratic, Figure 3d), which can be used for the implementa-tion of the above mentioned control approaches. Balancing the properties of these communication channels and the organization of managerial and operative processes with flexibility is domain dependent and has to be con-sidered individually for concrete applications.

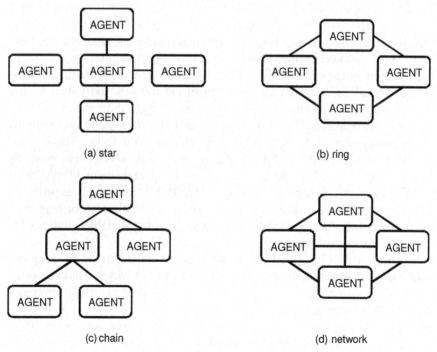

Figure 3. Interaction structures

Furthermore, there is a distinction between open and closed structures in analogy to operating systems [Tane1994]. In open structures agents are able to pronounce their membership, and any external agent is allowed to communicate with agents belonging to the structure. However, in closed structures, a managing entity decides on the membership of agents, as well as a representative entity routing the communication. While the realization of an open structure does not require sophisticated services, the implementation of a closed structure needs specific notions of communication and management, e.g., a closed structure with a high demand on availability will be managed in a distributed way. In the following, some dimensions of organizational structures will be discussed in more detail.

Organizational structures and structures in MAS are characterized by three dimensions: capabilities, duration, and decision-making. If the capability of an organizational structure were a synergetic fusion of individual skills, abilities and capabilities, it would be important to consider the type of designated synergy effects. If the organizational structure consisted of a homogenous set of agents with respect to their capabilities, the capabilities of this institution would enable a solution of the same problem sets at a larger scale or in a shorter period of time. These structures are similar to fundamental approaches in parallel computing [Quin1994], especially grid computing [RBGD2004]. As opposed to homogenous sets of agents, structures can also consist of agents with heterogeneous capabilities, in order to solve problems which cannot be solved by individual agents due to their limited range of capabilities. These heterogeneous structures introduce new challenges to the management of capabilities. Individual agents match capabilities to tasks autonomously, using algorithms which are hidden from other agents. These structures need algorithms and mechanisms for matching sets of heterogeneous capabilities with tasks. These challenges are researched in multiple fields, e.g., web service composition [MaLe2004] [Pis+2004], multiagent capability management [TiWo2003] [ScTW2004], and distributed planning [Durf1999]. Real applications usually require structures which consist mostly of a combination of heterogeneous and homogeneous sets of agents, thus allowing scalable solutions for a wider range of problems.

A further aspect of structures in MAS is the consideration of duration. Structures can persist over the complete life time of MAS. Thus, co-ordination mechanisms between agents can be considered at design time and consequently implemented statically into the agents. Such an approach enables an efficient co-ordination with only a small communication overhead, but it nevertheless limits the flexibility of the system. Dynamic structures allow for flexible reactions and the re-organization of MAS in changing environments. However, the efficiency of the necessary co-ordination is inferior to static structures, as additional communication efforts are required for forming, managing, and disbanding. The duration of structures may depend on goals, i.e., the structure may be disbanded once the goals of the structure have been reached. These can be described explicitly by joint intentions or system goals, or implicitly in utility functions of the agents, the MAS structure, or the system.

Table 1. Classification of economical structures

Economical Structures	Level	Capabilities	Duration	Decision Making
Cartel (e.g., OPEC)	horizontal vertical diagonal	homogeneous heterogeneous	short- to long-term	influence depends on resources
Collaboration (e.g., VW Sharan and Ford Galaxy	horizontal	homogeneous	short- to mid-term	democratic
Cooperation (e.g., DaimlerChrysler and Recaro/Lear)	horizontal vertical	homogeneous heterogeneous	short- to mid-term	hierarchic
Alliance (e.g. Star-Alliance: United Airlines, Lufthansa, etc.)	horizontal diagonal	homogeneous heterogeneous	long-term	globally democratic, locally autonomous
Department (e.g., Buying- and Sales-department)	horizontal vertical	homogeneous heterogeneous	short- to mid-term	hierarchic
Institution (e.g., EADS)	horizontal vertical diagonal	homogeneous heterogeneous	mid- to long-term	hierarchic, democratic or matrix
Location (e.g., stock market)	horizontal vertical diagonal	homogeneous heterogeneous	short- to long-term	market-based

The third dimension for MAS structures is how decisions are made how to form, manage, and disband structures. The scope ranges from decision makers appointed at design time to democratic selection algorithms during run-time [Sand1999]. Similar to the problem of design time vs. run-time in capability management, co-ordination efforts increase significantly in run-time approaches while the flexibility increases. Thus, the main criteria for choosing an appropriate level of decision making capabilities as well as capability management depends on the balance of flexibility and co-ordination efficiency.

These dimensions can be used for the classification of concrete structures. Groups or teams are typical representatives of organizational structures in MAS. In the context of the dimensions mentioned above groups consist of homogeneous sets of agents which are the basis for scalability or optimization of MAS. In general, groups are formed for higher efficiency, i.e., increased payoff for individual agents. These kinds of structures are discussed in coalition formation using approaches from game theory [Sand1999]. In contrast to groups, teams consist of heterogeneous agents, and are formed to solve specific problems. In this case, individual payoff is not the major selection criterion, but individual capabilities are used for forming a team. Team formation is consequently described using logic-based approaches [Wool2000].

These dimensions provide useful criteria for classifying structures. Table 1 shows representative types of structures. Additionally, a fourth dimension has been added which is specific to the economical domain. This fourth dimension is indicating up to three types of interaction: horizontal (interaction within the same market), vertical (interaction within different markets), and diagonal (horizontal and vertical interaction). From a decision-making point of view, there are three specific structures: alliances, institutions, and cartel. In a cartel, a group of enterprises which has a dominant position in the market is trying to dictate prices and conditions within this market. A single enterprise within such cartels has influence proportionally to its market share. In alliances, markets are often partitioned into regions; thus, each enterprise is deciding within its regional responsibility. Further decisions are made democratically. If an interaction between enterprises has a mid- or long-term perspective it can be institutionalized. In such an institution, internal organizations – including decision-making processes – are negotiated individually and domain dependent. Thus, the full range of decision-making policies is available.

References

[Aust1962]   Austin, J. L.: How To Do Things With Words. Oxford University Press, Oxford, 1962.

[Axel1997]   Axelrod, R.: The Complexity of Cooperation – Agent-Based Models of Competition and Collaboration. Princeton University Press, Princeton, New Jersey, 1997.

[BoGa1988]   Bond, A. H.; Gasser, L. (Eds.): Readings in Distributed Artificial Intelligence. Morgan Kaufmann Publishers, Inc., San Mateo, California, 1988.

[CoPe1979]   Cohen, P. R.; Perrault, C. R.: Elements of a Plan Based Theory of Speech Acts. In: Cognitive Science 3(1979), pp. 177-212.

[Cork1991]   Corkill, D.: Blackboard systems. In: Journal of AI Expert 9(1991)6, pp. 40-47.

[Dahr1968]   Dahrendorf, R.: Homo Sociologicus. Ein Versuch zur Geschichte, Bedeutung und Kritik der Kategorie der sozialen Rolle. 7. Aufl., Köln und Opladen, 1968.

[DaRJ2004]   Dash, R.; Ramchurn, S.; Jennings, N.: Trust-Based Mechanism Design. In: Proceedings of the Third International Joint Conference on Autonomous Agents & Multiagent Systems (AAMAS 04). ACM, New York, pp. 748-755.

[DaTo2004]   Dastani, M.; van der Torre, L.: Programming BOID Agents: A Deliberation Language for Conflicts between Mental Attitudes and Plans. In: Proceedings of the Third International Joint Conference on Autonomous Agents and Multi Agent Systems (AAMAS'04). New York, July 2004, pp. 706-713.

[DaDD2003]   Dastani, M.; Dignum, V.; Dignum, F.: Role-Assignment in Open Agent Societies. In: Proceedings of the Second International Conference on Autonomous Agents and Multiagent Systems (AAMAS'03). Melbourne, July 2003, ACM Press, 2003, pp. 489-496.

[Durf1999]   Durfee, E. H.: Distributed Problem Solving and Planning. In: Weiss, G. (Ed.): Multiagent Systems – A Modern Approach to Distributed Artificial Intelligence. MIT Press, Cambridge, Massachusetts, 1999.

[FaCa2004]   Falcone, R.; Castelfranchi, C.: Trust Dynamics: How Trust is Influenced by Direct Experiences and by Trust Itself. In: Proceedings of the Third International Joint Conference on Autonomous Agents & Multiagent Systems (AAMAS 04). ACM, New York, pp. 740-747.

[Ferb1999]   Ferber, J.: Multi-Agent Systems. Introduction to Distributed Artificial Intelligence. Addison-Wesley, Harlow, England, 1999.

[FiNi1971]   Fikes, R. E.; Nilsson, N.: STRIPS: A New Approach to the Application of Theorem Proving to Problem Solving. In: Artificial Intelligence 2(1971), pp. 189-208.

[GrMM1958]   Gross, N.; Mason, W. S.; McEachern, W.: Explorations in Role Analysis. New York, 1958.

[HiFU1994]   Hill, W.; Fehlbaum, R.; Ulrich, P.: Organisationslehre 1. Ziele, Instrumente und Bedingungen der Organisation sozialer Systeme. Verlag Paul Haupt, Bern et al., 1994.

[JaCL1951]   Jacobson, E.; Charters Jr., W. W.; Lieberman, S.: The Use of the Role Concept in the Study of Complex Organizations. In: Journal of Social Issues 7(1951)3, pp. 18-27.

[Kah+1964]   Kahn, R. L.; Wolfe, D.M.; Quinn, R. P.; Spoeck, J. D.; Rosenthal, R. A.: Organizational Stress. Studies in Role Conflict and Ambiguity. New York, 1964.

[KiKu1992]   Kieser, A.; Kubicek, H.: Organisation. 3. Auflage, de Gruyter, Berlin, New York, 1992.

[Lind2001]   Lind, J: Iterative Software Engineering for Multiagent Systems: The MASSIVE Method. Springer, Heidelberg, 2001.

[MaLe2004]   Martínez, E.; Lespérance, Y.: Web Service Composition as a Planning Task: Experiments Using Knowledge-Based Planning. In: Proceedings of the ICAPS 04 Workshop on Planning and Scheduling for Web and Grid Services. Columbia, Canada, 2004.

[Newe1962]   Newell, A.: Some Problems of the Basic Organization in Problem-Solving Programs. In: Proceedings of the Second Conference on Self Organizing Systems. Spartan Books, 1962.

[OmZa1999]   Omicini, A.; Zambonelli, F.: Tuple Centres for the Coordination of Internet Agents. In: 14th ACM Symposium on Applied Computing. San Antonio, Texas, February 1999.

[Pets2002]   Petsch, M.: Openness and Security in the FIPA Standard. In: Timm, I. J.; Berger, M.; Poslad, S.; Kirn, S. (Eds.): Proceedings of MAI '02: International Workshop on Multiagent Interoperability. 25th German Conference on Artificial Intelligence (KI-2002) Workshop (5). Aachen, 2002, pp. 13-26.

[Pis+2004]   Pistore, M.; Barbon, F.; Bertoli, P.; Shaparau D.; Traverso P.: Planning and Monitoring Web Service Composition. In: Proceedings of the ICAPS 04 Workshop on Planning and Scheduling for Web and Grid Services. Columbia, Canada, 2004.

[Quin1994]   Quinn, M. J.: Parallel Computing: Theory and Practice. McGraw-Hill, Columbus, Ohio, 1994.

[RBGD2004]   Rivera, F.; Bubak, M.; Gómez Tato, A.; Doallo, R. (Eds.): Grid Computing - First European Across Grids Conference. Santiago de Compostela, Spain, February 13-14, 2003, Revised Papers, LNCS 2970. Springer, Berlin, 2004.

[RoSt1981]   Roos Jr., L. L.;   Starke, F. A.:   Organizational   Roles.   In: Nystrom, P. C.; Starbuck, W. H. (Eds.): Handbook of Organizational Design. Vol. 1, Oxford, 1981, pp. 309-322.

[Sand1999]   Sandholm, T. W.: Distributed Rational Decision Making. In: Weiss, G. (Ed.): Multiagent Systems – A Modern Approach to Distributed Artificial Intelligence. MIT Press, Cambridge, Massachusetts, 1999.

[ScTW2004]   Scholz, T.; Timm, I. J.; Woelk, P.-O.: Emerging Capabilities in Intelligent Agents for Flexible Production Control. In: Katalinic et al. (Eds.): Proceedings of the International Workshop on Emergent Synthesis (IWES 2004). Budapest, Hungary, 2004.

[Scot1967]   Scott, W.G.: Organization Theory: A Behavioral Analysis for Management. Irwin, Homewood, Il1, 1967.

[Sear1969]   Searle, J. R.: Speech Acts: An Essay in the Philosophy of Language. Cambridge University Press, Cambridge, 1969.

[Tane1994]   Tanenbaum, A. S.: Modern Operating Systems. Prentice-Hall, London, 1994.

[ThJa2001]   Thoben, K. D.; Jagdev, H. S.: Typological Issues in Enterprise Networks. In: Journal of Production Planning and Control 12(2001)5, pp. 421-436.

[TiWo2003]   Timm, I J.; Woelk, P.-O.: Ontology-based Capability Management for Distributed Problem Solving in the Manufacturing Domain. In: Schillo, M. et al. (Eds.): Proceedings of the First German Conference on Multi-Agent System Technologies (MATES 2003), Erfurt, LNAI 2831. Springer, Berlin, pp. 168-179.

[Timm2004]   Timm, I. J.: Dynamisches Konfliktmanagement als Verhaltenssteuerung Intelligenter Agenten. DISKI 283, infix, Köln, 2004.

[Weis1999]   Weiss, G. (Ed.): Multiagent Systems – A Modern Approach to Distributed Artificial Intelligence. MIT Press, Cambridge, Massachusetts, 1999.

[Wool1999]   Wooldridge, M.: Intelligent Agents. In: Weiss, G. (Ed.): Multiagent Systems – A Modern Approach to Distributed Artificial Intelligence. MIT Press, Cambridge, Massachusetts, 1999, pp. 27-78.

[Wool2000]   Wooldridge, M. J.: Reasoning about Rational Agents. MIT Press, Cambridge, Massachusetts, 2000.

[Wool2002]   Wooldridge, M. J.: An Introduction to Multiagent Systems. John Wiley & Sons Ltd., Chichester, 2002.

3 Flexibility of Multiagent Systems

Stefan Kirn

Universität Hohenheim, Wirtschaftsinformatik II
kirn@uni-hohenheim.de

Abstract. The most important promise of multiagent technology is flexibility. Multiagent technology enhances the adaptability of IT systems in two ways: it facilitates "external" maintenance and it increases their own capabilities to perform necessary adaptations by themselves. These are important contributions to the competitiveness of enterprises as they increase their capabilities to react appropriately to changes in their markets, to meet their customers' demands better than before, and to take greater advantage of new market opportunities than would otherwise be possible. This contribution develops a formal framework for the description, and analysis of the flexibility of multiagent systems. It elaborates this framework in much detail and evaluates it on the basis of examples from the field of multiagent engineering.

3.1 Introduction

The development of a new software technology raises various questions about its practical benefits: For which type of design problems is it really well suited? Which requirements of an enterprise application does it better meet than (if any) other technologies? How does it enhance the robustness, scalability, and maintainability of software systems? Also: Why should any software engineer or software customer actually decide to pursue this new and possibly risky software technology?

With respect to multiagent technology, the answer of this book is: flexibility. The effective support of the adaptability of information is the most important strength of multiagent technology. This strength goes far beyond the capabilities of any other contemporary software technology and thus needs much more attention than it has attracted to date. This is important for enterprises which are increasingly challenged by the rapidly changing demands of their customers, by the continuously increasing competition in their markets, by (often dramatic) increases in the number of internal and external processes to be managed, and also by the growing impact of process technology on their competitiveness. Multiagent technology, which is essentially a software-based process technology, is thus of great relevance to any enterprise being faced with high flexibility demands.

How does multiagent technology achieve this high degree of flexibility? The theoretical foundations have already been introduced in Chapters I.1 and I.2. The autonomy of agents enables them to plan, perform and evaluate their actions according to their internal states, goals and resources. They are aware of the state and dynamics of their external environments and they are thus capable of individually exhibiting situated behaviors. They coordinate their actions with other agents belonging to the same multiagent system. Multiagent systems can employ a variety of organizational structures together with appropriately defined cooperation protocols in order to manage what has been called the micro macro link: the dynamic interplay between the individual agents on the micro level and the whole multiagent system on the macro level. Finally, multiagent systems are much more open than any other software system: new agents can always join an existing multiagent system (if this agrees) and members of a multiagent system may even withdraw at runtime.

This chapter starts with a review of selected flexibility concepts in different fields of literature (Section 3.2). We found that a production theory perspective is best suited for our purposes, leading to a set of six definitions of flexibility: qualitative flexibility, quantitative flexibility, problem solving flexibility, economic flexibility, time flexibility, and configuration flexibility. Formalizing this framework requires formal definitions of agents and multiagent systems. This is provided in Section 3.3. On this basis, Section 3.4 develops formal specifications for the flexibility definitions mentioned above. Section 3.5 presents initial considerations on the application of the framework in multiagent engineering. Section 3.6 summarizes the results.

3.2 Towards a Flexibility Framework for Multiagent Systems

Flexibility denotes the ability of a system (e.g., human being or machine, more or less complex biological, technical, or social systems) to be adaptable, i.e. to behave as required in different situations. Though flexibility is an important concept in many disciplines, it is still a vague concept in multiagent technology. This section therefore aims to establish an operational flexibility framework for multiagent systems.

Flexibility requires interactions between (at least) two systems: the system under consideration (agent a) and its counterpart, which we call its environment. Necessarily, the agent must be able to perceive information about the behavior of the environment and to react to the signals received from there. Flexibility further requires that the agent has to address at least one goal, e.g., to solve a problem, to complete a task, to survive physically, to display technical robustness, to act efficiently, etc. Flexibility is thus part of the agent's problem solving strategy. It may enhance its ability to achieve its goals, in particular if the achievement of these goals is somehow dependent on its environment. This may change its status over time, may conflict with the agent's goals, or may offer opportunities for (increased) synergies. Flexibility has thus much to do with situated behaviors (see I.1).

3.2.1 Contributions From Selected Fields

Flexibility is an important concept in many fields within and outside computer science. There are, thus, lots of specific definitions, concepts, and experiences, each inspired from very different perspectives. Multiagent engineering can draw from any of these, but within the context of this book the areas of software technology, machine learning, organizational theory, and production theory are of major interest.

The *software technology* perspective focuses on the engineering process, on requirements engineering and modeling, on engineering frameworks and tools, on implementation languages, on architecture patterns and software lifecycle management for agents and multiagent systems [Balz2001]. Flexibility imposes particular demands on the maintainability, adaptability to different application areas, configuration and integration management, testability, scalability and openness. In the field of multiagent systems, attention has mainly been put on requirements engineering and modeling, on single agent architectures, and on implementation issues. All other design phases, in particular the late phases like testing, configuration and integration management, and maintenance have not been considered yet. This is a relevant drawback as flexibility is just about the modification of already existing systems.

Machine learning [Weis1995] is a subfield of artificial intelligence. In that perspective, multiagent systems are societies of more or less autonomous intelligent systems (agents). Flexibility thus addresses the ability of agents and multiagent systems to adapt themselves (automatically) to dynamic changes in their environments. Changes in the system behavior through external actions (e.g., maintenance) are not considered. The machine learning perspective has much to do with autonomous action and it has particular advantages, if external access (e.g., by humans) is difficult or impossible.

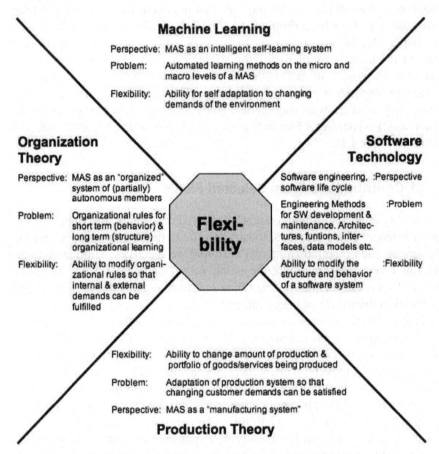

Figure 1. Selected approaches of semantic frameworks for flexibility

In an *organizational theory perspective* agents are considered as "artificial members" of multiagent systems. Membership establishes a temporal relation between an agent and a multiagent system. Organizational rules organize the division of labor, coordinate joint behaviors, and manage interactions within and between workflows [HiFU1994, p. 34] [KiGa 1998] [KiMu1998]. Flexibility denotes the ability of a multiagent organization to choose from given organizational alternatives (structures, rules, behaviors, workflows, roles, division of labor, information flow, etc.) to better meet external demands [KiKu1992, p. 379]. It is well understood that adaptation may cost time and money, may affect already established procedures, may be the source of confusion, failures, and other problems within the organization, and may also affect the interaction of the multiagent organization with its environment.

Production theory considers systems of production in enterprises and how they transform input into output. The relationships between input and output are formalized through production functions. These include specifications of the capabilities, behaviors, and interaction of the machines in use. In a production theory perspective, multiagent systems provide, typically on request, services to their environments. This is an interesting perspective as it simply focuses on the result of the behaviors of a multiagent system, which meets quite naturally the notion of flexibility introduced at the very beginning of this section. I.e. flexibility is the capability of a multiagent system to meet the changing demands of its environment (customers) and to react to changing internal situations in such a way that external demands can be fulfilled again. Below, we thus apply to the production-oriented perspective to develop a flexibility framework for multiagent systems.

In production theory and related fields there has been intensive discussion on definitions for flexibility.[1] Many definitions focus on the reactivity of companies and act on the assumption that environmental changes cannot be directly influenced and therefore have to be taken for granted [Zapf 2003, p. 90]. For this reason, flexible production processes will enable companies to react quickly and with goal-orientation to environmental changes [KüSc1990, p. 94]. This definition is often related to notions of (operational) flexibility or elasticity [Kalu1993, p. 1174]. Recent work emphasizes the active aspect of flexibility and argues that enterprises can also try to modify their environments according to their own needs [Schl 1996, p. 94] [Zapf2003, p. 90]. It is generally agreed that flexibility (due to internally or externally induced changes in environment) necessarily requires free resources that are not bound otherwise [Meff1985, p. 123] [Knof 1992]. Finally, an important contribution comes from Adam [Adam 1993] who has suggested an operational overall framework for the description and analysis of the flexibility of production automata in plants. This framework provides us with an appropriate conceptual basis for the development of our flexibility framework for multiagent systems.

---

[1]   Among others [Brow1984] [ChKi1998] [Dank1995] [MoSh1998] [BaSt1995] [StRa1995] [HyAh1992] [MaBr1989].

3.2.2 Conceptualization of a Flexibility Framework for Multiagent Systems

Referring to [Adam1993], the flexibility of a multiagent system is given through

- its service portfolio (i.e. the set of different services s_i it can offer as a reaction to received input, denoted as *qualitative flexibility QualFlex*),
- for each service s_i: how often can it deliver this service per unit of time (denoted as *quantitative flexibility QuantFlex*),
- the number of different (cooperative) problem solving processes that can produce a single service (denoted as *problem solving flexibility ProblSolvFlex*).

Obviously, the flexibility of an existing multiagent system depends on its current configuration, including the set of participating agents, the interaction patterns, its cooperation and coordination protocols, the cooperation language in use, etc.

Examples

- Multiagent system M_1 can offer a set of services s_i ($1 \leq i \leq m$), but each service only once a day. M_1 is thus less quantitative flexible than another multiagent system M_2 offering these services 10 times a day.
- After having been maintained, M_2 is able to produce the services s_j ($1 \leq j \leq n$), with $n > m$. The qualitative flexibility of M_2 is now greater than that of M_1.
- Though the quantitative flexibility as well as the qualitative flexibility of M_2 exceeds that of M_1, the problem solving flexibility of M_1 wrt a particular service s_k may be higher than that of M_2 iff M_1 can employ more different (cooperative) problem solving processes than M_2.

In general, flexibility is not free. It may require additional resources, may be risky for already established processes and services (e.g., due to bottleneck problems, limited scalability, etc.), and may in some cases even lead to confusion of the environment (e.g., because of delays of service deliveries, reduced service quality, etc.). We call these costs the *economic flexibility* of a MAS. Further, multiagent system adaptation may take some time. We call this the *time flexibility*[2] of a MAS. Economic flexibility and

---

[2] Time differs from other types of "economic" resources as it introduces a new dimension into the discussion, the time axis. Reasoning over time is distinct from reasoning over space, over monetary investments, etc. This has motivated the decision to treat time as a flexibility dimension on its own.

time flexibility may interact. E.g., adaptations under time pressure are often more expensive (and risky) than adaptations that can be performed calmly.

Finally, it may even be necessary to be able to modify the configuration of a multiagent system. This may change its internal structure, its interaction patterns, cooperation and coordination protocols, and existing membership agreements, but, possibly, also the exclusion of members from the multiagent system and the integration of new ones. We call this the *configuration flexibility* of a multiagent system. If the *configuration flexibility* equals $\varnothing$, the configuration of a multiagent system cannot be changed. We call this also static flexibility of a multiagent system.

To summarize:

- Adaptation denotes the process of fitting the behavior of a multiagent to the changed demands of its environment. This requires (at least): (i) that there is already an interaction between the system and its environment, (ii) that the behavior (demand) of the environment has changed (or is changing), (iii) that the MAS is able to sense this change and to reason about it, and (iv) developing new behaviors (displaying new services) expected to better meet the new demands of the environment.
- Adaptation may be performed within the current configuration of a multiagent system (static flexibility), or through modifications of its configuration (configuration flexibility).
- Adaptation is not free. It takes time to adapt a multiagent system and adaptation may require further resources. Let *curr* denote the status of the multiagent system before adaptation (i.e. "current") and let *adapted* denote its status after adaptation:

$$MAS_{curr} \ [\rightarrow QuantFlex_{curr} \times QualFlex_{curr} \times ProblSolvFlex_{curr}]$$
$$\rightarrow SetOfServices_{curr} \tag{1}$$

$$MAS_{curr} \times AdaptTime \times AdaptResources \rightarrow MAS_{adapted} \tag{2}$$

Remark

Sometimes, the same adaptation result may be achieved either within the current configuration (static flexibility), or through changes in the current configuration (modification flexibility). This must therefore be decided before an adaptation starts. The result of this decision may depend on available time and resources.

$$MAS_{adapted} \ [\rightarrow QuantFlex_{adapted} \times QualFlex_{adapted} \times ProblSolvFlex_{adapted}]$$
$$\rightarrow SetOfServices_{adapted} \tag{3}$$

The above formalization provides a generic framework within which one can give precise definitions of different types of flexibility each covering different (and relevant) flexibility perspectives. On that basis one can further develop methods and tools in order to describe, analyze, forecast, and design flexibility characteristics of multiagent systems. How this can be done in a particular case depends upon the concrete specification of the multiagent system, the services and resources available, the given environment(s), etc. The next step is thus to introduce a formal specification of agents, and multiagent systems (Section 3.3) in order to perform detailed elaborations of different definitions of flexibility (Sections 3.4 and 3.5).

3.3 Formalization of Agents and Multiagent Systems

In literature there are already numerous formalizations of agents, and multiagent systems. In this contribution we built upon the recent work of Burkhardt and Kirn ([BuAW2000] [Kirn2002]) in order to develop a conceptual specification of multiagent systems.

We define the concept of agents based upon their problem solving behavior. They perform their actions in a three-step cycle.

1. Information reception: agents observe (*sense*) their environments via sensors to identify the relevant information as *sensory_input* $\in$ *Sensory Inputs* and transfer them into one or more *perception* $\in$ *Perceptions*.

$$sense: SensoryInputs \rightarrow Perceptions \tag{4}$$

2. Information processing: in the second step the agent draws conclusions and updates his *internal_state* $\in$ *InternalStates*. The state *internal_state$_{new}$* is normally dependent on the state *internal_state$_{old}$* and a specific set of *perceptions*:

$$reason: InternalStates \times Perceptions \rightarrow InternalStates \tag{5}$$

The definition of *InternalStates* is based upon the environment model *EnvModel*, the *Goals*, and the *Commitments* (already promised services to be fulfilled in future) of the agent:

$$reason: (EnvModel_{old} \times Goals_{old} \times Commitments_{old}) \times Perceptions$$
$$\rightarrow (EnvModel_{new} \times Goals_{new} \times Commitments_{new}) \tag{6}$$

3. Actions: In the third step the agent fulfils its commitments by performing *action* $\in$ *Actions* in its environment:

$$act: Commitments \rightarrow Actions \tag{7}$$

The behavior of an agent can thus be described by sequences of the mappings *sense, reason* and *act*.

By definition, each agent is a member of the overall agent community. The agent community is given by:

$$AgentCommunity := (A \times C) \qquad (8)$$

where $A := \{a_1, ..., a_i, ..., a_n\}$ is the set of agents existing in the network and $C := \{c_{ij} \mid c_{ij} \to (a_i, a_j); 1 \leq i, j \leq n\}$ is the set of directed communication channels between pairs of agents.

Please note that $c_{ij} \neq c_{ji}$. C defines the overall connectivity of the agent society. Necessarily, interaction requires communication. Thus, c_{ij} also represents the set of possible interactions of the action(s) of agent a_i with the sensor(s) of agent a_j.

Multiagent systems are subsets of *AgentCommunity*. They are defined as

$$MAS_i \subseteq A \times C \qquad (9)$$

In accordance with literature, we assume that MAS_k is established only iff a cooperative problem solving process is required (dynamic definition). MAS_k declines, iff problem solving is completed.

We can therefore assume that if an agent accepts the invitation to join a cooperative problem solving process, it is immediately bound to this problem solving process. The binding of an agent can be static (static planning) or dynamic. If an agent decides to provide a specific service s_i to this problem solving process, this service s_i is bound to this process, too. This establishes a second level of binding.

The overall system behavior of a multiagent system is thus manifested in six steps:

Step I: Selecting agents $a_i \in A$ that will be invited to join cooperative problem solving.

Step II: Binding agents $a_i \in A$ to constitute MAS_k.

Step III: Selecting services $s_i \in SetOfServices$ needed for problem solving.

Step IV: Binding services $s_i \in SetOfServices$ to the process of problem solving.

Step V: Performing the problem solving process.

Step VI: Decline of the MAS_k.

Remark

This is a generic definition of a multiagent system, supporting our analysis of the flexibility framework introduced in Section 3.2. To this purpose, it abstracts from many conceptual and technical details (e.g., agent platform, common agent language, ontologies, coordination and cooperation protocols, directory services, etc.) needed to develop a concrete multiagent system.

3.4 Formalization of the Flexibility Framework

Building on the formal models of agency and multiagent systems in Section 3.3, we now formalize the flexibility framework of Section 3.2. Sections 3.4.1 to 3.4.5 assume static flexibility and give formal definitions for qualitative, quantitative, problem solving, economic, and time flexibility. In Section 3.4.6, we extend the analysis to the concept of configuration flexibility.

3.4.1 Qualitative Flexibility

Qualitative flexibility *QualFlex* denotes that set of services s_i, $1 \le i \le n$ (service portfolio) which a multiagent system can deliver to its environment. A quantitative measure of qualitative flexibility is the size of this set:

$$QualFlex: SetOfServices \rightarrow I\!N \tag{10}$$

$$qual\_flex := |SetOfServices| \tag{11}$$

This still simple definition ignores that the elements of *SetOfServices* may be different in many aspects. They may be unequal wrt their relevance, they may be requested in different frequency, at different times, in different quantities, etc. Depending on the requirements of a particular application it may thus be necessary to employ more sophisticated flexibility measures, e.g., such as statistical distribution functions.

Remark

In general, not all elements of *SetOfServices* are known. The set *SetOfServices* may even change over time. This may cause all well-known problems of incomplete, vague and non-monotonic knowledge. Similar considerations hold for all flexibility definitions below.

3.4.2 Quantitative Flexibility

Quantitative flexibility *QuantFlex* denotes how often a multiagent system can provide each of its services s_j per unit of time. Assumed, agent a_i can provide a set of services s_j $(1 \leq j \leq n)$ k times per unit of time. Then, a simple definition of quantitative flexibility is given through:

$$QuantFlex: SetOfServices_i \to SetOfServices_i \times |N \qquad (12)$$

$$quant\_flex(s_1,..., s_j, ..., s_n) := \{(s_j, k_j) \mid j := 1, ..., n, k \in |N\} \qquad (13)$$

This definition ignores that the elements of *SetOfServices* may be different wrt to their relevance for a given demand of the environment and that the quantitative output of service s_j may change over time.

Additional formalisms may thus be needed to get more appropriate specifications of *QuantFlex*.

Example

Assumed, agent a_i provides three services s_1, s_2 and s_3. Each service can be provided up to k_j times. This leads to *QuantFlex* := $\{(s_1, k_1), (s_2, k_2), (s_3, k_3)\}$. However, the triples *(100, 100, 100)* and *(1, 1, 10.000)* for k_j, $j := 1$, ..., *3* describe very different quantitative flexibilities that cannot easily be compared.

3.4.3 Problem Solving Flexibility

A multiagent system i may be able to produce a service s_i in different ways, i.e. through different sequences of activities. We call these sequences the problem solving patterns of a MAS i wrt a particular service s_j, denoted as *Patterns$_{i,j}$*. We can thus define:

$$ProblSolvFlex_i: Patterns_{i,j} \to |N \qquad (14)$$

$$probl\_solv\_flex_i(s_j) := |Patterns_{i,j}| \qquad (15)$$

Again, this is still a simple definition. It ignores, for example, that there may be different pre- and postconditions for each pattern, that they may require different quantities and qualities of resources, etc. This, however, depends on the underlying application and the concrete specification of the multiagent system under consideration.

If one aims to use this concept, a new reasoning component must be integrated into the architecture of a multiagent system. The inference process works as follows:

1. *Self observation*: The multiagent system has to keep track of all steps performed during problem solving.
2. *Evaluation*: The MAS evaluates these after the end of a problem solving process.

3. *Learning*: Store learning results as a new pattern in the problem solving pattern database.
4. *Monitoring*: As multiagent systems typically exist in dynamic environments, they are supposed to continuously monitor the applicability of the pattern in their databases.
5. *Use*: If necessary, employ an already existing pattern to solve a current task.

3.4.4 Economic Flexibility

We have already stated that flexibility cannot be taken for granted. Three main types of costs, all together denoted as potential expenses *pe,* can be identified:

1. *Resources R*: Flexibility may require additional resources (computing time, storage, bandwidth, access to external knowledge, etc.). These resources can be limited, they can cost money, they can be controlled by someone else, etc. If a multiagent system aims to involve such resources it may have to pay a price for it.
2. *Risks for current commitments CC*: As a result of changed internal structures and/or behaviors, the risk may arise that current commitments are broken (e.g., through a crash of ongoing problem solving processes, decreased performance, bottleneck problems, limited scalability, delays of service deliveries, reduced service quality, etc.). In such cases, these risks $Risk_{CC}$ have to be calculated in appropriate economic terms, e.g., in monetary equivalents.
3. *Changes of external behaviors E*: Flexibility may lead to changes in behaviors of the environment. This may require additional internal activities and may even complicate the internal planning and reasoning processes. This also can be (at least, in principal) mapped to appropriate (monetary) terms.

We call these costs the economic flexibility of a MAS. If *curr* denotes the current state of a multiagent system, *adapted* the state after adaptation, and M the additional costs (e.g., in terms of monetary equivalents), then a first definition of EconFlex can be given by:

$$M := R \times CC \times E \tag{16}$$

$$EconFlex: SetOfServices_{curr} \times M \rightarrow SetOfServices_{adapted} \tag{17}$$

$$econ\_flex(s_i) := \{ s_j \mid s_j := s_i \circ (r_x, cc_y, e_z) \wedge (r_x, cc_y, e_z) \in M \wedge$$
$$x = 1, ..., m, y = 1, ..., n, z = 1, ..., o)\} \tag{18}$$

Please note that different combinations of additional resources $(r_x, cc_y, e_z) \in M$ may transform a service s_i to the same new service s_j. This case can be considered as a combination of economic flexibility and problem solving flexibility.

3.4.5 Time Flexibility

Time flexibility denotes the amount of time necessary to perform required adaptations. This is of particular interest if a multiagent system needs to perform adaptations in very short time. May $t \in IN$ denote the number of units of time (e.g., seconds) needed to perform a requested adaptation of service s_i. Then, a simple definition of time flexibility is given by:

$$TimeFlex: SetOfServices_{curr} \times IN \to Boolean \tag{19}$$

This definition does only denote, that the MAS under consideration is able to perform a particular adaptation within time span t. This can be expressed through:

$$time\_flex(s_i, t) := \begin{cases} TRUE & iff\ "adaptation\ successful" \\ FALSE & otherwise \end{cases} \tag{20}$$

Remark

In the long term, multiagent systems must be able to perform necessary adaptations faster than changes occur to their environments.

3.4.6 Configuration Flexibility

According to the definitions in Section 3.3 a multiagent community *AgentCommunity* is given by:
- $A := \{a_1, a_2, ..., a_n\}$: set of agents, each able to sense, reason and act
- $C := \{c_{ij} \mid c_{ij} \to (a_i, a_j);\ 1 \leq i, j \leq n\}$: set of directed communication channels between pairs of agents a_i, a_j
- *AgentCommunity* $:= (A \times C)$
- Multiagent systems MAS_i are defined as subsets of *AgentCommunity*: $MAS_i \subseteq A \times C$

Configuration flexibility is a mapping from the current structure of a MAS to a new structure. For our model of multiagent systems, this is denoted by the following definition:

$$ConfigFlex: A_{curr} \times CC_{curr} \rightarrow A_{adapted} \times CC_{adapted} \qquad (21)$$

Let $\underline{A}$ be the set of agents which has been removed together with the set of agents which have been added and let $\underline{C}$ be the set of directed communication channels which has been removed together with the set of communication channels which have been added. Then we write:

$$config\_flex(MAS_i) := A \times C \qquad (22)$$

Iff $config\_flex(MAS_i) = \varnothing$ then MAS_i is called static flexible.

Remark

Section 3.3 provided a generic definition of multiagent systems. This abstracts from many conceptual and technical details (e.g., agent platform, common agent language, ontologies, coordination and cooperation protocols, directory services, etc.) needed to develop a concrete multiagent system. In a concrete, case, thus, the above definition must be extended to the conceptual model of the multiagent system(s) under development.

3.5 Applications and Further Research

The conceptual specification of multiagent system flexibility developed above can be used in many ways.

First, our flexibility framework provides software engineers with a new requirements engineering perspective, which, in turn, leads to a better understanding and much easier use of the advantages of multiagent technology. Thus, if software engineers are faced with high flexibility demands they can now (and have to) decide whether multiagent technology may be a relevant candidate for system development (or migration). This facilitates multiagent technology-driven innovations of enterprise software architectures, for making multiagent technology a tool for lots of software engineers, and for further innovations of the software engineering process as such.

After deciding to apply multiagent technology, this framework can further be used for what we call "flexibility engineering": the systematic design and implementation of adaptation strategies. The design process follows the definitions introduced above, and will further be driven by the specification of the concrete multiagent system architecture, including agent languages, coordination and cooperation protocols, etc.

Next, the framework may serve for testing. These are important tasks as multiagent systems control their external behaviors through bottom up strategies, without low or even any centralized control. In that perspective, the framework can also serve to restrict flexibility. This provides an interesting new approach for the control of emergent behaviors (which may not always be fully accepted in enterprise applications).

Finally, the framework can also be used to evaluate existing multiagent systems wrt their flexibility characteristics.

3.6 Summary

Flexibility is the most important characteristic of multiagent technology. We lack however substantial research in (MAS) flexibility engineering. This chapter aims to provide first theoretical foundations for such work.

To that purpose we compared flexibility definitions in four selected fields. From the results we learned that a production theory perspective together with its elaborated flexibility concepts can provide a valuable basis for our own theoretical work (e.g., [Adam1993]) on multiagent flexibility.

On this basis, Sections 3.3 and 3.4 developed and formalized a flexibility framework for multiagent systems which, of course, can also be applied to all other types of conventionally designed software systems.

Finally, Section 3.5 introduced some applications from the multiagent engineering perspective, arguing, that this framework may even establish a new field of research: the field of software flexibility engineering.

References

[Adam1993]   Adam, D.: Flexible Fertigungssysteme (FFS) im Spannungsfeld zwischen Rationalisierung, Flexibilisierung und veränderten Fertigungsstrukturen. In: Adam, D. (Hrsg.): Flexible Fertigungssysteme, Schriften zur Unternehmensführung. Gabler Verlag Wiesbaden 1993, pp. 5-28.

[Balz2001]   Balzert, H.: Lehrbuch der Software-Technik: Software-Entwicklung. Spektrum Akademischer Verlag, Heidelberg, Berlin, Band 1, 2.Auflage, 2000.

[BaSt1995]   Bateman, N.; Stockton, D.: Measuring the Production Range Flexibility of a FMS. In: Integrated Manufacturing Systems, 6 (1995) 2, pp. 27-34.

[BoGa1998]   Bond A.; Gasser, L. (eds.): Readings in Distributed Artificial intelligence. Morgan Kaufmann, California, 1998.

[Brow1984]   Browne, J.; Dubois, D.; Rathmill, K.; Sethi, S. P.; Stecke, K. E.: Classification of flexible Manufacturing Systems. In: The FMS Magazine (1984), pp. 114-117.

[BuAW00]   Burkhard, H.-D.; Andre, E.; Wachsmuth, I.: Softwareagenten. Unveröffentlichter Arbeitsbericht, Humboldt-Universität Berlin, 2000.

[Call1996]   Callon, Jack D.: Competitive advantage through information technology. Montreal, McGraw-Hill, 1996.

[ChKi1998]   Choi, S.-H.; Kim, J.-S.: A Study on the Measurement of Comprehensive Flexibility in Manufacturing Systems. In: Computers and Engineering, 34 (1998) 1, pp. 103-118.

[Dank1995]   Dankert, U.: Planung des Designs flexibler Fertigungssysteme. Betriebswirtschaftliche Forschung zur Unternehmensführung, Wiesbaden 1995.

[Dunc1995]   Duncan, N. B.: Capturing Flexibility of Information Technology Infrastructure: A study of Resource Characteristics and their Measure. In: Journal of Management Information Systems, 12 (1995) 2, pp. 37-57.

[HiFU1994]   Hill, W.; Fehlbaum, R.; Ulrich, P.: Organisationslehre 1 – Ziele, Instrumente und Bedingungen der Organisation sozialer Systeme. Verlag Paul Haupt Bern, 5.Auflage 1994.

[HyAh1992]   Hyun, J. H.; Ahn, B. H.: A Unifying Framework for Manufacturing Flexibility. In: Manufacturing Review, 5 (1992) 4, pp. 251-260.

[Jaco1974]   Jacob, H.: Unsicherheit und Flexibilität – Zur Theorie der Planung bei Unsicherheit. In: Zeitschrift für Betriebswirtschaft, 44 (1974) 5, pp. 299-326.

[Kalu1993]   Kaluza, B.: Betriebliche Flexibilität. In: Wittmann, W.; Kern, W; Köhler, R.; Küpper, H.-U.; v. Wysocki, K. (Hrsg.): Handwörterbuch der Betriebswirtschaft. Stuttgart 1993, pp. 1174-1184.

[Kies1969]   Kieser, A.: Zur Flexibilität verschiedener Organisationsstrukturen. In: Zeitschrift für Organisation (1969) 7, pp. 273-282.

[KiGa1998]   Kirn, St.; Gasser, L.: Organizational Approaches to Coordination in Multiagent Systems. Themenheft „Intelligente Agenten" der Zeitschrift it + ti, Heft 4, 1998, pp. 23-29.

[KiKU1992]   Kieser, A.; Kubicek, H.: Organisation. Walter de Gruyter Berlin, 3. völlig neubearbeitete Auflage 1992.

[KiMu1998]   Kirn, St.; Müller, H. J.: Artificial Agents in Human Organizations – Impact and Consequences. TU Ilmenau, Wirtschaftsinformatik 2, Arbeitsbericht Nr. 11, November 1998.

[Kirn2002]   Kirn, St.: Kooperierende intelligente Softwareagenten. Wirtschaftsinformatik, 44. Jahrgang, Heft 1, Februar 2002, pp. 53-63.

[Knop1992]   Knof, H.-L.: CIM und organisatorische Flexibilität. München 1992.

[KüSc1990]   Kühn, M.; Schneeweiß, C.: Zur Definition und gegenseitigen Abgrenzung der Begriffe Flexibilität, Elastizität und Robustheit. In: Schmalenbachs Zeitschrift für betriebswirtschaftliche Forschung (1990) 5, pp. 378-395.

[MaBr1989]   Mandelbaum, M.; Brill, P. H.: Examples of Measurement of Flexibility and Adaptivity in Manufacturing Systems. In: Journal of the Operational Research Society, 40 (1989) 6, pp. 603-609.

[Meff1985]   Meffert, H.: Größere Flexibilität als Unternehmenskonzept. In: Schmalenbachs Zeitschrift für betriebswirtschaftliche Forschung, 37 (1985) 2, pp. 121-137.

[MoSh1998]   Moodie, C. L.; Shewchuk, J. P.: Definition and Classification of Manufacturing Flexibility Types and Measures. In: The International Journal of Flexible Manufacturing Systems, 10 (1998) 4, pp. 325-349.

[Schl1996]   Schlüchtermann, J.: Planung in zeitlich offenen Entscheidungsfeldern. Neue betriebswirtschaftliche Forschung, Wiesbaden 1996.

[Schn1989]   Schneeweiß, C.: Der Zeitaspekt in der Planung. In: Hax, H.: Kern, W.; Schröder, H.-H. (Hrsg.): Zeitaspekte in betriebswirtschaftlicher Theorie und Planung, Stuttgart 1989, pp. 3-19.

[StRa1995]   Stecke, K. E.; Raman, N.: FMS Planing Decisions, Operations Flexibilities, and System Performance. In: IEEE Transactions on Engineering Management, 42 (1995) 1, pp. 82-90.

[Sund1994]   Sundermeyer, K.: Verteilte Künstliche Intelligenz. Künstliche Intelligenz Frühjahrsschule (KIFS-1994), Tutorial-Unterlagen, Berlin 1994.

[Weis1995]   Weiß, G.: Adaptation and Learning in Multiagent Systems: Some Remarks and a Bibliography. Adaption and Learning in Multiagent Systems 1995. pp. 1-21.

[WoJe1995]   Wooldridge, M. J.; Jennings, N. R.: Agent Theories, Architectures, and Languages: A Survey. In Wooldridge, M.J.; Jennings, N. R. (eds.): Intelligent Agents. Proceedings of the ECAI Workshop on Agent Theories, Architectures, and Languages. Amsterdam, August 1994. LNAI No. 890, Springer, Berlin 1995, pp. 1-39.

[Zapf2003]   Zapf, M.: Flexible Kundeninteraktionsprozesse im Communication Center. In: Gaul, W.; Heinzl, A.; Schader, M. (Hrsg.). Informationstechnologie und Ökonomie. Europäischer Verlag der Wissenschaften, Frankfurt (Main).

Part II

Application Examples I: Agent.Enterprise

1 Agent.Enterprise in a Nutshell

Peer-Oliver Woelk, Holger Rudzio

Universität Hannover, Institut für Fertigungstechnik und Werkzeugmaschinen
{woelk I rudzio}@ifw.uni-hannover.de

Roland Zimmermann

Universität Erlangen-Nürnberg, Lehrstuhl Wirtschaftsinformatik II
roland.zimmermann@wiso.uni-erlangen.de

Jens Nimis

Universität Karlsruhe (TH), Institut für Programmstrukturen und
Datenorganisation, nimis@ipd.uni-karlsruhe.de

Abstract. The manufacturing logistics domain is continually evolving towards ever more complex supply chain structures which call for increasingly flexible production capabilities. A concept is proposed which leverages agent technology's capabilities to provide flexibility in such a complex environment while at the same time it does not interfere with the manifold interdependencies and individual behaviors of actors in modern enterprise networks. The Agent.Enterprise concept is demonstrated in a prototype implementation which integrates various multiagent systems (MAS) into a multi-multiagent system (MMAS). It provides integrated yet distributed and flexible supply chain management, from inter-organizational coordination down to detailed shop-floor level production planning.

1.1 Introduction

Within the last years, technology for intelligent agents has been increasingly regarded as a promising approach to solve complex problems in real world business applications. Numerous publications including several books document this development. However, many of them primarily focus on technical aspects of agent technology and multiagent systems (e.g. software engineering and design issues) (e.g. [GiMO2003] [OdGM2004]). Other publications concentrate on applications of agent technology in very specialized domains, e.g. development of scheduling systems [BuJW 2004]. Hence, for the majority of large and complex problems in business environments agent technology seems to be a "promising approach" which has not yet proven its applicability as a widely accepted technology in industry.

The priority research program "Intelligent Agents in Real-World Business Applications" of the Deutsche Forschungsgemeinschaft aims at bridging the gap between current research trends in agent technology and their application to real-world problems. Doing so, multiple interdisciplinary research projects focus on two application domains: manufacturing logistics and healthcare management. Within this section we focus on the manufacturing logistics domain which is addressed in five projects which cover various aspects of the domain. While this chapter provides an overview of the application domain as a whole, specific application scenarios and business cases as well as related results are discussed in subsequent chapters.

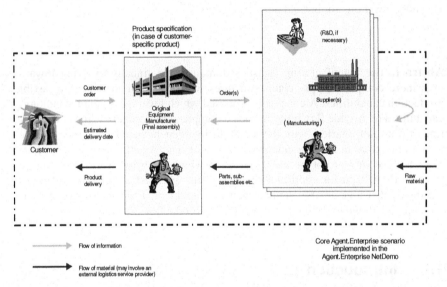

Figure 1. Scope of the Agent.Enterprise scenario

One of the main challenges for the priority research program is to identify and successfully implement real-world applications, in which agent technology provides benefits not yielded by conventional approaches. One benefit is for instance additional flexibility of processes which adapt quickly to changing customer demand. However, this has effects both on the internal and external processes of enterprises: Value chains are not restricted to internal processes but cover multiple enterprises in complex supply networks. Besides processes, which might be supported by agent technology, organizational structures and even organizational cultures are affected by the introduction of agent-based solutions.

The different aspects addressed in the research projects are integrated in one large application scenario termed *Agent.Enterprise*. It integrates inter-organizational supply chain solutions with intra-organizational manufacturing planning applications in one supply chain management control loop. An overview of the scenario domain is depicted in Figure 1: Multiple manufacturing facilities act together in a supply chain to provide goods to final customers. Besides information processes for communicating demand and fulfillment information, the physical processes of material transformation are considered in the scenario, too.

Based on this scenario a testbed for agent-based applications in the manufacturing logistics domain was designed and implemented conjointly by the research projects. It is termed *Agent.Enterprise NetDemo* and demonstrates the advantages of loosely coupling multiple agent-based solutions for supply chain management purposes as opposed to centralized traditional IT-system architectures (for details cf. II.1.4.3).

1.2   Challenges in the Application Domain

As addressed in the introduction of I.1, companies face a global market characterized by numerous competitors, a steadily increasing complexity of products, manufacturing technology, and business processes as well as a highly turbulent production environment. The business processes have to be highly efficient, need to provide flexibility, and are required to react to short-term changes of customer demand as well as unforeseen events during fulfillment. Furthermore, traditional long-lasting customer-supplier relationships are superseded by new business models, e.g. *Virtual Enterprises* and increased recognition of inter-enterprise supply chains [CaAF2003]. Such *systems* consist of networks formed by co-operating partners that are covering various companies (*Original Equipment Manufacturers (OEM)*, suppliers, sub-suppliers, etc.). The global optimization of corresponding business processes offers a vast potential for improvement of process flexibility and reduction of process costs. At the same time, various new problems arise: For instance, fluctuating demands multiply and create the so-called bullwhip effect. In addition, the global planning process is hindered by the fact that companies may not be willing to reveal their production data to potential competitors unless they are forced to do so by powerful OEMs (as it is common in the automotive industry).

Furthermore, the task of planning, operating, and monitoring of supply chains is getting more complex with an increasing number of participating enterprises, since heterogeneity and autonomy of partners, uncertainty of events, as well as an increased amount of necessary interaction have to be considered. Thus, negative consequences multiply (e.g. delays in suppliers' processes) due to latency of reaction to unforeseen events in supply chains. Planning reliability is decreased and it is increasingly difficult for enterprises to achieve cost-efficient production processes and thus, to maintain their profitability.

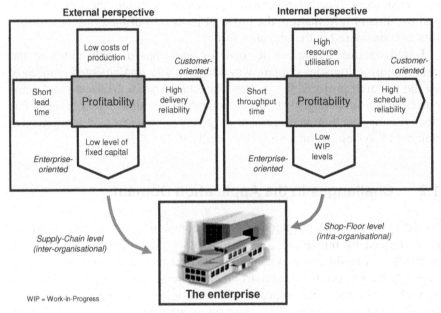

Figure 2. Key logistic performance indicators in the manufacturing logistics domain according to [WiCi2002]

Performance of supply chain processes is typically measured with respect to key performance indicators. Figure 2 illustrates typical key performance indicators of the manufacturing logistics domain as well as their desired states. For instance, *schedule reliability* on the shop-floor should be high to assure that orders are finished at their planned due date. This results in a high delivery reliability within a supply chain from an inter-organizational (external) perspective. Unfortunately, some of the desired states complement one another while other desired states are contradictory. For example, one desired state from an enterprise's internal (mostly technical) perspective is a low level of work-in-progress (WIP) and thus, a low level of fixed capital in a supply chain (external, mostly economic perspective). Low WIP level means short queues of orders waiting in front of each resource on the shop-floor. Since the ratio of queue time compared to the (fixed) processing time is decreasing, the overall throughput time of an order is comparatively short. On the other hand, short queues mean that queues may run out of waiting orders in some situations. Consequently, resources may become idle and resource utilization is reduced. Hence, the desired system states "low WIP level" and "high resource utilization" represent conflicting goals. These examples illustrate the complexity of planning tasks in the manufacturing logistics domain.

Further complexity in the management of a supply chain results from disruptive events which require fast reactions. However, inter-organizational order monitoring and so called *Supply Chain Event Management (SCEM)* are non-trivial issues as is shown in II.5 while the effects on process performance are significant.

1.3   Suitability of Agents in the Manufacturing Logistics Domain

Although agent technology is inherently suited to solve problems where conflicting goals (e.g. in production planning) have to be achieved (e.g. through negotiation), this feature alone does not justify its use: Other mechanisms such as optimization algorithms can also consider different constraints of a problem. In fact, further characteristics of a problem domain need to be considered before opting for an agent-based solution. Russel and Norvig provide a set of properties to describe domains and determine their suitability for intelligent software agent support [RuNo2003]. These properties characterize the task environment and are applicable to the manufacturing logistics domain as detailed below.

Each property provides one dimension of a graph (a hexagon) to characterize a typical task or problem in the manufacturing logistics domain (see Figure 3). The larger the resulting hexagon, the better suited is agent technology to the problem at hand and vice versa. The properties as applied to the manufacturing logistics domain are:

- *Observability*: If an environment is fully observable by an actor, the actor has access to all important information generated within the environment. In contrast, partially observable environments are common to multi-actor scenarios, since e.g. internal strategies of actors are regularly not accessible to other actors. In the past, enterprises mostly focused on in-house development and production with the consequence of *full observability* of these processes. Today, production is streamlined and focused on core competencies. Tasks such as design and production of subsystems and components (e.g. a brake system of a car) are completely outsourced to suppliers. Thus, an enterprise often has only limited visibility into processes of its suppliers although it is highly dependent upon them. Consequently, *observability* decreases significantly ("*partly*").

- *Predictability*: Assuming that the influence of an actor's behavior on the state of an environment is predictable, the environment is characterized as *deterministic*, else as *stochastic*. Due to the trend towards ever more complex global supply networks and customer-supplier relationships, demand as well as effects of disruptive events in manufacturing processes are increasingly hard to predict. Typical effects are the bullwhip effect or ripple effects of disruptive events in supply chains. Thus, business environments tend to be more stochastic than in the past.
- *Sustainability*: Actions of an actor which are independent from previous actions are termed *episodic* while actions that depend upon previous actions are characterized as *sequential*. Environments where *sequential* actions prevail demand tracing of effects of previous actions. Today, this is increasingly important in *Customer Relationship Management (CRM)* since long term development of individual relationships with customers is a primary goal. Strategic decisions such as the design of new products suited for customization are also affected by sequential behavior of customers.
- *Reliability*: A stable environment which does not change until a specific action of an actor takes effect is *static* otherwise *dynamic*. For instance, on a shop-floor, a machine failure prevents execution of the original production plan. Assuming that a new process plan is to be generated although it takes a few hours, the shop-floor situation may not be the same once the new plan is executed, because human actors have worked according to their individual plans in the meantime. *Dynamic* environments are common to many industries which face global competition, short product life cycles and fluctuating demand.
- *Continuity*: Describes, how time is handled in the environment: If each action is clearly associated to a specific time slot, the environment is *discrete*. Most environments tend to be *continuous* from the point of view of an observer since events occur at random points in time and may occur in parallel.
- *Interaction Density*: The number of communication channels required to solve a problem is determined by the number of actions and the intensity of interactions among them to find a solution (e.g. a production plan). Within a (theoretical) "single-actor" environment, an actor does not depend on communication with other actors. However, real business environments are "multi-actor" environments both on an enterprise level (departments, multiple machines and workers etc.) and on a supply

chain level (at least one customer, in most cases lots of partners in a supply chain).

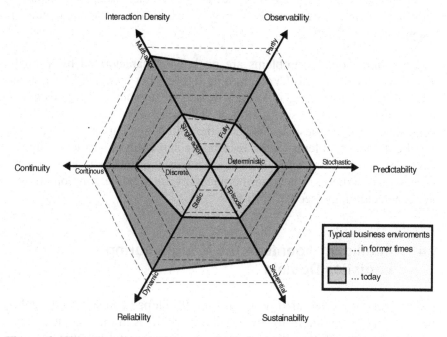

Figure 3. Changing task environments in the manufacturing application domain, criteria according to [RuNo03, pp. 41-44].

In the past, many of the influencing factors were rated as less critical. For instance, typical manufacturing processes provided better observability (in-house processes), higher predictability (smaller markets) and less sustainability (less intense customer relationships) (see Figure 3). Hence, IT-systems developed in the last decades were focused on solving problems with these characteristics while they are not suited to succeed in today's manufacturing logistics domain. The changed task environment in the manufacturing logistics domain requires different aspects of flexibility as introduced in I.3. Some examples are:

- A decrease of *predictability* of demand requires an increase in *quantitative flexibility* to adapt the output of a production or supply chain system to the changing demand.
- *Sustainability* which is ever more *sequential* (e.g. due to CRM activities) requires an increase in *I/O flexibility* to provide for instance customized products while maintaining a constant mix of input factors.

- *Dynamic* environments with a low reliability call for *process flexibility* to adapt e.g. production processes without changing the type of output. Furthermore, *defect flexibility* needs to be increased, for instance through event management techniques which handle disruptive events in a process.

Concluding, today's problems are no longer characterized by a small area around the origin of the diagram in Figure 3 but by much larger areas which requires an increase in various aspects of flexibility. Agent technology promises to provide such flexibility increases while existing technologies cannot provide these as easily. In the following chapters examples of specific domain problems within enterprises and within multi-level supply chains of the manufacturing logistics domain are analyzed according to these six properties to illustrate the necessity for flexible solutions based on agent technology (see II.2 to II.5).

1.4   Intelligent Agents in the Manufacturing Logistics Domain

The projects of the research program have developed concepts and implemented prototype systems to solve specific problems in the manufacturing logistics domain: Within these projects, evaluations and benchmark tests with typical scenarios were conducted in order to substantiate hypotheses and to compare behavior and results of MAS with traditional, mostly centralized solutions. Furthermore, the *Agent.Enterprise NetDemo* demonstrator was implemented conjointly as a proof-of-concept for an agent-based supply chain planning and monitoring system. With respect to the topics of scheduling and monitoring existing agent-based concepts and solutions are analyzed:

Scheduling

Problems of resource allocation in various industrial domains are one main focus area for agent applications. For instance, at DaimlerChrysler agents negotiate in order to control a manufacturing process in cylinder production [BuSc2000]. In the transportation domain, allocation of trucks to transportation routes and tours is optimized by negotiating agents in a solution provided by Whitestein Technologies [DoCa2005]. Distributed coordination of resource allocation in supply chain processes is considered in many research projects. For an overview see e.g. [WaGP2002]. Often, a wide range of different types of software agents is proposed for covering planning and execution of actions (e.g. [FoBT2000]).

Monitoring

Some providers of SCEM systems claim to use agent technology for providing flexibility within their solutions [PSIL2005]. This is an indicator for the suitability of agent technology to information logistics tasks in supply chains. Active research is conducted on information gathering agents although these are generally concerned with searching for information in Internet resources especially to prepare a transaction (e.g. comparing and combining offers) [Wag+2001] [ChLL2000]. A series of workshops on *Cooperative Information Agents (CIA)* is regularly organized since 1997 by Klusch [Klus2005]. Latest results have focused on aspects of information gathering based on the semantic web, interactive and mobile agents, agents in peer-to-peer computing, and recommender agent systems. However, agent-based monitoring in supply chains is seldom directly addressed by current research except by the project presented in II.5.

1.4.1 Agents for Particular Tasks in the Manufacturing Domain

The research projects which are involved in the *Agent.Enterprise* activities address the outlined problems. They offer services ranging from supply chain management and scheduling over shop-floor production planning and control to proactive monitoring services which guarantee reliability of supply chain processes in case of unforeseen disruptions. Table 1 gives an overview of the various MAS functionalities.

The DISPOWEB system presents a decentralized negotiation protocol for cooperative economic scheduling in a supply chain environment. These protocols are evaluated using software agents that maximize their profits by optimizing their local schedule and offer side payments to compensate other agents for lost profit or extra expense if cumulative profit is achievable. To further increase their income the agents have to apply a randomized local search heuristic to prevent the negotiation from stopping in locally optimal contracts. The developed search mechanism assures truthful revelation of the individual opportunity cost situation as the basis for the calculation of side payments and to protect the agents against systematic exploitation.

The IntaPS approach described in II.2 proposes a system architecture based on the application of cooperative agents for optimizing information logistics for process planning and production control. Evaluation and benchmarking of this approach shows its ability to consider the early stages of process planning. That means capacity information and due dates will be taken into account. Furthermore, process planning knowledge will be used for short term scheduling decisions at the shop-floor. Consequently, problems will be eliminated which result from delayed return of manufacturing knowledge and capacity data or other problems in information flows, e.g. due to the use of static process plans.

Table 1. Overview of involved projects and MAS functionalities

Project	Main MAS Functionality
DISPOWEB [DISP2005]	Negotiations among enterprises on supply chain level
IntaPS [Inta2005]	Integrated process planning and scheduling (with focus on discrete manufacturing)
KRASH/ControMAS[1] [KRAS2005]	Production planning and controlling (with focus on assembling industries)
FABMAS [FABM2005]	Production planning and controlling (with focus on batch production)
ATT/A4[2] [ATT2005]	Monitoring of orders including suborders in supply chains

MAS-based decentralized planning approaches produce better planning results than centralized job-shop algorithms. This is especially significant, if the decision space for a MSP problem is both complex and heterogeneous as it is in unit assembly environments. In these environments MAS provide good results in the decision space by taking time-dependent planning parameters into account. This is shown by the KRASH/ControMAS approach (see II.3). Additionally, in case of disruptive events waiting queues of production lines are handled more efficiently with MAS.

A third MAS for production planning with a focus on batch production is presented in II.4. However, it is currently not integrated in the *Agent.Enterprise NetDemo* demonstrator[3].

For agent-based monitoring and *Supply Chain Event Management (SCEM)* in multi-level supply chains (ATT) it is shown that this concept provides significant reductions of follow-up costs of disruptive events (see II.5). Currently available client-server-based SCEM systems generally do

---

[1] ControMAS is successor of the KRASH project.
[2] A4 is successor of the ATT project.
[3] Since FABMAS is not part of the *Agent.Enterprise NetDemo* demonstrator, specific aspects of batch production are not considered in the current *Agent.Enterprise* scenario.

not provide the necessary communicative abilities to realize inter-organizational monitoring and waste efforts on orders that do not encounter problems, thereby reducing efficiency of the SCEM systems. Experiments with a generic prototype and results from an industrial showcase substantiate these findings. For instance, within a showcase, potential cost reductions add up to nearly 100,000 Euros per quarter for a single logistics service provider (see II.5).

Detailed information concerning special challenges, which are addressed by the individual projects, their approach and the benefits achieved by the implemented MAS can be found in subsequent chapters. Nevertheless, some basic features of each system are illustrated in the context of the *Agent.Enterprise* scenario.

1.4.2 The Agent.Enterprise Scenario

All individual MAS solutions are integrated in the *Agent.Enterprise* scenario. The scenario comprises a simplified supply chain of a manufacturer of agricultural equipment (tractors etc.). Although the supply chain has limited complexity and the products represent models of tractors, trailers, etc., all criteria for an application to a real supply chain are fulfilled: For instance, the product structure of the tractor models is stored in a product database for product data management (PDM). Bills of material (BOM) for all products, process plans with estimated process times, and costs for manufacturing of some parts are available. Other parts are marked as supplied parts including a reference to the supplier(s). A typical supply chain management cycle of distributed supply chain activities for the scenario is shown in Figure 4.

The initial distributed supply chain planning (SCP) is performed by agents of the DISPOWEB system. After generating an initial plan of orders and suborders concerning prices and dates of delivery, software agents located at the different supply chain partners (shaded triangles) negotiate: They minimize costs and consider due dates of deliveries (①). These optimized delivery plans are used on the intra-organizational level within each enterprise to plan the production of goods on each stage of the supply chain in detail. The different intra-organizational MAS (e.g. IntaPS, ControMAS) are concerned with varying aspects of production planning (②). They require input from DISPOWEB agents and generate detailed plans for their production facilities in order to initiate their own "Plan-Execute-Control" cycle on the shop-floor level. These plans are the initial input for a controlling system on supply chain level (ATT).

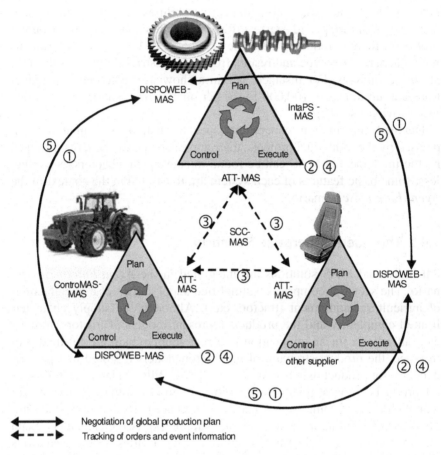

◆━━━━━━▶ Negotiation of global production plan
◆ - - - ▶ Tracking of orders and event information

Figure 4. MAS interaction within the Agent.Enterprise scenario

This MAS monitors orders on every stage of the supply chain using a distributed architecture in order to proactively detect events which endanger the planned fulfillment. In case of such an event (e.g. a disruption in a production cycle) the ATT system initiates communication with related partner enterprises and informs them of the event (③). This information can be used to trigger rescheduling of plans on an enterprise level (④) or, in case of major events, it results in renegotiation of the contracts on the inter-enterprise level of the DISPOWEB system (⑤). An overview of activities and corresponding actors in the supply chain is given in Table 2.

Table 2. Activities and actors in the Agent.Enterprise scenario

Step	Activity (Actor)
①	Negotiate initial plan of production among supply chain partners (DISPOWEB).
②	Operational assembly planning (KRASH/ControMAS). Production planning for mechanical parts (IntaPS).
③	Monitoring of orders and related suborders (ATT). Trigger internal planning systems in case of minor critical events (ATT). Next → ④ Trigger replanning by DISPOWEB agents in case of a severe critical event (ATT). Next → ⑤
④	Internal rescheduling in reaction to a critical event (KRASH, IntaPS). Next → ③
⑤	Renegotiate plan of production between supply chain partners due to severe critical event (DISPOWEB). Next → ②

1.4.3 Fundamentals of Agent.Enterprise Testbed Implementation

Since all MAS in *Agent.Enterprise* are evaluated individually with respect to their specific research problems and benchmarks, an evaluation of the *Agent.Enterprise* approach as a whole focuses on the technological integration of the various MAS. For this purpose, the *Agent.Enterprise Net-Demo* has been developed. It provides an open testbed for agent technology in the manufacturing logistics domain designed to be applied to complex manufacturing supply chains. Objective of the testbed is to prove the feasibility of managing supply chains cooperatively by multiple heterogeneous MAS and enabling comparative experiments with different research approaches in the context of the *Agent.Enterprise* scenario.

Therefore, the testbed features a bottom-up approach of loosely coupled MAS forming a supply chain according to the *Agent.Enterprise* scenario. This results in a so-called *multi-multiagent system* (MMAS). The MMAS incorporates three types of MAS as defined by the scenario: one for supply-chain-wide planning of orders (SCP role by DIPSOWEB), one specialized on intra-organizational production planning and scheduling (supplier-role by IntaPS and ControMAS), and one for supply chain monitoring (SCT role by ATT). Each enterprise (shaded triangles in Figure 4) in the supply chain is represented by three agents within the MMAS:

- one SCP-agent for supply chain (re-)planning of orders,

- one gateway agent for each enterprise which provides access to an enterprise's SCT-MAS for monitoring released orders and
- another gateway agent per enterprise as the link to the internal production planning MAS (supplier-role) of the different enterprises in the Agent.Enterprise supply chain (see Figure 5).

Gateway agents perform all necessary actions such as translating messages from the *Agent.Enterprise* format to the MAS-specific format and vice versa. For this purpose, a MAS-independent ontology (*Agent.Enterprise Interface Ontology*) has been designed. The mapping between the *Agent.Enterprise Interface Ontology* and the MAS-specific ontologies is realized by the gateway agent: In addition, interaction among gateway agents of different participating MAS is performed according to the *Agent.Enterprise Communication Protocol*, which consists of a number of nested FIPA-compliant agent communication protocols [SNSS2004]. FIPA-compliant ACL messages, which are sent from one participating MAS to another, are transmitted using a Hypertext Transfer Protocol (HTTP)-based message transport protocol. Thus, these messages can easily be transmitted via the Internet in a distributed environment.

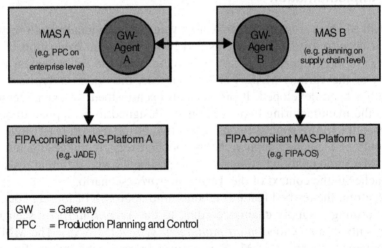

Figure 5. The Agent.Enterprise gateway agent concept

An important aspect of the testbed is loose coupling of the MAS: Due to the gateway agent concept, each participating MAS is executed without modification to its internal planning and coordination algorithms and data structures. The gateway agent concept also provides a fair degree of flexibility to the testbed. Currently, internal production planning is performed by the aforementioned MAS – developed within the different research projects of the research program – which assume the supplier roles. It would also be possible to develop gateway agents which implement a wrapper layer for conventional (non-agent-based) planning systems and link them to the *Agent.Enterprise* supply chain. This would allow experiments to compare conventional with agent-based coordination and planning approaches.

1.5   The Agent.Enterprise NetDemo's Portal and Benefits

To provide a wider audience with the opportunity to gather hands-on experience with agent technology applied to the manufacturing logistics domain, the testbed is accessible via the *Agent.Enterprise NetDemo* portal-website [NetD2006]. The portal visualizes interactions within the MMAS, provides the opportunity to initiate new experiments (e.g. placement of new orders) and allows to reset the simulation.

The welcome screen of the *Agent.Enterprise NetDemo* portal presents an overview of the participating MAS and offers links to examine them in detail (see Figure 6). Therefore, each participating MAS is visualized separately while it is situated in the context of the entire supply chain. In addition, the portal features a documentation of the *Agent.Enterprise* Communication Protocol as Agent-based Unified Modeling Language (AUML) diagrams as well as the *Agent.Enterprise* Interface Ontology (for download as Protégé file).

To our knowledge, the *Agent.Enterprise NetDemo* is currently unique – or at least exceptional – in two points: First, the MMAS underlines the feasibility of managing realistic complex supply chains with loosely coupled heterogeneous MAS. Its integration capabilities indicate the potential to exploit benefits of specialized agent-based solutions in larger contexts. Second, the portal is unique in that it provides a publicly available opportunity to user-driven experiments on agent technology in realistic commercial application scenarios.

Furthermore, the development of the testbed has also brought about important technological advancement, e.g. in the areas of MAS integration and agent-oriented software development methods. Some of the insights have already been published ([SNSS2004] [NiSt2004]) and/or influenced Part IV of this book.

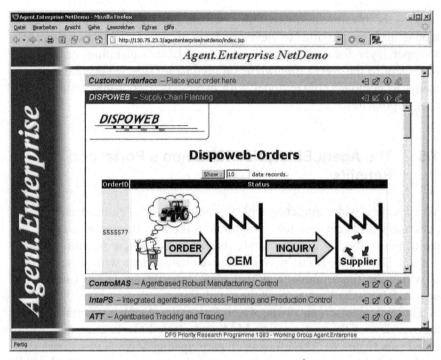

Figure 6. The Agent.Enterprise NetDemo portal-website[4]

1.6   Conclusion and Outlook

This chapter presented the *Agent.Enterprise* approach. It is based on two foundations: First, the application of cooperative software agents for optimizing scheduling in the field of concurrent process planning and production control. Second, a closed-loop control cycle in supply chains is realized by providing distributed monitoring and event management capabilities with dedicated MAS. Doing so, the challenges of today's manufacturing logistics environment are met by an integrated yet flexible and distributed concept of loosely coupled MAS. The *Agent.Enterprise NetDemo* demonstrator illustrates this ability as a proof-of-concept: Based on a prototypical implementation and a realistic application scenario, the presented research work confirms the ability of agent technology to solve real-world planning and control problems in supply chains.

---

[4] Here: detailed view of DIPSOWEB's SCP-MAS that currently builds an initial schedule for the production of a tractor ordered by a customer.

Detailed analysis of benefits to be achieved in the various specific problem domains is conducted in subsequent chapters. At this point, it is concluded that benefits of integrating all these MAS solutions will at least reach the level of cumulated individually realized benefits while overall supply chain flexibility is significantly increased with an MMAS approach. Hence, increasing requirements for flexibility in the manufacturing logistics domain, specifically regarding the dimensions defined in II.1.3, can be met with agent technology and realized with available software development resources. Based on these results we assume that agent technology today provides all means to provide additional flexibility to supply chain processes in the manufacturing logistics domain. Since single industrial-strength applications begin to emerge (see I.4) we predict that next-generation agent applications will provide industrial-strength solutions to various specific isolated problems. Although this isolation is required in the beginning to set up these systems, integration into MMAS is the logical next step since real-world supply chains are highly interdependent and complex. That complexity can be managed by MMAS is the main contribution and outcome of the *Agent.Enterprise* scenario and demonstrator.

References

[ATT2006]   Project Website "ATT" and "A4". http://www.wi2.uni-erlangen. de/index.php?id=253, accessed on 2006-01-31.

[BuSc2000]   Bussmann, S.; Schild, K.: Self-Organizing Manufacturing Control. In: Proceedings of the 4th International Conference on Multi-Agent Systems (ICMAS'2000). Boston, 2000, pp. 87-94.

[BuJW2004]   Bussmann, S.; Jennings, N. R.; Wooldridge, M.: Multiagent Systems for Manufacturing Control. Springer-Verlag, Berlin, 2004.

[CaAf2003]   Camarinha-Matos, L. M.; Afsarmanesh, H.: Elements of a Base VE Infrastructure. In: Journal on Computers in Industry 51(2003)2, pp. 139-163.

[ChLL2000]   Chun, I.; Lee, J.; Lee, E.: I-SEE: An Intelligent Search Agent for Electronic Commerce. In: International Journal of Electronic Commerce 4(Winter 1999-2000)2, pp. 83-98.

[DISP2006]   Project Website "DISPOWEB". http://dispoweb.wiwi.uni-frank furt.de/contact.php, accessed on 2006-01-31.

[DoCa2005]   Dorer, K.; Calisti, M.: An Adaptive Solution to Dynamic Transport Optimization. In: Proceedings of the Fourth International Joint Conference on Autonomous Agents and Multiagent Systems. ACM Press, New York, NY, 2005, pp. 45-51.

[FoBT2000]   Fox, M. S.; Barbuceanu, M.; Teigen, R.: Agent-Oriented Supply Chain Management. In: International Journal of Flexible Manufacturing Systems 12(2000)2/3, pp. 165-188.

[GiMO2003]   Giorgini, P.; Müller, J. P.; Odell, J. (Eds.): Agent-Oriented Software Engineering IV. 4th International Workshop, AOSE 2003, Melbourne, Australia. Springer (LNCS 2935), Berlin, 2003.

[Inta2006]   Project Website "IntaPS". http://intaps.org, accessed on 2006-01-31.

[Klus2005]   Klusch, M.: International Workshop Series CIA on Cooperative Information Agents. http://www.dfki.de/~klusch/IWS-CIAhome.html, accessed on 2005-02-15.

[KRAS2006]   Project Website "KRASH" and "ControMAS". http://www.ipd.uni-karlsruhe.de/KRASH, accessed on 2006-01-31.

[NetD2006]   Website "Agent.Enterprise NetDemo Portal". http://www.agententerprise.net, accessed on 2006-01-31.

[NiSt2004]   Nimis, J.; Stockheim, T.: The Agent.Enterprise Multi-Multi-agent System. In: Bichler, M.; Holtmann, C.; Kirn, S.; Müller, J. P.; Weinhardt, C. (Eds.): Coordination and Agent Technology in Value Networks. Proceedings of the Multi-Conference on Business Information Systems, ATeBA-Track (MKWI 2004). GITO Verlag, Berlin, Germany, 2004.

[OdGM2004]   Odell, J.; Giorgini, P.; Müller, J. P. (Eds.): Agent-Oriented Software Engineering V – 5th International Workshop AOSE 2004, New York. LNCS 3382, Springer, Berlin 2004.

[PSIL2005]   PSI Logistics: ABX LOGISTICS (Deutschland) GmbH. http://www.psilogistics.com/download/file/Referenzblatt_ABX_0507_en.pdf, accessed on 2005-10-21.

[RuNo2003]   Russel, S.; Norvig, P.: Artificial Intelligence – A Modern Approach. Prentice Hall, New Jersey, 2003.

[SNSS2004]   Stockheim, T.; Nimis, J.; Scholz, T.; Stehli, M.: How to Build Multi-Multi-Agent Systems. 6th International Conference on Enterprise Information Systems. Porto, 2004.

[Wag+2001]   Wagner, T.; Phelps, J.; Qian, Y.; Albert, E.; Beane, G.: A modified architecture for constructing real-time information gathering agents. In: Wagner, G.; Karlapalem, K.; Lesperance, Y.; Yu, E. (Eds.): Proceedings of the 3rd International Workshop on Agent Oriented Information Systems (AOIS). iCue Publishing, Berlin, 2001, pp. 121-135.

[WaGP2002]   Wagner, T.; Guralnik, V.; Phelps, J.: Software Agents: Enabling Dynamic Supply Chain Management for a Build to Order Product Line. In: Proceedings of International Conference on Internet Computing (IC2002). Las Vegas, 2002, pp. 689-696.

[WiCi2002]   Wiendahl, H.-P.; von Cieminski, G.: Logistic Manufacturing Cell Operating Curves – Modeling the Logistic Behavior of Cellular Manufacture. In: Production Engineering IX/2(2002), pp. 137-142.

2 Integrated Process Planning and Production Control

Leif-Erik Lorenzen, Peer-Oliver Woelk, Berend Denkena
Universität Hannover, Institut für Fertigungstechnik und Werkzeugmaschinen
{lorenzen I woelk I denkena}@ifw.uni-hannover.de

Thorsten Scholz, Ingo J. Timm, Otthein Herzog
Universität Bremen, Technologie-Zentrum Informatik
{scholz I i.timm I herzog}@tzi.de

Abstract. This chapter deals with the application of intelligent software agents to improve information logistics in the area of process planning and production control. Therefore, enterprises will be able to fulfill the requirement of flexible, reliable and fault-tolerant manufacturing. Fulfillment of these requirements is a prerequisite for successful participation in modern business alliances like supply chains, temporal logistics networks and virtual enterprises. Thus, agent-based improvements of information logistics enable enterprises to face the challenges of competition successfully. Conducted research activities focused on the development of agent-based systems for integrated process planning and production control. They led to the "IntaPS" approach which is presented in this chapter.

2.1 Introduction

Modern manufacturing is in need of flexible and adaptive concepts for process planning and scheduling to meet market requirements. However, today's industrial products are often characterized by a complex design, functionality, and necessary manufacturing and assembly processes. Computer systems for the support of process planning, production control, and scheduling tasks have to handle critical paths, bottlenecks, and risk of failures (e.g. machine breakdowns) within real-time. In this context, real-time means spontaneous reaction and re-planning in contrast to traditional re-planning where updated plans are computed e.g. in overnight batch-job runs of the planning system. Furthermore, with respect to manufacturing of complex and sophisticated products, the planning and scheduling tasks requires a high degree of knowledge about products and production processes. Therefore, computer-aided support for production planning and control systems is in need of formalized knowledge, which can be handled and processed adequately.

A promising approach to achieve the goal of flexible manufacturing is the application of intelligent agents. Since agents are able to collaborate and solve problems in a distributed manner, they are used for complex tasks, which can hardly be solved with a centralized approach and while exhibiting a natural distribution. In these domains agents can provide great benefit caused by the ability to react adequately to external influences (technical flexibility) and using the dynamic potential flexibility of a system (see I.3). In this context, the application of agent technology provides enterprises with opportunities to improve their competitiveness within the global economy. Especially small and medium-sized enterprises (SME) will benefit from this development, since many SME's focus on very specialized products in niche markets. These enterprises are affected by changing customer behavior in particular.

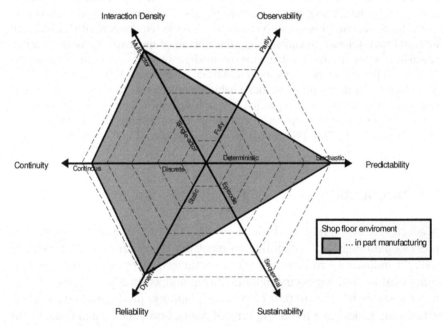

Figure 1. Properties of a shop floor manufacturing environment[1]

Furthermore, many SME's act as sub-contractors in supply chains instead of targeting the end-user market and face competition. Due to improved and reliable information logistics in the planning and execution of

---

[1] According to [RuNo2003].

manufacturing operations, these enterprises will meet this competition successfully (see II.1).

This chapter focuses on the development and application of agent-based systems for integrated process planning and production control in a shop floor environment. This meets to the IntaPS approach, which is presented in the following. According to Russell and Norvig [RuNo2003] and II.1.3 respectively Figure 1 points out properties of a shop floor manufacturing environment in the context of already described typical business environments.

A typical shop floor environment is characterized by a high amount of interaction density between all participants. Due to the fact that the shop floor environment is not fully observable and controlled by dynamic processes the predictability is basically influenced by stochastic events. Since most manufacturing processes depend on prior executed manufacturing steps the sustainability is very low. Manufacturing processes are continuous, which means that events may occur for a period of time without interruption and may also occur in parallel.

2.2 Conventional Approaches

With respect to the manufacturing domain, attention has to be drawn to process planning and production control. The traditional approach of separating planning activities (e.g. process planning) from executing activities (e.g. production control and scheduling) is characterized by definite borderlines [Ever2002, GaSl1999]. These borderlines result in a gap between involved systems, which implies a loss of time and information. This situation becomes obvious for instance in the strict spatial as well as temporal separation of process planning and production control. In most cases, static linear process plans are used for information exchange. Thus, the current situation in industrial applications is characterized by several problems. For example, information about the capacity and current load of resources as well as further economic aspects are not considered while conventional static process plans are generated. Resulting process plans are not flexible enough to be quickly adapted to unexpected situations at shop floor level (e.g. machine breakdowns, missing devices or broken tools etc.) [ToTe1998]. Thus, process plan modifications carried out on the shop floor level in case of unexpected events will lead to feasible, but not to optimal results. Furthermore, modifications carried out by centralized process planning groups are very time-consuming. This problem is intensified by the fact that complexity of new and innovative manufacturing processes as well as knowledge necessary for process planning increases. Due to well-trained workers, this knowledge is mostly available at shop floor level. Unfortunately, it often takes a long time until this knowledge is available at a centralized process planning group. Due to this lack of knowledge exchange, quality and reliability of planning results is reduced on a long-term basis [Deen2003]. Consequently, advantages of the application of innovative manufacturing technologies, which are often more suitable regarding economical as well as ecological aspects, remain unused.

These drawbacks become particularly obvious in decentralized jobshops with batch-job production. In this case, a lack of software support for process planning and scheduling activities in decentralized manufacturing can be spotted. In this context, a survey was carried out by IFW to determine the state of decentralization in industrial companies in Germany [Woel2003]. 75 companies from industries like mechanical engineering, automotive industry, and suppliers for automotive industry (enterprises with individual or batch-job production) answered a questionnaire concerning their efforts to decentralize managerial and manufacturing functions as well as their corresponding IT infrastructure. Approximately a quarter of them answered at each case: *(a)* "decentralization is no subject of interest", *(b)* "projects for decentralization are planned", *(c)* "projects are in progress", and *(d)* "projects had been carried out".

Most decentralization projects aim at reduction of lead time, higher flexibility, and robustness or cost reduction. Known obstacles are for example the lack of worker motivation to support decentralization measures and shortage of manpower for planning and executing decentralization projects. Despite these obstacles, most companies are satisfied with the results of decentralization: 37% stated that the goals of their projects are fulfilled. Only 3% acknowledged that they missed all of their goals. The measures taken by the companies deal for example with shifting tasks to the shop floor (e.g. scheduling tasks, detailed process planning tasks, and NC code generation), rearrangement of machines and resources at the shop floor, and the introduction of team production as well as further education of workers.

Another question referred to CAPP systems (computer aided process planning) used for computer aided process plan generation. Approximately 32% of the companies use the PP module of the SAP R/3 ERP system for process plan generation (see Figure 2; left). 21% use other commercial systems for this purpose. Another notable result is the fact that a quarter of all interviewed companies use proprietary software tools for process planning and 20% perform this task without computer support.

A similar situation characterizes the IT infrastructure for production control systems (see Figure 2; right). It is noteworthy that more than one-third of all interviewed companies use proprietary software (22%) or no software (17%) for this purpose.

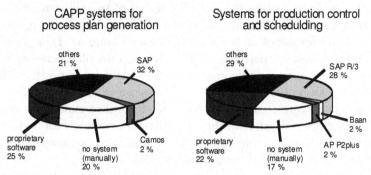

Figure 2. Survey on decentralization

These survey results emphasize the proposition of the lack of appropriate software tools to support necessary tasks like distributed process planning and production control. Thus, the assumption is affirmed that there is a strong need for new flexible information technologies and tools to support process planning and production control in a decentralized way as it is proposed in I.3.

2.3 Analysis and Model Building

The aim of integrating process planning and production control functionality to overcome the limitations discussed above is well known for several years. A very promising approach to improve information logistics in process planning and scheduling in batch job production is the use of multi-agent systems.

Not only with respect to the production engineering domain, the interests in agent technology and agent related topics have risen enormously in the last decade [JeWo1998]. Co-operative agents can act autonomously, communicate with other agents, are goal-oriented (pro-active), and use explicit, formalized knowledge [Weis1999]. Thus, the use of an agent-based approach with autonomously, co-operatively, and purposefully acting intelligent software units seems to be very promising to make possible short-term and flexible reaction in manufacturing.

Since numerous applications of software agents in the manufacturing domain focus on planning and scheduling tasks from a logistic point of view, the main topic of the research project IntaPS (Integrated process planning and production control) is set to the agent based integration of process planning and production control. The IntaPS approach is based on the application of co-operative agents and in-house electronic market-places. The basic architecture of IntaPS consists of two substantial components, which link information systems from earlier stages of product development and resources on the shop floor (see Figure 4). Today, centralized CAPP approaches perform all tasks for process plan generation at a single location (e.g. in a single instance of the CAPP program) [Ever2002]. In distributed system architectures these tasks are to be distributed among the involved software components. Since the benefit of multiagent systems results from emergent behavior through efficient communication, the strategy for system design should be not only to make the single agent as complex as necessary but also as simple as possible.

The following table lists typical activities which have to be carried out in process planning. The abbreviation behind each activity names the responsible entity:

Table 1. Responsibilities for process planning activities

Step	Activity	Responsibility
1	Determination/design of raw part	RLPP
2	Identification of machining tasks	RLPP
3	Divisions/sequencing of machining operations	(RLPP/)OA–RA
4	Selection of machine tool	OA-RA
5	Selection of cutting tools	RA
6	Selection of machining parameters	RA
7	Estimation of time and cost	RA
8	Generation of NC code	*
9	Documentation of process plan	OA-RA/SA

RLPP stands for 'Rough-level Process Planning' carried out by the centralized component. The sequence of machining operations and selection of machine tools are results of negotiations between order agents and resource agents (indicated by *OA – RA*). Known restrictions for sequencing are implied in the formal description of identified machining tasks generated by the RLPP (indicated by *(RLPP/)*). While calculating bids and offers during negotiations, resource agents evaluate their ability to perform requested machining tasks (indicated by *RA*). Thus, complete process plans (from the point of view of orders) and loading status (from the point of view of resources) are results of a negotiation. Since human users of planning systems like IntaPS prefer to have a bird-eyes view over the shop floor situation as a whole, service agents (indicated by *SA*) are used to gather information and to visualize them in the user interface for each user's request.

The activity of NC code generation is marked with an asterisk (*), since the performing entity depends on the organization of the individual company. If a company uses shop-floor-oriented programming procedures (SOP), the respective functionality has to be integrated into the resource agents. If a centralized CAM (Computer Aided Manufacturing) department generates NC codes, this department itself may be represented by a resource agent and other resource agents use its offered services. Some additional tasks performed by process planning groups in enterprises are not covered by the functionality of the IntaPS system, e.g. processing bill of materials (map design part list to manufacture/assembly bill of material), inspection planning (while inspection stations are not represented yet by resource agents), and consulting service for product design group to achieve a proper design-for-manufacturing. Nevertheless, the planner will be able to spend more time on these additional tasks due to time-saving generation of process plans and less efforts for manual interaction in case of re-planning. One important aspect of IntaPS is the structured modeling of the application domain. The modeling method consists of three phases: Conceptualization, analysis, and design.

During the first phase called *Conceptualization*, the analyzed domain is examined from a user-centric point of view. Typical use-cases as well as some basic communication requirements are identified. The objective of this phase is to get a basic idea of relevant interactions between participating entities. The results of this phase are documented using UML charts (Use-case diagrams, Message-Sequence-Charts) and are refined in the second phase.

The second phase is called *Analysis* and results in five mostly formalized models which serve as a basis for prototype implementation: These five models are:

- *Organizational model*: Description of the organizational structures in which the MAS has to be used (in this case: process planning department and shop floor of an enterprise) such as hierarchical structures, relationship between agents, their environment and agent society structure, identification of agents and roles.
- *Task model*: Determination of goals of the individual agents and their tasks.
- *Agent model*: Detailed model (e.g. represented as a UML class diagram) and (semiformal) textural description of the agents.

- *Coordination model*: Model of the agent interaction and coordination including specification of suitable communication protocols (e.g. based on state chart diagrams and detailed sequence message charts).
- *Expertise model*: Modeling knowledge of the domain, agents, and environment.

These models are mostly represented in UML. Some descriptions of individual agent properties contained in the agent model are based on semi-formal textual patterns.

The last phase is called *Design* and deals with the detailed design of the agents as well as the agent platform respectively the electronic marketplace. Thus, the third phase leads to implementation activities for the realization of the MAS and in this case to the IntaPS prototype.

In the context of the expertise model the Ontology Inference Layer (OIL) is used for the specification of an ontology which is common to all agents participating in the electronic marketplace. Formalization of necessary knowledge for rough-level process planning as well as for decentralized detailed planning is an important task of the IntaPS project. Therefore, common information models of the manufacturing domain are analyzed (Figure. 3).

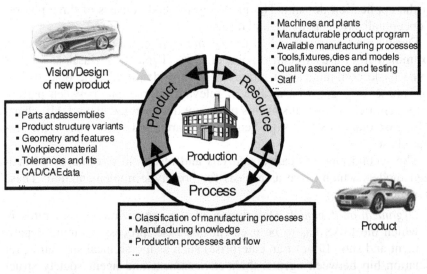

Figure 3. Relevant information models in the production engineering domain

Relevant information as well as other information concerning the domain is represented by three major information models: product model, resource model, and process model. These three major models depend on different well-known information models, which were adapted to the specific demands of IntaPS. For example, appreciable information models are: a formal description of manufacturing features from ISO 14649 'STEP-NC' [Weck2003], product structure definitions based on ISO 10303-4x 'STEP' [ISO10303-44], and a classification of manufacturing processes according to DIN 8580.

In case of the STEP-NC information model, STEP-NC-compliant manufacturing features are used for rough-level process planning. Since order agents need a well-structured description of manufacturing tasks to be carried out to execute the corresponding manufacturing order, they take advantage of STEP-NC. STEP-NC offers an object-oriented view to manufacturing tasks and describes manufacturing features like 'hole', 'pocket', or 'slot' instead of using a geometrical description of the tool path like conventional NC programming systems (e.g. so called G-code). Thus, the order agents build up an object-oriented task model for their corresponding work piece and are able to describe manufacturing tasks in a machine-independent way while tendering their request at the electronic market for a later decentralized detailed planning.

Furthermore, STEP-NC manufacturing features are used by resource agents for detailed process planning. During negotiations between order and resource agents, single manufacturing features like a dedicated instance of a pocket are analyzed by each involved resource agent. The single resource agent decides whether its corresponding resource (e.g. a specific machine tool) is able to process this manufacturing feature or not by evaluating its local knowledge base of contrivable manufacturing processes. If the agent decides, that its corresponding resource is able to process this manufacturing feature, the resource agent will offer its services to the order agent by submitting a proposal. Therefore, the resource agent requires information like estimated duration of the manufacturing process and uses the STEP-NC-based manufacturing feature and its attributes to calculate estimated processing times and machining parameters.

2.4 Design and Architecture

The IntaPS approach is based on a system of intelligent agents implementing integrated process planning and production control. The application architecture is derived from the previously introduced model and illustrated in Figure 4. In order to transform this architecture into a software system, agent architectures, agent decision, and coordination between agents behavior have to be designed.

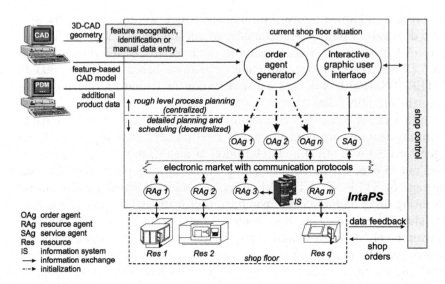

Figure 4. The IntaPS architecture

Central to the IntaPS approach a new and innovative agent architecture has been developed: *Discoursive Agents*. The *Discoursive Agents* approach specifies an architecture for agent behavior, knowledge representation, and inferences for application in eBusiness, esp. in the manufacturing domain. It strictly separates internal and external aspects due to privacy and security issues. We introduce a three layer architecture (cf. Figure 5) consisting of communicator, working on a low-level realization of speech acts; controller, determining general agent behavior; and executor, i.e. an interface to existing components, e.g. enterprise resource planning (ERP) systems and further information sources [Timm2001].

Nowadays, the communicator should be implemented with respect to standardization efforts like FIPA [PoCh2001]. In the case of the IntaPS research project, the communicator is realized on top of a FIPA compliant agent toolkit [BePR1999]. The executor has to be implemented according to its directly connected resources, e.g. machine tools. For evaluation purposes, the executor may serve as an interface to external simulation systems, e.g., eMPlant. While the communicator and executor layer is constructed in a straight forward manner, the design of the controller layer is more sophisticated implementing innovative concepts for agent-interaction in electronic marketplaces (open, adaptive communication (oac)), and decision making (conflict-based agent control (cobac), and capability management).

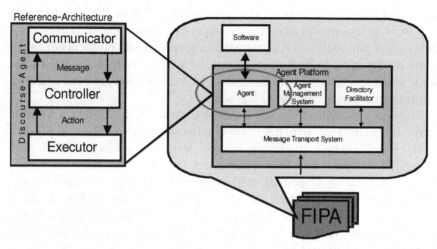

Figure 5. The discourse agent architecture

The controller layer determines the behavior, strategy, and state of the agent, i.e., an agent behaves in the way the functions and procedures in the controller are implemented resp. executed. It can only learn from experience acknowledged in the controller layer. The architecture presented here is based on the deliberative agent architecture BDI [RaGe1995]. The formal foundation is introducing a new multi-modal logic [Timm2004a], which integrates the formal approaches VSK-logic [WoLo2000] for inter-agent behavior and the LORA-logic [Wool2000] for deliberative agent behavior. In the following, we are presenting the core algorithms of the controller layer: open, adaptive communication (oac) for negotiation, capability management for fuzzy matchmaking, and conflict management for resolving conflicts of interest (cobac).

2.4.1 Open, Adaptive Communication

Common approaches to agent-oriented analysis and design like [WoLo2000] or [LuGI1997] lack an intuitive methodology to generate and customize agent communication protocols. Furthermore, communication protocols are often defined within a static structure, which cannot be directly adapted by the agents during runtime. In the manufacturing domain in the IntaPS project, where complex products are manufactured according to customer requirements, this kind of flexibility is required since negotiations about the products features will vary from customer to customer. Therefore, the agents collaborating have to be able to adapt their protocols according to the dialogue partner, their own state, the multiagent system's state, and experience of prior communications. Within the oac approach two main extensions of classical concepts are implemented: use of communication protocols is not restricted to a given set and protocols of opponents do not have to be known (open), as well as dialogues do not have static structures only, but are flexible and can be adapted, refined and even synthetisized during runtime (adaptive).

The oac approach is based on a probabilistic methodology, a Markov chain in analogy to dynamic belief networks [RuNo2003]. A Markov model is defined by a number of dialogue states Xi, and propabilities prob (Xi, Xj) for a transition from state Xi to state Xj. This model is highly flexible and allows adaptation, refinement and synthesis. It is easy to convert standard communication protocols, cg. Figure 6 into this formalization defining all transition probabilities as zero, if no transition exists in the protocol, as unity, if the Xj is definitely following Xi and splitting the probabilities for all possible branches.

$$
request^* \begin{cases} \xrightarrow{P_{RN}} not-understood \\ \xrightarrow{P_{RR}} refuse(reason) \\ \xrightarrow{P_{RA}} agree \end{cases} \begin{cases} \xrightarrow{P_{AO}^*} \alpha_0^* \xrightarrow{P_{OF}} & failure(reason) \\ \xrightarrow{P_{AO}^*} \alpha_0^* \xrightarrow{P_{OI}} & inform(Done(action)) \\ \xrightarrow{P_{AO}^*} \alpha_0^* \xrightarrow{P_{OI}} inform(iota\ x(result\ action)x) \end{cases}
$$

Figure 6. oac representation of FIPA-request protocol

The analysis and design of these protocols is done with minimum effort as only required protocol structures have to be defined and initial communication protocols be generated. The agents are modifying their protocols autonomously during simulation and application as follows:

- *Adaptation*: The execution of existing communication protocols leads to an adjustment of the selection probabilities (transition probabilities in the model) of the next action due to prior experience.
- *Refinement*: Within refinement an agent is extending protocols by adding new "states" Xi i.e. performatives out of a given set of basic communicative acts, e.g. FIPA-ACL [FIPA2000b]. Another method of refinement is to keep the states as they are, but to implement "new" transitions by setting zero transition probabilities to p>0, or to extinct certain transitions annulling their probabilities. Refinement is selected if an existing protocol tends not to lead to a satisfying result according to the agent's goals.
- *Synthesis*: The automatic generation of protocols is the desired methodology for the creation of new communication protocols. The basis for this method is a predefined set of dialogue "skeletons" as they are occurring within common communication protocols. The first step of the

synthesis is to select one of them as a core model. The necessary extension and customization of this rudimentary model follows the adaptation and refinement steps above.

2.4.2 Capability Management

Recent research projects deal with shop floor planning problems, e.g. by improving scheduling with respect to robustness and dynamic distributed environments. However, agent technology may be used to overcome existing traditional limitations in today's manufacturing systems, too [Mare2002]. The IntaPS approach is not bound to the restrictions of simple linear process plans [TWHT2001]. Since process plans are the result of agent communication, new alternative processing sequences can be found, e.g. in case of re-planning caused by unexpected machine breakdown. Order agents need knowledge about constraints related to the product's features and the necessary capabilities to manufacture these features. In addition, resource agents need knowledge about their capabilities. Thus, management of capabilities is important for negotiation of process plans. Currently, capabilities are only under consideration during design time, i.e. agents are implemented for a set of problem-solving methods. Even in adaptive approaches to agent design and implementations the skills and capabilities of agents are addressed to in a static manner. Requirements towards capabilities of agents are subject to change in dynamic environments, esp. if agents have the skill to form teams. In case of dynamic team formation, the set of capabilities can change significantly. Thus, the explicit representation of as well as inference on capabilities and set of capabilities are in question to build flexible multiagent systems. In the following, we address these problems with the term *capability management*.

In the IntaPS approach, a representation for capabilities based on 1st order logic has been chosen. Within these predicates, concept terms denote types of capability. The concept terms are organized in taxonomic hierarchies allowing for subsumption inference in order to achieve more flexible and "fuzzy" match-making between problem descriptions and capabilities [ScTW2004]. The capability management process is divided into four steps: a) identification of matching capabilities ("Is an agent capable to perform the action?"); b) generation of new composite capabilities ("Is a set of capabilities required?"); c) selection of the best-fit capability ("Which (composite) capability is suited best for a problem task?"); d) and learning new composite capabilities. It is implemented in the *Discoursive Agents* architecture assisting the option generation process (steps a and b) and the option filtering (step c). The learning process is triggered by new perceptions concerning the success of new, composed capabilities.

Additionally, capability management is used for team-formation in MAS. The process is based on the team-formation process proposed by [Wool2000]. Here, the basic assumption that all agents know the capabilities of one another is replaced by allowing agents to infer on their own as well as on other agents capabilities by using capability management.

2.4.3 Conflict Management

Agents representing machines within the IntaPS prototype are goal driven. In order to balance the various goals, e.g., produce or maintain, the agents need to implement a sophisticated conflict management. The conflict management (cobac) implemented in the *Discoursive Agents* architecture is based on BDI substituting the process of goal generation resp. option filtering. In the first step of the cobac algorithm options are generated on basis of accessible desires and current intentions. During the creation of a new option, a plan is selected for pursuing the desire in question using a plan allocation function. An evaluation function is assessing each option of the option set, using the desire assessing function and the current state of the plan, such that an option with an almost completed plan will receive high priority within the option filtering process. Next to the intention reconsideration, this evaluation function implements the commitment to an intention and should ensure that important and almost completed tasks will be finished first. In the next step the options are filtered. The filtering uses conflict assessment and resolution, i.e., for each pair of options, a synergy as well as a conflict value is calculated. Two options receive a high synergy value if they are pursuing similar desires and the plans are not contradictory, e.g. the post condition of plan A is not prohibiting the pre condition of plan B. A conflict and synergy potential is calculated as the sum of each conflict and synergy value and is used as a performance indicator within the process of conflict resolution. The conflict classification and resolution algorithm is motivated from the field of inter-personal conflict studies [Vlie1997]. A conflict taxonomy is introduced in [Timm2001], where each pair of options is classified as a leaf in this taxonomy. For each type of leaf, there is a resolution strategy taking the cooperation or conflict potential into account. E.g. if two objectives are very similar, they can be merged in a cooperative setting and two objectives pursuing conflicting post conditions can be removed.

2.5 System Description

In the previous section an outline of the basic algorithms has been provided. Based on this specification, an implementation of the concepts, esp. cobac, oac, and capability management has been realized. The implementation of these algorithms as well as necessary concepts for the simulation has been performed in Java. The architecture of the prototype has been designed in an open, modular manner, in order to enable integration of programming languages like Prolog for explicit knowledge representation and inference. The *Discursive Agents* architecture has been formalized and specified in multi-modal logic. A prototypical implementation has to be restricted in contrast to the specification with respect to decidability and complexity. The main bottlenecks are computing accessibility and estimating future states. In the IntaPS project, a prototypical implementation of the Discursive Agents architecture has been realized. This implementation transforms the theoretical concepts into Java in a straight forward manner. Doing so, any well-formed formulas with respect to the grammar may be expressed. Furthermore, elementary implementations for planning, dynamic conflict, and capability management have been integrated. The prototype also considers the branching temporal structures where states are represented as nodes in a tree, and the transition or edges are representing plans. Conventional temporal branching structures consider individual actions as edges instead of complete plans. However, this modification was chosen with respect to complexity and efficiency reasons.

The underlying agent toolkit is JADE [BePR1999]. The JADE agent is used as a super class for the Discourse Agent (communicator). The implementation of the controller layer focuses on the three algorithms cobac, oac, and capability management. As the formal specification of the algorithms is restricted to decidable parts of the multi-modal logic, implementation is directly following their formal model. There are only little modifications and extensions necessary with respect to the IntaPS domain.

Additionally for testing and evaluation purposes, a simulation manager has been implemented. It is designed as domain-independent controller for starting and deleting of agents, collecting results, logging agent behavior, and introspection of the system during runtime. The simulation manager interface allows the user of the prototype to specify simulation scenarios, e.g., the parameters of the involved agents, as well as further simulation parameters, e.g. duration of the simulation. In the IntaPS context, the configuration interface is used for the specification of complex shop-floors.

The above introduced implementation of intelligent agents is used in simulation as follows: The simulation manager is selecting a profile of an agent to be started. Resource agents are started with respect to the specified outline of the shop-floor in the scenario specification. Order agents may be started following a list of predefined orders or in a randomized manner. The profile specifies the parameters, knowledge base, and desires of an agent. After the agents have been started, they are initializing their local states and prepare for negotiations.

2.6 Evaluation and Benchmarking

2.6.1 Evaluation for User Domain Purposes

Prototype implementations like the IntaPS approach have to meet the challenge of being tested with realistic application scenarios. Whether they prove a better performance than conventional systems, industrial users will be interested in implementing them in enterprises (see Section 2.2). In case of the IntaPS approach, an evaluation concept has been developed using a simulated shop floor environment (Figure 7). The evaluation concept is based on reference data sets, which are part of a realistic scenario.

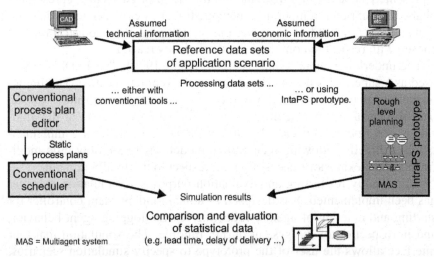

Figure 7. Evaluation concept of the IntaPS approach

Focus of this scenario is the manufacturing of a product that consists of self-manufactured components as well as bought components like screws or washers. The self-manufactured components are produced by using different production processes in a shop floor. Afterwards they are assembled to units first and finally to the complete product. The scenario contains further technical information about the products and orders (e.g. product type or data of manufacturing features) as well as economic and logistic information like due dates and order quantities.

Reference data sets will be processed in two different ways: With conventional tools as well as using the IntaPS prototype (Figure 7, right side). Using conventional tools (Figure 7, left side) sets of static process plans will be created using a standard process plan editor and scheduled by a conventional scheduler. The scheduled manufacturing orders are "manufactured" in a simulated ("virtual") shop floor environment. The "virtual" shop floor is realized using "Tecnomatix eM-Plant" (former SIMPLE++) and the common ERP-system "SAP R3". Simulation results are logged by these systems and are used for statistical analyses. In addition, the same reference data sets are processed using the IntaPS prototype.

As in the first case, "eM-Plant" and "SAP R3" logs all relevant events and simulation results. Finally, statistical data like average and maximum load of resources, lead times or delay of delivery will be compared and evaluated. This conduces the verification and validation of the IntaPS prototype. One of the current research activities of IntaPS deals with the identification of significant performance indicators that aim at the benchmark between agent-based and conventional systems of the job shop scheduling. Thereby, the user of the IntaPS MAS will be able to get advices how to improve the structure of the shop-floor (e.g. to identify bottleneck resources or changes in the product range).

Further developments aim at the integration of the existing IntaPS approach at the enterprise level into the supply chain level Agent.Enterprise scenario as described in II.1.

2.6.2 Algorithmic Evaluation

In the following, an empiric evaluation of selected algorithms of the IntaPS-approach (cobac, oac) is presented. The evaluation is based on a number of simulation runs of agents which use the given algorithms. Additionally, these algorithms are benchmarked with common state-of-the-art approaches from multiagent research.

2.6.2.1 Evaluation of Open Adaptive Communication

The open, adaptive communication is supposed to be especially suited for heterogeneous environments, in which an agent is not only part of the system, but also may become part of a new system. Electronic marketplaces with local communication-rules or -conventions pose a special challenge. Therefore, the evaluation is supposed to show that the discourse agents are capable of adapting to new environments. The evaluation is performed on an electronic marketplace with varying communication rules and conventions (conservative, communicative, aggressive). The success criteria of the discourse agents adoption is measured by the workload of the agent as well as how much it has "earned" in a virtual currency.

In order to gain statistically significant data, the simulation has been repeated 10 times with a conservative, learning agent in an aggressive market with 100 iterations each. Each of these repetitions has been randomized and statistically evaluated. The indexes of the results are shown in Table 2.

Table 2. Results of the oac-evaluation

Index	Results per iteration			
	0-10 iter.	11-25 iter.	26-50 iter.	51-100 iter.
average	21.472	37.030	49.262	53.322
standard deviation	1.348	2.472	2.101	1.250
significance (against non-learning agents)	+++	+++	+++	+++
probability	< 0.0001	< 0.0001	< 0.0001	< 0.0001
confidence intervals				
lower bound	20.508	35.262	47.759	52.428
upper bound	22.437	38.797	50.765	54.216

First, the average values of the 10 repetitions do not show a significant deviation to the single simulation indicating good reproduction. The standard deviation is smaller than 7% of the average values, emphasizing these results. The final row shows the 95% confidence intervals resulting from these values. The most prominent feature of these intervals is, that they are completely disjoint, i.e., the learning success is significant from interval to interval. For each interval, a t-test for covering the differences between learning and non-learning agents has been performed. Each has shown a most significant result ($p < 0.0001$). Verification of the total results with an analysis of variance also indicated highly significant differences both for the influence of learning and the learning success from interval to interval (cf. Figure 8b). For details, please refer to [Timm2004b].

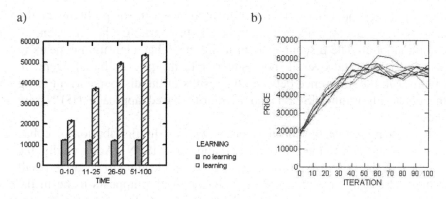

Figure 8. Results of the oac-evaluation

2.6.2.2 Evaluation of Conflict Based Agent Control

The evaluation of the cobac-algorithm is performed in the IntaPS-scenario. In order to assess the behavior of the cobac-algorithm, an evaluation with 1700 experiments and 163.200 decision cycles has been performed. Additionally, a state-of-the-art intention-selection algorithm based on dynamic priorities has been implemented in order to benchmark the cobac-algorithm.

Table 3. Results of the cobac-evaluation

Algorithm	Number of desires	Number of experiments	Average (balance)	Standard deviation
cobac	5	100	797.90	221.08
cobac	7	100	847.15	174.99
priorities	5	100	382.24	342.31
priorities	7	100	720.17	263.69

The cobac-algorithm as well as the priority intention selection algorithm are each tested with a set of generic desires (five desires) and an extended, set of partially composed desires (seven desires). The experiments have been used to assess the behavior of the cobac algorithm in different situations as well as to benchmark it against the priority intention selection. In Table 3 and in Figure 9, the results (balance) for both algorithms are shown.

The priority-controlled agent shows a significant statistical spread in the success parameters. Besides the balance shown in Table 3, especially the number of accepted but not processed orders is a major problem for the priority-based agent, since it fails to handle the backlog when it reaches a certain amount. The discourse agent using the cobac-algorithm appears to be more stable and overall more superior to the priority-based agent. In Figure 9a/b the difference between the results of the discourse agent using the cobac algorithm (ISCN) and a priority based approach (ISPN) are shown.

It is obvious, that the mean value as well as the distribution of cobac (ISCN) is superior to the priority based approach (ISPN). Additionally, the variance of the ISPN is significantly greater, also leading to negative result values. The main advantage of the cobac-algorithm appears to be in the ability to create composed goals on the basis of partially synergetic or conflictive goals. The resulting compromises are handling dynamic situations more efficiently. The alternative algorithm is only capable to achieve similar results by a significant increase of the pre-composed goals.

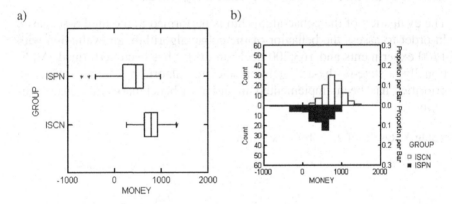

Figure 9. Results of the cobac-evaluation

2.7 Conclusions

Despite the fact, that agent-based applications are not state-of-the-art in manufacturing industry yet, the concept of intelligent software agents offers an enormous potential for the design of future collaborative manufacturing systems. This chapter presented the IntaPS approach based on the application of co-operative software agents for optimizing information logistics in the field of concurrent process planning and production control. Due to the approach of a wide integration and concurrency of planning and executing tasks, capacity information and due dates will be taken into consideration for the early stages of process planning. Furthermore, process planning knowledge will be used for short-term scheduling decisions at the shop floor. Therefore, problems will be eliminated, which result from time-delayed return of manufacturing knowledge and capacity data or other lacks of information flows e.g. from the use of static process plans.

In general intelligent software agents are a promising approach to improve information logistics in manufacturing enterprises. Thus, enterprises will be able to fulfill the requirement of flexible, reliable and fault-tolerant manufacturing. Fulfillment of these requirements is a prerequisite for successful participation in modern business alliances like supply chains, temporal logistic networks and virtual enterprises. Thus, agent-based improvements of information logistics enable enterprises to face the challenges of competition successfully.

Further information is available at http://www.intaps.org.

References

[BePR1999]   Bellifemine, F; Poggi, A.; Rimassa, G.: CSELT Internal Technical Report. In: Proceedings of PAAM. London, 1999, pp. 97-108.

[FIPA2002a]   FIPA Communicative Act Library Specification. Document Nr. SC00037J, 2002. http://www.fipa.org/specs/fipa00037/, accessed in October 2005.

[FIPA2002b]   FIPA: FIPA ACL Message Structure Specification. Document Nr. SC00061G, 2002. http://www.fipa.org/specs/fipa00061/, accessed in October 2005.

[Deen2003]   Deen, S. M.: Agent-Based Manufacturing. Springer-Verlag, Berlin et al., 2003.

[Ever2002]   Eversheim: Organisation in der Produktionstechnik - Arbeitsvorbereitung. 4. Auflage, Springer-Verlag, Berlin et al., 2002.

[GaSl1999]   Gaalman, G. J. C.; Slomp, J.: Towards an Integration of Process Planning and Production Planning and Control for Flexible Manufacturing Systems. In: The International Journal of Flexible Manufacturing Systems 11(1999), Kluwer Academic Publishers, Boston, pp. 5-17.

[ISO10303-44] ISO 10303-44: Industrial Automation Systems and Integration - Product Data Representation and Exchange - Part 44: Integrated Generic Resources: Product Structure Configuration. International Organization for Standardization, Geneva, 2000.

[JeWo1998]   Jennings, N. R.; Wooldridge, M. J.: Agent Technology: Foundation, Applications, and Markets. Springer, New York, 1998.

[LuGI1997]   Luck, M.; Griffiths, N.; d'Inverno, M.: From Agent Theory to Agent Construction: A Case Study. In: Müller, J. P et al. (Ed.):

	Intelligent Agents III. Springer Verlag, Berlin, LNCS 1193, 1997, pp. 49-64.
[Mare2002]	Marek, V.: Knowledge and Technology Integration in Products and Services. In: Proceedings Balancing Knowledge and Technology in Product and Service Life Cycle (BASYS). Kluwer Academic Publishers, Cancun, 2002.
[PoCh2001]	Poslad, S.; Charlton, P.: Standardizing Agent Interoperability: The FIPA Approach. In: Multi-Agent Systems and Applications, 9th ECCAI Advanced Course, ACAI 2001 and Luck, M. (Ed.): Agent Link's 3rd European Agent Systems Summer School, EASSS 2001, Prague, Selected Tutorial Papers. New York, NY, USA. Springer-Verlag Inc., 2001, pp. 98-117.
[RaGe1995]	Rao, A. S.; Georgeff, M. P.: BDI-Agents: From Theory to Practice. In: Proceedings of the First International Conference on Multiagent Systems. AAAI-Press, San Francisco, 1995, pp. 312-319.
[RuNo2003]	Russell, S. J.; Norvig, P.: Artificial Intelligence: A Modern Approach. Prentice Hall, New Jersey, 2003.
[ScTW2004]	Scholz, T.; Timm, I. J.; Woelk, P.-O.: Emerging Capabilities in Intelligent Agents for Flexible Production Control. In: Ueda, K. et al. (Ed.): Proceedings of the 5th International Workshop on Emergent Synthesis (IWES). Budapest, 2004, pp. 99-105.
[Timm2001]	Timm, I. J.: Enterprise Agents Solving Problems: The cobac-Approach. In: Bauknecht, K. et al. (Ed.): Informatik 2001 - Tagungsband der GI/OCG Jahrestagung. Wien, 2001, pp. 952-958.
[Timm2004a]	Timm, I. J.: Dynamisches Konfliktmanagement als Verhaltenssteuerung Intelligenter Agenten. DISKI 283, infix, Köln, 2004.
[Timm2004b]	Timm, I. J.: Selbstlernprozesse in der Agentenkommunikation, In: Florian, M. et al. (Ed.): Adaption und Lernen in und von Organisationen. VS Verlag für Sozialwissenschaften, Wiesbaden, 2004, pp. 103-127.
[ToTe1998]	Tönshoff, H. K.; Teunis, G.: Modular Shop Control Toolkit for Flexible Manufacturing. In: Production Engineering 2(1998), pp. 111-114.
[TWHT2001]	Tönshoff, H. K.; Woelk, P.-O.; Herzog, O.; Timm, I. J.: Integrated Process Planning and Production Control – A Flexible Approach Using Co-operative Agent Systems. In: Initiatives of Precision Engineering at the Beginning of a Millennium. Proceedings of 10th International Conference on Precision Engineering (ICPE), Yokohama. Kluwer Academic Publishers, Boston, 2001, pp. 857-861.
[Vlie1997]	Vliert, E. van d.: Complex Interpersonal Conflict Behavior – Theoretical Frontiers. Psychology Press, East Sussex, 1997.
[Weck2003]	Weck, M.: STEP-NC – A New Interface Closing the Gap Between Planning and Shop Floor. WZL, Aachen, 2003.

[Weis1999]   Weiss, G.: Multiagent Systems – A Modern Approach to Distri-
                buted Artificial Intelligence. The MIT Press, Cambridge, 1999.
[Woel2003]   Woelk, P.-O.: Survey on Decentralisation in Process Planning
                and Production Control-Short Summary. http://www.intaps.org/
                project/decsurvey.htm, accessed on 2003-07-25.
[WoLo2000]   Wooldridge, M.; Lomuscio, A.: Proceedings of the Seventh
                European Workshop on Logics in Artificial Intelligence (JELI-
                AI). Springer-Verlag, Berlin, 2000.
[Wool2000]   Wooldridge, M. J.: Reasoning about Rational Agents. The MIT
                Press, Cambridge, Massachusetts, 2000.
[WoJK2000]   Wooldridge, M.; Jennings, N. R.; Kinny, D.: The Gaia Method-
                ology for Agent-Oriented Analysis and Design. In: Autonomous
                Agents and Multi-Agent Systems 3(2000)3, pp. 285-312.

3 Benchmarking of Multiagent Systems in a Production Planning and Control Environment

Jan Wörner, Heinz Wörn

Universität Karlsruhe (TH), Institut für Prozessrechentechnik, Automation und Robotik, {woerner I woern}@ira.uka.de

Abstract. Multiagent systems (MAS) offer new perspectives compared to conventional, centrally organized architectures in the field of production planning and control. They are expected to be more flexible while dealing with a turbulent production environment with its environment-immanent disturbances. In this chapter, a MAS is developed and compared to an Operations Research Job-Shop algorithm using a simulation-based benchmarking scenario. Environmental constraints for a successful application of MAS are identified and classified to be applied to next generation priority-rules based decision algorithms in MAS-based production planning and control.

3.1 Introduction

Today, enterprises, especially manufacturing companies, have to face a global market characterized by numerous competitors, a steadily increasing vicissitude and complexity of business processes besides a highly turbulent production environment. Consequently, manufacturing systems have to provide the flexibility and reliability that is required to stay competitive.

Decentralized planning and controlling approaches offer interesting perspectives compared to conventional centralized architectures. In the scope of production planning and control (PPC), multiagent systems are expected to be more flexible than centrally organized systems. In II.1 the criteria to classify the environment of multiagent systems with regard to the application for manufacturing are described in detail.

The respective criteria to appraise the environment, in which the application oriented benchmarking of multiagent systems, this chapter deals with, is done, are shown in Figure 1. Due to the fact that the shop-floor scenario is limited to company internal processes at a first glance, the observability would be expected to be possible in every detail, however, by being integrated into a supply net, the possibilities of observing production parameters by machine data acquisition decreases.

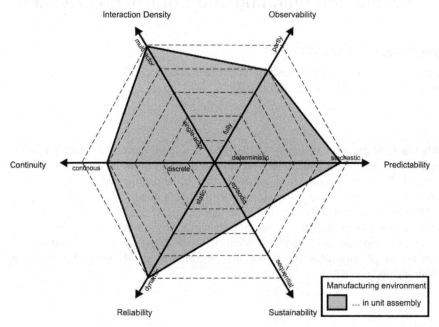

Figure 1. The environment of unit assembly in manufacturing according to Russels Criteria [RuNo2003]

In the manufacturing scenario mentioned above, the contacts between the different partners are increasingly isolated projects with high dynamics in the planning of the production process because of a growing vicissitude of the market and unpredictable production break downs.

To prove or disprove the thesis of MAS being more flexible and thus being able to increase the planning quality for well-defined shop floor scenarios, a simulation-based benchmarking platform on the basis of a real test case scenario was developed in the scope of the KRASH (Karlsruhe Robust Agent SHell) and the ControMAS (Control MAS) project. A performance measurement system is included to provide qualitative as well as quantitative results.

The platform is used to compare existing PPC approaches based on Operations Research (OR) algorithms with decentralized MAS approaches. Furthermore, different scenarios can be simulated with various levels of complexity. This makes it possible to set up a map that identifies application scenarios, where MAS provide a real benefit to potential industrial users. In the next step, abstract priority rules can be extracted from these results to gather further knowledge about the preferences of MAS.

After the description of existing approaches, initially, the respective simulation-based benchmarking platform is described. The developed MAS approach is presented in Section 3.3 and 3.4. Section 3.5 shows the results of the comparison of the centralized and decentralized planning approaches and draws conclusions of the results.

3.2 Existing Approaches for Unit Assembly Environments

Today, central approaches are used for production planning and control. The main advantage of the central approach, e.g. SAP APO is that all data is always available and the communication effort is very small. In a dynamic environment characterized by continuous manufacturing and almost non-predictable and not fully observable behavior of manufacturing units, the central approach does not achieve the required flexibility.

The transferability of the planning results upon an industrial shop floor environment is one of the major prerequisites. Thus the evaluation of the different approaches has to be performed on the basis of a real, or at least a realistic, production scenario. Besides industrial relevance, the application of a MAS has to be motivated. In technical literature e.g. [WeMe1999], [SWFM1995] or [Cav+1999], MAS are characterized to be more flexible (see I.3) and robust as described by Frey [FNWL2003] in a dynamic, turbulent production environment compared to centralized approaches.

In addition, they are able to handle complex production planning problems more effectively by dividing them into less complex partial planning problems. At that background, the scenario can be characterized by:

- sufficient production planning complexity,
- occurrence of short-term disturbances, e.g. machine failures,
- features like flexibility have to be key requirements.

A circuit breaker production plant represents the benchmarking environment. Within this plant, a production area ("Unit Assembly Area") is chosen, where components are assembled which will be used later in the final assembly. The area consists of 13 assembly lines. Six different component families and four sub-component families that are part of the components, are assembled. Thus, the test case represents a multi-level assembly. Material flow is controlled by a Kanban system [Ohno1993]. Raw material consumption in final assembly determines the production in component assembly. Orders in this area, including start dates, product IDs and quantities have been extracted in a simulation study beforehand. As a consequence, this part of the plant can be analyzed separately thus reducing the complexity of the task in a reasonable way. The correctness of the data was approved by a company running the production plant.

3.3 Multiagent System Approach for Unit Assembly Manufacturing

In this paragraph, the suitability of MAS in the range of production planning and control is analyzed, taking into consideration existing production planning and control approaches. A Kanban system is especially suitable for the integration of a MAS. Both systems are highly distributed, since Kanban consists of decentralized, self-controlling control cycles. To level the workload of the machines, a line balancing has to be performed. The main goal while setting up a Kanban system is the minimization of the internal buffer stock. The two parameters directly affecting the buffer stock are the maximum consumption rate of the raw material and the maximum replenishment lead time [Ohno1993].

The problem of minimizing the consumption rate is handled by a production smoothing (dispatching of a suitable product mix, so that the consumption rate of raw materials gets almost constant), whereas the replenishment lead time depends on internal production planning and control and the corresponding process structure (production of small lot sizes and material flow-oriented shop floor layout). In the case of disturbances, the standard deviation of the replenishment lead time has to be minimized (and thus its maximum). MAS are expected to deal with this task in a more effective manner due to their enormous flexibility.

3.4 Benchmarking Platform and Architecture

Solutions generated by MAS are expected to be more flexible and robust than conventional centralized approaches. On the other hand, centralized OR algorithms should provide better results in non-disturbed production environments, because of the huge number of experiences integrated in respective algorithms and methods. In addition, MAS are mostly developed within the scope of academic projects, thus there are only few perceptions related to real-world scenarios and the related shop floor complexity.

To prove or disprove the above assertion and compare the two varying approaches not only on a qualitative, but also on a quantitative basis a benchmarking scenario has to be defined and implemented. Cavalieri defines a benchmarking framework and provides a common platform [Cav+ 1999] [CGMT2000]. This means that the results of different planning approaches are comparable taking into account the requirements for qualified benchmarks. The developed benchmarking platform is used to perform the comparison task based on simulation and thus provides the necessary dynamical behavior.

The simulation model maps a real production scenario of a circuit breaker assembly. The planning task is a mixed-model assembly line balancing problem (MALBP) and a mixed-model sequencing problem (MSP). They differ in the planning horizon. The first one is a long-term and the second one a short-term decision problem [Scho1999].

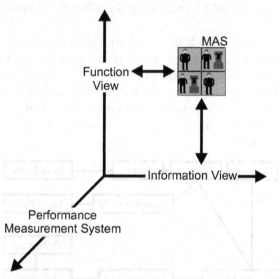

Figure 2. Platform components

The formal representation of the environment requires the definition of a meta-model. CIMOSA (Open System Architecture for CIM) (CIMOSA Association, 1996) was chosen as the modeling methodology, since it is publicly available, not restricted to a certain tool, and it is well-documented. eMPlant was chosen as the event-driven simulation tool including a building block library. The tool VICTOR (VIrtual FaCTORy lab) [Reit 1995] and [Reit1996] merges both CIMOSA and eMPlant. The modeling process is performed using CIMOSA elements which are mapped on the original eMPlant building blocks. Thus, an executable eMPlant model is automatically created. The CIMOSA model itself is represented in a textual format.

Cavalieri presents design guidelines for suitable production benchmarks [CaMV2003]. In addition, a highly sophisticated web-based modeling framework was developed enabling the user to define a scenario and respective processes which are stored in a test case library afterwards. Both, the static and the dynamic features of the environment are modeled. Additionally, measures of performance according to the criteria, shown in Figure 1, are defined. This approach provides a wide range of benchmarking scenarios representing various PPC problem classes. An interesting extension would be the integration of a simulation component which is able to map the non-deterministic dynamic behavior of the scenarios. The modular benchmarking platform (see Figure 2) consists of a process model (CIMOSA Function and Information View), a performance measurement system and interfaces for the MAS (accessing the CIMOSA Function and Information View).

The process model is built up by a building block library. This enables the user to create own scenarios by combining the building blocks in an adequate manner with standardized interfaces. The process structure of the building blocks is represented by the CIMOSA Function View. The information related to the scenario is mapped on the CIMOSA Information View. The definition of interfaces is based on a PPC database structure, presented in Figure 3.

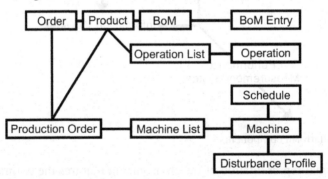

Figure 3. PPC database structure

The material flow in an economic environment and the possibilities of assigning orders to certain machines are given implicitly by the instantiation of this data structure as shown by Frey [Frey2003]. The technical specifications represented by database schemas are available at [DBRA 2005]. The required technical robustness of multiagent systems has been described by Frey [FNWL2003].

The following elements of the scenario's information view are mapped within the tables of a database as shown in Figure 3:

- The table *Product* contains product-specific data. The bill of materials lists all parts required for the assembly of the product whereas the operation list represents the single work steps of the product assembly.
- *Operation* is a table assigning operations to machines which are able to perform this particular work step (including a potential setup process).
- The *Order* table lists all customer orders. Besides product and quantity, due dates, or starting dates of the orders are defined.
- Based on the orders and other parameters, the *Production Order* table is the result of the planning process and finally determines production dates, facilities and quantities.
- The *Disturbance Profile* table is machine-specific and rests upon disturbance histories gathered from an MDA (Machine Data Acquisition) or a PDA (Production Data Acquisition) system and rules of thumb based on experiences.

The planning results are stored in the *Schedule* table. It contains the planning results of the PPC modules and the current status of the machines' waiting queues.

The CIMOSA Information View contains static information like master data, order data, production data and dynamic statistical data gathered during the simulation. Based on these data, performance measures like average buffer stock, consumption rates, throughput times, transportation times of the AGV system as well as processing times are implemented as shown by Frey and Wörn [FrWo2001].

Tailored interfaces enable other external MAS to access the benchmarking platform. In the first version of the benchmarking platform, the integration is performed using standardized interfaces of eMPlant, where the MAS has to be integrated directly by using the socket or C++ interface or implementing the MAS in the eMPlant-specific object-oriented programming language Simtalk.

This procedure is not too comfortable for the MAS developers, yet it is possible to use the discrete event mechanism of the simulation software. The second approach is a more sophisticated one. Its system architecture is depicted in Figure 4.

In this approach, the MAS is conceived as being decoupled from the benchmarking platform. Therefore it is not apparent for the MAS if it is working in a real application environment or inside of a simulation model. The current work is focusing on the synchronization of states and events on the basis of database triggers. They are used to synchronize the simulation and the MAS.

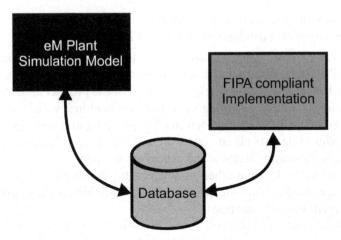

Figure 4. System architecture

In addition, numerous MAS which are working in one integrated scenario can be synchronized, too. In this case the agent systems are co-operatively dealing with different tasks. A scenario with numerous MAS is presented in II.1, Figure 4. The agent-oriented modeling of the scenario is performed by an abstract assign of agents to real objects.

Another major issue is the management of disturbances, since MAS are a promising technology to handle them more effectively as compared to existing approaches. Thus a complex parameterization of the scenario is possible.

The parameterization affects two dimensions, the complexity of the scenario and the homogeneity of the problem space. Both dimensions are expected to have an effect on the planning system. They can be varied by individually setting up the parameters like lot size, number of machines, workload, disruption profile and more.

The disruption interval is the time gap between the occurrences of two consecutive disruptions. Along with the disruption duration, it forms the disruption profile of a machine. During the simulation studies, these parameters have been varied continuously and a map has been set up marking those scenarios that prefer a MAS treatment.

3.5 Multiagent System

The developed multiagent system was intended to solve a mixed-model sequencing problem (MSP). With respect to the throughput time, the corresponding centralized OR algorithm produces optimum solutions for the non-disturbed case, whereas its performance is limited in the case of disruptions.

The problem of disturbance handling and MAS-based scheduling has been addressed by the MASCADA project at the KU Leuven. This project presents a MAS based on the PROSA (Product, Resource, Order and Staff Agent) architecture.

Jain and Foley analyze the effects of interruptions on flexible manufacturing systems and deduct guidelines for the development and implementation of schedules to cope with these uncertainties [JaFo2002].

In this case, a MAS was developed to handle a line balancing decision problem within an unit assembly manufacturing environment. The system operates on an intra-plant level, whereas there are interfaces to external suppliers and customers (orders). These interfaces have been used within the *Agent.Enterprise* scenario described in II.1. The developed system performs production planning and control tasks for unit assembly, however, the emphasis is set upon the execution functionality.

The MAS was directly integrated into the simulation environment due to performance and maintainability reasons. Additionally, an implementation based on FIPA-OS and JADE is available. Three algorithms for production planning and control have been implemented so far:

- Job-Shop (long-term planning horizon),
- MAS_pre (short-term planning horizon),
- MAS_act (no planning horizon).

These algorithms differ within the planning horizon. The planning horizon is part of the waiting queue which is "visible" to the algorithm and thus may be used for optimization purposes. "Job-Shop" is an MSP line balancing algorithm [Scho1999] and performs the planning task starting the simulation; consequently, it is not able to react to changes.

Having n machines, the order is assigned to the machine which obeys:

$$CD_{x,mx-1} = \min(CD_{i,mi-1}), \quad \forall i = 1...n \tag{1}$$

$CD_{i,j}$ Planned completion date of order i at machine i

N Number of machines that are able to process the current order

M Current position of the order within the waiting queue

The completion dates are calculated using the processing times of an order. In the non-disturbed case, this approach presents a forward scheduling algorithm which leads to an optimum solution with respect to the throughput time. MAS_pre assigns the orders to the production facility as soon as they are available. This leads to a short-term planning horizon. MAS_pre is able to react to changes within the planning horizon.

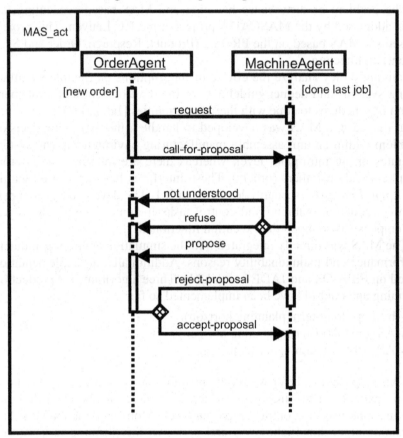

Figure 5. AUML diagram of the MAS_act approach

On the other hand, MAS_act is an exclusively reactive system. The machine agents ask for new orders as soon as they have finished the current order as shown in Figure 5. A performance comparison of both reactive and planning-based control architectures is also performed by Brennan [Bren2000]. Similar to the results presented in this chapter, the role of the planning horizon with respect to the performance of the system is analyzed. Both of the MAS approaches are communicating, using a protocol similar to the well-known ContractNet protocol [Paru1987].

The system consists of machine agents and order agents. Each machine agent represents a production facility and applies for an assembly order, if it is available. The order agent represents a production order and is responsible for the material and information flow of the system. Due to the reactive behavior of the MAS, the system is not able to reach general optimum solutions, as indicated by investigations [Frey2003]. Archimede and Coudert address this challenge by presenting the SCEP (Supervisor, Customers, Environment, Producers) framework for a reactive MAS that improves the range of co-operation, yet sustaining the ability to react to disturbances [ArCo2001].

The rating process for the machine agents in this project is based on a performance measurement number (PMN) as shown in Equation 2. The remaining processing time of an order is calculated on the basis of the current schedule and the processing time for each product. The primary goal of the planning strategy was the minimization of the throughput time and an effective line balancing of the various machines.

$$PMN = \frac{1}{\left(\sum_{i=1}^{n} RPT_i + MDT\right)\Big/60} \tag{2}$$

N   Number of Orders in the Waiting Queue of the Machine Agent

RPT_i Remaining Processing Time of Order i

MDT   Average Disruption Time

Besides the throughput time itself, its standard deviation is of interest, since it determines the predictability of the system. This is an important feature for a production planner, since MAS are assumed to act unpredictably due to their autonomy.

The performance is decisively affected by this performance measurement number. Similar to the Job-Shop algorithm, the processing time of the remaining orders in the waiting queue is calculated. The rating results in the inverse processing time and is scaled to 1, i.e. $0 \leq x \leq 1$, whereas 1 is the highest rating.

As a consequence, the order is assigned to that machine agent that will finish its order first. If the machine agent is disrupted, then the disruption time has to be considered in addition to the processing time. Normally, an estimated disruption time is unknown. To avoid this problem, each machine agent contains a disturbance history gathered during the simulation.

In reality, this information may be extracted from a MDA (Machine Data Acquisition) or a PDA (Production Data Acquisition) system. The global effects of several local balancing objectives in flexible manufacturing systems on performance measurement numbers like throughput time, make span, mean flow time and mean tardiness is analyzed by Kumar and Shanker [KuSh2002].

3.6 Benchmarking Results

3.6.1 Simulation Studies

Within the simulation studies, the complexity of the scenario and the homogeneity of problem space were continuously varied by changing the corresponding production parameters. Discrete values for disruption duration, number of operations, lot size, disruption interval and workload were chosen. It was investigated if the behavior of the MAS is continuous and predictable, depending on the environmental production constraints, or if the MAS performs non-deterministically.

The following sections will focus on disruption duration and lot size. Detailed explorations performed by Frey [Frey2003] point up that especially these two parameters are the most interesting comparing a central approach with the developed distributed MAS. For each configuration, represented by a tuple of the five parameters listed above in Table 1, the corresponding average throughput time and the standard deviation of the throughput time were analyzed, which led to more than 1000 simulation runs.

Table 1. Parameter units

Parameter	Unit
Disruption Duration	Minutes
Number of Operations	Number
Lot Size	Pallets
Disruption Interval	Processing time for one lot size
Workload	Factor, which extends the interval between the dispatching of two consecutive orders

Within the evaluation process, the results were abstracted with respect to only two parameters to reduce complexity of the results and increase their clearness. The scaled difference calculated by the amount of scenarios with the MAS performing better, minus the amount of scenarios with the Job-Shop algorithm performing better represents the final decision variable. The evaluation procedure may be described as the following:

- Choose two of the parameters.
- Fixing those two parameters, perform simulation runs with the other three varying.

- For these simulation runs, calculate the amount of scenarios where the MAS is performing better and subtract the amount of scenarios with the Job-Shop algorithm performing better.
- Scale the result, so that $-2 \leq x \leq 2$, x being the final decision variable.

The benchmarking results are presented in the form of area diagrams, the two axes mapping the two parameters mentioned above. The diagrams are intuitive graphical representations of the decision variable x. In addition, the color gradient enables the recognition of general tendencies concerning the behavior of MAS. Within the area diagrams, presented in Figure 6, the bright areas identify scenarios where a centralized Job-Shop algorithm produces better results concerning the average throughput time or its standard deviation ($x < 0$). The dark areas represent boundary conditions where the MAS is superior ($x > 0$).

3.6.2 Preliminary Analysis

The aim of the preliminary analysis is the limitation of the evaluation space. The effects of the number of additional machines and the variation of the disruption profiles are investigated to perform further evaluations on the basis of these results while fixing these two parameters.

In the first step, the complexity of the planning task was scaled up by increasing the number of operations which are necessary to assemble a product, introducing additional production facilities and extending the disruption intervals and duration for the individual machines. Similar machines that are able to handle the same operations were assigned the same disruption profiles. Surprisingly, the introduction of disturbances had almost no effect on the results.

On the contrary, the Job-Shop algorithm even produced better results. Closer investigations of results revealed the reason for this behavior. The production plant ran on its capacity limits. The workload of the machines is almost 100% during day shift. Consequently, there is no vacant capacity for rescheduling activities. When handling disturbances, vacant production capacities are one prerequisite for the successful use of reactive MAS. Otherwise, the Job-Shop algorithms always produce better results.

But even for this rather disadvantageous scenario for a MAS, it is clearly identifiable that the standard deviation of throughput time is decreasing with increasing complexity of the scenario. Small lot sizes increase the complexity of the planning process and offer more degrees of freedom. This leads to a more complex decision space. The results for the standard deviation of throughput time depending on the complexity of the system show the MAS producing almost constant throughput times. The standard deviation is obviously smaller compared to the centralized approach. Even if the average MAS results are worse than those of the Job-Shop algorithm, the standard deviation is normally smaller. In the next step, additional production capacity was introduced. It can be shown that no clear pattern is noticeable. The MAS performs well and gets slightly better when the interval between the dispatching of two consecutive orders is extended (resembles the factor increasing; as shown in Table 1), which leads to additional vacant production capacity.

Now the MAS have the opportunity to reschedule orders as soon as disturbances occur on one of the machines. But even now, the results got only slightly better compared to the centralized approach. Since redundant production facilities had the same disruption profile, rescheduling activities led to the effect, that the order was often disrupted on the machine which was chosen by the rescheduling algorithm. The superior planning quality of the Job-Shop algorithm and flexibility of the MAS nearly compensated each other. In the third step, both the complexity of the scenario and the homogeneity of the problem space were varied, so the MAS could fully benefit from its flexibility and its reactive behavior. The redundant machines got different disruption profiles representing different reliabilities. In reality, this corresponds to a mixed shop floor consisting of more than one generation of machines, as it is quite common.

In addition, the planning complexity was also increased. For this class of scenarios (different disruption profiles) the application of MAS makes a palpably impact. The results get better with decreasing lot sizes and increasing workflow factor, as supposed beforehand and explained above.

Due to the hitherto results, the rest of the evaluation process is performed on the basis of a scenario class without additional machines (i.e. the original circuit breaker assembly production plant) and different disruption profiles for the machines. This limits the evaluation space to a reasonable degree and the general features of MAS are expected to show up more evidently. In the following sub sections the two most interesting benchmarking criteria are presented.

3.6.3 Benchmarking of the Disruption Duration

The room for improvements of a decentralized MAS approach is positively affected by the disruption duration. While the centralized Job-Shop approach is not able to react to machine failures, the MAS can dispatch orders adaptively. However, vacant production capacity is a prerequisite. MAS produce steadily increasing results compared to the centralized OR algorithm. This assertion is also valid for the standard deviation of throughput time.

Furthermore, it is apparent that the MAS gets slightly better with the workload decreases. The factor 1.5, analyzed by Frey [Frey2003], leads to vacant production capacity. The standard deviation remains unaffected by the workload, which is defined by the dispatching mechanism.

3.6.4 Evaluation of the Lot Size Benchmarking Criteria

The lot size is an input variable for the production planning process. An order in the order list is split into $\frac{Order\ Quantity}{Lot\ Size}$ partial orders. The amount of partial orders is inversely proportional to the lot size. Small lot sizes entail many orders being dispatched which leads to a rise of complexity of the shop floor scenario.

Due to the huge amount of partial orders and the long planning horizon, the planned schedule increasingly differs from the real one in case of disturbances occur. The centralized Job-Shop approach is not able to regulate this deviation, as it can be derived from Figure 6.

The original goal of a line balancing algorithm, to minimize the completion dates by effectively balancing orders, is no longer feasible. This is caused by the missing consideration of disturbances in the planning process. The effect is even more obvious when looking at the standard deviation. The throughput time is calculated by summarizing processing and waiting time of the corresponding order. The waiting times for the machines are almost constant when using a MAS, which is caused by the highly effective treatment of waiting queues.

As a consequence, the completion dates can be estimated more precisely. Further analysis results, presented by [Frey2003] show that the dynamic dispatching of orders is handled slightly more efficient with decreasing workload. The MAS gets Non-deterministic vacant production capacity accessible, whereas the Job-Shop approach is not able to make use of it. The general advantage of MAS is caused by two factors. On the one hand, MAS can dispatch orders upon vacant machines dynamically. On the other hand, they are able to handle waiting queues more efficiently compared to centralized approaches. Depending on the order density, these MAS features come into conflict with each other, which leads to the almost constant behavior. This example once more points out several parameters affecting the behavior of a MAS at the same time. At this background, the flexibility of MAS elucidated in I.3 leads to better results of production planning and control in the described unit assembly manufacturing environment. Further research and development aim at the integration of a priority-rules-based approach at the enterprise level of the *Agent. Enterprise* scenario as described in II.1.

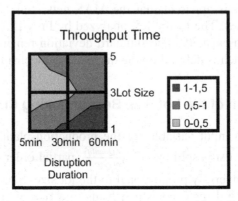

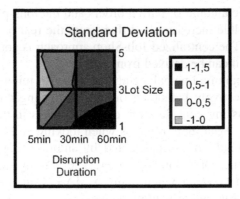

Figure 6. Average and standard deviation of the throughput time

3.7 Conclusion

MAS-based decentralized planning approaches produce better planning results than centralized Job-Shop algorithms when the decision space for a MSP problem is both complex and inhomogeneous. MAS facilitate good results in the decision space by taking into account time-dependent planning parameters. In addition, the waiting queues of the lines are handled more efficiently when disturbances occur. On the other hand, MAS normally provide less optimal solutions due to their local approaches of problem solving through negotiation. OR algorithms are highly sophisticated and effective in the non-disturbed case due to their much longer planning horizon and the global point of view. Yet, the corresponding re-scheduling algorithms that are applied in the case of disruptions are not sufficiently performing. The planning process for real industrial applications takes too much time to comply with real-time demands. The inhomogeneity of the problem space turned out to be the decisive factor for the suitability of a MAS in the scope of production planning and control.

In this case, the quality of the solutions is dynamically evolving and can not be predetermined. The other important factor is the complexity of the planning task. This structure and time complexity was mapped upon production parameters. During the evaluation, it was possible to assess the parameters according to their impact upon the results. Especially, the order was defined identically for all of the performance figures, throughput time, processing time and their standard deviations.

Two key features explaining the superiority of MAS in a turbulent production environment were identified in this chapter. First of all, MAS have the ability to "follow" good results. Due to the short planning horizon, the machine agents are able to consider time-dependent planning variables for their ratings, which lead to more precise results. The waiting queues of the lines are handled more efficiently when disturbances occur. The line balancing process is more effective and thus the medium throughput times and its standard deviations are smaller. The second factor is important with respect to the predictability of the results. These two key features affect each other, which finally explain the behavior of the MAS.

Another aspect, not being mentioned yet, is the maintainability of the different manufacturing systems. Due to its modular design, MAS are easier to maintain and the extensibility is guaranteed by the simple plug and play mechanisms of the respective agent platforms. This backs the explanations regarding flexibility in I.3 once again. On the other hand, the development effort to implement a MAS is higher, mainly caused by communication topics. However, MAS and rescheduling algorithms present a mean to guarantee robustness on the shop floor.

Standardization is a crucial task for the industrial propagation of agent-based technologies. This affects both the technological platform layer and the application layer. Standardized MAS solutions for well-defined PPC problems, including realistic and comprehensible benchmarks, are key factors for a successful dissemination and application in the future.

References

[ArCo2001]   Archimede, B.; Coudert, T.: Reactive Scheduling using a Multi-agent Model: The SCEP Framework. In: Engineering Applications of Artificial Intelligence 14(2001)5, pp. 667-683.

[Bren2000]   Brennan, R. W.: Performance comparison and analysis of reactive and planning-based control architectures for manufacturing. In: Robotics and Computer-Integrated Manufacturing 16(2000) 2-3, pp. 191-200.

[Cav+1999]   Cavalieri, S.; Bongaerts, L.; Macchi, M.; Taisch,, M.; Wyns, J.: A Benchmark Framework for Manufacturing Control. In: Proceedings of the 2nd International Workshop on Intelligent Manufacturing Systems. Leuven, 1999, pp. 225-236.

[CGMT2000]   Cavalieri, S.; Garetti, M.; Macchi, M.; Taisch, M.: An Experimental Benchmarking of two Multi-agent Architectures for Production Scheduling and Control. In: Computers in Industry 43 (2000)2, pp. 139-152.

[CaMV2003]   Cavalieri, S.; Macchi, M.; Valckenaers, P.: Benchmarking the Performance of Manufacturing Control Systems: Design Principles for a Web-based Simulated Testbed. In: Journal of Intelligent Manufacturing 14(2003)1, pp. 43-58.

[DBRA2005]   Database Specifications on RealAgentS, SPP 1083, http://www.realagents.org/public?ID=901&div1=879&action=open, accessed on 2006-01-31.

[FNWL2003]   Frey, D.; Nimis, J.; Wörn, H.; Lockemann, P.: Benchmarking and robust multi-agent-based production planning and control. In: Journal for Engineering Applications of Artificial Intelligence 16(2003), pp. 307-320.

[Frey2003]   Frey, D.: Simulationsgestützte Entwicklung eines Kanban-Systems in der Montage. Dissertation, 2003.

[FrWo2001]   Frey, D.; Wörn, H.: Development of a Complex Production Scenario for the Application of MAS in the Scope of Production Planning and Control (in German). In: Proceedings of the 3rd DFG colloquium of the German Priority Research Program on Intelligent Agents and Realistic Commercial Application Scenarios. Hameln, 2001.

[JaFo2002]   Jain, S.; Foley, W. J.: Impact of Interruptions on Schedule Execution in Flexible Manufacturing Systems. In: International Journal of Flexible Manufacturing Systems 14(2002)4, pp. 319-344.

[KuSh2002]   Kumar, N.; Shanker, K.: Comparing the effectiveness of workload balancing objectives in FMS loading. In: International Journal of Production Research 39 (2002)5, pp. 843-871.

[Ohno1993]   Ohno, T.: Toyota Production System. Productivity Press Incorporated, 1993.

[Paru1987]	Parunak, H.: Manufacturing Experience with the Contract Net. In: Huhns, M. N. (Ed.): Distributed Artificial Intelligence. Morgan Kaufmann Publishers, Los Altos, 1987.
[Reit1995]	Reithofer, W.: VICTOR – Designing the Factory of the Future. In: Proceedings of the 11th International Conference on CAD/CAM, Robotics and Factories of the Future (CARS& FOF). Pereira, 1995.
[Reit1995]	Reithofer, W.: Bottom-up Modeling with CIMOSA. In: Proceedings of the 2nd International Conference on the Design of Information Infrastructure Systems for Manufacturing (DIISM). Kaatsheuvel, 1996.
[Scho1999]	Scholl, A.: Balancing and Sequencing of Assembly Lines. Physica-Verlag, Heidelberg, 1999.
[SWFM1995]	Spieck, S.; Weigelt, M.; Falk, J.; Mertens, P.: Decentralized Problem Solving in Logistics and Production with partly Intelligent Agents and Comparison with Alternative Approaches. In: Nunamaker Jr., J. F.;. Sprague Jr., R. H (Eds.): Proceedings of the 28th Hawaii International Conference on System Sciences. Maui, 1995, pp. 52 ff.
[WeMe1999]	Weigelt, M.; Mertens, P.: Comparison of decentralized and centralized computer based production control. In: Baskin, A. B.; Kovacs, G. L.; Jacucci, G. (Eds.): Cooperative Knowledge Processing for Engineering Design, IFIP, Vol. 137. Kluwer, 1999, pp. 83-92.

4 Distributed Hierarchical Production Control for Wafer Fabs Using an Agent-Based System Prototype[1]

Lars Mönch, Marcel Stehli, Jens Zimmermann

Technische Universität Ilmenau, Institut für Wirtschaftsinformatik
{lars.moench | marcel.stehli | jens.zimmermann}@tu-ilmenau.de

Abstract. FABMAS is a hierarchically organized multiagent system for production control of semiconductor wafer fabrication facilities (wafer fabs). The production control of wafer fabs is challenging from a complexity and coordination point of view. Semiconductor manufacturing involves one of the most complex manufacturing processes ever used. In this paper, we describe the application domain and major design decisions that lead to the FABMAS system prototype. A detailed discussion of the suggested software architecture of the agent-based system is included. Furthermore, we present the results of computational experiments that show that FABMAS outperforms dispatching based production control schemes that are currently in use. The paper also discusses some limitations and drawbacks of the suggested approach and identifies areas of future research.

4.1 Introduction

Semiconductor manufacturing has been growing tremendously in the last decade. The goal of semiconductor manufacturing is the production of integrated circuits (ICs), also called chips, on silicon wafers. Today this domain consists of very complex manufacturing systems. The semiconductor manufacturing domain is characterized by several hundred of very expensive machines, hundreds of lots, a customer demand driven type of manufacturing, an over time changing product mix, sequence dependent set-up times, re-entrant process flows and a mix of single wafer, single lot, and batch processes. Here, a batch is defined as a set of lots that have to be processed at the same time on the same machine [MaSi2003]. Furthermore, the semiconductor manufacturing domain is characterized by stochastic events like machine breakdowns and the change of customer re-

---

[1] For more information on the FAB Multi Agent System (FABMAS) we refer to:
http://www.wirtschaft.tu-ilmenau.de/deutsch/institute/wi/wi1/projekt/start.html

lated due dates of the lots (cf. to [AtAt1995] [UzLM1994] [PfFo2005] for a more detailed description of semiconductor manufacturing problems).

Production control of semiconductor wafer fabs is challenging because of the complexity of the under laying production process and its stochastic and dynamical nature.

The motivation for the research described in this paper is driven by two different sources.

1. We find a high degree of automation on the shop floor in high-tech industries like semiconductor manufacturing. Data collection capabilities are highly developed within manufacturing execution systems (MES). Therefore, a computer-based decision support is highly desirable.
2. The capabilities of computers are increased in the last decade. There are huge improvements in hardware and software (for example, modern middleware). Furthermore, based on the improved computer performance we can observe a renaissance of computer intensive methods from Operations Research (OR) and Artificial Intelligence (AI).

Commercial production control software packages (mainly MES) applied to the semiconductor manufacturing domain have the following drawbacks:

1. They are based mainly on software technologies from the early 90s. The underlying architecture follows only in parts the client-server architecture.
2. An extension or further development of these information systems from a functional point of view is difficult.
3. A communication, i.e. information exchange, with other information systems on the shop floor and on other planning and control layers is complicated.
4. None of the currently used systems contains modern production control algorithms. There is no clear separation between the structure of the production control system and the production control schemes.
5. Most of the systems rely on centralized databases. However, for decision-making very often local data would be enough.

Techniques from Distributed Artificial Intelligence (DAI), especially multiagent systems (MAS) (cf. I.2), provide approaches that allow for the flexible collaboration of decentralized software systems ("agents") to solve superior tasks. That leads to the question which production control capabilities can be obtained through the collaboration of agents that work decentralized. Furthermore, it is challenging to investigate whether these decentralized systems equipped with cooperative capabilities may outperform more traditional production control systems.

The following coordination problems have to be solved in wafer fabs:

1. control of planned and dynamic bottlenecks, i.e. a starvation of planned bottlenecks has to be avoided, whereas appropriate scheduling and dispatching decisions have to be made for dynamic bottlenecks,
2. appropriate set-up and batching decision-making, i.e., the situation in front of downstream and upstream machine groups has to be taken into account during making scheduling decisions in front of parallel machines with sequence-dependent setup times or in front of a group of batching machines,
3. determination of enterprise-wide schedules is highly desirable instead of local optimization of schedules for selected machines because only in this situation global performance measures can be taken into account.

The semiconductor manufacturing domain is well suited to serve as a test-bed for the usage of techniques from DAI because it contains enough complexity (huge number of machines, products, and lots) as well as challenging coordination problems.

This chapter of the book is organized as follows. In the next Section, we discuss related literature. In Section 4.3, we describe our distributed hierarchical production control approach. The design and the implementation of our agent-based production control system is the topic of Section 4.4. We describe computational experiments in Section 4.5. Conclusions are presented and some future research topics are suggested in Section 4.6.

4.2 Related Work

Currently it seems that dispatching rules are the widely used production control approach in semiconductor manufacturing [PfFo2005]. Dispatching rules have the drawback that they are short-sighted in time and space. Usually, they support only one performance measure of interest. It is rather hard to work towards more global oriented goals. Furthermore, dispatching rules are only to a certain extent able to adapt to different situations like high load of the manufacturing system or tight due dates.

There are several prototypes for production control of wafer fabs described in the intelligent scheduling literature. The system LMS from IBM (cf. [SuFo1990] for more details), the system ReDS (cf. [Hada1994]), and the system MMST from Texas Instruments [FKKS1994] are examples for such prototypes. These systems are partially distributed and LMS uses also

functional agents. However, these prototypes rely on the software technologies from the early 90s (for example Lisp) and they are not in further
use in our days because of technical and also organizational reasons
[Kemp1994]. A more recent prototype of a knowledge-based scheduler
applied to wafer fabs is described in [MiYi2003]. Discrete event simulation and neural networks are used to make scheduling decisions in a situation-dependent manner. However, because of the time consuming simulation-based training data collection for the neural network this approach is
more appropriate for a static than for a dynamic environment.

Hierarchical production control approaches are quite popular in semiconductor manufacturing (cf. [SrBG1994] [VaRi2001] [VaRK2003]).
These approaches try to deal with the inherent complexity of wafer fabs by
using a hierarchical decomposition approach. However, the approaches described so far rely heavily on control theory and therefore are not able to
deal with individual lots. Hence, due date related performance measures
are not possible. They also do not exploit the distributed character of decision-making within hierarchies. The resulting systems are not distributed
from a software technology point of view.

Multiagent systems have attracted many researchers in the manufacturing domain. For more details, we refer, for example, to the survey papers
[ShNo1999] and [CaCa2004]. However, often only experiences with a
contract net type production control scheme are reported. Furthermore, the
domains of application are more related to low complexity (flexible)
manufacturing systems. A rigorous performance assessment is often
missed. It is at least questionable whether a complex manufacturing can be
controlled by a contract net type approach so that appropriate dispatching
rules are outperformed. The holonic manufacturing approach (see [McBu
2000] for a more detailed discussion) is going to reduce theses problems
by allowing agents to contain other agents. Following this approach we
can model hierarchical relationships with less effort.

Only one more recent agent-based production control system development effort [AEMS2005] in a very preliminary stage is reported in the literature for the semiconductor manufacturing domain. The system implements a starvation avoidance strategy based on negotiations among agents
that represent lots and machines. However, the system is described only on
a conceptual level, computational results are not reported.

A modified shifting bottleneck heuristic is described in [MaFC2002].
This heuristic decomposes the overall scheduling problem into scheduling
problems related to single groups of parallel machines. The view of the
overall problem is ensured by the concept of disjunctive graphs. An efficient implementation and some computational results of the shifting bottleneck heuristic are described in [MoRo2004]. The combination of a two-

layer hierarchical approach with the shifting bottleneck heuristic is described in [MoDr2005]. However, the distributed character of the approach is not used in [MoDr2005]. From the presented computational experiments it turns out that shifting bottleneck type solution heuristics are able to outperform dispatching rule based approaches in several situations.

So far, we described only related work with respect to solution techniques. However, scheduling on the shop floor is also limited by missing state of the art software systems and other infrastructure issues. We are far away from having an ultimate architecture for future production control systems. It seems to be possible that modern production control system will be agent-based and distributed. Therefore, it is highly desirable to develop ideas for leading edge production control systems.

Based on the discussed related literature it appear to be reasonable to compare an agent-based system with dispatching approaches and also with the centralized shifting bottleneck heuristic from a solution quality point of view. At the same time, it is necessary to compare issues like interoperability and data requirements to run a certain production control application.

4.3 Distributed Hierarchical Decision-Making in the Semiconductor Wafer Fabrication Domain

As suggested by Mesarovic [MeMT1970] and Schneeweiss [Schn2003] it turns out that hierarchical decomposition is a powerful tool to deal with complexity and uncertainty in systems. Generally, we say that two objects are in a hierarchical relationship if at least one of the following three conditions is valid [Schn2003].

1. The decision-rights of the two objects are different.
2. They make decisions at different points of time.
3. The information status of the two objects for decision-making is different.

Note that only the first condition is usually associated with rigid master-slave type hierarchical approaches. The notation of hierarchies suggested by Schneeweiss [Schn2003] is much more expressive. Consequently, we will use the term "distributed decision-making" when there are several decision-making units that make their decisions at different points of time and when the decision-making units have to collaborate to solve the overall problem.

Decision-making requires goals and a certain degree of pro-activity. On the other hand, communication abilities are required for the different decision-making entities in order to coordinate, i.e. harmonize, the distributed decisions. Therefore, as pointed out in [Schn2003] software agents (cf. a definition of agents in I.1) are an appropriate (software) tool to implement distributed decision-making systems if the resulting agent-based systems are enriched by more sophisticated coordination and optimization abilities.

Having this argumentation in mind, we will describe in a first step a distributed hierarchical approach to carry out production control for wafer fabs. Then, in a second step, we will identify the necessary agents in order to construct the distributed production control system.

Because of the multi-product, customer oriented type of wafer fabs we are interested in minimizing the total weighted tardiness (TWT) of the lots as performance measure. Note that this problem is NP hard [Lawl1977]. The quantity TWT is defined as follows:

$$TWT := \sum_{j=1}^{n} w_j \max(C_j - d_j, 0) \tag{1}$$

C_j Completion time of lot j

d_j Due date

w_j Weight factor that describes the importance of lot j (and the related customer)

n Number of lots already completed within a certain time horizon

Note that TWT is our primary measure of interest. However we have to measure the cycle time of the lots and the throughput too.

The suggested hierarchical approach contains three different layers. Based on our primary performance measure, we identify a top layer that has to take into account the due dates of the lots during its decision-making. The top layer works on aggregated routes. Each aggregated route consists of several macro-operations. A single macro-operation contains usually three to five consecutive process steps. All process steps of a macro-operation have to be performed in a single work area. A work area itself is defined as a set of groups of parallel machines that are nearby located on the shop floor. A wafer fab usually contains the lithography work area, the etching work area, the diffusion work area, and the implantation work area. The described situation is shown in Figure 1.

The top layer is used to determine start dates and end dates for single macro-operations of a lot with respect to a certain work area. Note that the result of the top layer is a rough schedule for all lots that takes the external due dates of lots into account. This schedule has to be refined by the other layers of the hierarchy. We use a simple infinite capacity approach that basically estimates waiting times as a multiple of the processing times to the macro-operations (cf. [MoDr2005] for more details on the top layer of the hierarchy).

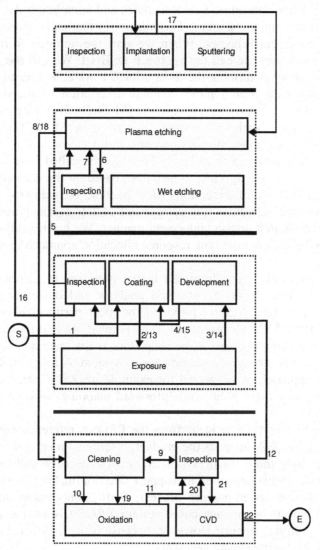

Figure 1. Decomposition of a wafer fab into different work areas

The start dates and end dates are necessary for the middle layer in order to determine detailed schedules for the lots. We assign a single decision-making unit to each work area. Hence, a distributed calculation of the schedules is possible. A shifting-bottleneck type heuristic is applied to the lots within each work area. The heuristic relies on the start dates and end dates of the top layer. We call this approach naive distributed shifting bottleneck heuristic (NDSBH). After determining a detailed schedule for one work area we can determine new start dates and completion dates for the lots in the remaining work areas. This allows for the implementation of iterative improvement schemes. When we start the iteration from a fixed bottleneck work area we call the approach DSBH-I. We call the approach DSBH-II when we determine the most critical work area dynamically and repeat the iteration. For a more detailed description of the distributed shifting bottleneck heuristic, we refer to [MoDr2005]. Compared to the centralized shifting bottleneck heuristic described in [MoRo2004] the distributed variant needs less memory and runs faster.

We have to consider a third layer. This layer is called base layer. The base layer is used to assign lots to machines based on the schedules of the middle layer. In case of exceptions (like machine breakdowns) that may lead to infeasible schedules, the assignment of lots to machines that are available is done in a dispatching-based manner. We use several dispatching rules and a contract net type resource allocation approach in this situation.

Several approaches are discussed in the literature to identify agents. There is a rich body on agent-based analysis and design approaches. Bussmann et al. [BuJW2001] provided the most pertinent ideas for the purpose of the FABMAS prototype. They pointed out that the analysis of the decision-making process of the shop floor is the main source in order to identify agents for a given manufacturing system. A role based analysis and design approach as suggested for example in [ZaJW2003] is not appropriate because there is no straightforward mapping between roles and decision tasks.

Furthermore, we borrow ideas from the PROSA reference architecture [Van+1998]. PROSA suggests the *p*roduct, *r*esource, *o*rder, and *s*taff *a*gent types. The first three agent types are called decision-making agents whereas staff agents are used to support decision-making agents in the course of their decision-making process. Staff agents encapsulate more centralized aspects in an agent-based system. PROSA is used as a starting point for identifying agents. However, because of its high level of granularity several refinements are necessary.

A decision-making agent is assigned to each decision-making unit in the hierarchical approach. We also have to consider the dynamic system entities as suggested by PROSA. Furthermore, the scheduling and dispatching schemes on the different layers of the hierarchy are used to identify staff agents.

We identify a manufacturing system agent as a specific decision-making agent. This agent has to determine the rough production schedules on the top layer. Therefore, it has to set certain parameters of the lot planning algorithm. In addition, this agent has to coordinate the distributed shifting bottleneck heuristic in the iterative case. The manufacturing agent is supported by a lot planning agent that determines the rough plans for the lots and additionally by a manufacturing system monitoring agent.

On the middle layer, we identify work area agents that are responsible for making detailed scheduling decisions for the lots within its work area. Each work area agent is supported by a work area scheduling agent that is responsible for determining detailed schedules based on the shifting bottleneck heuristic. We consider monitoring agents for each single work area.

In the base layer, we identify machine group agents that have to implement the schedules from the middle layer. They support a contract net type resource allocation scheme when the schedules from the middle layer are infeasible.

We also consider lot agents that represent individual lots on the shop floor. Batch agents are used for the representation of already formed batches.

4.4 Design and Implementation of the Agent-Based Production Control System

It turns out that we can use an agent-based system to implement our distributed hierarchical production control approach. The resulting agent-based system should support:

1. flexible representation of the process conditions of semiconductor manufacturing domain,
2. modeling capabilities for agent hierarchies,
3. capabilities to emulate a wafer fab represented by a discrete event simulation model for performance assessment of our agent-based production control system,
4. integration capabilities for legacy software in order to use more advanced heuristics for staff agents.

After developing a small complexity MAS prototype based on the JAFMAS framework using the Java programming language [MoSS2002], investigating some agent-based toolkits, and based on some not very optimistic information from the literature [Vrba2003], we decided to design and to implement our MAS based on the .NET framework mainly because none of the existing agent toolkits and agent frameworks support our four key requirements (for a more detailed discussion of this design decision we refer to [MoSt2005] due to space limitations). We decide to follow the FIPA standard for agent-based systems (cf. IV.7) as close as possible in order to ensure in principle interoperability of the FABMAS prototype with other MAS. Later, we generalized our agent system architecture in the *Manufacturing Agency* (ManufAg) agent framework [MoSt2005].

We follow a role based approach in order to design our single agent architecture. Roles are used to encapsulate the normative behavior repertoire of agents [OdPF2003]. Each single role is characterized by a set of possible behaviors. Transitions from a certain behavior to another behavior are possible. We present a corresponding UML class diagram in Figure 2.

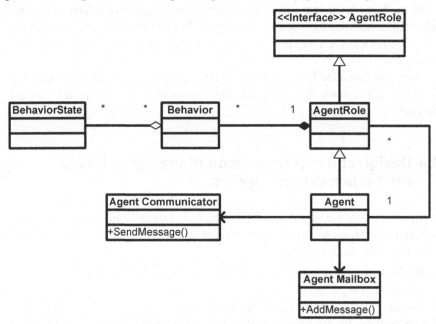

Figure 2. Single agent architecture

Our single agent architecture is somewhat similar to the layered architecture discussed in the literature. Decision-making agents are basically reactive agents, whereas the staff agents correspond to the local and cooperative planning layers in the layered approach. Each single agent contains an agent mailbox for incoming messages and has access to an agent communicator that is responsible for outgoing messages.

The agent-based system FABMAS consists of several runtime environments. The runtime environment contains

1. an Agent Container,

2. a Directory Service,
3. an Agent Management System,
4. an Agent Communicator.

The agent container as a collection of all active agents in the agent runtime environment contains the agents for production control (domain agents) and the system agents (e.g. agent management and directory service). An agent container is part of each runtime.

The agent directory service contains the information on the offered services of the agents during runtime. A directory service agent is located in each runtime. The directory service agents (of the different runtimes) interact and exchange information about the agent services of the MAS. Agents register their specifications as a service-entry at the directory service agent of the agent runtime where the agent is located and registered. Agents can ask the directory service agent looking for other agents with special services. Each agent can only ask his local directory service agent for the desired information. If the local directory service agent is not able to fulfill the inquiry the agent tries to find the information by interaction with the other directory service agents within the entire MAS. Hence, it is not necessary to establish a global directory service as a centralized information point in a distributed system.

An agent management system administrates the life cycle for all agents of its runtime. The creation of the agent, the observation of the agent behaviors, the provision of potentially mobility services and the removal of an agent if it is not any longer needed are the services of the agent that are represented by the agent management system.

For the communication between the agents an agent communicator is necessary. This agent communicator encapsulates direct and multicast communication capabilities. The relating agent communicator handles each communication act. When an agent is interested in sending a message then a message is stored in the outgoing mailbox and the agent communicator sends the message to the receiver agent that is addressed in the message.

In order to build a distributed agent hierarchy across different platforms, a unique identifier, called Hierarchy Identifier (HI), is introduced. This identifier is the organizational knowledge base for each agent. It provides the agents with a system wide unique hierarchy name that does not depend on the runtime where the agent is hosted. Furthermore, the HI stores the potential parent agent of a hierarchically organized agent and keeps track of its subsidiary child agents. The hierarchical organization of the agents is performed automatically as soon as an agent gets alive. The hierarchical organization system owned by each single runtime helps the agent to find its place within the hierarchy by looking for the appropriate parent and child agents. The used agent runtime environment is shown in Figure 3.

A single runtime environment is used for each work area. Each runtime environment contains all the agents that are related to the work area. Furthermore, a fixed runtime environment also contains the manufacturing system agent and the corresponding lot planning agent.

Each single runtime environment represents the data for decision-making locally. We use data replication and therefore redundancy in order to reduce the communication overhead. For example, the routes of the products are stored for each single runtime environment. We use data structures for lots and resources in order to maintain the necessary data.

Decision-making agents and staff agents interact in a rather generic way. For example, each decision-making agent has to set several parameters in order to use the algorithms that are represented by the staff agent.

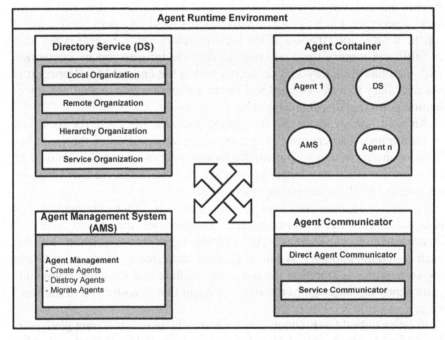

Figure 3. Agent runtime environment

We developed an ontology that contains the vocabulary for a meaningful communication of the different agents within FABMAS. The FABMAS ontology is described in [MoSt2003]. In order to use the ontology we developed the content language FABtalk [MoSt2004]. FABtalk is basically a context-free grammar that can be used to construct more complex meaningful statements during agent interactions. We convert the classes of the ontology in XML constructs that can be used by FABtalk.

Before presenting some computational results from performance assessment we are going to present some ideas of our implementation approach. We use basically an iterative, incremental approach. We started with the implementation of a small complexity MAS for production control using the Java programming language and the JAFMAS framework. The results and experiences made during this phase of the project are documented in [MoSS2002]. Based on these results we started with the design and the implementation of the described FABMAS architecture based on the C# programming language and the .NET remoting middleware. The suggested architecture is contained in a more general and abstract form in the ManufAg framework [MoSt2005]. At the same time, we developed all the necessary production control algorithms as stand-alone solutions (mainly by using the C++ programming language) and also the architecture for performance assessment [MoDr2005]. By using the concept of decision-making and staff agents the developed algorithms were later integrated with minimal effort in the FABMAS prototype. Because we have experience with the performance of all stand-alone algorithms the integration with FABMAS was quite straightforward. After implementing the infrastructure we developed a domain-specific ontology and a content language. After developing these prerequisites we were able to perform our performance assessment experiments. In summary, we agree with many observations from [WoJe1999] (for example, not every object should be modeled as an agent, building a MAS requires computer science knowledge), however, our picture on developing own agent-based systems (from scratch) is much more optimistic.

4.5 Performance Assessment of the Prototype

In this section we describe the results of simulation-based benchmark efforts for our agent-based system FABMAS. Simulation is used to emulate the manufacturing process of interest. We apply a performance assessment architecture that is already described in [MoRS2003]. The center point of the used architecture is a blackboard type data layer between the agent-based production control system and the simulation model. The data layer residents in the memory of a computer and is basically an object model. It acts as a mirror that contains the relevant business objects from the operative databases of the manufacturing execution system (MES) and the enterprise resource planning system (ERP). The blackboard type data layer is updated in an event-driven manner by the simulation system. We show the used architecture for performance assessment in Figure 4.

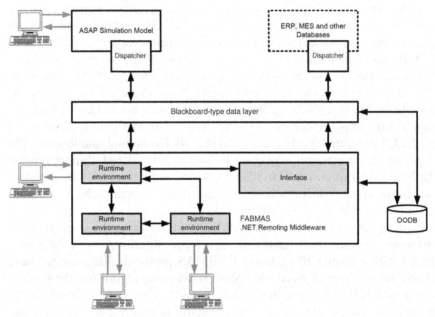

Figure 4. Architecture for performance assessment

We simulate 50 days. We do not include any machine breakdowns in our experiments. We use three different reference simulation models of wafer fabs in our experiments.

The first one is adapted from a small complexity model suggested by researchers from Intel [EIRT1997]. The original model contains only three work centers and two product routes with six steps. The process flow is organized in two layers. Among the machine groups, there is a batch processing one and a machine group with sequence-dependent set-up times. The model imitates some important features of wafer fabs. We call this model minifab model. Our first model contains three work areas. Each of them contains the machinery of the minifab model. The process flows are organized into two layers. The first work center is visited two times. Therefore, it contains 15 machines and two products with 24 process steps. We denote this model as model A.

The second model is a reduced variant of the MIMAC Testbed Data Set 1 [FoFL1995]. It contains two routes with 103 and 100 steps respectively. The process flow is highly re-entrant. The lots are processed on 147 machines that are organized into 38 work centers. Among the machines are batching machines. The model contains four work areas. We denote the second model by model B.

The third model is the MIMAC Testbed Data Set 1. It contains over 200 machines that are organized into over 80 work centers. The work centers form five work areas. The model contains two routes with 210 and 245 steps respectively. The third model is called model C.

We are interested in the performance measures TWT, cycle time (CT) and throughput (TP). All values for these measures are presented relative to the corresponding values obtained by a FIFO dispatched system. We expect that the performance of our approach depends on the due date setting and the load of the wafer fab. Furthermore, based on previous experiments with the centralized shifting bottleneck approach [MoRo2004] we investigate the dependency of the solution quality from various parameter settings of the hierarchical approach. We use different scheduling intervals τ_{up} for the top layer of the hierarchy. For the middle layer, we perform experiments with different scheduling interval τ_Δ and an additional scheduling horizon τ_{ah}, i.e., every τ_Δ time units we determine a schedule for a horizon of $\tau_\Delta + \tau_{ah}$. Furthermore, we are interested in the reduction of time for computation if we distribute the different agent runtimes (i.e., all the agents that are assigned to a certain work area) on different computers.

For due date setting, we use the relation

$$d_j := r_j + FF \sum_{i=1}^{n_j} p_{ji} \qquad (2)$$

r_j release date of lot j

p_{ij} processing time of step i of lot j

n_j number of process steps of lot j

The used experimental design for our experiments is summarized in Table 1.

Table 1. Experimental design

Factor	Level	Count
Model	A,B,C	3
Due Date Setting	Tight ($FF = 1.6$), Wide ($FF = 2.0$)	2
Load of the System	High, Moderate	2
Approach for Middle Layer	NDSBH, DSBH-I, DSBH-II	3
Production Scheduling Interval of the Top Layer	$\tau_{up} = \{2h, 4h\}$	2
Scheduling Interval of the Middle Layer	$\tau_\Delta = \{2h, 4h\}$	2
Additional Horizon	$\tau_{ah} = \{0h, 2h\}$	2
Computing	single computer, distributed	2

In a first series of experiments we change the settings for τ_Δ and τ_{ah}. We use model A and model B for these experiments. Furthermore, $\tau_{up} = 4h$ is valid. We present the corresponding TWT values in Table 2. We can see from Table 2 that we obtain the smallest TWT values for the combination $\tau_\Delta = 2h$ and $\tau_{ah} = 0h$.

The combination $\tau_\Delta = 4h$ and $\tau_{ah} = 2h$ also provides results of similar quality. Larger scheduling horizons lead to worse results. It is interesting to mention that we obtain a similar solution quality as for the shifting bottleneck heuristic implementation described in [MoRo2004].

Table 2. Solution quality for changing scheduling horizon

Approach	NDSBH		DSBH-I		DSBH-II	
Model	Model A	Model B	Model A	Model B	Model A	Model B
Scheduling Horizon						
2+0	0.6534	0.362	0.642	0.3677	0.5800	0.3733
2+2	0.754	0.4518	0.6809	0.4108	0.5481	0.5155
2+4	0.6846	1.2406	0.6149	1.3295	0.5882	1.0928
4+0	0.6033	0.4549	0.5915	0.4261	0.6359	0.3732
4+2	0.4751	0.4685	0.5068	0.4462	0.5271	0.3836
4+4	0.6136	1.1084	0.5639	1.5133	0.5623	1.5591
6+0	0.8364	0.5045	0.8521	0.4639	0.8738	0.5027
6+2	0.6488	0.5144	0.6437	0.4677	0.658	0.4339
6+4	0.5489	1.0226	0.6543	1.5081	0.6561	1.5943
8+0	1.1687	0.5892	1.2687	0.6972	1.2217	0.6589
8+2	0.9164	0.4452	0.8886	0.6172	0.9199	0.743
8+4	0.7979	1.3268	0.7391	2.0676	0.722	2.2628

In a second series of experiments we are interested in the solution quality that we can expect for different characteristics of the wafer fab. We consider model B. It hold $\tau_{up} = 2h$, $\tau_\Delta = 2h$, and $\tau_{ah} = 2h$. We present the corresponding results in Table 3. It turns out that tight due dates lead to larger improvements of TWT than wide due dates. In most cases we obtain better results for a high loaded system. The results for CT and TP are basically independent of the system conditions. The relative TWT values are rather high in case of wide due dates. This is mainly caused by TWT values close to zero for a FIFO dispatched system. The hierarchical approach performs not so well in this situation. We did experiments with other due date and slack-based dispatching rules (like, for example the earliest due date (EDD) and the critical ratio (CR) rule [AtAt1995]). In many situations, especially for tight due dates and a high load of the system, but not always, our approach was able to beat these dispatching rules.

We made a couple of experiments in order to find out how much we can gain from distributing the different decision-making entities of the work area layer on different computers in terms of speedup the computation.

The experiments were performed on a cluster of 2.4 GHz PCs with 256 MB RAM in a 100 Mbps Ethernet network.

Table 3. Solution quality for changing characteristics of the models

Approach		NDSBH			DSBH-I		
Measure		TWT	CT	TP	TWT	CT	TP
Load	Due Date						
High	Tight	0.5987	0.9895	1.0140	0.6187	0.9897	1.0102
	Wide	39.3131	1.0073	1.0064	47.4678	1.0049	1.0051
Mode- rate	Tight	1.0597	0.9956	0.9925	0.8796	0.9892	0.9962
	Wide	26.0175	1.0062	1.0013	139.106	1.0168	1.0013

According to the number of work areas in each of our three test models we use three, four, and five computers respectively. We show the savings in time required for computation in Table 4 for $\tau_{up} = 4h$, $\tau_{dh} = 0$, $\tau_{\Delta} = 2h$, and $\tau_{\Delta} = 4h$. We use NSBH in these experiments.

Table 4. Computational time savings due to distributed computing

Computational Time Saving (in %)	Model A	Model B	Model C
$\tau_{\Delta} = 2h$	21	35	34
$\tau_{\Delta} = 4h$	45	47	40

From Table 4 it turns out that the savings in case of a larger scheduling interval are greater. In the case of model C we run the algorithm on five different computers, hence the communication efforts are greater compared to model B. From the experiments it turns out that a distribution, especially in case of models of large-scale wafer fabs, offers some advantage.

4.6 Conclusions and Future Research

In this book chapter, we described an agent-based system that can be used for distributed hierarchical production control of wafer fabs. We use a proper hierarchical decomposition of the entire production control problem. We designed appropriate decision-making agents and related staff agents. We implemented the resulting agent-based system by using the C#

and the C++ programming languages. We performed a simulation-based performance assessment of the resulting production control system. It turns out that the new scheduling approach outperforms more traditional production control approaches like, for example, dispatching rules. We also compared our approach with a rather sophisticated centralized scheduling approach.

As a main result we conclude that our agent-based system produces approximately the same solution quality in term of total weighted tardiness, cycle time, and throughput as the centralized shifting bottleneck heuristic (cf. [MoDr2005]). It outperforms pure dispatching based production control approaches in case of a high system load and tight due dates in many situations. However, because of distributed determination of the schedules the agent-based production control is faster. Furthermore, it requires less memory. We come up with an architecture that leads to the required separation between structure of the production control system and the used production control algorithms. Clearly, it is rather easy to exchange production control algorithms during runtime of the production control system by simply remove an old staff agent and launch an appropriate new staff agent.

There are several future research needs. First of all, we have to include more adaptive system behavior in our production control system. Currently, we investigate the usage of fuzzy rules for the determination of sequences for scheduling machine groups within the distributed shifting bottleneck heuristic in a situation-dependent manner. A second research direction is a further extension of the suggested software architecture within the ManufAg agent framework [MoSt2005]. So far, we have implemented only the FABMAS prototype and a second prototype of a production control system applied to simple flexible manufacturing systems. However, in future research we also have to address the problem of modeling automated material handling systems (cf. [BaCS2004] for some preliminary steps into this direction).

References

[AEMS2005]   Agent-Enhanced Manufacturing System Initiative (AEMSI), 2005. http://www.altarum.org/-altarum/ESD/research_agent_complex.asp#aemsi.

[AtAt1995]   Atherton, L. F.; Atherton, R. W.: Wafer Fabrication: Factory Performance and Analysis. Kluwer Academic Publishers, Boston et al., 1995.

[BaCS2004]   Babiceanu, R. F.; Chen, F. F.; Sturges, R. H.: Framework for the Control of Automated Material-Handling Systems Using the Holonic Manufacturing Approach. In: International Journal of Production Research 42(2004)17, pp. 3551-3564.

[BuJW2001]   Bussmann, S.; Jennings, N. R.; Wooldridge, M.: On the Identification of Agents in the Design of Production Control Systems. In: Agent-Oriented Software Engineering. Springer, pp. 141-162.

[CaCa2004]   Caridi, M.; Cavalieri, S.: Multi-agent Systems in Production Planning and Control: An Overview. In: Production Planning & Control 15(2004)2, pp. 106-118.

[ElRT1997]   El Adl, M. K.; Rodriguez, A. A.; Tsakalis, K. S.: Hierarchical Modeling and Control of Re-entrant Semiconductor Manufacturing Facilities. In: Proceedings of the 35th Conference on Decision and Control. Kobe, Japan, pp. 1736-1742.

[FKKS1994]   Fargher, H. E.; Kilgore, M., A.; Kleine, P. J.; Smith, R. A.: A Planner and Scheduler for Semiconductor Manufacturing. In: IEEE Transactions on Semiconductor Manufacturing 7, pp. 117-126.

[FoFL1995]   Fowler, J. W.; Feigin, G.; Leachman, R.: Semiconductor Manufacturing Testbed Data Sets. Arizona State University, 1995.

[Hada1994]   Hadavi, K. C.: A Real Time Production Scheduling System from Conception to Practice. In: Zweben, M.; Fox, M. S. (Eds.): Intelligent Scheduling. Morgan Kaufmann, San Francisco, CA, 1994, pp. 581-604.

[Kemp1994]   Kempf, K.: Intelligently Scheduling Semiconductor Wafer Fabrication. In: Zweben, M.; Fox, M. S. (Eds.): Intelligent Scheduling. Morgan Kaufmann, San Francisco, CA, 1994, pp. 517-544.

[Lawl1977]   Lawler, E. L.: A "Pseudopolynomial" Time Algorithm for Sequencing Jobs to Minimize Total Weighted Tardiness. In: Annals of Discrete Mathematics 1, pp. 331-342.

[MaSi2003]   Mathirajan, M.; Sivakumar, A. I.: Scheduling Batch Processors in Semiconductor Manufacturing – A Review. Singapore MIT Alliance (SMA) 2003 Symposium, National University of Singapore. https://dspace.mit.edu/retrieve/3521/-IMST021.

[MaFC2002]   Mason, S. J.; Fowler, J. W.; Carlyle, W. M.: A Modified Shifting Bottleneck Heuristic for Minimizing Total Weighted Tardiness in Complex Job Shops. In: Journal of Scheduling 5(2002)3, pp. 247-262.

[McBu2000]   McFarlane, D. C.; Bussmann, S.: Developments in Holonic Production Planning and Control. In: Production Planning & Control 11(2000)6, pp. 522-536.

[MeMT1970]   Mesarovic, M. D.; Macko, D.; Takahara, Y.: Theory of Hierarchical, Multilevel Systems. Academic Press, New York, London, 1970.

[MiYi2003]   Min, H. S.; Yih, Y.: Development of a Real-Time Multi-Objec-
                tive Scheduler for a Semiconductor Fabrication System. In: In-
                ternational Journal of Production Research 41(2003)10, pp.
                2345-2364.

[MoDr2005]   Mönch, L.; Driessel, R.: A Distributed Shifting Bottleneck Heu-
                ristic for Complex Job Shops. In: Computers & Industrial Engin-
                eering 49(2005), pp. 363-380.

[MoRo2004]   Mönch, L.; Rose, O.: Shifting-Bottleneck-Heuristik für komple-
                xe Produktionssysteme: softwaretechnische Realisierung und
                Leistungsbewertung. In: Suhl, L.; Voss, S. (Eds.): Quantitative
                Methoden in ERP und SCM, DSOR Beiträge zur Wirtschaftsin-
                formatik 2, pp. 145-159.

[MoSt2003]   Mönch, L.; Stehli, M.: An Ontology for Production Control of
                Semiconductor Manufacturing Processes. In: Proceedings of the
                First German Conference on Multiagent System Technologies
                (MATES 2003), LNAI 2831. Springer, Erfurt, Germany,
                pp. 156-167.

[MoSt2004]   Mönch, L.; Stehli, M.: A Content Language for a Hierarchically
                Organized Multi-Agent-System for Production Control. In: Pro-
                ceedings Coordination and Agent Technology in Value Net-
                works. Essen, Germany, pp. 197-212.

[MoSt2005]   Mönch, L.; Stehli, M.: ManufAG: a Multi-Agent-System Frame-
                work for Production Control of Complex Manufacturing Sys-
                tems. To appear in Journal of Information Systems & E-Busi-
                ness Management.

[MoSS2002]   Mönch, L.; Stehli, M.; Schulz, R.: An Agent-Based Architecture
                for Solving Dynamic Resource Allocation Problems in Manu-
                facturing. In: Proceedings of the 14th European Simulation
                Symposium (ESS 2002). Dresden, 2002, pp. 331-337.

[MoRS2003]   Mönch, L.; Rose, O.; Sturm, R.: A Simulation Framework for
                Accessing the Performance of Shop-Floor Control Systems. In:
                SIMULATION: Transactions of the Society of Modeling and
                Computer Simulation International 79(2003)3, pp. 163-170.

[OdPF2003]   Odell, J.; Parunak, H. V. D.; Fleischer, M.: Modeling Agent Or-
                ganizations Using Roles. In: Software and Systems Modeling
                2(2003), pp. 76-81.

[PfFo2005]   Pfund, M. E.; Fowler, J. W.: Survey of Scheduling and Dis-
                patching Practice in Semiconductor Industry. Forthcoming.

[Schn2003]   Schneeweiss, C.: Distributed Decision Making. Springer, New
                York, Heidelberg, Berlin, 2003.

[ShNo1999]   Shen, W.; Norrie, D. H.: Agent-Based Systems for Intelligent
                Manufacturing: a State-of-the-Art Survey. In: Knowledge and
                Information Systems 1(1999)2, pp. 129-156.

[SrBG1994]   Srivatsan, N.; Bai, S. X.; Gershwin, S. B.: Hierarchical real-time
                integrated scheduling of a semiconductor fabrication facility. In:
                Control and Dynamic Systems 61, pp. 197-241.

[SuFo1990]   Sullivan, G.; Fordyce, K.: IBM Burlington's Logistics Management System. In: Interfaces 20(1990)1, pp. 43-64.

[UzLM1994]   Uzsoy, R.; Lee, C.-Y.; Martin-Vega, L. A.: A Review of Production Planning and Scheduling Models in the Semiconductor Industry, part II: Shop-Floor Control. In: IIE Transactions on Scheduling and Logistics 26(1994)5, pp. 44-55.

[Van+1998]   Van Brussel, H.; Wyns, J.; Valckenaers, P.; Bongaerts, L.; Peeters, P.: Refernce Architecture for Holonic Manufacturing Systems: PROSA. In: Computers in Industry 37(1998)3. Special Issue on Intelligent Manufacturing Systems, pp. 225-276.

[VaRi2001]   Vargas-Villamil, F. D.; Rivera, D. E.: A Model Predictive Control Approach for Real-Time Optimization of Reentrant Manufacturing Lines. In: Computers in Industry 45(2001), pp. 45-57.

[VaRK2003]   Vargas-Villamil, F. D.; Rivera, D. E.; Kempf, K. G.: A Hierarchical Approach to Production Control of Reentrant Semiconductor Manufacturing Lines. In: IEEE Transactions on Control Systems Technology 11(2003)3, pp. 578-587.

[Vrba2003]   Vrba, P.: JAVA-based Agent Platform Evaluation. In: Proceedings Holonic and Multi-Agent-Systems for Manufacturing (HoloMAS), 2003, pp. 47-58.

[WoJe1999]   Wooldridge, M.; Jennings, N.: Software Engineering with Agents: Pitfalls and Pratfalls. In: IEEE Internet Computing. May-June 1999, pp. 20-27.

[ZaJW2003]   Zambonelli, F.; Jennings, N.; Wooldridge, M.: Developing Multiagent Systems: the Gaia Methodology. In: ACM Transactions on Software Engineering and Methodology 12(2003)3, pp. 317-370.

5 Supply Chain Event Management With Software Agents

Roland Zimmermann, Stefan Winkler, Freimut Bodendorf

Universität Erlangen-Nürnberg, Lehrstuhl für Wirtschaftsinformatik II
{Roland.Zimmermann I Stefan.Winkler I
Freimut.Bodendorf}@wiso.uni-erlangen.de

Abstract. Operational fulfillment of supply chain processes in enterprise networks is regularly affected negatively by disruptive events. Event management promises to identify such problems in a timely fashion and significantly increase reaction time. A concept based on software agent technology is presented which enhances time and defect flexibility of supply chain processes. Evaluation of the concept indicates cost and cycle time reductions in multi-level supply chains which are not achieved by conventional approaches.

5.1 Introduction

During execution of fulfillment processes in supply chains stochastic problems occur which have a significant impact on the performance of enterprises and their supply chains: timeliness of fulfillment, quality measurements, costs and revenues of supply chain partners are affected negatively. Even small events in suppliers' processes result in deviations from globally planned and optimized schedules with serious impacts on supply chain performance. Nevertheless, negative consequences can be reduced, if event-related information is provided to supply chain partners at an early stage shortly after such events have occurred and corrective actions can be taken. Enhanced information provision increases *defect flexibility* of a supply chain system as defined in I.3.2 which results in lower follow-up costs of negative events.

However, a lack of reliable and accurate information on events and insufficient communication of event-related data between supply chain partners is observed. Thus, the supply chain control loop of planning, execution, and control (see II.1) is blocked regarding the *control* function in supply chains. The resulting information deficit at supply chain partners regarding event-related information will be referred to as the *Supply Chain Event Management (SCEM) problem* [Zimm2005].

Improved information management in supply chains is required to reduce the SCEM problem and increase the time for taking appropriate reactions to negative events. Consequently, *time flexibility* is increased: although increases in *time flexibility* refer to faster implementation of system modifications (see I.3.2), we argue that an increase in reaction time in a given situation (ceteris paribus) provides more time for system modifications and is thus a second aspect of *time flexibility*. The objective of information management is to provide a flexible SCEM solution for overcoming the information deficit and thereby improving the *time* and *defect flexibility* of a supply chain. To realize this objective supply chain partners ought to act proactive: first, partners in the supply chain have to "sense" what kind of information might be needed by themselves in the future and act proactive by pulling information from all available data sources including related partners. Second, information on disruptive events identified by a partner should be communicated to potentially interested supply chain partners proactively (information push). A SCEM solution has to enable and support both types of proactivity.

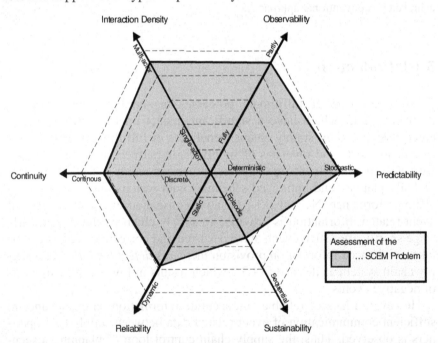

Figure 1. Characteristics of the SCEM problem, criteria according to Russel 2003.

The environmental properties (see II.1) of the SCEM domain are characterized in Figure 1: the *interaction density* among supply chain partners is high while at the same time a single partner only has restricted *observability* of (disruptive) events in the enterprise network.

Since stochastic events are at the core of the SCEM problem, *predictability* is very low. Disruptive events tend to be single occurrences without path-dependency: *sustainability* is rated primarily episodic. *Reliability* of the environment is dynamic in supply chains. Although events are discrete, their occurrence is *continuous* since it is unpredictable over time.

Following the line of argument in II.1, traditional IT-systems suited for problems which cover "small areas" in the criteria-graph of Figure 1 are not well-suited for the SCEM problem. However, agent technology is selected since it provides necessary flexibility features for SCEM such as autonomy, reactivity and proactiveness of behavior and social ability to communicate with other agents (or humans). These characteristics are agreed upon as being fundamental to the notion of a software agent (see I.1) [WoJe1995] [Jenn2001]. Proactivity as the primary requirement for a SCEM solution is inherently satisfied by agent technology: an agent is endowed with a goal it pursues. Furthermore, its advanced capabilities to engage in dialogs with other software agents enables it to proactively gather SCEM data and to decide on the necessity of proactively generating alert messages.

5.2 Conventional Approaches

Since the 1990s tracking-and-tracing systems are implemented within logistics service providers' networks [BSKP2002]. These systems provide on-demand information on transportation orders' status often via web-interfaces. However, such systems do not provide an assessment of an order's status in relation to its planned fulfillment [BSKP2002]. These issues are only addressed by SCEM systems. In the last years an increasing demand for SCEM systems [Bitt2000] [MoWa2001] [LoMc2002] is observed which is addressed by a growing number of available SCEM systems [ToRH2003]. Current SCEM solutions primarily focus on intra-organizational processes within single enterprises, while implementations with a true inter-organizational supply chain perspective are rare [Masi2003]. One reason is that current offerings of SCEM systems build upon centralized architectures which prevent the integration of multiple systems among different enterprises. This is illustrated by an initiative of the automotive industry to interconnect existing supply chain monitoring systems. In its official recommendation it points out that decentralized infrastructures are needed which aim at cooperation between enterprises. However, such solutions are not available [Odet2003].

Another major drawback of current SCEM systems is their lack of autonomous proactive behavior and their inability to participate in flexible dialogs with changing communication partners (e.g. for data gathering and alert exchange). However, some SCEM vendors are beginning to use agent-technology (or at least proclaim certain functions to be agent-based) [Barr2003]. This is an additional indicator for the suitability of agent technology to implement a SCEM system.

5.3 Analysis and Model Building

5.3.1 Supply Chain Event Management Process

All functions of the proposed SCEM solution are aggregated in a generic process for event management (see Figure 2). This process is applicable to every enterprise in a supply chain [BoZi2005] and realizes inter-organizational event management. The first activity is the *Monitoring decision* which is initialized by different triggers: queries from customers, alerts from suppliers and internally available critical profiles (CCP_j). Critical profiles are used to identify orders with a high probability of encountering disruptive events and thus focus monitoring efforts on high-risk orders [BoZi2005]. This allows preventing excessive communication and resource consumption due to proactive data gathering. Although it is possible that more than one type of trigger requires monitoring of the same order, the SCEM process is only initiated once for each order and continued until the order is finished.

A strategy for proactively gathering SCEM data in supply chains is used within the activity *Information gathering*. This activity is cyclically initiated as long as a monitored order is not finished (see Figure 2). Data is gathered both from internal data sources (e.g. an ERP system) and from external supply chain partners to assess suborders, as indicated by the two query variants. Since a status request for a suborder forces the queried supplier to monitor its own order and its related suborders, a cascading distributed data gathering mechanism is realized in a supply chain, if the SCEM process is implemented by every supply chain partner.

Interpretation of SCEM data analyses all gathered SCEM data and *Alert generation* decides whether and how to generate alerts. Both process steps use Fuzzy Logic mechanisms to imitate human assessment mechanisms

[ZWMB2005]. Alerts are directed to actors within an enterprise in order to initiate reactions to contain negative effects of disruptive events. Besides, alerts are sent to customers who will be affected subsequently by the effects of disruptive events (see Figure 1). After an order is finished and monitoring is terminated, results of monitoring activities are evaluated (*Evaluation of CCP$_j$*) to improve existing critical profiles and enhance the focus of SCEM efforts on potentially critical orders.

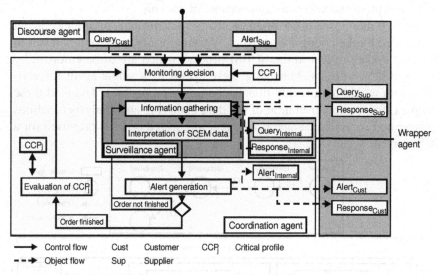

Figure 2. SCEM process and agent types

5.3.2 Agent Types

Four different agent types are defined (see Figure 3) that are responsible for different tasks in the SCEM process. A detailed explanation of associated roles is provided in [ZiWB2005]:

1. A *discourse agent* provides the interface to external supply chain partners.
2. The *coordination agent* coordinates initialization of monitoring processes and distributes their results.
3. A *surveillance agent* is responsible for creating an information product by gathering and interpreting SCEM data.
4. A *wrapper agent* hides heterogeneous data sources from a SCEM system and allows standardized access to these sources.

To realize the SCEM concept within a supply chain, each supply chain partner provides one agent society with a discourse and a coordination agent, as well as various surveillance and wrapper agents (see Figure 3) [Zim+2002]. A single coordination agent in each enterprise assures that initialization of monitoring efforts as well as management of external status requests and alerts is handled consistently within an enterprise. The coordination agent also allows gaining an overview of all monitored orders of an enterprise and serves as a management cockpit.

For each monitored order of an enterprise a dedicated surveillance agent is triggered by the coordination agent. Varying priorities of orders result in different update cycles in the SCEM process which are to be enforced by the surveillance agents. Managing these cycles by a single agent for various orders would require additional scheduling procedures. To avoid these complexities, an encapsulation of the data gathering and analysis functions in dedicated surveillance agents for each monitored order is proposed for a SCEM agent society.

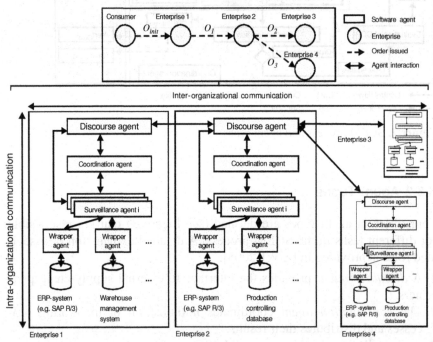

Figure 3. Agent society

Wrapper agents provide a standard interface to internal data sources for surveillance agents. An integration of theses abilities in surveillance agents would require a replication of all access details for each available data source in every surveillance agent. This redundancy is avoided by introducing wrapper agents.

5.3.3 Agent Interactions

Two main dimensions of communication are distinguished in the agent-based SCEM concept (see Figure 3):

- Interaction between enterprises which is referred to as *inter-organizational communication*: it is facilitated by discourse agents of the enterprises which exchange messages via the Internet. Every SCEM agent society has one discourse agent that serves as the single point-of-contact for external communication of SCEM data among enterprises.
- *Intra-organizational communication* within one enterprise: it refers to the interactions within one agent society between the various agent types that realize a SCEM system of a single enterprise.

Interactions among all agent types are based on requests for SCEM data and requests for activities to be performed for gathering or manipulation of this data. A suitable basic interaction protocol is the standardized FIPA "Request" interaction protocol [FIPA2002]. The content of the messages is defined based on a SCEM ontology which is discussed in detail in [ZKBB 2005]. Each agent type decides, based upon the message type, the sender and the content of a message, on an appropriate action, in order to fulfill its duties within the SCEM process (e.g. analysis of received data). Besides reactions to messages, every agent can decide proactively to take or initiate further actions in the event management process (e.g. send an alert).

The result is a distributed system of agent societies for monitoring critical orders across a supply chain with a combination of proactive SCEM data gathering (*pull mechanism*) and distribution of alerts (*push mechanism*). The implicit demand for information on disruptive events is satisfied with messages that are exchanged between supply chain partners.

5.4 System Description

5.4.1 Generic Prototype

A generic prototype with all agent types has been realized for conducting experiments in a laboratory environment[1]: each enterprise in a simulated supply chain hosts one agent society (see Figure 4). A single wrapper agent per enterprise is required to access a database that simulates the enterprise's ERP system which provides all internal SCEM data on orders. The main focus of the implementation is on SCEM features provided by coordination and surveillance agents, whereas only basic mechanisms of discourse and wrapper agents are realized. Every agent society is realized on its own instance of the FIPA-conform JADE agent platform. As in a realistic supply chain, agent platforms can be hosted on different computers to realize a physical distribution of SCEM systems. An additional agent type provides white and yellow pages services to all discourse agents of a supply chain: a global directory facilitator (GlobalDF, see Figure 4).

Within the generic prototype all agents rely on the SCEM ontology. The JADE agent platform selected for implementation of the generic prototype supports a special representation of ontologies based on Java Beans (JB) [CaCa2004]. Information on a certain instance of an ontological concept (e.g. a specific order) is represented as an instance of a JB class *Order*. Instantiation of ontological concepts define knowledge facts of an agent's knowledge base. Besides creating, accessing and manipulating the knowledge base with JBs, this representation is used by the JADE platform to define content of FIPA-ACL messages. Thus, knowledge is standardized among agents in a SCEM system, easily exchanged between agents, and always accessible through Java programming instructions.

To facilitate simulation of all orders in a supply chain during experiments a single data base aggregates all ERP systems of enterprises in a simulated supply chain. Each wrapper agent responsible for accessing internal data from its enterprise's ERP system has a restricted view on this database.

A simulator reflects changes in fulfillment processes in the ERP system. These changes are identified by agents of the SCEM system. Most functions are integrated in a special agent type: a simulator agent that has direct

---

[1]   This prototype is also integrated in the Agent.Enterprise NetDemo environment to demonstrate use of agent-based SCEM in a Multi-MAS environment.

access to both the ERP system and an experiments data base (see Figure 4).

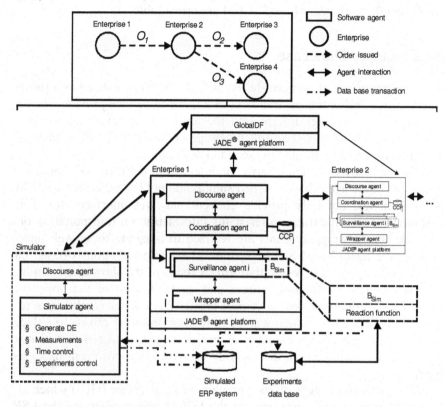

Figure 4. Architecture of the MAS

This agent initiates new experiments by starting all agent societies and triggers monitoring through requests to *Enterprise 1* which it transmits via an additional discourse agent. During execution of fulfillment processes it generates disruptive events for selected orders of the supply chain. It stores these disruptive events and its effects on process times (delays) in the ERP system for discovery by the agents of the SCEM systems. As soon as a surveillance agent has identified a new disruptive event and its corresponding delay, a reaction mechanism (*B_Sim* in Figure 4) is triggered that calculates how much of the delay can be reduced depending on the remaining reaction time. The results of this reaction are stored in the ERP system, and measurements (e.g. time point of identification of disruptive event, reaction consequences) are stored in the experiments data base. All delays in suborders that cannot be coped with propagate to the next customer level of the supply chain. Such propagation is assured by the simulator agent. In case several suborders are delayed, a maximum delay is assumed for the main order. Thus, propagating disruptive events are simulated and effects of agent-based SCEM are measurable.

5.4.2 Industry Showcase

A second prototype of an agent-based SCEM system is realized as a showcase within a real-world environment of a logistics service provider (LSP). The prototype provides insight into the ability to integrate agent-based SCEM concepts into existing fulfillment processes and IT-infrastructures. The showcase is documented in detail in [BoZi2005].

Industrial carriers which receive suborders from the LSP and which are integrated in the agent-based SCEM solution do not have their own SCEM agent societies, but only provide conventional web-interfaces for their customers. These interfaces offer status information on transportation orders. Dedicated wrapper agents are realized to integrate these web interfaces in the agent-based SCEM system. The implementation is based on the FIPA-compliant FIPA-OS platform. A focus of the showcase is on integration of real-world data sources and on realization of the proactive monitoring of orders based on critical profiles. The latter results from requirements of the LSP which wanted to focus monitoring efforts to reduce its main problems: large amounts of irrelevant and outdated data that it gathers in its databases but that nobody uses for proactive event management.

The coordination agent offers a graphical user interface (GUI) which allows a user to monitor and manage the SCEM agent society of the LSP (see Figure 5). A user can manually start surveillance agents to monitor certain orders, access detailed information of a specific surveillance agent, and terminate observation tasks. The GUI provides a short overview of all currently active surveillance agents with their monitored order's identifier, predicted duration of the order, and an aggregated status that indicates whether the order is on time, late, critical, or finished. Configuration and management of critical profiles is also managed by this GUI.

If a user decides to monitor a specific order or if an order is identified as potentially critical by a profile, the coordination agent instantiates and initializes a surveillance agent. The surveillance agent monitors the fulfillment process across the entire supply chain from order reception to order delivery. The system uses a series of milestones which divide the fulfillment process into individual sub-processes defined by the LSP.

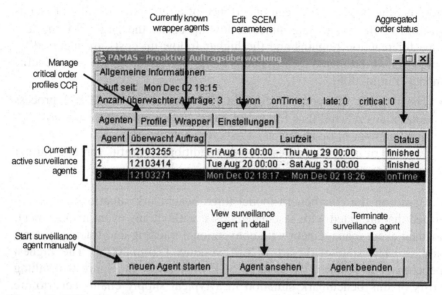

Figure 5. GUI of coordination agent

Based on the order's milestone plan which defines when a milestone is supposed to be completed, each surveillance agent identifies any deviations. All deviations are registered by the agent and displayed to the user upon request. The main GUI provided by each surveillance agent employs a traffic light metaphor. To indicate the status of a monitored order the agent differentiates between states of single milestones and an aggregated status of an order. This order status indicates whether an order is fulfilled on time, late, or critical. Proactive alerts to actors are provided by the agents through warning emails and an automatic display of a surveillance agent's GUI to an actor ("pop-up").

5.5 Evaluation and Benchmarking

5.5.1 Analytical Cost-Benefit-Model

Evaluation of the agent-based SCEM concept is guided by the question: *How much can follow-up costs of disruptive events be reduced by a SCEM system?* A theoretical cost-benefit-model presented in [Zimm2005] provides hypotheses on the specific benefits of agent-based event management in multi-level supply chains. At the core of the model is the assumption that the time ΔT between occurrence of a disruptive event and identification of the event determines follow-up costs: the larger ΔT the less time for reaction remains and the higher follow-up costs are incurred by supply chain partners. Two hypotheses are derived from the cost-benefit-model [Zimm2005]:

- The number of update cycles (SCEM cycles) in the SCEM process determines ΔT and thus follow-up costs of disruptive events. A cost-optimal number of update cycles exists for each order.
- The use of critical profiles provides additional benefits through further reductions of ΔT and associated costs.

Based on the cost-benefit-model three benchmark situations are established that are rated with associated costs: without any event management, manual event management with conventional tracking-and-tracing systems and isolated state-of-the-art SCEM systems [Zimm2005]. The highest benchmark is realized by isolated SCEM systems. In Figure 6 resulting costs of this benchmark situation in a typical supply chain scenario are compared to the agent-based approach.

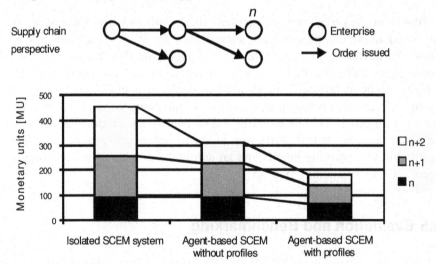

Figure 6. Cumulated costs of SCEM scenarios

Two conceptual differences determine the additional benefits of agent-based SCEM compared to isolated SCEM systems:

- Inter-organizational proactive data gathering and alerts assure that an agent-based SCEM system of a customer gains advance knowledge on disruptive events that will threaten its processes in the future. Since such inter-organizational communication is seldom realized today in SCEM systems [Masi2003] isolated SCEM systems can only identify disruptive events as soon as they eventually affect the enterprise's processes. Additional reaction time which is quantified by a reduction of ΔT provides additional reductions of follow-up costs of up to 50% according to scenario calculations with the cost-benefit-model (see Figure 6 middle column).

- Critical profiles allow focusing monitoring efforts on potentially critical orders thereby enhancing efficiency of event management activities. Based on data of the logistics service provider (see *industry showcase*) realistic critical profiles are identified [BoZi2005]. Since focused monitoring with such profiles decreases costs of monitoring the number of cost-optimal update cycles per order is increased [Zimm2005]. This results in an additional reduction of costs of up to 40% compared to the benchmark "isolated SCEM system" which adds to the benefits from inter-organizational communication (see Figure 6 right column).

In addition to these monetary effects Figure 6 indicates more fair distribution of remaining negative effects of disruptive events among supply chain partners. Most benefits are realized by customers and customers of customers in a supply chain. This is considered a fair constellation, since in the situation with isolated SCEM systems most costs are incurred by those partners not responsible for an initial disruptive event.

5.5.2 Experimental Results

Experiments conducted with the generic prototype are used to validate the hypotheses of the cost-benefit-model. All experiments are conducted with the simulator presented above. The mechanism for reducing a delay assumes that to a certain extent the planned duration of fulfillment processes can be reduced. However, this reduction is limited to a predefined threshold, since in reality fulfillment processes (e.g. a production process) always have some minimum duration (e.g. for working on a product).

Depending on when event information becomes available, the intensity of a reaction changes: the earlier information is available the more intense is the reaction and vice versa. A linear function is selected for calculating the exact extent of a reaction. However, in real-world scenarios different reaction functions to calculate a reaction might also be realistic.

Within experiments, disruptive events are inserted by the simulator during fulfillment of a suborder which is placed with *Enterprise 4* (see Figure 7). All orders in the supply chain have the same planned duration of five days. An initial advance planning horizon for *Enterprise 3* is 15 days. A maximum reduction of 10%, which is 12 hours, is defined for every enterprise.

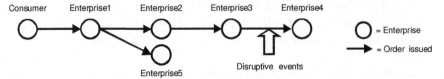

Figure 7. Supply chain configuration

In Figure 8 results of an experiment are depicted where a disruptive event occurs very early during fulfillment at *Enterprise 4* (within the first day of the planning horizon) and results in an initial delay of 100 hours. Measurements are taken at *Enterprise 3* for different numbers of SCEM cycles.

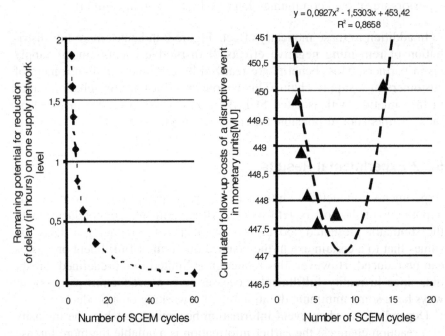

Figure 8. Impact of SCEM cycles – experimental results

Since a very precautious reaction function with only 10% maximum reduction is selected, the maximum reduction at *Enterprise 3* with its 120 hours cycle time is 12 hours. The potential for reduction of the delay which remains after implementation of different SCEM cycle configurations is depicted in Figure 8 (left side). The results state that an increase in

SCEM cycles results in a sharp decline of the remaining delay similar to behavior predicted by the theoretical cost-benefit-model. In the experiments the minimum number of SCEM cycles per order is an average of 2.5 which results from fixed intervals between data gathering rounds and the specific fulfillment duration of an order. An increase of SCEM cycles allows realizing nearly the maximum reduction of 12 hours at *Enterprise 3* that is represented by nearly zero remaining potential for reduction in Figure 8. Similar reductions are realized on following supply chain levels (not depicted here): on average, the reductions of delays are even larger since information is available earlier for customers in supply chains as predicted by the cost-benefit-model.

In Figure 8 right side the experimental results are rated with costs both for follow-up costs of the delay and costs for each SCEM cycle [ZiWB 2005]. This results in a clear indication of a cost-optimal number of SCEM cycles as predicted by the cost-benefit-model.

5.5.3 Showcase Assessment

An assessment of the industry showcase provides insight into the impact of agent-based SCEM on real-world processes and associated costs. For instance, the prototype provides significant improvements compared to the manual monitoring processes currently implemented at the LSP. A conservative estimation of process times for a single manually conducted SCEM cycle results in a cumulated 125 seconds for finding status information on a certain order and assessing this information. Associated costs are approximately 1.15 Euro per manual SCEM cycle since average costs of personnel are 34 Euro per hour [ZiWB2005]. The showcase prototype provides the same information automatically in a matter of seconds and without manual intervention. Although no direct cost measurements are available for the prototype it is assumed that every update cycle costs at most 4 Euro Cent [ZiWB2005]. The difference between manual and automatic data gathering efforts is more than 1 Euro per SCEM cycle.

Costs associated with reactions to disruptive events largely determine benefits of SCEM. For the LSP a process analysis has been conducted which exemplifies a method to determine cost functions for different reactions [Zimm2005]. In the analysis reactions to severe disruptive events within orders of important European customers are in the focus: a second delivery has to be triggered since the initial delivery is definitely not arriving at the planned delivery date. Typical reasons for this reaction are - as stated by experts of the LSP - damages during transportation and incorrect routing of goods (e.g. to another country).

In every case where a new (second) delivery is initiated due to a disruptive event, internal activities within the administration of the LSP take about one hour and consist of devising a plan for reaction and creating a new delivery note. The internal warehouse processes are well designed with a very short reaction time: picking and packaging is finished about 20 minutes after the delivery note is received in the warehouse, if goods are available on stock. Packaged goods then wait for pick-up by a carrier.

Four variants depending on the remaining time for reaction exist. For instance, if only about one day remains a dedicated direct courier with a small and fast transportation vehicle can reach most locations of central Europe within about 24 hours. The required cycle times associated with processes of the alternatives determine how long each alternative is viable for a specific order's fulfillment. For each alternative the associated costs are gathered in interviews with experts of the LSP.

Based on the process analysis and associated costs a cost function is devised (see Figure 9). It illustrates use of the cheapest alternative available for each point in time between beginning of fulfillment of an order and its planned delivery date.

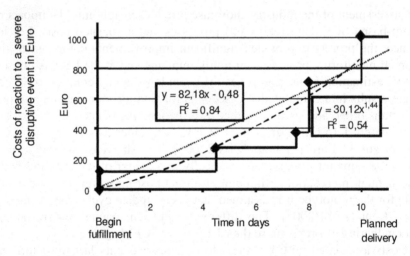

Figure 9. Cost function

In the example, a planned cycle time for orders of 10 days is assumed which is realistic for deliveries to central European countries outside the European Union. For instance, only before four and a half days of fulfillment have passed is a second regular transport by truck viable with lowest costs of 119 Euro.

The step-wise cost function illustrates realistic alternatives for the LSP in relation to the remaining reaction time during an order's fulfillment.

Two statistical trends based on a linear and a non-linear trend are depicted. In the example the linear function provides better statistical results and underlines the viability of using linear cost models for assessing the benefits of event management in supply chains (e.g. reaction function in experiments). The cost function in Figure 9 indicates a cost reduction potential for follow-up costs compared to the worst case (after day 10) of more than 80% for early disruptive events.

5.6 Conclusions

The role of agent-based SCEM in the *Agent.Enterprise* scenario is to close the control loop in supply chain management: while production planning is conducted by several other MAS, the SCEM MAS effectively controls order fulfillment in multi-level supply chains and gives feedback event-related information to actors and planning systems.

It is shown that an agent-based concept is suited to reduce negative effects of disruptive events in supply chains. While agent technology supports the autonomy of supply chain partners it also offers mechanisms to both pull and push event-related information. Hence, the initial information deficit is significantly reduced which is reflected by improved process measurements (e.g. reduced delays) and reduced follow-up costs of disruptive events. Follow-up costs of disruptive events costs serve as an indicator for *defect flexibility*. To this end the *defect flexibility* (see I.3.2) of a supply chain is increased by the reduction in follow-up costs of disruptive events (up to 50% compared to existing SCEM concepts). With respect to the concept of *time flexibility*, the increase in reaction time realized with agent-based SCEM is a second indicator for measuring the improvement in flexibility of a supply chain system to adapt to unpredictable events in its processes. In experiments (see above), significant increases in reaction time are realizable which depend on the point-in-time when an event occurs and on the type of reaction function.

References

[Barr2003]   Barrows, T.: Using the SCOR Model to Map Collaborative Multi-Agent Systems (MAS) Business Environments. Presentation at Supply-Chain-World-Australia/New Zealand Exe Technologies, 2003.

[Bitt2000]   Bittner, M.: E-Business Requires Supply Chain Event Management. AMR Research, Boston, 2000.

[BoZi2005]   Bodendorf, F.; Zimmermann, R.: Proactive Supply Chain Event
                Management with Agent Technology. In: International Journal
                of Electronic Commerce 9(2005)4, pp. 57-90.
[BSKP2002]   Bretzke, W.; Stoelzle, W.; Karrer, M.; Ploenes, P.: Vom Track-
                ing & Tracing zum Supply Chain Event Management - aktueller
                Stand und Trends. KPMG Consulting AG, Duesseldorf, 2002.
[CaCa2004]   Caire, G.; Cabanillas, D.: JADE Tutorial - Application-defined
                Content Languages and Ontologies. TILab S.p.A., 2004. http://
                jade.tilab.com/doc/CLOntoSupport.pdf, accessed on 2005-03-
                31.
[FIPA2002]   Foundation for Intelligent Physical Agents, FIPA Request
                Interaction Protocol Specification, 2002. http://www.fipa.org/
                specs/fipa00026/ SC00026H.pdf, accessed on 2004-09-24.
[Jenn2001]   Jennings, N. R.: An Agent-Based Approach for Building Com-
                plex Software Systems. In: Communications of the ACM
                44(2001)4, pp. 35-41.
[LoMc2002]   Lockamy, A.; McCormack, K.: Supply Chain Event Manage-
                ment Best Practice Models. Presentation held at Supply Chain
                World - Conference and Exhibition 2002. http://www.logis-net.
                co.kr/wwwboard/data/1/scmpractice.pdf, accessed on 2005-04-
                18.
[Masi2003]   Masing, N.: Supply Chain Event Management as Strategic Per-
                spective – Market Study: SCEM Software Performance in the
                European Market. Diploma thesis, 2003. http://www.cata.ca/files
                /PDF/Resource_Centres/hightech/reports/studies/Supply-
                ChainEventMgt.pdf, accessed on 2005-04-18.
[MoWa2001]   Montgomery, N.; Waheed, R.: Supply Chain Event Management
                Enables Companies to Take Control of Extended Supply Chains.
                AMR Research, 2001.
[Odet2003]   Odette, Supply Chain Monitoring, Version 1.0, Recommenda-
                tion May 2003. http://www.odette.org/html/scmopr.htm, ac-
                cessed on 2005-04-19.
[ToRH2003]   Tohamy, N.; Radjou, N.; Hudson, R.: Grading Order Fulfillment
                Solutions. TechStrategy Report. Forrester Research, 2003.
[WoJe1995]   Wooldridge, M. J.; Jennings, N. R.: Intelligent Agents: Theory
                and Practice. In: Knowledge Engineering Review 10(1995)2,
                pp. 115-152.
[Zim+2002]   Zimmermann, R.; Butscher, R.; Bodendorf, F.; Huber, A.; Görz,
                G.: Generic Agent Architecture for Supply Chain Tracking. In:
                The 2nd IEEE International Symposium on Signal Processing
                and Information Technology. IEEE-Press, Marrakesh, 2002, pp.
                203-207.
[Zimm2005]   Zimmermann, R.: Agent-based Supply Network Event Manage-
                ment. PhD thesis, Nuremberg, 2005. To appear in Whitestein Se-
                ries on Agent Technologies, Birkhäuser, Basel, 2005.

[ZKBB2005]   Zimmermann, R.; Käs, S.; Butscher, R.; Bodendorf, F.: An Ontology for Agent-Based Monitoring of Fulfillment Processes. In: Tamma, V.; Cranefield, S.; Finin, T. W.; Willmott, S. (Eds.): Ontologies for Agents: Theory and Experiences. Whitestein Series in Software Agent Technologies, Birkhäuser, Basel, 2005.

[ZWMB2005]   Zimmermann, R.; Winkler, S.; Meyreiss, C.; Bodendorf, F.: Assessment of Supply Chain Event Management Data by an Agent-based System with Fuzzy Logic. Submitted to ASIM 2005.

[ZiWB2005]   Zimmermann, R.; Winkler, S.; Bodendorf, F.: Agent-based Supply Chain Event Management – Concept and Assessment. Accepted for HICSS 2006.

6 Trust-Based Distributed Supply-Web Negotiations

Tim Stockheim

Universität Frankfurt, Lehrstuhl für BWL, insb. Wirtschaftsinformatik und Informationsmanagement, stockheim@wiwi.uni-frankfurt.de

Oliver Wendt

Technische Universität Kaiserslautern, Lehrgebiet Wirtschaftsinformatik und Operations Research, wendt@wiwi.uni-kl.de

Wolfgang König

Universität Frankfurt, Lehrstuhl für BWL, insb. Wirtschaftsinformatik und Informationsmanagement, koenig@wiwi.uni-frankfurt.de

Abstract. This chapter presents a decentralized negotiation protocol for cooperative economic scheduling in a supply chain environment. These protocols are evaluated using software agents that maximize their profits by optimizing their local schedule and offer side payments to compensate other agents for lost profit or extra expense if cumulative profit is achievable. To further increase their income the agents have to apply a randomized local search heuristic to prevent the negotiation from stopping in locally optimal contracts. We show that the welfare could be increased by using a search strategy similar to Simulated Annealing. Unfortunately, a naive application of this strategy makes the agents vulnerable to exploitation by untruthful partners. We develop and test a straightforward mechanism based on trust accounts to protect the agents against systematic exploitation. This "Trusted" Simulated Annealing mechanism assures truthful revelation of the individual opportunity cost situation as the basis for the calculation of side payments.

6.1 Introduction

Real-life supply chain management (SCM) is closely related to problems caused by the diverging interests of the actors (enterprises) and the distributed structure of the underlying optimization (scheduling). Increasing outsourcing of former in-house processes and more intense customer relationships shifted the demands of SCM from hierarchical coordination to a more heterarchical, partially market-based coordination. But when assuming long-term relationships of selfish, independently acting units many of the influencing factors such as *observability* and *interactivity* can no longer be considered as uncritical. New coordination concepts and protocols have to be taken into account in order to increase the efficiency of cooperative production processes that are planned by independent organizational units.

One way to address these needs is to employ a holonic multiagent system (MAS), in which the process structure is mapped onto single agents [Eyma2001]. Each agent – operating a single production facility – maximizes its own profit by determining an optimal internal schedule. To streamline the production process and to avoid penalty costs due to processing bottlenecks or late delivery, agents have been programmed to carry out economic scheduling. Accordingly, they employ "outsourcing contracts" to reduce their production load and to optimize their schedules. The negotiation has to be seen as a second inter-agent schedule optimization process, leading to social contract equilibrium of the MAS based on prices calculated according to the production load. Due to the fact that the calculation of the agents' prices cannot be directly monitored by the contract partners, a trust protocol has been included to foster truthful bidding. Another characteristic problem in this context is the unwillingness of actors to reveal sensitive but (in terms of system optimization) valuable information. By implementing an incentive compatible mechanism to avoid exploitation by competitors our decentralized supply chain optimization system is able to deal with such agency problems, too. We address the revelation issue by introducing a trust account mechanism, which helps to prevent individual long-term exploitation. The trust mechanism is directly integrated with the schedule optimization procedure, similar to [PSEP2002].

Russel and Norvig provide a set of properties to describe domains and determine their suitability for intelligent software agent support [RuNo2003]. These properties characterize the task environment and are applicable to the manufacturing logistics domain as detailed below. In the context of the already described typical business environments presented in II.1, the DISPOWEB-approach (see Figure 1) addresses among others the following requirements:

- It increases the flexibility of resources, e.g. industrial facilities, leads to more and more heterogeneous tasks, which are processed on a single resource. Allocation mechanisms could thus not rely on discrete time-windows but need to handle tasks that start and finish on a *continuous time line.*
- Resulting from adding more and more features/variants into existing and new product lines, the number of participants with a need of coordination and communication increases. The resulting requirement for *I/O*

flexibility need to be inherently implemented into new coordination frameworks.

• Taking into account asymmetric information and opportunistic behavior requires the development of "stable" mechanisms. In the presented approach the decrease in *observability* of supply chain partners is addressed by implementing trust accounts into the protocols.

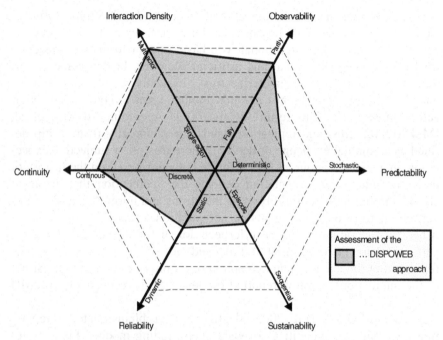

Figure 1. Characteristics of the DISPOWEB approach[1]

Concluding, today's automation requires SCM systems to increase their potential in all six areas around the origin of the diagram in Figure 1. Agent technology promises to provide such flexibility (see I.3) but should not be considered as a silver bullet to solve real-life problems. DISPO-WEB makes use of agent technology to implement a concept of decentralized optimization. Moreover it provides a certain level of "fairness" to the participants.

After depicting the theoretical foundations of our holonic MAS in the next section, we deliver a detailed description of the combined trust and scheduling protocol. In the analysis of our experimental results the usefulness of the mechanism is demonstrated by applying it to settings based on

---

[1] Criteria according to [RuNo2003, pp. 41-44].

purely selfish, altruistic or mixed agent "strategic worlds". As benchmarks, we employ individual income distribution and global welfare.

6.2 Agents and Trust in the Manufacturing Logistics Domain

Besides sociological, psychological, behavioral, and philosophical dimensions of trust [CaBG2002] artificial intelligence research considers the cognitive aspect of human rationality to have a major formative impact on trust as a concept in human and artificial societies. In this context Castelfranchi and Falcone characterize trust "basically as a mental state, a complex attitude of an agent x towards another agent y about the behavior/ action relevant for the result" [CaFa2001]. According to Mui et al. [MuHM2002] trust and reputation stand in a reciprocity relationship defined as a "mutual exchange of deeds", where trust is "a subjective expectation an agent has about another's future behavior based on the history of their encounters" and reputation denotes the "perception that an agent creates through past actions about its intentions and norms". Based on this definition, trust between agents in computational models can be established by "accounting" the historic behavior of the agents. For the most part, reputation factors consist of direct and indirect reputation components representing the agent's own perception of its prospective contract partner or the interaction cognition reported by other agents respectively [MuMH 2002].

Jurca and Faltings [JuFa2003] identify three problems related to reputation reporting in competitive software agent trading models: First, by reporting information the agent provides a competitive advantage to other agents; second by reporting positive ratings the agent slightly decreases its own reputation with respect to the average reputation of the other agents; and third, the agents could be thus tempted to give negative reputation ratings to improve their own situation. By implementing a combined trading and side payment scheme employing reputation-information trading agents, the model compensates for these drawbacks. Applying reputation and trust mechanisms in SCM, Padovan et al. [PSEP2002] implement an electronic market that employs a simple reputation mechanism based on direct and indirect reputation in order to exclude fraudulent participants from negotiation. The implementation of centralized and decentralized trust mechanisms in a market organized along the value chain, integrating risk premiums for potential loss in contracts, leads to improved system reliability for both cases. In a similar model [Eyma2001] use genetic algorithms to vary the agents' behavior. By analyzing decentralized coordination in the supply chain, they instruct their agents to take information about the reputation of a potential transaction partner into consideration and use it to choose the appropriate partner. Franke et al. [FrSK2005] analyze the impact of direct discounted reputation on supply webs. In this model, strong reputation stimulates the formation of monopolies and stable supply chains. The well known bullwhip effect is observed to antagonize this reputation effect.

Sabater [Saba2003] presents the SuppWorld scenario with a market structure, in which agents acquire the input products for a given manufacturing process while aiming to maximize their revenue. Using different negotiation tactics and enabled to form coalitions for the exchange of reputation information, they act in a simulative economy. Relying on the ReGreT system, which takes an individual (direct) and a social (indirect) view of reputation into account, Sabater introduces an ontological meaning enabling a differentiation of reputation with respect to crucial aspects of the supply chain such as delivery on time or quality reliability [JoSi2001] [SiJo2002] and systemically evaluates the impact of reputation on the SCM framework.

6.3 A Model-Based Approach to Evaluate Negotiation Protocols in the Manufacturing Logistics Domain

Based on the arguments in the preceding section, prototype systems have been developed in this project in order to solve specific problems in the manufacturing logistics domain. Within this project, evaluations and benchmark tests with typical Operations Research scenarios were conducted in order to compare the different outlined negotiation protocols.

The global problem, which is similar to the Economically Augmented Job Shop Scheduling problem [Cone2003], is decomposed into Weighted Job Interval Scheduling Problems (WJISP). The optimization of the WJISP in the multiagent system is conducted by using Simulated Annealing (SA). Depending on the properties of a typical setting, e.g. smaller intervals, other optimization approaches may be able to improve the performance of the individual agents (cf. [GoKu1998] [DaSe2003] [Elen 2003]). The assumptions of the DISPOWEB-model are summarized in the following paragraphs:

- *Each job is composed by a number of subtasks to be executed sequentially (other inputs are not critical)*: Although we adopted this classical job shop scheduling assumption for our multiagent scheduling model, it is unrealistic to assume only one predecessor for each task. The relaxation requires the WJISP's release times to be defined as the maximum of all contract times over all suppliers.

- *Closed model with deterministic jobs*: We assume every task to be known to the agents, i.e. they only renegotiate existing contracts. Extending to a dynamic model with emerging tasks is straightforward, however: Whenever a new service or product request has to be priced, the agent's WJISP defined by its current portfolio of contracts is extended by two additional contracts.
- *Immediate delivery*: Our negotiation model assumes the supplier's due date and the customer's release time to be identical. This assumption can easily be relaxed by introducing intermediary logistics agents for storage or transport. The negotiation protocol does not have to be altered with respect to a potentially different internal scheduling calculus applied by these agent types.
- *Static costs for task outsourcing*: Currently we assume an outsourcing option to be available for all tasks and every agent at all times, meeting whatever deadline the customer will require. While this simplification reduces the problem's complexity it is true that in most economies for almost any product or service a substitute will be available at any time for a price below infinity.
- *Unlimited compensation budgets*: We assume each agent to have unlimited financial resources for side payments. Since the side payments only serve to compensate for economic value generated by relaxing the agent's scheduling constraints or to collaboratively escape suboptimal plans, the sheer number of re-contracting steps applied keeps the probability of persistent financial loss very low.

The resulting set of possible optimization problems is obviously not a simple mapping of a real-world problem. Such an approach would not only exceed the resources of this project but make a benchmarking (in terms of comparable results) almost impossible. While our approach preserves the complexity that is typical scheduling problems, it is stronger structured (less flexible), deterministic, and the single tasks are more predictable in terms of processing time than typical real-world optimization problems. Due to the fact that our agents do not consider situation dependent properties of other agents, e.g. their current workload, this does not restrict our analysis of the protocol.

6.3.1 The Multiagent System Negotiation Protocol

Each agent optimizes a WJISP defined by the tasks' execution times and time windows that are specified by supply and delivery contracts. Besides this optimization of the internal schedule, an agent tries to achieve a wider temporal action space by offering compensation payments and/or selling free slack time to contract partners.

As mentioned in the assumptions, the payoff function of the consumer is higher for earlier deliveries. A schedule with less slack time thus results in earlier delivery times and increases the payments that can be distributed among the agents.

For every given plan an agent can calculate its opportunity cost or benefit incurred or gained by a specific agent from moving the contract time (defining due date for the supplier and release time for the customer respectively). Since widening of the interval always leads to a relaxed WJISP, the new WJISP always has the same or lower cost while narrowing the interval generates a WJISP with the same or higher cost.

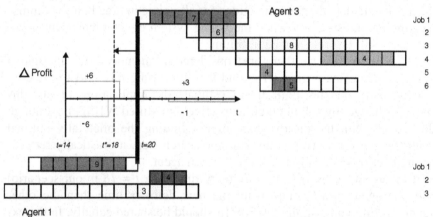

Figure 2. Time dependent prices of the multiagent WJISP

Consider, for example, agent 3 in Figure 2. Re-contracting the release time of job 1 (the upper one) from $t = 20$ to $t = 23$ or even later would decrease the remaining interval such that the scheduling of this task becomes impossible. On the other hand, the resources freed by this would allow for scheduling of the (currently outsourced) second task in the optimal solution leading to total cost of 15 instead of 14 monetary units (MU), i.e. a cost increase of 1 MU. Relaxing the contract to $t = 18$ or earlier would allow for scheduling both, the first and the second task thus yielding an additional profit of 6 MU. For agent 1 a contract time of $t = 17$ or earlier renders job 1 impossible but in turn allows for scheduling the third task (third from top) causing a total cost increase by 6 MU. When relaxing the deadline to (at least) 21 however, all tasks can be scheduled by agent 1 (starting with the third one).

Assuming both agents had agreed on delivery time of $t = 20$ adding the respective cost deltas indicated in Figure 2 to their agreed price would define time-dependent price functions representing the agents' opportunity cost or benefits. By communicating this function to the partner, each agent could calculate an optimal re-contracting step. In our case, agreeing on $t = 18$ would lead to a total surplus of 6 MU that could be shared by the two agents.

When calculating the price functions showing the optimal contract time for this task, we have to assume all other contracts to be kept unchanged. This in turn means, the re-contracting operation for task 1 now leads to outdated price functions for all other tasks of agent 1 and agent 2, i.e. updating would be required to determine whether their contracting time is still optimal.

Of course, this raises the question whether it is really efficient to have the agent calculate the price functions for all points in time before communicating them, especially when the whole system of interdependent negotiations is still far from any equilibrium.

As an alternative we therefore considered a "memory-free" alternative randomly choosing a time offset and then proposing this shift to the contracting party, making both agents estimate the implications of just this specific change (by solving their respectively modified WJISPs). Although this comes with the disadvantage of not finding the bilaterally optimal contract time for a given contact in one search step, it drastically reduces the number of WJISPs to be solved by each agent.

If the agents agree on a new delivery time (e.g. $t = 18$ in our scenario) and one agent profits more from the new delivery time than the other agent's additional cost, the total profit should be shared equally. In the example agent 2 makes a side payment of 3 MU to agent 1, leading to a situation where both agents profit from the change of the delivery contract.

6.3.2 Selfish Agents

To evaluate the decentralized economic scheduling protocols outlined above, we modified the Fisher & Thompson 6x6 Job Shop Scheduling Problem [FiTh1963], by introducing an outsourcing price of 50 MU per unit of required processing time. Besides the size of this example, which allows for concise presentation of the findings, it is one of the three initial benchmarks published for the JSSP.

Figure 3 shows the total welfare surplus obtained via 50,000 selfish re-negotiation trials, defined as the total cost of the (heuristic) solution of the final WJISPs compared to the total cost of the agents' initial WJISPs' solution. We ran 200 independent simulations, yielding the individual sequences of dots (left chart), whereas the black line shows the average improvement over all simulation runs up to a given number of negotiations. While the right chart in Figure 3 depicts the final distribution after 50,000 negotiation trials averaging the values of the achieved welfare in this setting results in 4,210.16 MUs. Table 1 in Section 6.3.5 provides an overview of averaged welfare values of each analyzed setting.

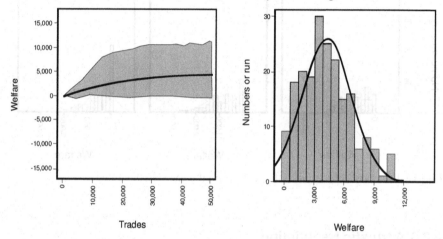

Figure 3. Welfare distribution for agents applying the selfish strategy

Implied by the selfishness of the protocol no agent will ever accept any proposal making him worse off compared to the current schedule, so there is no downside risk of any decrease in welfare, neither on a social scale nor for any individual agent. However, as the income distribution of Figure 4 shows, the distribution of benefits from negotiation is significantly skewed towards later tiers of the supply chain, leaving almost no benefits for agent 1 and agent 2.

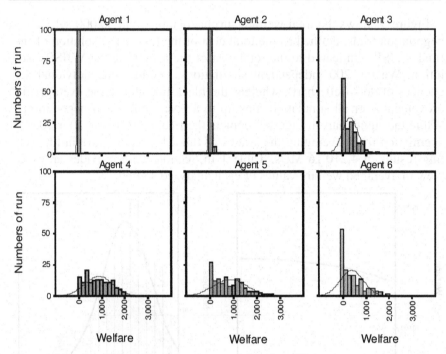

Figure 4. Income distribution of agents applying the selfish strategy

6.3.3 Altruistic Negotiation

Due to the complexity of the global scheduling problem relying purely on improvement steps will not lead to optimal schedules. We therefore introduce a mechanism that accepts delivery times which temporarily make both agents worse off. Similar to the agents' internal optimization we used a SA-like approach such that the agents accept contract changes depending on virtual temperature and amount of monetary loss. This allows the agents to search for globally superior solutions even if no direct improvements could be achieved.

As we see from Figure 5 an altruistic strategy (with a Simulated-Annealing-based acceptance criterion for non-profitable transitions) applied by all agents (no defecting agent) leads to worse results for the initial negotiation steps, but this temporary loss is compensated for by a significant increase in total welfare after 20,000 renegotiations, almost doubling the expected benefits of the selfish strategy.

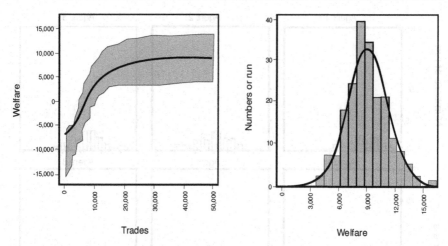

Figure 5. Welfare distribution for negotiation applying the altruistic strategy

While in the setting with solely altruistic agents the profits is almost equally distributed (with a slight advantage of the agents at the end of the supply chain), the introduced altruism is extremely prone to exploitation: Figure 6 depicts the distribution of income when agent 4 exaggerates its true cost by 20 %. While the defecting agent generates extraordinary profits the other agents may be worse off in the end compared to their initial plans. Most of their side payments finally end up at agent 4, not returning anything to them.

As shown in Figure 6 it is very easy for an agent to increase its income by pretending to have higher costs. To avoid such exploitation our agents use a memory that stores the aggregated side payments. How the agents use this memory is detailed in the following section.

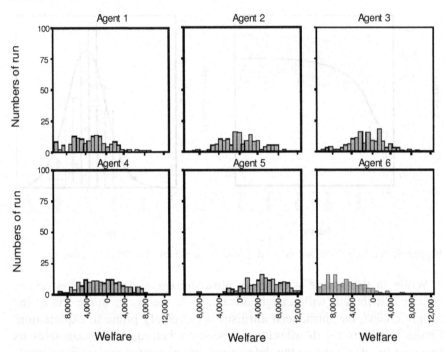

Figure 6. Income distribution of the agents applying the altruistic strategy but agent 4 defecting (exaggerating true cost by 20 %)

6.3.4 Avoiding Exploitation via Trusted Annealing

Agents who try to maximize their profits at the expense of other agents systematically underestimate their profits or overestimate the costs of a new delivery time. In light of the consumers' willingness to pay for earlier deliveries, the agents should, at least in the long run, increase their joint income by agreeing to new delivery times. So, each agent should limit its side payment to the other agent. The left side of Figure 7 shows the agents' true cost and benefit from a given re-contracting proposal. The right side illustrates that *agent b* will overcompensate the loss of *agent a* by a side-payment of 3 monetary units, yielding a profit of 2 MUs for both agents (rights side). All side payments are cumulated in accounts that are associated to the negotiation partners. Based on these accounts, a trust limit can be used to restrict the re-contracting if a certain level of side payments has been spent. In case both agents are truth-telling their mutual trust accounts of cumulated payments will fluctuate around zero, since the probability that it is always the same agent incurring the negative effects of recontracting is very low. On the other hand, if *agent a* is consistently cheating by exaggerating losses and hiding profits, side-payments from *agent b* to *agent a* will be higher on average than payments from *a* to *b*, leading to an ever increasing negative balance on *agent b*'s trust account for *agent a*. By selecting a trust limit *agent b* decides at which negative balance he will start to reject any re-contracting incurring further side payments to *agent a*. He will resume side-payments, however, once *agent a* proposes sufficient contract changes to reduce this deficit.

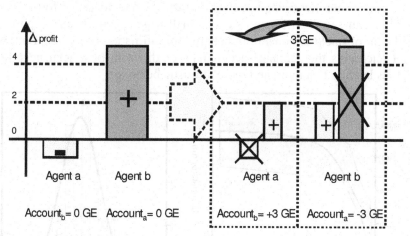

Figure 7. Trust accounting for a truthful agent vs. a defecting agent

Based on the trust account each agent grants the other agents a temporary advantage hoping for a system wide efficiency increase from which he could benefit in later periods. In our application trust only acts as the result of aggregate reputation. The advantage of the integration of trust accounts in the economic WIJSP lies mainly in three points:

- A more convincing economic interpretation of the WIJSP can be achieved by introducing the trust accounts and simulating the outcome of varying system participants' behavior.
- The decomposition of the WJSSP into separate instances of the WJISP reduces the computational complexity of the optimization tasks to be solved. While enabling the economic agents to generate tentative partial solutions by solving the WJISP, trust has to be introduced into the decentralized system to grant the incentive compatibility of the scheduling mechanism.
- Similar to the pure Simulated Annealing approach, our trust mechanism for decentralized economic scheduling is a nature inspired optimization process and therefore easier to integrate into real world scenarios.

The trust accounting mechanism used in our model does not employ a composed reputation index using, for example, indirect reputation like most MAS reputation applications do. This is not necessary due to the equilibrium property of the system introduced by the SA negotiation process. In addition the use of indirect trust could inhibit the detection of optimal scheduling solutions in the iterated bilateral negotiation strategies by blocking whole clusters of negotiation partners. On the other hand, the use of indirect trust could help to identify regularly cheating agents earlier at the risk of further increasing information flow and negotiation effort.

As we can see from Figure 8 even small trust accounts do not pose a significant obstacle to generating benefits for altruistic agents: After a few initial rejections the accounts accumulate credit from beneficial negotiation thus leading to a more and more altruistic behavior.

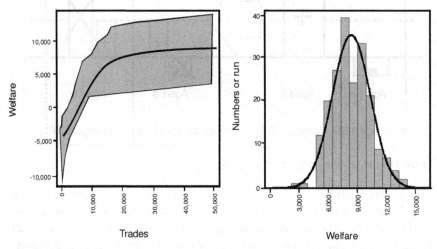

Figure 8. Trusted annealing: result granting maximum credit 100

To prevent the exploitation by a defecting agent it is advisable to use a low initial setting for trust accounts. Too much initial goodwill allows the defecting agent to withdraw this goodwill.

As Figure 9 illustrates, trusted annealing safely prevents exploitation by a defecting agent. However, the problem of a strong bias in welfare distribution, as we have seen in the selfish case, prevails: Agent 0 and agent 1 hardly participate in any gains. Although this results partially from the fact that they do not have a supply side to renegotiate with (but only customers), it nevertheless raises the question if it is possible to implement any "distributional fairness" criterion by a purely decentralized protocol or whether this requires communication to a central intermediary.

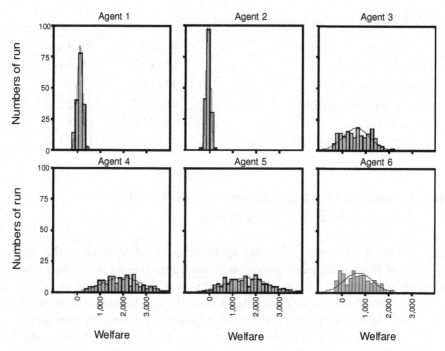

Figure 9. Income distribution of the agents granting maximum credit 100 and agent 4 defects (trusted annealing)

6.3.5 Overview of Results

This section provides a short overview of the simulation's results (Table 1). The negotiations that rely on purely selfish strategies achieve the lowest averaged welfare. To improve the quality of decentralized planning agents could cooperatively apply an altruistic SA protocol, temporarily allowing for decreases in solution quality (and profit) for the sake of escaping local contract optima which are far from a globally optimal solution. Trust accounts can be introduced, without a considerable decrease of the solution quality.

Trying to increase profits by giving false information is a pattern that has to be considered in distributed manufacturing environments. Assuming that agents use a selfish strategy to defend themselves against exploitation in such settings the Trusted Annealing protocol could increase the welfare dramatically. Obviously, if a setting with solely altruistic agents is possible a (slightly) higher welfare could be achieved.

Table 1. Overview of the cumulated welfare values

	Welfare	Std. Dev.
Selfish agents	4,210.16	174.04
Altruistic agents	9,174.02	137.58
Altr. and defecting agent(s)	9,029.24	221.52
Trusted Annealing	9,107.21	147.92
Trusted Annealing with defecting agent(s)	7,584.11	171.13

6.4 Coupling Trust-Based Negotiation With Scheduling Support Systems

An important issue for real world applications of SCM-MAS is the integration of the automated negotiation process into human controlled business environments. One way to achieve this is to employ Negotiation Support Systems (NSS), which are able to close the gap between the necessity of human involvement and automated decision processes, by introducing hybrid systems like SILKROAD. "In hybrid negotiation systems, structured or formalized tasks are automated, and decision support mechanisms are used to assess unstructured tasks, whereas humans interactively control the execution of the negotiation and perform the exception handling" [Stro2001]. The outlined trust-based scheduling system could propose the acceptance or rejection of the manufacturing tasks according to the trust account of a proxy agent coupled to a specific production facility. The decision itself has then to be acknowledged by the human control agents, whereas the trust-accounting of the SCM-MAS is corrected corresponding to the human's decision. The overall performance of the NSS should then be near to the distribution calculated in our setting.

One drawback of our protocol could be a high sensitivity to the additional parameters introduced by the Simulated Annealing approach or the interleaving of contract renegotiation (cooperative action) and the agents' internal optimization of the WJISPs defined by these contracts. Cooling too fast or too low a starting temperature will rather emulate the selfish strategy while cooling too slow or too high an initial temperature will yield contracts which are not even locally optimal.

The same holds for the number of internal search steps trying to adapt the solution of the old WJISP to the new version after a re-contracting step. Too small numbers will generate "noisy" estimates of a re-contracting step's cost impact on the two agents involved, increasing the number of false acceptance or rejection decisions. A high number reduces this error at the price of overall computational resources spent. Although there is a significant benefit of additional computational effort here, 250 steps per re-contracting step already allow for adequate estimates of the cost difference and thus produce a low rate of erroneous acceptance or rejection.

6.5 Conclusion

Due to the growing number of applications of MAS in the production planning domain, decentralized scheduling mechanisms are of increasing interest especially in supply chain environments. A main problem while bringing optimizing software to work in real supply chains is the unwillingness of business participants to reveal sensitive information to a central planning institution. In the decentralized negotiation protocol presented here, agents are neither urged to reveal their internal planning state nor their exact utility function to other agents but nevertheless reach a solution of high quality.

We have shown how the quality of decentralized planning significantly improves when agents apply an altruistic SA protocol, temporarily allowing for decreases in solution quality (and profit) for the sake of escaping local contract optima which are far from a globally optimal solution. To limit this altruism's vulnerability to exploitation, trust accounts can be introduced, fortunately almost without sacrificing solution quality.

The downside of our approach is the high number of negotiation steps necessary to achieve good solutions. However, with ever decreasing cost of information and communication technology, we believe this will pose no major obstacle.

A number of future extensions could help to further improve the model's solution quality or usability for real-world applications:

- Up to now our model assumes agents either to be truth-telling or defecting. An important extension could be the analysis of a trust discounting protocol, also allowing to protect against agents dynamically changing their behavior from altruistic to selfish in later stages of the negotiation process.
- Although the application of a SA re-negotiation process defines a probability distribution over the agents' strategy space and the incorporation of trust accounts modifies this probability distribution based on the historic behavior of the other players, it is highly unlikely that this mixed strategy and its evolution during the re-contracting game is optimal. A rigid game theoretic analysis could help to further improve solution quality.

- As discussed in the simplifying assumptions, multiple inputs to tasks are worthwhile extensions. The introduction of tasks simultaneously requiring multiple resources should also be considered for future extensions.

References

[CaBG2002]   Carter, J.; Bitting, E.; Ghorbani, A. A.: Reputation formalization within information sharing multiagent architectures. Comp Intelligence 18(2002)4, pp. 45-64.

[CaFa2001]   Castelfranchi, C.; Falcone, R.: Social trust: A cognitive approach. In: Castelfranchi, C.; Tan Y.-H. (Eds.): Trust and Deception in Virtual Societies. Kluwer Academic Publishers, 2001, pp. 55-90.

[Cone2003]   Conen, W.: Economically-augmented job shop scheduling. In Giunchiglia, E.; Muscettola, N.; Nau, D. (Eds.): International Conference on Automated Planning & Scheduling (ICAPS). AAAI Press, Trento, Italy, 2003.

[DaSe2003]   Dauzère-Pérès, S.; Sevaux, M.: Using lagrangean relaxation to minimize the weighted number of late jobs on a single machine. Naval Research Logistics 50(2003)3, pp. 273-288.

[Elen2003]   Elendner, T.: Scheduling and combinatorial auctions: Lagrangean relaxation-based bounds for the WJISP. Technical Report 570, Manuskripte aus den Instituten für Betriebswirtschaftslehre. Christian-Albrechts-Universität zu Kiel, 2003.

[Eyma2001]   Eymann, T.: Co-evolution of bargaining strategies in a decentralized multi-agent system. In: Proceedings of the AAAI Fall 2001 Symposium on negotiation methods for autonomous cooperative systems. North Falmouth, MA, November 03-04, 2001.

[FiTh1963]   Fisher, H.; Thompson, G.: Probabilistic learning combinations of local job-shop scheduling rules. In: Muth, J.; Thompson, G. (Eds.): Industrial Scheduling. Prentice Hall, Englewood Cliffs, New Jersey, 1963, pp. 225-251.

[FrSK2005]   Franke, J.; Stockheim, T.; König, W.: The impact of reputation on supply chains: An analysis of permanent and discounted reputation, In: Journal of Information Systems and e-Business Management 3(2005)4, pp. 323-341.

[GoKu1998]   Gordon, V.; Kubiak, W.: Single machine scheduling with release and due date assignment to minimize the weighted number of late jobs. Information Processing Letters 68(1998), pp. 153-159.

[JoSi2001]   Jordi, S.; Sierra, C.: REGRET: A reputation model for gregarious societies. In: Proceedings of the 4th Workshop on Deception

Fraud and Trust in Agent Societies. Montreal, Canada, 2001, pp. 61-70.

[JuFa2003]   Jurca, R.; Faltings, B.: An incentive compatible reputation mechanism. In: Proceedings of the IEEE Conference on E-Commerce CEC03. Newport Beach, California, USA, 2003.

[MuHM2002]   Mui, L.; Halberstadt, A.; Mohtashemi, M.: Notions of reputation in multi-agents systems: a review. In: Proceedings of the 1st International Joint Conference on Autonomous Agents. Bolonga, Italy, 2002.

[MuMH2002]   Mui, L.; Mohtashemi, M.; Halberstadt, A.: A computational model of trust and reputation. In: Proceedings of the 35th Hawaii International Conference on System Science (HICSS). Big Island, 2002.

[PSEP2002]   Padovan, B.; Sackmann, S.; Eymann, T.; Pippow, I.: A prototype for an agent-based secure electronic marketplace including reputation tracking mechanisms. In: International Journal of Electronic Commerce 6(2002)4, pp. 93-113.

[RuNo2003]   Russel, S.; Norvig, P.: Artificial Intelligence – A modern approach. Prentice Hall, New Jersey, 2003.

[Saba2003]   Sabater, J.: Trust and reputation for agent societies. PhD thesis. Institute for Artificial Intelligence Research, Bellaterra, 2003.

[SiJo2002]   Sierra, C.; Jordi, S.: Reputation and social network analysis in multi-agent systems. In: Proceedings of the first International Conference on Autonomous Agents and Multiagent Systems. Bologna, Italy, 2002, pp. 475-482.

[Stro2001]   Ströbel, M.: Design of roles and protocols for electronic negotiations. Electronic Commerce Research 1(2001)3, pp. 335-353.

Part III

Application Examples II: Agent.Hospital

1 Agent.Hospital – Health Care Applications of Intelligent Agents[1]

Stefan Kirn, Christian Anhalt
Universität Hohenheim, Wirtschaftsinformatik II
{kirn I canhalt}@uni-hohenheim.de

Helmut Krcmar, Andreas Schweiger
TU München, Lehrstuhl Wirtschaftsinformatik
{krcmar I schweiga}@in.tum.de

Abstract. In SPP 1083 the *Hospital Logistics* group studies the applicability of agent-based information systems in health care business scenarios by identifying problems, analyzing requirements, elaborating the state of the art of conventional and agent-based systems, specifying and designing multiagent applications, and evaluating their application. This chapter includes a survey of both the projects forming the group and their collaboration in order to integrate the systems designed by them into the agent testbed named *Agent.Hospital*. Therefore, two exemplary (hospital) processes are presented involving each project's multiagent application. Also, the ontology *OntHoS* and agent infrastructure services used in *Agent.Hospital* are shown.

1.1 Introduction

Driven by the requirements coming from patients, the domain of health care is characterized by complexity, dynamics, variety, and fragmentation of distributed medical prevention, diagnosis, treatment, and rehabilitation processes. Among other aspects, shared decision-making, combined with different skills and roles of health care professionals, and incompleteness and asymmetry of information results in an environment requesting high

---

[1] This chapter is based on the paper "Paulussen, T. O.; Herrler, R.; Hoffmann, A.; Heine, C.; Becker, M.; Franck, M.; Reinke, T.; Strasser, M.: Intelligente Softwareagenten und betriebswirtschaftliche Anwendungsszenarien im Gesundheitswesen. In: Dittrich, K.; König, W.; Oberweis, A.; Rannenberg, K.; Wahlster, W. (Eds.): INFORMATIK 2003 Innovative Informatikanwendungen. GI-Edition Lecture Notes in Informatics, P-34. Köllen Verlag, Bonn, 2003, Vol. 1, pp. 64-82."

demands on information systems applied to reach advanced levels of automation.

Multiagent technology is assumed to be one possible solution to meet requirements coming from complex and dynamic environments. Due to their adaptability and flexibility, agent-based information systems have the potential to significantly improve the competitiveness of enterprises. Their application should allow more effective and efficient (logistic) processes and may also generate new customer welfare by making product improvements available.

Against this background, health care, and especially hospital logistics, was chosen as one exemplary application domain used in the German Priority Research Program "Intelligent Agents and Their Application in Business Scenarios." A special interest group named *Hospital Logistics* has been founded, including all (sub-) projects referring to the application of agent-based inter- or intra-hospital information systems.

Each project has its own specific research question and considers, examines, and analyses specific organizational parts of different hospitals. A nearly complete model of a virtual hospital was generated by the combination of the projects' partial models. Both the partial models and the developed multiagent systems of each project form the agent technology testbed *Agent.Hospital* (cf. [KHHK2003a] [KHHK2003b]), which is addressed and introduced in this chapter.

The chapter is organized as follows: First, the sub-domain hospital is presented by exemplarily identifying domain specific problems in Section 1.2. Based on this, Section 1.3 presents the goals of the single subprojects. Section 1.4 deals with the development of the ontology *OntHoS*, whereas the agent testbed *Agent.Hospital* is described in detail in Section 1.5. Giving two selected examples, the interaction of the subprojects is shown in Section 1.6. A summary and an overview regarding Part III of this book conclude this chapter.

1.2 Hospital Logistics as an Object of Investigation

Due to rising costs, economic ways of acting gain more and more importance in the domain of health care. Among other aspects, this is reflected in the abolishment of the principle of coverage of all hospital costs, i.e. all costs of a hospital were met by the health insurance scheme in 1993. It is also reflected by the introduction of the diagnosis related groups (DRGs) in 2002^2, which succeeded other case-based models of remuneration. DRGs particularly force health care institutions to act economically, as they are now liable for their actions (cf. [Rych1999] [Jast1997]). They also encourage competition between hospitals. Further, the rapid development of new methods of treatment and diagnosis, the application of new medications, and the progress in medical engineering induce an increasing differentiation and specialization of health care service providers. As a result, the demands on networking between all actors participating in fragmented and distributed treatment processes rise. Increasing mobility of patients, change of the age structure, and patients' incremental claims to quality of treatments intensify this situation.

Hospitals can be defined as social organizations with the purpose of improvement of the patient's state of health [Dlug1984]. The main differences between logistics in production and hospitals are based on the fact that not lifeless material is managed, but diseased people. A hospital is thus a service enterprise where production and consumption of services coincide [Greu1997] [Herd1994]. The patient is directly involved in his treatment and its success [DuWi1997].

A hospital is partitioned into semi-autonomous functional areas, where patients pass through according to their particular diseases [Schl1990]. These areas are either organizationally assigned directly to certain (single) departments or can be deployed to several departments as centralized service units [Schm1999], as radiology or operating theatres normally are. Although functional centralization enables more efficient exploitation of rooms and resources and thus more flexibility, the autonomy of functional areas induces the necessity of a comprehensive coordination among the medical departments.

Especially when deploying centralized operating theatres, coordination may become complex. In such cases, scheduling is usually carried out by requests coming from different departments, finally verified and, if required, corrected by a physician in the role of a coordinator. After this verification, the schedule is forwarded to the central operating theatre department assigning the staff, e.g., nurses, to the surgical operations. This multilevel scheduling process is carried out in many hospitals manually, i.e. without IT support. Causes for this are different and contradicting interests and priorities of the involved actors resulting in requirements not capable by conventional systems. Even without considering emergency cases, this manual planning approach results in complex coordination processes.

---

[2] Germany.

Additionally, in contrast to the production domain, there is the problem that the patient's disease is not or only partially known at the time of his admission. Therefore, procedures such as examinations and treatments cannot be predetermined completely [Wend1987]. The lack of accompanying information can be reduced progressively only by multiple and sequential diagnoses, resulting in changes and adaptations of the processes. Further, complications and emergency cases induce partially heavy disruption in regular hospital processes [Schl1990].

In order to react flexibly to those uncertainties, treatments are assigned to patients by a ward's physician and forwarded to the particular functional area by requests. The functional areas then call the patients from the wards depending on their workload. Coordination among different functional areas, which may help avoiding idle time for both patients and the functional areas, is unusual or does not exist [PJDH2003]. Thus, an optimized exchange of information between these units, or even better, between all actors participating in specific treatment process is one of the main challenges of hospital logistics.

Similar problems also exist in hospital emergency centers, whose processes are characterized by cooperation of different clinical departments and handling of various medical data [KnRS2000]. Here emergency physicians coordinate the interaction of different departments in order to perform examinations and emergency or ambulant treatments. Unlike in previously described functional areas, the availability of resources primarily forms the requirements to be met. When locating and calling/using these resources, e.g., medical staff or equipment, both disruptions of running medical processes and effects on already scheduled appointments have to be considered.

An additional challenge becomes obvious if clinical trials are taken into account. In order to prove the effectiveness of therapeutic methods, particularly the application of medication, it is not only necessary to carry out experiments with animals, but also tests on humans. As information systems vastly support scheduling, their usage becomes more and more crucial for the allocation of clinical trials (which are, of course, profitable). Their application may reduce scheduling times, increase planning reliability, optimize structures and processes, and significantly improve the quality of documentation. Furthermore, they may help in integrating clinical trials into the regular operation of hospitals. This is characterized by considerable complexity, as the design of trials allows only marginal flexibility regarding the selection of patients, medication, and documentation.

Currently existing hospital information systems are not capable of mitigating the exemplarily described problems and meeting the outlined challenges. In particular cooperation, coordination, and communication between all actors participating in treatment processes are not supported sufficiently.

Also, the localization of patients, professionals, and resources still takes place by beeper, pagers, and announcements. Thus, localization, identification, and information about availability are still not manageable in an automated way. Direct personal communication is needed, which is time-consuming and characterized by an unacceptable error rate.

Furthermore, access to electronic patient records, which is restricted to preserve the privacy of personal data, does not have the necessary flexibility in terms of context sensitive composition and analysis of medical data. Although clinical data systems and paperless records are very common nowadays [BWWD2002], they are in general still passive and quite inflexible. Retrieving data, even from patient records, is time-consuming [Ginn2002] and also implies the risk of overlooking important information.

At least from an inter-hospital perspective, proprietary data exchange formats complicate and avoid the integration of, e.g., fragmented treatment processes. Even standards like CEN, ISO, or HL7 do not lead to adequate interoperability, as they are not existent, not used, or not usable due to their incompatible software realization.

1.3 Aims and Approaches of Participating Projects

The *Policy Agents* project (cf. III.2) aims at the solution to the described scheduling problem for operating theatres. Using an agent-based planning system, scheduling for operating theatres can be largely automated [CzBe2002]. Special project focus is on the explicit consideration of the departments' and persons' interests. For this purpose a software agent with a person specific preference profile represents each actor. These software agents negotiate autonomously in finding schedules and try to reach an efficient resource allocation well below the usual transaction costs (see also [BeKS2001] [CzBe2002] [CzBe2003]).

The *MedPAge* project (cf. III.4) deals with planning, controlling, and coordination of clinical processes across boundaries of functional areas. A patient-centered approach is chosen, which models both the hospital's resources and the patients as autonomous software agents. On the basis of preference functions, agents representing patients negotiate autonomously with each other for scarce hospital resources. As a coordination mechanism a market mechanism is implemented, in which the resource allocation is improved until Pareto optimality is reached [PJDH2003] [AwPa2001].

The focus of the *EMIKA* project (cf. III.7) is the real-time coordination of patient logistics in radiology in order to integrate acute emergency cases preferably without delay into the current schedule and to analyze these in terms of time accuracy. In a decentralized implementation with localizable devices (e.g., RFID[3] chips), software agents act as shadow objects of the devices. They identify their physical environment and the context of use in order to generate a state model of the reality. Thereon, they decide autonomously whether the current schedule can be met or new planning is necessary. Permanent dynamic feedback between reality and the information system is established via the interaction with mobile devices without central control of the system [SaEM2002].

The *ADAPT* project (cf. III.5) focuses solutions to the described problems regarding clinical trials. The main goal is the construction of an agent-based simulation system that simulates processes relevant to the implementation of clinical trials [HHPA2003]. For that purpose adequate simulation models were implemented, which map necessary and participating actors. These models were based on an actor-centered view and were implemented by an agent-oriented approach. The developed prototype supports medical personnel and other staff of participating departments dealing with analysis, evaluation, and scheduling of the clinical trials [HeHK2002].

The *ASAinlog* project (cf. III.6) tackles questions in hospital information logistics regarding the use of patient records. There are two main aims: (1) All persons involved in the treatment process are to be provided with relevant and context-sensitive information at the right point in time and at the right place; (2) Processes for cooperation and coordination are to be effectively supported regarding information needed for cooperation, i.e. context-sensitive medical data. Central elements of the solution are active medical documents implemented as composite software agents. They encapsulate both data of patients and elementary agents that interpret and concatenate these medical and administrative data.

In the *AGIL²* project (cf. III.3), e.g., treatment processes are modeled using a Java based tool (AGILShell), which was developed in the first phase of the project and can be deployed for the design and implementation of multiagent systems. The pursued approach comprises three steps: (1) domain experts model existent processes; (2) analysis of processes in order to identify application scenarios for agents; (3) optimization of processes through integration of agents. Based upon existent processes of the previously described projects, an "agentified" process is elaborated by interdisciplinary cooperation. In this process, agents carry out tasks that were

---

[3]   RFID – Radio Frequency Identification.

previously done by humans. The described approach improves the quality of the software, since the user is actively involved [BACR2001] [Sta+ 2001].

In order to take advantage of all described approaches, full integration and coordination of the individual projects through the consortium Hospital Logistics is necessary. The need for support and coordination is implemented on the basis of the cooperation platform RealAgentS (http://www. realagents.org) [AnKi2003].

1.4 Development of the Common Ontology OntHoS

One of the first steps in the direction of an integrated scenario was the establishment of a task force in March 2002. Its aim was the development of an ontology crossing the boundaries of the individual projects. It was recognized that the developed multiagent systems were based upon different knowledge representations and slightly different terms, blocking complex interactions between the systems. In order to abolish this deficit, the ontology *OntHoS* for the domain hospital and nursing was developed.

OntHoS was modeled using a widely used ontology and knowledge engineering tool, Protégé. It allows the domain expert to model the formal definition of concepts and terms of the application domain and provides support for programmers regarding agent implementation. For that purpose, a defined ontology can be transformed into Java code. The advantage of this approach is the absence of an additional error-prone manual transformation process between model and implementation.

One problem of the collaborative development of an ontology is the integration of overlapping concepts. Therefore the domain was divided into a set of concept categories. As a result, a consensus regarding the underlying hierarchy was found (cf. Figure 1). At several places, one tried to use established ontologies or parts of it, e.g., the *temporal concept*, which is mainly based upon the Dharma Guideline Model [Dhar2005]. Nevertheless, most of the categories could not be based upon existing ontologies. For these reasons, each project elaborated suggestions, which were discussed within the group and, if necessary, adapted. As a result, the ontology *OntHoS* is capable of expressing message contents of all project agent systems.

The concept classes used in *OntHoS* are described as follows (cf. [BHHK2003]):

- *Temporal concept*: The defined terms are domain-independent definitions of temporal concepts, e.g., date, fixed or relative points in time,

time intervals, or duration. In addition, more abstract terms such as "today" or "now" are defined, which need reference points of time for interpretation.

- *Medical concept*: Terms within this concept define medical knowledge. These range from symptoms, diagnoses, and therapies to a representation structure for formalizing clinical guidelines. Knowledge bases for a particular scenario can be developed by the insertion of instances of a defined class or term.

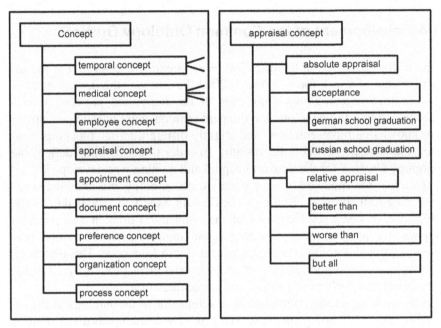

Figure 1. *OntHoS* – main hierarchy level of the ontology and base concepts (left) and concept hierarchy of appraisals (right)

- *Employee concept*: This concept group unites terms for the description of clinical staff, e.g., qualifications and roles.
- *Appraisal concept*: For planning and scheduling in hospitals and for making decisions terms for expressing evaluations are needed. In order to be as flexible as possible it is only distinguished between absolute and relative appraisals. Absolute appraisals are, e.g., school grades, relative appraisals are terms like "better than."
- *Appointment concept*: For the scheduling of treatments and examinations additional terms – not included, e.g., in the temporal concept – are necessary, e.g., *appointment task, appointment time, etc.* We dis-

tinguish between previously agreed upon appointments and appointment suggestions to be evaluated.

- *Document concept*: Format and contents of different typical clinical documents such as findings or patient records are described. Standards for hospital information systems are also to be taken into account.
- *Organizational concept*: In order to model a hospital, underlying organizations and their units are to be described. There are usually functional units that provide services such as examinations and treatments. Additionally, there are wards, administration, and special units, e.g., a pharmacy or an external orthopedic service. All units have resources and provide several types of services (see process concept).
- *Process concept*: Processes can be described as sequences and alternatives of atomic actions. A simple basis process representation was chosen, which can be extended in order to support domain modelers with different kinds of model languages, e.g., modeling using EPCs (Event-driven Process Chains) or Petri nets. Atomic actions of these processes are either medical or logistic actions. Medical actions are subdivided into examinations, treatments, or nursing. Many actions need to be carried out by special functional units and others need special resources or persons (see object concept or employee concept).
- *Object concept*: In contrast to the terms described above, which refer to abstract, non-existent concepts, object concepts define all real objects and persons. Real objects are, e.g., rooms, medical or technical devices, or drugs. Objects can be relevant resources for actions or they can be subject to appraisals. Persons like patients and clinical staff are subclasses of this concept, whereas their tasks, qualifications, and roles are partly described by the employee concept.

1.5 Agent Technology Testbed Agent.Hospital

Agent.Hospital is a testbed for agent-based information systems in health care, supporting both the development and the evaluation at the level of modeling and implementation. At the model level a framework for different partial models of health care is provided. At the implementation level, infrastructure services and multiagent-based modular health care services exist. As the integration of additional partial models and multiagent applications has been one requirement right from the beginning, *Agent.Hospital* is designed to be an open framework. Thus, only open standards for, e.g., application integration, are used.

Figure 2 illustrates the architecture of *Agent.Hospital*. Currently, the following integrated supply chains are implemented: Clinical trials, radiotherapy (ADAPT), emergency patients (AGIL), lung cancer treatment (ASA*inlog*), angina pectoris (MedPAge), gall stone treatment (MedPAge and Policy Agents), operating theatre processes (Policy Agents), and radiological processes (EMIKA). Further information, as detailed process models, can be retrieved from http://www.realagents.org.

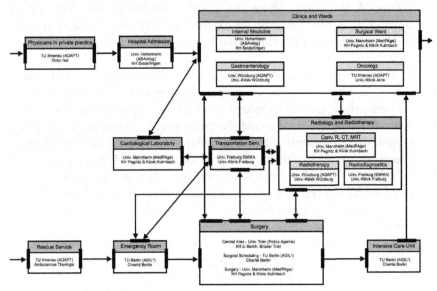

Figure 2. Architecture of and supply chains in *Agent.Hospital* (as of 2003)[4]

Several infrastructural services are provided by *Agent.Hospital* coupling the subsystems of the individual projects. These comprise the following services (for a detailed description see [KHHK2003b]):

*   *Agent.Hospital Directory Facilitator (AHDF)*: Directory service for the registration and supervision of *ServiceAgents* and for display of registered agents and their services.
*   *Agent.Hospital TimeService (AHTS)*: a time service that allows for the registration of several groups of *ServiceAgents* and for their discrete timing.

---

[4] Please note that some allocations of projects have changed, e.g., ADAPT is now located at the Universität Hohenheim, ASA*inlog* at TU München.

- *Agent.Hospital Ontology Repository (AHOR)*: A repository for domain and task ontology of the health care domain. This service supports the exchange of task ontology and the access to the common domain ontology *OntHoS* [BHHK2002].

- *Agent.Hospital Knowledge Base (AHKB)*: A knowledge base for the health care domain. It is comprised of an A-box and a T-box. The T-box contains all terms of the domain ontology and structures for formulating concepts. The A-box aggregates instances of terms and concepts of the T-box, which helped in modeling representative scenarios of the health care domain.

- *Agent.Hospital Actor Agent (AHAA)*: An additional common element of *Agent.Hospital* relevant for coordinating the services. Instances of actor agents represent patients with their basic personal data and individual time schedule.

- *Agent.Hospital CVS (ACCVS)*: A repository for the administration of source code of *ServiceAgents*. It supports the exchange of commonly usable modules and interface classes between the developers.

Most of these services are based on and extend existing infrastructural services of the FIPA-compatible Java Agent Development Framework JADE.[5] Afterwards they were reintegrated in JADE.

Besides the infrastructural services, *Agent.Hospital* contains *ServiceAgents* of the individual projects. These implement gateways among the organizational units of the domain model and provide their functionalities in the form of an agent service to the remaining organizational units and their representing agents. By the deployment of FIPA-compatible gateway agents for the functional integration of the technically different multiagent systems, a standard at the level of communication was established. This enables the cross-project usage of common interaction protocols, agent communication languages, and knowledge representation languages (for a detailed description see [KHHK2003b]).

The central integration element of *Agent.Hospital* is *AHDF*, as it implements the mediation of the services. The main task of the *AHDF*, and also the differentiating criterion regarding the global DF (Directory Facilitator) of the *Agentcities*[6] network, is the bundling of services of the same context to an application-specific services forum. The implemented functionality of the *AHDF* is domain independent and allows for the deployment in the production domain within the SPP 1083 (cf. II.1).

---

[5] Cf. http://jade.tilab.com/
[6] Cf. http://www.agentcities.net/

Finally, *Agent.Hospital* is implemented as part of the *Agentcities* community. As a result, five new *Agentcities* platforms have emerged: Aachen, Ilmenau, Würzburg, Freiburg, Hamburg, all integrated by the common directory service *Agent.HospitalDF*.

1.6 Selected Agent.Hospital Application Scenarios

Two cross-project application scenarios demonstrate the interaction of the projects' multiagent systems within the *Agent.Hospital* framework: (1) clinical trials and (2) diagnosis and treatment of colon cancer. Except for the ADAPT project, in these scenarios the acronyms of the projects are similarly to the names of the developed multiagent systems. The ADAPT projects consists of two applications named DAISIY (Deliberative Agents for Intelligent Simulation Systems) and SeSAm (Shell for Simulated Agent Systems). Although both systems are part of *Agent.Hospital*, SeSAm is used additionally for simulating the *Agent.Hospital* real world environment, in which the other multiagent systems are situated.

1.6.1 Clinical Trials

The goal of (controlled) clinical trials is the deduction of a general statement regarding the benefit-risk ratio of treatments on the basis of study results, which have to be reproducible within a given probability. Besides strong medical and statistical requirements to be fulfilled by hospitals when performing clinical trials, additional challenges for the participating hospitals exist. So, besides the determination of the required patients needed during a certain time period, a hospital has, e.g., to calculate whether sufficient resources are available. If shortages jeopardizing trial execution are identified, the hospital is obligated to, e.g., employ additional trial nurses or documentalists. Usually, such decisions are made intuitively, which may lead to inefficiencies and errors – due to the complexity of trials.

Figure 3 illustrates an exemplary section of the integrated scenario process "clinical trials." The description is based upon the extended EPC. The tight bipartite alternation of events and functions is abolished in order to simplify the representation.

In general, at the beginning of clinical trials a lot of diagnostic and therapeutic measures need to be coordinated and scheduled. Also resources like equipment and staff need to be assigned and possibly informed. The process given in Figure 3 focuses on this first phase. It illustrates both US (ultra sound) and MRI (magnetic resonance imaging) examinations and related surgery.

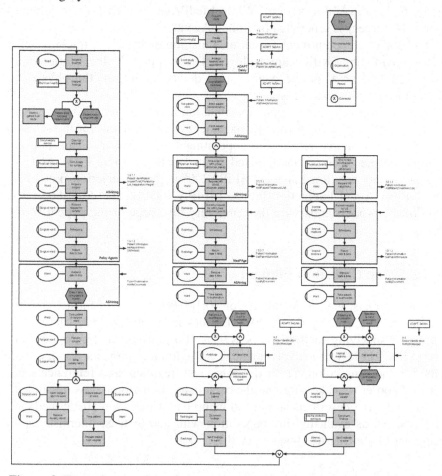

Figure 3. Exemplary section of a process of the integrated scenario "clinical trials"

As a first step, the eligibility of the patient for the trial is checked. The DAISIY-system evaluates the data provided by the SeSAm-system with specific inclusion and exclusion criteria of the clinical trial. If the patients meet the study requirements, an individual study plan is generated for the measures to be taken by the service *RequestStudyPlan*. The trial's documentalist can insert individual appointments. After the medium-term study plan is planned for the patient (usually a study cycle of four weeks), the electronic patient record is extended applying the ASA*inlog* service *AddNewDocument*. The multiagent systems of MedPAge and Policy Agents start their operative planning and scheduling of binding appointments based on this information, i.e. they are triggered by the active patient records of the ASA*inlog* system. While MedPAge schedules the examinations, the surgery is scheduled by Policy Agents.

If the actual appointment for an examination approaches, tracking services provided by EMIKA are deployed. They support the localization of a particular bed or a mobile examination device or inform the physician about the current appointment.

In case of, e.g., an emergency examination involving the resource MRI, the responsible systems for the management of the trial and for the scheduling of the resource reschedule appointments if necessary. This is performed on the basis of standardized agent languages (here FIPA-ACL – Agent Communication Language [FIPA2005a]) and interaction protocols (e.g., FIPA Agent Interaction Protocol [FIPA2005b]). The described section of the process ends with the temporary discharge of the patient from the hospital.

1.6.2 Colon Cancer Treatment

Colon cancer is, with an incidence of 40:100,000, the third most frequent carcinoma in Germany [Psch1998]. Besides medical relevance (the probability of surviving for five years is 95%-100% at best and below 6% at worst [Psch1998]), the involvement of all individual projects was a criterion for choosing colon cancer diagnosis and treatment as a reference scenario. In order to make sure that the exemplary scenario process illustrated in Figure 4 and described on the following pages maps a realistic medical process, it was evaluated in cooperation with anesthetists, internists, and surgeons of the Charité Hospital, Berlin.

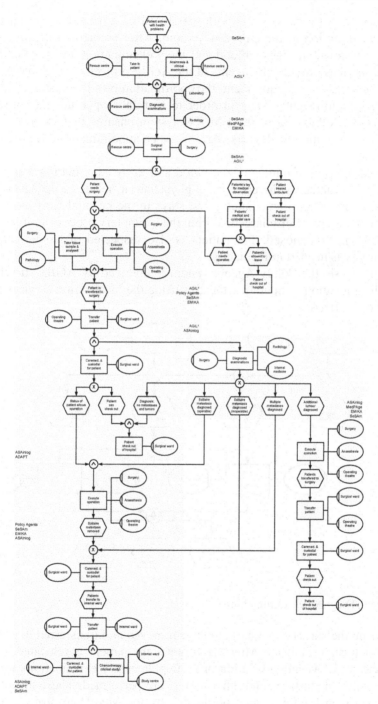

Figure 4. Integrated scenario "colon cancer treatment"

The scenario process starts with the arrival of a patient at the hospital and his admission to the emergency room. After an anamnesis, an emergency physician arranges a blood and x-ray examination using the coordination services provided by agents of the AGIL² project. As the emergency room lacks radiology equipment, the coordination task is transferred to the MedPAge multiagent system in order to rearrange appointments of, e.g., (central) radiology. Also, the EMIKA system ensures that the necessary staff and examination devices, despite other appointment schedules, are available.

Based upon the findings of the blood and x-ray examination a surgical council is initiated by the emergency physician. It decides whether the patient is operated on immediately, first stays in the hospital for further observation, or can be discharged. Within the exemplary process an intestinal obstruction is diagnosed. The patient is also suspected of having cancer. So, surgery is needed immediately.

In this case, the Policy Agents system is involved by AGIL.² It schedules the allocation of operating theatres using the localization services provided by EMIKA.

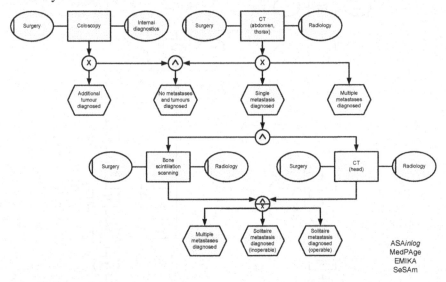

Figure 5. Diagnostic examinations

During the surgery a tissue sample is removed and transferred to pathology for further analysis. After the surgery, the patient is relocated to the surgical ward. Meanwhile, additional supplementary examinations for the exclusion of metastases and other tumors are performed. These diagnostic measures (see Figure 5) are coordinated by the MedPAge project, while the patient is scheduled in regular intervals by the EMIKA agents for check-ups in radiology.

If there are no metastases or tumors, the patient is cured and needs no further therapy. If there are metastases, their number and localization give clues about further actions. If there is a single metastasis, it will be removed in follow-up surgery if possible (coordination via Policy Agents). If there are several metastases in a single organ, or in several organs, or if the single metastasis cannot be removed due to its localization, additional surgery makes no sense. The patient will be treated with chemotherapy.

For clinical trials only those patients are suited that fulfill special study requirements. During the process it will continuously be checked whether the patient meets these requirements and can participate in a study. The ADAPT project chooses patients for a clinical trial and optimizes the accomplishment of the trial (cf. Figure 4). If the patient meets the requirements and if the patient agrees to participate, he becomes a trial patient for chemotherapy.

The previously described projects interact with the agents of the ASA*inlog* project during the entire process. These agents manage and provide relevant data in terms of active documents, forming the active patient record. The interactions between the multiagent systems ASA*inlog*, Med-PAge, and EMIKA are illustrated in Figure 6.

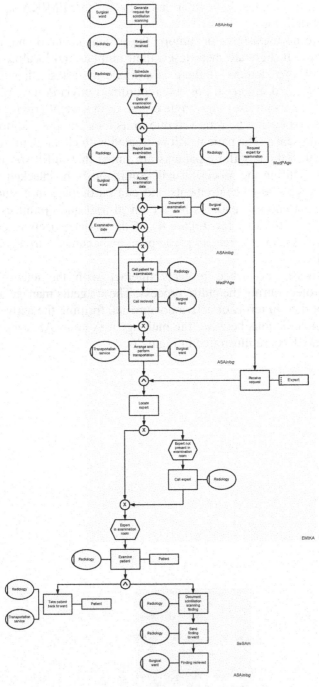

Figure 6. Detailed diagnostic examination in the example scintigraphy

1.7 Summary and Outlook

The goal of the *Hospital Logistics* consortium is the deployment of intelligent software agents in realistic business application scenarios in the health care domain, especially in hospitals. In this chapter, the cooperation between the projects forming this group is shown. A selection of the problems identified is given, trying to illustrate the challenges regarding information systems used in this domain. Also, the aims of the projects have been described in brief.

As both problems and goals of all projects showed high interdependencies, the group decided to integrate both their partial models and developed multiagent systems into the agent testbed *Agent.Hospital*. This testbed, developed in cooperation with the *Technology* consortium of SPP 1083 [Kre+2003], is described by (1) the ontology *OntHoS* used for agents communication, (2) the organizational structure of *Agent.Hospital*, (3) the main infrastructural services, and (4) two application scenarios.

In Part III of this book, all projects participating in *Agent.Hospital* and thus outlined in this chapter were described in detail. With the information given in this chapter the overall domain specific situation can be considered when looking at specific research questions addressed by the projects.

References

[AnKi2003]   Anhalt, C.; Kirn, S.: Koordinations- und Kooperationsunterstützung im SPP 1083 – das Zentralprojekt RealAgentS. In: Dittrich, K.; König, W.; Oberweis, A.; Rannen¬berg, K.; Wahlster, W. (Eds.): INFORMATIK 2003. Springer, LNI P-34, Berlin, 2003, pp. 83-86.

[AwPa2001]   Awizen, M.; Paulussen, T. O.: Modellierung von Kommunikationsprotokollen für die dezentrale, agentenunterstützte Koordination von Krankenhausprozessen. In: Bauknecht, K.; Brauer, W.; Mück, Th. (Eds.): Wirtschaft und Wissenschaft in der Network Economie - Visionen und Wirklichkeit. Österreichische Computer-Ges., 2001, pp. 883-888.

[BHHK2003]   Becker, M.; Heine, C.; Herrler, R.; Krempels, K.-H.: OntHoS - an Ontology for Hospital Scenarios. In: Moreno, A.; Nealon, J. (Eds.): Applications of Software Agent Technology in the Health Care Domain. Whitestein Series in Software Agent Technologies (WSSAT), Birkhäuser Verlag Basel 2003, p. 87-103.

[BeKS2001]   Becker, M.; Krempels, K. H.; Schiffelholz, S. D.: Artifizielle
                Policy-Agenten zur Terminkoordination im Akutkrankenhaus.
                In: Informatiktage. Bad Schussenried, 2001.

[BACR2001]   Beuscart-Zéphir, M.; Anceaux, F.; Cinquette, V.; Renard, J.: In-
                tegrating Users' Activity Modeling in the Design and Assess-
                ment of Hospital Electronic Patient Records: The Example of
                Anesthesia. In: International Journal of Medical Informatics 64
                (2001) 2-3, pp. 157-171.

[BWWD2002]   Burke, D.; Wang, B.; Wan, T.; Diana, M.: Exploring Hospitals'
                Adoption of Information Technology. In: Journal of Medical
                Systems 26 (2002) 4, pp. 349-355.

[CzBe2002]   Czap, H.; Becker, M.: New Scheduling Approach for Hospital
                Operating Theatres. In: European Journal of Medical Research,
                5 (2002) 1, pp. 16-17.

[CzBe2003]   Czap, H.; Becker, M.: Multi-Agent Systems and Microeconomic
                Theory: A Negotiation Approach to Solve Scheduling Problems
                in High Dynamic Environments. In: Proceedings of 36th Annual
                Hawaii International Conference on System Sciences (CD-
                Rom). 2003.

[Dhar2005]   Dharma Guideline Model. http://smi-web.stanford.edu/projects/
                eon/DharmaUserGuide, accessed on 2005-09-21.

[Dlug1984]   Dlugos, N.: Eine Untersuchung zur Reorganisation in Kranken-
                häusern mit einer empirischen Studie im Bereich des betrie-
                blichen Transportwesens. Brockmeyer, Bochum, 1984.

[DuWi1997]   Duesing, W.; Winter, U. J.: Der Weg vom Krankenhaus zum
                Gesundheitszentrum. In: Winter U. J. et al. (Eds.): Modernes
                Krankenhausmanagement. Thieme, Stuttgart et al., 1997, pp. 38-
                43.

[FIPA2005a]   FIPA FIPA ACL Message Structure Specification. http://www.
                fipa.org/specs/fipa00061/, accessed on 2005-09-21.

[FIPA2005b]   FIPA FIPA Application specification. http://www.fipa.org/repo
                sitory/applicationspecs.php3, accessed on 2005 09 21.

[Ginn2002]   Ginneken, A.: The Computerized Patient Record: Balancing Ef-
                fort and Benefit. In: International Journal of Medical Informatics
                65 (2002) 2, pp. 97-119.

[Greu1997]   Greulich, A.: Prozeßmanegement im Krankenhaus, Vol. 8., De-
                cker, Heidelberg, 1997.

[HHPA2003]   Heine, C.; Herrler, R.; Petsch, M.; Anhalt, C.: ADAPT – Adap-
                tive Mutli Agent Process Planning & Coordination of Clinical
                Trials. In: Proceedings of the 2003 Americas Conference on In-
                formation Systems. 2003, pp. 1823-1834.

[Herd1994]   Herder-Dorneich, P.: Ökonomische Theorie des Gesundheitswe-
                sens: Problemgeschichte, Problembereiche, Theoretische Grund-
                lagen. Nomos, Baden-Baden, 1994.

[HeHK2002]   Herrler, R.; Heine, C.; Klügl, F.: Appointment Scheduling
                Among Agents: A Case Study In Designing Suitable Interaction

Protocols. In: Proceedings of 2002 Americas Conference on Information Systems. 2002, pp. 1456-1463.

[Jast1997]   Jaster, H. J.: Qualitätssicherung im Krankenhaus. In: Jaster, H. J. (Ed.): Qualitätssicherung im Gesundheitswesen. Thieme, Stuttgart, 1997.

[KHHK2003a]   Kirn, S.; Heine, C.; Herrler, R.; Krempels, K. H.: Agent.Hospital Agent-Based Open Framework for Clinical Applications. In: Kotsis, G.; Reddy, S. (Eds.): Proceedings of the 12th IEEE International Workshops on Enabling Technologies: Infrastructure for Collaborative Enterprises (WET ICE 2003 Post-Proceedings), 2003, pp. 36-41.

[KHHK2003b]   Kirn, S.; Heine, C.; Herrler, R.; Krempels, K.-H.: Agent.Hospital – Agentenbasiertes offenes Framework für klinische Anwendungen. In: Uhr, W.; Esswein, W.; Schoop, E. (Eds.): Wirtschaftsinformatik 2003 Medien – Märkte – Informationen. Proceedings of the 6th International Conference on Wirtschaftsinformatik, Physica, Heidelberg, 2003, pp. 837-857.

[KnRS2000]   Knublauch, H.; Rose, T.; Sedlmayr, M.: Towards a Multi-Agent System for Proactive Information Management in Anesthesia. In: Proceedings of the Agents-2000 Workshop on Autonomous Agents in Health Care. 2000.

[Kre+2003]   Krempels, K.-H.; Nimis, J.; Braubach, L.; Pokahr, A.; Herrler, R.; Scholz, T.: Entwicklung intelligenter Multi-Multiagentensysteme - Werkzeugunterstützung, Lösungen und offene Fragen. In: Dittrich, K.; König, W.; Oberweis, A.; Rannenberg, K.; Wahlster, W. (Eds.): INFORMATIK 2003. Köllen, Bonn, 2003, pp. 31-46.

[PJDH2003]   Paulussen, T.O.; Jennings, N. R.; Decker, K. S.; Heinzl, A.: Distributed Patient Scheduling in Hospitals. In: Proceedings of the 18th International Joint Conference on AI. 2003, pp. 1224-1229.

[Psch1998]   Pschyrembel Klinisches Wörterbuch. (258. Ed.). de Gruyter, Berlin, 1998.

[Rych1999]   Rychlik, R.: Gesundheitsökonomie und Krankenhausmanagement: Grundlagen und Praxis. Kohlhammer, Stuttgart, 1999.

[SaEM2002]   Sackmann, S.; Eymann, T.; Müller, G.: EMIKA – Real-Time Controlled Mobile Information Systems in Health Care Applications. In: Bludau, H.-B.; Koop, A. (Eds.): Mobile Computing in Medicine. Köllen, Bonn, 2002, pp. 151-158.

[Schl1990]   Schlüchtermann, J.: Patientensteuerung: am Beispiel der Radiologie eines Krankenhauses. Josef Eul Verlag GmbH, Bergisch Gladbach, 1990.

[Schm1999]   Schmidt-Rettig, B.: Profitcenter-Organisation und Prozessorganisation – Konflikt oder Konsens? In: Eichhorn, S.; Schmidt-Rettig, B. (Eds.): Profitcenter und Prozessorientierung: Optimierung von Budget, Arbeitsprozessen und Qualität. Kohlhammer, Stuttgart, 1999, pp. 207-216.

[Sta+2001]   Staccini, P.; Joubert, M.; Quaranta, J.; Fieschi, D.; Fieschi, M.:
                Modeling Health Care Processes for Eliciting User Require-
                ments: A Way to Link a Quality Paradigm and Clinical Infor-
                mation Systems Design. In: International Journal of Medical In-
                formatics 64 (2001) 2-3, pp. 129-142.

[TYWA1996]   Thompson, D.; Yarnold, P.; Williams, D.; Adams, S.: Effects of
                Actual Waiting Time, Perceived Waiting Time, Information De-
                livery, and Expressive Quality on Patient Satisfaction in the
                Emergency Department. In: Annals of Emergency Medicine.
                1996, pp. 657-665.

[Wend1987]   von Wendt: Patientensteuerung an Computer-Tomographen. In-
                stitut für Industrie- und Krankenhausbetriebslehre der Westfäli-
                schen Wilhelms-Universität Münster, 1987.

2 Artificial Software Agents as Representatives of Their Human Principals in Operating-Room-Team-Forming

Marc Becker, Hans Czap

Universität Trier, Lehrstuhl für Wirtschaftsinformatik I
{marc.becker I hans.czap}@uni-trier.de

Abstract. The scheduling of centralized operating theatres in large hospitals can be regarded as an archetypal cooperative decision problem. Multiagent systems (MAS) form an appealing paradigm for solving such problems. In a MAS-setting, each involved individual can be represented by an intelligent software agent that carries the specific constraints and the main preference-structures of his human principal. The scheduling can then be done by inter-agent negotiations, resulting in a cooperative solution, which optimizes "social welfare" and medical and organizational resource allocation simultaneously. For measuring human preference structures a concept based on conjoint analysis is introduced, that deduces individual utility functions suitable for inter-agent negotiations from human preference statements. Aggregation of individual preferences to find a final compromise schedule is then done by a distributed negotiation mechanism, based on the Nash-Bargaining-Solution of game theory.

2.1 Introduction

The scheduling of centralized operating theatres in large hospitals can be regarded as a typical cooperative decision problem suited for delegation. Typical features of the problem are:

- a low involvement of participants, which enforces delegation;
- it is time consuming for those responsible for the scheduling – also an argument to strengthen automation;
- it features a high degree of repetition, which essentially counts for the possibility of learning by feedback.

The process of scheduling use of operating rooms involves different parties: surgeons, anesthetists and operating room nurses. Each one, in general, belongs to different – relatively autonomous – organizational units. Optimizing the cooperation of working teams composed of human individuals, derived from these different units is the main focus of this scheduling approach.

Individuals, but also organizational units, have particular preference structures, resulting in conflictive goals and therefore leading to conflicts of interests between them. These conflicts should be resolved in a fair manner. In addition, environmental influences worsen the problem of simply resolving different interests: Hospitals operate in a highly dynamic and complex environment generating the need to adapt very fast and flexible to environmental variables and their changes.

The Policy-Agent (PA)-Project presented in this paper assumes each involved individual to delegate the negotiation process to an intelligent software agent. These software agents strive in finding a compromise schedule obeying hard medical constraints while simultaneously resolving individual conflicts of interest.

Next section shows details of scheduling operation theaters as they are typical for German hospitals. The subsequent section discusses the general design of the PA-MAS, their tasks and interactions. Thereafter, focus has been laid on providing solutions to two central problems of negotiating software agents crucial to the MAS-approach chosen: The delegation- and the coordination-problem. Delegation and coordination are detailed in Sections 2.4 and 2.5. Last section shows empirical results of the solution provided.

2.2 Application Scenario

Traditionally, each medical department had its own operating room. This has been changed in hospital organizations where operating rooms are combined to form a centralized operating theatre, establishing thus an independent organizational unit to be used by different medical departments. This allows for a better utilization of rooms, devices and personnel as well as to higher flexibility in planning and reacting to emergencies. On the other hand, scheduling complexity rises dramatically causing the need for automated planning systems.

The conventional manual planning process relies heavily on direct communication between different departments and follows in a sequential manner strict formal rules, which lead to a reduction of complexity:

In the first step, each medical department gets the assignment of specific operating rooms for their daily disposal. Next, the department heads make a preliminary schedule of planned operations. This preliminary schedule will obey department specific preferences (department policies) but not any interdependencies. The plans at next stage are transmitted to the operating theatre coordinator, who first checks compatibility with scarce resources. Then he decides about needed anesthetists and makes an assignment. If incompatibilities occur, the coordinator has to contact the involved departments and negotiate a compromise solution. Finally, the plans are handed to the nurse personnel who have to assign the needed nurses. Again, incompatibilities respectively a shortcut of available operating room personnel has to be resolved by negotiation.

The presented scheduling process shown so far has some severe shortcuts since it does not allow counting for the existing interdependencies in an adequate manner, leading to frequent interactions of the responsible coordinator. Also, those who are at the end of this sequential process only have reduced possibilities to change the presented schedule. This is the cause of major job dissatisfaction of nurse personnel, yielding to specific problems in planning their demand and resulting in frequent overtime work [CzBe2003].

2.3 Multiagent Solution

The scheduling problem presented here leads to different requirements for a MAS:

- First, human-to-human interaction should be reduced to a minimum, thus reducing the needed time to resolve incompatibilities by phone.
- Second, sequential processes imply time-consuming feedback cycles, if any incompatibilities arise. Therefore, the planning procedure should happen in a simultaneous way, where any constraints are obeyed immediately.
- Third, a MAS should take care of the organizational and individual interests of the involved parties whenever possible. This will give strong evidence for the acceptance of the planning system and will allow a better degree of staff satisfaction.

In the PA-MAS these requirements are met by a two-stage-scheduling approach:

- In the first stage, the agent system creates a preliminary plan without respect to individual preferences. Only medical and organizational demands and constraints are taken into account. Therefore known scheduling approaches and algorithms can be used. The scheduler-component interacts with the planner via dialogs and offers him sub plans for modification, reordering or to place them into a Gantt-chart [BKNP2003].

Sub plans consist of a set of actions, selected with respect to the constraints of the concepts of the used ontology OntHoS from the resource database [BHHK2003].

- In the second stage, the preliminary plan is improved by agent negotiation. In this stage, the agents of the involved individuals try to achieve the best realizable working schedule for their principals. Using a negotiation approach based on the Nash-Bargaining-Solution the final schedule optimizes "social welfare", i.e. respects the individual preferences of the involved staff, without satisfying medical or efficiency goals.

In the following focus is laid on detailing the second stage of the scheduling process, thereby addressing two central problems of this stage: the delegation relationship between human principal and artificial agent as well as the design of the coordination mechanism required to efficiently resolve preference conflicts in team forming.

2.4 Delegation

In contrary to standard maximization problems, the solution of negotiation problems typically depends not only on decisions taken by one party. Rather, the result depends on actions resp. decisions taken by any of the involved parties during the negotiation process. Thus, all participants try to maximize their individual utility functions, but they control a subset of relevant variables only. Solving negotiation problems, therefore, implies the willingness to accept concessions and compromises by each involved participant. From an information economic standpoint, this requires more knowledge than the information transferred in fixed goal structures i.e. new goals must be flexible generated during the course of negotiations (compare to I.3.5.4).

Therefore the negotiating individuals need not only to know which alternative they prefer, i.e. their (ordinal) preference ordering, they also need to know how much they prefer one alternative over the other. This requires a utility function that has to be valid on an interval scale of measurement at least, thus allowing for intra-individual utility comparisons, while still maintaining an easy measurement approach. In the PA-Project this is done by using conjoint analysis as method of utility measurement [BCPS2005] [CBPS2005]. The needed adaptation to overtime preference changes is handled by combining a learning mechanism with a traditional measurement approach (compare to I.3.4.3).

2.4.1 Conjoint Analysis

Conjoint analysis (CA) aims at statistically revealing the additional information that is hidden in ordinal preference statements. In CA, decision alternatives are described by a number of attributes, each attribute being made up of certain levels. CA demands some effort in constructing the survey; especially the correct determination of attributes and attribute levels for the specific application is crucial [LuTu1964].

The alternatives – in the application of scheduling hospital operating theatres are the possible assignments of anesthetists, nurses and surgeons to time slots and operations – should be ranked by the individual. In general, since the number of all possible alternatives is far too large, only a subset will be presented for ranking. This subset is called the set of *stimuli*. Addelman has shown that in order to allow an uncorrelated statistical estimation of part-worths, the set of stimuli must fulfill the condition of "orthogonal frequencies". This condition requires every attribute level to appear with all levels of the other attributes in proportional frequency to their number of appearances in the whole sample. Designs that hold this condition are called *Orthogonal Main-Effect Plans (OMEPs)* [Adde1962]. In the PA-MAS, an algorithm based on suggestions by Jacroux is used for design reduction. This method guarantees computation of a minimal *OMEP*, which consists of the smallest sample size still allowing uncorrelated estimation of part-worths [Jacr1992].

Having decided on the set of stimuli the next step is the analysis of the principal's preference structure. Therefore, the principal has to evaluate the presented stimuli by ranking them according to his preferences:

- A limited number of stimuli is presented to the principal at once and has to be brought by him into the right order.
- Every additional stimulus is inserted into the existing order by pair wise choice, i.e. the principal repeatedly decides between the new stimulus and an already sorted one just by stating his preference between the two alternatives.

Relying on the fact, that through the ordering of multi-attributive objects (or alternatives) more information than a simple ordinal ranking is generated, the relative importance of each attribute level can be calculated and expressed as part-worth-utility (short: part-worth). This is done by analyzing the occurrence of the different attribute levels within the ranking. Combining the part-worths by means of an additive utility function an interval scaled total utility function – sufficient for agent negotiation applications – is generated:

The part-worths for the different attribute levels are calculated based on the order of the stimuli revealed by the principal. Assuming an additive utility function, the principal's total utility for a multi-attributive a_0 is represented by the sum of its part-worths:

$$u(a_0) = \sum_{j=1}^{J} \sum_{m=1}^{M_j} \beta_{jm} * x_{jm} \qquad (1)$$

$u(a_0)$ Total utility of alternative a_0

β_{jm} Part-worth of level m of attribute j

x_{jm} $\begin{cases} 1 \text{ if level } m \text{ of attribute } j \text{ occurs in } a_0 \\ 0 \qquad\qquad\qquad \text{else} \end{cases}$

Estimating the part-worths is done by an ordinary least square regression (OLSR). In doing so, to each ranked stimulus a_i a number z_i corresponding to the rank-level is assigned (most preferred stimuli get the highest number). By OLSR the part worth utilities β_{jm} are calculated, such that the sum of squared errors becomes minimal:

$$\min \quad \sum_{i \in set \ of \ stimuli} (z_i - u(a_i))^2 \qquad (2)$$

In addition, the resulting β_{jm} will undergo a process of normalization [Klei2002].

2.4.2 Preference Adaptation

Considering the fact that individual preferences may change over time, a utility function that was determined by CA once cannot be regarded as statistically valid forever. Instead, an agent system that is supposed to be in use for a longer period must be able to adjust dynamically to changes within the principal's preferences. That is, it needs to detect if the agents utility function still represents the principals preferences correctly and to adjust it in case it does not.

To accomplish this task, some user interaction is required. As, obviously, intelligent agents are supposed to make their principals' lives easier, too much interaction is not beneficial. Research has shown that while most users are willing to give some short feedback about the quality of the agent's work, they consider a longer procedure as frustrating and annoying [ScAm2004]. Keeping that in mind, a procedure for permanently monitoring the quality of the agent's utility model, while reducing communication with the principal to a minimum, has been designed.

The learning process proposed in this section is based on the main idea that in order to facilitate easy communication, the principal only needs to respond to a single question after selected negotiations done by the agent.

For this, he must evaluate the result of the negotiation (a_p) $(a_p = primary$ $assignment)$ together with the next possible alternative (a_s), which might be the outcome of negotiation $(a_s = secondary\ assignment)$. Note that in the light of the agents' meaning a_p is the best possible result achievable during negotiation, whereas a_s is the second best one, that is the best possible assignment if a_p would not have been included in the set of possible alternatives. Consequently, the utility assignment expressed by the part-worths β_{jm} represents a preference order of the agent that states $a_p \succ_a a_s$ or $a_p \sim_a a_s$. (The symbols $\succ_a$, $\sim_a$ indicate the preference ordering of the agent, whereas $\succ_p$, $\sim_p$ that of the principal).

In order to get feedback, the agent presents both alternatives, a_p and a_s to his principal and asks for a ranking of these. Clearly, if the principal decides $a_p \succ_p a_s$, or $a_p \sim_p a_s$ and this coincides with the agent's preference order on these two alternatives, there is no need to change anything. In all other cases, the preference order the agent had learned needs some adjustment.

In the following, a method is proposed for adaptation of the part-worths in order to count for the discrepancy in preference orders of agent and principal with respect to a_p and a_s, i.e.

$$(a_p \succ_a a_s \ and \ (a_p \prec_p a_s \ or \ a_p \sim_p a_s \ )) \ or$$
$$(a_p \sim_a a_s \ and \ (a_p \prec_p a_s \ or \ a_p \succ_p a_s)) \tag{3}$$

In order to handle this situation, the reduced design that led to the actual part-worths β_{jm} is augmented by the alternatives a_p and a_s (if these alternatives are not already included in the reduced design), and the principal is asked to rank theses additional stimuli with respect to the others. Since there are at most two additional *stimuli* to be ranked, the necessary effort remains limited. The resulting utility function correctly will state the principal's preferences with respect to the alternatives of the reduced design and also provides a better approximation for the unknown utility function based on the complete set of alternatives.

2.5 Coordination

Every coordination mechanism, realized for solving conflicts of interest between human beings or in this case their artificial representatives, has to address the so called bargaining problem of economics. Below the general bargaining problem is detailed. Thereafter the Nash-Solution of the bargaining problem, that forms the foundation of the negotiation mechanism used in the PA-Project is illustrated and interpreted in the light of modern bargaining theory. Last, the used negotiation mechanism is exemplified.

2.5.1 The Bargaining Problem

The Edgeworth Box shown in Figure 1 illustrates the simplest form of the bargaining problem: a two person (P_1, P_2) two goods (X_1, X_2) pure exchange economy. The length of the Edgeworth Box represents the total amount of X_1 available in the economy, while the height of the box shows the total amount of X_2. Any point within the box represents a possible distribution of X_1 and X_2 between P_1 and P_2. Assuming conventional shaped indifference curves for both P_1 and P_2, example indifference curves, labeled $I_{j(Py)}$ $(j = 1..7, y = 1, 2)$ are superimposed onto the box. Index j corresponds to higher levels of utility, i.e. P_1 is happier on $I_{7(P1)}$ than on $I_{6(P1)}$.

Given an initial endowment c $(c_{1(P1)}, c_{2(P1)}, c_{1(P2)}, c_{2(P2)})$ both individuals can increase their utility by bargaining. Every point in the shape $S = (a, b, c, e)$ is at least as good as c for both P_1 and P_2. At every point outside of S at least one individual achieves a worse result than at the point of initial endowment. Therefore, these points are not eligible solutions in a negotiation between P_1 and P_2. Instead of accepting a negotiation result outside of S at least one individual prefers staying with its initial endowment c, thus making c the so called conflict point of the negotiation game (S, c). Bargaining between rational individuals will continue in S until no individual can make better without reducing the utility level of the other, i.e. a so called Pareto optimal solution is reached.

In the example above every point on line (a, d, b) is Pareto optimal and thus a possible solution to the game (S, c). Due to Pareto efficiency, every solution point on line (a, d, b) is a stable one, since in any case at least one individual will not make further concessions in bargaining. These points are allocation efficient in the sense, that there is no waste of utility potential. Thus, while every form of negotiation between rational individuals must have a solution located on line (a, d, b)[1], the exact solution point at

---

[1]   The so called "core solution" of game theory.

which negotiating individuals arrive remains subject to the concrete course of the bargaining process. The behavior of the involved individuals, therefore, turns out to be widely indeterminate and subject to normative reasoning.

Every coordination mechanism designed to solve coordination problems – either implicitly or explicitly – gives an answer to the problem of the indeterminacy of a bargaining solution.

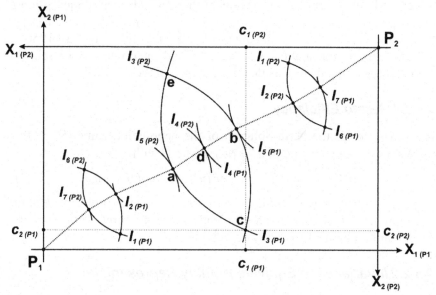

Figure 1. Simple bargaining problem

Typically, indeterminacy of bargaining is reduced by explicitly introducing additional concepts like justice or fairness to the bargaining process. Applying these constructs, the solution point a – all surplus given to P_2, nothing to P_1 – or vice versa the solution point b most likely will be excluded, while on first look solution point d – surplus divided between P_1 and P_2 – seems to be the most reasonable one. Due to the non-metrical nature of utility this choice remains difficult. Truly, point d looks like a fifty/fifty split of surplus, but implicitly this solution assumes equal relevance of utility-gain of P_1 and utility-gain of P_2 [NeMo1947].

In general, individual utilities are not comparable. Therefore, any definite solution to the bargaining problem must address the problem of the impossibility of inter-individual utility comparisons. In the PA-Project a negotiation mechanism based on the Nash-Bargaining-Solution is used, as this solution relies explicitly on a concept of fairness.

2.5.2 The Nash-Bargaining-Solution

Given a two-person negotiation situation, where P_i are the involved persons having utility function u_i $(i = 1, 2)$. Let $c = (c_1, c_2)$ be the point of conflict and S the set all possible solutions (u_{1j}, u_{2j}). The ordered pair (S, c) designates the (two-person) negotiation game. In 1950 Nash characterized a fair bargaining solution of (S, c) by four axioms. Requiring S to be a closed and convex set, it can be shown there is only one unique solution point $\hat{u}(S, c) = max (u_1-c_1) * (u_2-c_2), (u_1, u_2) \in S$, that simultaneously fulfills all four axioms, the so called Nash-Bargaining-Solution [Nash1950].

Below, these four axioms are presented and interpreted in the sense of modern bargaining theory, as they are adopted in the PA-Project.

2.5.2.1 Pareto Efficiency

If $\hat{u} = (\hat{u}_1, \hat{u}_2)$ is the Nash-Solution of the negotiation game (S, c), then there does not exist any point $u' = (u'_1, u'_2) \in S$ with:

$$(u'_1 > \hat{u}_1 \text{ and } u'_2 \geq \hat{u}_2) \text{ or } (u'_1 \geq \hat{u}_1 \text{ and } u'_2 > \hat{u}_2) \qquad (4)$$

Clearly a bargaining solution, i.e. a solution to the problem of utility distribution, also should be an efficient allocation. Pareto efficiency is a minimum requirement for every bargaining solution.

2.5.2.2 Invariance to Equivalent Utility Representations

Since a utility-function u is determined up to linear transformations only, the solution of a bargaining game must be independent of this kind of transformation, i.e. if u_i is transformed to $u_i' = a_i + b_iu_i$, $b_i > 0$, $(i = 1, 2)$ and a corresponding transformation applies to any point in S yielding the bargaining problem (S', c') the resulting optimal solution $\hat{u}'$ equally corresponds to $\hat{u}$.

Game theory has shown that confining utility theory to simple ordinal preferences – as done in classical economics – is not sufficient in negotiations. Negotiations require the individual decision maker to regularly evaluate different alternatives and to give concessions in order to arrive at a compromise solution. For this, at least the strength of individual preferences must be known requiring at least cardinal-interval scaled utility functions. Also this axiom excludes direct inter-individual utility comparisons from the bargaining solution.

2.5.2.3 Symmetry

A negotiation game is called symmetric, if point of conflict $c = (c_1, c_2)$ results in identical payoffs, $c_1 = c_2$, and if $(u_1, u_2) \in S$ implies $(u_2, u_1) \in S$. Clearly, as Nash requires, symmetric games should have an optimal solution $\hat{u} = (\hat{u}_1, \hat{u}_2)$ with identical payoffs $\hat{u}_1 = \hat{u}_2$, which is a matter of fairness. As a consequence, in the case of symmetry two rational individuals will get to a definite and unique solution of the bargaining problem corresponding to point d in Figure 1.

2.5.2.4 Independence of Irrelevant Alternatives

If, instead of (S, c) having the optimal solution $\hat{u} = \hat{u}(S, c)$, the bargaining problem (S', c) is considered, where $S' = S \cup \{u'\}$, $u' \notin S$, and $u' \neq \hat{u}$ holds (i.e. u' is an irrelevant alternative), the augmented problem (S', c) has the same optimal solution $\hat{u}$ as the original one (S, c).

In negotiation terms this axiom requires the players to gradually narrow down the set of alternatives under consideration to smaller and smaller subsets of the original negotiation set, gradually eliminating outcomes as unacceptable (and therefore irrelevant), until just the (optimal) solution remains.

2.5.3 Policy-Agents Negotiation Mechanism

The negotiation problem of the PA-Project differs somewhat from the simple bargaining treated so far. Any solution involves not only two components but rather consists of an assignment of at least one surgeon, one anesthetist, two nurses, an operating room, a time-slice and a patient. Scheduling is known to belong to the class of NP-complete problems, thus, in the light of the huge set of alternatives, algorithmic complexity is prohibitive.

Also, in contradiction to standard negotiations about the allocation of normal goods, in the presented application the negotiators are "negotiation goods" themselves, as their allocation in the final schedule affects not only their own utility functions but also the utility functions of at least some of the other involved negotiators.

These problems are solved by a negotiation approach using arbitration agents. As the solution space is too large for allowing all agents to negotiate over all alternatives simultaneously, it is necessary to divide up interaction. A two stage approach is followed: First, an initial assignment of people and rooms calculated by conventional methods is performed. This initial assignment is basis of improvements during second step, where the agents negotiate with each other in order to arrive at a solution which is allocation efficient as well as fair in sense of the Nash criterion.

In order to reduce algorithmic complexity we assume the operating room, the anesthetist, the surgeon and the patient to be given by the initial assignment and not subject to any negotiations of second step, i.e. the nurses are assumed to be interchangeable. Remember that there are two nurses for every operation.

Assume there are n operation theatres. For an initial assignment of nurses $N = 2*n$ nurses are needed. In the case of 10 operating rooms,[2] 20 nurses must be assigned. In order to reduce negotiation-complexity further, negotiating groups had been formed, which sequentially try to find improvements. For example, in the simplest case the assignment $(n_1, n_2) \rightarrow R_1$ and $(n_3, n_4) \rightarrow R_2$, where n_i designates nurse i $(i = 1,..,4)$ and R_j room j $(j = 1, 2)$, may be questioned in order to arrive at an assignment, let's say $(n_1, n_4) \rightarrow R_1$ and $(n_2, n_3) \rightarrow R_2$ the agents consider to be better.[3] The optimal assignment will be calculated by the arbitrator-agent based on Nash-Solution theory.

Next, the actual assignment with respect to room R_1 and R_3 may be negotiated, i.e. $(n_1, n_4) \rightarrow R_1$ and $(n_3, n_5) \rightarrow R_3$. The algorithm will proceed to negotiate the assignment of pairs of rooms (R_j, R_k) as long as there is a change of assignment during a complete cycle of all $\binom{n}{2}$ combinations.

2.6 Results

The pair wise allocation procedure of the last paragraph, in general, cannot arrive at the optimal solution. Therefore, some calculations (cf. Figure 2-5) have been performed in order to compare pair wise allocation, i.e. considering the assignment of four agents to pairs of rooms (R_i, R_j), against the simultaneous assignment of six agents, corresponding to triples of rooms (R_i, R_j, R_k) and finally of eight agents, corresponding to quadruples of rooms. In addition, the number of rooms is varied from two to ten.[4] The re-

---

[2]   The analysed hospital runs 10 operating theatres.

[3]   Knowing the utility-functions of the nurse-agents, negotiation overhead further is reduced by introducing an arbitration agent, who optimizes allocation of these four agents.

[4]   Nine different basic planning scenarios result from these variations. Each of these is tested with twelve randomized scheduling scenarios resulting in 108 simulations for each algorithm.

sults are compared to a heuristic procedure which first composes working teams based on the part-worth utilities and afterwards assigns these teams to the scheduled operations.

In order to allow the efficiency of the chosen approach different criteria are evaluated:

- the average percentage of possible utility reached (PUR) by the agents is shown. This figure would be 100 % for an agent that could dictate the negotiation result without caring for the other agents;
- the standard deviation of this utility, measuring the distribution of individual utilities;
- the minimal utility reached, i.e. the utility achieved by the individual who makes the worst deal.

If one identifies "mean degree of satisfaction" with "average percentage of possible utility reached", which is at least strongly correlated, Figure 2 shows surprisingly good results of the negotiation procedure and far outreaches the heuristic approach. Also, the additional effort to choose larger groups of agents (consisting of 6 or 8 agents) for negotiation instead of the minimal four ones does not pay for. Results are only slightly better, but completion time rises significantly (cf. Figure 3).

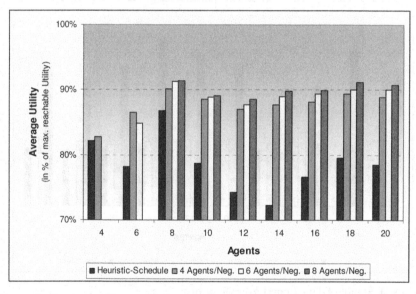

Figure 2. Average utility reached

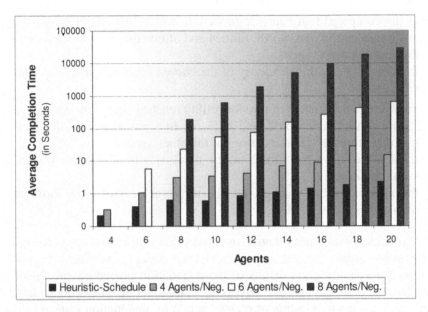

Figure 3. Average completion time in seconds

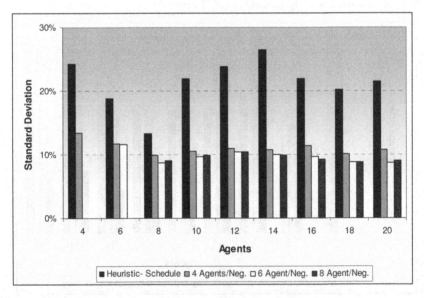

Figure 4. Standard deviation of average utility

Figure 4 shows the standard deviation of average utility. Standard deviation of utilities at the different negotiation scenarios remains nearly constant at about ten percent across the whole experimental range. Compared to the heuristic approach, the negotiation procedures significantly work better.

Figure 5 shows the average minimal utility reached as well as the range of minima encountered over all scenarios. The negotiation procedures manage to maintain a minimum utility-level of about 60% PUR in average, i.e. even the "loser" of the coordination game regularly receives at least 60% of the utility he could obtain if he was in charge of the coordination process all alone.

The absolute lower bounds of the negotiated utility ranges, i.e. the worst cases over all test-scenarios still lie at around 50% PUR. Again this is significantly better than the results generated by the heuristic procedure, were the lower bounds regularly fall under 10% PUR and average minimal utility constantly declines below 30% PUR for $n > 8$.

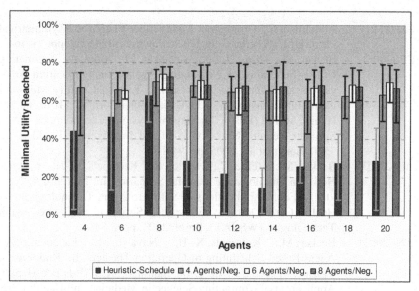

Figure 5. Minimal utility reached

2.7 Conclusion

In solving the problem of optimized working team allocation during medical operations different evaluation criteria must be met. A MAS approach should be efficient from a technical as well as an economical point of view.

Technical efficiency includes both the efficiency of computation and the efficiency of distribution and communication. In the PA-Project efficient distribution and communication is achieved by the use of arbitration agents minimizing negotiation overhead. Computational efficiency results through successive four agent negotiation.

Economical efficiency combines efficient resource allocation with efficient utility distribution. For the application domain considered in the PA-Project efficient utility distribution means the presentation of a solution to the bargaining problem. The results presented show the adequacy of the chosen algorithm based on the Nash-Bargaining-Solution.

References

[Adde1962]   Addelman, S.: Orthogonal Main-Effect Plans for Asymmetrical Factorial Experiments. In: Technometrics 4(1962)1, pp. 21-46.

[BCPS2005]   Becker, M.; Czap, H.; Poppensieker, M.; Stotz, A.: Estimating Utility–Functions for Negotiating Agents: Using Conjoint Analysis as an Alternative Approach to Expected Utility Measurement. In: Eymann, T.; Klügl, F.; Lamersdorf, W.; Klusch, M.; Huhns, M. N. (Eds.): Multiagent System Technologies 2005. Springer Lecture Notes on Artificial Intelligence (LNAI), vol. 3550. Berlin et al., 2005, pp. 94-105.

[BHHK2003]   Becker, M.; Heine, C.; Herrler, R.; Krempels, K.-H.: a) Ont-HoS - an Ontology for Hospital Scenarios. In: Moreno, A; Nealon, J. (Eds.): Applications of Software Agent Technology in the Health Care Domain. Whitestein Series in Software Agent Technologies (WSSAT). Basel, 2003, pp. 87-103.

[BKNP2003]   Becker, M.; Krempels, K.-H.; Navarro, M.; Panchenko, A.: Agent Based Scheduling of Operation Theaters. In: Rudomin, I; Vazquez-Salceda, J.; de Leon Santiago, JLD (Eds.): e-Health: Application of Computing Science in Medicine and Health Care. Mexico-City, 2003, pp. 220-227.

[CzBe2003]   Czap, H.; Becker, M.: Multi-Agent Systems and Microeconomic Theory: A Negotiation Approach to Solve Scheduling Problems in High Dynamic Environments. In: Proceedings of 36th Annual Hawaii International Conference on System Sciences (CD-Rom). Hawaii, 2003.

[CBPS2005]   Czap, H.; Becker, M.; Poppensieker, M.; Stotz, A.: Utility-Based Agents for Hospital Scheduling: A Conjoint-Analytical Approach. In: Proceedings of AAMAS Workshop - MAS*BIO-MED'05 (Multi-Agent Systems for Medicine, Computational Biology, and Bioinformatics). Utrecht, 2005, pp. 1-15.

[Jacr1992]   Jacroux, M.: A Note on the Determination and Construction of Minimal Orthogonal Main-Effect Plans. In: Technometrics 34(1992)1, pp. 92-96.

[Klei2002]   Klein, M.: Die Conjoint-Analyse: Eine Einführung in das Verfahren mit einem Ausblick auf mögliche sozialwissenschaftliche Anwendungen. In: ZA-Information 50(2002), pp. 7-45.

[LuTu1964]   Luce, R. D.; Tukey, J. W.: Simultaneous Conjoint Measurement: A New Type of Fundamental Measurement. In: Journal of Mathematical Psychology 1(1964), pp. 1-27.

[Nash1950]   Nash, J. F.: The Bargaining Problem. In: Econometrica 18(1950) pp. 155-162.

[ScAm2004]   Schiaffino, S., Amandi, A.: User – Interface Agent Interaction: Personalization Issues. In: International Journal of Human-Computer Studies 60(2004), pp. 129-148.

[NeMo1947]   Von Neumann, J.; Morgenstern, O.: Theory of Games and Economic Behavior. Princenton University Press, Princeton, 1947.

3 Agent-Based Information Logistics

Thomas Rose, Martin Sedlmayr

Fraunhofer Gesellschaft, Institut für Angewandte Informationstechnik
{thomas.rose I martin.sedlmayr}@fit.fraunhofer.de

Holger Knublauch

Stanford School of Medicine, Stanford Medical Informatics
holger@smi.stanford.edu

Wolfgang Friesdorf

Technische Universität Berlin, Institut für Psychologie und Arbeitswissenschaft
wolfgang.friesdorf@awb.tu-berlin.de

Abstract. Situated and context-sensitive information logistics surface as decisive requirement for supporting critical care units, because information relevant for patient treatment stems from heterogeneous as well as distributed data sources. Immediate treatment starts with an incomplete and almost empty array of information which fills continuously over time by examinations conducted by organizationally as well as geographically distributed departments. Agent technology and multiagent systems appear as a promising enabling technology to improve information logistics in intensive care units. However, an overall development methodology is required that enables an engineering process from the capture of know-how about clinical processes towards a model-based generation of multiagent systems. This contribution reports on an agile development methodology used for the design, implementation and testing of applications for agent-based information logistics.

3.1 Introduction

Decision-making in critical care units requires the integration of information from various clinical data sources, such as the patient, the laboratory, the surgery and the clinical personnel. However, information management and processing is aggravated by the highly heterogeneous and distributed nature of the current clinical data and information repositories in addition to complex, dynamic working processes. Furthermore, critical situations such as the arrival of emergency patients demand a context-sensitive provision of information in a timely fashion: the time from entering the emergency room to the beginning of the operation can be less than 15 minutes. Hence, intelligent clinical information logistics should provide help in collecting, preparing and presenting data as well as reducing tedious pager or phone calls. Up to this point in time, there is unfortunately no system available that provides the flexibility and comprehensiveness of support for the treatment of emergency care patients.

Agents and in particular multiagent systems (MAS), with their ability to provide intelligent and proactive services within a distributed environment, have a huge potential to improve the management of clinical information logistics. In the clinical information space, autonomous agents can proactively collect, integrate and analyze relevant patient data, and condense and communicate the most relevant information to the responsible decision makers.

The objective of AGIL (Agent-based Information Logistics for Operation Theatre Management in Anesthesia) has been the development of a generic development methodology for the capture of know-how about clinical information processes and the support of certain clinical procedures by autonomous agents. The development methodology is supported by the AGIL-Shell which supports a seamless development process from process capture via generation of operational code for a multiagent system up-to testing scenarios. Specific attention has been devoted to the support of clinical processes that can be characterized by their complexity of information flow and communication processes. The approach has been validated by developing a prototype of a multiagent system for emergency care units.

Following our methodology, one first acquires a semi-formal model of the existing clinical processes. This model will be used for the identification of information bottlenecks and potential agent application scenarios. Based on the existing process, one then designs an "agentified" process, in which agents fulfill tasks like theatre management, decision-support, notification services, information filtering, and patient tracking. Many of the agents are ergonomically designed to run on small mobile computer devices. A prototype of our agent system has been successfully implemented in Java following an Extreme Programming methodology.

The clinical setting and processes

A closer look at the clinical processes frequently reveals geographical and organizational distribution as major cause for unnecessary bottlenecks [HuJF1995] [KnRS2000]. Distribution is caused by the high level of specialization that characterizes modern health care. As illustrated in Figure 1, an average patient will most likely be treated by staff from different departments such as anesthesia, surgery, laboratory, and administration. Although all these departments operate on a shared object (the patient) they do not necessarily share data, information and knowledge about this object. Patient data are typically distributed across many types of individual and incompatible media such as paper-based forms, telephone calls, fax messages, and departmental information systems. The still most common way of maintaining a patient data record is to collect the various forms and notes in a paper-based patient record that is moved together with the patient's bed. The sheer amount of these data prevents clinicians from quickly getting a comprehensive overview of the patient's state. As a result, physicians might be unable to access relevant information or simply be not aware of critical process attributes.

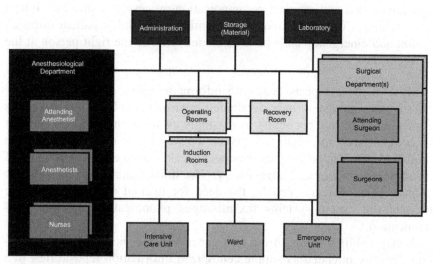

Figure 1. Processes and responsibilities are distributed among several clinical departments and locations

Generalizing this scenario, the following properties describe the clinical processes.

- *Distribution*: Tasks, concerns, organization and know-how are distributed among various human agents and departments. Since all of the clinical units have to deal with only certain aspects of the patient, data and information are also distributed. Accordingly, patient data are distributed across various types of media, such as fax messages, data sheets or insular clinical information systems. Besides diversity in formats, there are also diverging standards for semantic descriptions in terms of ontologies.

- *Parallelism*: The tasks mentioned above run concurrently, as do the surgical procedures.
- *Non-determinism*: Since patients are complex and little-understood biological system, the prediction of the outcome of surgical procedures is difficult. Unexpected emergency cases happen, as do incidents in anesthesia.
- *Self-organization*: Responding to the uncertainty, the clinical staff has to react in a flexible manner. Although there is a strict hierarchy in terms of commands, the personnel acts to a certain extent self dependent. Many decisions in theatre management are a matter of negotiation, since resources are limited.
- *Communication-intensity*: The properties mentioned above demand for sophisticated and efficient communication processes among the clinical personnel. Commands, requests, intentions, schedules, patient information and emergency calls have to be delivered to the right person at the right time.

Most of these aspects deal with information flow and processing between (human) agents in a distributed environment. Decision-makers in clinical domains are becoming increasingly aware of the potential benefits of computerized information logistics. However, the current situation in most hospitals can be characterized as a weakly coupled agglomeration of incompatible media and terminology. The information flow between the clinical units is aggravated by the need for manual data transformation between the various systems, fax messages, phone calls and verbal communication.

A major shift is needed from first generation Hospital Information Systems, mainly intended as simple centralized information repositories, to a distributed environment composed of several interconnected agents which actively cooperate in maintaining a full track of the patient's record and supporting care providers in all the phases of patient management [LaFS1995].

In order to implement an operational information backbone that monitors the flow of information and actively notifies members in the process chain, clinicians commonly call for the support of their workflow by means of simplified communication and data presentation [HaKK2001], i.e. medical pathways ought to be accompanied and supported by intuitive information services. A major step in this direction is taken by the various efforts towards medical standards for data and information exchange, such as HL7 and UMLS [BeMu1997]. The utilization of these standards allows one to replace more and more paper-based forms by digital counterparts, leading to a shared data backbone that can be exploited for the implementation of advanced information services. On the other hand, this data backbone bears the risk of an overload of information flow. The focus of these services therefore shifts to the critical issue of how to provide the clinicians in charge with exactly that piece of information which they require to execute their actual task. In other words, clinicians aim to reduce the manual collection and translation of medical data required, while by the same time preventing data overload by means of smart information filtering and brokering services.

Hence, agent technology appears as an attractive enabler for improving information logistics due to agent properties, such as responsiveness, mobility, and their ability to learn. However, the question arises of how to capture know-how about the processes and how to use agent technologies and its characteristics in clinical information logistics. AGIL addressed these issues by the development of an overall engineering method for process capture and evolutionary system implementation.

3.2 An Agile Development Method

Prior to developing any computer system, the people involved in the project must agree on a methodology to define what roles specific people play, what decisions they must reach, and how and what they will communicate [Cock1997]. Methodologies typically suggest a selection of modeling and programming languages, and corresponding tools. This section describes a novel methodology for developing multiagent systems, which has been adopted for clinical information agents. Our basic observation is that such systems should be developed in a rather explorative style in a close collaboration between domain experts and technicians (Section 3.2.1, [Knub2002]). In order to make this collaboration work, we propose a simple and intuitive, yet sufficiently formal process metaphor as the central modeling language (Section 3.2.2, cf. [RFKR2002). We describe a modeling tool with which clinical processes can be modeled, analyzed and incrementally enhanced by agents (Section 3.2.3, [KnRo2001]).

3.2.1 Modeling as an Iterative, Collaborative Effort

General-purpose software methodologies are insufficient for developing multiagent systems, particularly because the complex communication scenarios of agents require specific modeling primitives. Therefore, researchers have extended approaches from Software Engineering, leading to the emerging field of Agent Oriented Software Engineering (AOSE, see

[CiWo2001] for a recent overview). Existing AOSE methodologies, like GAIA [WoJK2000] and DeLoach [Delo1999], define a systematic sequence of activities that guide the developers through classical Software Engineering phases like requirements analysis, design, implementation, and test. A major goal of these systematic, rather "waterfall-based" approaches is to ensure that development processes become reproducible and (at least apparently) plan-able, and that design models are not constrained by implementation details. However, the general weakness of these AOSE approaches is the overhead when models need to be changed. DeLoach's approach is divided into seven successive phases, with intermediate models between each phase. GAIA's design model is relatively decoupled from the implementation, i.e. the entire design (perhaps even the analysis) has to be revised in order to develop a model that can actually be implemented. In these methodologies, customer feedback is available late, so that systematic methods are suitable only when requirements are relatively stable.

In our opinion, the assumption of relatively fixed requirements is unrealistic with clinical multiagent systems, because the complexity of potential agent interaction scenarios and the emerging behaviors within a multiagent system can make pre-planning very difficult.

In order to elicit the requirements for a clinical system, software engineers will have to interact closely with domain experts, who are the only ones able to assess potential agent features, benefits and pitfalls. Since agents have to execute tasks on behalf of various types of human actors (e.g., anesthetists, laboratory nurses, and administrative staff), many individuals with different backgrounds and partially contradicting requirements need to be interviewed. In decentralized domains like clinical care, it is almost impossible to find a single individual that will be able to overview all potential agent scenarios in a comprehensive up-front design. "As a consequence, users such as the medical or administrative personnel of a hospital must be allowed to select the applications most suitable for their needs and requirements" [LSTO1997]. Furthermore, the close involvement of highly specialized domain experts such as clinicians requires a different level of collaboration than supported by waterfall-based methods. Most of the AOSE approaches rely on quite formal modeling artifacts, which lead to a considerable cognitive gap between the engineers and the clinical experts, so that the domain experts or end users are relatively excluded from the phases. This, however, is crucial in health care, where domain experts and decision makers usually only possess shallow computer knowledge and require hands-on experiments to clarify their requirements.

Due to these reasons, we argue that clinical multiagent systems can (and probably should) be developed in a rather feedback-driven style in a close collaboration between technicians and domain experts. While so-called agile methodologies like Extreme Programming (XP) [Beck1999] have gained a rapidly growing attention in mainstream software technology during the last years, their achievements have until recently not been transferred to the domain of multiagent systems. XP proposes a set of values and principles, which can help to produce experimental prototypes rapidly and to use customer feedback to make the prototypes mature and turn them into robust and well-tested systems. A key value of XP is simplicity that suggests keeping models and modeling meta-models as simple as possible, so that direct communication with customers is supported and the team does not spend valuable resources for features that are later rejected by the customers. We have adapted XP to agents (see [Knub2002] for details) and successfully applied the resulting methodology for the development of a clinical multiagent system.

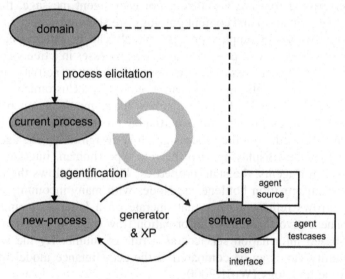

Figure 2. Rapid development of prototypes through constant feedback loops

The development process modifies incrementally the various models to meet the clinical requirements. The application scenario and agents therein are designed collaboratively by clinical staff and computer technicians by means of a simple process modeling framework. It is often convenient to first acquire a model of the existing clinical processes (without agents), and then to identify where agents can help to improve those processes. This leads to a new "agentified" process design, which then can rapidly be translated into an executable system.

Building blocks for the implementation of certain process patterns are used in the process of "agentifying" for the reuse of code.

3.2.2 A Modeling Tool for Process Analysis and Agent Design

The AGIL-Shell is a tool that can be used to model clinical processes, to analyze them in order to detect potential agent scenarios, and to design these agents. This tool provides various graphical views of the processes and agents.

- *Process Graph*: The main view of AGIL-Shell is a graph in which domain experts and engineers can define processes by arranging activities and media as nodes, and by representing the media flow and the sequence of activities by means of edges. For each activity, the name and the performing role are visualized. For each agent message, the command (performative) and content ontology are shown.
- *Process Explorer*: Complex process models can be quickly navigated along their hierarchy of processes and sub-processes in a tree view.
- *Customizer*: The properties of the currently selected activity, process, message, agent or ontology class can be edited by a Customizer.
- *Community Viewer*: This graph displays the communication pathways between the roles involved in a particular process. The graph is automatically derived from the process graph at design time. The agents are shown as nodes displaying also the role type (human, interface agent, etc.) and, for agents, the state properties. This view allows the identification of information bottlenecks. Nodes with many incoming and outgoing arrows represent roles that operate on a large accumulation of data. These pivotal points of information flow might benefit most from agent-based information services as a rule of thumb. By the way, the community view can be compared to the acquaintance model from the GAIA methodology [WoJK2000].

Beside these views, other types of graphical visualization of (clinical) processes can be derived from the meta-model. For example, the sequence of activities allows extracting a life-cycle view in which only those activities are shown which are performed by a given technical or human agent. Such views allow for the crosschecking of the design with the human process participants, who can – from their local point of view – assess whether their daily routine is sufficiently covered by the overall process.

A large chunk of the executable source code can be generated from the process models, because it contains sufficient information about the types of agents, the (potential) message flow between them, the services they are expected to provide, and the ontologies they rely on. Parts of the agent source code are test cases in the sense of Extreme Programming, which check whether agents correctly expose the desired functionality.

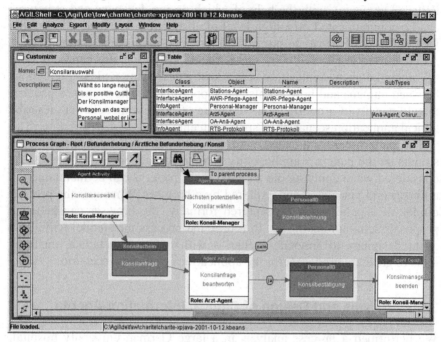

Figure 3. A screenshot of the process and agent modeling tool AGIL-Shell

The individual process models describe the information flow within single scenarios like the reception of emergency patients. The main purpose of these scenarios is to identify the types of agents and their services, so that the implementation can commence. The identified agent application scenarios can also serve as templates for other scenarios in related modeling projects. This allows designing clinical agent systems from reusable modules, which suits to the modular architecture of modern hospitals: Although most hospitals are made of similar units such as emergency rooms and laboratories, their spatial distribution, size and internal policies can vary noticeably. A simple approach for building customized clinical systems is to copy selected process models into a process repository that can be browsed during modeling to identify parts that might be reused. Such a process repository can serve as a portal to clinical best practices and thus also serves as a tool for knowledge management.

For advanced and semi-automated support for the identification of potential agent application scenarios we propose an approach similar to the Design Patterns [GHJV1995] from object-oriented software engineering.

Design Patterns describe solutions and best practices for frequently recurring problems and thus provide modeling knowledge that can be exploited by others. Design Patterns additionally define a terminology (a so-called Pattern Language), with the help of which design decisions and structures can be communicated on a high level of abstraction. We have adapted the idea of Design Patterns to our process-oriented multiagent system design. As elaborated in [WoJK2000], these Agent Design Patterns can help identify potential agent application scenarios by describing typical interactions between humans and how agents can support them. The proposed patterns mainly consist of a configurable template of process models that describe typical application scenarios of specific agent types.

The patterns are annotated with semantic metadata that specify constraints on the pattern's applicability and the consequences that need to be considered when applying the pattern. These patterns can be maintained in a library and visualized and explored by a browser. Whenever the preconditions of a pattern can be captured formally, the browser can generate proposals semi-automatically. In future, the process metamodel will allow agent designers to annotate scenarios with optional metadata, enabling tools to generate proposals for the application of an agent scenario.

3.2.3 Analysis and Design of Clinical Information Agents

We performed a process analysis in a large German university hospital, which has led initially to the design of about 30 sub-processes with 160 agent activities and 32 different agent types which were nearly doubled in later iterations. Our analysis was performed to identify process bottlenecks in which agents can be introduced to optimize the logistics of clinical information. We investigated structure, information flow, and involved personnel in an emergency department by a participative process analysis, as described in [MaFr2000]. The basic idea was to let process participants capture the existing processes themselves, because the complex organizational web and the different parallel tasks can only be disassembled by people with sufficiently deep domain knowledge. The analysis was done by a practitioner supported by involved physicians, and took several months. The findings of this analysis were captured in a process model using the AGIL. Then, the same tool was used to incrementally redesign this process model with agents.

Our process analysis focused on the treatment of emergency patients. Emergency units are in Germany typically staffed by an attending anesthetist. Anesthetists are also involved in nearly all surgical procedures, so that they need to communicate and collaborate intensively with various other departments. Further, since anesthetists require a comprehensive overview of patient data to decide on a treatment plan, and since a main task during anesthesia is to maintain protocols and other formal "paperwork", anesthesiology is a particularly promising application area for agents. Computer support in anesthesia is additionally promising because the practices of anesthesia are repeated over and over again, so that clinical guidelines have become standard.

3.2.4 An Extreme Programming Case Study

We have used our approach to develop a prototypical clinical multiagent system for emergency rooms in Java. Our case study was conducted as XP courses for Computer Science students at the University of Ulm, Germany in 2001 and 2002. The courses took place in a single office with 5 PCs and involved each 8 students, a coach, and a medical doctor, who was permanently on-site to provide clinical knowledge. The courses took 7 days, the first two of which were used to introduce the students to XP, agents, and the tools (IntelliJ, JUnit and CVS). For the reminder of this subsection we will present the basic principles of Extreme Programming and report on major findings identified during the course with regard to our development methodology.

- *40-hour-week*: The practical work itself was done during one 40-hour week. The students were explicitly not encouraged to work overtime. After the course, the students reported that they used to be quite exhausted after a full day of pair programming, but were very disciplined and concentrated while in the office. Nevertheless, the atmosphere was very relaxed and enjoyable and thus stimulated creativity and open, honest communication. This helped to prevent communication barriers between technicians and the clinical expert.
- *Planning game*: At the beginning of each day, the team jointly defined the features that were to be implemented next. Since the process models (story cards) described the phases of a patient's treatment on its way through the hospital in a rather sequential style, we found it most useful to implement the agents in their order of appearance within the process. We locally focused on those agents that – according to the domain expert – promised the most business value.
- *Pair programming*: Each pair of programmers had to develop and test their individual agent in isolation. The students found pair programming very enjoyable and productive. The intense communication helped to spread a basic understanding of the clinical processes among the programmers. We changed pairs almost every day.

- *Testing*: Agents are typically rather small and loosely coupled systems that solve their tasks in relative autonomy. As a consequence, writing automated test cases is quite easy for agents, because the single agents have a small, finite number of interaction channels with external system units. Many tests therefore consisted of sending a test message to the agent and of checking whether the expected reply message was delivered back and whether the agent's state has changed as expected. The students found testing quite useful to clarify requirements although it was considered to be additional work by some. During the course, the students have implemented 76 test cases, amounting to 4909 lines of code, while the 43 agent source code classes amount to 5673 lines. The students enjoyed using JUnit very much, because correct test runs improved motivation and trust in the code. We found specifying and implementing tests extremely important, because it clarified several misunderstandings between the domain world and the programmers.
- *Collective ownership*: Since each pair only operated on the source package of a single agent, there was barely any overlapping. Only ontology classes (which describe the content of agent messages) had to be modified by various teams. Coordination of these changes was accomplished very informally by voice and the code versioning system CVS.
- *Coding standards*: In the beginning of the project, we defined a project-wide coding standard that was very easy to follow, because the Java tool we used provides automated code layout features. Thus it was very simple to shift implementation tasks between the pairs and to change pair members regularly.
- *Simple design*: The students were explicitly asked to focus on programming speed instead of comprehensive up-front designs. This seemed to be sufficient because the agents were rather small units with few types of tasks to solve. Despite the focus on simplicity, experienced students almost automatically identified some useful generalizations of agent functionality. Our initial process model underwent several evolutionary changes. Despite the various small changes, the overall design remained quite stable throughout the project, so that our process modeling framework proved to be appropriate.
- *Refactoring*: Since the agents were rather small units, they were very easy to maintain and refactor. Even if an agent evolved into a performance or quality bottleneck after a series of refactorings, it was possible to completely rewrite it from scratch without risking the functionality of the overall system. IntelliJ's refactoring support was valuable.
- *Continuous integration and short releases*: The agents were uploaded onto the CVS server and integrated at least every evening. Since the students were only allowed to upload those agents that passed all test

cases, there were almost no integration problems. Agent interactions were tested and presented on a beamer with the help of a small simulation environment that could trigger external events.

- *On-site customer*: In the questionnaires that were filled out by the students after the course, the presence of the domain expert was deemed very positive. He was asked to provide clinical knowledge regularly, at least once an hour, so that expensive design mistakes were prevented. His presence did not even mean an overhead for him, because he could use the "spare time" for other types of work on his own laptop.
- *Metaphor*: Many communication bottlenecks and misunderstandings between clinicians and developers are due to different terminology and perceptions. Metaphors, which map clinical domain concepts onto symbols the engineers are acquainted with, can help. For example, the process of anesthesia, with its induction, monitoring, and extubation phases can be compared to aviation, where take-off, cruising, and landing are the main activities. This metaphor helped us to draw some insightful parallels between the requirements of clinical monitoring devices and cockpit technology.

3.3 Discussion

In a clinical environment, one has to deal with a plethora of software and hardware units. However, the level of interoperability is rather low and often the integrating factor still remains to be a nurse copying values from one printout into the next form by hand. Agent technology does have the potential to integrate information islands caused by missing interfaces, incompatible data formats and the like.

The inherent modularity of agents allows one to customize a clinical information infrastructure to a hospital's individual requirements and prerequisites. The co-ordination mechanisms found in multiagent systems offer a high level of flexibility, e.g. when unexpected emergency patients need to be treated.

A major challenge for the engineering for this kind of software is requirements elicitation, because intimate knowledge of the work processes is required. Our methodology exploits ideas from agile software development approaches such as Extreme Programming in the face of uncertain requirements. It builds upon collaboration with domain experts and human creativity driven by rapid feedback. We support collaborative requirements elicitation by means of an iterative, tool-supported modeling approach that allows one to capture existing and agentified processes in a format that is sufficiently simple to be understood and maintained by domain experts.

Interestingly, we have experienced that the concept of agents are a useful and well-perceived communication metaphor for discussions with users and domain experts during the requirements elicitation and design phase. It can be used in addition to process or rule-based approaches. It seems to be more natural to think along the concepts of subjects talking and interacting with each other instead of abstract processes and activities, especially in very dynamic and "chaotic" environments. Yet this new modeling paradigm has to be investigated further.

We enable creativity by means of a searchable repository of reusable agent design patterns and other types of process modeling knowledge. Our tool, called AGIL-Shell (Agent-based Information Logistic), is used for process and agent modeling and can automatically generate source code for a variety of agent platforms (native Java, Java Enterprise, JADE/FIPA-OS). This tool proved helpful for the creation of prototypes used in simulations to verify the targeted processes. The elicited process and agent models can be synchronized automatically with executable agent source code, so that rapid feedback is ensured.

A special focus should be put on human-agent interaction. Trust and co-operation are two important topics even more pressing in a critical, safety concerned environment. In a time critical situation, the interaction between man and agent need to be without hesitation. Especially here, the pro-active aspects can be utilized. Trust of a user in an agent's decisions and activities is a vital precondition to the delegation of work. The most sophisticated and verified MAS will be useless if the user does not trust the system.

The aspect of co-operation goes even further. A user agent may accompany a user during some period of time. It can become an assistant much like a secretary or butler, adjusting and learning about the preferences and peculiarities of its user. It can initiate actions in the interest of its user even without the human knowing. In a hospital environment one could think of a patient's advocate reminding the staff to treat a patient who is sitting in the waiting room for long.

3.4 Conclusion

We have developed an agile methodology for the development of MAS, in particular multiagent systems that support the collaboration of distributed work groups like clinical departments.

Classical engineering principles appear inappropriate due to the complexity and dynamics of processes, and due to uncertain clinical requirements. Instead, we have successfully applied an Extreme Programming approach, which explicitly involves communication and evolution into the process. The communication was based on a simple, yet sufficiently formal process modeling metaphor. Code generation and the various practices of XP, which help to reduce the cost of change, supported evolution. The implementation process has led to many process improvements and a prototypical clinical information system.

Using the concept of software-agents in the analysis and design phase of an (agile) software engineering approach is an efficient and natural way to discuss with customers and users, because entities that communicate and interact seem a more natural mapping than processes and information flow of traditional pure-process oriented approaches.

References

[Beck1999]   Beck, K.: Extreme Programming Explained: Embrace Change. Addison-Wesley, 1999.

[BeMu1997]   van Bemmel, J. H.; Musen, M. A. (Eds.): Handbook of Medical Informatics. Springer-Verlag, Heidelberg, 1997.

[CiWo2001]   Ciancarini, P.; Wooldridge, M. (Eds.): Agent-Oriented Software Engineering. Springer-Verlag, Berlin, Heidelberg, New York, 2001.

[Cock1997]   Cockburn. The Methodology Space. Humans and Technology Technical Report TR.97.03, 1997.

[Delo1999]   DeLoach, S. A.: Multiagent Systems Engineering: A Methodology and Language for Designing Agent Systems. In: Proceedings of Agent Oriented Information Systems. Seattle, OR, 1999.

[GHJV1995]   Gamma, E.; Helm, R.; Johnson, R.; Vlissides, J.: Design Patterns: Elements of Reusable Object-Oriented Software. Addison-Wesley, 1995.

[HaKK2001]   Hartung, E.; Kobelt, F.; Kutz, N. et al.: Patientendaten-Managementsysteme. In: Anästhesiologie und Intensivmedizin 42(2001) pp. 89-111.

[HuJF1995]   Huang, J.; Jennings, N.; Fox, J.: An Agent-based Approach to Health Care Management. In: Applied Artificial Intelligence: An International Journal 9(1995)4, pp. 401-420.

[Knub2002]   Knublauch, H.: Extreme Programming of Multi-Agent Systems. In: Proceedings of the First International Joint Conference on Autonomous Agents and Multi-Agent Systems (AAMAS). Bologna, Italy, 2002.

[KnRo2001]   Knublauch, H.; Rose, T.: Werkzeugunterstützte Prozessanalyse zur Identifikation von Anwendungsszenarien für Agenten. In: Proceedings of the Verbundtagung Verteilte Informationssysteme auf der Grundlage von Objekten, Komponenten und Agenten (vertIS). Bamberg, Germany, 2001.

[KnRS2000]   Knublauch, H.; Rose, T; Sedlmayr, M.: Towards a Multi-Agent System for Pro-active Information Management in Anesthesia. In: Proceedings of the Agents-2000 Workshop on Autonomous Agents in Health Care. Barcelona, Spain, 2000.

[LaFS1995]   Lanzola, G.; Falasconi, S.; Stefanelli, M.: Cooperative Software Agents for Patient Management. In: Proceedings of the 5th Conference on Artificial Intelligence in Medicine in Europe (AIME). Pavia, Italy, 1995.

[LSTO1997]   Leisch, E.; Sartzetakis, S.; Tsiknakis, M.; Orphanoudakis, S. C.: A Framework for the Integration of Distributed Autonomous Healthcare Information Systems. In: Medical Informatics 22(1997)4, pp. 325-335.

[MaFr2000]   Marsolek, I.; Friesdorf, W.: TOPICS – Together Optimizing Processes in Clinical Systems. In: Komplexe Arbeitssysteme – Herausforderung für Analyse und Gestaltung. GfA Press, 2000, pp. 369-371.

[RFKR2002]   Rose, T.; Fünffinger, M.; Knublauch, H.; Rupprecht, C.: Prozessorientiertes Wissensmanagement. In: Künstliche Intelligenz 1(2002), pp. 19-24.

[WoJK2000]   Wooldridge, M.; Jennings, N.; Kinny, D.: The Gaia Methodology for Agent-Oriented Analysis and Design. In: Journal of Autonomous Agents and Multi-Agent Systems 3(2000)3, pp. 285-312.

4 Agent-Based Patient Scheduling in Hospitals

Torsten O. Paulussen, Anja Zöller, Franz Rothlauf, Armin Heinzl

Universität Mannheim, Lehrstuhl für ABWL und Wirtschaftsinformatik,
{paulussen I zoeller I rothlauf I heinzl}@bwl.uni-mannheim.de

Lars Braubach, Alexander Pokahr, Winfried Lamersdorf

Universität Hamburg, Fachbereich Informatik, Verteilte Systeme und Informationssysteme {braubach I pokahr I lamersd}@informatik.uni-hamburg.de

Abstract. Patient scheduling in hospitals is a very complex task. This complexity stems from the distributed structure of hospitals and the dynamics of the treatment process. Hospitals consist of various autonomous, administratively distinct units which are visited by the patients according to their individual disease. However, the pathways (the needed medical actions) and the medical priorities (the health condition of the patients) are likely to change due to new findings about the diseases of the patients during examination. Moreover, the durations of the treatments and examinations are stochastic. Additional problems for patient scheduling in hospitals arise from complications and emergencies. Thus, patient scheduling in hospitals requires a distributed and flexible approach. To this end, a flexible, agent-based approach to patient scheduling is developed in this chapter. After a description of the addressed patient scheduling problem, the proposed mechanism for patient-scheduling is presented and evaluated.

4.1 Introduction

In this chapter, an agent-based coordination mechanism for patient scheduling in hospitals is described. Patient scheduling is concerned with the optimal assignment of the patients to the scarce hospital resources [Schl1990], where the goal of the patients is to minimize their stay time and the goal of the resources is to minimize their idle time. However, patient scheduling in hospitals resolves as a very complex task. Hospitals consist of several autonomous, administratively distinct wards and ancillary units [DeLi2000] [KuOP1993], which are visited by the patients for their treatments and examinations in accordance with their illness [Schl 1990]. However, the pathways (the needed medical actions) and the medical priorities (the health condition of the patients) are likely to change due to new findings about the diseases of the patients during examination

[PJDH2003]. Further, the durations of the treatments and examinations are stochastic [BrWo1991] [RoCh2003]. Additional problems for patient scheduling in hospitals arise from complications and emergencies, which are in urgent need for treatment [PJDH2003]. Due to this, patient scheduling in hospitals requires an approach which is distributed, in order to leave the authority at the responsible units, and flexible, to be able to react to new information in a timely manner.

For this reason, a multiagent based approach was chosen for this problem, because it allows the representation of every coordination object as a single autonomous agent with own goals [WeGo1996]. Further, the agents can react with the needed flexibility to changes (as new information about the health status of a patient becomes available) and disturbances (emergencies and complications) through proactiveness and responsiveness [Jenn2001]. In this context, the notion of flexibility refers to the term "technical flexibility", that is, the ability to react adequately to external influences (see I.3).

The remainder of this chapter is structured as follows. Section 4.2 elaborates the patient scheduling problem in hospitals. Based upon this, the conceptual framework of the proposed multiagent system is developed in Section 4.3. In Section 4.4, a prototypic implementation of the coordination mechanism is evaluated and benchmarked against the status quo of patient scheduling in hospitals. This chapter closes with conclusions and an outlook to future work in section 4.5.

4.2 The Patient Scheduling Problem in Hospitals

Hospitals are service providers with the primary aim to improve the health state of their patients, where the treatment of the patients is the main value adding process in hospitals [Fein1999] [GrTT997]. Hospitals consist of several autonomous, administratively distinct wards and ancillary units [DeLi2000] [KuOP1993] [PJDH2003]. During hospitalization, the patients reside at the wards and visit the ancillary units for treatments according to their individual disease, where the *treatment process* comprises the medical tasks which must be performed for the patients during hospitalization.

The service provision in a hospital can be viewed from a patient (or job) perspective and from a resource perspective. While the patients focus on the sequence of their medical tasks with the goal to minimize their stay time, the resources focus on the treatments and examinations within the resources with the goal to minimize their idle times [DeLi2000] [KuOP1993].

The *patient scheduling* is now concerned with the (optimal) temporal assignment of the medical tasks for the patients to the (scarce) hospital resources [Schl1990]. However, the patient scheduling problem in hospitals is confronted with a high degree of uncertainty. The patients arrive continuously at the hospital and the necessary medical treatments are often not completely determined at the beginning of the treatment process. Moreover, the new findings during diagnostic examinations might change the (medical) priority of the patients, invoke additional treatments or examinations, and make other medical actions obsolete [PJDH2003]. Further, the service times of treatments and examinations are stochastic [BrWo1991] [RoCh2003]. Finally, complications and arrivals of emergency patients – which are in urgent need for treatment – result in schedule disturbances.

To be able to handle the process dynamics in a distributed environment, hospitals commonly use a very flexible approach for patient scheduling which can be compared to a first-come first-served priority rule. Typically, a ward physician prescribes the necessary treatments and examinations for the patients. These prescribed medical tasks are send as treatment requests to the ancillary units. Based upon these requests the ancillary units order the patients from the wards when they deem appropriate [DeLi2000] [KuOP1993]. This allows the units to react very flexible to changes with very low communication needs. If, for example, an emergency patient needs to be inserted, the next patient will simply be called from the ward later, leaving this patient available to other ancillary units.

However, because there is no inter-unit coordination, this procedure cannot resolve resource conflicts, which occur if the same patient is requested by more than one ancillary unit at the same time [DeLi2000]. Because the ancillary units only have a local view, that is, they do not – and cannot – take the whole pathway of the treated patients into their scheduling consideration, no inter-unit process optimization can be undertaken (i.e., the medical tasks for the patients cannot be scheduled and coordinated in an efficient manner). This causes undesired idle times as well as overtime hours for the hospital resources and extended patient stay times.

4.3 Conceptual Framework

In this section, the conceptual framework of an agent-based coordination mechanism for patient scheduling is developed. As described previously, the patient scheduling problem is concerned with the optimal assignment of the treatments and examinations of the patients to the scarce hospital resources; where the goal of the patients is to minimize their stay time and the objective of the resources is to minimize their idle time. In order to achieve this assignment in a goal-driven manner, the proposed coordination mechanism relies on the economic concept of mutual selection. In this context, the patients and resources can be identified as the coordination objects, which are modeled as autonomous agents; where the patient-agents try to acquire the needed medical services, that is, treatment or examination time slots, from the resource-agents. Because a resource is generally demanded by several patients, each resource-agent auctions off the medical services (time slots) of its hospital resource. In order to participate in the resource auctions, the patient-agents need utility functions, which enable them to determine the values of the required time slots and thus to generate the bids for the time slots.

4.3.1 Health-State Dependent Utility Functions

In the proposed auction-based coordination mechanism, the patient-agents compete with each other over the scarce hospital resources in order to achieve the objectives of their corresponding patients as good as possible. This kind of coordination problem represents a worth-oriented environment [RoZl1994], in which the degree of goal achievement can be evaluated through a utility function cf. [PJDH2003]. The usage of continuous utility functions (instead of single values assigned to specific goals) allows the coordination objects to relax their goals, that is, to compromise in order to reach a better overall solution cf. [RoZl1994].

In contrast to the domain of electronic commerce or industrial production control, the bid-price for a resource time slot in hospitals can neither be based on the patient's willingness to pay for a time slot nor be derived from cost accounting, respectively. The preferences of the patient-agents rather have to be based upon medical priorities, that is, the health state of the patients [PJDH2003]. Because the patient-agents have to reason about the execution time of their treatments, time-dependent utility functions are developed which capture the health state development of the patients [Pau+2004]. In these utility functions the disease of a patient is viewed as disutility (decrease in quality of life) [HoRu1991] [PJDH2003]. Because the loss of utility adds up as long as the disease is not cured, this disutility over time can be viewed as opportunity costs for not curing the disease right away [PJDH2003]. Thus, the utility functions of the patient-agents are modeled as (opportunity) cost functions.

For the construction of these utility (or cost) functions, a cardinal measurement of the health state is required. Hospitals currently use numerous health state or priority measures, like the APACHE II score (*Acute*

Physiology and Chronic Health Evaluation) in intensive care units cf. [KDWZ 1985], or a simple 1 to 6 priority scale to indicate the priority of cardiac patients (as observed in the performed field studies). In order to achieve inter-agent comparable priorities, the various used measures need to be expressed through one single health measure. For this reason, this work proposes a health state measure which was inspired by the (macro-economic) concept of *years of well being* [Torr1987], which already incorporates the notion of time. Here, a health state H of 1 denotes total health and 0 refers to death. In order to determine the value of a health state H for a certain disease, it must be determined (by a decision maker) what time period xT of total health ($H=1$) equals one specific time period $1T$ with this disease, i.e.

$$1T \times H = xT \times 1 \Leftrightarrow H = x. \tag{1}$$

Through this, the health state of a patient can be described in time units [PJDH2003]. For example, [Torr1987] determined a health state of 0.7 for a middle angina pectoris; in other words, that suffering one year from a middle angina pectoris equals 0.7 years of total health.

Because the loss of utility adds up as long as the disease is not cured, this disutility over time can be viewed as opportunity costs for not curing the disease right away [PJDH2003]. These opportunity costs $C(t)$ equal the difference between the achievable health state through treatment z and the patient's health state development over time without treatment $H(t)$. Because a treatment might not be able to restore total health, the achievable health state z might be lower than 1 (total health). In [Torr1987], for example, the health state after a kidney transplantation has a value of 0.84.

Further, the health state of a patient can either remain constant or can decrease over time. In case of a decreasing health state a linear reduction is assumed for practical reasons, i.e., $H(t)=s-bt$, where s denotes the initial health state and b the decrease rate [PJDH2003]. From this, the costs $C(t)$ are

$$C(t) = \int_0^t z - H(\tau)\,d\tau = at + \frac{b}{2}t^2; a = z - s. \tag{2}$$

In other words, the initial health state a might also be viewed as the *severity* and the decrease rate b as the *criticality* of the patient's illness. Figure 1 shows an exemplary course of an illness with linear reduction of the health state, resulting in a quadratic, convex opportunity cost curve.

Finally, the achievable health state through treatment (z) might decrease. Because a decrease of the achievable health state due to late treatment would result in a lifelong decrease of the quality of life for the patient, these patients are treated immediately as emergency patients.

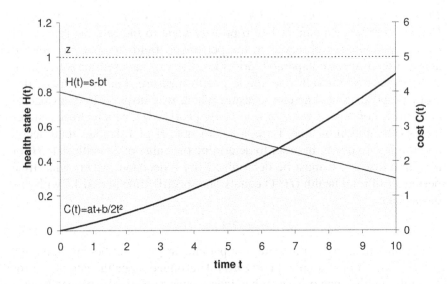

Figure 1. Linear reduction of the health state

After the determination of the time dependent utility function, it is necessary to consider the case of *stochastic treatment durations*. Because the service times of the medical tasks might be stochastic, it is necessary for the patient-agents to consider this uncertainty in the bargaining process. For this reason, the cost function $C(t)$ has to be extended to a cost function $\tilde{C}(\mu,\sigma)$ based upon the expected mean μ and variance σ^2 of the starting time distribution $\varphi(t,\mu,\sigma)$. To calculate the value of $\tilde{C}(\mu,\sigma)$, the starting time distribution $\varphi(t,\mu,\sigma)$ has to be weighted with the cost function $C(t)$ of the patient agent, i.e.

$$\tilde{C}(\mu,\sigma) = \int_{-\infty}^{\infty} \varphi(t,\mu,\sigma)C(t)\,dt. \qquad (3)$$

Based upon decision theory the variance of the envisaged starting time for a task is viewed as risk (of delay), where a linear opportunity cost curve indicates risk neutrality, because the benefit from the chance to start earlier compensates (in case of a symmetric distribution function) the disutility through the chance of a delayed start. A convex opportunity cost function on the other hand indicates risk adversity, because the possible gains from an early start are outweighed by the possible losses due to a delayed start [Schn1991]. This should be illustrated by the following example equation, using a normal distribution and the described health state dependent cost function. The expected costs $\tilde{C}(\mu,\sigma)$ for a patient agent for a timeslot with a mean starting time μ and variance σ^2 can now be calculated by

$$\tilde{C}(\mu,\sigma) = \int_{-\infty}^{\infty} \frac{1}{\sqrt{2\pi}\sigma} e^{-\frac{(t-\mu)^2}{2\sigma^2}} \left(at + \frac{b}{2}t^2 \right) dt = a\mu + \frac{b}{2}\left(\mu^2 + \sigma^2\right) \quad (4)$$

where the variance σ^2 is only influenced by b. With regards to decision theory, the health decrease rate b can be interpreted as the determinant of the agent's attitude to risk, that is, for $b=0$ the agent is risk neutral and for $b>0$ the agent is risk adverse [Schn1991].

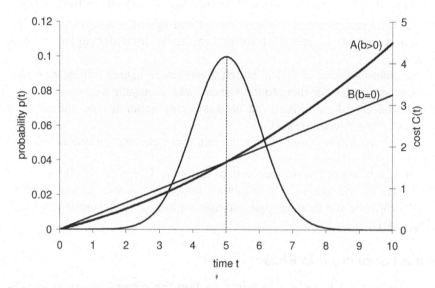

Figure 2. Stochastic treatment duration

This is illustrated in Figure 2, where curve A shows a risk adverse and curve B a risk neutral preference or cost function of the patients. However, if the starting time distribution is not symmetric, even risk neutral patients are sensitive to different variances.

Because the service times of the treatments and examinations in a hospital often do not correspond to a normal distribution, discrete distribution functions are used in this work. Therefore, the expected cost for a treatment results as the sum of the cost-values $at + b/2 \times t^2$ of each time point (the n classes of the distribution) weighted by its probability p, i.e.

$$\tilde{C} = \sum_{i=1}^{n} p_i \left(at_i + \frac{b}{2}t_i^2 \right) \quad (5)$$

4.3.2 Coordination Mechanism

For the assignment of the treatments and examinations of the patients to the scarce hospital resources, a market inspired coordination mechanism (based upon the Contract Net Protocol [Smit1980] [DaSm1983]) is used. In this coordination mechanism the resources auction off their time-slots. Consequently, a resource time-slot is assigned to the patient-agent with the highest bid. The rational for this is, that the patient-agent who gains the highest utility from a specific time-slot is willing to pay the highest price for it (up to the expected utility).

In detail, the proposed coordination mechanism consists of four phases:

1. the *subscription phase*, where the patient-agents subscribe to the required resource-agents to inform them about their demanded medical tasks,
2. the *announcement phase*, in which the resource-agents initiate new auctions and announce them to the subscribed patient-agents,
3. the *bidding phase*, where the patient-agents generate and submit their bids for the needed time slot,
4. and the *awarding phase*, where the winner of the auction is determined.

Thus, this coordination mechanism turns the Contract Net Protocol on its head, as the potential contractors (resource-agents) announce their availability and the manager (patient-agents) bid for their pending tasks cf. [Durf2001].

4.3.2.1 Subscription Phase

In order to participate at a resource auction the patient-agents must subscribe to the required resource-agents, that is, inform the resource-agents about the required treatments and examinations. However, to be able to subscribe to a resource-agent the patient-agents first must identify the resources capable of performing the needed treatments and examinations. Because the capabilities of the resources might overlap, i.e., different resources might be able to perform the same treatment, a *yellow page service* is used at which the resource-agents advertise their capabilities, and the patient agents inform themselves about the adequate resources. This allows the agents to flexible incorporate changes in the hospital environment (see also I.3).

When a resource-agent receives a subscription from a patient-agent it informs the subscriber about the duration of the requested medical task. Because the service times of the medical tasks are stochastic, the resource-agent submits an array containing a discrete (empirical) distribution function, which is generated from historical task durations.

The subscription phase is somewhat distinct from the bidding and awarding phase. A subscription of a patient-agent is only needed if the treatment pathway of the corresponding patient is altered, that is, when a new treatment or examination is needed or an already registered medical task becomes obsolete. Thus, the main purpose of the subscription phase is to avoid unnecessary broadcast messages when a resource agent initiates a new auction, which is described next.

4.3.2.2 Announcement Phase

The announcement phase initiates the actual auction mechanism. A resource-agent opens an auction for a new treatment or examination if its associated hospital resource has (almost) finished the current medical task. Similar to the current practice in hospitals, this allows the resource to react in an efficient manner to complications and emergency patients: if a treatment takes longer than expected or an emergency patient (who has not yet been entered into the information system) needs urgent treatment, the resource-agent just does not open a new auction until the exception is handled. Obviously, for this to work, the resource-agent needs some external input in order to update its beliefs about the state (busy or idle) of its physical resource.

In order to open a new auction, the resource-agent informs all subscribed patient-agents about the new auction and queries their envisaged starting time. In response, each contacted patient-agent replies the time at which the patient it represents is expected to be available. This can either be immediate if the patient is idle or later, otherwise. If the patient is not idle, the corresponding patient-agent transfers an array containing a distribution function of the finish time of the medical task the patient is currently engaged in. Based upon this information, the resource-agent computes the expected finish time distributions for all participating patient-agents. Then, the resource-agent submits these finish time distributions to the participants and calls for proposals (bids). This call for proposals initiates the bidding phase.

4.3.2.3 Bidding Phase

In the bidding phase the patient-agents generate and submit bids for the prescribed medical procedures to the resource-agents. To be able to evaluate their current schedule and to calculate bid-prices for time slots, the patient agents rely on the utility functions described in Section 4.3.1. Based upon these utility functions the agents generate the bid-prices by calculating the expected loss of utility (cost of waiting) if they would loose a specific auction. In other words, the price a patient-agent is willing to bid for a specific time slot corresponds to the expected disutility the patient-agent would suffer if it does not win the auction. Therefore, the patient-agent has to determine the value of its own schedule with and without winning the desired time slot. To determine the schedule in case of loosing the auction, the finish time distributions of the other participating patient-agents are considered as block time of the corresponding resource. After the bids are generated, they are submitted (proposed) to the auctioneer.

4.3.2.4 Awarding Phase

The last step of the coordination mechanism is the awarding phase. After the auctioneer (the resource-agent) has received the proposals containing the bids of the patient-agents, it awards its time slot to the patient-agent which causes the lowest harm to all other agents. In the case a patient-agent wins in more than one auction – as a patient-agent generally participates in multiple simultaneous auctions –, it must decide which award it should accept. Here, the patient-agent chooses the resource it gains the highest utility out of. If an awarded resource time slot is rejected by the patient-agent, the corresponding resource-agent awards its auctioneered time-slot to the next best bidder until one patient-agent accepts the award or all participants rejected the time-slot.

4.4 Evaluation and Benchmark

For the evaluation and benchmark of the proposed coordination mechanism, a prototypic multiagent system was implemented. To test and evaluate the prototype under real-world conditions a simulation environment was built, that allows simulating different scenarios by varying several parameters, such as the hospital size, the divergence of treatment durations, or the probability of emergency cases. Additionally, in order to benchmark the proposed coordination mechanism against the status-quo patient scheduling in hospitals, a priority rule based strategy was also implemented.

4.4.1 Prototype Realization

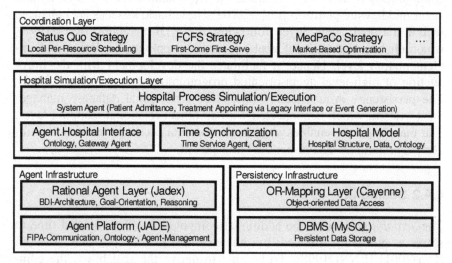

Figure 3. Prototype implementation

The prototype implementation is organized in three separate layers: The coordination layer, the hospital layer, and the infrastructure layer (see Figure 3). The coordination layer is comprised of the different coordination mechanisms, each of which can be applied to perform the treatment scheduling. The coordination mechanism described in the previous sections and the alternative strategies used for benchmarking have been designed and implemented using agent-oriented tools and concepts. More details about the concrete realization of the coordination mechanisms can be found in [Pau+2004] [BrPL2004].

The hospital layer is designed to support the execution of the coordination by providing the facilities to perform simulation runs or to run the system as an application. When a simulation run is initiated, the information from the hospital model is used to create the hospital infrastructure consisting of initial patient and resource agents. During the run, the system agent uses different random distributions to approximate real arrival rates of patients and other occurrences like emergencies. It therefore decides at when next arrival or emergency will take place. The system agent is conceived to emulate all simulation external occurrences. Hence, for running the system as application instead of simulation it is merely required to adapt the system agent to react on some user interface and set-up the time service with real time.

The infrastructure layer provides system-level services for the implementation such as agent management and execution, as well as persistency. Basic agent services as the agent lifecycle management, agent communication and search facilities are provided by a FIPA-compliant agent middleware platform [PoCh2001]. These basic services are enhanced with a rational agent layer following the BDI-metaphor [RaGe1995], which enables the usage of goal-oriented concepts at the design and implementation level. Hence, it facilitates the development with the introduction of high-level agent-oriented programming concepts [PoBL2005]. The persistency infrastructure consists of a relational database management system, which is connected with an object-relational mapping layer. The mapping layer enables object-oriented data access by making the underlying relational database model transparent.

4.4.2 Scalability

The *scalability* denotes the additional computation effort (needed time to solve a problem) invoked by an increase of the problem size cf. [Durf2001] [LNND1998]. To be able to derive the scalability, the complexity of the test problems should only differ with respect to the problem size. For this, the open shop benchmark problems of [Tail1992] were used. In these problems the amount of jobs equal the amount of resources; thus the number of tasks is $n \times n$, where n denotes the number of resources or jobs, respectively.

The Taillard open shop benchmark consists of six different problem sizes (4×4, 5×5, 7×7, 10×10, 15×15, 20×20), each comprising ten problem instances (the used problems are available from [Tail1992]). Figure 4 shows the (logarithmic) mean run time of the proposed coordination mechanism ("Auctions") for each problem size ($n \times n$), and a curve representing a quadratic scaling ("$O(n^2)$") for comparison. Through comparison of the empirical run times of the proposed mechanism with the calculated $O(n^2)$ curve it can be stated, that the proposed mechanism approximately scales quadratic with the problem size.

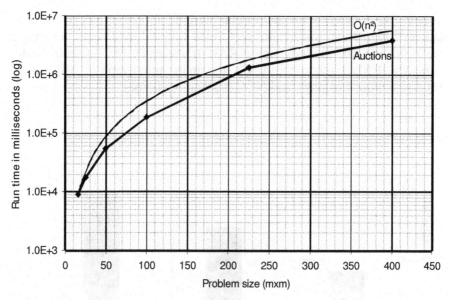

Figure 4. Scaling of Taillard n×n open shop problems

4.4.3 Continuous Patient Arrival

This subsection investigates the performance of the proposed coordination mechanism in a dynamic environment, where the patients arrive continuously at the hospital. To analyze the suitability, the mechanism is compared against a coordination mechanism using a *first-come first-serve* (FCFS) priority rule in three different scenarios:

1. short inter-arrival intervals with few medical tasks for each patient;
2. short inter-arrival intervals with many tasks; and
3. long inter-arrival intervals with many tasks.

A test of long inter-arrival intervals with few tasks was omitted, because pre-tests have shown that the problem was too easy (almost no resource conflicts occurred).

The setup of the tests is a follows. In all tests the last patient doesn't arrive after the 400th minute. The *short* inter-arrival intervals where uniformly drawn from of the interval [1,10] (minutes), and the *long* inter-arrival intervals were randomly chosen between [1,60]. Because these tests are designed to analyze and compare the effect of short versus long inter-arrival intervals on the performance of the coordination mechanism separately, a uniform distribution of the inter-arrival intervals in both tests was chosen. The treatments for the patients were drawn out of a database containing 3393 actual, historically performed hospital treatments, involving the following six ancillary units: RAD (radiology), ECG (electrocardiography), ENDO (endoscopy), CT (computer-tomography), MR (magnetic-resonance-imaging), and NUC (nuclear-medicine).

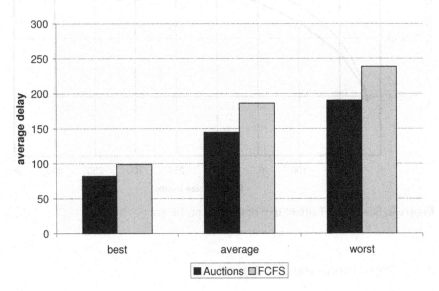

Figure 5. Results "short-few"

For the test with the *few* medical tasks up to three treatments were assigned, and for the tests with *many* treatments one to seven treatments where drawn out of the treatment-database cf. [KuOP1993]. Thus, the most tasks have to be scheduled at the test with short inter-arrival intervals and many tasks. The best, average and worst achieved results (average patient idle time) of the test runs are given in Figure 5 (short-few), Figure 6 (short-many), and Figure 7 (long-many).

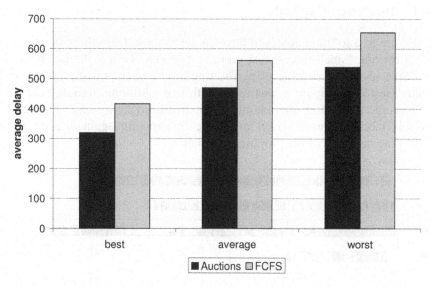

Figure 6. Results "short-many"

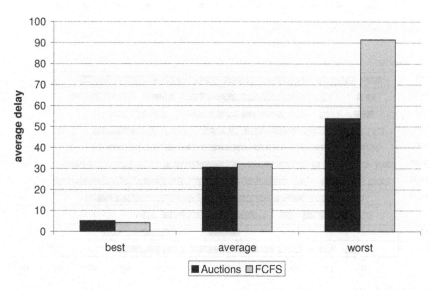

Figure 7. Results "long-many"

4.4.4 Resource Capacity

In Figure 8, a solution achieved through the proposed coordination mechanism for one "small-many" test problem is given. To test the handling of multiple resources capable of performing the same treatment, the "small-many" test from Figure 8 was rerun with two additional radiological and endoscopic units, and one additional electrocardiography unit. The result of this modification is given in Figure 9, showing again a good load balancing behavior of the proposed mechanism.

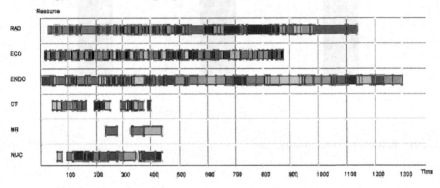

Figure 8. Single resource capacity.

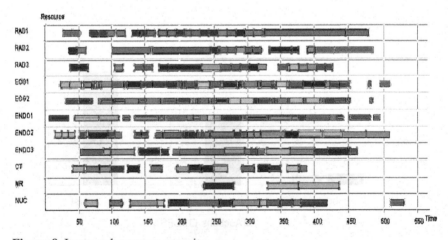

Figure 9. Increased resource capacity

4.4.5 Emergencies

To test the behavior of the proposed mechanism in case of emergencies, simulations were run with different emergency probabilities (the chance that an arriving patient is an emergency). Here, each emergency patient receives only one task, but this task must be performed immediately. Using the simulation setup of the previous subsection, tests with an emergency probability of 5, 10, 20, 25, and 50 percent were performed with the proposed coordination mechanism as well as with the first-come first-served mechanism. While normal patients do not arrive after the 300th minute, emergency patients can arrive until the 600th minute (the occurrence of emergencies must be bounded, because the system would run infinitely otherwise). Figure 10 shows a schedule with emergency patients (dark bars).

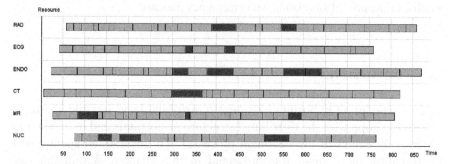

Figure 10. Resource allocation with emergency patients

The results in percentage improvement of the idle time of the patients by the proposed coordination mechanism over the first-come first-served priority rule are given in Figure 11. Here, the achieved improvement over the hospital benchmark decreases with an increase in the emergency probability. However, this is plausible, because an increase of unpredictable tasks consequently reduces the scheduling potential of any scheduling approach.

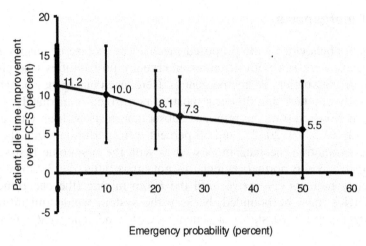

Figure 11. Results of simulation with emergency patients

4.5 Conclusions

Patient scheduling in hospitals requires a distributed and flexible approach in order to cope with the distributed structure of hospitals and to handle the inherent dynamics of the treatment processes. To this end, an agent-based coordination mechanism was presented in this chapter. Within this approach the patient-agents compete with each other over the scarce hospital resources. Through a decentralized auction mechanism the resource time slots are assigned to the patient-agents who gain the highest utility out of these time slots.

Because the utility of a patient in a hospital cannot – or at least should not – be based on the patient's willingness to pay for a specific resource time slot, it is important to develop utility functions which adequately represent the health stateover time. To this end, a novel health-state dependent utility function was introduced. Through these utility functions, the patient-agents can generate their bids for the time slot auctions at the resource-agents.

The proposed coordination mechanism significantly improves the current patient scheduling practice in hospitals (modeled as a first-come first-serve priority rule), while providing the required flexibility.

Currently the proposed coordination mechanism considers the health state of the patients as the only determinant of the patients priority. Thus, future research should address the question how the utility function of the patient agents can be adapted to handle multiple preferences. Here, the multi-attributive utility theory [Schn1991] might provide a good starting point. In this work, the proposed coordination mechanism was benchmarked against the status quo patient scheduling in hospitals. In future work, this benchmark will be extended to consider state of the art scheduling heuristics and meta-heuristics, e.g. genetic and evolutionary algorithms. Finally, the proposed mechanism will be evaluated in a real hospital. Here it is essential to integrate the existing legacy systems of the hospital. However, an agent-based system is assumed to be well suited for this, because the legacy systems can be encapsulated through agents, and thus easily be integrated into the framework cf. [Jen+2000].

References

[BrPL2004]   Braubach, L.; Pokahr, A.; Lamersdorf, W.: MedPAge: Rationale Agenten zur Patientensteuerung. In: KI – Zeitschrift für Künstliche Intelligenz: Forschung, Entwicklung, Erfahrungen. Schwerpunktheft ‚Anwendungen von Softwareagenten' (2004)2, pp. 34-37.

[BrWo1991]   Brahimi, M.; Worthington, D. J.: Queueing Models for Out-Patient Appointment Systems – A Case Study. In: Journal of the Operational Research Society 42(1991)9, pp. 733-746.

[DaSm1983]   Davis, R.; Smith, R. G.: Negotiation as a Metaphor for Distributed Problem Solving. In: Artificial Intelligence, 20(1983)1, pp. 63-109.

[DeLi2000]   Decker, K. S.; Li, J.: Coordinating Mutually Exclusive Resources using GPGP. In: Autonomous Agents and Multi-Agent Systems, 3(2000)2, pp. 133-157.

[Durf2001]   Durfee, E. H.: Distributed problem solving and planning. In: Luck, M.; Marik, V.; Stepankova, O.; Trappl, R. (Eds.): Multiagents systems and applications. Springer-Verlag, Berlin, 2001, pp. 118-149.

[Fein1999]   Feinen, R.: Patientenbezogene Organisation von Behandlungsprozessen. In: Eichhorn, S.; Schmidt-Rettig, B. (Eds.): Profitcenter und Prozessorientierung: Optimierung von Budget, Arbeitsprozessen und Qualität. Kohlhammer, Stuttgart, 1999, pp. 188-199.

[GrTT1997]   Greulich, A.; Thiele, G.; Thiex-Keye, M.: Prozeßmanagement im Krankenhaus. In: Schriftenreihe zum Managementhandbuch Krankenhaus, vol. 8. v. Decker, Heidelberg, 1997.

[HoRu1991]   Horvitz, E.; Rutledge, G.: Time-Dependent Utility and Action Under Uncertainty. In: Seventh Conference on Uncertainty in Artificial Intelligence. Morgan Kaufmann, San Mateo, 1991, pp. 151-158.

[Jenn2001]   Jennings, N. R.: An agent-based approach for building complex
                software systems. In: Communications of the ACM 44(2001)4,
                pp. 35-41.
[Jen+2000]   Jennings, N. R.; Faratin, P.; Norman, T. J.; O'Brien, P.; Odg-
                ers, B.: Autonomous Agents for Business Process Management.
                In: International Journal of Applied Artificial Intelligence,
                14(2000)2, pp. 145-189.
[KDWZ1985]   Knaus, W. A.; Draper, E. A.; Wagner, D. P.; Zimmermann, J. E.:
                APACHE II: A Severity of Disease Classification System. In:
                Critical Care Medicine 13(1985)10, pp. 818-829.
[KuOP1993]   Kumar, A.; Ow, P. S.; Prietula, M. J.: Organizational Simulation
                and Information System Design: An Operations Level Example.
                In: Management Science 39(1993)2, pp. 218-240.
[LNND1998]   Lee, L. C.; Nwana, H. S.; Ndumu, D. T.; De Wilde, P.: The
                Stability, Scalability and Performance of Multi-Agent Systems.
                In: BT Technology Journal 16(1998)3, pp. 94-103.
[Pau+2004]   Paulussen, T. O.; Pokahr, A.; Braubach, L.; Zöller, A.; Lamers-
                dorf, W.; Heinzl, A.: Dynamic Patient Scheduling in Hospitals.
                In: Bichler, M.; Holtmann, C.; Kirn, S.; Müller, J.; Wein-
                hardt, C. (Eds.): Mulitkonferenz Wirtschaftsinformatik, Agent
                Technology in Business Applications. Essen, 2004.
[PJDH2003]   Paulussen, T. O.; Jennings, N. R.; Decker, K. S.; Heinzl, A.:
                Distributed Patient Scheduling in Hospitals. In: Proceedings of
                the International Joint Conference on Artificial Intelligence.
                Acapulco, Mexico, 2003, pp. 1224-1232.
[PoBL2005]   Pokahr, A.; Braubach, L.; Lamersdorf, W.: Jadex: A BDI Rea-
                soning Engine. In: Bordini, R.; Dastani, M.; Dix, J.; Seghrou-
                chni, A. (Eds.): Multi-Agent Programming, Kluwer (to appear in
                2005).
[PoCh2001]   Poslad, S.; Charlton, P.: Standardizing Agent Interoperability:
                The FIPA Approach. In: 9th ECCAI Advanced Course, ACAI
                2001 and Agent Links 3rd European Agent Systems Summer
                School, EASSS 2001, Prague, Czech Republic. Springer, Hei-
                delberg, 2001.
[RaGe1995]   Rao, A.; Georgeff, M.: BDI Agents: from theory to practice,
                Systems (ICMAS'95). MIT Press, 1995.
[RoCh2003]   Robinson, L. W.; Chen, R. R.: Scheduling doctors' appoint-
                ments: optimal and empirically-based heuristic policies. In: IIE
                Transactions 35(2003), pp. 295-307.
[RoZl1994]   Rosenschein, J. S.; Zlotkin, G.: Rules of Encounter. MIT Press,
                Cambridge, 1994.
[Schl1990]   Schlüchtermann, J.: Patientensteuerung. Verlag Josef Eul, Ber-
                gisch Gladbach, 1990.
[Schn1991]   Schneeweiß, C.: Planung. Springer-Verlag, Berlin, 1991.

[Smit1980]   Smith, R. G.: The Contract Net Protocol: High-Level Communi-
                cation and Control in a Distributed Problem Solver. In: IEEE
                Transactions on Computers 29(1980)12, pp. 1104-1113.
[Tail1992]   Taillard, E.: Benchmarks for basic scheduling problems. In:
                European Journal of Operations Research 64(1992), pp. 278-
                285.
[Torr1987]   Torrance, G.-W.: Utility approach to measuring health-related
                quality of life. In: Journal of Chronic Diseases (1987)6, pp. 493-
                600.
[WeGo1996]   Weinhardt, Ch.; Gomber, P.: Domänenunabhängige Koordinati-
                onsmechanismen für die dezentrale betriebliche Planung. In: In-
                formation Management (1996)1, pp. 6-16.

5 Adaptivity and Scheduling

Rainer Herrler, Frank Puppe

Universität Würzburg, Lehrstuhl für Künstliche Intelligenz und Angewandte Informatik, {herrler | puppe}@informatik.uni-wuerzburg.de

Abstract. The structures in health care are currently changing. Clinical management and physicians have the obligation to both ensure quality of care and to work more cost effectively. The optimization of the system respecting these contrary goals is a big challenge. New information technology and computer applications like adaptive agent based assistance agents may be one way to optimize the system. Additionally organizational changes regarding resources or processes may also enhance the system. In many cases the effects of optimization ideas are difficult to foresee. This chapter describes the possibilities of multiagent simulation for experimentation and optimization of adaptive scheduling in hospitals. It presents a specialized agent based construction kit for hospital simulation and describes the results of realized example scenarios.

5.1 Introduction

This chapter addresses the problem of coordinating and scheduling logistical issues in hospitals, in particular those pertaining to treatments and examinations. Despite the introduction of clinical information systems in recent years, the execution schedule of medical tasks is often determined by ad-hoc decisions and typically costly factors such as patient treatment duration, efficient resource loadings or balanced working hours are not optimized. Often simple waiting queues (first-in first-out) in front of functional units can be found to determine the execution sequence. If appointments are made, they are individually negotiated by telephone. Even though this is one particular solution, it is suboptimal and is likely to cause unnecessary delays and result in an uneven distribution of work amongst the functional units.

Some properties of hospital patient scheduling hamper manual or central problem solving. Firstly patient scheduling is *inherently distributed*. Several organizational units - traditionally autonomous and different in their nature - are involved and make their own decisions regarding appointments. The patients on the other hand are very individual, suffer from different diseases with different severities and often need immediate care.

Our patients of a clinic in particular, have *individual preferences* and restrictions. In fact many of the patient constraints are hard to formalize in detail and furthermore they are dynamic and subject to future change. Centralized systems can hardly represent all of the constraints and keep them up to date. Complexity is also an issue, as the processes are *interdependent* and patients may compete for the same resources. Compared to other scheduling domains, patient scheduling has very *dynamic* demands. Current schedules may become obsolete by sudden changes: durations of task execution may be unpredictable; emergencies have to be treated urgently and patients may not appear on time. A system that successfully deals with these problems has to provide the capability for efficient, dynamic rescheduling.

Considering these problem characteristics we arrive at the following conclusion: A scheduling system has to be distributed and individually configurable, and it has to perceive the changes of the environment and be able to adapt to these situations very quickly. The natural properties of agents deal very well with these circumstances: They are situated in an environment; they reason about changes in the environment, they act autonomously and interact socially with each other to solve problems. These properties can also be summarized as the adaptivity of an agent.

As we have illustrated, optimization of patient scheduling is very promising and the agent paradigm fits well for these problem properties. The projects of the priority research program SPP 1083 followed two basic approaches to provide solutions for the problem domain.

- *Introduction of agent based scheduling systems*: This approach comprises the development of an agent based scheduling assistance system. These systems can improve patient scheduling by endowing patients as well as functional units with assistance agents for appointment negotiation. (see III.4; [HeHe2004a]) The interaction between software agents is faster, cheaper and less problematic (if frequently repeated) than human interaction. The prerequisite for the application of software agents is that the system should be continually up-to-date and in close contact with their human counterparts. Then agents can perform a more exhaustive search for 'good' solutions than humans. Even if this could also be realized by a centralized scheduling system, an agent based solution reflects more closely the existing organization and therefore can better deal with the inherent uncertainties in the clinical environment.
- *Agent based simulation of hospital processes*: The second approach deals with the development of hospital simulations to evaluate scheduling questions. Effects on global evaluation parameters like staytime and average unit load are the result of dynamic interactions between humans

or between software agents and humans. Multiagent simulation is very helpful when predicting the overall effects of different strategies of agent based scheduling assistance systems. These effects can be examined under normal as well as stress conditions, and important influences upon the system can be determined. Building simulations is effort intensive therefore powerful tools and methodologies are needed to create credible and useful simulations.

Both approaches apply agent technology to improve the ability to manage scarce resources in hospitals. The combination of system development and simulation based evaluation is very promising. Whilst III.4 has already discussed scheduling systems, this chapter will consider agent based simulation more closely.

In the next section the required basics of agent based adaptive scheduling and scheduling in hospitals are discussed in more detail. Furthermore aspects of adaptivity in agent based scheduling are treated. III.5.3 deals with the state of the art in hospital simulation, the role of pathway models for scheduling and simulation and finally presents a novel agent construction kit for hospitals. III.5.4 presents case studies that have been realized and the first results of these simulations.

5.2 Adaptivity Aspects of Agent Based Scheduling in Hospitals

Scheduling examples are known from everyday life. Besides the clinical application mentioned above, the bandwidth reaches from finding a time for a joint meeting to more complex problems like production scheduling or the scheduling of shift plans. Fundamentally, scheduling deals with the temporal *assignment* of activities or tasks to limited resources [Saue2000] [Bla+1996] [Pine1995]. Scheduling also determines time-intervals of task execution. Usually non-linear constraints and optimization-criteria have to be regarded. Due to the exponential size of the solution space these problems usually cannot be solved by an exhaustive search algorithm. Therefore approximate methods like algorithms of operations research or artificial intelligence have been applied in the past. These approaches provide representations and heuristic problem solving algorithms. Much research about scheduling can be found in the manufacturing domain, where production tasks have to be assigned to resources [Hest1999] [Schm2000] and due times have to be considered.

Whereas scheduling in the manufacturing domain can often be delegated to one central system some application domains require distributed systems. Supply chain management across several enterprises and inherently distributed organizations like hospitals lack the possibility of central planning. A basic property of these domains is that the knowledge about the problem is distributed and usually cannot be shared by reasons of distributed responsibilities, missing communication infrastructure, data security, or protecting a company's intellectual property. Since no central planner can be realized and authorized to collect the necessary knowledge about the problem, distributed problem solvers look for partial solutions and have to solve conflicts by interaction and negotiation about a suitable solution.

Even within hospitals we find very different kinds of scheduling, each problem showing their own specific properties. In the following these types are introduced to show the typical properties, which also affect the necessity for adaptivity and therefore possible solution approaches:

- *Shift scheduling*: This problem deals with the creation of shift plans. The resource allocation of daily shifts with personnel can be treated as the temporal assignment of shift roles to available nursing staff. Typical properties of this problem are that schedules have to be created *periodically* and for a *fixed planning period* of *discrete* time (days). Usually there is *no need for rescheduling* because unforeseen employee absence (e.g. because of illness) can be compensated by a spare employee. Complex constraints are considering functional issues (e.g. number of nurses of various qualifications per shift), legal issues (e.g. max nightshifts in series), logical issues (e.g. nurse cannot be assigned to two jobs at the same time) and preferences of the staff (e.g. nurse x prefers to work just the early shift). Central planning for shift scheduling is reasonable, because the staff as well as the constraints are very constant. [HePu2004]

- *Appointment scheduling*: Appointment scheduling in hospitals deals with the temporal assignment of examinations, treatments and transport actions (tasks) to certain resources or functional units. In contrast to the previous example, schedules cannot be created periodically. Appointment requests are generated *continuously* and have to be responded in time. Additionally, appointment scheduling deals with an *open planning period* and *continuous* time. Constraints are typically task execution orders, capacities of functional units and minimal stay times of patients. Due to the high probability of unforeseen changes (unexpected task durations, emergencies, etc.) the task execution has to be monitored and tasks have to be rescheduled in case of changes. As already mentioned scheduling knowledge in hospitals is inherently distributed and changes occur quickly, so central systems do not have access to the necessary information and lack adaptivity to comprehensively solve the problem. In a distributed agent based system the problem can be split into small negotiation tasks between task requesters and service providers.

- *Surgery-team-scheduling*: Surgery-team-scheduling is more like organizing meetings than bilateral appointments. It deals with the creation of surgery teams and the temporal assignment to certain resources (e.g. rooms). In contrast to appointment scheduling for patients it involves more people (and therefore objectives from different origins). The systems are very dynamic, since the durations of surgeries are hardly predictable. Typically schedules have to be created *periodically* every day for a *fixed planning period* of *discrete* time. Typical problem constraints are: considering availability of team members, required qualifications of team members and room preferences. An agent based approach providing coordinator agents for each task and different team member agents seems also very suitable, because of the dynamics and distribution.

Table 1. Properties of different scheduling problems in hospitals

	Shift scheduling	Appointment scheduling	Surgery-team-scheduling
Assignment	Shift roles to nurse	Task to functional units/ resources	Task to time
Scheduling times	Periodically (monthly)	Continuous	Periodically (daily, for the next day)
Period length	Fixed	Unlimited	Fixed
Assigned time	Discrete (days)	Continuous	Continuous
Dynamics	Few changes	Many changes, rescheduling	Few changes, but often delays
Complexity of constraints	Many constraints, many interdependencies	Few constraint types, interdependencies	Few constraint types but high number, interdependencies
Knowledge distribution	Slow changing knowledge, centralized	Inherently distributed, spread and changing knowledge	Inherently distributed, spread and changing knowledge

In Table 1 the properties of scheduling problems in hospitals are summarized. Because of their different properties different kinds of solutions are required. Whereas central predictive scheduling works well for

shift scheduling, it has problems when dealing with appointment scheduling and surgery-team-scheduling. Distribution and adaptivity are central to
these problems. With an agent based approach, agents take care of their
own goals and considers the individual local constraints in planning a
schedule. Global conflicts of the schedule have to be negotiated between
the agents. Using this approach the natural distribution of information can
be kept and a practical solution can be generated as well. Furthermore,
agents are capable of quick adaptation to dynamic changes and emerging
conflicts can be solved locally between some of the agents. The principal
drawbacks of an agent based approach to scheduling are that the amount of
necessary information exchange compared to central approaches might be
very high and a more exhaustive search for a solution could be performed
on a central system. Nevertheless, central solutions are not applicable in all
problem domains.

As shown adaptivity and distribution is central to dynamic scheduling
problems like appointment scheduling and surgery-team-scheduling.
Adaptivity is supported by the key properties of intelligent agents. According to several definitions in the literature [WoJe1995] [Ferb1995]
these typical attributes of agents are: situatedness, autonomy, reactivity,
social ability, pro-activity, mobility and learning. In the following, three
aspects of adaptivity supported by agent based scheduling and their relation to the key properties are described:

- *Adaptation to the dynamic environment*: Agents are situated in an environment and are constantly aware of their local situation by their abilities for perception. By interaction with the user or other agents (social
  ability), they can efficiently detect if plan execution is out of synchronization with the schedule, and react promptly. Additionally intelligent
  agents can adapt their behavior and respond to the behaviour of other
  agents. In negotiation they may anticipate certain situations and therefore parameters (like e.g. negotiation thresholds) may be learned.
- *User adaptation*: Software agents can act pro-actively and goal-directed
  based upon the individual configuration and goals of their users. With
  regard to scheduling this includes an individual definition of preferences
  and constraints. Very sophisticated agents may also be able to learn user
  preferences, react accordingly and thus improve the usability of the
  system.
- *System adaptation*: System adaptation means the ability to adapt the
  multiagent system to another situation (e.g. another hospital). This property is supported by the modular design of agent systems. Communication interfaces and protocols for interaction have to be explicitly defined. On the one hand this makes agents candidates for substitution and

on the other hand reusable in different scenarios. They are not statically linked to a domain and are flexibly looking for interaction partners. System adaptation can also be reached by introducing interface or proxy agents to connect the agent system to legacy systems.

5.3 Simulation Toolkit for Hospitals – Hospital Extension of an Agent Simulation Tool

If applications like the ones described in III.4 or [HeHe2004a] are to be evaluated some problems arise. Often a test in the real world is not applicable for reasons of cost or security (see also V.2 Simulation and Evaluation). Also different management decisions for optimization can be taken concerning resources, processes or scheduling strategies. However, certain prognoses on effects and side-effects of probable optimization steps are debatable in most cases. Simulation models help to get better estimations of effects and are therefore useful to support decisions or to design and evaluate novel information systems [Ouel2003]. It would seem that multi-agent simulation in contrast to traditional simulation techniques is especially suited for realizing models of dynamic, distributed systems [SiUr 2001] [KOPD2004] Experiments can be performed quickly, cheap and safely inside the computer.

Nevertheless tool support is crucial for creating experiments. Principally you have to decide between using a general purpose simulation framework and using a domain specific simulation tool. Unspecific tools are usually very versatile but the creation of models is more complicated and time-consuming. Often the application of these tools is a job for simulation experts or programmers. Using domain specific simulation tools typically facilitates fast and easy model creation. Even domain experts may be able to make experiments with simulation models. The drawback of specific tools is that they are not very flexible if the user wants to realize unforeseen use cases.

Specialized but also flexible simulation tools would also be desirable for modeling the scheduling of hospital patients. The organizational structure and the processes in hospitals are not just different from department to department but also from hospital to hospital. The effects of changes may be dependent on hospital specific parameters. Therefore simulation results can not be generalized and the adaptation of the model for different hospitals is necessary. The creation and modification of models to realize new scenarios should be as easy as possible and on the other hand the model should be prepared for future needs.

In this section basic ideas of the hospital simulation are described and a novel construction kit for scheduling scenarios based on the established agent simulation tool SeSAm is presented. This kit is supposed to ease modeling work and provides specialized editors for modeling clinical pathways. Two simulation models are presented in the area of radiation therapy and internal medicine.

5.3.1 State of the Art in Hospital Simulation

Simulation is much more widespread in the manufacturing domain than in health care. Reasons might be that hospitals have neglected cost pressure for many years and that clinical processes are usually more complex and more varying than manufacturing processes. Nevertheless one can find some approaches for hospital simulations in the literature and there are even commercial applications. Task scheduling as well as efficient resource utilization are a very promising field for optimization and therefore tackled very often. For example [ErDO2002] use simulation for the evaluation of a novel appointment system in an outpatient clinic. Agent based approaches for task scheduling in hospitals have also been presented by Decker and Paulussen [DeLi1998] [Pau+2004]. These systems were also evaluated using simulation. Some approaches [Rile1999] [AlCe1999] were initially designed for usage as a decision support system. Within these systems different strategies can be evaluated respecting the given circumstances. Sibbel and Urban have presented an ambitious project for creating an agent-based hospital simulation system and already have the aim of creating a visual general purpose construction kit [SiUr2001]. Many providers of commercial simulation systems have realized the need for simulation in health care and are offering specialized extensions (e.g. Flexsim or Promodel). The major problem of many existing simulation models and systems for hospital simulation is that they do not represent the patient process in its whole complexity. Often a very reduced and simplified set of the actual processes is used. This is critical, because the load of resources may also be influenced by the neglected tasks, and the associated interdependencies between processes may play an important role.

5.3.2 The Role of Clinical Pathways for Appointment Scheduling and Simulation

Clinical Pathways – sometimes also referred to as clinical guidelines – describe the patient processes or task structures in a standardized manner. The introduction of DRG's (Diagnosis Related Groups) for reasons of quality assurance and accounting forced health care officials and physicians to formalize pathways. This pressure generally improved the availability of systematic process descriptions and, as a side effect, the results can be utilized for automated task scheduling and for the creation of realistic simulation models. Nevertheless physicians are usually reluctant to rigidly formalize processes. Another problem is that hampers formalization, is that medical processes are manifold and formal representations from computer science or economic science lack expressivity (if kept simple) or are too complicated to be used by physicians. That is the reason why pathways are often described textually following a structured template. Sometimes descriptive diagrams are used but often without strong semantics. These semi-formal pathway representations are a first step but further formalization has to be made to utilize these pathways in simulation and planning. To acquire the necessary knowledge about pathways in internal medicine, several existing approaches for representing pathways have been examined and the suitability for the simulation purposes was evaluated. Partial order plans are easy to handle by planning algorithms, but as a limitation all specified actions have to be executed and alternatives can not be represented. Decker [Deck1996] has developed the TAEMS framework for the representation of task structures. This framework has useful features, like the representation of required resources or task alternatives. It is suited to planning but for simulation purposes it lacks the possibility of stochastic branching. A further representation for clinical pathways is the Asbru-Language [MiSJ1996].

This representation is very detailed and also allows specifying knowledge about medical decisions. This makes dealing with the language very complicated and the lack of visual modeling makes the work difficult for a medical domain expert. Due to the specific requirements of the project a pragmatic pathway representation was developed. It can be seen as an extension of partial order plans, which integrates task order restrictions, stochastic branches, alternatives as well as complex temporal constraints. A visual editor eases modeling work and guarantees concise pathways (see Figure 1). The appropriateness of the representation has been proved in a case study, where a set of the most common gastroenterological pathways have been implemented.

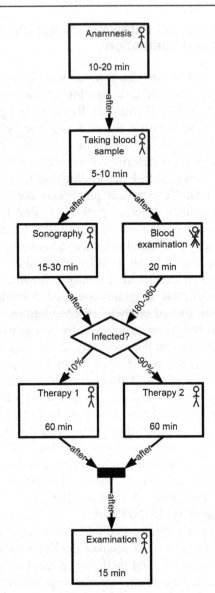

Figure 1. A simplified pathway diagram

5.3.3 A Hospital Simulation Toolkit Based on an Established Agent Simulation Tool

The hospital simulation kit is based on the multiagent simulation environment SeSAm[1] (ShEll for Simulated Agent systeMs). SeSAm already provides many useful features like

- *Visual agent modeling*: Simulation models in SeSAm are constructed completely by visual programming. Editors for the agents' properties are available and the agent behavior is described by UML activity graphs. Agent modelers do not have to learn syntactic notations of a programming language.
- *Integrated simulator*: The integrated simulator interprets and executes the declarative agent model in a time stepped manner. Internal compilation ensures maximal performance.
- *Experimentation support*: For deriving results from simulation, analysis functions can be defined, which record evaluation parameters during simulation. These can displayed in different types of charts (block chart, series charts) or alternatively logged to a file for later processing. Additionally experiment scripts can be defined to execute various simulation runs in a batch job.
- *Extensibility*: A flexible plug-in mechanism allows third party developers to include their own functionality. Interfaces to the SeSAm core and user interface make almost every kind of extension possible. Many useful extensions like database support and ontology support are available.

Despite all the advantages the major drawback is that SeSAm is a general purpose tool and it means still a lot of work to realize complex behavior like negotiation and scheduling from scratch. Therefore the basic idea of the hospital simulation toolkit is to provide a domain specific extension. This extension contains reusable agents, components and corresponding specialized editors. In the following these agents and components are described in more detail.

- *Pathway modeling tool*: SeSAm already provides activity graphs for modeling the agents' behavior. Nevertheless it is advantageous to specify the patient processes separately. As previously described an editor for pathway libraries was implemented. This editor can be used as a small stand-alone tool that can be used by physicians. New pathway libraries are saved as XML-files and can be used by the hospital extension to get realistic treatment requirements within the simulation model.

---

[1] A more detailed description of SeSAm can be found in Chapter V.2 Simulation and Evaluation

- *Time-feature*: The basic SeSAm simulator simulates tick by tick and it does not provide any concrete time model. Using this module for adjustable time, the user can specify the desired relation between a simulation tick and simulated minutes. The time advance can be changed dynamically to speed up simulations during the night or to skip weekends.
- *Timetable-feature*: This feature can be used by *patient agents* as well as by *functional units* to keep their confirmed appointments. Each timetable is associated with exactly one agent. Based on the contents of the timetable an agent might select his next actions. The timetable is also consulted when seeking for appointment proposals or deciding if a proposal will be accepted. Primitive behavior functions allow setting and removing new appointments, as well as asking for the next appointment or getting all appointments of a specific date. During the simulation run, a graphical timetable shows the current appointments of the selected agent (see Figure 2, right).
- *Serviceprovider feature*: This feature provides new properties for organizational units like laboratories, wards and functional units. These entities can be configured in a corresponding user interface. Here the modeler specifies a list of services (examination names) and daily opening hours (see Figure 2, top). Patient agents are able to search for the services and depending on the configuration they can either request an appointment from the functional unit or queue immediately. The service provider feature offers basic scheduling functions to search for suitable appointments and for calculating, if the current simulation time is within the opening times.
- *Patient-feature*: This feature provides new means for modeling patient-agents. Patients generally suffer from any disease. This feature allows the selection of an according pathway from a pathway-library, which is specified with the previously mentioned editor. Patients with pathways associated with severe diagnoses are treated as emergencies. Primitive behavior functions are available to set the state of a task (preconditions fulfilled, task finished) and to determine the next possible tasks. Depending on the desired scenario scheduling functions can be called to negotiate all upcoming tasks with the respective functional units or scheduling can be omitted to directly queue at the functional unit. As an additional functionality the patient feature contains the medical record, showing a protocol of all executed tasks and accumulating the value of the overall waiting times, for statistical evaluation purposes.

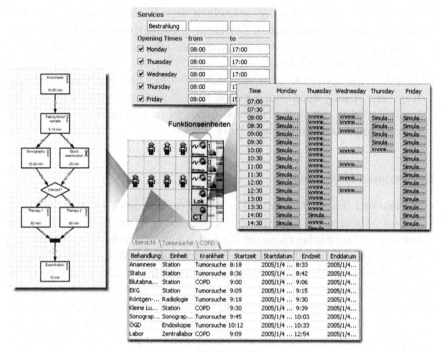

Figure 2. Components of the SeSAm Hospital Extension[2]

5.3.4 Setting up the Virtual Hospital

In the previously described toolkit components are used to construct hospital simulation models. In this section we want to describe supported model parameter in more detail. Model parameters can be divided into measurable evaluation variables and configuration parameters. Some parameters are static environmental parameters and some parameters can be influenced to optimize the system.

Hospital configuration

- *Number and kind of resources*: The number and kind of functional units have an influence on waiting times and average load of resources. The original situation of the exemplar hospital can be modeled by placing predefined agents on a two-dimensional layout sketch of the hospital.

---

[2] Patients and organization units have different new features, specialized to realize scheduling scenarios.

- *Individual configuration of opening times*: Each functional unit may have different opening times. Different opening times may be subject to simulation experiments, because they are easy to realize compared to introducing a new resource.
- *Probabilistic duration of treatment activities*: The expected treatment times are usually determined by the type of task and are specified in the treatment plan. Steps that may be taken to reduce the duration on employing more staff and parallelizing actions.

Environmental parameters

- *Patient mix and arrival rate*: The term "patient mix" denotes the distribution of patients by disease and emergency. It has effects on the upcoming tasks and therefore the load of functional units. The patient mix and the arrival rate of patients are environmental parameters, which are dependent upon the geographical infrastructure and can hardly be influenced for optimization.
- *Reliability of patients to be on time*: The best schedule is not working if patients do not appear in time. Therefore the simulation results regarding the quality of schedules are also dependent upon the reliability and average lateness of the patients. One factor that significantly influences the reliability is the classification as either in-patient or ambulatory treatment.
- *Probability of device failure*: Not just patients but also devices of functional units might be unreliable. Thus the probability of device failures is also an environmental parameter that has effects on patient treatment.

Different types of scheduling

There are many possibilities for how appointments are scheduled and the pathways that are executed. This is highly dependent on organizational and infrastructural circumstances and the means of execution often changes with the introduction of new information technology. The scheduling type also may vary from unit to unit within one hospital. Essentially there are the following types:

- *On-line scheduling*: On-line scheduling means task selection without any predictive planning. Incoming patients or medical samples are put on a queue and are treated one by one. The queue can be managed either by the first-come first-served strategy or priority driven. Priorities might be medical priorities (e.g. emergencies) as well as coordination heuristics. The on-line scheduling strategy needs very little organization and is applicable, if the tasks are very short or the patient's presence is not required (e.g. blood samples in the laboratory).

- *On-line scheduling with call*: To reduce waiting times in on-line scheduling and to make simultaneous queuing at several units possible, some functional units register a patients request and call him, if he is likely to be treated soon. In this case a lead time for the patient to come to the functional unit has to be communicated. This strategy is especially suited for inpatient treatment, if tasks are of unpredictable duration.
- *Predictive scheduling*: Predictive scheduling means that appointments are made in advance. Discrepancies between the actual execution and the schedule have to be compensated by a local waiting queue. Ambulatory patients usually get predictive appointments. Additionally, important and expensive tasks are also often scheduled in advance because a constant load of the resources is cost-relevant and desirable. If confidence of the schedule is of importance, buffer times may be introduced to compensate variable durations of tasks.
- *Predictive-reactive scheduling*: The drawback of predictive scheduling is that it does not deal very well with uncertainties. Waiting times (for patients) and idle times (for functional units) could be avoided, if the task execution was monitored and a dynamic rescheduling process was started after growing discrepancies.

Evaluation parameters

Evaluation parameters are those parameters, which are not initially defined, but result from the simulation. Those are:

- *Average staytime of patients*: This parameter summarizes the average staytime of patients from admission until dismissal. Staytime is an important cost factor, because in most cases the hospitals get a flat rate for each pathway. Therefore the average patient staytime regarding a single pathway is very interesting as well.
- *Waiting times*: Regarding patient satisfaction, waiting times for queuing in front of functional units is also of interest. Especially waiting times related to certain functional units can show bottlenecks in the supply.
- *Resource load*: The load of resources like functional units can be defined by the number of executed treatments a day. Another approach is to compare the relation between active time and idle time. If a functional unit is allowed to do overtime, the number of necessary additional working hours indicates another measure of the load.

- *Number of reschedules*: Hospital configuration and scheduling strategies have influence on the number of reschedules. Whereas the positive aspect of reschedules is that patients have reduced waiting times, the drawback is that frequent reschedules might be annoying for patients as well.

Based on these "adjusting screws" and "indicators" of the hospital simulation toolkit one can realize various experiments answering scheduling or resource questions. For example, a hospital could examine the effects on the average staytime if it were to introduce priority-driven selection of patients. Another hypothesis might be that modern information technology (e.g. automatic phone calls) allows a higher grade of dynamic rescheduling and optimized throughput. Experiments can show how many patients (average arrival date a day) can be treated for a given situation or how many additional working hours would be necessary to deal with a given situation.

5.4 Realized Case Studies

In this section two example simulation models based on the framework are presented in detail. The first example deals with the optimization of radiation therapy (containing rather simple pathways) the second presents the ambitious attempt to depict a rather comprehensive part of a gastroenterological unit.

5.4.1 Simulation of a Radiation Therapy Clinic

Regarding the treatment of cancer radiation therapy plays an important role besides surgery and chemical therapy. Ambulatory patients are usually sent by their local general practitioner.

After their arrival a couple of appointments are made for examinations and adjustment of radiation devices. The scheduling of the first appointment is most critical because it has to be performed at short notice and many constraints (e.g. minimum delay between examinations, etc.) have to be considered. After the first examination in the outpatient department one of three possible treatment plans (clinical paths) is selected. The path determines, which treatment tasks (listed in Table 2) are executed in which order. Different functional units or resources are responsible for task execution: a radioscopy device, where a suitable patient position for radiation can be determined and a further unit to make computer tomography pictures, and finally there are four devices for radiation therapy, each having its own schedule. The first exposure in these units is for adjustment and takes longer than the following daily exposures and there are reserved time intervals for adjustment. As soon as the patients have passed the adjustment, the phase of daily exposures starts for an average treatment time of 30 days. A medical assistant is responsible for the scheduling after the patient's admission. He sends appointment requests to the different functional units and monitors the compliance of the path constraints. Since the times given in Table 2 are just average times, the execution time of single tasks may differ from the pre-planned schedule. A simulation model depicting this scenario was built upon the SeSAm Hospital Framework. It simulates the described scheduling and treatment in the radiation therapy department. Patients with random paths are generated by the simulation. The arrival rate and the random distribution of the paths can be specified by the modeler. Furthermore he can modify the number and opening hours of functional units. By running the simulation evaluation parameters like average stay time, patient throughput and the average load of devices can be measured and shown as a series chart.

Table 2. Table with task durations and order restrictions

	Task	Cond.	Involved resource (amount/opening times)	Duration
1	Pre-localization	before 3	Simulator (1/8:00-17:00)	~20 min
2	Simulation	before 4		~30 min
3	CT	before 2	CT (1/8:00-15:00)	~30 min
4	Adjustment	before 5	Radiation therapy (4/8:30-17:00)	~15 min
5	Exposure			~10 min

For the validation of the model an actual state model has to be created and resulting evaluation parameters are to be compared with reality. In the simulation of the radiation therapy we were able to reproduce real world phenomena like periodical oscillations of the load of certain devices and verify that the maximum patient quantity was consistent with reality. Having validated the actual state model, different simulation experiments can be performed, comparing the original model with alternative settings. Possible questions for a comparison are:

- *Calculation of the maximum load*: The amount of patients can be influenced by modifying the arrival rate, so one can determine the amount of patients that can be treated for a given resource configuration.

- *Effects of buffer times*: Buffer times in the schedule allow a flexible reaction to unexpected changes (like device breakdown or emergencies). On the other hand buffer times might also have negative effects on patient throughput, if the general load is very high.
- *Strategies for dealing with device breakdowns*: If one of the four radiation devices breaks, the available time slots for treatment are reduced. Two strategies might counter this shortage: A second shift can be introduced at one of the working devices or all working devices extend their opening hours and the staff is apportioned to the rest.
- *Strategies to assign patients to radiation devices*: Patients may be treated at one of the four radiation devices. If assigned to one of them, all consecutive treatments have to be performed at this device. This leads to typical periodical oscillations of the load. It's desired to avoid big variations. Effects of different assignment criteria can be evaluated within the simulation.

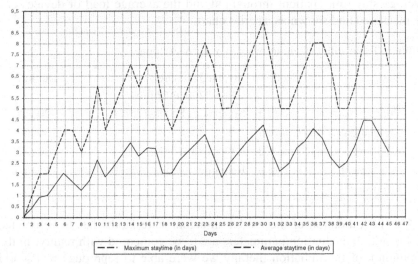

Figure 3. Chart with patient staytime during the simulation of the current situation[3]

Effects of these model changes on the average waiting time of a patient or the load of devices can be easily observed with the analysis charts. Figure 3 shows the average and maximum staytimes according to the real situation. We can observe an average treatment time (from admission until all examinations are finished) of about three days up to a maximum of ten

---

[3]   Variations in the staytime are mainly weekday-dependent.

days (including weekends). An important observation is, that the series chart is not constantly growing, showing us that this resource configuration can handle the current patient arrival rate. The simulation of alternative configurations has shown that the clinic can treat up to three additional patients a day resulting in a slight increase of the average staytime. If more than three additional patients would arrive, other changes – like for example extending working hours – have to be made to compensate the increased patient number.

Another experiment showed how the clinic could balance the load of his devices more effectively (see Figure 4). A new assignment strategy considering the current load and already scheduled dates was evaluated and compared with the current situation. We observed that the periodical variations got better and the maximum load could be reduced with the new strategy.

These two examples show the possibilities given by the toolkit. By using the building blocks similar experiments concerning other questions are quickly realized.

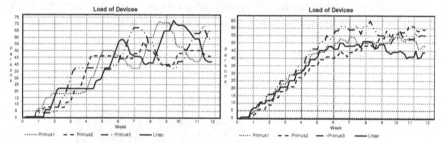

Figure 4. Analysis of the device load[4]

5.4.2 Simulation of Complex Pathways in Internal Medicine

As a second example we realized a simulation model of a clinic for internal medicine. In contrast to radiation therapy there are quite a lot of pathways and patients usually stay in the hospital for several days. Patients in internal medicine tend to be elderly and suffer multiple medical complaints. Therefore one or more pathways are assigned after the initial diagnosis. We have currently collected data about 16 pathways that occur in 46 combinations (multiple complaints). During their stay patients are assigned to a ward that performs the task of care and medication. The patients have to visit several functional units like the sonographic and endoscopic labo-

---

[4]   The left graph shows the current situation, at right side describes the effects of a new strategy.

ratory, the radiological unit or the intracardiac catheter lab. Additionally samples are sent to the central lab or the microbiological unit. On-line scheduling and waiting queues are used to determine the execution sequence of upcoming examination and treatment tasks. The resulting stay-times and waiting hours of patients can be measured as results of the simulation. Figure 5 shows the average patient staytime according to some suffered diseases. We validated this model by a comparison of the simulation results with the actual staytimes. A current project in progress examines the effects of more sophisticated scheduling strategies in this scenario, especially the application of predictive-reactive scheduling. As a prerequisite to introduce these new scheduling methods some hypotheses concerning the communication infrastructure and the outreach ability of patients have to be made. These hypotheses are usually not realistic in the current situation, but the introduction of electronic agent based assistance systems can satisfy the necessary requirements. Thus the simulation can show the potential of the new technology.

Although this scenario has very different characteristics compared with radiation therapy the toolkit also offered useful instruments for the implementation of the model. The variety of configuration possibilities makes it flexible to implement different types of scenarios.

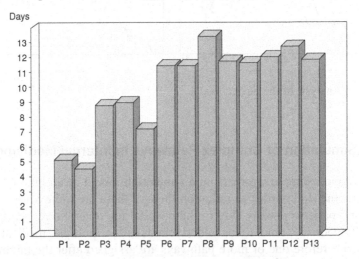

Figure 5. Evaluation of the average patient staytime in days[5]

---

[5] The staytime is separately calculated for every occurring combination of diseases (P1,...,Px). The picture shows just a part of the possible disease-combinations.

5.5 Conclusion and Outlook

Clinical management and physicians are constantly facing the problem of balancing the quality of care against cost efficiency. New information technology and computer applications like agent based assistance agents may be one way to optimize the system. Additionally organizational changes regarding resources or processes may also enhance the system. In many cases the effects of optimization ideas are difficult to foresee. Multi-agent systems are very useful for performing experiments with distributed and dynamic systems like hospital organizations, because their abstraction provides an intuitive and realistic model paradigm. A specialized construction kit for hospital simulations was presented that allows implementing simulations in a fast and simple manner. In summary, this simulation is useful for system developers as well as hospital management for the following reasons:

- discovering the properties of different systems designs (system developer),
- providing a testbed for developing agent applications (system developer),
- supporting management decision-making (management).

A thoroughly validated, realistic model presents credible predictions for the real world system. Creating big and comprehensive simulation models means a lot of modeling work but is also a big challenge. A specialized simulation environment allows the effort to be concentrated on the variable factors like the organizational configuration and the clinical pathways. Whereas the structural part is of limited complexity, the main effort lies in acquiring knowledge of clinical pathways. This problem has been addressed with the development of a new pragmatic pathway representation that meets the requirement of process simulation.

Regarding a comprehensive simulation framework, some challenges remain for the future work. In the current state of development, process costs and the occupation of single employees are not examined. We also have a very good long term perspective to increase the detail level of the simulations. The increased utilization of clinical information systems makes more real world data available for the configuration and validation of simulation models.

References

[AlCe1999]   Alvarez, A. M.; Centeno, M. A.: Enhancing simulation models for emergency rooms using vba. In: Proceedings of the 1999 Winter Simulation Conference.

[Bla+1996]   Blazewicz, J.; Ecker, K.; Pesch, E; Schmidt, G; Weglarz, J: Scheduling Computer and Manufacturing Processes. Springer, 1996.

[DeLi1998]   Decker, K.; Li, J.: Coordinated Hospital Patient Scheduling. In: Proceedings of the Third International Conference on Multi-Agent Systems, (ICMAS98). Paris, France, July 1998, pp. 104-111.

[Deck1996]   Decker, K.: Taems: A framework for environment centered analysis & design of coordination mechanisms. In: O'Hare, G.; Jennings, N. (Eds.): Foundations of Distributed Artificial Intelligence, Chapter 16. Wiley Inter-Science, 1996, pp. 429-448.

[ErDO2002]   Erdem, H. I.; Demirel, T.; Onut, S.: An Efficient Appointment System Design For Outpatient Clinic Using Computer Simulation. In: Proceedings of the 2002 Summer Computer Simulation Conference.

[Ferb1995]   Ferber, J.: Multi-agent Systems. Introduction to Distributed Artificial Intelligence. Addison-Wesley Professional, 1995.

[HeHe2004a]   Herrler, R.; Heine, C.: A4care: Persönliche Assistenzagenten für die Klinische Pflege. In: Künstliche Intelligenz 19(2004)3, pp. 56-58.

[HeHe2004b]   Herrler, R.; Heine, C.: The adapt toolkit-supported engineering process for agent based applications. In: Proceedings of the Tenth Americas Conference on Information Systems (AMCIS 2004). New York, 2004, pp. 1794-1805.

[HeHK2002]   Herrler, R.; Heine, C; Klügl, F.: Appointment scheduling among agents: A case study in designing suitable interaction protocols. In: AMCIS 2002 Proceedings, Dallas, pp. 1456-1463.

[HePu2004]   Herrler, R.; Puppe, F.: Computerunterstützte, doppelt interaktive Schichtplanung für Pflegepersonal. In: Abstraktband des Internationalen wissenschaftlichen Kongress für PflegeInformatik ENI2004. Innsbruck, 2004.

[Hest1999]   Hestermann, D.: Wizard: A system for predictive, reactive and interactive multi-resource scheduling. In: Proceedings der Konferenz Planen und Konfigurieren (PuK 1999).

[Jenn2000]   Jennings, N. R.: On agent-based software engineering. In: Artificial Intelligence 177(2000)2, pp. 277-296.

[KOPD2004]   Klügl, F.; Oechslein, C.; Puppe, F.; Dornhaus, A.: Multi-Agent Modelling in Comparison to Standard Modelling, In: Simulation News Europe 40(2004), pp 3-9.

[KlHO2003] Klügl, F.; Herrler, R.; Oechslein, C.: From simulated to real environments: How to use SeSAm for software development. In: Schillo, M. (Ed.): Multiagent System Technologies - 1st German Conferences MATES (LNAI 2831), 2003, pp. 13-24.

[KOPD2002] Klügl, F.; Oechslein, C.; Puppe, F.; Dornhaus, A.: Multi-agent modelling in comparison to standard modelling. In: Giambiasi, N.; Barros, F. J. (Eds.): AIS'2002 (Artificial Intelligence, Simulation and Planning in High Autonomy Systems), pp. 105-110.

[KPRT1998] Klügl, F.; Puppe, F.; Raub, U.; Tautz, J.: Simulating multiple emergent behaviors - exemplified in an ant colony. In: Adami, C.; Belew, R.; Kitano, H.; Taylor, C. (Eds.): Proceedings of Artificial Life VI, Los Angeles. MIT Press, 1998.

[MiSJ1996] Miksch, S.; Shahar, Y.; Johnson, P.: Asbru: A task-specific, intention-based, and time-oriented language for representing skeletal guidelines. SMI Technical Report No. SMI-96-0650, 1996.

[Ouel2003] Ouelhadj, D.: A Multi-Agent System For The Integrated Dynamic Scheduling of Steel Production. PHD-Thesis, University of Nottingham, August 2003.

[Park2001] Parker, M. T.: What is Ascape and why should you care? In: Journal of Artificial Societies and Social Simulation - JASSS 4(2001)1.

[Pau+2004] Paulussen, T. O.; Zöller, A.; Heinzl, A.; Pokhar, A.; Braubach, L.; Lamersdorf, W.: Dynamic patient scheduling in hospitals. In: Coordination and Agent Technology in Value Networks. Multikonferenz Wirtschaftsinformatik, Agent Technology in Business Applications. Essen, 2004.

[Pine1995] Pinedo, M.: Scheduling: Theory, Algorithms and Systems. Prentice-Hall, New Jersey, 1995.

[Rile1999] Riley, L. A.: Applied simulation as a decision support system tool: The design of a new internal medicine facility. In: Proceedings of the 32nd Hawaii International Conference on System Sciences, 1999.

[Saue2000] Sauer, J.: Knowledge-based systems in scheduling. In: Leondes, C. T. (Ed.): Knowledge-Based Systems: Techniques and Applications. Academic Press, San Diego, pp. 1293-1325.

[Schm2000] Schmidt, G.: Scheduling with limited machine availability. In: European Journal of Operational Research 121(2000), pp. 1-15.

[SiUr2001] Sibbel, R.; Urban, C.: Agent-Based Modeling and Simulation for Hospital Management. In: Saam, N. J.; Schmidt, B. (Eds.): Cooperative Agents, Applications in the Social Sciences. Dordrecht, Boston, London, pp. 183-202.

[WoJe1995] Wooldridge, M.; Jennings, N. R.: Intelligent agents: Theory and practice. In: The Knowledge Engineering Review 10(1995)2, pp. 115-152.

6 Active, Medical Documents in Health Care

Andreas Schweiger, Helmut Krcmar

Technische Universität München, Lehrstuhl für Wirtschaftsinformatik
{schweiga | krcmar}@in.tum.de

Abstract. Distributed and heterogeneous information systems can be observed in health care. In order to implement the vision of seamless health care, the boundaries of institutions need to be closed. Furthermore, information needs to be provided to the members of the health care team according to the principle of information logistics for the effective and efficient support of treatment processes. Since health care can be understood as a complex, adaptive system, an agent-based approach for an information system being capable of reacting flexibly to changes in its environment is an adequate solution. After the identification of characteristics of the health care domain the solution concept of active, medical documents is described, complemented by an analysis and development approach for a corresponding agent-based system.

6.1 Introduction

The current discussion in health care focuses on the improvement of patient orientation and quality of medical care. In order to achieve these goals, information technology is attached a considerable value. Medical information is usually distributed among several information systems at different locations, since sundry participants are involved in treatment processes. In order to allow for a seamless and consistent treatment process a uniform maintenance for medical information seems to be adequate. This idea reflects the transition from electronically stored medical information within a single institution to a universally accessible information folder across the borders of institutions and service providers in health care. In order to meet this requirement, we describe an agent-based implementation concept based on active, medical documents and a possible development process. The results were elaborated on within the ASA*inlog* subproject of the German Priority Research Program "Intelligent Agents and Their Application in Business Scenarios".

The remainder of this chapter is structured as follows. In Section 6.2 we start by giving an overview of different implementations of electronic medical documents. We attach a description of a vision of seamless health care. As a result we postulate the need for a uniform medical patient archive.

Section 6.3 describes health care systems as complex adaptive systems. Additionally, we identify deficits in information logistics in health care: health care is characterized by inherent distribution, heterogeneity, and multi-contextuality of information. Information systems for usage within an institution are supplemented through special applications. This accounts for distribution and heterogeneity of information and demonstrates the need for an integrative solution. Software agents are capable of collecting, opening, and preprocessing of data from heterogeneous and distributed data sources. The members of the health care team act at different locations and with distinct intentions and needs. Software agents exhibit proactive and autonomous behavior which is capable of mapping the requirements of the personnel. A hospital is characterized as an open and dynamic environment. This is determined, in some cases, by an ad hoc unknown treatment process, as the diagnosis is established during the hospital stay. The requirement of flexibility is driven by unpredictable resource and personnel conflicts due to emergency situations. Software agents are capable of reacting to such changes in their environment. Proactive behavior is not supported by current hospital information systems. The use of functionalities such as context-based information retrieval would foster the work process of the health care team.

Section 6.4 starts by illustrating the advantages of deploying agent-based systems and their suitability when facing the described problems in information logistics. The core of the proposed agent-based solution is the concept of an active, medical document, which is implemented as a composite software agent. This component encapsulates both medical and coordinative and administrative information. Furthermore, this document allows for the integration of access rights mechanisms. Information is extracted from various sources by dedicated agents and aggregated into the medical document at run-time. This procedure allows for taking into account different ontologies as they exist when integrating various service providers in health care. The active part of the document checks e.g. for current appointments and points to upcoming examinations. Another agent visualizes the aggregated contents and takes into account varying display properties. The analysis of information is carried out at the storage location of relevant data. Only the results of the information collection process are reported back to the document. Processing intensive operations are relocated to the original location of information. The idea of an active, medical document is supplemented by the concept of active, dynamic activity areas which allow for modeling information logistics within a treatment process and take into account treatment processes across boundaries of institutions.

For building an agent based system in the described application domain, the continuous development process described as follows is deployed. The ethnography-based analysis approach, "Needs Driven Approach", provides guidelines as a starting point for an extensive requirement process. The approach's deployment results in the description of domain models. These are transformed to constructs of software engineering by mapping elements of a defined meta-model to elements of agent-based systems. This process is ensued by the application of an architecture-based method for the construction of multiagent systems. This development process identifies the following steps: domain modeling, specialization of a pattern architecture, construction of fragments of the system, integration, and integration and allocation of the subsystems. The proposed approach combines the results of socio-scientific and engineering disciplines. We conclude our contribution and give an outlook to further work in Section 6.6.

6.2 Vision

6.2.1 Patient Records

Before outlining the benefits of deploying a visionary electronic health record, it is important to define what is meant by this term. Medical records comprise not only medical and administrative information, but also co-ordinative data. In line with Waegemann [Waeg1999] we distinguish between several stages of the implementation of an electronic health record (cf. Figure 1):

- An *Automated Medical Record* is defined as being in parallel with paper based documentation. We observe incremental steps in computerization within an institution.
- A *Computerized Medical Record* denotes a completely paperless system within a single institution.
- If all medical data are integrated into a single record within an institution, we refer to it as a *Provider-based Electronic Medical Record*. All information that is distributed among different information systems is integrated into a single information folder.
- *Electronic Patient Records* extend this idea by aggregating information that is distributed among several institutions. The borders across institutions are bridged by a single information repository.
- An *Electronic Health Record* places the focus of the treatment process on the patient in order to allow him or her to control the access to and

modification of the data of an electronic health record. Furthermore, the patient is capable of adding additional information such as wellness and general health information.

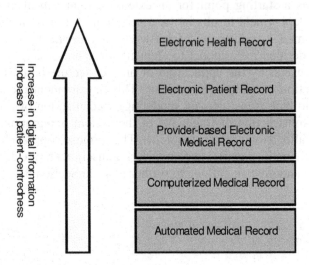

Figure 1. Types of patient records

We aim for an integrative solution across several institutions which allows the patient himself or herself to view or add information that is captured during the treatment process. The electronic health record is designed as a life-long collection of all health related data. Studies clearly show that a significant number of patients is interested in viewing health related information [Ros+2005]. We can clearly conclude that there is an obvious trend towards integrated, patient-centered health records.

6.2.2 Vision

Up until now information systems in health care were mostly reactive systems. In order to support the treatment process and its varying requirements we describe an agent-based medical document that comprises all stages of the treatment process. As an example, consider the following scenario:

A patient consults his general practitioner. Using an identification card which allows access to his medical record, the patient's medical information is retrieved from several and possibly locally distributed information systems. The general practitioner is able to view all medical information about the patient and, using the current description of the patient's illness, provide a diagnosis. When a hospital admission is necessary, the process of admission is automatically negotiated taking into account the current capacity of relevant hospitals. Once at the hospital, assignment to a ward has been previously arranged. The responsible physician has all relevant information which were extracted from hospital information systems of previous hospitalizations together with medical data provided by the general practitioner's information system. After diagnostic evaluation, the patient is assigned a surgery date. However, due to an emergency case, the scheduled surgery needs to be rescheduled. Once surgery has been performed, the results are inserted into the hospital information system. Suggestions for further treatment and medication are dynamically deduced from the patient's health condition. The results of the hospital stay are aggregated and visualized by the general practitioner who provides the patient with nutritinoal advice.

Current information systems are not capable of dealing with the requirements that are described in the previous scenario. There are inherent deficits in information logistics that need to be addressed in order to bring the described scenario to implementation.

6.3 Health Care Systems

6.3.1 Characteristics

Health care is characterized by inherent distribution of information. Typical hospitals are organized into compartments dealing with specialized tasks. Many departments deploy special information systems to meet particular requirements. As a result, there is a typical variety of information systems each storing medical data about patients. Their integration is often implemented using standards like HL7 [Arbo2005]. The potential interoperability within institutions is no longer a problem. Nevertheless, the aggregation of information that is stored in distributed information systems across the borders of institutions needs to be collected.

New research results in treatment processes generate information that needs to be taken into account during the treatment process. Additionally, new methods for treatment and diagnosis generate more data-volume intensive information. As a result, the members of the health care team need to cope with a vast amount of data and information.

The members of the health care team are usually highly specialized in terms of their tasks. These tasks are performed at different locations. Further, the performed tasks differ in terms of goals and tasks need to be co-ordinated in order to accomplish the delivery of effective treatment to the patient. A treatment process consists of several parts, each of which is looked after by one of the health care professionals. All these actors need to cooperate and to communicate in order to achieve the improvement or stabilization of a patient's state of health. As mentioned, the total number of the participating actors is quite significant. Therefore, the demand for personal assistance provided by an adequate information system is high. The relationship between the actors in terms of communication, coopera-tion, and coordination needs to be supported by information systems in or-der to allow for efficient and dynamically changing processes.

Health care is characterized by open and dynamic environments. Flexi-ble treatment processes demand flexible support of the health care team. Current information systems provide static guidance for the health care team members.

For the development of agent-based information systems we need to provide modeling techniques for the described complex system. One ap-proach is described in the following section.

6.3.2 Health Care as a Complex Adaptive System

According to Tan et al. [TaWA2005] health care can be understood as a complex adaptive system. A complex adaptive system is defined as "a collection of individual, semiautonomous agents that act in ways that are not always predictable and whose actions seek to maximize some measure of goodness, or fitness, by evolving over time" [TaWA2005, p.38]. Treat-ment processes are inherently complex, since many different actors with mutually dependent tasks participate. Additionally, the actual treatment process is also characterized by inherent complexity. As there are numer-ous diseases requiring varying therapeutical interventions, and, as patients may react in different ways to different treatments, the "perfect" treatment process cannot always be determined in advance and must be flexible to be applied in a changing environment.

Tan et al. [TaWA2005] described the health care system in terms of the chaos theory. Chaos theory describes systems with nonlinear equations. The output of an equation is put into the next equation. The result of this process yields nonlinearity after several iterations. A chaos system con-tinuously changes and evolves and is therefore an appropriate model for health care as a complex adaptive system [TaWA2005, p. 41]. Because of these characteristics, a health care system cannot be entirely controlled, but can rather only be potentially guided [TaWA2005, p. 43].

After the identification of characteristics of the health care system, which complicate the development of adequate information systems, we propose in the following sections an agent-based solution to the deficits in information logistics in health care.

6.4 Building an Agent-Based Solution

6.4.1 Suitability of Agents

As outlined above, health care is characterized by special properties that make it difficult to develop adequate information systems. These systems must be capable of improving the patient-centeredness and the efficiency of treatment processes while taking into account the flexible adaptations to the patient's health situation. Current research results make us confident that agent-based systems are capable of dealing with the intricacies of complex health care systems (see e.g. [ZaSc2004] [Zach2004a] [Zach 2004b] [More2003] [MoIS2003] [MMGP2002] [BHHS2003]).

The inherent distribution of health care information systems can be adequately tackled by agent-based systems. Software agents can be advantageously deployed for collecting, preprocessing, and interpreting distributed information. Information logistics is a typical application domain for multiagent systems [JeSW1998, p. 27].

Software agents are capable of providing support for managing extensive data volumes. Due to their proactive behavior they can be assigned to collect relevant data and make this data available at the current point in time.

Paper-based medical documents are not only deployed for documentation reasons but also for the coordination between physicians and other members of the health care team. Therefore, an electronic equivalent of paper-based documents must be able to support the communication between the members of the health care team. The concept of an active, medical document implemented as a composite software agent is capable of providing such requirements. Furthermore, software agents are capable of flexible reactions to previously undetermined environmental changes. Hospitals are attached the same characteristics: Various diseases need to be tackled dynamically, since treatment processes are not fully predetermined at the beginning. In addition, emergency cases disturb scheduled appointments and cause rescheduling. The patient's changing health state makes dynamically adapted treatment processes necessary.

As outlined above, health care systems and especially treatment processes in hospitals are inherent complex adaptive systems. Such systems evolve over time through self-adaptation without central control [TaWA 2005, p. 39]. Multiagent systems as such lack a central control because they are inherently distributed. Health care systems modeled as complex adaptive systems can therefore be implemented by an agent-based paradigm. According to Jennings [Jenn2001] multiagent systems are an adequate means for the development of complex distributed systems.

6.4.2 Active, Medical documents

A patient record, regardless of whether it is paper or digital form, serves documentation purposes and at the same time serves as a medium for cooperation and communication within the team. For example, the physician orders an x-ray examination. A nurse arranges an appointment with the radiology department. Following completion of the x-ray, findings and therapy measures are documented in the medical record. This described application highlights the central role of the health record. Due to its central role, the health record needs to be adequately mapped to a software implementation. For this purpose, we propose an approach based upon active, medical documents. Such documents are constructed as composite software agents and are composed of administrative and medical data of the patient. Additionally, other agents enrich the functionality of the health record. They deal with the collection of relevant medical data, the preprocessing for presentation of relevant data and the extraction of data to medical personnel. Furthermore, the agents monitor and trigger appointments, control complex treatment processes, associate similar disease patterns and recommend potential therapies. Additionally, agents grant access to medical data or parts of it. Figure 2 illustrates an excerpt of the described concept. We assume a composite agent to be an aggregate of internal service agents. The specialized service agent ViewManager is responsible for displaying relevant information at the user interface. Before displaying, all information needs to be collected and extracted from various data sources. A DataRetrievalManager is responsible for delegating data retrieval tasks to external search agents. These migrate to the location of the data to be retrieved and extract these. Data may be previously preprocessed and is reported back to the DataRetrievalManager. This manager collects data from the search agents and composes them. A DataWrapper agent is the single point of contact for accessing the medical document. After checking the access rights, the previously described process for data retrieval is triggered.

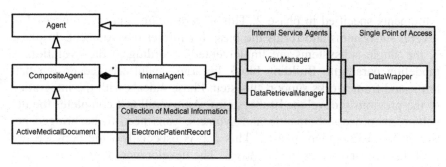

Figure 2. Structure of an active, medical document

A further dedicated service agent controls the process supporting the treatment of the patient. As already outlined, flexible adaptations to determined processes can arise due to emergency situations or a change in health status. Having these considerations in mind, we identify flexibility in terms of production theory. Furthermore, process flexibility is implemented due to a need to change treatment in order to achieve the required outcome, i.e. recovery or stability of the disease. Additionally, changing requirements of the environment result in the selection of potential actions of agents. Therefore, technical flexibility can be observed.

6.4.3 Continuous Development Process

One of the biggest impediments for the penetration of agent-technology is the lack of adequate development methods [LMSW2004, p. 20]. Luck et al. [LMSW2004, p. 20] argued, that basic principals of software engineering need to be deployed when constructing agent-based systems. But these need to be augmented in order to meet the requirements of the agent paradigm. Although there are some established development approaches, Luck et al. [LMSW2004, p. 20] conclude that they are not yet fully mature.

After describing the advantages of using active, medical documents, we describe a continuous development process for agent-based systems to be deployed in the health care scenario. The proposed development process unites socio-scientific (ethnographic) approaches of domain analysis and engineering (architecture-based) methodologies for the design and implementation of software systems. The basic idea is the seamless integration of analysis, design, and implementation methods throughout the development process.

As illustrated in Figure 3 the development process begins by modeling the requirements of the system by means of domain analysis. A general or domain specific pattern architecture is specialized according to the requirements specified in phase 2. This pattern architecture is comprised of several subsystems and forms the basis for further development. In phase 3, the single subsystems are implemented according to the evolutionary modeling paradigm. Building block libraries, agent-oriented design patterns, and frameworks support this step. Phase 4 deals with the integration of the previously developed subsystems. An overall test completes the development process. Semantic and syntactic gaps need to be bridged between the development phases. This gap is especially wide between domain models and architecture models. The development process is simplified by providing transformation rules between the models.

For domain analysis, phase 1, we propose the deployment of the Needs Driven Approach (NDA) [ScKr1996] [Schw2001]. This approach is based on ethnography and exhibits the prerequisite as an observation-based mechanism for capturing work processes and their related elements. The observation is guided by a set of focus areas, which are derived as follows [ScKr1996]: Tasks, processes, structure of interaction, means of work, locations the work is performed in, adoption of technology and structure of informational memory.

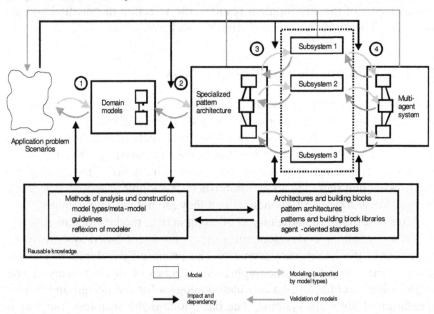

Figure 3. Phases for the development of a multiagent system

The original NDA is refined by detailing guidelines for the observation of the domain to be analyzed. These guide the analysis engineer in capturing the requirements step-by-step [ScKr2005]. The guidelines are separated into several stages and comprise the following five sections (cf. Figure 4). To begin, the work setting, such as rooms, organizational structure and involved actors, must be described. This allows the observer to acquire an orientation within the domain which is needed for gathering further information. The results of these observations are captured in floor plans, organization charts and a list of actors. In section two of Figure 4 the description of tasks and locations where actors accomplish these tasks follows. Users and their tasks are depicted in use case diagrams. By creating these diagrams for different locations, users are mapped to rooms, and the tasks performed in those rooms are identified. This follows an observation of partial work flow and its integration in section three of Figure 4. The treatment process in health care is the focus as it represents the central building block of this domain. Process models describe actions and their dependencies. Actors, necessary material and tools are associated with these actions. Parts of the interaction between actors are often already known at this point as they are provided implicitly by the description of the observed work processes. In section four (Figure 4) these interaction parts are completed, put into a new perspective by detaching them from the work processes, and then described in interaction diagrams. These diagrams constitute an integral part of the Needs Driven Analysis much the same as interactions play an important role in health care (i.e. the collaboration of different health care professionals is essential to deliver a specific treatment). Furthermore, interactions and processes are closely linked. Therefore, the association between interactions and processes is described in detail in section five (Figure 4). By separating processes and interactions, the complexity of diagrams is reduced. The described guidelines provide a general starting point of the requirements analysis. They allow the analyst to get quickly into the field of domain analysis. The guidelines are generally verbalized and are therefore capable of being applied to other domains. Thus, they provide an open framework for requirements analysis.

Since health systems are inherently distributed, there is also the need for modeling processes across the boundaries of institutions. For this purpose, the concept of active, dynamic activity areas [ScKr2004] can be employed. These areas provide an adequate means for interrelating parts of the process models and describing flexible work processes thereby enabling the integration of cross-institutional work flow. An activity area is comprised of actors, their tasks, and the necessary data and tools, e.g. medical devices. It contains explicit or implicit knowledge about the processing of tasks, their decomposition, their forwarding, and delegation. Activity areas are dynamic in terms of adding, removing, or changing the involved actors, i.e. affecting their migration. Actions such as making-up and finishing interactions, changing the process knowledge, and the integration of new data sources or devices all add further dynamic aspects. These activity areas are heterogeneous with respect to their properties, e.g. the used data and its storage.

Figure 5 exemplifies activity areas for a section of the health care domain. Consider a patient visiting an internal medicine ward within a hospital. The patient's activity area, as well as the activity area of the ward including physicians, nurses, information systems, and medical devices, are merged. The information exchange between physicians regarding the medical information about the patient is facilitated by active, medical documents. Additional information about the patient's health status is extracted from clinical information systems. Results of the physical examination, which are relevant for treatment decisions, are shared with a general practitioner via active, medical documents.

- Observe those locations, tasks are performed in.
- Create adequate room models via floor plans.
- Observe the formal organizational structure.
- Map these structures to organizational charts.
- Identify relevant actors.

- Identify actors' tasks.
- Observe the location in which actors perform their tasks.
- Define use case diagrams.

- Describe steps of (partial) work processes that actors perform to accomplish their tasks.
- Identify work material and tools, that actors use to accomplish their tasks.
- Merge the partial processes of the individual actors to complete treatment processes.
- Define process diagrams.

- Observe interaction relationships between actors.
- Classify interaction relationships (e.g. formal or informal)
- Create interaction diagrams.

- Observe the association between interactions and processes.
- Describe informal organizational structure.

Figure 4. NDA-guidelines for the requirements engineer

The concept of activity areas allows for the explication of integration and cooperation between different institutions and thus adds further expressive power to domain analysis. By means of this concept, separated work processes, as identified in the analysis phase, are connected by merging activity areas of different institutions thereby bridging the gap between the boundaries of organizations. This modeling technique reflects the observable trend from separated information systems to integrated health information systems [KuGi2001] [Waeg1999]. The concept of an active, medical document can be embedded seamlessly into activity areas. Since search agents collect relevant medical data and extract these from various, locally distributed information systems, information is able to be shared among different institutions.

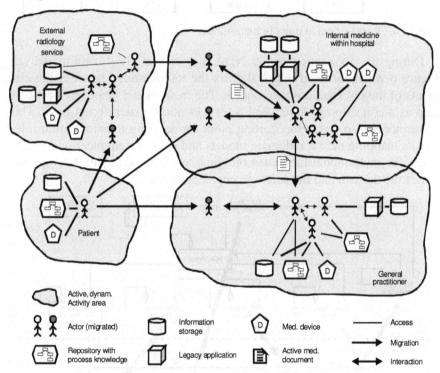

Figure 5. Active, dynamic activity areas

Reinke [Rein2003] described a method for an architecture-based construction of multiagent systems (ArBaCon), depicted in Figure 3. Through the application of the NDA approach in several case studies, we have concluded that this approach is especially suited for capturing the specialties of the health care domain. Since ArBaCon models are described exclusively as pure or enhanced UML constructs, there is the need to transform gathered NDA domain models into constructs of software engineering, in order to apply ArBaCon for the remainder of the development process.

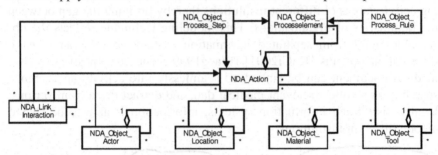

Figure 6. Object-oriented domain meta-model

During the application of the NDA in a case study a meta-model (cf. Figure 6 was conceived which defines the interrelations between the elements of the obtained domain models. The meta-model identifies a process step as a collection of associated actors, location, material and tools. This meta-model also forms the starting point for defining transformation rules for the mapping between domain models and software engineering models. Thus, the meta-model facilitates bridging semantic and syntactic gaps between the domain and the software engineering area.

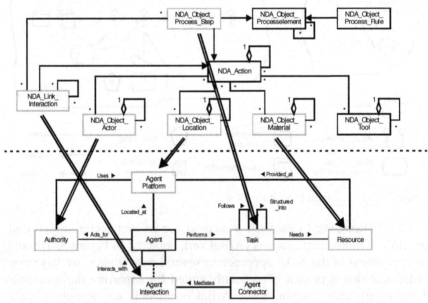

Figure 7. Transformation rules between domain models and constructs of software engineering

As depicted in Figure 7 domain elements are mapped to constructs of software engineering. According to this mapping, an actor of the domain is represented by the authority on behalf of which an agent acts. Locations are mapped to agent platforms which can reside on locally distributed nodes. Identified process steps are carried out through the agent's tasks. Material such as documents are represented by resources which the agents use when performing their tasks. Applying these transformation rules, the seamless integration of elaborated domain models using description techniques, which are similar to the domain into the ArBaCon method, is facilitated.

6.5 Evaluation

As described by Hevner et al. [HMPR2004], a fundamental element of the applied design science approach in information systems includes an evaluation of the constructed solution. The goal of the evaluation is to show the usefulness of the described agent-based approach.

As an evaluation method, a comparison to current information systems is a reasonable approach. According to the requirements for information systems in health care, these systems need to provide information in compliance with the principle of information logistics. This principle is defined as follows [Augu1990]: The right information is provided at the right point of time, in the right amount, at the right place, and in necessary quality. Current information systems are usually isolated solutions exhibiting export functionality. As a result, electronic information exchange is usually restricted to special data formats, if any. Agent-based systems allow for the integration of non-agent applications and the extraction and provision of relevant data. Therefore, software agents enable the vision of seamless health care. Furthermore, software agents allow for the reorganization and rescheduling of treatment processes according to changes in timetables and the patient's health status. Thus, an agent-based solution provides added value in comparison to current information systems in two dimensions.

6.6 Conclusion and Outlook

This chapter described the deployment of agent-based systems in health care. We began by giving definitions for different forms of electronic patient records. Since more and more patients are interested in viewing their medical data, the trend towards an electronic health record is gaining support not only by the needs of medical personnel, but by the demands of patients as well. Electronic Health Records maximize the self-determination of patients and extend the boundaries of electronic communication. We identified the missing data interchange between heterogeneous information systems as the prevailing challenge regarding the provision of integrated and seamless health care which includes the communication across boundaries of institutions. Furthermore, information logistics, i.e. the communication, cooperation, and coordination processes needs to be supported adequately by information systems. We showed that health care systems can be understood as complex adaptive systems and can be modeled by multiagent systems. Therefore, we propose an agent-based solution for future information systems in health care. Our agent-based solution focused on the provision of an adequate system to meet the complex demands of communicating and coordinating treatment. We described the concept of an active, medical document which is implemented as a composite software agent. For the development of an agent-based system we described a process model which unites socio-scientific and engineering methods in order to analyze the domain and build an agent-based system step-by-step. In order to bridge syntactic and semantic gaps between domain models and models of software engineering, we defined transformation rules. These transformation rules map domain model elements to constructs of agent-based engineering.

The outlined approach for the construction of multiagent systems for deployment in health care is currently being applied. The basis of the resulting prototype is formed by the implementation of an agent-based active, medical document. Using this approach, a hospital information system is embedded into the agent system. Active documents will be enriched for the support of flexible, dynamically changing treatment processes. Furthermore, the patient is empowered by giving web-based access to all medical data and by allowing the addition of personal health-related data. Finally, data consistency and persistency need to be tackled in an extended implementation.

References

[Augu1990]   Augustin, S.: Information als Wettbewerbsfaktor: Informations-
              logistik - Herausforderung an das Management. Verlag TÜV
              Rheinland, Köln, 1990.
[BHHS2003]   Beer, M.; Hill, R.; Huang, W.; Sixsmith, A.: An agent-based ar-
              chitecture for managing the provision of community care - the

INCA (Intelligent Community Alarm) experience. In: AI Communications 16(2003)3, pp. 179-192.

[Arbo2005]   Health Level Seven, I., Ann Arbor, MI: Health Level Seven Internetseite, 2005. http://www.hl7.org/, accessed on 2005-03-15.

[HMPR2004]   Hevner, A. R.; March, S. T.; Park, J.; Ram, S.: Design Science in Information Systems Research. In: MIS Quarterly 28(2004)1, pp. 75-106.

[Jenn2001]   Jennings, N. R.: An Agent-Based Approach for Building Complex Software Systems. In: Communications of the ACM, 44 (2001)4, pp. 35-41.

[JeSW1998]   Jennings, N. R.; Sycara, K.; Wooldridge, M.: A Roadmap of Agent Research and Development. In: Autonomous Agents and Multi-Agent Systems, 1(1998)1, pp. 7-38.

[KuGi2001]   Kuhn, K. A.; Giuse, D. A.: From Hospital Information Systems to Health Information Systems: Problems, Challenges, Perspectives. In: Methods of Information in Medicine 40(2001)4, pp. 275-287.

[LMSW2004]   Luck, M.; McBurney, P.; Shehory, O.; Willmott, S.: Agent Technology Roadmap: Overview and Consultation Report. http://www.agentlink.org/roadmap/, accessed on 2005-04-07.

[More2003]   Moreno, A.: Agents applied in health care. In: AI Commu-nica-tions, 16(2003)3, pp. 135-137.

[MoIS2003]   Moreno, A.; Isern, D.; Sánchez, D.: Provision of agent-based health care services. In: AI Communications 16(2003)3, pp. 167-178.

[MMGP2002]   Mouratidis, H.; Manson, G.; Giorgini, P.; Philp, I.: Modeling an agent-based integrated health and social care information system for older people. Paper presented at the International Workshop on Agents applied in Health Care at the 15th European Conference on Artificial Intelligence (ECAI), Lyon, France, 2002.

[Rein2003]   Reinke, T.: Architekturbasierte Konstruktion von Multiagentensystemen. Dissertation, Universität Potsdam, 2003.

[Ros+2005]   Ross, S. E.; Todd, J.; Moore, L. A.; Beaty, B. L.; Wittevrongel, L.; Lin, C.-T.: Expectations of Patients and Phy-sicians Regarding Patient-Accessible Medical Records. In: Journal of Medical Internet Research 7(2005)2, Article e13.

[Schw2001]   Schwabe, G.: Bedarfsanalyse. In: Schwabe, G.; Streitz, N.A.; Unland, R. (Eds.): CSCW-Kompendium: Lehrbuch zum computerunterstützten kooperativen Arbeiten. Springer, Berlin et al., 2001, pp. 361-372.

[ScKr1996]   Schwabe, G.; Krcmar, H.: Der Needs Driven Approach: Eine Methode zur bedarfsgerechten Gestaltung von Telekooperation. In: DCSCW 1996, pp. 69-88.

[ScKr2004]   Schweiger, A.; Krcmar, H.: Multi-Agent Systems for Active, Dynamic Activity Areas. In: AMCIS 2004, pp. 242-245.

[ScKr2005]   Schweiger, A.; Krcmar, H.: Designing Multi-Agent Systems - The NDA-Approach Applied in Health Care. In: AMCIS 2004, pp. 1011-1019.

[TaWA2005]   Tan, J.; Wen, J. H.; Awad, N.: Health Care and Services Delivery Systems as Complex Adaptive Systems. In: Communications of the ACM 48(2005)5, pp. 36-44.

[Waeg1999]   Waegemann, C. P.: Current Status of EPR Development in the US. In: Toward An Electronic Health Record Europe. London, 1999, pp. 116-118.

[Zach2004a]   Zachewitz, L.: Konsistenzsicherung in agentenbasierten Informationssystemen. In: 16. GI-Workshop über Grundlagen von Datenbanken. Heinrich-Heine Universität Düsseldorf, Monheim, pp. 118-122.

[Zach2004b]   Zachewitz, L.: MEDUSA: A Multiagent System for Establishing Electronic Healthcare Records. In: 16th European Conference on Artificial Intelligence (ECAI 2004), Workshop 7: Second Workshop on Agents Applied in Health Care. Valencia, Spain, 2004, pp. 31-37.

[ZaSc2004]   Zachewitz, L.; Schwolow, A.: MEDUSA: Agentensystem zur intra- und interinstitutionellen Zusammmenführung von Patienteninformationen. In: Interdisziplinärer Workshop KIS / RIS / PACS. Schloss Rauischholzhausen, 2004.

7 Self-Organized Scheduling in Hospitals by Connecting Agents and Mobile Devices

Torsten Eymann

Universität Bayreuth, Lehrstuhl Wirtschaftsinformatik (BWL VII)
torsten.eymann@uni-bayreuth.de

Günter Müller, Moritz Strasser

Universität Freiburg, Institut für Informatik und Gesellschaft
{guenter.mueller | moritz.strasser}@iig.uni-freiburg.de

Abstract. This chapter describes the conceptualization and realization of a real-time managed mobile information system in healthcare. The particular application addressed is a dynamic, self-organized scheduling of the treatment of patients. Building blocks for this project are locatable, interactive Personal Digital Assistants (PDAs) to connect medical staff and patients; physical resources are connected by locatable Radio Frequency Identification (RFID) chips. These physical objects are represented in the information system by software agents. The multi-agent platform EMIKA implements a negotiation-based schedule system to enable a dynamic planning process. The EMIKA-System has been developed to prototype level and functionally tested in a real-time laboratory [SaEM2002]. Lessons learned from the realization pertain to technical functionality and to privacy and security issues.

7.1 Problem Definition and State of the Art

In classical information systems, a centralized scheduler using allocation rules creates an optimized appointment plan; however, due to the high dynamics of the hospital environment, the appointments have to be constantly adapted. This way scheduling becomes a continuous, never-ending process. Especially in life-crucial environments, as in hospitals, any hold-ups can have severe consequences. This chapter addresses a flexible real-time reaction to hold-ups. Scheduling patient logistics can be regarded as an ill-structured task [Schl1990], since it requires the assessment of treatment priorities and the allocation of resources, e.g. doctors' time and availability. Unforeseeable hold-ups due to emergencies, delayed patients and varying treatment times prevent a complete advance mapping of the entire tasks and thereby a reliable planning of individual treatment schedules. Various planning goals compete with one another. A minimum throughput time of patients and a maximum allocation of resources cannot be simultaneously optimized [Gäfg1990]. Different scheduling mechanisms work in parallel. Outpatients are summoned to prefixed appointments; emergency patients always lead to a real-time adaptation of whatever schedule exists at that point in time and inpatients are summoned from the wards in the event of under-allocated resources [ScCZ1996]. All three scheduling types have in common that, for treatment, patients need resources in the form of a doctor and diverse medical equipment.

The approach to handle this complexity of scheduling in EMIKA[1] is to divide the complex task into several less complex subtasks [CyMa1963]. The divided tasks, however, remain loosely connected, in order to buffer goal conflicts and to model a highly dynamic and complex environment like a hospital for three reasons:

1. There are three types of patients with conflicting scheduling strategies: Outpatients require planning reliability to be able to coordinate the appointments with their activities outside the hospital (predictive scheduling). Inpatients are summoned directly in the course of time when the required resources are available (dispatching). Through urgent appointments (emergencies) or cancellations, the already existing and optimized appointment sequences must be additionally amended (reactive scheduling). Other projects using software agents focused on improving predictive scheduling concepts, which try to generate an optimized patient flow sequence under several scheduling constraints and optimization parameters well in advance of the real treatment execution time (see III.3 and III.4). The EMIKA project can acknowledge such optimized sequences and incorporates changes initiated by real-time events.

2. Optimizing schedule sequences: Even when only a limited number of auxiliary conditions are observed, this is an NP-hard problem due to the exponential number of alternate solution paths [GaJo1979]. The non-observance of dependencies on other appointments, the full utilization of the resources and the aims of the actors would create further disruptions in a 'domino effect' and thereby lead to a generally less efficient coordination result.

3. Because the requirements and general conditions in a hospital are not precisely known in advance, uncertainty is inherent in the system and makes exact planning almost impossible. Job-shop scheduling using

---

[1] *Echtzeitgesteuerte mobile Informationssysteme in klinischen* Anwendungen (Real-time mobile Information Systems in clinical Applications) – Institut für Informatik und Gesellschaft, Abt. Telematik (http://www.telematik.uni-freiburg .de/emika/)

deterministic data cannot be applied, as hospital processes cannot assume having a given quantity of orders, production facilities and constant processing time [KuRo1995].

7.2 A Layered Realization of Agent-Based Mobile Healthcare Information Technology

Supporting hospital procedures with information systems requires having a constant up-to-date picture of the locations and intentions of hospital resources and actors. In the EMIKA experimental system, the actors and resources are modeled using software agents, which get their information about the physical reality through a networking infrastructure employing PDA and RFID tags to track resources. The emerging multiagent system coordinates through self-organizing behavior, evaluating the opportunities and limitations of this approach. Why agents and multiagent systems are beneficial for such environments can be found in Part I. "What Agents Are And What They Are Good For?" of this book.

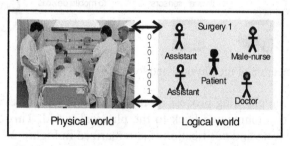

Figure 1. Physical and logical world

EMIKA divides the application scenario into the *physical* world and its information system model, the *logical* world as seen in Figure 1. The physical world encompasses the concrete, tangible hospital environment, which is occupied by patients, physicians and other hospital staff. Parameters of the physical world, such as the location of a resource, the current task of a physician and the waiting time of a patient are sensed by information technology and modeled using digital data structures of the logical world. The projection of the physical world generates a logical mirror image, which is closer to reality the more often the projection is made – preferably in real time [HoNE2004]. At the same time, the complex real world data is retrieved in digitalized form – the mirror image is always a simplified model. The logical mirror image enables hold-ups and alternative treatment paths to be identified and is the precondition for further flexible reactions (see I.3).

The *modus operandi* of the logical world is automated decision making, after having analyzed the detected states and processes of the physical world. The "logical world" of patient logistics detects and relays where queues build up before surgeries, which treatment takes longer than expected, and which resources or staff members are currently available or occupied. The procedures which are necessary for continuous planning, making appointments and coordination of processes handle this information [Cor+2003].

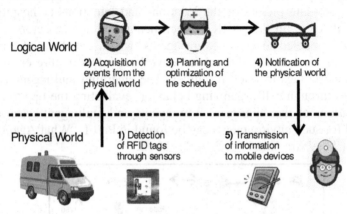

Figure 2. Connection of the physical and logical world

Executing the planning process alone has little effect however, if the results are not communicated back to the physical world. This cycle of detection, processing and notification is summarized in Figure 2.

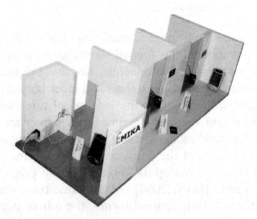

Figure 3. EMIKA scale model

EMIKA's research efforts combine simulations, prototypical and empirical methods. A scale model of a hospital department, shown in Figure 3, has been equipped with realistic information technology for the purpose of a technical and functional evaluation. The scale model allows for the testing of the hospital logistic processes and their coordination without affecting the extremely sensitive hospital procedures. The technical configuration of the model comprises RFID readers on the door frames and RFID tags on all movable resources, whose change in location can be recorded in the physical sphere and transmitted to the information system. The resources generate a data stream when they pass through the doors, which yields location information through pre-processing in the receiver process and logical interconnection with the previous location.

7.2.1 Communication Layer

RFID readers are attached to the door frames (see Figures 3 and 4). The passing of an RFID chip fixed to a mobile object ("tag") through an RFID reader produces a "passing" event. The reader sends a signal on a standardized frequency (here 13 MHz) which is received by the passive tag that has no power supply of its own. The electrical impulse is sufficient enough to stimulate the tag processor which then sends back an identifying bit string of up to 128-bit. The RFID reader forwards this identification to an information system for further processing.

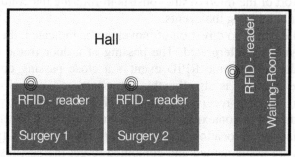

Figure 4. Plan of the scale model

Such passing and location information can also be gained via other channels. In the EMIKA prototype, additional infrared data can be processed. Infrared (IrDA) beacons are fixed in the rooms in such a way that a certain area is covered (see Figure 5). Objects with infrared receivers can receive and send data at any time as long as they are within the range of an IrDA beacon. Alternative location detection methods like triangulation with radio cell-based wirelessnetworks e.g. Bluetooth, W-LAN, GSM, UMTS and satellite navigation systems e.g. GPS or GALILEO do not provide the required accuracy for indoor positioning in the EMIKA-System.

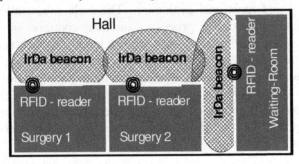

Figure 5. Combination of RFID and IrDA technologies

7.2.2 Middleware Layer

The amount of information generated by the hardware is huge and ambiguous. On the one hand, continuous identification data is transmitted from the RFID readers, which does not however result in any change in condition in the physical world. Only the first contact between reader and RFID tag marks the actual incident (entering or leaving a room). The transformation effort of the middleware consists in filtering the continuous data stream and only relaying the events.

Furthermore, since no direction of movement is indicated, the event data can be ambiguously interpreted. The passing of a door frame in both directions produces the same RFID event – a close passing or a turning-around in the doorway is also thereby not recognized as such. To handle this problem, the data received from the RFID reader must be pre-processed with the aid of context knowledge in such a way that a clear as possible determination of location is reached. In the EMIKA prototype, different solutions are implemented and combined to get the best results for location information.

To illustrate the problem, a map of the scale model is shown in Figure 4. There is an RFID reader at the door between surgery 1 and the hall. If an individual passing event is discovered at this door, it is not clear whether the carrier has moved from the hall to surgery 1, or vice-versa. The current realization relies on a history, which is adjusted after each event. For example, if the last position was surgery 1, a new reader event at the door would change the location information to the hall.

This mode of operation seems trouble-free as long as all reader events are detected. In a real operating environment, however, it is possible that through concealment, movement beyond the range or the passing of several tags at the same time, reader events are lost. The resulting inconsistency between the last entry in the history of the object and the actual situation increases with each lost event.

In order to solve this problem, a graph of the environment models the rooms as states and the doors as edges. In the case of lost events, the possible paths between the last reader event and the actual measured event are examined. The approach can be illustrated using Figure 6. For example, if a reader event is lost when the object leaves the hall towards the waiting-room, the location information becomes inconsistent. If the ensuing reader events were waiting-room/hall and hall/surgery 1, the intersection of both events would be the hall. From this, it can be concluded that the object is now, after the last event, in surgery 1. Nevertheless, if the error frequency is relatively high and many reader events are omitted, the reliability of the position determination inevitably decreases or becomes impossible.

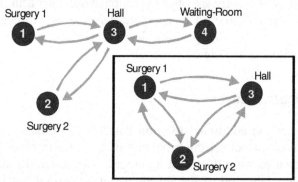

Figure 6. Environment graph

In particular, cycles in the environment graph are a problem (see box in Figure 6). A known position in *surgery 1* and a lacking reader event at the door between *surgery 1* and *surgery 2* leads to a situation in which the next event (door *surgery 2/hall*) cannot be interpreted: there is not enough information to decide in which direction this door has been passed. A remedy for this problem is the application of two or more RFID tags attached to the mobile objects.

Figure 7 shows a multi-tagged object passing an RFID reader fitted on the wall. The object is fitted with four differently positioned tags. On the assumption that every person enters a room forwards, it is possible to determine the direction of movement of the object on the basis of the chronological order of the contact of two side tags. The reader quality of the tag data can offer further information regarding the movement: a tag, which is held almost parallel to the induction lines of the reader (this is label 1 in Figure 7) is activated more quickly than the more badly positioned label 2. Only when the carrier moves further forward does the situation change and the identification of label 2 becomes "visible".

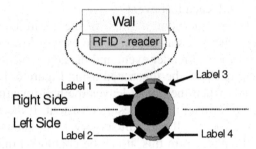

Figure 7. Object fitted with multiple tags

A directory service compares the recorded identification of the hardware with the address of a software object (or a database entry). In the EMIKA prototype, data management is carried out decentralized through the individual agents. The recorded position data is therefore sent directly to the respective agents via messaging protocols.

7.2.3 Application Layer

On the basis of the additional location data, the information system can now *immediately* detect arising problems such as, for instance, long waiting queues or a missing doctor in a surgery. The reaction time increases and a flexible adaptation of the schedule can be carried out in real-time [EySM2003].

7.2.3.1 Negotiation of Priorities

The currently prevailing planning variable for optimizing scheduling and reservations is time duration. The waiting periods of patients in hospital should be minimized; the utilization of medical equipment should be maximized (see also III.4).

In EMIKA, a virtual time-dependent monetary substitute in the form of time points is introduced as coordination variable and constitutes the direct connection to the optimizing time variable. The time points enable the evaluation of the time required in hospital. The patients pursue the strategy of completing all their treatment in the shortest time. Through the selection of the most cost-favorable resource at a point in time in each case, overall "costs" are minimized. Compensation for waiting periods spent includes the throughput time into the optimizing strategy in which the patients experience constantly increasing priority. All hospital resources try to arrange their appointments as closely together as possible and to treat the highest priority first, calculated in time points gained. This creates a demand and time-dependent price function which signalizes the actual capacity of the resources. With increasing utilization, the price for the remaining capacity increases. A comparison of the prices of two corresponding resources by the patients leads to a relative control function, which prefers cheaper (less requested) resources.

Predictive scheduling takes place in order to build up an optimized treatment sequence, which defines the order in which the patients should arrive at the hospital. The effect of changes in scheduling (e.g. emergencies) is that they tend to rearrange the sequence; without disturbances, we just have to preserve that given order. A First-in-First-out condition guarantees that the pre-arranged, optimized sequence persists until no further event (e.g. emergency) occurs and changes of the scheduled sequence become necessary. A given sequence for the scheduling is considered in a market-based coordination [Eyma2003] as auxiliary condition with the result that patients of the same group, with the same needs and in the same situation, obtain reservations in the sequence in which they enter into the system (hospital). The compensation of the waiting period ensures that those patients of a group, which are in the system (hospital) earlier, always have a higher budget than the patients from the same group entering later.

The goal of the dispatching strategy is to schedule inpatients when resources are in low demand. Instead of the price level falling to near zero at idle times, the inclusion of inpatients aims at keeping utilization continuous. Inpatient bids are set so low that they are not considered during a constant flow of outpatients. In the market mechanisms, inpatient bids are constantly included, but raise only slightly during waiting times. Only when the resource prices fall lower than a flexible and endogenously emergent threshold are those bids automatically taken into account. With the capability to predict a future abundance of resource capacity, it may be possible to call patients directly from the wards. For the experiment shown here, we assume a near-zero transport time.

Through reactive scheduling, a "normal" process is adapted according to the situation. Existing appointments are replaced and individual decisions and plans change. As the emergency patients arrive with a higher budget, the respective emergency resources react by raising their prices over a threshold where normal outpatient bids can no longer compete. This leads to an almost exclusive availability of the emergency resources for emergency patients. The various and individual payment reserves lead to a partitioning of the market in layers according to available budget. Once the emergency patients have been treated, the high-priced demand disappears and the market re-integrates.

Treatment coordination is achieved through direct negotiation between software-agents, which signal the desired schedules (goals) on behalf of the actors involved in each case. The negotiation parameter (which indicates scarcity and priorities) basically is time, perceived as busy times of hospital resources and waiting times for patients.

7.2.3.2 Connection to Physical World

The first step for communication with external devices is the transfer of data out of the information system onto the external units. Basically, two ways of addressing can be pursued, either that of the person or the location. If the hospital staff is equipped with personal, mobile end devices (PDAs, beepers), a direct communication with this end device is the best way. After the planning system has figured out which person has to either actively make or passively confirm an alteration, the end device allocated to this person is addressed. If such a direct allocation is not possible (e.g. in the case of patients), the location at which the person presently finds himself can also be addressed instead of the person himself [Zuge2003].

A special aspect is the change of plans for devices which cannot act by themselves in the physical world. A wheelchair or a mobile diagnostic apparatus required at another location cannot move itself. In this case, the transport order must be sent to the external device of a transport service assistant, who then performs the necessary change in the physical world.

Figure 8. Notification of the user about a rescheduling

The external units and internal objects of the information system must be able to communicate with each other via a common interface. In EMIKA, this is realized via Java sockets which transport XML-based messages. Moreover, the addressing of the external units on the systems level takes place via permanently allocated IPv4 addresses.

The wireless transfer of information to a PDA or a Tablet-PC also takes place in the hospital via customary radio technologies. In order to guarantee the necessary reachability, RFID cannot currently be implemented, as the time of the next connection is uncertain. Technologies with higher reachability and thereby also higher energy expenditure and exposure are Wireless LAN and Bluetooth. The deployment of mobile telephone technologies like GSM, GPRS or UMTS do not offer any guarantee of reachability in closed buildings, such as hospitals, due to their screening effect.

When the information has finally been received by the persons in the physical world, they can evaluate and confirm the received data (cf. Figure 8), but also alter or ignore it on the basis of their own knowledge. Even ignoring provides the system in turn with further information (e.g. the notified doctor could have no opportunity to reply due to an emergency) and thereby initiates a feedback to the renewed rescheduling process.

7.2.4 Simulating Self-Organized Scheduling in the Application

The realization of the prototype alone does provide some insight into the technical feasibility of connection agents and mobile information technology, and thus the vertical link between the physical and the logical world. However, the horizontal adaptation within the logical world can only be evaluated using agent-based simulation (see V.2 for a discussion of agents in simulations). In the following section, we have used an agent-based simulation of the patient logistics application, which was realized using the SeSAM toolkit (see III.5).

In the logical model of the hospital environment, each patient and each resource is represented by a software-agent. Treatment coordination is achieved through direct negotiation between these software-agents, which signal the desired schedules (goals) on behalf of the actors involved in each case. Using the time-dependent monetary substitute, EMIKA creates an internal economic market platform for treatment schedules [StEy2004].

A waiting room, an emergency treatment room and two "normal" treatment rooms were modeled as resources in the simulation. In the course of the simulation, the hospital environment generates a set number of inpatients, a constant stream of outpatients and a random number of emergency patients at irregular intervals (see Figure 9).

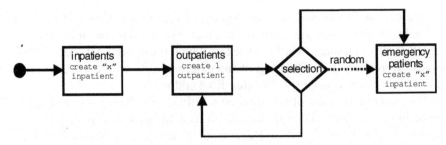

Figure 9. Modeling of the hospital environment

The various patient types are represented by various groups of patient agents (see Table 1). The outpatients, who require treatment in any of the three treatment rooms; the inpatients, who can be directly summoned for treatment and the emergency patients, who require treatment in the emergency treatment room only. Each individual software agent represents a group-specific strategy, which is determined according to medical objectives through individual needs, starting budget and waiting-time compensation.

Table 1. Parameter of the individual groups of patient agents (TU = time unit)

	Outpatients	Inpatients	Emergency
appointment in room	A, B or C	A, B or C	A
starting budget	10 TU	10 TU	20 Tu
waiting-time compensation	1 TU	O,1 TU	5 TU

Any number of patient agents can stay in the waiting room. From there, they negotiate with the resources (treatment rooms) for reservations and increase their budget through spent waiting periods until they obtain a reservation (see Figure 10). Each patient agent can carry out negotiations with those resource agents, for which a medical treatment possibility exists.

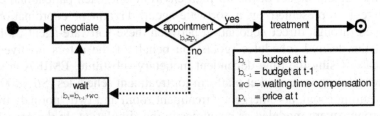

Figure 10. Structure of the patient agents

A treatment room can only be visited by one patient at a time and if he has previously reserved it. The agents of the resources receive information as to how many patients require a resource of their type, on the basis of which they can make an initial price offer (see Figure 11). The vacant resources offer their capacities on the market for treatment schedules through price offers. The patient agents compare the offers of resources suitable to them and make an individual decision. The offer prices sink constantly if no patient has responded to the offers (a_{t-1} = no).

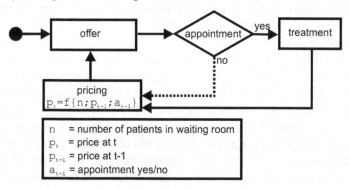

Figure 11. Structure of the resource agents

Experiment No. 1 - The individual negotiations between patient agents and resource agents subsequently lead to a dynamically coordinated procedure, in which treatment sequences are produced and carried out according to the situations arising.

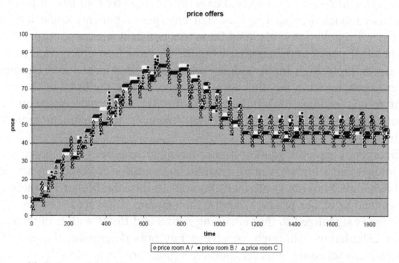

Figure 12. Prices with various patient numbers – above, below and full capacity

If the waiting room fills up, the prices increase, so as to fall again with a lower flow of patients. In the experiments, the market-based coordination mechanism reacts flexibly to the changing situations and enables a continuously adapted order of priority of the treatment rooms. In the course of the experiments, the prices for a treatment schedule of the same length alter depending on the demand (number and type of the patients in the waiting room). Lower prices give incentive to make appointments for "less" demanded treatment rooms.

The individual resources reach their full utilization by booking new appointments through negotiations. The resources accordingly vary their prices depending on the demand and their own capacity. In a preliminary capacity experiment, the hospital environment of the simulation was modeled through three periods with various amounts of patients; time tact 0-500 resources operated above capacity, time tact 500-1000 resources operated below capacity and time tact 1000-1400 resources operated at full capacity. The prices of the resources continuously rise in Figure 12 with an amount of patients which lies above their capacities, fall in the case of a lower amount of patients and remain in a dynamic equilibrium when the amount corresponds exactly to their capacities. The price value of the dynamic equilibrium average is correlated to the actual waiting periods. The dynamic prices thereby reflect, as expected, the actual capacities of the resources. The prices of all treatment rooms show a typical structure for the actual utilization for each situation.

Experiment No. 2 - In a second experiment, the environment of the hospital was modeled in such a way that emergency patients came into the system at irregular intervals in addition to a constant stream of outpatients.

The clear peaks in the centre of Figure 13 show how emergencies (with correspondingly high input budget) remove the treatment room equipped for emergencies from the allocation dynamic, in that the price of the treatment room becomes prohibitively high for the other patient agents. On conclusion of the emergency treatment, however, the treatment room re-enters into the "market".

Emergency patients acquire higher payment reserves via a larger starting budget and a higher waiting-period compensation, whereby an accelerated schedule booking is attained. Parallel to this, the higher payment reserves lead to higher prices, whereby the demand is lowered. The resource shortage is signalized to the remaining actors and flows with it in their decision calculation. Although the emergency only determines the price for its treatment schedule, indirect shortage signals are transmitted to the other patients, which influence the choice of their appointment. Through the increased prices, the emergency signalizes the shortage of the emergency treatment room and works as control function.

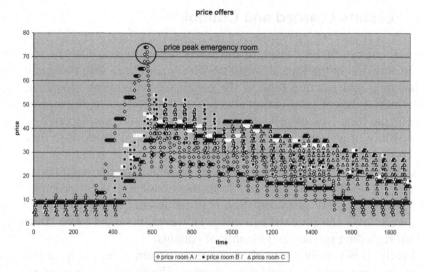

Figure 13. Prices with constant stream of outpatients and random number of emergency patients

Experiment No. 3 - In a third experiment, a set number of inpatients were additionally generated (Figure 14). Inpatients only occupy resources when free capacities are available, so that other processes are not disrupted. The inpatients were treated in the experiment between the time tact 0-250, 700-800 and from time tact 1100, which leads to a higher usage of resources in general compared to the previous experiment.

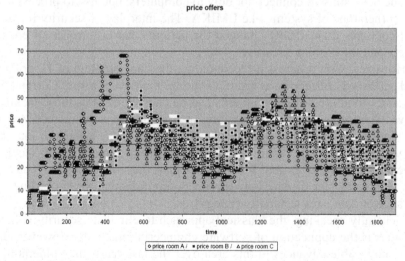

Figure 14. Prices with constant stream of outpatients, set number of inpatients and random number of emergency patients

7.3 Lessons Learned and Outlook

A preliminary, obvious result of the EMIKA prototype is that the amount of information in the logical world positively correlates with the quality of scheduling and reaction time in the physical environment. However, the pure availability of information also has its downside. A still unsolved aspect is the total lack of privacy. An EMIKA-like solution depends on the availability of as much information as possible and it would lose function if privacy were demanded [EyMo2004].

Connectivity and communication are essential for the automated processing of accumulated data and to manage patient care procedures. The efficient availability of information is of paramount importance for keeping workflows and processes running. However, there are some considerations regarding privacy and identity of patients:

Firstly, it is possible to track many signals from a source, regardless of time, location and communication channel. The result is a privacy threat: the human user's actions can be fully observed, his goals preferences derived from the observations. By sharing information between different receivers, even more characteristics and their interdependencies are made available until we recognize "the transparent user".

Secondly, it is possible to construct different profiles or "digital identities" by combining a purposeful or accidentally selected set of received signals. This is an inverse situation to that above and the threat is not to privacy, but to accountability.

The possibility to connect not only to computers, but also to processes is the cornerstone of systems like EMIKA. The interplay of security for data and code has dramatically changed the patterns and occurrence of errors, safety and the ensuing security.

However, with progressing technology, the hard problem of IT privacy and security is further away from a solution than ever before. Current approaches to address these problems can be characterized as those tackling privacy concerns, and those providing security and trust guarantees. As for the former, identity management systems have been designed and deployed [MuGJ2001].[2] With regard to the latter, a plethora of security mechanisms have been realized. In particular, these mechanisms focus on the secure transfer of data between peers (confidentiality) and on the assurance of data's respectability (integrity).

Generally speaking, the classical approach to eliminate security vulnerabilities is the application of software engineering methods. However, despite noticeable advances in this area over the last years, the vulnerability

---

[2]   See http://www.iig.uni-freiburg.de/telematik/atus/index.html for details.

rate in classical systems keeps increasing. There is no indication that this does not also apply to EMIKA-like systems.

Traditionally, known security threats are remedied by devising security policies, which in essence describe threatening events that should not occur. Security mechanisms, namely authentication, authorization, and accounting (AAA), then ensure that these policies are followed by prohibiting undesirable events from taking place. Just by way of evidence, AAA policies are expressed in this manner: authentication protocols prevent communicating partners from committing transactions with wrong partners (in particular, with an adversary); authorization techniques preclude illicit users from accessing resources to which they do not have the right; finally, accountability mechanisms avoid repudiation of the actions of a user.

However, to anticipate and describe each and every unwanted scenario is an infeasible exercise in EMIKA, where emergent, at design time unforeseen behavior plays an essential role. In this setting, one simply does not know what action to forbid, or which chain of actions will lead to a security threat. This supports the assumption that, although security policies based on prohibitions should not be disregarded, they are insufficient to actually provide a thorough account for security in highly dynamic systems [Mue+2005].

A promising approach to address this problem is based on the idea of commands. Instead of only specifying threatening situations, security policies expressed by means of commands also characterize situations that should occur, i.e. goals that should be accomplished. As an example, consider the downloading of a software module as a system extension. A reasonable policy is that it seamlessly integrates into the system and eventually fulfils the desired task. But by only stating the desired outcome of its execution, nothing is stated for instance about the access permissions (authorization) of the downloaded module, to prevent it from accessing unrequired but sensitive system data.

The research project EMIKA implemented concepts to allow self-organization of complex tasks on the basis of economic coordination measures. The agents signal their individual preferences using a criteria derived from economic concepts, which is basically related to money and budgeting.

Self-organization of life-saving resources is technically possible and its future realization in a real environment looks promising [Mue+2003]. Apart from the required set of building blocks, EMIKA has also shown that the coordination metrics is anything but simple and is the main source of any acceptance issue. In this case study, we have used a substitute of money to define scheduling priorities. In principle, making life-saving decisions on the basis of available budget leads to long-winded ethical discussions. However, arguments pro money are that scheduling decisions are required to be made transparent and software designers and users are free to define what the currency is – call it "health points" or "medicoins".

The continuous data-gathering process consequently leads to a dynamically updated mapping of the reality. This saves time to react and improves the probabilities that the reaction is adequate to the arisen problem. A self-organization of the dynamic treatment process by means of mobile technologies and software agents seems at least functionally obtainable. The main acceptance issue can be found in the long-lasting tradition to protect patient's privacy and the resistance to schedule according to market strategies based upon prices. For future work regarding privacy, a new concept of liveness properties is about to be introduced and tested.

References

[Cor+2003]   Coroama, V.; Hähner, J.; Handy, M.; Rudolph-Kuhn, P.; Magerkurth, C.; Müller, J.; Strasser, M.; Zimmer, T.: Leben in einer smarten Umgebung: Ubiquitous-Computing-Szenarien und Auswirkungen. Technical Reports 431. ETH Zürich, Institute for Pervasive Computing, Zürich, 2003.

[CyMa1963]   Cyert, R. M.; March, J. G.: A behavioral theory of the firm. Blackwell Business, Cambridge, Mass., 1963.

[Eyma2003]   Eymann, T.: Digitale Geschäftsagenten – Softwareagenten im Einsatz. Springer Xpert.press, Heidelberg, 2003.

[EyMo2004]   Eymann, T.; Morito, H.: Privacy Issues of Combining Ubiquitous Computing and Software Agent Technology in a Life-Critical Environment. Paper presented at IEEE International Conference on Systems, Man and Cybernetics. Hague, Netherlands, 2004.

[EySM2003]   Eymann, T.; Sackmann, S.; Müller, G.: Hayeks Katallaxie: Ein zukunftsweisendes Konzept für die Wirtschaftsinformatik? In: Wirtschaftsinformatik 45(2003)5, pp. 491-496.

[Gäfg1990]   Gäfgen, G.: Gesundheitsökonomie. Nomos, Baden-Baden, 1990.

[GaJo1979]   Garey, M. R.; Johnson, D. S.: Computers and intractability: a guide to the theory of NP-completeness. Freeman, San Francisco, 1979.

[HoNE2004]   Hohl, A.; Nopper, N.; Eymann, T.: Automatisierte und Interaktive Kontextverarbeitung zur Unterstützung der Patientenlogistik. Paper presented at Workshop on Mobile Computing in Medicine. Stuttgart, 2004.

[KuRo1995]   Kurbel, K.; Rohmann, T.: Ein Vergleich von Verfahren zur Maschinenbelegungsplanung: Simulated Annealing, Genetische

Algorithmen und mathematische Optimierung. In: Wirtschaftsinformatik 37(1995)6, pp. 581-593.

[MENS2004]   Müller, G.; Eymann, T.; Nopper, N.; Seuken, S.: EMIKA System: Architecture and Prototypic Realization. IEEE International Conference on Systems, Man and Cybernetics edn. Hague, Netherlands, 2004.

[MuGJ2001]   Müller, G.; Gerd tom Markotten, D.; Jendricke, U.: Benutzbare Sicherheit – Der Identitätsmanager als universelles Sicherheitswerkzeug. In: Müller, G.; Reichenbach, M. (Eds.): Sicherheitskonzepte für das Internet. Springer Xpert.press, Heidelberg, 2001, pp. 135-146.

[Mue+2003]   Müller, G.; Kreutzer, M.; Strasser, M.; Eymann, T.; Hohl, A.; Nopper, N.; Sackmann, S.; Coroama, V.: Geduldige Technologie für ungeduldige Patienten: Führt Ubiquitous Computing zu mehr Selbstbestimmung? In: Living in a Smart Environment. Springer, Heidelberg, 2003.

[Mue+2005]   Müller, G.; Accorsi, R.; Höhn, S.; Kähmer, M.; Strasser, M.: Sicherheit im Ubiquitous Computing: Schutz durch Gebote? In: Mattern, F. (Ed.): Der Computer im 21. Jahrhundert – Perspektiven, Technologien, Wirkungen. Springer, Heidelberg, 2005.

[SaEM2002]   Sackmann, S.; Eymann, T.; Müller, G.: EMIKA – Real-Time Controlled Mobile Information Systems in Health Care Applications. In: Bludau, H. B., Koop, A. (Ed.): Mobile Computing in Medicine. Köllen, Bonn, 2002, pp. 151-158.

[ScCZ1996]   Scheer, A. W.; Chen, R.; Zimmerman, V.: Prozeßmanagment im Krankenhaus. In: Adam, D. (Ed.): Krankenhausmanagment. Schriften zur Unternehmensführung. SzU, Wiesbaden, 1996.

[Schl1990]   Schlüchtermann, J.: Patientensteuerung, 26th edn. Eul, Bergisch Gladbach, Köln, 1990.

[StEy2004]   Strasser, M.; Eymann, T.: Self-organization of schedules using time-related monetary substitutes. In: Bichler, M. et al. (Ed.): Coordination and Agent Technology in Value Networks. Conference Proceedings Multi-Konferenz Wirtschaftsinformatik, Essen, 2004. GITO-Verlag, Berlin, 2004, pp. 45-58.

[Zuge2003]   Zugenmaier, A.: Anonymity for Users of Mobile Devices through Location Adressing. Rhombos-Verlag, 2003.

Part IV

Agent Engineering

1 The Engineering Process

Ingo J. Timm, Thorsten Scholz
Universität Bremen, Technologie-Zentrum Informatik
{i.timm | scholz}@tzi.de

Holger Knublauch
Stanford School of Medicine, Stanford Medical Informatics
holger@smi.stanford.edu

Abstract. Engineering highly flexible software systems for real-world applications on the basis of intelligent agents and multiagent systems is a challenging task. Conventional software engineering provides established methodologies and tool support. Additionally, knowledge engineering captures the necessary aspects of integrating knowledge in intelligent agents. However there is still a gap between software and knowledge engineering methodologies. State-of-the-art approaches of agent-oriented software engineering partially integrate these approaches. Nevertheless, challenges for the engineering process of agent technology remain open and therefore are addressed in this section on agent engineering.

1.1 Introduction

A key prerequisite for running successful software projects is the use of adequate software engineering techniques. Software engineering provides adequate methodologies supporting the development process of realistic large scale applications. Furthermore, software engineering tools are required for economically efficient engineering processes aiming for commercial applications.

Modern business processes and the increasing importance of networks demand for new paradigms for the architecture of complex software systems. Traditional software architecture and methodologies like object-oriented design have been originally developed for monolithic, static, and closed systems. However, most systems are now distributed, dynamic and open. The *multiagent systems paradigm* offers a more suitable approach to understand, represent and model such complex systems. *Agents* are autonomous computer systems that are situated in an environment to fulfill tasks. *Multiagent systems* are societies of agents that share the same environment and communicate with each other. In this introductory chapter we give an overview of the state of the art in multiagent system development, and set the stage for the remaining chapters in this book.

The multiagent paradigm shift can be regarded as a gradual evolution from existing software engineering approaches. On the micro level, agents can be regarded as objects that encapsulate a state and expose behavior. Agents also need to be implemented in some programming language and interact with conventional (typically object-oriented) systems. In the first section of this chapter we therefore refer to basic methodologies of software engineering (Section 1.1). On the macro level, multiple communicating agents form new types of organizations which are not easily captured and designed with the help of conventional methodologies. Higher levels of abstraction are needed that go beyond the level of objects and their methods. Furthermore, agents need to agree on domain formalizations including semantics to be able to communicate in a meaningful way. We therefore take a look into methodologies, languages and tools from the field of knowledge engineering (Section 1.2). Based on this background, Section 1.3 introduces state-of-the-art approaches in agent-oriented software engineering, and Section 1.4 discusses their limitations and challenges. Here, the remaining chapters of the agent engineering part of this book are introduced, which are addressing these challenges.

1.2 Software Engineering

Software should fulfill requirements of customers with respect to their specific context and environment. Software engineering is a structured process of transforming customer demands into software systems, which meet the requirements defined within the process. Software engineering covers requirements analysis, design, implementation, testing, and delivery of software systems (cf. Figure 1) [Boeh1995]. The software development process is not necessarily completed with delivery of the system but may also include maintenance and revision.

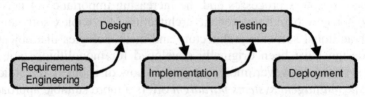

Figure 1. The software development life cycle typically runs through various stages.

The history of software engineering may be divided into phases, and development methodologies evolved from approaches taken in earlier phases. In the pre-history of software engineering, development mostly consisted of pure "hacking", i.e. systems have been implemented *ad hoc* without structured design phases. As size and complexity of software systems increased, these unstructured approaches soon turned out to be inadequate, as they were incomprehensible to non-programmers and failed to analyze requirements correctly. One of the first structured approaches to software engineering, the *waterfall-model*, considers successive stages: Analysis of *a priori* requirements, design, implementation, and testing. The shortcomings of this approach may be found in difficulties to capture all requirements correctly in advance. Furthermore, there is no feedback between the various stages. As an improvement, the iterative waterfall model contains pre-defined loops. However, these feedback loops may lead to a model drift, i.e., improved models may cause substantial change in the code resp. implementation. Many variations of this idea, e.g. the *Rational Unified Process*, increase the importance of feedback. Nevertheless, they all suffer from the fact that it is difficult to synchronize models and implementation while the system evolves.

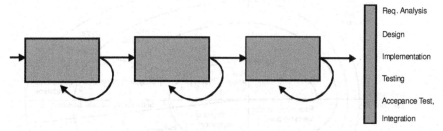

Figure 2. The eXtreme programming approach

Modern approaches in software engineering try to overcome the problems of insufficient feedback loops. The integration of models and implementation is proposed by *model-driven architectures* using a higher level of abstraction. In this approach, the models are used to drive code generation for various target platforms. The most widely used modeling language for model-driven architecture is the Unified Modeling Language (UML). UML defines visual notations such as use case diagrams, class diagrams and sequence diagrams. UML is now widely supported by engineering tools and can be used for various stages during the development. Where the predefined modeling elements alone are not sufficient, the expressivity of UML can be extended by means of extension mechanisms like stereotypes or metaclasses. This makes it possible to build new languages on top of UML, for example to optimize it for the design of multiagent systems.

The major bottleneck of model-driven architecture is the difficulty to develop appropriate tools which convert the high level design models into executable code. As a result, the vision of "pure design" is often unrealistic and low level programming is still needed.

In addition to systematic, structured development methodologies, many software developers have applied *rapid prototyping* and (later) *agile development* approaches such as eXtreme Programming (cf. Figure 2). These approaches focus on testing, less design effort and very fast implementation cycles. The basic assumption of these approaches is that software will naturally evolve when it has been exposed to user feedback. However, software engineering in this context is restricted to small systems and small developer teams and the reusability of developed models is limited.

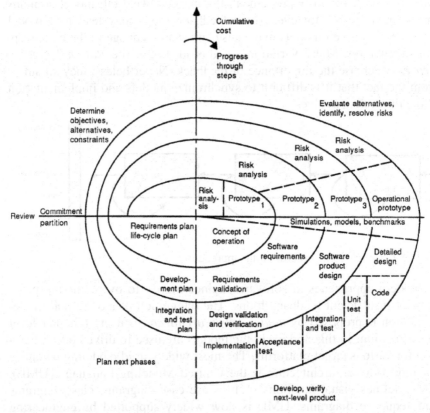

Figure 3. The spiral model[1]

---

[1]   See [Boeh1988].

Nevertheless, agile methodologies are an attractive option for subsystems, even if the general process follows a more systematic development model. Also, the popularity of agile approaches has resulted in improved tools and techniques for software testing. For industrial applications validation or even verification of software systems is crucial. Most modern development tools such as Eclipse or IntelliJ provide built-in facilities to build and execute software tests.

The agile approaches as described above are mainly motivated and introduced for the implementation level. However, large-scale software projects require a sophisticated management of the development process. Boehm introduced an iterative software engineering process, the spiral model, to integrate the benefits of rapid prototyping and structured system development [Boeh1988]. Additionally to the implementation and validation, there are three more major process steps, which consist of definition of system goals and evaluation of alternatives, risk analysis, and planning of the next cycle (cf. Figure 3).

The software engineering of intelligent agents or multiagent systems requires specific extensions but significant results from conventional software engineering may be incorporated. Summarizing, lessons learned for multiagent systems are

- numerous structured engineering processes exist for the development of large-scale software systems,
- standards like UML should be reused wherever possible,
- domain-specific extensions for multiagent systems are required, and
- many problems may only be solved with iterations and validation.

1.3 Knowledge Engineering

While software engineering explores the development of arbitrary software systems, the field of knowledge engineering provides methodologies and tools for creating a distinct class of software systems, the so called *knowledge-based systems* [Feig1977]. Similar to agent research, various definitions for knowledge-based systems exist. In a nutshell, knowledge-based systems can be described as systems that encode a formal representation of (asserted) human knowledge, and use this knowledge to infer new knowledge to expose "intelligent" behavior. The architecture of knowledge-based systems typically separates between the representation of the knowledge and the inference engines or other components to fulfill knowledge-based tasks.

Historically, one of the main challenges in knowledge engineering has been acquiring, encoding, and representing knowledge in a machine-understandable way. The origins of knowledge representation can be traced back to formal logic and the efforts to build a solver for any problem (general problem solver). In the early 70ies, object-centered knowledge representations have been introduced to cope with increasing complexity of real-world problems. Especially, frame-based representations have been developed, enhancing interactions between knowledge and software engineering leading to object-oriented approaches.

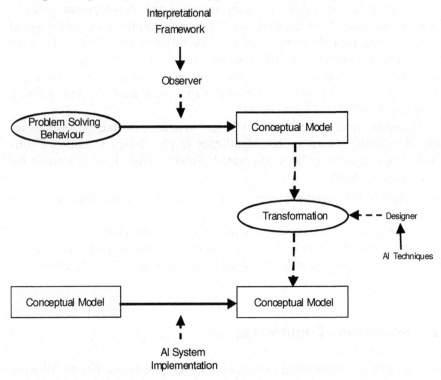

Figure 4. Knowledge engineering approach

More sophisticated knowledge-based systems have been based on highly specified problem-solving methods with specific knowledge bases. Problem-solving in this context exceeds conventional method-design in software engineering. This development led to the establishment of a new research area in knowledge engineering: knowledge acquisition. The key question here is not how to represent knowledge, but how to gather knowledge from a human expert. A general approach to knowledge acquisition is found in Figure 4 [WiSB1992, p. 9] where problem solving behavior in the real world is analyzed and interpreted for a conceptual model. For the implementation of a knowledge-based system, this model has to be transformed into a design model, which is implemented as a software system in the next step. Furthermore, approaches with enhanced complexity are required for problem solving facing uncertainty and possibly incorrect decisions.

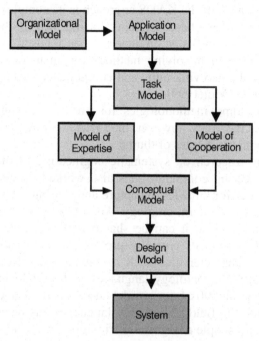

Figure 5. KADS models for the knowledge engineering task

Knowledge bases and problem-solving methods require high implementation efforts, and the engineering efforts of knowledge-based systems could be significantly reduced by reusing priory developed knowledge or methods. Therefore, strong efforts have been spent within the 80ies and early 90ies to evolve a standardized engineering process. One of the main achievements of these efforts is the "Knowledge Analysis and Design Support" (KADS), providing types of knowledge, relations between components, and model-building process. The model-building process contains the creation of seven different models: organizational, application, task, expertise, cooperation, conceptual, and design model (cf. Figure 5, [WiSB 1992, p. 11]. The philosophy of KADS is to provide a structured process of creating these models in a semi-formal or formal way, such that they may be integrated in a straight forward way. Common KADS framework integrates three types of knowledge models: task, inference, and domain, which should be sufficient for the description of application-related knowledge [WiSB1992]. The task knowledge refers to problem-solving capabilities. The inference knowledge describes the reasoning steps in a functional way. The domain knowledge includes structure and contents of domain knowledge. The relations between the components define their role in the inference process.

The main bottleneck of the KADS approach is its complexity and design effort building knowledge-based systems. Facing these problems, the next step in evolution of knowledge engineering has focused on the development of isolating problem-solving methods for an increased reusability. This leads to problem-solving units and components for knowledge modeling [FBMW1990] [Mott1999].

Summing up, some methodologies for knowledge engineering have been suggested in the 90ies, however, the focus lays now on languages and tools, together with some rules of thumb.

Parallel to the research on systematic engineering methodologies, the knowledge engineering community has also worked on defining suitable modeling languages for knowledge capture and sharing. The central notion in these languages is the term ontology. An *ontology* is a formal representation of concepts so that it can be shared between human or software agents. Ontology languages typically provide means to define concepts/ classes and their characteristics such as properties, restrictions and instances. Many different ontology languages such as KIF have been suggested in the 1980s and 90s, but no widely used standard emerged.

In recent years, the field of ontology languages has received a significant boost as many people recognized its importance for developing multi-agent systems and other web-based applications in the context of the so-called Semantic Web. The Semantic Web is a large-scale effort supported by the World Wide Web Consortium and its president Tim Berners-Lee, with the aim of making internet content more accessible and "comprehensible" to software agents. One of the cornerstones of the Semantic Web is the Web Ontology Language (OWL) and its base language RDF. OWL and RDF are Web-based knowledge representation languages that allow users to define domain concepts, properties, logical relationships and individuals in a machine-readable format. OWL and RDF ontologies can be uploaded on the Web and shared between applications or agents. The formal underpinnings of OWL in a variant of logic called Description Logic can be exploited to drive automated reasoning tools for classification and consistency checking tasks. Due to its clean foundation on formal logic and well-defined Web-based standards, the Semantic Web therefore serves as a powerful infrastructure or habitat for agent-based systems.

Ontology languages and methodologies have been supported by generations of modeling tools. While many of these tools are limited to "academic" prototypes and research projects, some of them have established a solid position in their niche. The currently most widely used knowledge modeling tool with support for OWL and RDF is Stanford's Protégé system [KFNM2004], which provides a customizable user interface for defining ontologies and to invoke reasoners. While – like UML-based tools – Protégé is a general purpose tool for many domains, the architecture of Protégé makes it easy to integrate additional services optimized for agent design or simulation.

Knowledge engineering is an important task for the development of intelligent agents or multiagent systems. However, only few approaches for successful adaptation may be identified. The lessons learned for multiagent systems are, that:

1. there is a large number of approaches for the specification of models,
2. ontologies may be a powerful mechanism to capture domain experts knowledge,
3. ontologies may be used for reasoning at run-time,
4. the Semantic Web is a natural infrastructure for agents,
5. formal logic may be used to support the construction of consistent knowledge models (consistency checking, classification).

These experiences have been taken into consideration within the development of agent-oriented software engineering methodologies. In the following, we will give an overview over these methodologies.

1.4 Approaches to Agent Oriented Software Engineering

In the previous sections software and knowledge engineering have been introduced. As mentioned before, the design of large scale multiagent systems requires a sophisticated engineering process which integrates aspects of knowledge as well as software engineering. In the last years, multiple approaches to AOSE have emerged which differ basically in the target architecture of the agents or in the stages considered in the process of engineering, e.g., design, requirements analysis, etc. A first survey on AOSE methodologies has been introduced by Müller [Muel1997]. However, the research field of AOSE has recently gained more significance in the agent community. As a result, there is a good selection of books summarizing or reflecting the current state of the art, e.g., [BeGZ2004] [WeJa2005] [Lu AD2004] [OdGM2005] [Gar+2003].[2]

In the following we present a brief overview on AOSE methodologies which are distinguished according to Bergenti et al. as: special purpose methodologies and general methodologies for agent-based system development [BeGZ2004]. Special purpose methodologies benefit from their close connection to specific domains and problems. Their shortcomings arise from the difficulties of transferring the tools and methods to other situations. The general methodologies for agent-based system development are not restricted to a specific application area or a specific part of the system, but should be applicable to the most problem domains and the development of multiagent systems.

The main variation of AOSE methodologies is the different starting points and their "disciplinary background". Weiß and Jakob identify four main starting points for AOSE: agent technology, requirements engineering, object-orientation, and knowledge engineering [WeJa2005]. Four representatives, one for each starting point, are introduced in the following: GAIA for agent technology [WoJK2000], Tropos for requirements analysis [CaKM2002], MaSE for object orientation [DeLo2004], and MAS-CommonKADS for knowledge engineering [IGGV1997].

1.4.1 GAIA

The focus of agent technology-based approaches like GAIA lies on agent specific abstraction, e.g., group, organization, role, and methods for specification of coordination and communication [WeJa2005]. GAIA is one of the first methodologies proposed for the analysis and design of multiagent systems [CJSZ2004] introduced by Wooldridge et al. 2000. The original version considered benevolent agents interacting in closed multiagent systems (MAS). The methodology compromises of three phases: requirements specification, analysis (role model, interaction model), and design (agent model, service model, acquaintance model). Further phases from software engineering, e.g., testing, were not considered. The shortcomings of GAIA were addressed by Zambonelli et al. who extended GAIA with respect to organizational abstractions [ZaJW2003]. In consequence, the extended GAIA is more suited for designing and building systems in complex and open environments. Juan et al. extended GAIA by a sophisticated approach called ROADMAP for requirement specification [JuPS2002]. The main benefits of this extension are a dynamic role hierarchy, models to explic-

---

[2]   For advanced reading, please refer to these books.

itly describe the agent environment, and the agent knowledge [CJSZ2004]. Even with these extensions, GAIA is limited to the software engineering phases requirements specification, analysis, and design. Implementation and testing are not considered. Knublauch applied agile software engineering to the GAIA methodology in order to compensate this shortcoming [Knub2002].

1.4.2 Tropos

The Tropos methodology is focusing on requirements engineering as specific starting point [WeJa2005]. Therefore, it is intensively linked to techniques and formalisms of the requirements engineering field (Bresciani et al. 2004). Agent-oriented requirements engineering parallels goal-oriented requirements engineering (cf. IV.2; [MyCY1999]). The Tropos approach uses object oriented modeling techniques, i.e., UML, and has been specifically designed for the development of BDI agents within the JACK agent platform [NoRi2001]. There is a framework for Tropos, which provides techniques for formal analysis, i.e., the verification of requirement specifications. The specification language is based on the temporal language KAOS [Lems2001]. The Tropos methodology consists of five phases: early requirements, late requirements, architectural design, detailed design, and implementation. It is inspired by modeling socially based MAS and therefore focuses on organization theory, strategic alliances, and social patterns. This focus is reflected in the differentiation between early and late requirement analysis. In the second phase of requirement analysis, there is the description of dependencies between actors. Architectural design is used for a first sketch of the system, where goals and tasks are assigned to the system resp. sub-goals and sub-tasks are assigned to actors. The resulting models are detailed out in the next phase. Even if the Tropos methodology uses an explicit implementation phase, there is no focus on the steps after the model building.

1.4.3 Multiagent Systems Engineering

While object-orientation is a significant feature in the Tropos methodology, it becomes the essential starting point for the MaSE methodology (Multiagent Systems Engineering). Object-oriented methods are not only integrated but extended to agent specific software engineering. Nearly all existing object-oriented principles and techniques are applied and adapted to the specific requirements of AOSE. In this context, domain independency of the approach is emphasized, such that MaSE is a *general* methodology for developing multiagent systems, introduced by DeLoach et al. [DeWS2001]. There are no restricting assumptions for the agent architectures, communication, or implementation language [WeJa2005]. The MaSE methodology is based on UML and has a strong focus on analysis and design. As a result of the analysis phase, models for goal hierarchies, use cases, sequence diagrams, concurrent tasks, and role models are created. These models are used within the design phase which is the next step in the MaSE methodology. In the design phase, models for agent classes, conversations, agent architectures, and deployment are specified. Compared to the GAIA method, MaSE and GAIA both gather the same type of information in the analysis phase, just in different models [BeGZ2004].

1.4.4 MAS-CommonKADS

As has been pointed out in the introduction of this chapter, there are close interactions between the fields of knowledge engineering and AOSE. Especially, the previously introduced KADS methodology for knowledge engineering has been specifically designed for modeling knowledge domains including actors, organizations, and interactions. This close relationship to agent engineering seems to be advantageous for developing agents or multiagent systems. Therefore, it is not surprising, that one of the first structured approaches to AOSE has emerged as an extension of the KADS approach. This approach was introduced nearly simultaneously in a two-fold way as MAS-CommonKADS [IGGV1997] and as CoMoMAS [Glas1996]. Both approaches integrate two phases analysis and design of the software engineering process only. Although, the original approach in the variation of CommonKADS also included the implementation step [ScWB1993]. Depending on the modeling language used within MAS-CommonKADS or CoMoMAS, there has been a formal syntax or semantics included to some extent. In consequence, the main application areas are knowledge-centered domains. The approach seemed promising; however, it failed to integrate tools, especially like agent platforms, such that significant implementation effort arose.

1.5 Challenges for Agent Oriented Software Engineering

The main benefit of multiagent systems as proposed in this book is flexibility, which is realized by a high degree of autonomy and emergent organization as well as dynamic negotiation. Each software engineering process may be structured by the following tasks: requirements engineering, specification resp. design, implementation, and testing. A significant paradigm shift has been introduced by object orientation in conventional software engineering. For AOSE, it is in question if a similar paradigm shift has occurred which is connected to increasing efforts for requirements engineering and specification while implementation efforts decrease significantly. Hints supporting this claim are the strong focus on requirements engineering, model building, and formal languages applied to MAS. In either case, special requirement arises for the engineering process of multi-agent systems, such that conventional approaches to software engineering are not sufficient. Knowledge engineering on the other hand, is not an exclusive option for AOSE as it fails in lack of supporting tool or method support.

In principle, AOSE could benefit from both engineering technologies: from the strong tool and methodology support in software engineering and the advantageous know-how about model building, knowledge representation, and inference in knowledge engineering. Schreiber and Wielinga stated a strong relationship between these areas but until today, there is no convincing approach bridging the gap between them in an integrated AOSE approach [ScWi1996].

The development of multiagent systems faces specific challenges leading to a general engineering process. As in software engineering, there are different approaches to organize the development phase: sequential, agile, and iterative processes. In any of these processes, we identified a set of seven process steps: requirements engineering, interaction design, architectural design, semantics specification, dependability specification, tool and platform selection, and validation (cf. Figure 6). In concrete software development, there might be a variation of the ordering of these steps, especially interaction and architectural design should be intertwined.

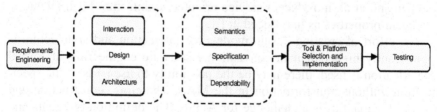

Figure 6. Mandatory process steps in AOSE

In the following, we are discussing the major challenges according to this process, separating AOSE from conventional software and knowledge engineering.

The first challenge in AOSE is the construction of an adequate requirements specification. Following conventional approaches to requirements engineering, flexibility and emergent behavior of MAS cannot be modeled adequately. The consideration of requirements engineering in context of agents and multiagent systems is twofold: On the one hand, requirements analysis may be applied for identifying agents within a domain; on the other hand, the notion of agents and multiagent systems may be used for performing a requirements analysis. Bieser et al. are investigating requirements analysis as an independent approach for analysis of a domain. The decision if agent technology is applied as a solution remains open. However, goal-oriented requirements engineering may be a good compromise between technology independency and requirements specification for MAS.

In MAS, multiple agents are interacting with each other. Therefore, static specification of agent relationships is not sufficient. Obviously, the design of interaction differs from interface design in conventional software engineering significantly. As the structure and process of interaction is a significant feature of multiagent's flexibility, the challenge for AOSE arises from the interaction design. Interaction has to be restrictive enough to enable reliable system behavior and should be permissive enough to allow for flexibility or emergent behavior. Within IV.3, Krempels et al. introduce different concepts of interaction within MAS. Furthermore, characteristics of interaction are discussed with respect to performance and design and implementation of large scale multi-multiagent systems.

Interaction is essential for MAS design, but not sufficient to establish the agents` design. Intelligent agents differ essentially from conventional software objects. Consequently the architectural design of intelligent agents is a key challenge for AOSE. It is the basic feature to enable the transformation of the requirement specification into software. In IV.4, Lockemann et al. introduce a service-oriented architecture for implementing agent properties as introduced in I.1.

The effort of creating design models for interaction and architecture is significantly higher than in conventional software engineering. If formal specification is used, there may be the possibility to use parts of the specification without transformation in the MAS. Therefore, construction and usage of semantics is a challenge for AOSE. The definition of agents and multiagent systems requires explicit knowledge representation. In multiagent systems we may identify three different parts of a knowledge-base for an agent:

- environment,
- agent interaction and opponents, and

• internal state.

The interdependencies of knowledge and MAS are discussed within Chapter IV.5 on semantics for agents. Here, Scholz et al. introduce fundamental concepts for semantic consideration of intelligent agents, multi-agent systems, as well as the interaction and communication between agents.

MAS are highly dynamic systems allowing for flexible adaptation to concrete situations. On the other hand, software systems for real-world applications have to act in concordance with the requirements specification. From this contradiction a further challenge arises. The problem is to construct agents and MAS being flexible and dependable. In IV.6, Nimis et al. introduce approaches for ensuring reliability within MAS.

Experiences gathered in the knowledge engineering domain suggest, that complexity and variation of applications require efficient methods and reusable modules. Thus, another challenge is the tool support for specification and implementation as well as standardization of agent related technology. For commercial applications, the reusability of agents but also MAS is important. Therefore, Braubach et al. deal with existing standards and available tools in Chapter IV.7 on Tools and Standards.

After implementation of a system, it is important to evaluate, validate or verify the system with respect to the requirements. Testing of software as long as it is not based on model checking or formal verification is not considered within current AOSE approaches adequately [WeJa2005]; [BeGZ 2004]. In highly distributed systems testing is complex and suffers from concurrency [Ried1997]. Therefore, the challenge for testing MAS is discussed in IV.8. As there are no significant approaches in AOSE; Timm et al. present a general approach from software engineering and artificial intelligence and their application in AOSE.

In consequence, we are focusing on the specific requirements of agents and multiagent systems in the following chapters in Part IV: requirements engineering (cf. IV.2), interaction design (cf. IV.3) and architectural design (cf. IV.4), semantics (cf. IV.5), dependable agent systems (cf. IV.6), tools and standards (cf. IV.7), as well as testing (cf. IV.8).

Further Reading

As mentioned before, there is a set of good textbooks and collections on AOSE. The book of Bergenti et al. [BeGZ2004] focuses on a detailed and technical description of different approaches to AOSE methodologies. Here, special as well as general purpose development methodologies are presented. Weiß and Jakob [WeJa2005] compare AOSE methodologies in a consistent way using a comprehensive scenario. As a final recommendation, the book of Luck et al. [LuAD2004] presents a technical view to AOSE, where existing methodologies play a minor role.

References

[BeGZ2004] Bergenti, F.; Gleizes, M.-P.; Zambonelli, F. (Eds.): Methodologies and Software Engineering for Agent Systems. Kluwer Academic Publishers, Boston, Dordrecht, London, 2004.

[Boeh1988] Boehm, B. W.: A Spiral Model of Software Development and Enhancement. In: IEEE Computer 21(1988)5, pp. 61-72.

[Boeh1995] Boehm, B. W.: A Spiral Model of Software Development and Enhancement. In: IEEE Engineering Management Review 23 (1995)4, pp. 69-81.

[CaKM2002] Castro, J.; Kolp, M.; Mylopoulos, J.: Towards Requirements-Driven Information Systems Engineering: The Tropos Project. Information System, Elsevier, 2002.

[CJSZ2004] Cernuzzi, L.; Juan, T.; Sterling, L.; Zambonelli, F.: The Gaia Methodology. In: Bergenti, F.; Gleizes, M.-P.; Zambonelli, F. (Eds.): Methodologies and Software Engineering for Agent Systems. Kluwer Academic Publishers, Boston, Dordrecht, London, 2004, pp. 69-87.

[DeLo2004] DeLoach, S. A.:The MaSE Methodology. In: Bergenti, F.; Gleizes, M.-P.; Zambonelli, F. (Eds.): Methodologies and Software Engineering for Agent Systems. Kluwer Academic Publishers, Boston, Dordrecht, London, 2004, pp. 107-126.

[DeWS2001] DeLoach, S. A.; Wood, M. F.; Sparkman, C. H.: Multiagent System Engineering. In: International Journal of Software Engineering and Knowledge Engineering 11(2001)3, pp. 231-258.

[Feig1977] Feigenbaum, E. A.: The Art of Artificial Intelligence: Themes and Case Studies of Knowledge Engineering. In: Reddy, R. (Ed.): Proceedings of the 5th International Joint Conference on Artificial Intelligence (IJCAI 1977). Cambridge, MA, August 1977, pp. 1014-1029.

[FBMW1990] Fensel, D.; Benjamins, V. R; Motta, E.; Wielinga, B. J.: A Framework for knowledge system reuse. In: Proceedings of the International Joint Conference on Artificial Intelligence (IJCAI-99). Stockholm, Sweden, July 31-August 5, 1990.

[Gar+2003] Garcia, A.; Lucena, C.; Zambonelli, F.; Omicini, A.; Castro, J. (Eds.): Software Engineering for Large-Scale Multi-Agent Systems. Springer, Berlin, Heidelberg, New York, 2003.

[Glas1996] Glaser, N.: Conceptual Modelling of Multi-Agent Systems. In: The CoMoMAS Engineering Environment Series: Multiagent

Systems, Artificial Societies, and Simulated Organizations 4(1996), p. 288.

[IGGV1997]   Iglesias, C. A.; Garijo, M.; González, J. C.; Velasco, J. R.: Analysis and Design of Multiagent Systems using MAS-Common-KADS. In: AAAI'97 Workshop on Agent Theories, Architectures and Languages, Providence, RI, July 1997. (An extended version of this paper has been published in Intelligent Agents IV: Agent Theories, Architectures, and Languages, Springer Verlag, 1998.)

[JuPS2002]   Juan, T.; Pierce, A.; Sterling, L.: ROADMAP: Extending the Gaia methodology for Complex Open Systems. In: Proceedings of the 1st ACM Joint Conference on Autonomous Agents and Multi-Agent Systems. ACM Press, 2002, pp. 3-10.

[Knub2002]   Knublauch, H.: Extreme Programming of Multi-Agent Systems. In: Proceedings of Autonomous Agents and Multi-Agent Systems (AAMAS 02). The Association for Computing Machinery Inc., Bologna, Italy, July 2002, pp. 704-711.

[KFNM2004]   Knublauch, H.; Fergerson, R. W.; Noy, N. F.; Musen, M. A.: The Protégé OWL Plugin: An Open Development Environment for Semantic Web Applications. Third International Semantic Web Conference, Hiroshima, Japan, 2004.

[LuAD2004]   Luck, M.; Ashari, R.; D'Inverno, M.: Agent-Based Software Development. Artech House, Boston, London, 2004.

[Mott1999]   Motta, A.: Reusable Components for Knowledge Modelling. IOS Press, Amsterdam et al., 1999.

[Muel1997]   Müller, H.-J.: Towards Agent Systems Engineering. In: International Journal on Data and Knowledge Engineering, Special Issue on Distributed Expertise 23(1997), pp. 217-245.

[MyCY1999]   Mylopoulos, J.; Chung, L.; Yu, E. S. K.: From Object-Oriented to Goal-Oriented Requirements Analysis. Communications of the ACM 42(1999)1, pp. 31-37.

[NoRi2001]   Norling, E.; Ritter, F. E.: Embodying the JACK Agent Architecture Source. In: Proceedings of the 14th Australian Joint Conference on Artificial Intelligence. Lecture Notes in Computer Science 2256. Springer, London, 2001, pp. 368-377.

[OdGM2005]   Odell, J.; Giorgini, P.; Müller, J. P. (Eds.): Agent-Oriented Software Engineering V. Springer, Berlin, Heidelberg, New York, 2005.

[Ried1997]   Riedemann, E. H.: Testmethoden für sequentielle und nebenläufige Software-Systeme. B. G. Teubner, Stuttgart, 1997.

[ScWi1996]   Schreiber, G.; Wielinga, B. J.: SWI: Making knowledge technology work. In: IEEE Expert 11(1996)2, pp. 74-76.

[ScWB1993]   Schreiber, G.; Wielinga, B.; Breuker, J. (Eds.): KADS: A Principled Approach to Knowledge-Based System Development. Academic Press, London et al., 1993.

[Lems2001]   van Lamsweerde, A.: Goal-Oriented Requirements Engineering: A Guided Tour. In: Proceedings of the 5th IEEE International Symposium on Requirements Engineering (RE'01), pp. 249-263.

[WeJa2005]   Weiß, G.; Jakob, R.: Agentenorientierte Softwareentwicklung. Springer, Berlin, Heidelberg, New York, 2005.

[WiSB1992]   Wielinga, B.; Schreiber, A.; Breuker, J.: KADS: A Modelling Approach to Knowledge Engineering. In: Knowledge Acquisition 4(1992), pp. 1-162.

[WoJK2000]   Wooldridge, M.; Jennings, N. R.; Kinny, D.: The Gaia Methodology for Agent-Oriented Analysis and Design. Autonomous Agents and Multi-Agent Systems 3(2000)3, pp. 285-312.

[ZaJW2003]   Zambonelli, F.; Jennings, N. R.; Wooldridge, M.: Developing Multiagent Systems: The Gaia Methodology. In: ACM Transactions on Software Engineering Methodology 12(2003)3, pp. 317-370.

2 Requirements Engineering

Thomas Bieser, Hendrik Fürstenau, Stephan Otto, Daniel Weiß

Universität Hohenheim, Wirtschaftsinformatik II,
{tbieser I fuersten I ottosn I d-weiss}@uni-hohenheim.de

Abstract. This chapter investigates requirements engineering (RE) for agent-based systems and in this context discusses the assumption that requirements engineering methods and tools are independent of the used technology. For this purpose, specific needs of agent-based systems that must be considered during requirements engineering are examined. As a possible approach for the fulfillment of the discussed needs, the capability of methods of goal-oriented requirements engineering (GORE) to support requirements engineering for agent-based systems is investigated.

2.1 Introduction

The development of agent-based systems requires the use of appropriate processes, methods and tools of software engineering (SE). Accordingly, the engineering of agent-based information systems usually follows a software process [WeJa2005]. While these software processes may vary greatly, they typically consist of several phases, such as requirements engineering, information system design, implementation, test and maintenance. These phases generally are interdependent, as their successful completion relies on deliverables provided by previous phases [Balz2000]. Therefore, phases of software processes may not be completed properly or in time, if required deliverables are missing, incomplete or inappropriate. It is a well-known fact that such problems regularly result in increased cost or significant delay of software development [Boeh1981].

As an early step of SE, requirements engineering (RE) deals with requirements of stakeholders concerning the information systems to develop. For this purpose, requirements are collected and brought into a specification the developer is capable of building the desired system upon. In that way RE provides crucial deliverables for the following phases of information systems design and implementation. As a consequence, RE is considered as a critical prerequisite for efficient and successful software projects, because inadequate or incomplete results of RE may lead to technological and economic risks in software development [Part1998].

A general assumption in RE is that procedures, methods and tools of RE are fully independent of the technologies used later on to design and implement the system. In the context of a new technology, such as agent technology, this leads to two questions: Does this new technology demand, according to new design opportunities, the development of currently unavailable RE methods? Does the new technology by itself introduce new types of requirements, which have not been considered so far in RE as it is performed today? It is the purpose of this chapter to investigate these two questions in detail.

This chapter is structured as follows: To obtain a basic understanding we sum up the state of the art in RE and discuss specific aspects of agent-based technologies which must be considered during RE in Section 2.2. Section 2.3 discusses goal-oriented requirements engineering (GORE) methods as a common approach to engineer requirements for agent-based systems. Respective methods are introduced in Section 2.3.1 and evaluated regarding their capability to support the phases of RE in Section 2.3.2. Furthermore their capability to specify relevant criteria of the organizational environment of information systems is investigated in Section 2.3.3. Section 2.4 summarizes the results of this chapter and discusses possible perspectives for further research in this area. Section 2.5 lists the references used in this chapter.

2.2 Agent-Oriented Requirements Engineering

A sophisticated RE is considered an important prerequisite for successful software projects, as a lot of mistakes and failures during system development are the direct causes of inadequate requirements elicitation and analysis [IbRe1996]. A systematic and prioritized requirements-elaboration prevents these problems by supporting early discovery of unsuitable requirements and thus limits the costs of error correcting, which usually grow exponentially over time during development [Boeh1981] [NaKu1991].

2.2.1 Phases and Methods of Requirements Engineering

Even though there is overall consensus on the importance of RE, the definitions of the requirements process and its activities are not standardized [Kava2002]. The variety of proposed approaches for RE ranges from two activities (problem analysis and product description [Davi1993], requirements elicitation and requirements analysis [Grah1998]) to four activities (elicitation, negotiation, specification documentation and verification/validation [Pohl1996]) all the way to a framework consisting of eight activities (eliciting, elaborating, structuring, specifying, analyzing, negotiating, documenting and modifying [vanL2004]).

A further process model presented by [HiDa2003] adds more detail to a process model proposed by the SWEBOK [AbMo2004]. This model is mappable to the Sommerville Model [Somm2005] and thus combines most aspects of the other approaches. Therefore, we will base our further analysis on its five phases and introduce them shortly:

- *Phase of requirements elicitation*: Includes the learning, uncovering, extracting, surfacing and/or discovering of needs of customers, users, and other potential stakeholders. Techniques used in this phase may be interviews, scenarios, prototypes, facilitated meetings and/or observations [AbMo2004], as well as group elicitation, cognitive techniques or contextual techniques [NuEa2000]. The result of this phase is a deeper understanding of the stakeholder needs, which may be incrementally detailed during the further process.
- *Phase of requirements modeling*: Is used to create and analyze models of requirements. The aim of the modeling is an increasing understanding of the respective requirements, as well as an identification of incompleteness and inconsistency. For this purpose, especially the modeling of essential properties of the system environment and/or the application domain in terms of data, structures, rules and behaviors is considered as useful [Broy2004]. Furthermore, the provision of appropriate model-representations improves the ability to communicate about requirements with stakeholders. This phase is closely connected to the triage phase.
- *Phase of requirements triage*: In this phase, subsets of the requirements ascertained by the requirements elicitation are determined, which are considered as appropriate to be addressed in specific releases of a system. This may be done by requirement prioritization, resource estimation and requirement selection [Davi2003]. Also integrated in this phase are the analysis and understanding of the requirements, their overlaps and conflicts as well as the negotiation about the requirements priority with the stakeholders to obtain a consistent set of requirements [Somm2005]. Thus this phase is closely connected to the modeling phase.
- *Phase of requirements specification*: Includes the documentation of the desired external behavior of a system. The specification notation or language used for this purpose may be formal, semi-formal or informal, ranging from logic to natural language [NuEa2000]. In this phase, the focus lies on the ability to communicate with the system designers and

developers without losing sight of the other requirements' stakeholders. This phase results in a representation of the user requirements that system designers and developers are capable of understanding.

- *Phase of requirements validation/verification*: Comprises the determination of reasonableness, consistency, completeness, suitability, and lack of defects in a set of requirements. The purpose of requirements validation is to certify that the requirements are acceptable descriptions of the system to be implemented (the stakeholders´ intention). Techniques which can be used may be review and/or testing [PaEM2003]. In contrast, requirements verification checks requirements specifications for internal consistency through mathematical proofs or inspection techniques [HoLe2001]. Thus this phase will be closely connected to the specification, because its result is a consistent, thorough and best suiting specification.

While the above enumeration of phases may convey the impression that the order of the requirements process is sequential, the introduced activities are usually intertwined or run in parallel [HoLe2001] [HiDa2003] [Somm2005].

These phases serve as a generic framework for the engineering of requirements, whereas RE as part of SE must face several challenges. In particular, the need of businesses to respond quickly to new opportunities and challenges must be taken into account. Accordingly, SE and, hence, RE paradigms and methods are affected by several change drivers [Somm 2005]:

- need for rapid software delivery,
- increasing rate of requirements changes,
- need for improved ROI on software,
- new approaches to system development.

Especially the effects of the last key change driver can be observed when looking at the ongoing changes in SE over the last 30 years. These effects do not affect only single, but all entities involved in software development and maintenance, because these entities overlap to some extent or depend on each other. Thus "[…] one must focus on individual aspects […]" in the SE process [LeRa2002]. Nevertheless, closer connection and integration of the RE and remaining development processes seems desirable to "[…] address the system development challenges of the 21st century […]" [Somm2005].

This seems particularly true for agent-oriented software engineering (AOSE). Here, processes and methods for the engineering of agent-based systems must be capable of meeting the special needs driven by agent-based technologies. However, the decision for the use of specific technologies, such as agent-based technologies, usually comes after the initial RE phase. Thus, methods are needed, which on the one hand allow the engineering of requirements independent of specific technologies, but on the other hand are able to supplement requirements specific to the used technologies. For this purpose, additional technology-specific requirements must be integrated with already elicited technology-independent requirements.

2.2.2 Agent-Oriented Requirements

Methods of goal-oriented requirements engineering (GORE) seem capable of meeting the needs just mentioned. In fact, these methods are an outgrowth of agent-oriented development and are already used in AOSE [ArWo2002] [Hein2005].

2.2.2.1 Functional and Non-Functional Requirements

Aspects of information systems, which may be used as requirements, are proposed by different quality models and standards. As a well-known standard, the ISO/IEC 9126 standard defines top-level characteristics as requirements concerning the capability of the application:

- to provide defined functions (*functionality*),
- to provide a specified performance level under specified conditions (*reliability*),
- to be understood, learned, used and attractive to the user (*usability*),
- to provide appropriate performance with given resources (*efficiency*),
- to be modified for corrections, improvement or adaptation (*maintainability*),
- and to be transferred to different environments (*portability*).

These requirements furthermore are refined in several sub-characteristics [ISO2001].

In general, one distinguishes functional and non-functional requirements [ThDo1990] [Chun1993]. Functional requirements determine the available behaviors and functions as a result of installing and interacting with the system. In contrast, non-functional requirements (NFR) determine available properties and qualities as a result of installing and interacting with the system [Jack1998]. Reliability, usability, efficiency, maintainability and portability are considered as non-functional requirements.

As functional requirements depend on specific aspects of the respective domain and individual application, no general assumption about them can be made. Thus, in the following we focus on non-functional requirements.

2.2.2.2 Linking Requirements and Flexibility

Agent technology is a candidate for system design whenever a high degree of flexibility is needed. Therefore, before mapping the aforementioned top-level requirements to the specific capabilities of agent-based systems, we take the intermediate step of examining the relative importance of the non-functional requirements for flexibility. Flexibility has several aspects. *Technical flexibility* is the ability of a system to react adequately to external influences with its current functionality and configuration. *Economic flexibility* is the adaptability of a system to changing demands under the assumption that additional resources are to be involved. *Static flexibility* is all flexibility potential that remains fixed within a given period of time. *Dynamic flexibility* is the capability of changing flexibility potential at run-time.

The various aspects of flexibility will indeed contribute to the fulfillment of ISO/IEC 9126 requirements types. *Maturity,* as a sub-characteristic of reliability, addresses the avoidance of failures as a result of faults in the software. Here dynamic, static, and technical flexibility may be useful. *Fault tolerance,* as another sub-characteristic of reliability, can be achieved through dynamic and technical flexibility. *Portability* requires a high degree of flexibility to react in different environments and situations and encompasses all four identified dimensions of flexibility. *Adaptability* as a sub-characteristic of *portability* describes "[…] the capability of the software product to be adapted to different specified environments without applying actions or means, other than those provided for this purpose for the software considered." [ISO2001]. These issues are addressed by technical, static, and dynamic flexibility. *Coexistence,* as a further sub-characteristic, also addresses technical, static, and dynamic flexibility. Finally, the capability of systems to adapt to users may have effects on *usability* and may benefit from dynamic and static flexibility.

2.2.2.3 Relating Agent Properties and Flexibility

The third and last step is to relate the aspects of flexibility to agent properties and, as a result, determine how the non-functional requirements can exploit the potential of agent technology. According to [WoJe1995] there are four high-level requirement categories [DeIm2005] that can be seen as building blocks for flexibility in agent-based systems: proactivity, i.e. sociability, autonomy and reactivity. These requirements in turn, are connected to aspects of agent-based technologies, as already discussed in previous chapters, such as goals, situated behavior and autonomy.

Goals, reactivity and proactivity

In the agent-technology context, a goal is an "[...] information that describes situations that are desirable." [RuNo2003]. Goals are defined as the consistent and achievable subset of desires whereas desires are inputs to the agent's deliberation process [SiRG2001]. Thus, information about goals is required to implement proactive or reactive behavior that enables agents to act flexibly and provide flexibility.

Goals should thus be the fundamental concept underlying the requirements engineering methods for agents. These methods should consider how the intended system would meet organizational goals [DeIm2005]. The interesting question is whether the organizational goal concepts used by these methods will ever be matched by the more technology-oriented goal concept used by agent-based system. In general, it seems that the goal concept in the RE domain is semantically richer than the technology-oriented one, since more complex goals, which are typical for human beings, are considered and cannot be integrated directly into agent-based systems yet.

Situated behavior and sociability

An agent should be able to "[...] continuously interact with, or to be embedded in its environment." [Weis2003]. This situatedness refers to the agent's capability to use its environment as an information source, by perception of the environment or communication with other agents to better cope with situations where the agent has no complete world-model of [GoWa2003]. Thus it has to interact with other agents in an organizational setting, something that can be seen as a capability to communicate, coordinate and cooperate in a social context. This in turn enables flexibility through the ability to deal with dynamic situations and environments.

Here, requirements regarding organizational aspects and aspects of interaction must be considered in RE. This may be done using already existing common RE methods, such as scope definition or stakeholder analysis. To some degree, respective requirements are also the subject of GORE methods. The open question yet is if these methods are sufficient to handle the respective requirements.

Autonomy

The concept of autonomy suffers from a major problem, in that "[…] it is difficult to limit it in a definition." [HeCF2003]. It is "[…] one of the most used but least operationalized words in the fields of intelligent agents and multi-agent systems." [LuDM2003].

This is a major problem for the connection to the RE domain: How can the domain elicit requirements or adapt methods to capture a requirement which is not really clear, even though different methods exist to elicit uncertain knowledge? Therefore, as long as the concept of autonomy is not concretized, it cannot be supported in RE methodology appropriately.

2.3 Goal-Oriented Requirements Engineering

As we just saw, while there is no direct connection between high level requirements, such as those provided by ISO/IEC 9126, the requirement of flexibility, and design aspects of agent systems, it seems possible to identify indirect links between these levels of requirements, in particular between high-level requirements and the requirement for flexibility, as well as between the requirement for flexibility and design aspects of agent systems. We also noted that goals seem to be the key to the process of requirements engineering with agents. We refer to such a process as Goal-Oriented Requirements Engineering (GORE). This section gives an introduction.

2.3.1 Overview

The main problem within the requirements engineering process lies in the fact that customers' expectations are often vague, incomplete, inconsistent or expressed informally [DeIm2005]. To better cope with this fact and to build a sound basis for further system development, the concept of early requirements engineering was brought into play which is "[…] concerned with the understanding of a problem by studying an organizational setting […]" [CaKM2001]. Thus the intentions of stakeholders are captured by forming them into goals because "[…] the study of contemporary requirements engineering […] methodologies indicates that modeling of organizational goals constitutes a central activity of the RE process." [Kava2002]. Furthermore "Goals have been recognized to be among the driving forces for requirements elicitation, elaboration, organization, analysis, negotiation, documentation, and evolution." [vanL2004].

According to their significant new description element, the early requirements engineering methods focusing on goals form a special branch of requirements engineering named "Goal-Oriented Requirements Engineering" (GORE). They represent an extension of the classical RE methods and better support the early-requirements phase: "Previously the world to be modeled consisted just of entities and activities." [DeIm2005].

Goals are the core concept in terms of modeling the stakeholders' interests and concerns, organizational goals, reasons for the later system to exist or hint on the alternatives for the subsequent development decisions. Agents on the other hand are seen as entities with goals. GORE methods try to serve both goal concepts. Some of the more noteworthy methods are:

- KAOS [DaLF1993] [vaDL1998] [vanL2000],
- EKD (Enterprise Knowledge Development) [KaLo1998],
- AGORA (Attributed Goal-Oriented Requirements Analysis) [KaHS 2002],
- GBRAM (Goal-Based Requirements Analysis Methodology) [Ant+ 2001],
- Albert I & II (Agent-oriented Language for Building and Eliciting Real-Time requirements) [DDDP1994].

Each method focuses on a different part of the RE-process as far as functions, phases or modeling elements are concerned.

In the following section we will first show how far the methods are usable during the RE phases defined in Section 2.2.1 and then analyze from a perspective of meta-modeling which types of organizational goals are currently supported by existing RE methods. To complete this analysis we consider further GORE methods and also methods from the related research field of Agent-oriented Requirements Engineering (AORE) with the case of i* [Yu1997] and Agent-oriented Software Engineering (AOSE) with the case of Tropos [CaKM2001].

2.3.2 Goal-Oriented Requirements Engineering Methods in the Requirements Engineering Phases

Based on a review of the documentation of existing GORE methods, further research conducted by [NuEa2000] [KaLo2004] and especially the work done by [Hein2005] we analyze the capability of methods of GORE to support the previously presented phases of RE. While an objective assessment of the capabilities of these methods is intended, the level of detail of the available documentation of some methods is not always adequate for this purpose. In these cases a more subjective decision, whether a method seems to fulfill the basic needs of a certain RE phase, was brought about.

- *Phase of requirements elicitation*: According to the results of [Hein 2005] the phase of requirements elicitation is the quantitatively best supported phase. It is found that in relative comparison EKD facilitates better than Tropos, i* and AGORA. On the other hand KAOS does not support this phase at all. [KaLo2004] comes to the same result. None of the methods explicitly stress a certain method for the elicitation of customers or stakeholder needs as requested in the definition.

- *Phase of requirements modeling*: In the underlying analysis papers, the modeling phase is connected with either the elicitation or the triage phase and called "negotiation". To come to a judgment of whether a method supports modeling or not we refer to the next section in this paper which deals with the question of goal modeling from a meta-modeling perspective.

- *Phase of requirements triage*: The results of the aforementioned "negotiation" phase are directly connected to this phase according to the fact that the triage phase is concerned with the communication with stakeholders and/or actors about the elicited and modeled goals and requirements in terms of deliberation. [Hein2005] comes to the conclusion that for this phase no single method is best suited, even though Tropos and i* have rudimentary support for negotiation with the stakeholders. [KaLo2004] underlines this impression because they do not associate any of the analyzed methods with this phase.

- *Phase of requirements specification*: The results from [Hein2005] show that this phase is supported best in comparison to the other phases. In detail, the support of KAOS for this phase is considered best followed by Tropos, NFR and GSC. [KaLo2004] also considers GBRAM as a suitable method to support this phase. Furthermore, Albert I & II facilitate this phase in a formally defined way.

- *Phase of requirements validation*: According to [Hein2005] and [KaLo2004] this phase is the worst supported phase in terms of activities explicitly advised in this phase's definition. GSN implicitly supports this phase according to the formal specification notation. This also applies for Albert I & II, GBRAM and NFR, which do allow an evaluation of the impact of decisions. URN and AGORA are assumed to support this phase best.

Table 1 sums up the discussed results[1]:

---

[1] s = suited; cs = conditionally suited; na = not appraisable.

Table 1. GORE methods per RE phase

	Elicitation	Modeling	Triage	Specification	Validation
GSN	na	s	s	s	cs
AGORA	s	s	s	s	s
i*	s	s	s	na	na
GDC	s	s	s	na	na
NFR	cs	s	cs	s	cs
GBRAM	na	s	s	s	cs
EKD	s	s	s	cs	na
GCS Method	na	na	cs	s	na
KAOS	s	s	na	s	na
ALBERT I&II	na	cs	na	s	cs
URN	cs	s	s	s	s
Tropos	s	s	s	s	na

2.3.3 Mapping of Requirements Through Goal-Oriented Requirements Engineering

As stated in the previous sections, goals and organizational aspects are important elements of requirements engineering for agent-based systems. To analyze the capability of GORE methods regarding the modeling of such goals and organizational aspects, we take a closer look at these elements using a meta-modeling perspective.

Meta-models apply in many research fields, such as the evaluation of object-oriented analysis methods [Stra1996] or Model Driven Architectures [KlWB2003]. In scientific literature the term "meta-model" is used in very different ways. But in general a meta-model can be understood as a models' model, also called an object model.

According to [Stra1996] language based and process based meta-models are distinguished. *Language-based meta-models* represent the syntax, semantic and notation of the object models [KaKu2002]. The *syntax* describes the elements and rules for creating models using grammar. *Semantics* represent the meaning of a modeling language and for this purpose consist of a semantic domain describing domain-specific meaning and a semantic mapping to connect syntactical elements and domain-specific elements. Finally, the visualization of the respective modeling language is defined by the *notation*. In contrast, *process-based meta-models* define single modeling steps that need to be done when creating object models. In this chapter, we use language-based meta-models.

2.3.3.1 Goal Meta-Model

The term "goal" is used to convey several meanings, including human tasks, problem-solving outcome or desired states. Therefore it seems difficult to identify a uniform notion of goals in requirements engineering. It is however possible to distinguish enterprise, process and evaluation goals as abstract types of goals [KaLo2004]:

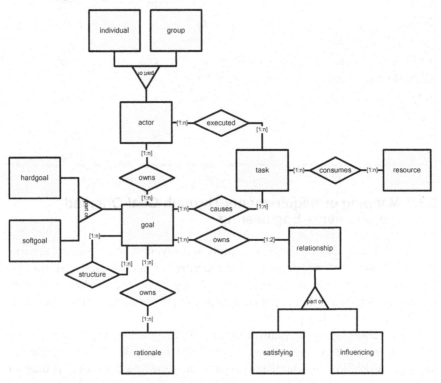

Figure 1. Goal meta-model

Enterprise goals describe wishes a company wants to achieve and can be business wide or single actor goals. *Process goals* designate any demand to be satisfied or issue to be discussed. *Evaluation goals* in contrast aim to assist requirements engineering validation signifying the stakeholders' criteria against which a system specification can be assessed [KaLo2004] [Mylo1992]. For the purpose of this chapter, we focus on enterprise goals and thus assess the capability of GORE methods regarding their capability to model these.

The underlying elements of the enterprise goal meta-model are:

- Goal: In general goals designate an aimed state or development that arrives as the effect of decisions [Hein1976] [Bidl1973]. Therefore goals have a guiding action character; the aiming and fulfilling intention is an integral part [Fres1992].
- Actor: An actor normally has at least one goal. The goal achievement leads to concrete tasks. An actor represents a role [Balz2000] [Jeck 2004] that can be taken by persons or groups, and interacts with other actors again.
- Resource: Generally spoken, resources characterize means or instruments to solve certain tasks. At the most, resources subsume working fund, basic materials, persons or information [Gabl2000].
- Relationship: Between the goals, diverse interdependency relations exist that provide information on which way the implementation of a specific goal influences the others: they can be either satisfying (complementary), neutral or influencing (concurrent) [BeDS2000].
- Rationale: The rationale is the explanation for the fundamental reasons [Kuep1975].

An analysis of the before mentioned GORE methods has shown that especially AGORA, I*, NFR, EKD and GBRAM address the business focus the most, wherefore the focus will be constricted to them.

The analysis shows that i* accomplishes most of the specified criteria, whereas EKD and GBRAM meet them less. None of the studied methods address actors on the level of individuals or groups. Although i* exclusively caters to the needed resources, it leaves out the rationale for the specified goals. Thus the "why"-question suffers noticeably. Measured by the defined characteristic values, both GBRAM and EKD handle the goal term undifferentiated. They also do not address the necessary single tasks and activities for achieving the specified goals.

Table 2. GORE methods per goal element

	AGORA	i*	NFR	EKD	GBRAM
Goals				✓	✓
Time referenced	✓				
Hardgoal		✓			
Softgoal		✓	✓		
Prioritized	✓	✓	✓		
Contribution	✓	✓	✓		
Rationale	✓			✓	✓
Actors	✓	✓		✓	✓
Individual					
Group					
Tasks		✓	✓		
Resources		✓			
Relationship					✓
Satisfying and/or	✓	✓	✓	✓	
Influencing conflict support	✓	✓	✓	✓	

2.3.3.2 Company Organization Structure Meta-Model

On eliciting goals the organizational context may not be disregarded, as a poor understanding of the surrounding domain is a primary cause of project failure [CuKI1988]. Therefore a deep understanding of the needs, interests, priorities and abilities of the various actors and players is indispensable [Yu1997]. Therefore the characteristic elements of an organizational meta-model need to be defined [RoMu1997] [HiFU1994] and modeled in a semantic data model [Balz2000]:

- Role: In research literature a consistent understanding of this term does not exist yet. Therefore we define in this context a role to be the minimal qualification for the execution of a task (e.g. special skills), transferred competences, privileges and responsibilities.
- Job: A job combines several tasks and delegates them to a person permanently. One task comprises different single activities that need to be processed. Activities are elements of any processes. Various relations (e.g. technical assignment or substitute regulations) exist between single jobs. Jobs that perform tasks together are often centralized to departments.

- Job type: Job types represent jobs with the same competences. One job type can comprise several roles whereas one role can be referenced by several job types.
- Task responsible: A task responsible is at least one person, as only persons can carry competences and responsibilities. It is also possible that one job is executed by two or more persons, which can be both internal and external [HiFU1994] [Thom1992]. As external persons (e.g. customers or freelancers) need to be modeled too, we abandon the obligation of attaching a person to a job.
- Organizational unit: Single units are combined to organizational units, which on their part build the company organization structure. They can be differentiated as permanent and temporary. Temporary organization units normally lie orthogonal to the permanent units and allow building structures such as projects or committees.
- Connecting paths: As jobs always only accomplish sub-tasks they need to be connected in the sense of cooperation and coordination. Therefore several connecting paths are established, on which either physical objects or information is exchanged. Consequently we differ between routes of transport and information paths. The issue of routes of transport is normally subsumed under the term "materials logistics."

Information logistics on the other hand must supply jobs with their required information and support the information exchange between jobs.

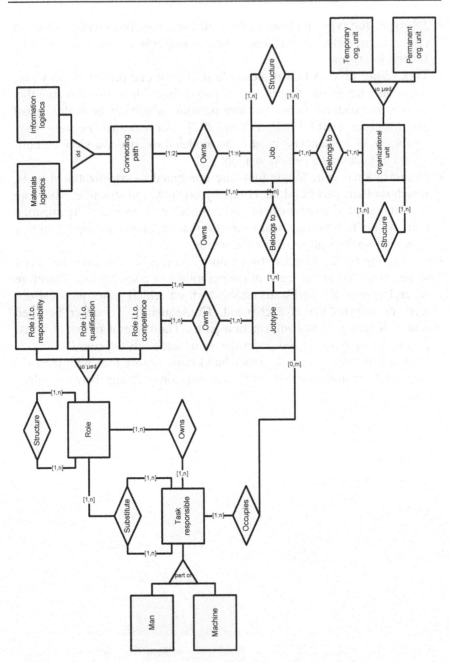

Figure 2. Organization structure meta-model

For the analysis of existing GORE methods in reference to the ability to capture organizational structures to a sufficient extent all methods have been taken into account, as the consideration of these structures is not bound to a special type of method as was the case in the goal-focused analysis. The formal organizational elements worked out of the evaluated methods are presented in Table 3.

Table 3. GORE methods per formal organizational element

	GSN	AGORA	i*	GDC	NFR	GBRAM	EKD	GSC Method	KAOS	ALBERT I & II	URN	Tropos
Role			✓				✓				✓	✓
Qualification												
Competence												
Role hierarchy												
Job												
Job hierarchy												
Job type												
Task responsible		✓					✓				✓	✓
Organizational unit												
Permanent												
Temporary												
Hierarchy												
Connecting paths												

Vertical column annotations: GSN — "Organizational modeling not supported"; AGORA — "Organizational aspects not explicitly modeled, but stakeholders included"; GDC — "Organizational aspects not explicitly modeled, but stakeholders included"; NFR — "Organizational modeling not supported"; GBRAM — "Organizational modeling not supported"; GSC Method — "Organizational modeling not supported"; KAOS — "Organizational modeling not supported"; ALBERT I & II — "Organizational modeling not supported".

As a first result it is obvious, that eight of the evaluated methods do not picture the organizational reality at all, as can be found in Workflow-Management-Systems, for instance as a counter example. Only four methods, namely i*, EKD, URN and Tropos, contain the option to sufficiently map at least some of the needed elements. Single roles can be modeled and connected to task responsibles that appear in a non-nearer specified role.

2.4 Conclusion and Further Research

In this chapter, some questions that arise in the context of requirements engineering for agent-based systems were discussed. Thus a notion about the demands that suitable RE methods must face was developed to see if existing methods comply with these needs. Therefore we presented the different phases and methods of RE to get a basic understanding of agent-based RE in general. In a second step we analyzed flexibility as the major advantage of agent systems and split it up into more operationalizable constituents: goals, situated behavior and autonomy. Because of the goal-orientation of MAS, we restricted our view to the methods of Goal-Oriented Requirements Engineering and their capability to manage relevant requirements.

We found out that not all introduced phases of requirements engineering are covered by all discussed GORE Methods. The AGORA method is suited best to support all RE phases. Furthermore, not all relevant aspects regarding goals and organizational requirements are handled adequately by all GORE methods. Here, the i* method provides the best support for modeling goals and further organizational aspects.

The most significant capability of agent-based systems is to provide flexibility. This capability comprises *technical, economic, static* and *dynamic flexibility* as the capability of changing flexibility potential at runtime, which characterizes the ability to adapt to changes in different ways. None of the analyzed GORE methods directly support these dimensions of flexibility. Instead they focus, among other aspects, on the derived characteristics, such as goals.

GORE methods can be considered as independent of the underling technology insofar as they focus on requirements from a very abstract point of view. Thus, they are in a way suitable for RE for agent-based systems, as they focus on the description of requirements by defining goals and the environment of a system. By this, they allow the identification of technologically independent requirements, while concrete technical requirements of a system are not considered. However, this abstract point of view may not be suitable to capture all relevant types of requirements. This becomes apparent when looking at the requirements discussed in connection with flexibility. They are omitted by the GORE methods presented above. Yet, we showed that indirect links between high-level requirements, flexibility requirements and concrete design aspects of agent systems, such as goals and organizational environments, can be identified. Thus, flexibility requirements can be represented only indirectly by goals and organizational environments in GORE methods.

Further research in this line will pursue the development of new GORE methods for better addressing the agent-based requirements. While a first step towards the identification of new requirements was done in this chapter, there is still a lot of analysis necessary to better define aspects of flexibility. However, as the current focus of GORE methods is not suitable to capture all types of requirements, additional RE methods may be needed to capture these very requirements.

References

[AbMo2004]   Abran, A.; Moore, J.W.: Guide to the Software Engineering Body of Knowledge. IEEE Press, 2004.

[Ant+2001]   Anton, A. I.; Carter, R. A.; Dagnino, A.; Dempster, J. H.; Siege, D. F.: Deriving Goals from a Use Case Based Requirements Specification. In: Requirements Engineering Journal 6(2001), pp. 63-73.

[ArWo2002]   Arazy, O.; Woo, C. C.: Analysis and Design of Agent-Oriented Information Systems. In: The Knowledge Engineering Review 3 (2002), pp. 215-260.

[Balz2000]   Balzert, H.: Lehrbuch der Software-Technik: Softwareentwicklung, 2nd ed. Spektrum, Heidelberg, 2000.

[BEds2000]   Bea, F.; Dichtl, E.; Schweitzer, M.: Allgemeine Betriebswirtschaftslehre, vol.1, 8th ed. UTB, Stuttgart, 2000.

[Bidl1973]   Bidlingsmaier, J.: Unternehmensziele und Unternehmensstrategien. Gabler, Wiesbaden, 1973.

[Boeh1981]   Boehm, B.: Software Engineering Economics. Prentice Hall, New Jersey, 1981.

[Broy2004]   Broy, M.: Architecture Driven Modeling in Software Development. In: Proceedings of the 9th IEEE International Conference on Engineering Complex Computer Systems Navigating Complexity in the e-Engineering Age (ICECCS´04). IEEE Press, pp. 3-12.

[CaKM2001]   Castro, J.; Kolp, M.; Mylopoulos, J.: A Requirements-Driven Development Methodology. In: Dittrich, K. D.; Geppert, A.; Norrie, M.C. (Eds.): Advanced Information Systems Engineering. Lecture Notes in Computer Science 2068. Springer, 2001, pp. 108-123.

[Chun1993]   Chung, L.: Representing and Using Non-Functional Requirements: A Process-Oriented Approach. PhD Thesis, University of Toronto, DKBS-TR-93-1, 1993.

[CuKI1988]   Curtis, B.; Krasner, H.; Iscoe, N.: A Field Study of the Software Design Process for Large Systems. In: Communications of the ACM 31(1988)11, pp. 1268-1287.

[DaLF1993]   Dardenne, A.; van Lamsweerde, A.; Fickas, S.: Goal-directed requirements acquisition. In: Science of Computer Programming 20(1993), pp. 3-50.

[Davi1993]   Davis, A. M.: Software Requirements: Objects, Functions and States. Prentice Hall, New Jersey, 1993.

[Davi2003]   Davis, A. M.: The Art of Requirements Triage. In: IEEE Computer 3(2003), pp. 42-49.

[DeIm2005]   De Antonio, A.; Imbert, R.: Combining Requirements Engineering and Agents. In: Mate, J. L.; Silva, A. (Eds.): Requirements Engineering for Sociotechnical Systems. Information Science Publishing, Hershey, 2005, pp. 68-83.

[DDDP1994]   Dubois, E.; Du Bois, P.; Dubru, F.; Petit, M.: Agent-oriented Requirements Engineering: A Case Study using the ALBERT Language. In: Verbraeck, A.; Sol, H. G.; Bots, P. W. G. (Eds.): Proceedings of the 4th International Working Conference on Dynamic Modelling and Information Systems. 1994.

[Fres1992]   Frese, E.: Handwörterbuch der Organisation, 3rd ed. Poeschel, Stuttgart, 1992.

[Gabl2000]   Gabler-Wirtschafts-Lexikon. Gabler, Wiesbaden, 2000.

[GoWa2003]   Görz, G.; Wachsmuth, I.: Einleitung. In: Görz, G.; Rollinger, C. R.; Schneeberger, J. (Eds.): Handbuch der künstlichen Intelligenz, 4th ed. Oldenbourg, München, 2003.

[Grah1998]   Graham, I.: Requirements Engineering and Rapid Development. Addison-Wesley, Boston, 1998.

[Hein1976]   Heinen, E.: Grundlagen betriebswirtschaftlicher Entscheidungen – Das Zielsystem der Unternehmung, 3rd ed. Gabler, Wiesbaden, 1976.

[Hein2005]   Heine, C.: Goal oriented Requirements Engineering Methods for Developing Agent Systems. In: it – Information Technology 1(2005), pp. 20-27.

[HeCF2003]   Hexmoor, H.; Castelfranchi, C.; Falcone, R.: A Prospectus on Agent Autonomy. In: Hexmoor, H.; Castelfranchi, C.; Falcone, R. (Eds.): Agent Autonomy. Kluwer, Boston, 2003, pp. 1-10.

[HiDa2003]   Hickey, A. M.; Davis, A. M.: Requirement Elicitation and Elicitation Technique Selection: A Model for Two Knowledge-Intensive Software Development Processes. In: Proceedings of the 36th Hawaii International Conference on System Science. IEEE Press, 2003.

[HiFU1994]   Hill, W.; Fehlbaum, R.; Ulrich, P.: Organisationslehre. UTB, Stuttgart, 1994.

[HoLe2001]   Hofmann, H. F.; Lehner, F.: Requirements Engineering as a Success Factor in Software Projects. In: IEEE Software 4(2001), pp. 58-66.

[IbRe1996]   Ibanez, M.; Rempp, H.: European Software Process Improvement Training Initiative – European User Survey Analysis. TR 95104, 1996.

[ISO2001]   ISO/IEC 9126: Software Engineering – Product Quality – Part 1: Quality Model. 2001.

[Jack1998]   Jackson, M. A.: A Discipline of Description. In: Requirements Engineering Journal 2(1998), pp. 73-78.

[Jeck2004]   Jeckle, M.: UML 2 glasklar. Hanser, München, 2004.

[KaHS2002]   Kaiyia, H.; Horai, H.; Saeki, M.: AGORA: Attributed Goal-Oriented Requirements Analysis Method. In: 10th Anniversary IEEE Joint International Conference on Requirements Engineering. IEEE Computer Society, 2002, pp. 13-22.

[KaKu2002]   Karagiannis, D.; Kühn, H.: Metamodelling Platforms. In: Bauknecht, K.; Min Tjoa, A.; Quirchmayer, G. (Eds.): Proceedings of the Third International Conference EC-Web 2002 - Dexa 2002, Aix-en-Provence, France, September 2-6, 2002. Springer, Berlin, p. 182.

[Kava2002]   Kavakli, E.: Goal-Oriented Requirements Engineering: A Unifying Framework. In: Requirements Engineering 4(2002), pp. 237-251.

[Kava2004]   Kavakli, E.: Modeling organizational goals: Analysis of current methods. Proceedings of the 2004 ACM Symposium on Applied Computing, Nicosia, CY. ACM, New York, 2004, pp. 1339-1343.

[KaLo1998]   Kavakli, E.; Loucopoulos, P.: Goal driven business analysis: An application in electrivity deregulation. CAiSE'98, Pisa, 1998.

[KaLo2004]   Kavakli, E.; Loucopoulos, P.: Goal Driven Requirements Engineering: Analysis and Critique of Current Methods. In: Krogstie, J.; Terry, H. T.; Siau, K. (Eds.): Information Modeling Methods and Methodologies. IDEA Group, Hershey, 2004, pp. 102-124.

[KlWB2003]   Kleppe, A.; Warmer, J.; Bast, W.: MDA Explained: The Model Driven Architecture: Practice and Promise. Addison-Wesley, Boston, 2003.

[Kuep1975]   Küpper, H.-J.: Das Rationalprinzip. In: WiSt – Wirtschaftswissenschaftliches Studium 4(1975), pp. 95-97.

[LeRa2002]   Lehman, M. M.; Ramil, J. F.: Software Evolution and Software Evolution Processes. In: Annals of Software Engineering 14 (2002), pp. 275-309.

[LuDM2003]   Luck, M.; D'Inverno, M.; Munroe, S.: Autonomy: Variable and Generative. In: Hexmoor, H.; Castelfranchi, C.; Falcone, R. (Eds.): Agent Autonomy. Kluwer, Boston, 2003, pp. 11-28.

[Mylo1992]   Mylopoulus, J.: Conceptual Modelling and Telos. In: Loucopoulos, P.; Zicari, R. (Eds.): Conceptual Modelling, Databases and CASE: An Integrated View of Information Systems Development. Wiley, New York, 1992, pp. 49-68.

[NaKu1991]   Nakajo, T.; Kume, H.: A Case History Analysis of Software Error Cause-Effect Relationships. In: Transaction on Software Engineering 8(1991), pp. 830-838.

[NuEa2000]   Nuseibeh, B.; Easterbrook, S.: Requirements Engineering: A Roadmap. In: 22nd International Conference on Software Engineering (ICSE'00), Future of Software Engineering Track. ACM Press, Limerick, 2000, pp. 35-46.

380   T. Bieser et al.

[PaEM2003]   Paetsch, F.; Eberlein, A.; Maurer, F.: Requirements Engineering and Agile Development. In: 12th International Workshop on Enabling Technologies: Infrastructure for Collaborative Enterprises (WETICE´03). IEEE Press, 2003, pp. 308-314.

[Part1998]   Partsch, H.: Requirements Engineering systematisch: Modellbildung für softwaregestützte Systeme. Springer, Berlin, 1998.

[Pohl1996]   Pohl, K: Process-Centered Requirements Engineering. Wiley, 1996.

[RoMu1997]   Rosemann, M.; zur Muehlen, M.: Modellierung der Aufbauorganisation in Workflow-Management-Systemen: Kritische Bestandsaufnahme und Gestaltungsvorschlaege. In: Jablonski, S. (Ed.): Proceedings of the EMISA-Fachgruppentreffen. Darmstadt, 1997, pp. 100-118.

[RuNo2003]   Russel, S.; Norvig, P.: Artificial Intelligence: A modern Approach, 2nd ed. Prentice Hall, New Jersey, 2003.

[SiRG2001]   Singh, M. P.; Rao, A. S.; Georgeff, M. P.: Formal Methods in DAI: Logic-Based Representation and Reasoning. In: Weiss, G. (Ed.): Multiagent Systems – A Modern Approach to Distributed Artificial Intelligence. MIT Press, Cambridge, 2001, pp. 331-376.

[Somm2005]   Sommerville, I.: Integrated Requirements Engineering: A Tutorial. In: IEEE Software 1(2005), pp. 16-23.

[Stra1996]   Strahringer, S.: Metamodellierung als Instrument des Methodenvergleichs - Eine Evaluierung am Beispiel objektorientierter Analysemethoden. Shaker, Aachen, 1996.

[ThDo1990]   Thayer, R. H.; Dorfman, M.: System and Software Requirements Engineering. IEEE Computer Society Press Tutorial, 1990.

[Thom1992]   Thom, N.: Stelle, Stellenbildung und -besetzung. In: Frese, E. (Ed.): Handwörterbuch der Organisation, 3rd ed. Schäffer, Stuttgart, 1992.

[vaDL1998]   van Lamsweerde, A.; Darimont, R.; Letier, E.: Managing conflicts in goal-driven requirements engineering. In: IEEE Transactions on Software Engineering 11(1998), pp. 908-926.

[vanL2000]   van Lamsweerde, A.: Requirements Engineering in the Year 00: A Research Perspective. In: 22nd International Conference on Software Engineering (ICSE´00). ACM Press, Limerick, 2000, pp. 5-19.

[vanL2004]   van Lamsweerde, A.: Goal-oriented Requirements Engineering: A Roundtrip from Research to Practice. In: Proceedings of RE'04, 12th IEEE Joint International Requirements Engineering Conference. IEEE Press, 2004.

[Weis2003]   Weiß, G. (Ed.): Multiagent Systems – A Modern Approach to Distributed Artificial Intelligence. MIT Press, Cambridge, 2003, p. 603.

[WeJa2005]   Weiß, G.; Jakob, R.: Agentenorientierte Softwareentwicklung. Springer, Berlin, 2005.

[WoJe1995]   Wooldridge, M.; Jennings, N.: Intelligent Agents: Theory and practice. In: The Knowledge Engineering Review 2(1995), pp. 115-152.

[Yu1997]   Yu, E.: Towards Modelling and Reasoning Support for Early-Phase Requirements Engineering. In: Proceedings of the 3rd IEEE International Symp. on Requirements Engineering (RE' 97). Washington, 1997, pp. 226-235.

3 Interaction Design

Karl-Heinz Krempels, Otto Spaniol

RWTH Aachen, Lehrstuhl für Informatik IV
{krempels I spaniol}@informatik.rwth-aachen.de

Thorsten Scholz, Ingo J. Timm, Otthein Herzog

Universität Bremen, Technologie-Zentrum Informatik
{scholz I i.timm I herzog}@tzi.uni-bremen.de

Abstract. Interaction is one of the core challenges in multiagent systems. It enables agents to share their knowledge, to do competitive or cooperative planning, coordination or bargaining, to interact with their principals, and to simple act. Interaction has to be restrictive enough to enable reliable system behavior and should be permissive enough to allow for flexibility or emergent behavior and performance. Obviously, the design of interaction differs from interface design in conventional software engineering significantly. Agents may also be designed for use in changing, respective unknown environments.

3.1 Introduction

The main benefit of MAS might be found in the provided flexibility. This flexibility is similar to the properties of emergence, which have been discussed from the early days of MAS research on. As one of the key challenges for engineering MAS is interaction design. Conventional design and implementation of distributed systems consists of standardizing interaction and consequently implementing strict interfaces. The approach of Web Services incorporates flexible links of consumer to provider services. Nevertheless, there is no "slack" in their interaction, which allows for solving dynamically emerging problems.

Interaction design should enable a system engineer to avoid a possible rigid design character of distributed interacting system components. This Chapter will introduce the fundamental concepts and general approaches used in agent interaction design, the agent interaction capabilities, and types of agent interactions.

This chapter is organized as follows: We introduce the foundations of agent interaction with special focus on categories of application domains. On this basis, different properties of communication resp. interaction mechanism evaluation are discussed. The following sections are focused on different types of interaction infrastructures, i.e., shared memory and message passing. Subsequently, agent communication languages are briefly introduced. The question of mechanism design resp. design of interaction in AOSE is discussed following the four AOSE methodologies introduced in IV.1. Concluding, challenges for the design of interaction in heterogeneous multiagent systems are identified.

3.2 Foundations of Agent Interaction

A collection of agents becomes an agent society only if the agents can interact. As mentioned earlier, the autonomy of the individual agents results in loose coupling among the agents. Weiss [Weis1999, p. 3] identifies four major characteristics of multiagent systems that have a direct bearing on the interaction between agents:

- Each agent has just incomplete information and is restricted in its capabilities.
- System control is distributed.
- Data is decentralized.
- Computation is asynchronous.

In other words, there is no "natural" central authority to which the agents can turn to organize the cooperation – if they need such an authority they would have to find one of their own, an agent, to take on this responsibility.

The characteristics of multiagent systems as described above imply that the agents are organized in a distributed way, i.e., they have their own knowledge bases as well as their own control cycles. Depending on the application of the multiagent system, the agents will have to solve problems either cooperatively or competitively, and this will determine the kind of required interaction. Rosenschein and Zlotkin distinguish between three different categories of application domains [RoZl1994]: *task-oriented (TOD)*, *state-oriented (SOD)*, and *worth-oriented (WOD)* domains. These domains are organized in a three-tier theoretical model, where *WOD* are the most general and *TOD* the most specific kind of domains.

- *TOD*: multiagent systems are mainly used for distributed problem solving under the assumption that all required resources are available, i.e., agents are cooperatively solving problems or tasks which cannot be solved by a single agent or entity.

- *SOD*: the challenge for agents in these domains arises from efficient and effective negotiation about bottleneck resources, and agents have to transform an initial state to one of their goal states. In contrast to *TOD*, these domains are characterized by conflicts and competition over limited resources.
- *WOD* are a generalization of *SOD*, where every state is associated with a function assessing the private value for the agents (the "worth" to an agent). This allows for the application of decision or game theoretic approaches to agent coordination. *SODs* may be implemented as *WOD* where all none-goal states are assessed a value of 0.

For multiagent design, it is crucial to clarify the type of domain before specification of interaction issues. Interaction control in *TOD* settings should mainly rely on behavior whereas monetary assessments as in auction protocols seem less suitable. In *WODs* conflicting recommendations may be proposed so that structured and monetary-based communications are the first choice for interaction design. Open negotiation does not take advantage of the possibility to evaluate individual states by each agent. Therefore, a pattern-based interaction control seems superior for this case.

In consequence, interaction may be evaluated with respect to the change of value for an agent. The resulting question for the interaction design is the choice of the adequate interaction control for a specific situation.

As introduced in I.2, there are two basic concepts for realizing agent interaction: shared memory and message passing. Message passing results in a looser coupling of agents, leaving them more latitude and thus better flexibility in their actions. Consequently, in recent research and applications of multiagent systems message passing is the predominant method for agent interaction. Notice, that none of the research projects presented in Parts II and III utilized a shared memory approach.

3.3 Interaction in Multiagent Systems

Cooperative distributed problem solving has been one of the starting points for distributed artificial intelligence research in the 80ies. The study of how loosely-coupled networks of problem solvers could work together to solve problems beyond individual capabilities has been in focus of research [DuLC1989]. Cooperation has been necessary, because no single agent is assumed to have sufficient expertise, resources, or information to solve a problem solely. The basic assumptions of this approach are that agents are benevolent, share common goals at least implicitly, and there is no potential for conflicts of interest between agents.

In real-world business scenarios the assumption of benevolent agents or cooperative settings does not hold. Furthermore, it is assumed that multi-agent systems are "societies" of self-interested actors, which do not necessarily share common goals. A reason for this may be found in the fact, that agents in a multiagent system have been designed and implemented in a different way and thus do not share common goals. Therefore encounters between such agents resemble games where agents have to act strategically in order to achieve their goals. Since agents are designed with autonomous behavior they must be capable of dynamically coordinate their actions and cooperate with other agents at run-time of the system. In contrary classic distributed systems have their coordination and cooperation potential hardwired at design time [Wool2002].

A simplified approach would distinguish between two types of multi-agent systems: cooperative and competitive. However even in cooperative settings coordination mechanisms based on competition, e.g. auction protocols, may be applied.

For evaluation purposes, the assessment of efficiency is crucial. In order to make a well-founded decision, a set of evaluation criteria is required to support the decision process. Rosenschein and Zlotkin introduced a set of five attributes of negotiation mechanisms, which may assist in the selection of concrete mechanisms [RoZl1994]. The first property, *efficiency*, is related to an agent's usage of resources with consideration of global and Pareto optimality (cf., e.g., [Krep1990]). The *stability* of a negotiation mechanism is closely related to the definition of strategies in equilibrium, i.e., no individual agent should have an advantage of acting incentively [FuTi1991]. This aspect is accompanied by the property *symmetry*, which is addressed to the problem, that interaction mechanisms should not be arbitrarily biased against an agent. Two further properties deal with complexity issues: *simplicity*, the overall computational complexity for an individual agent but also for the community of agents should be in balance with benefits of cooperation between agents and the *distribution* property suggests that there should not be a central decision maker for applying the negotiation mechanism. Sandholm has proposed similar evaluation criteria for the choice of interaction control in [Sand1999]. In his approach, *social welfare* measures the "global good" of all agents, i.e., the payoffs or utilities in a given solution and is closely related to the next criterion, the *Pareto efficiency*. This criterion measures also the "global good", but does not require inter-agent utility comparisons. In contrast to these global efficiency criteria is the local *individual rationality*. Here, the payoff of an agent from a negotiated solution should be no less than the payoff it would have if it would not participate in the negotiation. The next criterion is *stability* which Sandholm defines on the basis of the Nash Equilibrium, i.e., strategies resp. dominant strategies. The last two efficiency criteria are addressed to complexity: *computational efficiency* within an agent as well as *distribution and communication efficiency*.

While the evaluation criteria of Rosenschein and Zlotkin as well as Sandholm form an abstract basis for the assessment of interaction mechanisms, the challenge here lies on the formulation of criteria, which may be applied to practical settings of multiagent system applications. These settings for evaluation are given by agents in a multiagent system, a problem associated with a payoff-function for its solution, and a cost-function associated with agents indicating their effort for participating in the solution. Mandatory categories for the evaluation are *efficiency*, *reliability*, and *complexity*. The *efficiency* might be measured by individual and global outcome, e.g., individual rationality, global welfare, and Pareto efficiency. The main criteria for *reliability* range from stability defined as resistance against manipulation on basis of non-cooperative game theory to symmetry which indicates that both sides of an interaction reach comparable payoffs. The third category, *complexity*, is regarded to technical efficiency, i.e., aspects as computation, communication, and speed up through distribution are considered.

3.4 Shared Memory

The oldest cooperation model and for a long time the mainstay of controlled agent interaction has been the *blackboard system*. It follows the natural metaphor of a group of human specialists seated next to a large blackboard. The specialists work cooperatively to solve a problem, using the blackboard for developing the solution. Problem solving begins with the problem and initial data written onto the blackboard. The specialists watch the blackboard, looking for an opportunity to apply their expertise to the evolving solution. When a specialist finds sufficient information to make a contribution, he records the contribution on the blackboard.

The metaphor is abstracted to the architecture of Figure 1, with the blackboard as a common workspace, and the specialists represented by so-called knowledge sources having their processing machinery and implementation hidden from direct view. The basic assumption is that each knowledge source is an expert on some aspects of the problem and can contribute to the solution independently of the other sources. Knowledge sources are triggered into action in response to blackboard and external events, and may add, modify or remove information on the blackboard. Rather than continuously scanning the blackboard, a knowledge source subscribes to certain kinds of events. Obviously then, a control component separate from the knowledge sources is needed for managing the blackboard and, more importantly, the course of problem solving.

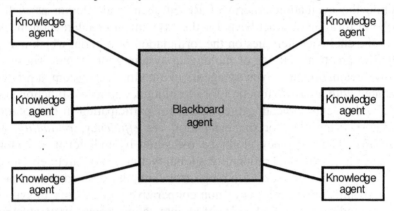

Figure 1. Blackboard system, basic distributed solution.

Blackboard systems have several drawbacks that make them less attractive for modern multiagent systems. They require a centralized blackboard and control component, problem solving is purely sequential, and the need for synchronous communication contradicts the autonomy of agents. A distributed approach that relies on a planning and execution strategy is referred to as "task sharing" or "task passing" [Durf1999]. Another distributed option would introduce a special agent to control the blackboard, like illustrated in Figure 2.

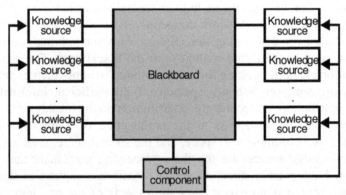

Figure 2. Blackboard system

The main properties of multiagent systems using a shared memory approach may be found in the assumption that any agent is using the same problem representation, the agents are interacting cooperatively, there is no need for direct or private interaction, and there is no need for pro-active behavior. In problem domains where cooperative problem solving is in question, i.e., task-oriented domains, shared memory approaches may be an efficient approach for coordination and interaction. However the shared memory approach could evolve to a bottleneck and therefore has a negative influence on scalability.

3.5 Message Passing

In contrast to the shared memory approach, the message passing approach is characterized by more complex message structures, separation of internal and external representations, and is often speech-act based. Message passing seems essential as an interaction infrastructure whenever the assumption of cooperative behavior does not hold or where the underlying technical infrastructure is a distributed system. Furthermore, message passing is more suitable for scaling up or distributing multiagent systems. However, the individual effort for handling communication is considerably higher compared to shared memory approaches. This results from the required naming schema for the identification of agents in distributed systems, the routing overhead needed for message delivery, and the encoding for different communication and representation layers.

The naming schema must allow the identification of an agent and its communication addresses. Furthermore, the naming schema must be implemented by directory services used for agent and service discovery, and must hide the logical underlying communication protocols, e.g. HTTP, WAP, IIOP, and the used physical communication infrastructures, e.g Ethernet, ATM, Bluetooth, etc. In heterogeneous distributed systems the gap among platforms with different implemented protocols must be closed with the help of gateways that support many protocols at the corresponding logical or physical communication layer, and are able to translate the protocol of an incoming message to one that will be understood by the message receiver.

Routing of messages is necessary to determine the way on which a message will be delivered from the sender to the receiver. If a message is delivered to the receiver without the intervention of an intermediate agent or gateway, the message is delivered directly and the two communication parties communicate in *direct* mode. The *indirect* communication mode involves intermediate benevolent parties, which support the communication demand of the former parties. These definitions can be carried over to interactions.

Due to the discussed naming schema and message routing the message format becomes more complex. Furthermore, the separation of internal and external representation of the message content requires a few consecutive encoding and decoding steps, corresponding to the appropriate abstraction layer. This leads to a kind of virtual envelope that contains elements for the identification of an agent, message routing information and content description, e.g.: agent identifier, agent communication addresses, encoding language, content language, the type of the message, a time stamp of the message, etc.

3.5.1 Conversations

The possibility for more sophisticated interaction between technical components makes up for the complex message structure. Just take the difference between interaction among objects and agents. Interaction among objects is restricted to the reciprocal invocation of public methods and limited object protocols in the form of well-defined sequences of method calls. Agents are supposed to interact at a higher level: An agent is able to decide by itself when and whether an external requested action is to be processed, and is also able to process a message based on its internal knowledge base and domain vocabularies, i.e., does more than strictly executing the body of a method.

Agents that communicate via the message passing mechanism can completely hide their internal knowledge base and reasoning engines from the other agents. Therefore, the message passing approach is more suitable for interactions in *SOD* and *WOD*.

Since communication among agents is of a more sophisticated quality we will in the remainder refer to the communication among two or more agents as a *conversation*.

As matter of principle, the interaction among agents should follow a limited number of institutionalized, i.e., generic (conversation) patterns. The design of these patterns is an important objective of the design of an agent society architecture. Typical conversation patterns are contract nets, auctions, bargaining, etc. If existing interaction patterns do not suffice and new patterns cannot be designed in advance, the conversation could be controlled by the agents' behavior, that is, guided by a problem solving method or a utility function.

3.5.2 Pattern-Based Conversations

Conversations are considered in real life as part of the normal acquaintance. Usually a conversation has a goal, varying from a simple announcement to complicated negotiations. One can either observe conversations among humans to identify patterns that are used for specific situations, or should design the pattern with a special objective in mind, e.g. efficiency, a limitation of time, participants etc. The representation of conversations as directed graphs, containing a node for each participant of the conversation and a directed edge for interaction taken, would simplify the recognition process. The edges could be labeled to reflect the chronological order of the interactions among the participants.

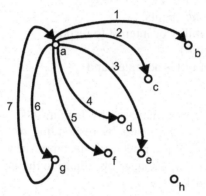

Figure 3. Conversation pattern represented as DG

In Figure 3 we observe that participant a interacts with all the other participants excepting the participant h. This justifies the assumption that participant a holds the role of a coordinator. Depending on the conversation context, its role could be:

- a coordinator for a call for proposals in a contract net or in an auction, if and only if the messages 1 to 6 were sent simultaneously,
- a coordinator in a leader election algorithm, notifying the participants b to g that the participant g becomes leader, and receiving its commitment therefore,
- a sentinel requesting from the participants b to g the time of their last interaction with participant h, etc.

The most widely used truly distributed interaction protocol is the contract net protocol. The protocol is modeled on the contracting mechanism used by businesses to govern the exchange of goods and services and achieves a satisfactory overall "social" outcome if the agents pursue only their self-interest [Sand1999].

The protocol provides a solution for the so-called connection problem: finding an appropriate agent to work on a given task. An agent wanting a task solved is called the manager, agents that might be able to solve the task are called potential contractors. The manager

- announces a task that needs to be performed,
- receives and evaluates bids from potential contractors,
- awards a contract to a suitable contractor and
- receives and synthesizes results.

From a contractor's perspective the process is to

- receive task announcements,
- evaluate own capability or interest to respond,
- respond (decline, bid),
- perform the task if bid is accepted and
- report the results.

Any agent can act as a manager by making task announcements, and any agent can act as a contractor by responding to task announcements. This flexibility allows for further task decomposition: a contractor for a specific task may act as a manager by soliciting the help of other agents in solving parts of the task.

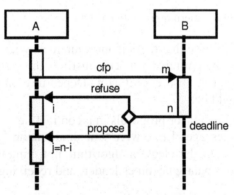

Figure 4. Conversation pattern represented in AUML

Conversations can be described in a formal fashion. Take the conversation pattern in Figure 4 which is part of a contract net. Therefore we assume that participant *a* holds the proactive role of a coordinator and corresponds to node *a* in Figure 3. We assume further that the interactions *1* to *6* take place simultaneously. The conversation participants *b* to *g* hold the reactive role of a simple conversation participant. In Figure 4 the participant b is representative of this reactive role and the initiator a of the former, proactive one.

More complex conversation patterns could consist of many simpler conversation patterns, as the one in Figure 3. With the help of the observation method it seems that only simple patterns could be identified, and for complex patterns the observation sense of someone will be overextend. As simple patterns we could consider the patterns of conversations of type question-answer, request-agree/refuse and auction mechanisms. More complex conversation patterns that are harder to recognize, may be because the conversation patterns contain an embedded negotiation strategy, a game strategy, or are part of a problem solving method should be cooperatively designed by domain and problem solving experts. This enables the pattern designers to take into account also the functional and non-functional requirements, resulting from the requirements analysis, as well as limitations of suitable problem solving methods, e.g. stability, the space and time complexity of algorithms, etc. At this point it's a good time to remind us that a conversation among technical components, e.g., intelligent agents should not be an end in itself, and that it should be an essential part of the problem solving method of competitive or cooperative participants.

It can happen that for a complex problem no suitable conversation patterns can be found. In this case the interaction designer could try to compose a new conversation pattern, lets name it a conversation meta pattern, using well known patterns for generic situations. When a conversation pattern was recognized, it should be analyzed with the objective to determine the roles of the conversation participants, e.g. initiator, responder, arbitrator, etc. In the case of a designed conversation pattern, the roles of the participants are well known before the conversation pattern is design. The roles of conversation participants could be specified with the help of rules, that define the proactive, reactive, or possibly alternating behavior of a participant in a conversation, depending on preceding interactions.

3.5.3 Behavior-Based Conversations

A large part of conversations among technical systems could be assigned to corresponding patterns or will be designed based on known conversation patterns. Complex conversations that are not covered by existing patterns have to be controlled by the agents' behavior. An agents' behavior is guided by a problem solving method or a utility function.

In case of behavior-based conversation control, the behavior of an agent is guided with respect to its capabilities, e.g. communication, interaction, mobility, adaptability, etc., by one or more utility functions of the agent. A utility function could influence the agents' behavior in a direct way, in the sense that the agents' behavior change is the immediate effect of the value change of the utility function. In other words, the agents' behavior follows the utility functions graph, on which we can imagine virtual triggers for actions of the agent, which finally determines the agents' behavior. The utility function itself could be influenced in this case by interactions of the agent with other agents (incoming messages), by changes of internal states of the agent, which could depend on other utility functions, finite state machines, probabilistic networks, by events recognized by the agent with the help of its sensors, etc.

Furthermore, an agents' behavior could be influenced in an indirect way when the agent adapts its behavior as consequence of changes of its environment. In this case the agent seems to have a more reactive than proactive behavior. As example we could consider a mobile agent that would like to do a complex computation, and therefore, would move from time to time to a known agent platform with a low system load. The mobile agents' behavior will be influenced directly, that means that the agent will stop its computation and will move to another agent platform, when the agent received a message containing a movement request, and then moves as rational effect of this message. The same agent could be influenced in an indirect way, when one more agent will arrive on the same agent platform, causing a very high load. The former agent, will recognize the high platform load, and will move as a result of this to an agent platform with a lower load.

From an observer's point of view an agent's behavior, influenced directly by conversations and environmental changes, is perceived as reactive behavior because it produces an immediate effect. It is difficult for the observer to associate a delayed action of an agent with one of many possible preceding causes, and therefore, to perceive a delayed action as part of the agents' reactive behavior. In this case, or when the agents' behavior is influenced more by the agents' internal states, which are determined by different control mechanisms and are invisible to the observer, the behavior is perceived as proactive. Due to the nondeterministic change of an agents' environment, it is difficult to predict its behavior and also the flow of its conversations influenced thereby. In highly dynamic environments, like instant and ad-hoc networks, it seems to make sense to reduce the message types used in interactions and conversations to a few very generic ones that would be useful to most interactions among agents.

In cooperative problem solving methods, all the participants have to contribute in some way to the final solution. If the problem could be decomposed into different tasks, one agent should do this job and assign these tasks to the other cooperating agents. Furthermore, an agent or a group of agents should orchestrate the cooperation. The interactions among these agents as well as the conversation flow could be specified in a way similar to the one in parallel systems. Depending on the common problem and its decomposition capabilities, the required conversations will be made based on one of the possible interaction structures, known also from parallel systems: full meshed, mesh, torus, ring, cube, and hypercube. Characteristics that have to be considered for efficiency reasons are: connectivity, diameter, narrowness, and expandability of these structures.

3.6 Agent Communication Languages

FIPA/ACL specifies messages between agents by communicative acts syntactically (message model) as well as semantically (formal model) [FIPA2002a] [FIPA2002b]. Communicative acts are classified with respect to their semantic perspective and use performatives in analogy to speech act theory. The performatives *request, inform, confirm,* and *disconfirm* are the basis from which another 18 performatives are derived [Timm2004]. The formal model of a message is associated with a performative and uses the semantic language SL [Sade1992]. It consists of a logical expression, a feasibility precondition and a rational effect. The logical expression is the formal representation of the message. The semantics of the message is specified in analogy to AI planning by pre-conditions as indicators if an action is applicable, and by an effect describing world-state changes after the execution of the action. Unlike AI planning though, SL defines a rational effect, i.e., if the agents behave rationally, the effect will be achieved. However, with respect to irrational behavior, SL allows explicitly for effects not consistent with the rational effect.

Sequences of messages form a complex behavior resp. course of action. A sequence of messages is called *conversation* if the messages are related with respect to a goal, semantic or temporal context. In message passing there are three main approaches for conversations: unilateral, bilateral, or multilateral. Unilateral conversation is used for messages, which do not require responses, e.g., expressive acts or communication with the environment. Bilateral and multilateral conversations require the response of the communication partners and they are distinguished by the number of communication partners. In a bilateral setting, there is exactly one initiator and one responder while in the multilateral setting there is no restriction on the number of responders. A special case in bi- and multilateral conversation is the dialog, which is characterized by a sequence of messages alternating between initiator and responder(s).

The challenge in conversations is to select specific actions resp. performatives for achievement of a goal, e.g., contracting another company for production and delivery. This situation is similar to AI-planning in that conversations are instantiations of plans. In order to achieve a library of reusable conversation patterns, the FIPA standardizes a set of interaction protocols including *request*, *query*, *contract-net* and others. Interaction protocols reduce the complexity of the plan space drastically by limitation of the number of possible actions. For example, the FIPA-Request protocol uses 6 out of 22 possible performatives, *request, refuse, agree, failure, inform-done*, and *inform-result* with a plan length of three actions [FIPA2002c]. This reduces the combinatorial complexity in the plan space by a factor of almost 50 (6^3 vs. 22^3). The actual reduction is even higher, since for each possible expansion there are no more than three possible actions. With the help of this reduction, the efficient integration of possible answers of an agent opponent in the communication process becomes feasible without the need for complex plan recognition algorithms.

A fundamental assumption for successful communication is that all communication partners are capable of understanding the content of the message, i.e., sender and receiver are able to decode messages with the same semantic conclusions. However, this assumption has a strong impact on system design and is leading to problems known from early distributed expert systems. Hence, the Knowledge Sharing Effort (KSE) in the framework of DARPA standardization created context description protocols for knowledge interchange in expert systems. The main efforts were KIF [GeFi1992] as a knowledge representation and KQML [FiLM1997] [Fin+1995] as a knowledge exchange protocol. Due to the strong relationships between distributed expert systems and MAS, these developments have been widely used in DAI and had a considerable impact on the evolution of a standard agent communication language. The result, the FIPA agent communication language (FIPA-ACL) is standard in nowadays MAS implementations and is used by the majority of agent researchers. FIPA-ACL consists of three main specifications: Communicative acts, interaction protocols, and content languages [FIPA2001a] [FIPA2001b] [FIPA2002d] [FIPA2003]. Although FIPA does not demand the use of a specific content language, mandatory requirements for content languages are defined in the standardization. Any content language has to provide three modeling concepts: propositions, objects, and actions. Additional requirements are a normative definition, a "good" level of syntax allowing for parsing, clear and intuitive but not necessarily formal semantics, and the provision of usage examples. A fundamental assumption for content languages is that they incorporate the agent context, i.e., beliefs, abilities, and wants [Wool2001]. A standard approach in DAI is to use multimodal logics, e.g., with KD45 semantics [RaGe1995]. However, ontology languages like OWL [Bec+2004] [PaHH2004] can easily be adapted to the requirements and additionally offer a well structured representation of knowledge disregarding the semantics of beliefs, abilities, and wants. Further aspects regarding the semantics of the content of an interaction are discussed in IV.5.

3.7 Design Methodologies

Interaction design is accounted by existing AOSE methods as part of the system development process, and is always considered very close to the analysis and identification of roles. In this section, the interaction design part of several established AOSE methods is addressed.

3.7.1 Generic Architecture for Information Availability

The Generic Architecture for Information Availability (GAIA) [Zam+2003] method recommends the analytical identification and deduction of the roles of the final target system from the problem domain description. Simultaneously the necessary interactions among the role holders are designed, and therefore, to each role the required technical and organizational authorizations, restrictions and obligations are assigned. The set of identified roles are combined in a role model and the defined interactions in an interaction model. However, the resulting MAS design has a rigid character and therefore, it seems that the use of pattern based interaction control seems to be the more suitable solution.

3.7.2 Multiagent Systems Iterative View

In contrast to GAIA, the Multiagent Systems Iterative View (MASSIVE) [Lind2001] does not consider in advance a given technology for the implementation of the target system. This would be one of the results of the iterative design. In MASSIVE the interaction design is based on a task model and a role model. The task model contains an hierarchical task-tree with all the tasks, resulting from the requirements to the target system. The role model contains all roles of the target system. Each role is composed of a group of atomic tasks and their corresponding activities.

Interaction design covers in MASSIVE the specification of the necessary interactions among the role holders, and the definition of the interaction flow with the help of interaction protocols. In MASSIVE the use of pattern based interaction control is also suitable, but the resulting designs do not have the rigid character of GAIA models.

3.7.3 Multiagent System Engineering

The Multiagent System Engineering (MaSE) [DeWS2001] recommends a two-phase design approach. As part of the first phase – the analysis phase, a set of UML sequence diagrams is deduced from use cases of the problem domain and for each involved entity, a role is defined and assigned to it. Further, a set of tasks is defined, providing solutions for all the identified requirements of the target system. In the system design phase – the second phase of MaSE, the interactions are designed based on the already specified sets of roles and tasks. The conversations, at which an identified role should be involved, are also derived from the UML sequence diagrams. For each conversation of a role the interaction protocols for the conversation initiator and the conversation praticants, as responder, are defined.

The interaction design in MaSE is made on the basis of an instruction, and therefore it seems that the pattern-based interaction control approach is more suitable. Existing interaction protocols can be used in MaSE as communication components, and the interaction becomes a mean to end of the problem solving method.

3.7.4 Tropos

Tropos [GKMP2003] is a generic AOSE method that accentuates the early and late requirements analysis, and the consistent use of concept definitions in the whole development process. The interaction design in Tropos is part of the architecture design phase. In this phase the target system is composed of many subsystems, represented as actors.

The actors are interconnected among themselves with dependency edges, representing data and control flows. This model could be improved in the way that data flows for input, output and control for each actor is specified.

The generic interaction design in Tropos accords a favor for goal-based interaction design, resulting in a more adaptive and flexible architecture of the target system. However, if this is not one of the main non-functional requirements of the target-system, the interaction design could also be made pattern-based, resulting in a pattern-based interaction control, and in the integration of interaction protocols.

3.8 Challenges

In MAS, the core feature is the interaction of autonomous agents. However methods from software- and knowledge engineering are not sufficient to cope with the high degree of flexibility which is inherent in multiagent systems. As the structure and process of interaction is a significant feature of multiagent's flexibility, the challenge for AOSE arises from the interaction design. Interaction has to be restrictive enough to enable reliable system behavior and should be permissive enough to allow for flexibility or emergent behavior. As mentioned before, AOSE methodologies address interaction design especially for the identification and analysis of roles. Nevertheless, effective and efficient interaction requires the match of application requirements and available interaction mechanisms.

The concepts and challenges, which have been, introduced mostly deal with homogeneous, self-contained multiagent systems. Nevertheless, in real-world business applications, especially in logistics, a wide range of conventional as well as multiagent systems are applied. In most cases, these systems are highly heterogeneous, which poses new challenges towards the integration process. For example, information systems within a supply chain are naturally distributed and are developed spatially separate. Even if multiagent systems are applied within delimited areas which implement standards like FIPA, it cannot be assumed that the different multiagent systems use a homogeneous implementation of interaction. Heterogeneities within the interaction behavior as well as the semantics of the communication (cf. IV.5) require a strong focus on the interaction design of these multi-multiagent systems.

These challenges are found especially in the integration of the multiagent systems in the manufacturing domain to the *Agent.Enterprise* Net-Demo (cf. II.1), which have been developed distributed. The subsequent integration of multiple multiagent systems poses specific challenges to AOSE methodologies supporting the interaction design process. These challenges consist of: Definition of the multiagent system interfaces; Definition of the interaction semantics; Selection or definition of interaction protocols; Assurance of interaction behavior.

The first challenge, the definition of the multiagent system interfaces is addressed to the question, which agents are going to interact with other agents in other multiagent systems. Since the integration aspects are complex towards semantics, interaction behavior, and security, a good choice for such a multiagent system interface is the definition of a special agent, serving as a gateway for the system [SNSS2004].

The next challenge to interaction design for the integration of heterogeneous multiagent systems is the selection and definition of interaction protocols. In order to tackle this challenge, the real-world process of information-, material-, and decision-flow has to be analyzed and appropriate interaction protocols, which map the processes, have to be selected. Since these processes are in most cases complex, a composition of standard interaction protocols might be the appropriate solution. For example, this has been done for the *Agent.Enterprise* NetDemo, where first the different roles within the integrated multi-multiagent system have been identified. The next step is the specification of the interactions between these roles, and the final step the composition of the specific FIPA interaction protocols to the global supply-chain interaction protocol (cf. II.1).

The third challenge, the definition of interaction semantics, has a strong similarity to the challenges found in the semantic web. Here, the integration of different ontologies is the major problem. Even There are numerous approaches addressed to this question (i.e., mediator technology (cf. [Wied1992] [Gar+1997] [Wach2003]), federated/global schemas (cf. [LaRo1982] [Tem+1987]), shared ontologies (cf. [StTi2002]), which offer different degrees of flexibility for the integration process. In *Agent.Enterprise*, the global schema approach has been used, where an ontology as a specification of the semantics for the interaction has been jointly developed by the participating projects. Nevertheless, the more flexible approach is the use of context based mediator technology [Wach 2003], but its adoption to agent technology was not in the focus of the *Agent.Enterprise* development.

The last challenge is aimed to the development process itself. Ensuring the interaction behavior in a distributed, heterogeneous multi-multiagent system is crucial to the overall systems behavior. If one multiagent system within the multi-multiagent system shows incorrect interaction behavior, this may have a negative impact on the overall systems performance. In the *Agent.Enterprise* NetDemo, the behavior of the sub-systems has been ensured by time-consuming distributed tests. More sophisticated approaches for validation of the interaction behavior are discussed in IV.8.

Further Reading

[Mire2002]   Mirel, B.: Interaction Design for Complex Problem Solving –
                Developing Useful and Usable Software. Morgan Kaufmann
                Publishing, San Francisco, California, 2002.
[RoZl1994]   Rosenschein, J.; Zlotkin, G.: Rules of Encounter. MIT Press,
                Cambridge, Massachusetts, 1994.
[RuNo2005]   Russel, S.; Norvig, P.: Artificial Intelligence – A Modern Ap-
                proach. Prentice Hall, New Jersey, 2005.
[Weis1999]   Weiss, G.: Multiagent Systems – A Modern Approach to Distri-
                buted Artificial Intelligence. MIT Press, Cambridge, Massachu-
                setts, 1999.
[Wool2002]   Wooldridge, M.: An Introduction to Multiagent Systems. John
                Wiley & Sons, Chichester, England, 2002.

References

[Bec+2004]   Bechhofer, S.; van Harmelen, F.; Hendler, J.; Horrocks, I.; Mc
                Guinness, D. L.; Patel-Schneider, P. F.; Stein, L. A.: OWL Web
                Ontology Language Reference. 2004. W3C Recommendation.
                http://www.w3.org/TR/owl-ref/, accessed in December 2004.
[DeWS2001]   Deloach, S. A.; Wood, M. F.; Sparkman, C. H.: Multiagent Sys-
                tem Engineering. In: International Journal of Software Engi-
                neering and Knowledge Engineering 11(1998)3, pp. 231-258.
[Durf1999]   Durfee, E. H.: Distributed Problem Solving and Planning. In:
                Weiss, G (Ed.): Multiagent Systems. A Modern Approach to
                Distributed Artificial Intelligence. The MIT Press, Cambridge,
                London, 1991, pp. 121-164.
[DuLC1989]   Durfee, E. H.; Lesser, V. R.; Corkill, D. D.: Trends in Coopera-
                tive Distributed Problem Solving. In: IEEE Trans. Knowl. Data
                Eng. 1(1989)1, pp. 63-83.
[Fin+1995]   Finin, T; Weber, J.; Wiederhold, G.; Genesereth, M.; Fritz-
                son, R.; MacKay, D.; McGuire, J.; Pelavin, R.; Shapiro, S.;
                Beck, C.: Specification of the KQML Agent-Communication
                Language. Technical report, the DARPA Knowledge Sharing
                Initiative External Interfaces Working Group. 1995.
[FiLM1997]   Finin, T.; Labrou, Y.; Mayfield, J.: Software Agents, chapter
                "KQML as an Agent Communication Language." AAAI Press/
                The MIT Press, Menlo Park, California, 1997, pp. 291-316.
[FIPA2001a]   FIPA CCL Content Languages Specification. Document Nr.
                XC00009B, 2001. http://www.fipa.org/specs/fipa00009/, access-
                ed in December 2004.

[FIPA2001b]   FIPA RDF Content Languages Specification. Document Nr. XC00011B, 2001. http://www.fipa.org/specs/fipa00011/, accessed in December 2004.

[FIPA2002a]   FIPA ACL Message Structure Specification. Document Nr. SC00061G, 2002. http://www.fipa.org/specs/fipa00061/, accessed in December 2004.

[FIPA2002b]   FIPA Communicative Act Library Specification. Document Nr. SC00037J, 2002. http://www.fipa.org/specs/fipa00037/, accessed in December 2004.

[FIPA2002c]   FIPA Request Interaction Protocol Specification. Document Nr.: SC00026H, 2002. http://www.fipa.org/specs/fipa00026/, accessed in December 2004.

[FIPA2002d]   FIPA SL Content Languages Specification. Document Nr.: SC00008I, 2002. http://www.fipa.org/specs/fipa00008/, accessed in December 2004.

[FIPA2003]   FIPA KIF Content Languages Specification. Document Nr.: XC00010C, 2003. http://www.fipa.org/specs/fipa00010/, accessed in December 2004.

[FuTi1991]   Fudenberg, D.; Tirole, J.: Game Theory, MIT Press, 1991.

[Gar+1997]   Garcia-Molina, H.; Papakonstantinou, Y.; Quass, D.; Rajaraman, A.; Sagiv, Y.; Ullman, J. D.; Vassalos, V.; Widom, J.: The TSIMMIS Approach to Mediation: Data Models and Languages. J. Intell. Inf. Syst. 8(1997)2, pp. 117-132.

[GeFi1992]   Genesereth, M. R.; Fikes, R. E.: Knowledge Interchange Format Version 3.0 - Reference Manual. Technical Report 94305, CS Department, Stanford University. Stanford, California, 1992.

[GKMP2003]   Georgini, P.; Kolp, M.; Mylopoulos, J.; Pistore, M.: The Tropos Methodology: an overview. In: Bergenti, F.; Gleizes, M. P.; Zambonelli, F. (Eds.): Methodologies and Software Engineering for Agent Systems. Kluwer Academic Publishing, New York, 2003, pp. 1-20.

[Krep1990]   Kreps, D. M.: A Course in Microeconomic Theory. Princeton University Press, 1990.

[LaRo1982]   Landers, T; Rosenberg, R.: An Overview of MULTIBASE. In: Schneider, H. (Ed.): Proceedings 2nd International Symposium for Distributed Databases. North Holland Publishing Company, Berlin, 1982, pp. 153-183.

[Lind2001]   Lind, J.: Iterative Software Engineering for Multiagent Systems: The MASSIVE Method. Springer-Verlag, Heidelberg, 2001.

[PaHH2004]   Patel-Schneider, P. F.; Hayes, P.; Horrocks, I.: OWL Web Ontology Language Semantics and Abstract Syntax. W3C-Recommendation. http://www.w3.org/TR/owl-semantics/, accessed in December 2004.

[RaGe1995]   Rao, A. S.; Georgeff, M. P.: BDI-Agents: From Theory to Practice. In: Proceedings of the First International Conference on

Multiagent Systems. AAAI-Press, San Francisco, California, 1995, pp. 312-319

[RoZl1994]   Rosenschein, J.; Zlotkin, G.: Rules of Encounter. MIT Press, Cambridge, Massachusetts, 1994.

[Sade1992]   Sadek, M. D.: A study in the logic of intention. In: Proceedings of the 3rd Conference on Principles of Knowledge Representation and Reasoning (KR'92). Cambridge, MA, 1992, pp. 462-473.

[Sand1999]   Sandholm, T. W.: Distributed Rational Decision Making. In: Weiss, G. (Ed.): Multiagent Systems – A Modern Approach to Distributed Artificial Intelligence. MIT Press, Cambridge, Massachusetts, 1999, pp. 201-258.

[SNSS2004]   Stockheim, T.; Nimis, J.; Scholz, T.; Stehli, M.: How to Build a Multi-Multi-Agent System: The Agent.Enterprise Approach. ICEIS 4(2004), pp. 364-371.

[StTi2002]   Stuckenschmidt, H.; Timm, I. J.: Adapting Communication Vocabularies Using Shared Ontologies. In: Cranefield, S. et al. (Eds.): Proceedings of the Second International Workshop on Ontologies in Agent Systems. Workshop at 1st International Conference on Autonomous Agents and Multi-Agent Systems. Bologna, Italy, 15-19 July 2002, pp. 6-12.

[Tem+1987]   Templeton, M.; Brill, D.; Dao, S. K.; Lund, E.; Ward, P.; Chen, A. L. P.; MacGregor, R.: Mermaid – A front end to distributed heterogeneous databases. In: Proceedings of the Institute of Electrical and Electronics Engineers (IEEE) 75(1987)5, pp. 695-708.

[Timm2004]   Timm, I. J.: Dynamisches Konfliktmanagement als Verhaltenssteuerung Intelligenter Agenten. DISKI 283, infix Köln, 2004.

[Wach2003]   Wache, H.: Semantische Interpretation für heterogene Informationsquellen. DISKI - Dissertationen zur Künstlichen Intelligenz, vol. 261. infix Köln, 2003.

[Weis1999]   Weiss, G.: Multiagent Systems – A Modern Approach to Distributed Artificial Intelligence. MIT Press, Cambridge, Massachusetts, 1999.

[Wied1992]   Wiederhold, G.: Mediators in the Architecture of Future Information Systems. IEEE Computer 25(1992)3, pp. 38-49.

[Wool2001]   Wooldridge, M.: Intelligent Agents: The Key Concepts. Multi-Agent-Systems and Applications 2001, pp. 3-43.

4 Architectural Design

Peter C. Lockemann, Jens Nimis

Universität Karlsruhe (TH), Instiut für Programmstrukturen und
Datenorganisation, {lockemann I nimis} @ipd.uka.de

Lars Braubach, Alexander Pokahr, Winfried Lamersdorf

Universität Hamburg, Fachbereich Informatik, Verteilte Systeme und Informationssysteme, {braubach I pokahr I lamersd} @informatik.uni-hamburg.de

Abstract. This chapter introduces a reference architecture that provides a methodical framework for the implementation of software agents. The central concept is a layered architecture where each layer offers a well-defined service to the higher layers, and where each of the agent properties of I.1 is unambiguously associated with a single layer. The design method proceeds in three phases: A first phase examines the functional service characteristics in order to determine which responsibilities should be assigned to single agents and which to collections of agents. The second phase structures the individual agent into the layers along the non-functional properties. The third phase augments the layered structure by the interactive capabilities of agents.

4.1 Introduction

A requirements specification must be turned into a working software and hardware system. This is a multi-step task. Perhaps the most decisive step is the first, architectural design. Since it is an accepted doctrine that mistakes are much cheaper to correct when caught in the early stages than when discovered in the late stages, good architectural system design has enormous economical potential. Consequently, architectural design should follow a rigorous methodology rather than intuition.

Buschmann et al. [Bus+1996] describe such a methodology which they call *pattern-oriented software architecture.* Generally speaking, *a pattern for software architecture (or architectural pattern for short) describes a particular, recurring design problem that arises in specific design contexts, and presents a well-proven generic scheme for its solution. A pattern expresses a fundamental structural organization schema for software systems, describes their constituent components, specifies their responsibili-*

ties, and includes rules and guidelines for organizing the relationships between them and the ways in which they collaborate.

The definition is general enough to cover many levels of detail starting from architectural design on the level of programming-in-the-very-large all the way down to individual components and objects. It is also general enough to cover a wide range of software with differing requirements. Nonetheless, as pointed out in IV.1.5, agent-oriented software engineering poses its own challenges. To meet the challenges, IV.4 combines the principle of pattern-orientation with the specifics of agent-oriented software.

The focus of this chapter is the individual agent. This focus does indeed include the interaction between agents: It is well-known that in distributed systems – and multiagent systems are distributed systems – the communication between the components takes place on a functionally trivial physical level so that all higher-level interaction must be realized as part of the components themselves. However, before designing the individual agents one must first identify the responsibilities within the multiagent system, and then determine the constituent components by deciding which responsibilities to relegate to different agents and which to encapsulate within a single agent. The remainder is devoted to the architectural patterns that can be applied to the individual agent.

4.2 Service-Oriented Design

4.2.1 Responsibilities and Services

The principle underlying all methods for architectural design is *separation of concerns* [Vog+2005]. The methods differ to what is considered a concern and how to separate such concerns. Starke equates concerns with responsibilities of pieces of software [Star2002]. In particular, he calls a piece of software with focused, well-defined and guaranteed responsibilities a (software) *component*.

Generally speaking, given a requirements specification for an entire system the design task is to construct a collection of components, with each one assigned a *responsibility* that is to be matched by its *competence*.

Responsibility and competence are hazy terms. Lately, the term service has become accepted to describe the responsibilities and competences of software systems as they enter into more dynamic relationships prevailing in distributed systems. More precisely, a *service* is the range of tasks that a component offers to its outside world and is capable of performing. Realizing an overall responsibility by a set of narrower responsibilities would then be the same as collecting a set of services into a larger service. A useful interaction is that one where a component may draw on a service of another component to gain a competence it does not own by itself. Consequently, interaction between software components is by one component requesting a service from another component and the other component fulfilling the request.

A metaphor may illustrate the perspective (Figure 1). Since a service is the result of assigning a responsibility to a component, a service represents an *obligation* for the component. But likewise, the component calling on the service (the *service client*, or *client* for short) has an obligation to provide the called component (the *service provider*, or *server* for short) with all the information needed to render the desired action. In other words, interaction between two components involves mutual obligations and may be formulated as something akin to a service level agreement.

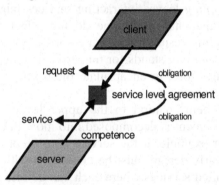

Figure 1. Service metaphor

The service perspective makes good sense for agents as well, since I.1, with Property 2, reflects on the central role of the notion of service in agents.

4.2.2 Service Organization

Architectural design that is based on the notion of service is referred to as *service-oriented design*. The result of service-oriented design is a collection of service providers that enter into client-server relations among themselves. This raises two major design issues:

1. What are the service providers?
2. What is the cohesion among the service providers?

To turn to the first question, Vogel et al. [Vog+2005] relate the principle of separation of concerns to another widely-used design principle, divide-and-conquer. Starting from the specific needs of a given external world, the principle essentially imposes a top-down system view. It is a recursive process because it decomposes a given service into lesser responsibilities, and these again, until one reaches services that do not warrant further decomposition. The result is a service hierarchy, or more generally a service heterarchy if the same service is the result of more than one service decomposition. Figure 2 illustrates a heterarchy.

Divide-and-conquer is basically an analytic method. The synthetic equivalent is a bottom-up view that starts from a pool of existing components and determines an organization of the interactions that can be proven to result in the desired overall system responsibility. In practice both methods are combined into a so-called middle-out approach.

To answer the second question, we follow Vogel [Vog+2005] and distinguish between loose coupling and strong cohesion. Operationally speaking, *loose coupling* leaves interacting services fairly independent of another, implying that changes to one do not affect the other. Consequently, loose coupling results in separate software components. On the other hand, *strong cohesion* stands for numerous interdependencies, and it is recommended, therefore, to encapsulate these services within one and the same software component.

Loose coupling seems natural to the upper levels of the heterarchy where a given requirement is decomposed into more limited but still fairly coarse services. For example, if the service is to be provided by a multi-agent system, the early design must be concerned with breaking the services into more limited services where each can be meaningfully assigned to a unit realized either by an agent or a group of agents, and where the original service can be obtained by proper interaction between the smaller units. This is indicated in Figure 2. The figure also shows that ultimately a level is reached where strong cohesion takes over. In our example the services below this level are encapsulated within individual agents (which may already pre-exist and become part of a middle-out design).

Indeed though, as we proceed further down with decomposition we come across basic services needed by many if not all components above. Consequently, we encounter another barrier across which to apply loose coupling. Since experience indicates that on the lowest levels services are domain-independent and common to different service implementations, we relegate these services to separate providers referred to as a *resource managers*. Resource managers are usually collected into a framework (or platform). In our case, a common platform would be provided at every location where agents are to be installed, without becoming part of the agent proper. This is again indicated in Figure 2. If such a platform is capable of dealing with the differences between local computer systems, operating systems, data formats and the like, i.e., if the platform can overcome the heterogeneity between different systems, and if it can take care of the message exchange in a distributed system, the platform is referred to as a *middleware*.

4.2.3 Service Characteristics

So far we deliberately left open how to characterize the concerns that guide the decomposition and influence the choice between loose coupling and strong cohesion. We now introduce a hypothesis that makes use of the different aspects of a service:

- *What* is the service? More precisely, what is the collection of related functions that the service provider makes available to a client? We refer to the collection as the *service functionality*. Functions are specified in terms of their syntactical interfaces (signatures) and their semantic effects, the latter often expressed by their input-output behavior and the effected change of state. Functionality is what a client basically is interested in.
- *How good* are the qualities of service? The qualities are expressed in terms of attributes that determine, beyond the functionality, the usefulness of a service to a client. The attributes are collectively referred to as the *non-functional properties* of a service.
- *How* is the service attained? To answer the question one has to get at least a rough idea on how to *implement* the service.

In our hypothesis we claim that divide-and-conquer starts with *functional decomposition*. Functional decomposition is primarily guided by service functionality, whereas the non-functional properties are just passed along. Decomposition comes to an end when all derived units are decided to be agents, usually on pragmatic grounds such as reusability, cost, maintainability that are known to induce strong cohesion further down. The resulting service collection forms the (multiagent) society architecture.

Once the level of individual agents has been reached, our thesis is that the non-functional properties are the ones that are responsible for the strong cohesion. Consequently, we start a process of conscious *assignment of the non-functional properties*. Properties that cannot, or not entirely, be taken care of on one level are propagated to the next lower level where the process is repeated. If needed, the functionality is adjusted by subordinate functional decomposition. Keller, in his dissertation [Kell2003], cites empirical evidence that confirms the importance of the non-functional properties in a system architecture. The prevailing architectural pattern for cohesive decomposition is the *layers pattern*. Higher layers build their service not from interaction among lower peers but by calling the lower-level services and incorporating their results on the higher level. The result is a (layered) agent architecture.

Finally we reach the framework (or platform) containing the resource managers. Preferably, platforms should be used that are tailored to the specific needs of agents.

Figure 2 summarizes the design principles of this chapter.

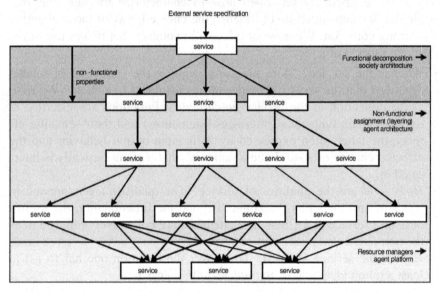

Figure 2. Design model for multiagent systems

4.2.4 Agent Services

The last step in developing our design model is to clearly identify which agent properties of I.1 refer to functionality and which can be equated with non-functional qualities.

Properties 2 and 8,

(2) *A software agent offers a useful service. Its behavior can only be observed by its external actions, its internal processes remain encapsulated,*

(8) *An intelligent software agent may have to possess social ability, that is, is capable of interacting with other agents to provide its service,*

are common properties that offer a link to the functional properties to the service an agent provides. What these properties are is determined by the application domain of the agent:

(1) *A software agent is a computer system that is situated in some environment.*

In other words, there must be some part of agent software that will have to reflect the application domain and will have to be specifically designed for this domain.

On the other hand, all other agent properties of I.1.3 qualify as non-functional properties.

(3) *A software agent is capable of autonomous action in its environment in order to meet its design objectives, i.e., to provide its service.*

(4) *As a corollary to Property 3, the autonomy of a software agent is determined by its own goals, with goal deliberation and means-end assessment as parts of the overall decision process of practical reasoning.*

(5) *An intelligent software agent is reactive, that is, it continuously perceives its environment, and responds in a timely fashion to changes that occur.*

(6) *An intelligent software agent achieves an effective balance between goal-directed and reactive behavior.*

(7) *An intelligent software agent may be proactive, that is, take the initiative in pursuance of its goals.*

(9) *An intelligent software agent may be able to learn.*

These properties sound generic, that is, they apply to a software agent no matter what its domain is. Ideally then, it should be possible to devise an architectural framework that reflects these non-functional properties and need "only" be augmented to cover the specific functionality.

Property 8 states that agents do not act in isolation but offer their services to other agents. These will expect the properties of

- *Performance*: Services must be rendered with adequate technical performance at given cost. Performance is a prerequisite for the *scalability* of multiagent systems, that is, continuous growth in the number of agents without deterioration in overall functionality and qualities. In turn, scalability is prerequisite to keep multiagent systems open systems.
- *Reliability*: The service must guarantee its functionality and qualities to any client, under all circumstances, be they errors, disruptions, failures, incursions, interferences within or outside the agent. Reliability must always be founded on a failure model. There may be different models for different causes.

- *Security*: Services must remain trustworthy, that is, show no effects be-yond the guaranteed functionality and qualities in the face of failures, errors or malicious attacks.

An agent can pursue goals or even learn only if it possesses an internal memory. In particular it may need the non-functional property of

- *Durability*: The agent may have unlimited lifetime, hence the memory data must remain durable unless and until explicitly overwritten.

4.3 Agent society architecture

We start with the first stage of our design model in Section 4.2.3, develop-ment of an agent society architecture. Obviously, determining the individ-ual constituent agents that make up the multiagent system depends on the overall service the system is intended to provide, and this is highly do-main-specific. All we can do at this point is to sketch some methods that allow to derive a decomposition of the overall requirements into indepen-dent services, and to distribute them to separate autonomous entities.

4.3.1 GAIA

The GAIA methodology is founded on the view of a multiagent system as a computational organization consisting of a collection of roles that enter into certain relationships to one another, and that take part in systematic, institutionalized patterns of interactions with other roles. GAIA deals with both the macro (societal) level and the micro (agent) level aspects of de-sign [WoJK2000].

GAIA, as most other agent-oriented methodologies, assumes that an ini-tial requirements specification is already available. From this requirements specification the roles and the interactions between them have to be de-rived. Roles are described by properties such as responsibilities, permis-sions and activities. Interactions are captured as protocols describing the purpose and course of an interaction between two or more roles. In a sec-ond step, from the roles and interactions the required services can be de-rived. Agent types are designed, supporting one or more roles, by using the functionality of the services.

The basic methodical idea of GAIA, its two dimensions of responsibili-ties and interaction protocols, will be the foundation of the reference archi-tecture in Section 4.4.

4.3.2 Tropos

Tropos [Bre+2004] is a methodology that supports all activities of the software engineering process ranging from application domain analysis to the final system design. Hence, Tropos supports four main development phases: Early Requirements, Late Requirements, Architectural Design, and Detailed Design.

Tropos takes a global view where an agent society is an organization in which the agent application is one actor embedded into an environmental setting consisting also of other actors which need not necessarily to be software systems. Within the Early Requirements phase the stakeholders and their intentions are analyzed, whereby, stakeholders are described as social actors that depend on one another for goals to be fulfilled. These goals are identified by a goal-oriented analysis and are refined into goal-hierarchies that possibly offer alternative ways of goal achievement. The Late Requirements analysis focuses on the software system being developed. This system is introduced as one actor within the organization and the dependencies to other actors along with its system goals need to be identified. These dependencies represent the system's functional and non-functional requirements. The purpose of the Architectural Design phase is to subsequently elaborate the system's global architecture in terms of subsystems (actors) interconnected through data and control flows (dependencies). The Detailed Design phase deals with the description of the individual agents where it applies one particular architectural pattern, the BDI agent model [Wool2002]. Beliefs, plans, goals, and additionally the communication relationships are specified in detail leading to a natural transition into the Implementation Phase in which a mapping from the models to code has to be carried out.

4.3.3 Prometheus

Like Tropos, the Prometheus methodology [PaWi2004] covers both the design of an agent society and of its constituent agents and assumes that the individual agents follow the architectural pattern of the BDI model. The basic construct is the behavioral description of individual intelligent agents. The methodology is divided into three layers of different abstraction, System Specification, Architectural Design, and Detailed Design.

Tropos comes closest to the design philosophy of Section 4.2 as the main objective of the System Specification phase is to identify the overall services (here called functionalities) that the planned application should support. For that purpose use cases and the overall system goals are identified and refined into initial functionality descriptors. Within the Architectural Design phase these descriptors in connection with other artifacts such as agent acquaintances and data coupling diagrams are employed to derive the relevant agent types of the system, that is, the necessary agent types are directly derived from the functionalities. In this process well-established software engineering principles such as coherence and coupling are used to decide which functionalities should belong to which agent types. The identified agent types together with their interrelationships are composed into a global system overview diagram, which shows the static structure of the multiagent system and is somewhat comparable to a class diagram of the traditional UML modeling for object-oriented systems. At the Detailed Design stage the internal behavior of the agents is described in the form of descriptors for the constituting elements such as beliefs, plans, and goals.

4.4 Individual Agent Architecture

4.4.1 Layering

We now turn to the second part of our design model, design of the architecture of an individual agent. It would be most convenient if we could develop an architecture that covers all agents no matter what their service and where only certain details must still be filled in for a concrete agent. Such an architecture is called an architectural framework or a *reference architecture*. Alternatively, one could interpret a reference architecture as a set of guidelines for deriving a concrete architecture.

To develop a reference architecture there must be enough generic properties, both functional and non-functional. We observed earlier this is indeed the case for agents. Hence, there is a good chance to find a suitable reference architecture.

Our design model of Section 4.2.3 foresees an abstract implementation as a layered architecture that is derived by refinement. Refinement is the conscious assignment of the non-functional properties to different levels of abstraction, where the levels may additionally be determined by functional decomposition. Ideally, we develop an architecture where we can associate a non-functional property with a specific layer. The question of *"How is the service attained?"* is answered not by an interaction pattern among peers but by constructing functionality and quality attributes of a layer from those found on the next lower layer.

The design model itself needs some further refinement. We add two rules:

- We assume that Properties 1 to 4 suffice to construct the basic layered structure, since they are the ones shared by all agents. Properties 5 to 9 of intelligent agents should only have an influence on the internals of some of the common layers.
- We divide each layer into two sections, one that characterizes those aspects that apply irrespective of the application domain, and another that accounts for the domain. If we succeed, the first section can essentially be made part of a common agent platform whereas the second remains to be filled according to the domain characteristics.

4.4.2 Reference Architecture

Although we concentrate on the agent properties we are aware that software agents need a kind of "substrate" that supplies them with the necessary ingredients to be able to function at all. The substrate includes the typical operating systems functionality, data management facilities as offered, e.g., by relational database systems, and data communication services such as HTTP or IIOP. We include these facilities in the reference architecture as the domain-independent part of the bottom layer L1.

Also part of the bottom layer are all mechanisms that reflect Property 1 that a software agent is situated in some environment, and Property 2 that the agent interacts with its environment by externally observable actions. Consequently, layer L1 must include the sensors and effectors necessary for the interaction. Which ones are effectively needed depends, of course, on the domain being served.

Property 2 implies that an agent is an active component. We decide to locate all mechanisms that make an agent an executable component, i.e., the agent runtime environment, on the next higher layer L2. The basic computing infrastructure on layer L1 serves as the foundation of the environment. The environment is at the core of agent behavior and can often be found as the central part of agent development frameworks. Take as an example of a core service the life cycle management of an agent. It makes sense to locate Property 3, to be capable of autonomous action, on layer L2 as well. To allow an agent to control its own behavior independent of the progress of other agents, the runtime environment should enable each agent to run in its own control thread.

Property 4 states that the external actions are a result of goal deliberation and means-end assessment. There is a considerable gap between the signal level of sensing and effecting the environment and deriving the necessary actions by practical reasoning. Therefore, as first step commensurate with the level of the runtime environment we translate the signals into processes that can be handled by a software agent.

Layer L3 is the next step towards satisfying Property 4. To offer "a useful service" (Property 2), the agent must have some understanding of its environment, i.e., the application domain and its active players. The understanding is reflected on layer L3 by the world model of the agent. To link the world model and the sensed observations, and after adapting the model if necessary to translate the changes to effected actions, the agent may make use of ontologies that reflect the overall community knowledge. Consequently, there are two sections to layer L3, a section for managing the ontologies, and a section that deals with the world model.

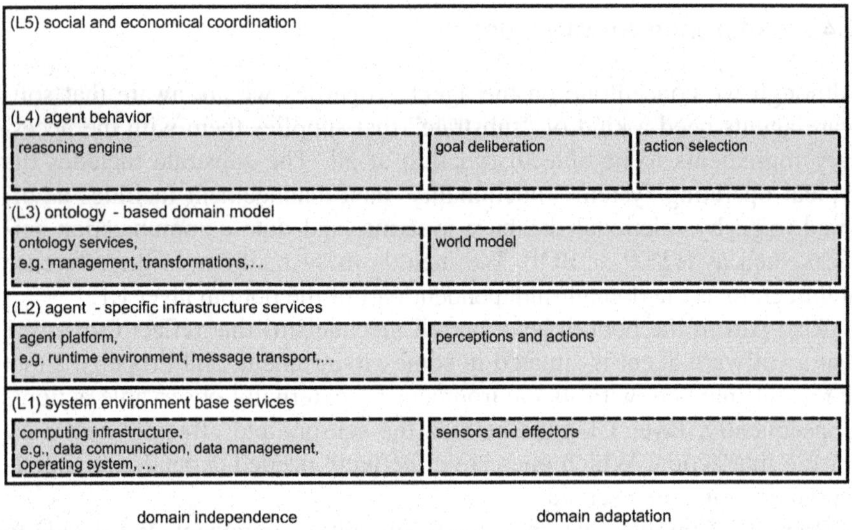

(L5) social and economical coordination	
(L4) agent behavior	
reasoning engine	goal deliberation · action selection
(L3) ontology - based domain model	
ontology services, e.g. management, transformations,...	world model
(L2) agent - specific infrastructure services	
agent platform, e.g. runtime environment, message transport,...	perceptions and actions
(L1) system environment base services	
computing infrastructure, e.g., data communication, data management, operating system, ...	sensors and effectors
domain independence	domain adaptation

Figure 3. Reference architecture for agents

Layer L4 is the one where ultimately the agent behavior according to Property 4 is realized. The layer must include all mechanisms necessary for goal deliberation and means-end assessment. Goal deliberation has more of a strategic character, means-end assessment is more tactical in nature and results in a selection among potential actions. The goals may originate from a single principal or, if the agent serves many clients, from several principals. Particularly in the latter case the goals may sometimes be in conflict so that the agent must reconcile them. Since both, goal deliberation and means-end assessment make use of the world model of layer L3, the rules for practical reasoning and the world model must match in structure, e.g., distinction between facts, goals and means, and in formal- ization, e.g., use of a symbolic representation.

Being situated in an environment can often mean working for some common goal. The agent may then have to pursue some common goal over and above its own goals. We decide to differentiate in the architecture between the goals of the individual agent and the communal goals. The former are located on layer L4, the latter on layer L5. On L5 the actions are derived according to the more abstract social and economical princi- ples governing the community as a whole. Figure 3 summarizes the refer- ence architecture for agents.

4.4.3 Localizing Agent Intelligence

The reference architecture just derived provides the framework where ac- cording to the design principle of Section 4.4.1 some of the details are still to be filled in by considering Properties 5 to 9 of intelligent agents.

Property 5 states that an intelligent software agent is reactive, that is, it continuously perceives its environment and responds in a timely fashion to changes that it observes. Clearly, meeting the property affects the action selection on L4 and the agent platform on L2.

In particular, the need for reactivity may cut short goal deliberation. That there is an interaction between the two, but that the interaction may in fact be rather complicated, is reflected by Property 6 that requires an intel- ligent software agent to achieve an effective balance between goal-directed and reactive behavior. In particular the balance may result in the revision of goals and may thus also affect the world model.

Proactivity of an agent (Property 7), i.e., being able to take the initiative in pursuance of its goals, is closely related to autonomy and, hence, is al- ready technically solved by the runtime environment of layer L2. Having control over its own progression, the agent can continuously pursue its own goals without the need for external events to trigger the activities. An effect can also be expected on level L4 where there may be a need to rec- oncile long-term and short-term goals.

Property 8 introduces another aspect of intelligence in a software agent, the capability of interacting with other agents. This is an extension to the reasoning behind layer L5: While pursuing common goals the agent may communicate with other agents to elicit certain responses or to influence their own goals, i.e., it may take a more proactive role than just adjusting its own behavior. To do so, it ought to be aware of the social and economi- cal constraints that direct the interaction. On a technical level, the commu- nication should follow appropriate interaction protocols, hence Property 8 has also an effect on layer L2. Further additions to L2 deals with the directory services of service-oriented architectures, or specific communication formats such as speech act based messages.

Finally we should localize Property 9, an agent's capability to learn. Effects can be expected on layers L3 because the world model must be able to reflect past experiences and conclusions, L4 because goal deliberation and means-end assessment should now include machine learning techniques, and particularly L5 where past experiences may alter the coordination strategies. Figure 4 summarizes the responsibilities of the layers for the various properties.

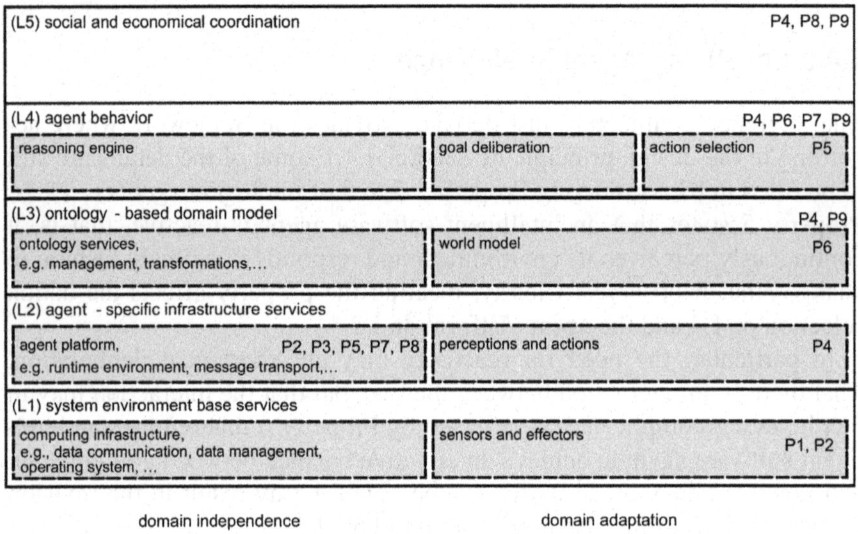

(L5) social and economical coordination		P4, P8, P9
(L4) agent behavior		P4, P6, P7, P9
reasoning engine	goal deliberation	action selection P5
(L3) ontology - based domain model		P4, P9
ontology services, e.g. management, transformations,...	world model	P6
(L2) agent - specific infrastructure services		
agent platform, P2, P3, P5, P7, P8 e.g. runtime environment, message transport,...	perceptions and actions	P4
(L1) system environment base services		
computing infrastructure, e.g., data communication, data management, operating system, ...	sensors and effectors	P1, P2

domain independence   domain adaptation

Figure 4. Assignment of agent properties to the layers of the reference architecture

4.4.4 Reinterpreting the Jadex Architecture

There are several so-called agent architectures that fall somewhere between the fairly abstract level of our reference architecture and the concrete architecture of a domain-specific agent. Such architectures usually reflect a certain philosophy or view of agents by their designers. We claim that these architectures fit into the reference architecture, but occupy only a very few layers for which they serve as a refinement. As a consequence, these architectures are incomplete and must be augmented by implementations for the remaining layers.

Perhaps the most popular among the agent architectures is the belief-desire-intention (BDI) model. To study how the model fits into the reference architecture we examine a software framework for agents that follows the BDI model, the Jadex reasoning engine [BrPL2005] [PoBL2005a]. Jadex is intentionally conceived as pure reasoning engine, factoring out basic aspects of agent management. Hence, Jadex is realized as a rational agent layer that sits on top of a middleware agent infrastructure that corresponds to layers L1, L2 (and optionally L5) (Figure 5). Currently, Jadex has been tested on three different middlewares: JADE [BBCP2005], Diet[1] and on a simple standalone layer.

The Jadex reasoning engine uses a world model that is based on beliefs and belief sets. The beliefs are stored and managed within a container called belief base in the form of single and multi-valued facts (Property P1). In contrast to other BDI systems such as Jason[2] and dMars [IKLW1998] that employ a formal representation of beliefs, in Jadex an object-centered perspective was chosen. The reasoning engine can inspect the knowledge base by posing queries in a declarative and set-oriented language similar to OQL. This part of Jadex clearly occupies layer L3.

Means-end reasoning (Property P4) follows the "classical" BDI mechanism as proposed by Rao and Georgeff [RaGe1995]. For a given goal or event the relevant plans are searched within the library of plan templates. In a second step it is checked which of those options are applicable in the current context by evaluating their preconditions. Finally, from the list of applicable plans a candidate is selected (e.g., via meta-level reasoning) and executed. Thereafter, affected mental attitudes such as fulfilled goals are updated accordingly. Since BDI was originally conceived to address real-time decision making by alleviating the unacceptably slow reaction times of traditional planning systems, Jadex naturally addresses Property P5 as well.

While goal deliberation (Property P4) is considered neither in current BDI theories nor in other available agent frameworks, the Jadex reasoning engine introduces new concepts such as explicit goals and goal deliberation mechanisms (see e.g. [BPLM2004]), and enhances the original BDI architecture by allowing the integration of extensions such as goal deliberation strategies into the interpreter [PoBL2005b]. The foundation for such extensions is a generic goal lifecycle that introduces explicit goal states allowing a uniform treatment of different kinds of goals during the agent's lifetime, and thus goes some way towards meeting Property P7 [BPLM2004]. As an example, the Easy Deliberation strategy handles con-

---

[1]   See http://diet-agents.sourceforge.net/ for details.
[2]   See http://jason.sourceforge.net/ for details.

flicts between goals given relative order of goal importance [PoBL2005c]. The relationship between goal deliberation and action generation (Property P6) is not fixed within the architecture but heavily depends on the used deliberation strategy which determines the computational costs.

In summary, Jadex primarily addresses Properties P4, P5, P6 and somewhat P7. In our reference architecture these properties are located on layers L3 and L4. Consequently, Jadex can be considered a refinement of layers L3 and L4 (see Figure 5).

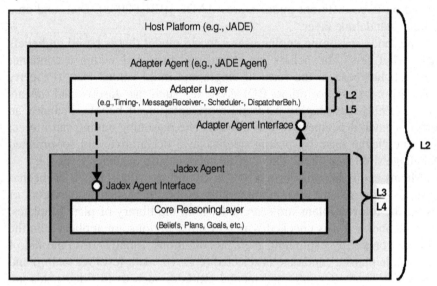

Figure 5. Jadex as a refinement of the reference architecture

4.4.5 Reinterpreting the InteRRaP Architecture

As a second example we consider InteRRaP [Muel1996]. InteRRaP has as its main objective the integration of reactivity, goal-orientation, and cooperation into a single model. Hence, InteRRaP seems to focus on Properties 6 (effective balance between goal-directed and reactive behavior) and 8 (social ability). Now, if we examine Figure 4, we would then expect that the InteRRaP model would in particular fill in more details of the layers L4 and L5. Figure 6 shows the InteRRaP architecture.

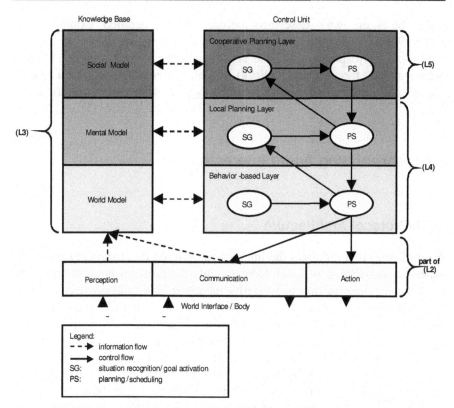

Figure 6. InteRRaP as a refinement of the reference architecture

The core is the control unit. It is divided into three layers, the Behavior-based Layer, the Local Planning Layer and the Cooperative Planning Layer. The Behavior-based Layer reflects the short-term reactive behavior of the agent, the Local Planning Layer is responsible for the longer-term goal-directed behavior. Together the two constitute Layer L4 of the reference architecture. The balance between goal-directed and reactive behavior is achieved by dividing the two layers into two functional components each, SG (situation recognition and goal activation) and PS (planning and scheduling). Each SG component examines its specific knowledge base, and then hands its conclusions to the PS component. If PS has insufficient information it turns to the PS component on the next lower layer which, probably with the help of its SG partner, determines the shorter-term actions and then notifies the SG component one layer up.

The third layer, Cooperative Planning Layer, corresponds to Layer L5 of the reference architecture. Like the other two layers it contains both, an SG and a PS component, and interacts with the Local Planning Layer in exactly the same way described before. For a detailed example see [Muel1996].

In close correspondence to the control unit the knowledge base is also organized into three-layers, a World Model, a Mental Model and a Social Model. All three can be seen as part of Layer L3 in the reference architecture.

4.5 Incorporating Agent Interaction

4.5.1 Protocol Architecture

A set of rules that regulates the interaction between two (or more) agents is called an *interaction protocol*. Conceptually the protocol must be enforced by some mechanism that is located – as a sort of virtual connector – between the agents (Figure 7). In fact, though, as noted in IV.3 in the prevailing form of interaction, conversations, there is no "natural" central authority to which the agents can turn to organize the cooperation. Rather it is up to the individual agents themselves to incorporate the mechanisms for organizing and controlling the information exchange if it is above the physical layer. In other words, each agent contains software that reflects its contribution to the protocol, and altogether the protocol is realized in a distributed fashion across the agents. Hence, we have to augment the agent reference architecture of Section 4.4 by further elements.

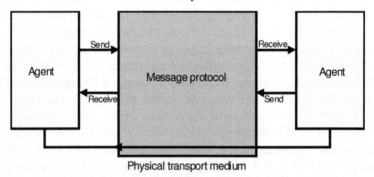

Figure 7. Design architecture for a multiagent system

Conversations are based on (asynchronous) message exchange. As is well-known from telecommunications, the corresponding communication software follows the layers pattern and, hence, is referred to as a protocol stack. Figure 8 illustrates the protocol mechanism for the ISO/OSI reference model [Stal2005].

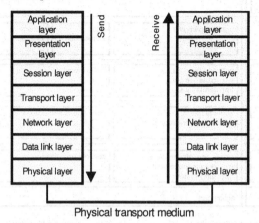

Figure 8. ISO/OSI data communications reference architecture

What does the protocol stack within an agent look like? Taking our cues from the ISO/OSI model, the lower four layers – the transport system – are oblivious to the purpose of the message exchange, let alone the application domain. Consequently, the mechanisms necessary for physical communication can be located on layer L1. Property 8, *An intelligent software agent may have to possess social ability, that is, is capable of interacting with other agents to provide its service*, is already preconditioned towards interaction and was associated with layer L5. Hence, we would expect that the conversation protocols are primarily reflected in that layer. Protocols govern a sequence of message exchanges between the agents. Hence, what we need in between is a layer that is geared towards agent messages. Layer L2 seems the right layer. Interaction depends on some common understanding among the agents, i.e., a shared world model and ontology. Layer L3 thus must provide suitable mechanisms for proper message encoding. Layer L4 controls the behavior of the individual agent and, hence, does not seem to contribute anything to the coordination per se, so it does not participate in the protocol stack.

Figure 9 outlines the protocol stack within an agent and may be seen as an extended reference architecture for agents. Clearly, protocol layers L1 and L2 are domain-independent. Even layer L5 can be formulated in a domain-independent way as long as one employs generic interaction protocols. However, some interaction protocols are intimately related to the agent architectures on layers L3 and L4. Just consider the InteRRaP architecture of Section 4.4.5.

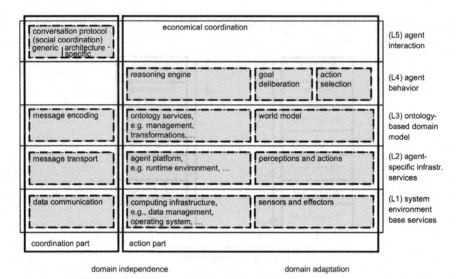

Figure 9. Agent implementation architecture for a multiagent system

4.5.2 Example: Contract Net

The most widely used conversation protocol is the *contract net* protocol. An agent – called the manager – seeks other agents – called (potential) contractors – to contribute to the solution of a task. In doing so the manager announces a task that needs to be performed, receives, and evaluates bids from potential contractors, awards a contract to a suitable contractor, and receives and synthesizes results. On the other hand, the contractor receives task announcements, evaluates its own capability or interest to respond, responds (declines or bids), performs the task if the bid is accepted, and reports the results. Figure 10 gives an example, the FIPA contract net protocol (see below).

The protocol must be translated into the detailed protocol stack spanning layers L5, L3, L2 and L1. These stacks will have to reflect the responsibilities each agent assumes within the protocol. For example, Dinkloh and Nimis use Figure 10 as the basis of a finite-state automaton that is turned into the implementation of protocol stacks for both, initiator and participant [DiNi2003]. The protocol determines the message exchange based on a higher-level communication language, FIPA-ACL, which obviously must also be provided on layer L2 at the location of each agent. The contract net itself defines the layer L5 protocol.

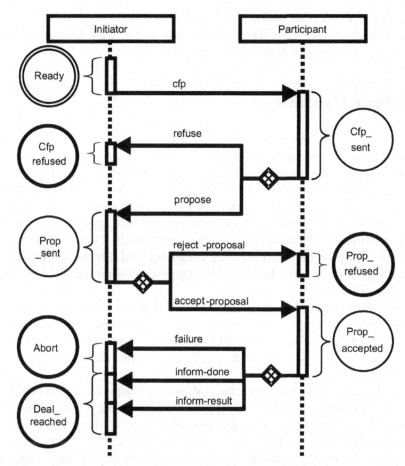

Figure 10. FIPA-Contract Net Protocol

4.5.3 Living Systems Technology Suite

The layered communication model of a commercial development and run-time suite, Living System® Technology Suite (LS/TS) by Whitestein Technologies AG, closely parallels the protocol stack of Figure 9 and may thus also serve as a proof of concept for our reference architecture. LS/TS distinguishes four levels in a so-called tiered model. The Interaction Tier deals with basic messaging including rendezvous policies. It is followed by the Linguistic Tier for the classification of message types (speech acts). Both correspond to Layer L2 in the protocol stack. The next level, the Domain Tier, represents the topic of conversations, with the knowledge captured in domain ontologies, and corresponds to Layer L3. The upper-most Tier, the Social Tier, represents the structure of the conversation such as roles, protocols, and matches the responsibilities of Layer L5.

4.6 Agent Platforms

Finally we take a look at the platform section of Figure 3. Clearly, layers L1 and L2 of our reference architecture are fairly generic and thus domain-independent. Furthermore, its services appear useful to any agent no matter what its specific purpose. Hence according to Section 4.2.3, these layers are prime candidates for the agent platform (or framework) section. Such a platform would be provided at every location where agents are to be in-stalled, without becoming part of the agent itself. Hence, a platform (framework or middleware) imposes a standard, and it is the responsibility of each location to provide a suitable mapping between the local systems and the middleware.

FIPA (Foundation for Intelligent Physical Agents) proposes a reference architecture for an agent middleware, and a good number of mature im-plementations exist for it. We shall briefly cover it in this section in order to demonstrate that agent developers can safely concentrate on the coordi-nation protocols.

The FIPA reference architecture is shown in Figure 11. It assumes that layer L1 is provided by standard system software so that it can concentrate on layer L2. It consists of a number of related specifications. Basic among them are the FIPA Abstract Architecture Specification [FIPA2002a] and the FIPA Agent Management Specification [FIPA2002b]. Both together define an agent management system for the lifecycle management of the local agents, and a directory facilitator for registering external services.

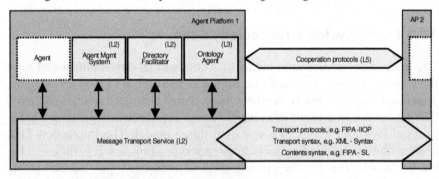

Figure 11. FIPA-Agent Management Reference Model

The platform core of the FIPA architecture, however, is the message transport system on layer L2. The architecture offers standards for various transport protocols, transport syntaxes and contents syntaxes. In particular, FIPA introduces an agent communication language (ACL, see IV.3).

Relegating the basic message exchange mechanisms to a platform allows agent designers to concentrate on the purposeful agent interaction which, as we saw before, is the subject of agent layer L5. For this purpose, the FIPA architecture offers specific interaction protocols such as the FIPA-Contract Net interaction protocol.

4.7 Conclusions

Architectural design of software, although deemed important by the community, often remains a neglected topic [Kell2003]. Good architectural design, though, tends to isolate the various issues to be concerned with, and localizes them within specific software parts. The foremost benefit is in a division of work, well-defined responsibilities and a well-controlled development process. If encapsulated in a reference architecture, one can also gain a blueprint along which to organize similar development processes. The purpose of this chapter was to demonstrate that such an approach is entirely feasible for the development of software agents.

Further Reading

[Bus+1996]   Buschmann, F.; Meunier, R.; Rohnert, H.; Sommerlad, P.; Stal, M.: Pattern-Oriented Software Architecture – A System of Patterns. John Wiley & Sons, New York, 1996.

[Muel1996]   Müller, J. P.: The design of intelligent agents: a layered approach. Springer-Verlag, Heidelberg, 1996.

[Star2002]   Starke, G.: Effective software architectures – a practical guide (in German). Carl Hanser, München, 2002.

References

[BBCP2005]   Bellifemine, F.; Bergenti, F.; Caire, G.; Poggi, A.: JADE – A Java Agent Development Framework. In: Bordini, R.; Dastani, M.; Dix, J.; El Fallah-Seghrouchni, A. (Eds.): Mutli-Agent Programming. Kluwer, Dordrecht, 2005.

[BPLM2004]   Braubach, L.; Pokahr, A.; Lamersdorf, W.; Moldt, D.: Goal representation for BDI agent systems. In: Bordini, R. H.; Dastani, M.; Dix, J.; El Fallah-Seghrouchni, A. (Eds.): Proceedings of the Second International Workshop on Programming Multi-agent Systems: Languages and Tools (PROMAS 2004). Springer Verlag, Heidelberg, 2004, pp. 9-20.

[BrPL2005]   Braubach, L.; Pokahr, A.; Lamersdorf, W.: Jadex: A BDI Agent System Combining Middleware and Reasoning. In: Unland, R.; Calisti, M.; Klusch, M. (Eds.): Software Agent-Based Applications, Platforms and Development Kits. Birkhäuser, Basel, 2005, pp. 143-168.

[Bre+2004]   Bresciani, P.; Perini, A.; Giorgini, P.; Giunchiglia, F.; Mylopoulos, J.: Tropos: An Agent-Oriented Software Development Methodology. In: Autonomous Agents and Multi-Agent Systems 8(2004)3, pp. 203-236.

[Bus+1996]   Buschmann, F.; Meunier, R.; Rohnert, H.; Sommerlad, P.; Stal, M.: Pattern-Oriented Software Architecture – A System of Patterns. John Wiley & Sons, New York, 1996.

[DiNi2003]   Dinkloh, M.; Nimis, J.: A Tool for Integrated Design and Implementation of Conversations in Multiagent Systems. In: Dastani, M.; Dix, J.; El Fallah-Seghrouchni, A. (Eds.): Proceedings of the First International Workshop on Programming Multiagent Systems: Languages and Tools (PROMAS 2003). Lecture Notes in Artifical Intelligence 3067. Springer Verlag, Heidelberg, 2004, pp. 187-200.

[FIPA2002a]   Foundation for Intelligent Physical Agents: FIPA SC00001L – FIPA Abstract Architecture Specification. 2002. http://www.fipa.org/specs/fipa00001, accessed on 2005-11-30.

[FIPA2002b]   Foundation for Intelligent Physical Agents: FIPA SC00023K – FIPA Agent Management Specification. 2002. http://www.fipa.org/specs/fipa00023, accessed on 2005-11-30.

[Kell2003]   Keller, F.: The role of architectural descriptions for the software development process (in German). Ph.D. thesis. Universität Potsdam, 2003.

[IKLW1998]   d'Inverno, M.; Kinny, D.; Luck, M.; Wooldridge, M. J.: A Formal Specification of dMARS. In: Singh, M. P.; Rao, A. S.; Wooldridge, M. (Eds.): Proceedings of the 4th International Workshop on Intelligent Agents IV, Agent theories, Architectures, and Languages. Lecture Notes in Computer Science 1365. Springer-Verlag, Heidelberg, 1998, pp. 155-176.

[Muel1996]   Müller, J. P.: The design of intelligent agents: a layered approach. Springer-Verlag, Heidelberg, 1996.

[PaWi2004]   Padgham, L.; Winikoff, M.: Developing Intelligent Agent Systems: A Practical Guide. John Wiley & Sons, New York, 2004.

[PoBL2005a]   Pokahr, A.; Braubach, L.; Lamersdorf, W.: Jadex: A BDI Reasoning Engine. In: Bordini, R.; Dastani, M.; Dix, J.; El Fallah-

	Seghrouchni, A. (Eds.): Multi-Agent Programming. Kluwer, Dordrecht, 2005, pp. 149-174.
[PoBL2005b]	Pokahr, A.; Braubach, L.; Lamersdorf, W.: A Flexible BDI Architecture Supporting Extensibility. In: Skowron, A.; Barthes, J. P.; Jain, L.; Sun, R.; Morizet-Mahoudeaux, P.; Liu, J.; Zhong, N. (Eds.): Proceedings of the 2005 IEEE/WIC/ACM International Conference on Intelligent Agent Technology (IAT-2005). 2005, pp. 379-385.
[PoBL2005c]	Pokahr, A.; Braubach, L.; Lamersdorf, W.: A Goal Deliberation Strategy for BDI Agent Systems. In: Eymann, T.; Klügl, F.; Lamersdorf, W.; Klusch, M.; Huhns, M.: Proceedings of the Third German Conference on Multi-Agent Technologies and Systems (MATES 2005). Lecture Notes in Artifical Intelligence 3550. Springer Verlag, Heidelberg, 2005.
[RaGe1995]	Rao, A. S.; Georgeff, M. P.: BDI-agents: from theory to practice. In: Lesser, V. R.; Gasser, L. (Eds.): Proceedings of the First International Conference on Multiagent Systems. The MIT Press, Cambridge, 1995, pp. 312-319.
[Stal2005]	Stallings, W.: Business Data Communication – 5th edn. Pearson Prentice-Hall, Upper Saddle River, 2005.
[Star2002]	Starke, G.: Effective software architectures – a practical guide (in German). Carl Hanser, München, 2002.
[Vog+2005]	Vogel, O.; Arnold, I.; Chugtai, A.; Ihler, E.; Mehlig, U.; Neumann, T.; Völter, M.; Zdun, U.: Software Architecture – foundations, concepts, practice (in German). Elsevier Spektrum Akad. Verlag, München, 2005.
[WoJK2000]	Wooldridge, M. J.; Jennings, N. R.; Kinny, D.: The Gaia Methodology for Agent-Oriented Analysis and Design. In: Autonomous Agents and Multi-Agent Systems 3(2000)3, pp. 285-312.
[Wool2002]	Wooldridge, M. J.: An Introduction to Multiagent Systems. John Wiley & Sons, New York, 2002.

5   Semantics for Agents

Thorsten Scholz, Ingo J. Timm, Otthein Herzog
Universität Bremen, Technologie-Zentrum Informatik
{scholz I i.timm I herzog}@tzi.de

Günter Görz, Bernhard Schiemann
Universität Erlangen-Nürnberg, Lehrstuhl für Informatik 8
(Künstliche Intelligenz) {goerz I schiemann}@informatik.uni-erlangen.de

Abstract. In the previous chapters design issues have been discussed with respect to architecture and interaction. These chapters are focused on techniques and methodologies. However, an explicit semantics of agent architectural and interaction behavior is required for the analysis and implementation of complex real-world systems. Additionally, the adaptation of a multiagent system to real-world domains requires the formal specification of knowledge. In this chapter, we introduce semantics from a general perspective with special focus on agent technology, e.g., semantics for communication. Finally, we introduce formal semantics for representation of intelligent agents and multiagent systems.

5.1 Introduction

The definition of agents, multiagent systems as well as multi-multiagent systems is a key challenge in agent engineering. The specific characteristic of agent engineering, comparable to developing distributed knowledge-based systems with complex interaction, requires sound and formal specification of the system. The advantage of formalizing agent behavior in a logical framework consists in providing a descriptive level that abstracts from the agent's architecture as well as from algorithmic details. An example for such an abstract description was mentioned earlier: the modal logic proposed for modeling BDI agents. In computer science, this level of abstraction is well known as the specification level of an information processing system and is distinguished from its implementation level. Generally, it turns out to be much easier to prove that the system's specification matches our expectations about the functionality of the system (i.e. the agent's behavior) than to prove the same for the system implementation. According to [SiRG1999], the challenge lies in developing "techniques for ensuring that agents will behave as we expect them to – or at least, will not behave in ways that are unacceptable or undesirable."

Any formalization of deliberative agents establishes a balance between the expressiveness of the formalism and its computational complexity. [RaGe1995], for instance, describe a simple BDI-logic that is decidable in linear time. Often, however, the price for a logical formalism sufficiently expressive to capture particular type of agent behavior is prohibitively high. In this case, an agent that is reasoning in the formalism would not be able to act rapidly enough under the temporal constraints of its environment. Although such a logic may be useful for the purpose of analysis, it is certainly not suited as a basis for building actual agents. To clarify this point, [SiRG1999] distinguish two different objectives which can be followed by the developer of an agent formalism.

- Specification: External Use of the Formalism. This is the objective of the agent designer who uses a logical language to specify the agent's behavior. Tools from logic (e.g. model checking) are applied to analyze whether the specification is consistent.
- Reasoning: Internal Use of the Formalism: The agent's deliberation processes are implemented by reasoning within the formalism. This is the objective followed by most work on MAS.

In multiagent systems a third aspect is accompanying them: Interaction, i.e., the internal use of the formalism for interaction of the participating agents within a system. This area of research is comparable to the Semantic Web. In both domains, the Semantic Web as well as the interaction in multiagent systems, ontologies are the key technology for ensuring semantically sound interaction of heterogeneous autonomous entities. Additional problems in the multiagent domain arise from the connection of deliberation cycle with its underlying knowledge representation and the semantics of transferred information within messages. Here mediation between ontologies is required.

In this chapter, semantics from a general perspective with special focus on agent technology is introduced. Starting from an abstract view on the foundations of semantics defined as meaning and reference, communication aspects and foundation of logics are discussed. In the following, interaction and reasoning are described in abstract agent context. Here, the focus lies on specific approaches to the semantic description of dynamic behavior like temporal logic, situation calculus, or non-monotonic reasoning. As a logical basis for interaction in distributed systems, i.e., agents resp. multiagent systems, ontologies are introduced as a building block for interaction semantics. For the flexibility of multiagent systems as well as for the interaction of heterogeneous systems, one of the key challenges lies in the integration of heterogeneous ontologies, which is discussed in the subsequent section. In the second part of the chapter, the focus lies on semantics for agent architectures. Here, recent trends in formalization as well as an unified approach to the formal foundation of agent deliberation is presented. For multiagent systems it might be of interest to analyze the systems semantics, i.e., the dynamic change of the multiagent system.

5.2 Semantics: Foundation, Communication, and Reasoning

This section gives a brief introduction to the question of semantics, i.e., the problem of assigning meaning to linguistic expressions, formal as well as "natural" ones, i.e., those of everyday common language, in its application to agents and multiagent systems (as introduced above and in accordance with [Wool2000]). As we want to understand agents' actions as meaningful w.r.t. some goal agents are supposed to achieve, we have to deal with the interpretation of the (external) relation of agents to their environment as well as with the question how the symbolic structures on which the agents' operations depend are meaningful in relation to their internal symbolic representations of the environment. In the following, we are focusing on semantics from an internal, agent-local point of view, i.e. semantics applied to agents for communication, reasoning, and action planning. The question for meaning comes up on the object- and meta-level, i.e. for knowledge representation and reasoning in agents on the one hand, and also with reasoning about rational agents. The latter aspect is closely tied to the tasks of specification and verification: We want to define agents in a way that they do what we mean and we want to show that their "behavior" conforms to that definition.

5.2.1 Foundation of Semantics

For our discussion of semantics, we assume the framework of logic in its most general sense, just as Allen Newell expressed in 1981 that "*there is no non-logical knowledge representation*": "*Just as talking of programmer-less programming violates truth in packaging, so does talking of non-logical analysis of knowledge.*"

According to a long-standing tradition, logic has been considered as the basis of any theory of argumentation. Traditionally, logic deals with the doctrines of concept formation, judgment (expressing assertions), and reasoning. In computer science, there are different uses of logic. It is used as a tool

- for the analysis, design and specification of modeling tasks and
- formalisms,
- a representation formalism itself, and
- a programming language (Prolog).

As a reason for its widespread use, usually it is stated that standard logic has the advantage of a clear and well-defined semantics. So, what is the background for this claim, and what is semantics all about? Semantics is the investigation of the meaning of linguistic expressions or of signs in general, and in particular of the validity conditions of sentences and propositions.

5.2.1.1 Semantics: Meaning and Reference

The question for semantics has always been closely tied to the use of human language. The function of language has clearly been stated by Plato as "somebody communicates something to somebody else", a view which has been prevailing till this day. He describes semantics in terms of a picture theory, i.e., a unique relation between names and things. A modern version of picture theory can be found in Wittgenstein's "Tractatus Logico-Philosophicus" (1921), where each element of a declarative sentence stands for something, be it an object or a quality or a relation, etc.; the connectives and the way the words are put together correspond to the way the objects and qualities and so on are related in the world - understood as the totality of facts and not of things.

Within this framework, all prevailing problems can be formulated which come up with any attempt to answer the two fundamental questions of semantics: The substance-related or ontological question "What are meanings?", and the functional or epistemological question "How can signs mean (something)?" Considering the relation between names and things, either names have been regarded as a particular kind of things, which leads to an external relation between things, or things have been regarded as special kind of names (representations) resulting in an external relation between signs. A third answer has been that names are a priori assigned to (in individual actions) accessible individual things as individual instances of sign schemata, resulting in an internal relation between language and world.

Thorough investigations have shown that both of the external answers taken separately lead to extreme difficulties in explaining communication. Therefore, the need for a combination of both approaches became obvious.

The canonical solution is due to Frege's (1892) theory of "Sinn" (meaning) and "Bedeutung" (reference). The meaning of a proposition governs its linguistic understanding ("by which"), and it is required to assess its validity in the world ("whereabout"). The transition from names - playing a significative, extensional role - to statements (propositions) - playing a communicative, intentional role - is provided by propositional functions, which in turn are represented by predicative expressions. Hence, predicative expressions are to be explained in a meaning-related way, i.e. intentionally, and in a reference-related way, i.e. extensionally, as well.

This claim can be satisfied by means of two equivalence relations between predicative expressions, because, according to the modern theory of abstraction as conceived by Frege, each function is obtained by abstracting over its representing terms. The first one, synonymy, is an analytic equivalence relation which holds due to terminological rules or meaning postulates and which leads to concepts. As an intentional abstraction, it encompasses our knowledge of language. On the other hand, general (material) equivalence is empirical, hence synthetic, and comprises knowledge of the world.

5.2.1.2 Including Communication

In order to cope with the communicative aspect, the so called semantic triangle, *sign, meaning, reference,* is extended to a pragmatic quadrangle by including the distinction between speaker and hearer, which in particular allows to take into account the difference between speaker-reference and hearer-reference, which is important for the function of names. Then the pragmatic context of linguistic expressions, their use (token) or type of use, resp., provides a foundation for the determination of their meaning. In Wittgenstein's words: "The meaning of a word is its use in the language". The primacy of pragmatics, expressed by "communication is action", leads to a foundation of semantics where meaning is rooted in a theory of action. The recent theory of speech acts (see below), which also plays an essential role for agent communication, is justified exactly by such a pragmatic foundation.

5.2.1.3 Pragmatic Foundation of Logic

Referring to our introductory remarks about the general logical framework, immediately the question comes up whether there is a pragmatic foundation for logic itself. What would be symbolic actions which allow to assign a meaning to composite logical expressions? In fact, dialogical logic provides an answer; an approach, which, often referred to as "logic as game", has recently gained considerable popularity. Dialogical logic sets up a framework for two-person games, where two partners play games about the validity or truth (if truth-value definiteness is given) of composite logical formulae. For each connective and each quantifier rules are given which define the moves, attacks (doubts), and defenses for formulae composed with the resp. connective. The justification of these rules is precisely a pragmatic one: executing a move is an action. In further abstraction steps games can be turned into formal developments in a tableau calculus, reaching the level of a full formalization. Logical truth of a formula, i.e. truth by its form alone, is given if such a tableau can be closed. Among many publications, readers interested in a detailed exposition are referred to [LoLo1978].

Dialogical logic has the advantage of covering constructive ("intuitionistic") and classical logics as well up to the level of modal logic. It comprises the traditional proof-theoretic exposition of logic - although in a top-down fashion due to the tableau method - and, because of its pragmatic foundation, without the need to refer to Hilbert-style axioms. Model theory plays primarily an exhibitory role as models are constructed by successful tableau proofs, and model theoretic methods are nevertheless important tools on the meta level, but it is not required as a foundational discipline in Tarski's sense. Tarski's approach attempts to introduce truth in a purely formalistic way as illustrated by his famous example: The sentence "Snow is white" is true if and only if snow is white. But pushing the problem of truth to the meta-level leads to a vicious circle as long as one does not leave the formalism.

5.2.2 Foundation of Semantics

The most popular formalization of rational agency is the belief-desire-intention (BDI) model which is based on the assumption of the primacy of beliefs, desires, and intention in rational action. It is rooted in the philosophical tradition of understanding practical reasoning in humans and has been developed in its present form by Michael Bratman [Brat1987].

For agents, conceived as computational systems in its broadest sense, formal theories have been developed that allow to reason about their actions – often referred to as "behavior" in an anthropomorphic terminology. Those theories can be understood as defining the semantics of such systems, i.e. they allow to interpret a given state of affairs and the agent's reasoning in a logical precise way. To build such theories, rational action has to be reduced to its operationalizable aspects and the theory has to provide justifications for the adequacy of the required abstractions. In particular, for the BDI model, a logical language has to be designed which extends standard logic with representations for beliefs, desires and intentions in the first place. LORA (Logic of Rational Agents) is such a language, originally developed by Rao and Georgeff and presented in depth in [Wool 2000]. In addition to the BDI component, it contains a temporal component to represent the dynamics of agents and their environments, and an action component to represent the agents' actions and their effects.

5.2.2.1 Logic for Multiagent Systems

In order to provide a concise and efficient notation, in general a modal logic framework is chosen, which can be understood as a class of specialized languages for representing the properties of relational structures, as, e.g. temporal relations. So, e.g., LORA is a first-order branching time logic, containing modal connectives for representing the beliefs, desires, and intentions of agents, as well as expressions in a dynamic-logic style for representing and reasoning about the actions agents perform. It is well known that the satisfiability problem for first-order logic is only semi-decidable, and the corresponding problem for modal logics is even worse. So there will presumably never be practical theorem-proving methods for such logics. But that does not mean that designing it is a useless enterprise at all. In general, it can play a threefold role in the engineering of agent systems: as a specification language, as a programming language, and as a verification language. As for specification, it helps to give precise definitions and to identify inconsistencies in designs. For programming and verification, it is an indispensable tool for formalization, even when in terms of execution the language has to be weakened or incomplete inference algorithms must be used.

An important feature of logical models of multiagent systems is that they must be able to represent the information-state of each agent containing knowledge and belief, and that they allow to explore the relation between both. In particular, the representation of shared knowledge is essential for reasoning and, in particular, planning. To express the knowledge/belief distinction in a clear and succinct way, modal operators in their epistemic reading have been a well proven tool.

5.2.2.2 Agent Communication

In the following, we will focus on the issue of agent communication in general, i.e., the linguistic framework of agent communication languages, and on the role of formal ontologies. One important feature is that they ensure semantic compatibility w.r.t. to the conceptualization of the objects and their properties agents have to deal with, the conceptual representation of the environment itself, and w.r.t. to their operations in the environment. The purpose of this presentation is to complement the theoretical exposition of LORA and similar languages as given in Section 5.3 (see also [Wool2000]), to which the interested reader is referred to, from an application-oriented point of view.

Agents are supposed to be autonomous in the following technical sense that they have control over both their state and their "behavior". Therefore, it is not possible, that an agent can "invoke a method" in another agent as in object-oriented programming. Agents cannot force other agents to perform some action and they cannot directly access the internal state of other agents, in particular not write any data into it. But they can exchange messages with each other, i.e., communicate. In our understanding of communication as a special form of action, agents can perform communicative actions to convey messages to other agents in order to influence their internal state and their future actions, let it be communicative or other ones.

5.2.2.3 Speech Acts

Speech act theory, originally conceived in the philosophy of language by Austin, Searle, and others, has at its center precisely the notion of communication as action. Usually, three different aspects of speech acts are distinguished: the elocutionary act - making an utterance -, the illocutionary act - the action performed in saying something -, and the perlocution - the effect of the act. Subsequently, a typology of speech acts has been elaborated which are associated with corresponding performative verbs, comprising representatives, directives, commissives, expressives, and declarations. Furthermore, in order to perform speech acts successfully, general conditions on communication situations were identified, among which sincerity is an important one. In a framework of systems like agents, which shall be able to plan how to autonomously achieve goals, such plans must include communicative actions. So, Cohen and Perrault [CoPe1979] and others gave an operational account of speech acts in terms of AI planning techniques, and which later on has been generalized in embedding speech act theory in a more general theory of intentional rational action for agents.

5.2.2.4 The Meaning of Agent Communication Language Expressions

The semantic question we are facing is how to assign meaning to the expressions of agent communication languages. The actual agent communication language, based on speech acts, is FIPA-ACL; it has been standardized in 1995 by the Foundation of Intelligent Physical Agents. The FIPA standard defines an unambiguous format for messages in a LISP-like syntax, 20 performatives (such as "inform", "query", "confirm", etc.) to stipulate the intended interpretation of messages, and it does not mandate a specific object language for message content. In general, it is assumed that the content is given by a logical expression. Here is an example of a FIPA-ACL message (from [Fipa2001]):

```
(inform
    :sender     agent1
    :receiver   agent2
    :content    (price good2 150)
    :language   s1
    :ontology   hpl-auction)
```

The formal semantics of FIPA-ACL is defined in terms of a "Semantic Language" SL, a quantified multi-modal logic containing modal operators for referring to the beliefs, desires and intentions of agents and expression types in a dynamic-logic style for representing agent's actions. It was inspired by previous work of Cohen, Levesque, Sadek, and others. The semantics definition of FIPA-ACL provides a translation semantics which maps each ACL expression to a corresponding SL formula which in turn is a constraint that the sender of the message must satisfy.

Intuitively, the example message encodes an inform speech act directed from agent1 to agent2, containing a predicate term expressed in the language SL. Whereas the meaning of the logical symbols in the content expression is defined in SL, the interpretation of its non-logical symbols is provided by a formal ontology, in our case "hpl-auction". The actual wording suggests strongly that the given predicate expression gives a price information for a good named "good2" of 150 currency units, but its precise meaning has of course to be taken from the formal ontology where the concept of "price" will be located within a terminological hierarchy and will possibly carry some further attributes.

5.2.2.5 Formal Ontologies: Meaning of Content Words

Whereas the problem of semantics of logical symbols has been addressed above, we will now broach the issue of formal ontologies, dealing with the non-logical symbols ("content words"), and the important role they play for agent systems. The term ontology, which in philosophy denotes the doctrine of "what there is", is used here in a much more restricted way.

Formal ontologies consist of (formal) definitions of the concepts and relations in a domain, in our case the agents, their environment, and the tasks they have solve in it. A formal ontology defines, which and in which way objects, substances, aggregates, changes, events, actions, time and place specifications, etc., are available for knowledge representation and reasoning. For this purpose, within a logical framework a basic inventory of linguistic expression types is required, which enables representations of

- Concepts (also: classes, categories) resulting from predication and abstraction, represented by predicates;
- Relations among concepts resulting from terminological (predicator) rules and are represented in a super-/sub-concept hierarchy;
- Assigned properties ("roles", attributes) to concepts, represented by (binary) relations.
- Further content-based relations between concepts are laid down by rules ("axioms").

Furthermore, languages for the representation of formal ontologies need to provide a suitable vocabulary for conceptual modeling; this question will be discussed in more detail below. Formal ontologies resemble a lot to terminological systems, hierarchical dictionaries and thesauri, but usually they convey more information than those which capture the use of terms, but not more. Usually, empirical, encyclopedic knowledge is not contained in dictionaries, but is an essential component of formal ontologies.

5.2.2.6 Reference and Application Ontologies

Among formal ontologies, at least two kinds can be distinguished, reference and application ontologies. Reference (or foundational) ontologies account for a generic, universal conceptual inventory, i.e. a representation language and fundamental distinctions, and for foundational relations like parts and wholes (mereonymy), similarity, dependence, connection, inherence, and temporal order. Today, instead of just a single "upper level", often a small set of foundational ontologies is provided, and current work aims even at a foundational ontologies library.

Application ontologies provide conceptual models of particular application domains; the formal ontologies presented in this volume are of this type. For a general overview of formal ontologies in agent architectures see also [SyPa2004].

Building a formal ontology is still more an art than a science, although for scientific domains like physics or biology a lot can be adopted from fundamental work in the philosophy of science. Many formal ontologies have been constructed upon empirical evidence within the framework of ordinary language. Recently, methods of systematic conceptual construction based on epistemic criteria have been proposed, among which the OntoClean methodology in combination with the DOLCE reference ontology (Descriptive Ontology for Linguistic and Cognitive Engineering) by Guarino et al. is the most advanced [GuWe2004] [Gan+2002]. For already existent ontologies, they provide a systematic approach to the construction and remodeling of ontologies.

Experience has shown that basic conceptual modeling constructs such as instantiation, generalization, association, aggregation have been used in a less rigid and systematic way in many cases. Therefore, the distinction between particulars and universals, class-instance-of and membership, subsumption and instantiation, part-of and part-whole relations, as well as composition, disjunction, identity, etc., need to be made compatible among different ontologies before they can be combined.

5.2.2.7 Semantic Content in Formal Ontologies

The question for semantic content in formal ontologies has to be answered in a twofold way: On the one hand, the ontology representation language offers epistemological constructs the semantics of which has to be defined similar to languages of formal logic as indicated below for the case of de-scription logics. On the other hand, starting with some primitive concepts, the structure and attribution of domain concepts as represented by means of these epistemological constructs makes up a definition of the semantics of the given domain. In our case, these are the concepts and roles which define the agents' "world", i.e., the epistemological and operational categories which constitute the conditions of all possible perceptions and actions. Those are the (only) formal linguistic means agents have at their disposal for the representation of states of affairs and of situations or world-states as a whole.

5.2.2.8 Computational Logic

To enable a computational device such as an agent to make use of the rep-resented knowledge it must be equipped with some kind of an inference mechanism. For our logical framework, this means that we have to address the computational aspects of logic. Given a formal logical language with its syntax and semantics and the subsequent expressive power, first of all the reasoning problem has to be specified. Investigations of the reasoning problem are aimed at its decidability and computational complexity. Fi-nally, a problem solving procedure, i.e. a specific implementation solving the reasoning problem, has to be provided, and the problems to be ad-dressed at this level are its soundness and completeness and the practical aspects of complexity.

Of course, an ideal computational logic should be expressive, and have decidable reasoning problems for which sound complete and efficient reasoning procedures are available. Unfortunately, as one might expect, the field of logic is not an ideal world at all. As we know, even the question for decidability cannot be answered positively for full first-order logic. Therefore, for practical purposes, specialized logic-based representation formalisms are needed. Among them, a family of sublanguages of first-order logic named "Description Logics" has been developed, which explore the "most" interesting expressive decidable logics with classical semantics, and which can be equipped with "well-behaving" reasoning procedures [Baa+2003].

5.2.2.9 Description Logics as Ontology Languages

Description Logics (DLs) are structured fragments of classical first-order logic which offer expressive means according to the requirements for formal ontologies as described above: concepts arranged in subsumption hierarchies, properties (roles) and individuals (instances). They can be characterized as sound and complete logics which are suitable to formalize theories and systems for expressing structured information and for accessing and reasoning with it in a principled way. The representation is object-oriented and done at the predicate level; there are no variables in the formalism. For structured descriptions, a restricted set of epistemologically adequate language constructs is provided to express complex relational structures of objects. Of particular importance is the distinction between conceptual (terminological, "T-Box") knowledge and knowledge about instances (assertional, "A-Box"). For reasoning, automatic classification to determine the subsumption – i.e., universal (material) implication - lattice plays a central role.

Constructions of conceptual models begin with a small set of primitive concepts and roles. Further concepts are defined by composite expressions which express sufficient and necessary conditions. Compositional operators are negation (complement), conjunction, disjunction, and value and existential restrictions for roles. The semantics of this language which has become familiar under the name "ALC " is defined model-theoretically, i.e. by associating a set-theoretical expression, denoting its interpretation in a domain, with each syntactic construct as shown in Table 1. This procedure can be justified by introducing a predicative set theory through abstraction, taking the pragmatic foundation of logic for granted. For the syntax of DL, a simple variable-free notation has been established, derived from frame languages and standard logic.

Table 1. Syntax and semantics (with a brief explanation) of ALC[1]

A	$A^{\mathcal{I}} \subseteq \Delta$	Primitive concept
R	$R^{\mathcal{I}} = \Delta \times \Delta$	Primitve role
$\top$	Δ	Universal concept (top)
$\bot$	$\varnothing$	Empty concept (bottom)
$\neg C$	$\Delta \setminus C^{\mathcal{I}}$	Complement
$C \sqcap D$	$C^{\mathcal{I}} \cap D^{\mathcal{I}}$	Conjunction
$C \sqcup D$	$C^{\mathcal{I}} \cup D^{\mathcal{I}}$	Disjunction
$\forall R.C$	$\{x \mid \bigwedge_y . R^{\mathcal{I}}(x,y) \rightarrow C^{\mathcal{I}}(y)\}$	Universal quant. (value restr.)
$\exists R.C$	$\{x \mid \bigvee_y . R^{\mathcal{I}}(x,y) \wedge C^{\mathcal{I}}(y)\}$	Existential quant. (exist. restr.)

A DL knowledge base consists of a T-Box (usually a formal ontology) and an A-Box which describes a certain situation in terms of its instances. Figure 1 gives an example.

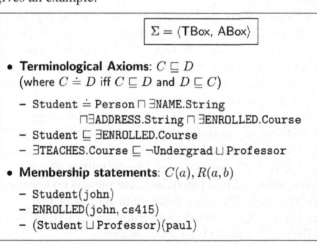

Figure 1. Example of a DL knowledge base[2]

As for reasoning, the fundamental inference relation is concept satisfiability, i.e. the proof that a concept expression has a model. All other kinds of inferences can be shown to be reducible to concept satisfiability: subsumption, general satisfiability, instance checking, retrieval, and realiza-

---

[1] C and D denote concept expressions, either concept names or composite expressions.

[2] With the "subset" sign partial definitions are introduced, giving necessary conditions. The equal sign introduces complete definitions, specifying necessary and sufficient conditions (example due to E. Franconi).

tion. For DLs, tableaux provers have become a de facto standard for proof procedures. For comprehensive overview of DL, see [BaHS2005].

On top of ALC, a variety of more expressive DLs have been developed and investigated. A particularly important DL is called SHIQ, which adds to ALC [Bec+2004]:

- qualified number restrictions,
- "General Inclusion Axioms" (GCI),
- transitive and inverse roles,
- role hierarchies, and
- data types ("concrete domains"), e.g. real numbers.

The importance of this DL is due to the fact that it provides the basis for OWL-DL, a version of the (Semantic) Web Ontology Language OWL (cf. [AnHa2004] [Bec+2004]). In fact, for OWL-DL (qualified) number restrictions and nominals, i.e. classes with a singleton extension, have to be added [HoSa2005].

For the Semantic Web, a hierarchy of standardized representation languages based on XML has been proposed: The basic layer is given by XML plus namespaces plus data types (XMLSchema). The second layer consists of RDF (Resource Description Framework), a language to express associative triples (subject-predicate-object) which can be combined to associative networks as directed labeled graphs. RDF offers as modeling primitives instance-of, subclass and properties with range, domain, and cardinality restrictions. This layer is enriched by RDFS (RDFSchema), which provides a limited modeling vocabulary and allows to organize it in a typed hierarchy with facilities for the definition of classes and subclasses, and of roles and role hierarchies, but there is no commitment to an inference mechanism. The logic layer, built on top of that, is exactly the place where OWL-DL is located as an extension to RDFS(FA), a sub-language of RDFS with a First Order style semantics.

OWL as a standardized language guarantees a stable future for a very expressive description logic. Future layers will deal with extensions like rules and defaults which go definitely beyond DL, sacrificing at least completeness or even decidability.

5.2.2.10 Temporal Logic

An extension already mentioned is the possibility to represent and process temporal statements. A common approach to deal with time in logic is to use versions of modal logic. Temporal operators like 'always' and 'sometimes' are defined in analogy to 'necessary' and 'possible'. An example of a theorem of such a temporal logic would be "If always Q then sometimes

Q". Augmenting 'always' and 'sometimes' with other modalities such as "P" for past ("It has at some time been the case that...") and "F" for future ("It will at some time be the case that...") leads to modal languages known as tense logics; they have been pioneered by Arthur Prior et al. In the simplest cases, time is regarded as consisting of a linear sequence of states, whereas in more advanced logics (as LORA) branching time is introduced in order to represent possible futures. Further extensions introduce binary temporal operators as 'since' and 'until'. From a semantic point of view, of course the various axiomatizations of temporal operators are to be questioned for their adequateness; otherwise temporal logics are just modal logics (for a detailed account of temporal logic see [OeHa1995]). To plan actions in a changing world, in most cases a metric representation of time is required: actions occur in time, they have durations, and frequently they occur concurrently. For this purpose, metric temporal logics have been developed.

5.2.2.11 Situation Calculus

For planning, understood as an inference task, a first attempt to take situations into consideration was to add a further argument position to any situation-describing predicate. Unfortunately, the desired abstractions cannot be expressed adequately in this simple way. Therefore, situation calculus was designed by McCarthy, Kowalski, and others, a second-order language specifically suited for representing dynamically changing worlds. As such, it is incomplete, but nevertheless a useful tool for semantically characterizing actions and their properties. Appropriate extensions of logic programming for situation calculus are available (cf. [Reit2001]).

As an outlook, let us briefly mention two practical requirements which are important for agent systems, but which force us to leave the secure semantic grounds we have been in up to now: Non-monotonic reasoning and acting under uncertainty. The investigation of semantic problems in these areas is still a research challenge.

5.2.2.12 Non-Monotonic Reasoning

Reasoning with incomplete knowledge is another important issue in agent systems, and its general importance is also reflected by the fact that it is addressed by a future layer in the Semantic Web language hierarchy. So, in a next step, we will have to deal with non-monotonic reasoning (for a comprehensive overview see [BrDK1997]). Examples are reasoning with defaults, revising beliefs, or asserting and retracting formulae in a knowledge base. In a dynamic world, an agent will have to revise appropriately his beliefs when it is facing any of the following situations:

- new information from the outside world has to be assimilated,
- premises turn out to be erroneous or change over time,
- assumptions made during problem solving are violated,
- an obvious contradiction is encountered, ...

This brings up an entirely new situation compared to standard logic and its semantics, where the monotonicity property holds: If a formula p follows from a set of premises Q, then p also follows from any superset of Q. As your set of beliefs grows, so does the set of conclusions that can be drawn. In contrast to common sense reasoning, conclusions are never withdrawn. In agent systems, as long as we insist on the consistency of knowledge bases, in the case of contradictions we have to identify the source of conflict and withdraw any belief depending on conflicting assumptions or inconsistent data. As in many cases the knowledge available only suffices to formulate general rules that usually apply, but also allow for exceptions, an agent might be forced to revise a general assumption if it encounters an individual which instantiates an exception.

5.2.2.13   Belief Revision and Reason Maintenance Systems

To support approaches to the belief revision problem, computational tools have been developed: Reason Maintenance Systems (RMS). In them, data dependencies are represented explicitly in a network composed of assertions and justifications. In fact they are data dependency network management systems, pursuing the goal to keep the knowledge base consistent. Because this task is common to a variety of applications, it has been separated from the problem specific algorithms and encapsulated in a module of its own. Basically, two kinds of RMS are to be distinguished:

- justification-based, which maintain a single actual context, and
- assumption-based which allow for multiple contexts.

5.2.2.14   Uncertainty and Bayesian Inference

The last requirement to be briefly addressed in this section is the need of agents to acting under uncertainty. In the real world, an agent can never be completely sure. In many cases, there is a certain degree of uncertainty due to incompleteness and incorrectness in the domain model. The fact that many domain rules will be incomplete because too many conditions would have to be enumerated, or some conditions are unknown, has been called the qualification problem. But nevertheless, agents have to make rational decisions, taking into consideration that their knowledge leads in the best case to a "degree of belief" for the truth of assertions.

For reasoning under uncertainty, the concept of subjective probability in combination with Bayes' rule has become the most important approach: Bayesian inference uses probability theory to make probabilistic inferences. But its application is justified only if the required probability distributions can be obtained, which is often very hard in practice (and in many cases neglected). Bayes' rule allows to compute the a posteriori probability distribution for (a set of) query variables or hypotheses, given exact values for the probabilities of some evidence variables (e.g. gained through perception):

$$P(H|E) = P(E|H) * P(H) / P(E)$$

$$i.e., Posterior = Likelihood * Prior / Evidence \qquad (1)$$

In general, instead of a logical approach, agent systems can be defined by means of decision theory, where rational decisions of agents are made by considering action benefits vs. the certainty of success. Decision theory is a normative theory of action in that it tells an agent what it should do in principle, but the actual implementation of the utility optimization function imposes nevertheless a hard problem: it seems to require an unconstrained search over the space of all actions and their results which is extremely expensive. And the difficulties increase if we are not only considering one action, but a sequence of actions as in planning. Another problem is that for utility functions the same difficulty holds as for probability distributions: they are hard to obtain in practice.

5.3 Merging Ontologies

Nowadays, autonomous software agents (short: agents) communicate via a standardized format using FIPA-ACL [Fipa2001]. In the content field of the FIPA-ACL message format, assertions are applicable. These assertions are elements of the *A-Box* of a formal ontology. Before starting, every agent gets a local copy of the *T-Box* (see Section 5.2.2.9 for explanation of *T-Box*). To ensure consistency of the assertions w.r.t. the *T-Box*, ontology merging is applied. The structure of this section is as follows. In the second paragraph we shed light on the problem of ontology merging and explain it by an example. Then, in the third paragraph, we show some existing ideas, frameworks and algorithms that can be applied to the problem. We close with a brief discussion of still missing features for this task.

In human-agent interaction concepts might be added to or changed in the local copy of the *T-Box* of one agent. If this change is unknown to other agents (its communication partners), it will generate an ontology exception. Let us look at an example:

In the ATT-Multi-Agent-System (MAS, see II.2), this problem occurs if a new kind of disruption (as an explanation for supply chain delays in delivering) is added. Think of a logistics company where a truck and its freight are stolen. Before this situation occurred, no local copy of the *T-Box* contained a concept "theft" because nobody thought about thefts. So, a human disponent adds this concept to his copy of the *T-Box* and informs his agent (here a Surveillance-Agent (SA1) of ATT-MAS) that it must update its local copy. In this case the SA1 informs the SA of its customer (SA2) that (corresponding to an order containing this freight) a disruption of the type "theft" has occurred. As explained above, assertions are used in communication and therefore SA1 sends SA2 an instance of "theft". Without ontology merging capabilities, SA2 will generate an ontology exception (meaning "message not understood").

Applying the following approaches to (semi-automatically) merge ontologies to agent communication is a possibility to improve inter-agent "understanding".

Before merging ontologies it is necessary to have the same understanding of basic ontological aspects. The *OntoClean* methodology already introduced in Section 5.2.1 enables this.

The *OntoMorph* method [Chal2000] was originally designed to translate knowledge bases from one formalism to another. It uses two mechanisms: syntactic and semantic rewriting. Syntactic rewriting (via patterns) works as central part of this system. Semantic rewriting finds (through reasoning) subclass-superclass relations and then applies syntactic rewriting to them. The Rosetta [Bock2005] agent based translation scenario uses the OntoMorph method in the implemented wrapper agents.

The *prompt* tool is member of the Protege plugin family[3] and allows authors to merge ontologies semi-automatically. Based on lexical analysis, pairs of related terms of the source ontologies are computed. *Anchor-PROMPT* [NoMu2000] takes these pairs as input. It interprets the formal ontology as a graph where nodes represent concepts and edges represent roles. *Anchor-PROMPT* computes paths in the resulting graph and these paths are used to find equivalence classes. A cumulative similarity score

---

[3]   http://protege.stanford.edu/download/plugins.html

(based on heuristics) and analysis of the path assigns matching candidates. These are presented to the user for merging.

Looking at these approaches, one can see that there are still open problems in the field of ontology merging. If we look closer at the *OntoMorph* methodology, the syntactical matching leads to similarity of "car" to "carpenter". Additionally this method is not designed to create one ontology out of several others. *Anchor-PROMPT* needs similarity in the way the ontologies to be merged were modeled. It is significant that the approaches do not use reasoning capabilities to assist the merging task. As explained in Section 5.1, domain ontologies (formal ontologies) correspond to description logics such that reasoners like RACER [HaMo2001] can be used to answer queries referring to *T-Boxes*. It is still an open research question to integrate reasoner feedback with ontology merging. There exist some problem classes related to the given example that need not to be worked out by merging ontologies. For these problems might fit other solutions like aligning order translating ontologies. A short overview of other methodologies gives [StTi2002].

5.4 Semantics for Agent Architectures

In I.1 to I.3, properties of Intelligent Agents, MAS, and especially flexibility have been introduced in an informal way. The main properties, i.e., autonomous behavior and flexibility of agents and multiagent systems, are new challenges for the design and the implementation of these systems. There are various approaches for the formalization of the definition and specification of MAS and their properties [RaGe1995] [LePi1999] [DuLM2003] [GeNi1987]. In this chapter, formal concepts for agents, MAS, and their properties are introduced in a general manner allowing for specific extensions resp. specializations. In the previous section formal languages are discussed in context of interaction and decision making in agents. This section is focused on architectural and decision making issues within agents.

5.4.1 Recent Trends in Formalization

The majority of formal approaches are focused on enabling intelligent behavior within agents [vHWo2003] [WoJe1995] [RaGe1998] [FiGh2002] [NiTa2002] [Timm2001]. As introduced before, design of intelligent agents is often based on an explicit, cognitive model of beliefs, desires, and intentions (BDI). The underlying idea is that an agent is creating an explicit world model (beliefs) on the basis of observations and its actions. Additionally, it contains a set of objectives (desires or persistent goals) and a set of goals which are currently pursued (intentions). The agent pursues its goals by autonomously created plans. BDI-agents are "the dominant force" in formal approaches [Inv+2004, p. 5] for which [Wool2000a] already identified three major reasons:

- It is based on a widely accepted theory of rational actions of humans.
- They are successful in a great number of complex applications.
- There is a large family of well-understood, sophisticated, and formalized approaches available.

However, modeling heterogeneous MAS requires the abstraction of individual agents' behavior. The model of the system should only include those actions, which are perceivable to other agents or which change the environment. Standard BDI approaches do not focus on system behavior but on agent internal knowledge representation and decision making. Wooldridge and Lomuscio introduce VSK as a formal model for MAS based on multimodal logic [WoLo2000a]. VSK integrates an environment depending visibility function (visibility) and an agent depending perception function (see). These concepts realized as modalities enable varying virtual environments for specific agents. A third modality is used for representation of the local state of agents (knowledge). However, the interaction of desires, beliefs, and intentions is not handled explicitly. Semantically, VSK is based on multi-modal sorted first-order logic [WoLo2000a] and for temporal aspects it includes the possible worlds semantics, i.e., beliefs resp. propositions about knowledge follow weakS5 (KD-45) modal system [MeHV1991]. In spite of the convincing concept of VSK, the underlying multi-modal sorted first-order logic suffers from the well-known problems introduced before.

5.4.2 Agents on a Meta Level

In the following the basic concepts for agents are introduced on a meta-level. As a starting point, we use the formalization concept introduced in [Kirn2002]. Agents as the core concept of this book are the building blocks for multiagent systems. In I.1, agents are introduced with basic properties. One of the main properties is, that agents are situated in an environment (cf. I.1.2.2, Property 1) and act upon information they perceived from the environment. A general approach to formal agent behavior has to be based on these three phases, perceive, reason, do.

Perceive

For each agent agt, there exists a unique environment env(agt), which is principally visible for it. Agents observe their environment via sensors in order to identify the relevant information constituting its perceptions perc(agt):

$$perceive : env(agt) \rightarrow perc(agt) \qquad (2)$$

The environment is not constant but changing from agents' actions or external events. For concrete situations at time t, the notion should be extended to

$$perceive : env(agt,t) \rightarrow perc\ (agt,t) \qquad (3)$$

Reason

Reasoning is the core functionality of agents. It enables agents to process perceptions and change their internal state. Depending on the agent's internal architecture and state design, it is able to deliberate, plan, or select appropriate actions for execution. Let loc(agt) denote the local state of agent agt. The reasoning process may be formalized by:

$$reason : loc(agt) \times perc(agt) \rightarrow loc(agt) \qquad (4)$$

To be more precise, reasoning has to be specified in context of time:

$$reason : loc(agt,t) \times perc(agt,t) \rightarrow loc(agt,t+\Delta) \qquad (5)$$

The local state of an agent may be constituted by highly complex structures. There are several aspects, which have been discussed in order to specify this structure. The above mentioned reasoning in BDI logics uses beliefs, desires and intentions for this purpose. Kirn proposes the definition of commitments and goals as mandatory properties of a local state [Kirn2002].

Additionally, in several formalizations, an explicit state transformation function is introduced for updating the agent's local state. For building an intelligent agent, this function has to be specified analogously to belief revision functions [ChGM2002] [MaDK2002].

Do

In the third step the agent is selecting an action act(agt) according to its internal state, which is performed in its environment:

$$do : loc(agt) \rightarrow act(agt) \qquad (6)$$

The behavior of an agent can thus be described within a temporal context as follows:

$$do:\ loc(agt,t) \rightarrow act(agt,t) \tag{7}$$

Summarizing an agent can be defined as a tuple, consisting of the three decision functions perceive, reason, do, as well as the accompanying concepts environment, perceptions, local states (including initial state loc0), and actions:

$$Agt = \langle env,\ perc,\ loc,\ perceive,\ reason,\ do,\ loc_0 \rangle \tag{8}$$

5.5 Unifying Formalisms

In agent research, a common approach includes the formal description and semantic explication of agent behavior. As a formal basis the behavior and architecture will be described following the BDI approach [RaGe1991] and their specializations Lora [Wool2000], VSK [WoLo2001], and discourse agents [Timm2004]. The Lora logic is focused on internal decision behavior of rational agents. States of the global system are considered implicitly. For a specification of a multiagent system it is advantageous to explicitly model the relationships of agents as well as local and global states. As mentioned before, the VSK logic is addressed to describe these issues as well as the perception-relation between environment and specific agents. Due to the individual advantages of VSK and Lora, the formal model of discourse agents integrates both aspects: sophisticated decision making and system perspective.

In agent design, a major challenge is the specification of agent behavior. Therefore, the core element of agent architectures is the control cycle, where generic actions are activated resp. executed as a consequence of internal state-transformations or external perceptions. The control cycle of an agent should specify the pro-active as well as reactive behavior. The control flow of discourse agents is illustrated in Figure 2. It differs from conventional BDI approaches in the reflection phase where an agent adapts its internal state with respect to external perceptions. Here, it explicitly differentiates between adaptation of beliefs, i.e., the core knowledge base of an agent, desires, i.e., persistent goals, strategy, and plans. The possibility to adapt desires and strategies should enable the multiagent system to become more flexible, even on a long-term strategic level. The reflection of plans is an explicit approach for learning from recent plan execution for future situations and behavior and, therefore, a mid-term adaptation of agent behavior.

In the following semantics of an intelligent agent is introduced following the meta-level conceptualization as introduced before: perceive, reason, do. In VSK agents are defined by perception (*perceive*), local state transformation resp. deliberation (*reason*), and action selection (*do*). These three elements form the abstract behavior of an agent: The agent perceives its environment, it adapts its local state with respect to new information as well as deliberation on desires and intentions, and it selects an action which is adequate in the current setting. In virtual as well as physical environments agents usually do not have complete access to all information in the environment. For example, messages sent between agents are not accessible to agents which do not participate in the interaction. These aspects are also discussed in context of "visibility" within section system semantics (Section 5.4). In the last section, perception is defined on the basis of env(agt) (Equation 2) to emphasize the agent-dependent view on the environment. Each agent has a perception function (*see*) which maps environmental states to a set of perceptions. The underlying idea is that an agent using malfunctioning sensors is not capable of perceiving all accessible information. However, if its sensors are fixed, it would be able of perceiving the information. In software MAS, data packages delayed through the network could lead to restricted views on the environment even if the environment is fully accessible.

The second step of agent behavior is to adapt its local state considering the accessible and perceived environmental states as well as its local state. The state transformation is realized by the *next* function mapping.

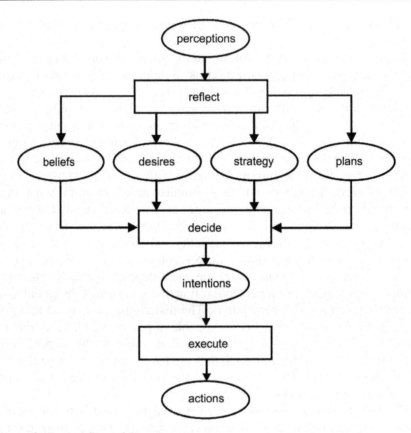

Figure 2. Control flow of discourse agents

Finally the agent has to select an action to be performed in the environment. However an agent may select the *null* action which determines that the agent is not changing the environment willfully. The action selection is one of the core aspects of intelligent behavior in agents; [WoLo2000a] are not requiring detailed behavior for flexibility reasons, such that agents using different internal inferences (reactive, deliberative agents) may be formalized in this framework. Following the conceptualization introduced in the last section, *do* is executed without changing its internal state. Here, this formalization differs from [WoLo2000b] and [Timm2004], where deliberation and, consequently, change of internal state takes also place in the *do* function. The formal definition of an agent following VSK is summarized as follows:

$$Ag = <L, \text{ } see, \text{ } next, \text{ } do, \text{ } l_0> \tag{9}$$

$L = \{l_0, ..., l_m\}$:   set of possible agent's states

$see : E^2 \rightarrow P$:   function for perceiving environmental states

$next : L \times P \rightarrow L$:   local state transformer function

$do : L \rightarrow Act$:   action selection function

$l_0 \in L$:   initial state of the agent

In this definition, the *see* function is dependent on the concrete design of an agent, i.e., its sensors. Therefore, only the two major functions *next* and *do* will be discussed in more detail in the following sections.

5.5.1 Belief Revision (Next)

One of the major design principles in the BDI framework is the notion of beliefs for knowledge acquired by the agent. In competitive environments an agent may not have access to all information or may even perceive intentionally incorrect information from opponents. Therefore, in contrast to conventional knowledge based systems, it is assumed that information resp. knowledge within an agent may be uncertain, fuzzy, incomplete, or incorrect. *Beliefs* are propositions of a specific agent about the environment, opponents, or itself. Therefore the validity of beliefs may change due to internal reasoning or external perceptions. In consideration of the concrete model of BDI, the local state of an agent may vary from consisting of beliefs only to more complex models which include beliefs, desires, intentions, strategies, and plans. Summarizing, there are two main challenges for agents resp. multiagent belief revision: Handling of uncertain, fuzzy, incomplete, or incorrect knowledge between states or within states.

The first step in the decision process of a BDI agent is to reflect its internal state and update the models of the environment and opponents with respect to recent perceptions. A completely autonomous or automatic adaptation to the environment is a non-trivial task and is handled in current AI research projects, e.g., [ChGM2002] [MaDK2002]. The elementary challenge for an intelligent agent is to compute input information (perception) and the resulting changes to the knowledge base (beliefs). The concrete formulation of belief revision depends on the language for knowledge representation used within the agents. Many approaches in agent research utilize multi-modal logic in combination with branching temporal structures. Here, belief revision is performed as follows: Each iteration of belief revision creates a new state as a clone of the current state. Inconsistent beliefs to the current perceptions are removed. The advantage of this approach is that each state is consistent and usual inference mechanisms may be applied. The discourse agents specification proposes this approach as a first step. However, inconsistent perceptions or exceptions in the beliefs may not be handled easily.

On top of the reflective behavior the local state of an agent is transformed again by the deliberation process. In common BDI approaches deliberative behavior is characterized by *intention reconsideration, generation of options* resp. intentions, and *filtering of these options*. In the discourse agents architecture, filtering is specialized to a specific conflict management approach.

Intention reconsideration is the function for deciding on an intention commitment in the current situation. Following [RaGe1991], three types of commitments may be differentiated:

- *Blind commitment*: An agent pursues an intention until the agent beliefs that the intention has been satisfied.
- *Single-minded commitment*: An intention will be removed if the agent comes to the conclusion, that there is no action sequence resp. plan to satisfy the intention.
- *Open-minded commitment*: An agent keeps the intention as long as it beliefs that it is possible to satisfy the intention.

Even if open-minded commitment does not seem to be an adequate means in concrete business applications, it may be advantageous to use this commitment. Here, computing temporal structures with all possible worlds emerging from the current situation is impossible, even computing a significant number of possible worlds may be hard. With open-minded commitment agents would be enabled to continue pursuing an intention even if they are not capable of calculating an action sequence within a plan.

The next step in the BDI approach is the *generation of options*, e.g., creation of goal sets. Many approaches in literature introduce this as an indeterministic function which is not specified in detail. In discourse agents, conflict management is used for creating alternative goals, the so called options. The generation of options is considering those desires which are not already pursued with an intention. For the remaining desires, accessibility is computed. A desire is classified as accessible, if the agent beliefs that it is possible to achieve this desire in at least one possible world. For each accessible desire, a plan is allocated. The step of plan allocation for desires is used to support the analysis of interdependencies between options. An additional step in discourse agents is the assessment of options. In conventional BDI approaches, there is no numeric evaluation of options.

This evaluation enables an adequate application of BDI in worth-oriented domains as introduced in IV.3.

On the basis of this evaluation, *filtering of options* may be performed by, e.g., conflict management or priority based selection. As a result of the reasoning, a new local state is created containing revised beliefs and an extended or updated set of intentions.

5.5.2 Action Execution (Do)

The executive behavior (do) ensures action execution on the basis of intentions, i.e., an action sequence is generated resp. planned with regard to the intention selection in the reasoning process. This process is shown schematically in Figure 3.

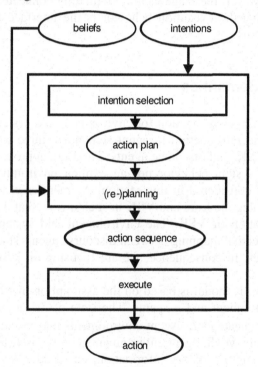

Figure 3. Executive behavior of discourse agents

In the first step, the evaluation of the intentions is updated due to the current situation in the environment and the agent's local state. With respect to these evaluations, an intention is selected for execution. In case of the discourse agents architecture, the intentions already contain a plan which is revised according to the current state. In conventional BDI approaches a new plan is generated on the basis of active intentions and the current state. Depending on the concrete specification and implementation of an agent, actions of a plan may be executed iteratively or some actions may be executed and the next decision cycle with perception, reason, do is started.

In a formal model, the *do* function is a mapping from an agent local state to an action. The action execution is performed within the environment, cf. next section. However, if the design of an agent is in question, there are various approaches to specify and implement the execution module. In physical agents, the action execution model is normally an interface to the actuators. In software agent settings, the execution is usually limited to communication. In the context of this book, agents may represent physical entities. However, these agents are not directly connected to real-world entities, such that the execution behavior is the interface for connecting simulation systems.

5.6 System Semantics

In the following, a formalization for environment and system semantics is presented. In the introduction to agent semantics, three logics were discussed: Lora, VSK, and discourse agents. The Lora approach includes neither a specific system behavior nor an explicit environment model and therefore is not considered in this section. As mentioned before, the discourse agents integrate Lora and VSK in such a way, that discourse agents are a specialization of VSK. The environment and system semantics is therefore an injective mapping between discourse agents states and all possible VSK states. In consequence, we are focusing on VSK logic in this section.

The formal VSK model is based on the assumption that there is exactly one agent environment and n agents. The state of the environment is expressed by a predicate $e \in E$. Agent environments may contain different aspects. In software MAS, agent environments can be used for communication and providing mandatory information, e.g., addresses or service descriptions. Furthermore they may include rules valid for any agent, e.g., social laws [ShTe1995].

This global environment can be partitioned into virtual sub-environments, which are accessible to groups, resp. structures or individual agents. Accessibility is realized by visibility functions which are part of the environment and each of them is associated with one agent, i.e., vis_i is the visibility function for agent i. This approach can also be used for the physical or logical movement of the agents, i.e., if an agent moves from one virtual environment to another, this is realized by a dynamic modification of its visibility function. The visibility functions define anything which is accessible to the agent and not what an agent actually perceives, i.e., it is sensor-independent. Formally, the visibility function behaves like an equivalence relation on environmental states, i.e., it returns a set of states which are indistinguishable with respect to accessibility.

Next to visibility and states, agent actions, e.g., communication acts, are part of the environment within the formal model of VSK. For each agent, there is a set of actions specified in the environment. These sets include those actions executed in the environment and exclude those which are used for internal reasoning. Additionally, a *null*-action is defined for doing nothing.

The transformation of states is realized by a mapping from the Cartesian product of the agent actions and an environmental state to an environmental state. This formulation implements a discrete instead of a continuous environment. The formal definition of an environment is given by:

$$Env = <E, Act_1, ..., Act_n, vis_1, ..., vis_n, \tau, e_0> \qquad (10)$$

E $E = \{e_0,...,e_m\}$: set of all possible environmental states

Act_i Act_i : set of actions of agent i

τ $\tau : E \times Act_1 \times ... \times Act_n \rightarrow E$: state transformer function

e_0 $e_0 \in E$: initial state of the environment.

For applications it is useful to define the agent environment with respect to the FIPA standardization, i.e., service directories, and agent management and communication can also be mapped to the formal environment model [Timm2004].

For a systemic view on semantics of MAS, it is necessary to define the complete MAS formally. In the VSK framework a MAS contains the agent environment and the agents. With respect to the formal definitions in the previous sections the formal definition of a MAS is given by:

$$MAS = <Env, Ag_1, ..., Ag_n> \qquad (11)$$

The global state of a MAS is specified by the environmental state as well as the local states of each agent ($g = <e, l_1, ..., l_n>$). Temporal resp. dynamic behavior of a system are defined implicitly. VSK uses an inductive approach for building the temporal structure. The initial state of a system is based on agents and the environment starting in their initial states ($e_0, l^0_1, ..., l^0_n$). However, the initial state of the system includes a first synchronization of the agents with the environment and a transformation of their local state. As mentioned before, agents do not have total perception of the environment. Accessibility and perception of the environment depend on the agent specific authorization which is formally represented by an agent-specific visibility function. The initial global state is derived from the initial environmental state and the initially transformed local states of the agents. New global states are achieved by agents' actions, i.e., the environmental state is transformed with respect to the actions and the local states are synchronized as described above. Formally, VSK defines "runs" for MAS, which are potentially infinite sequences of global states:

1. The initial global state is defined by

$$g_0 = <e_0, next^1(see^1(vis^1(e_0))), ..., next^n(see^n(vis^n(e_0))))>$$

2. Given $g_t = <e_t, l^1_t, ..., l^n_t>$ with $t \in N_0$:

$$t : g_{t+1} = <e_{t+1}, l^1_{t+1}, ..., l^n_{t+1}>$$

is defined by:

a) $e_{t+1} = \tau(e_t, do^1(l^1_t), ..., do^n(l^n_t))$ and

b) $l^i_{t+1} = next^i(l^i_t, see^i(vis^i(e_t))) \; \forall i \in \{1, ..., n\}$.

Further Reading

For further reading on VSK refer to [WoLo2000a], [WoLo2000b], [WoLo2000c], [WoLo2001], and [Wool2000b]. An adaptation to the FIPA specification and extension to deliberative behavior can be found in [Timm2004].

References

[AnHa2004]   Antoniou, G.; van Harmelen, F.: A Semantic Web Primer. The MIT Press, Cambridge, MA, 2004.

[BaHS2005]   Baader, F.; Horrocks, I.; Sattler, U.: Description Logics as Ontology Languages for the Semantic Web. In: Hutter, D.; Stephan, W. (Eds.): Mechanizing Mathematical Reasoning: Essays in Honor of Jörg H. Siekmann on the Occasion of his 60th Birthday. Lecture Notes in Artificial Intelligence, vol. 2605. Springer-Verlag, Berlin, 2005, pp. 228-248.

[Baa+2003]   Baader, F.; Calvanese, D.; McGuiness, D.; Nardi, D.; Patel-Schneider, P. (Eds.): The Description Logic Handbook. Theory,

Implementations and Applications. Cambridge University Press, Cambridge, 2003.

[Bec+2004]   Bechhofer, S.; van Harmelen, F.; Hendler, J.; Horrocks, I.; Mc-Guinness, D. L.; Patel-Schneider, P.F. Lynn Andrea Stein [...]: OWL Web Ontology Language Reference. W3C Recommendation, 2004-02-10. http://www.w3.org/ TR/2004/REC-owl-ref-20 040210/.

[Bock2005]   Bockting, S.: A Semantic Translation Service using Ontologies. 2005.

[Brat1987]   Bratman, M. E.: Intentions, Plans and Practical Reasoning. Harvard University Press, Cambridge, Massachusetts, 1987.

[BrDK1997]   Brewka, G.; Dix, J.; Konolige, K.: Nonmonotonic Reasoning. An Overview. In: CSLI Lecture Notes, vol. 73. CSLI Publications, Stanford, CA, 1997.

[CaJo2002]   Castelfranchi, C.; Johnson, W. L. (Eds.): Proceedings of the First International Joint Conference on Autonomous Agents & Multiagent Systems (AAMAS 2002) – Part 1. Bologna, Italy, July 15-19, 2002.

[Chal2000]   Chalupsky, H: OntoMorph: A Translation System for Symbolic Knowledge. In: Principles of Knowledge Representation and Reasoning. 2000, pp. 471-482

[ChGM2002]   Chopera, S.; Ghose, A.; Meyer, T.: Iterated Revision and the Axiom of Recovery: A Unified Treatment via Epistemic States. In: Harmelen, F. van (Ed.): Proceedings of the 15th European Conference on Artificial Intelligence (ECAI2002). Lyon, France, July 2002. IOS Press, Amsterdam, the Netherlands, 2002, pp. 541-545.

[CoPe1979]   Cohen, P. R.; Perrault, C. R.: Elements of a plan based theory of speech acts. In: Cognitive Science 3(1979), pp. 177-212.

[DuLM2003]   Dunne, P. E.; Laurence, M.; Wooldridge, M.: Complexity Results for Agent Design Problems. In: Annals of Mathematics, Computing & Teleinformatics 1(2003)1, pp. 19- 36.

[Fipa2001]   FIPA 97 Part 2 Version 2.0: Agent Communication Language. Document Nr. OC00003A, 2001. http://www.fipa.org/specs/fipa 00003/.

[FiGh2002]   Fisher, M.; Ghidini, C.: The ABC of Rational Agent Modelling. In: Castelfranchi, C.; Johnson, W. L. (Eds.): Proceedings of the First International Joint Conference on Autonomous Agents & Multiagent Systems (AAMAS 2002) – Part 1. Bologna, Italy, July 15-19, 2002, pp. 849- 856.

[Gan+2002]   Gangemi, A. et al: Sweetening Ontologies with DOLCE. In: Knowledge Engineering and Knowledge Management. Ontologies and the Semantic Web. 13th International Conference, EKAW 2002, Siguenza, Spain, October 1-4, 2002. Springer-Verlag, Berlin, 2002, pp. 166-181.

[GeNi1987]   Genesereth, M. R.; Nilsson, N.: Logical Foundations of Artificial Intelligence. Morgan Kaufmann Publishers, San Mateo, CA, 1987.

[GuWe2004]   Guarino, N.; Welty, C.: An Overview of OntoClean. In: Staab, S.; Studer, R. (Eds.): Handbook on Ontologies. Springer-Verlag, Berlin, 2004, pp. 151-159.

[HaMo2001]   Haarslev, V.; Möller, R: RACER system description. In: Proceedings of the International Joint Conference on Automated Reasoning, IJCAR'2001, Siena, Italy, Lecture Notes in Computer Science, June 18-23, 2001. Springer-Verlag, Berlin, 2001.

[Harm2002]   Harmelen, F. van (Ed.): Proceedings of the 15th European Conference on Artificial Intelligence (ECAI2002). Lyon, France, July 2002. IOS Press, Amsterdam, the Netherlands, 2002.

[HoSa2005]   Horrocks, I.; Sattler, U.: A Tableaux Decision Procedure for SHOIQ. In: Proceedings of the Nineteenth International Joint Conference on Artificial Intelligence IJCAI-05, Edinburgh, UK. Morgan Kaufmann, San Francisco, 2005, pp. 448-453.

[Inv+2004]   d'Inverno, M.; Luck, M.; Georgeff, M.; Kinny, D.; Wooldridge, M.: The dMARS Architecture: A Specification of the Distributed Multi-Agent Reasoning System. Autonomous Agents and Multi-Agent Systems 9(2004)1-2, pp. 5-53.

[Kirn2002]   Kirn, S.: Kooperierende intelligente Softwareagenten. In: Wirtschaftsinformatik 44(2002)1, pp. 53-63.

[LePi1999]   Levesque, H. J.; Pirri, F.: Logical Foundations for Cognitive Agents. Springer, Berlin, 1999.

[LoLo1978]   Lorenzen, P.; Lorenz, K.: Dialogische Logik. Wissenschaftliche Buchgesellschaft, Wiesbaden, 1978.

[MaDK2002]   Mateescu, R.; Dechter, R.; Kask, K.: Tree Approximation for Belief Updating. In: Proceedings of the Eighteenth National Conference on Artificial Intelligence and Fourteenth Conference on Innovative Applications of Artificial Intelligence (AAAI/ IAAI), Edmonton, Alberta, Canada, July 28 – August 1, 2002. AAAI Press, Menlo Park, CA, 2002, pp. 553-559.

[MeHV1991]   Meyer, J.-J. C.; Hoek, W. van d.; Vreeswijk, G. A. W.: Epistemic Logic for Computer Science: A Tutorial (Part One). In: Bulletin of the European Association for Theoretical Computer Science 44(1991), pp. 242-270.

[NiTa2002]   Nide, N.; Takata, S.: Deduction Systems for BDI Logics Using Sequent Calculus. In: Castelfranchi, C.; Johnson, W. L. (Eds.): Proceedings of the First International Joint Conference on Autonomous Agents & Multiagent Systems (AAMAS 2002) – Part 1. Bologna, Italy, July 15-19, 2002, pp. 928-935.

[NoMu2000]   Noy, N F.; Musen, M. A.: Anchor-PROMPT: Using Non-Local Context for Semantic Matching. 2000.

[OeHa1995]   Oehrstroem, P.; Hasle, P.: Temporal Logic. From ancient Ideas to Artificial Intelligence. Kluwer Academic Publishers, Dordrecht, 1995.

[RaGe1991]   Rao, A. S.; Georgeff, M. P.: Modelling Rational Agents in a BDI-Achitecture. In: Proceedings of the Second International Conference on Principles of Knowledge Representation and Reasoning (KR & R-91). Morgan Kaufmann Publishers, San Mateo, CA, 1991, pp. 473-484.

[RaGe1995]   Rao, A. S.; Georgeff, M. P.: BDI-Agents: From Theory to Practice. In: Proceedings of the First International Conference on Multiagent Systems. AAAI Press, San Francisco, CA, 1995, pp. 312-319.

[RaGe1998]   Rao, A.; Georgeff, M.: Decision procedures for BDI logics. In: Journal of Logic and Computation 8(1998)3, pp. 293-342.

[Reit2001]   Reiter, R.: Knowledge in Action: Logical Foundations for Specifying and Implementing Dynamical Systems. The MIT Press, Cambridge, MA, 2001.

[ShTe1995]   Shoham, Y.; Tennenholtz, M.: On Social Laws for Artificial Agent Societies: Off-Line Design. In: Artificial Intelligence 73 (1995)1-2, pp. 231-252.

[SiRG1999]   Singh, M. P.; Rao, A. S.; Georgeff, M. P.: Formal Methods in DAI: Logic-Based Representation and Reasoning. In: Weiss, G. (Ed.): Multiagent Systems – A Modern Approach to Distributed Artificial Intelligence. MIT Press, Cambridge, Massachusetts, 1999.

[StTi2002]   Stuckenschmidt, H.; Timm, I. J.: Adapting Communication Vocabularies Using Shared Ontologies. In: Cranefield, S. (Ed.): Proceedings of the Second International Workshop on Ontologies in Agent Systems. Workshop at 1st International Conference on Autonomous Agents and Multi-Agent Systems. Bologna, Italy, July 15-19, 2002, pp. 6-12.

[SyPa2004]   Sycara, K.; Paolucci, M.: Ontologies in Agent Architectures. In: Staab, S.; Studer, R. (Eds.): Handbook on Ontologies. Springer-Verlag, Berlin, 2004, pp. 343-363.

[Timm2001]   Timm, I. J.: Enterprise Agents Solving Problems: The cobac-Approach. In: Bauknecht, K.; Brauer, W.; Mueck, Th. (Eds.): Informatik 2001 - Tagungsband der GI/OCG Jahrestagung, September 25-28, 2001. Universität Wien, 2001, pp. 952-958.

[Timm2004]   Timm, I. J.: Dynamisches Konfliktmanagement als Verhaltenssteuerung Intelligenter Agenten. DISKI 283, infix, Köln, 2004.

[vHWo2003]   van der Hoek, W.; Wooldridge, M.: Towards a Logic of Rational Agency. In: International Logic Journal of the IGPL 11(2003)2, pp. 133-157.

[Weis1999]   Weiss, G. (Ed.): Multiagent Systems – A Modern Approach to Distributed Artificial Intelligence. MIT Press, Cambridge, Massachusetts, 1999.

[Wool2000a]   Wooldridge, M. J.: Reasoning about Rational Agents. The MIT Press, Cambridge, Massachusetts, 2000.

[Wool2000b]   Wooldridge, M.: Computationally Grounded Theories of Agency. In: Durfee, E. (Ed.): Proceedings of the Fourth International Conference on Multi-Agent Systems (ICMAS 2000). IEEE Press, July 2000.

[WoJe1995]   Wooldridge, M.; Jennings, N. R.: Intelligent Agents: Theory and Practice. In: The Knowledge Engineering Review 10(1995)2, pp. 115-152.

[WoLo2000a]   Wooldridge, M.; Lomuscio, A.: A Logic of Visibility, Perception, and Knowledge: Completeness and Correspondence Results. In: Proceedings of the Third International Conference on Pure and Applied Practical Reasoning (FAPR-2000). London, UK, September 2000.

[WoLo2000b]   Wooldridge, M.; Lomuscio, A.: Multi-Agent VSK Logic. In: Proceedings of the Seventh European Workshop on Logics in Artificial Intelligence (JELIAI-2000). Springer-Verlag, Berlin, 2000.

[WoLo2000c]   Wooldridge, M.; Lomuscio, A.: Reasoning about Visibility, Perception, and Knowledge. In: Jennings, N. R.; Lesperance, Y. (Eds.): Intelligent Agents. VI Springer-Verlag Lecture Notes in AI Volume, March 2000.

[WoLo2001]   Wooldridge, M.; Lomuscio, A: A Computationally Grounded Logic of Visibility, Perception, and Knowledge. In: Logic Journal of the IGPL 9(2001)2, pp. 273-288.

6 Towards Dependable Agent Systems

Jens Nimis, Peter C. Lockemann

Universität Karlsruhe (TH), Instiut für Programmstrukturen und
Datenorganisation, {nimis | lockemann}@ipd.uka.de

Karl-Heinz Krempels

RWTH Aachen, Lehrstuhl für Informatik IV
krempels@i4.informatik.rwth-aachen.de

Erik Buchmann

Universität Magdeburg, Institut für Technische und Betriebliche
Informationssysteme, buchmann@iti.cs.uni-magdeburg.de

Klemens Böhm

Universität Karlsruhe (TH), Instiut für Programmstrukturen und Datenorganisation, boehm@ipd.uka.de

Abstract. If an environment depends on the services of a multiagent system it should do so only if it can justifiably place reliance on this service. If so, the system appears to the environment reliable, or dependable. It is well-known that dependability should be designed right into a system rather than added as an afterthought. Particularly due to the high degree of distribution and the autonomy of agents, multiagent systems pose numerous and often novel challenges but also offer new opportunities to deal with dependability. This chapter examines the important issues and discusses how appropriate solutions can be associated with specific layers of the reference architecture of IV.4. Specifically, a distinction is made between unintentional and intentional failures, the former resulting in a suite of solutions referred to as error processing, the latter in measures called trust management.

6.1 Introduction

Designs are incomplete if they assume that nothing can ever go wrong. Or expressed the other way round: Chances that something outside the norm can occur should be taken into account right from the beginning and made an integral part of system design rather than – as happens only all too often – added as an afterthought.

Consider the job-shop example of II.3 where several agents interact following the Contract Net Protocol (Figure 1).

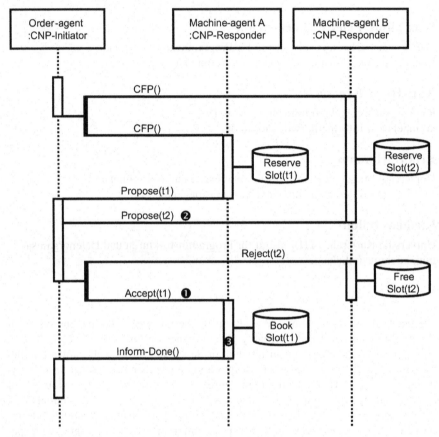

Figure 1. Scenario using the contract net protocol

Suppose that the protocol has progressed to the point where the order-agent accepts the offer of machine-agent A. Suppose further that the accept message never reaches agent A due to a communication failure (1). If no precautions are taken, agent A forever holds the resources reserved for the order-agent, while the order-agent never gets his order fulfilled. Or earlier on, suppose that machine-agent B submitted a proposal that would be the best if the order-agent could just understand B's choice of wording (2). Again, without some sort of precaution the order-agent would pay more than necessary. Or more towards the end, assume that machine-agent A breaks down while processing the order, or takes longer than promised because it encounters some shortage (3). The order-agent would be expected to find some way around the problem if it were designed to handle such a contingency.

Informally speaking, we call a multiagent system *dependable* if it maintains its service according to specifications even if disturbances occur that are due to events endogenous to the system. We call a multiagent system *robust* if it continues its service according to specifications once it dealt with exogenous events (events in the application environment) it was not specifically prepared for (Figure 2). An endogenous event within the multiagent system may be perceived by a single agent as an internal fault, namely if the event arises within the agent, or as an external fault, namely if the event is due to a disturbance in some other agent or the underlying technical platform.

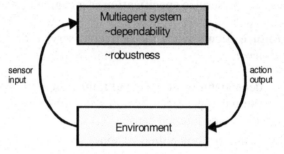

Figure 2. Dependability and robustness

In this chapter we concentrate on the dependability of multiagent systems. Accordingly, we study the mechanisms that an agent or the entire multiagent system maintains in order to guarantee that all services are rendered according to specification even when disturbances occur. We distinguish two major classes of disturbances or malfunctions: Those that are unintentional, that is, where all agents within the multiagent system are innocent victims, and those that are intentional, that is, where one or more agents as a consequence of their autonomy pursue intentions contrary to the overall interests of the system. Sections 6.2 through 6.6 cover unintentional malfunctions, Section 6.7 addresses intentional malfunctions. Since there are a good number of countermeasures that differ in the malfunctions they deal with, we take a systematic approach by associating each of them with a layer of the reference architecture of IV.4.

6.2 A Dependability Model

6.2.1 Failures and Dependability

We base our dependability model on (some of) the definitions of Laprie [Lapr1985] [Lapr1992].

- Computer system **dependability** is the *quality of the delivered service* such that *reliance* can *justifiably* be placed on this service.
- The **service** delivered by a system is the system behavior *as it is perceived* by another special system(s) interacting with the considered system: its user(s). The service **specification** is an agreed description of the expected service.
- A system **failure** occurs when the delivered service deviates from the specified service.

Accordingly, dependability, service and failure are notions that describe a component's external appearance. Failures should be avoided, but if one occurs there must be some internal cause.

- The cause – in its phenomenological sense – of any failure is a **fault**. Upon occurrence, a fault creates a **latent error**. For example, a programmer 's mistake is a fault; the consequence is a latent error in the written software (erroneous instruction or piece of data).
- A latent error becomes an **effective error** when it is activated in the course of providing a service and leads to failure. For example, the fault discussed before becomes effective upon activation of the module where the error resides *and* an appropriate input pattern activating the erroneous instruction, instruction sequence or piece of data.

Ideally, faults do not occur. Or at least, we should make sure that only very few faults occur in a software component, in our case an agent. We speak of *fault avoidance* as the collection of all measures that reduce the number of faults. Fault occurrences may be prevented by, e.g., advanced construction methods, better training in programming or by testing. Autonomy and concurrency poses specific issues to software agent testing which are discussed in detail in IV.8.

Latent errors are not recognized as such. Consequently, only effective errors can be subject to treatment. Accordingly, a *dependability model* describes the service, the effective errors occurring within the system, which ones are dealt with and how (*error processing*), and what the ensuing failures are. Figure 3 outlines the basics of the dependability model.

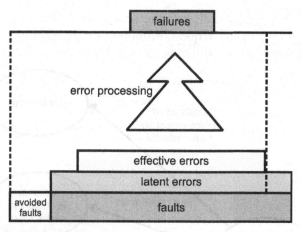

Figure 3. Faults, errors and failures

6.2.2 Dependability Model for Unintentional Faults

The dependability model from above assumes that faults are *unintentional*. To make the model operational we need to refine what processing of unintentional errors is all about. Error processing will have to take note of the nature of the effective error which in turn has something to do with the nature of the underlying fault.

As noted before, an endogenous disturbance within the system takes either of two forms. It is an *internal* fault if it is due to causes purely internal to the component under consideration. For example, if we consider a layer in the reference architecture of IV.4, an internal fault may be due to a programming fault or faulty parameter settings within the code of that layer. It is an *external* fault if it occurs outside the component. External faults fall into two categories.

- *Infrastructure failures*: Infrastructure is all the hardware and software the component depends on to function. Examples are processor and memory hardware, operating systems, file systems, data communication systems, but also the agent platforms.
- *Peer failures*: Peers are components on the same level of service. Peers fail if they do not deliver on a request. For example, the connection to it has been lost or its own infrastructure failed (*total failure*), or it came to a regular end but ran into unfavorable conditions that kept it from reaching the desired objective (*unfavorable outcome*, see Pleisch and Schiper [PlSc2004]).

Error processing may itself be more or less successful, and this will affect the result of a service request. From the service requestor's viewpoint the returned states fall into different classes (Figure 4).

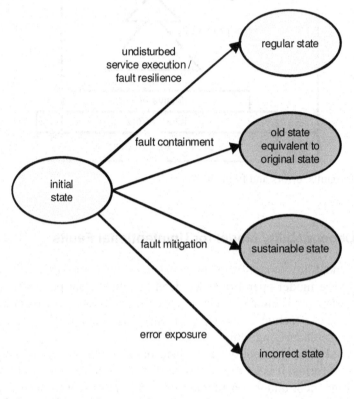

Figure 4. States after service provision

At best, the fault may have no effect at all, i.e., the state reached after servicing the request is identical to the regular state. Or the state is still the old state, i.e., the state coincides with the state prior to the request because the fault simply caused the request to be ignored. A bit worse, servicing the request may reach a state that while no longer meeting the specification may still allow the service requestor a suitable continuation of its work (sustainable state). All three states meet the definition of dependability. At worst, the outcome may be a state that is plainly incorrect if not outright disastrous.

To distinguish between the states we introduce the following notions. We speak of *fault tolerance* if a service reaches one of the three dependability states. Specifically, under *fault resilience* the correct state is reached, under *fault containment* the old state and under *fault mitigation* the sustainable state. Otherwise we have *error exposure*.

Our goal is to relate the dependability model to the layered reference architecture. Therefore, Figure 5 shows two layers where the lower layer provides a service requested by the upper layer. Clearly, fault resilience and fault containment fall to the provider. Fault containment is achieved by *recovery*. Typical techniques for fault resilience are recovery followed by *retry*, or *service replication*. Fault mitigation requires some action on the provider's part as well, such as partial recovery. Since fault containment, fault mitigation and fault exposure lead to irregular states, the requestor must be informed by *error propagation*. In case of fault containment the requestor will simply resume work in some way. In case of fault mitigation the requestor may have to transfer by *compensation* to a state from where to resume regular work. Fault exposure leaves the requestor with no choice but to initiate its own error processing.

One may argue that compensation may only mask part of a fault so there still is some error exposure. Consequently, error processing may span more than one layer. Nonetheless we will base the subsequent discussion on the simpler model of Figure 5.

6.2.3 Intentional Faults: Trust and Reputation

The dependability model of Section 6.2.2 assumes that peers are cooperative and if they fail it was not by intention. However, in an environment of agents peers are autonomous and, hence, may very well decide to pursue their own interests, with the effect of *intentional* non-delivery. Such *uncooperative behavior* is not immediately recognizable by the requesting agent.

In our introductory example one could imagine such an uncooperative behavior by a malicious machine-agent. It could outbid all other agents without ever intending to deliver the promised goods, but rather in the hope of harming the requesting order-agent or its principal.

Dealing with intentional faults must follow a model that differs from Figure 5. For one, these faults are exclusively peer failures. Second, they usually are not immediately recognizable. Take the agent from above that pursues objectives that are not in line with the agent system. Or take an agent that behaves selfishly, i.e., refuses to follow the specified protocol in order to gain benefits from others without service in return. For example, a selfish agent (also known as free rider or freeloader) would demand prepayment but would not return the commodities it was paid for.

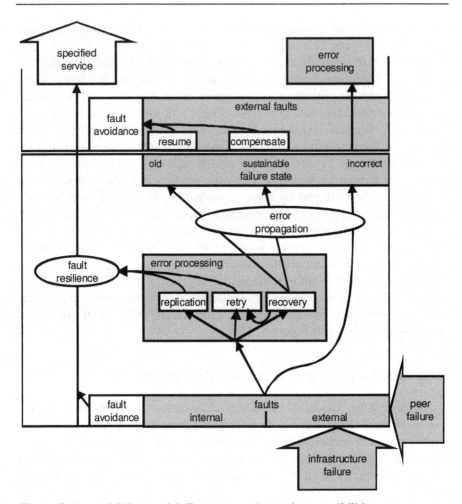

Figure 5. Dependability model: Error processing and responsibilities

Instead we need a model that offers remedies of a *preventive* nature. The prevailing concepts are *trust* as an individual agent's opinion of some other agent, and *reputation* as the general opinion of a society of agents towards a certain agent (see [Mars1994] for an exhaustive analysis of trust and reputation).

More precisely, trust is the subjective belief of one agent in another agent's willingness and ability to follow the protocol of the multiagent system to process a certain request. The definition implies that:

- Trust is unidirectional, i.e., an agent that trusts another one might not be trusted from the other side in turn.

- Trust is subjective. Each agent computes trust individually. Thus, one agent could trust another agent while others do not.
- Trust is bound to a certain domain of interest. For example, one would trust a baker to bake fine biscuits, but not to roast tasty steaks.
- Trust is based on belief, not on a comprehensive set of facts. Therefore the notation of trust gives statistical guarantees at best, and contains the risk of fraud.

In general, it is quite easy (or inexpensive in economic terms) to estimate a trust factor from an incomplete set of data, e.g., the outcome of the last interactions with a certain agent. By contrast, it would be very expensive to provide a complete database of all interactions with that agent in the past, and there may not even be enough interaction in a multiagent system with a high degree of fluctuation. Only the agent society as a whole may be able to do so. This explains the importance of reputation.

- Reputation is the aggregated trust value of many agents in a specific domain of interest.
- Reputation is shared among the agents. In particular, each agent has the same information about the standing of a certain other agent, but decides individually if it deems that agent trustworthy or not.
- Reputation is expressed in a generalized, normalized manner. Agents that wish to exchange reputation information have to agree on a common set of domains and measures.

6.3 Layered Agent Dependability Model

6.3.1 Single Layer

Figure 5 demonstrates that fault processing may not always be effective when confined to a single layer. Instead it must often be spread across layers. As the discussions in IV.4 demonstrate, the next higher level cares less about certain details but has available to it a wider context. E.g., it follows a sequence of statements rather than a single one, or considers a larger database, and thus may be in a better position to process the failure. Consequently, a layered reference architecture not only is attractive to structure the normal function of a complex piece of software but should also help to organize and localize the various dependability issues. Hence, we use the layered reference architecture of IV.4 for organizing the dependability of agents.

In order to discuss the responsibilities of each layer we use an abstraction of the dependability model of Figure 5 that borrows from the Ideal Fault Tolerant Component of Anderson and Lee for software component architectures [AnLe1981, p. 298].

As Figure 6 illustrates, a layer can be in one of two operation modes. During normal activity the component receives service requests from layers higher up, eventually accomplishes them using the services of the next lower layer components and returns normal responses. It may also draw on the services of other components on the same layer or receive service requests from such components.

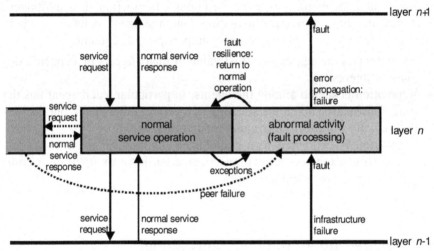

Figure 6. Abstract dependability model for a single layer

If the lower layer fails to service the request, this can be interpreted on the current layer as the occurrence of an external fault. The mode changes to abnormal activity where the fault is interpreted and treated. Fault processing follows the model of Figure 5. Propagated errors are signaled as a failure to the next higher layer. Otherwise the layer returns to normal mode and tries to resume normal operation.

Abnormal activity mode may also be the result of failures within the same layer. If it is a peer failure that is recognized as such and requires immediate counteraction it is treated as an external fault. If a peer failure remains unrecognized it will propagate upwards as part of a normal service response and may then induce an internal fault higher up.

If the failure within the same layer is a malfunction within the same component it is treated as an internal fault. A typical mechanism for signaling such a malfunction is (in Java terminology) by throwing exceptions. Exceptions can also be used to model a situation where a fault was not activated further down and thus remains unrecognized while crossing a layer in normal mode and moving upwards as a normal service response. Only on a layer higher up the fault is detected as such. Take a missing Web page whose loss may only be noticed close to the user level.

Another failure within the same layer is a peer failure that is recognized as such and requires immediate counteraction. On the other hand, if a peer failure remains unrecognized it will propagate upwards as part of a normal service response and may then induce an exception higher up.

6.3.2 Multiple Layers

Given the reference architecture for agents, we will now have to augment each layer by the model of Figure 6. For each layer we should identify the faults originating from it, determine which faults whatever their origin can be taken care of within the layer and which ones are to be passed upwards – hopefully in mitigated form – to the next higher layer where the principle repeats itself.

For the rest of this section we give a structured overview of the various faults that may occur on each layer, and short summaries of some of the approaches to cope with them. For this purpose we take a developer's point of view and go through the layers in order of increasing abstractness. Figure 7 depicts failures and approaches and thus summarizes the following subsections. A deeper discussion of some selected approaches is given in Sections 6.4 to 6.6.

6.3.3 System Environment Base Services Layer (L1)

Layer L1 encompasses all services general to a computing environment, notably the hardware, the operating system, the data management and due to the distributed system organization, data communication. Consequently, all failures occurring are infrastructure failures.

The individual agent is affected by hardware and operating system failures. Operating systems have a built-in dependability that allows them to recover from hardware failures, usually by built-in redundancy features such as parallel processors, mirrored disks, repeated disks writes, RAID storage. The operating system will show a failure only if such measures are ineffective. If the failure is catastrophic the system will stop executing altogether. If the failure is non-catastrophic such as excessive waiting or unsuccessful disk operation, a failure will be propagated upwards with a detailed description of the cause.

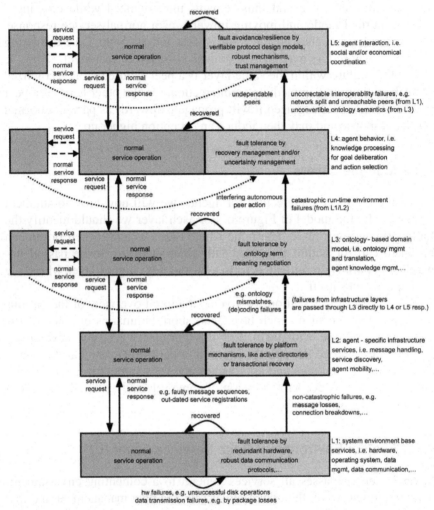

Figure 7. Dependability in the layered agent architecture

Data communication rests on a communication infrastructure, like the Internet with HTTP or IIOP running over TCP/IP. Hence, all faults typical for classical data communication (e.g., package loss/duplication/reordering, or network partition) will occur. Almost all of them are internally resolved by any of the numerous protocols, i.e., modern data communication is inherently dependable (see for example [Hals1996]). This leaves very few failures to be propagated upwards, such as network delays, connection loss, non-correctable transmission failures, unreachable destination, or lifetime expiration. Some dependability aspects are subject to agreement and become quality-of-service (QoS) parameters, e.g., transmission reliability with respect to loss and duplication (at-least-once, at-most-once, exactly-once, best effort), or order preservation. Qualities outside the agreement must be controlled on the next higher layer and if deemed unsatisfactory will raise an exception there.

Note that a catastrophic failure cannot be recognized by the affected agent but will only be detected by other agents where it is translated into an unreachable destination ("node is down!").

6.3.4 Agent-Specific Infrastructure Services Layer (L2)

Layer L2 is purely mechanistic: It offers those infrastructure services that are specialized towards the specific needs of agents, but it restricts the services to those that can safely ignore the domain semantics and the goals and intentions of the agents. It provides the services as part of platforms. Examples are agent development/runtime frameworks like JADE [BBCP 2005] or LS/TS (Living Systems® Technology Suite [Whit2005]). Typical services concern message handling and exchange, trading and naming, or agent mobility. To give an example, message handling is in terms of the FIPA-ACL messages with their numerous higher-level parameters, where in particular the message content may be expressed in terms of the FIPA-ACL communicative acts.

Now think of an uncorrectable data transmission failure on the communication layer. It can result in a message loss on the platform layer. Some of the multiagent development frameworks have rudimentary mechanisms to deal with such situations. As an example, JADE allows to specify a time-out interval within which a reply to a given message must be received. If the time-out expires before the expected message has been received, an exception method is invoked that determines a contingency behavior as defined by the developer. The behavior could be a retry, requesting a resend of the original message.

Such a behavior could solve the problems caused by the lost accept message (1) in our introductory example, where the successful progression of the protocol is blocked. The machine-agent would experience a time-out which it would follow with resending the proposal provided the transmission problem is of a non-permanent nature.

Or take trading, locating an agent that offers the services needed by another agent. The yellow pages functionality of FIPA's Directory Facilitator implements such a function. Typical problems are incorrect or outdated agent service registrations or implementation faults in the frameworks themselves. Outdated entries can internally be resolved by an active Directory Facilitator that periodically checks for availability of the registered services. Otherwise the upper layers must be notified of the failure to execute the needed agent service, where most probably the coordination layer (L5) would have to handle it by finding an alternative peer to provide a similar and available service.

6.3.5 Ontology-Based Domain Model Layer (L3)

The borderline between layers L2 and L3 is fundamental in nature: While L2 is devoid of domain semantics L3 is tailored towards dealing with the domain semantics. L3 is also highly specific in that the layer deals foremost with static aspects while the dynamics are left to layer L4. Consequently, any unresolved failures from below are best passed directly through to layer L4.

Aside from programming faults the only problems that may arise on layer L3 are peer failures in connection with ontologies. For example, in an exchanged message the partner agent does not share the ontology of the agent under consideration so that there is a mismatch in the meaning attributed to a certain term. But even if sender and receiver share the same ontology, different coding into and decoding from the transport syntax can be a source of errors. The ontology mismatch problem is addressed by various approaches like Mena et al. [MeIG2000] that try to negotiate the meaning of the ontological terms during the course of the agents' interaction. Just think of failure (2) of the introductory example, where the proposal needs a reformulation or translation to be understood by the receiving order-agent.

6.3.6 Agent Behavior Layer (L4)

This layer deals with the agent functionality and itself has a more or less complicated internal structure that is based on certain assumptions, i.e., the way knowledge and behavior of the agents are presented and processed. Clearly then, layer L4 should be the layer of choice for all faults whose handling requires background knowledge on the domain, the goals and the past interaction history. Consequently, most of the error processing will fall under the heading of fault resilience. This is true even for catastrophic infrastructure failures. Suppose the agent temporarily loses control when its platform goes down, but regains it when the platform is restarted. Recovery from catastrophic failure is usually by backward recovery on the platform layer. The resulting fault containment should now be interpreted in light of the agent's prior activities. If these were continuously recorded the agent may add its own recovery measures, or judge itself to be somewhat uncertain of its environment but then act to reduce the uncertainty.

In our example, the order-agent after an elapsed period of time could become uncertain, if either failure (3) occurred, meaning that a shortage delayed the delivery of the ordered goods, or if only the message that should indicate the completion of its production has been lost. The order-agent could reduce the uncertainty by enquiring with the producing machine-agent. If the delay would be confirmed or if no information would be provided it could become necessary to involve the interaction layer L5 to find an alternative provider to reassign the manufacturing.

6.3.7 Agent Interaction Layer (L5)

Whereas Layer L4 is the most critical for dependable functioning of the single agent, layer L5 must ensure the dependable performance of the entire multiagent system. The interaction between the agents and, hence, dependability aspects involve two issues. The first is a technical issue dealing with the interaction protocol that organizes the collaboration under the assumption that each participating agent supports the common goal. The second issue is one of trying to ensure that the agents are indeed supportive of one another and, hence, deals with trust and reputation (see Section 6.6).

IV.3 refers to the communication between and, hence, coordinated interaction of agents as a conversation. From the perspective of the first issue conversations follow a – usually predefined – conversation protocol. Successful conversation imposes a common convention on the message sequence and meaning. A number of approaches deal with this issue by supporting the protocol design process. Paurobally et al. [PaCJ2003], Nodine and Unruh [NoUn1999], Galan and Baker [GaBa1999] and Hannebauer [Hann2002] present approaches in which they enrich a specification method for conversation protocols by a formal model that allows them to ensure the correctness of the protocol execution analytically or constructively.

At run-time conversations are threatened by uncorrectable interoperability failures that are passed upwards from lower layers. The infrastructure layers may pass up network splits and unreachable peers, the ontology layer semantic disagreements, the agent behavior layer unforeseen behavior of peer agents. Layer L5 may itself discover that peers respond in mutually incompatible ways. Techniques of fault resilience seem essential if the user is not to be burdened. For example, the agents may search for alternative services that are either very similar to the one originally needed, or they may attempt to agree on a new protocol with different peer roles or peers.

6.3.8 Errors Passed Through to the User

A multiagent system may not be able to automatically handle each and every fault, and probably should not even be designed to do so, particularly if the outcome of the failure has a deep effect on the MAS environment and it remains unclear whether any of the potential therapies improves the environmental situation. Consequently, a careful design should identify which errors should be passed as failures up to what one could conceptually see as an additional "user" layer. Agents would indicate unrecoverable problems to the user and request his or her corrective input. To give a somewhat extreme example, if the user detects that the failure of the MAS has financial consequences for him or her, he or she may have to decide on litigation. V.3 discusses these and similar consequences for the principals of agents.

6.4 Layer L2 Techniques: Resilience and Recovery

As noted above, layer L2 has no knowledge of the domain semantics and the goals and intentions of the agents. Therefore all it can do is make sure that somehow the correct state is mechanistically reached (fault resilience), or an earlier, correct state is preserved (fault containment by recovery), or a state is reached that combines several old states into one that is well-defined (fault mitigation).

6.4.1 Resilience by Replication

A well-known resilience technique is process replication. In case a process fails a functioning replica substitutes it. Specifically, in multiagent systems the replicated entities are agents.

In replication the content of the replicates remains transparent to the system. Clearly then, replication is a technique below layers L3 to L5 and above layer L1. Agent replication that fits this characterization was introduced in Pleisch and Schiper [PlSc2004] or in Kumar and Cohen [KuCo2000]. And indeed, replication will result in fault resilience only if the replicas do not fail at the same time and for the same reason. Consequently, agent replication will protect against infrastructure failures such as hardware, operating system, or middleware failures provided the agents are hosted on different subsystems, or communication link failures. Replication will neither protect against unfavorable outcomes, application failures, nor against programming faults if the programs have been replicated as well.

Clearly, the risk of losing a service is inversely proportional to the rate of replication. Economics dictate a suitable balance. The following approach allows a choice of balance by using availability categories and restore times. Given these, one can compute the lower and upper bounds of the needed availability of the needed replications. If the lower bound exceeds the availability of the best host available, one must resort to a cluster that consists of several hosts, where their number depends on the desired availability category. Replicas of an agent are created on all of the hosts of the cluster. In case of a failure, a replica substitutes for the failed service-providing agent. One host in the cluster acts as a leader with the task of deciding which replica to choose. To avoid the leader to become a new single point of failure, the leader should dynamically be selected from the member hosts of the given cluster, e.g., with an adapted leader election-algorithm that protects against link failures [Garc1982].

A service provider agent has to acquire a lease time from the leader and, if necessary, must renew it before expiration. Fault resilience is now achieved in two phases. During the first, once the leader detects the expiration of a lease time it starts a new replica of the respective service provider agent. The second phase starts immediately after the chosen replica has been launched and becomes available. If the failing agent is still up and running it will itself detect its inability to acquire a fresh lease time. Possible reasons could be a communication link failure, the quality of the provided service, etc. For a predefined period of time it is possible for this agent to submit the results it computed to its successor. After expiration of this deadline the agent terminates itself irrespective of a potential recovery. Whenever the failure of the erroneous agent has become final the started replica takes over the service provision and during this time adopts the identifier of its predecessor.

Resilience comes at a price. The approach causes an increased communication load for the whole system due to the required synchronization for the leader election algorithm, the acquisition and renewal of the lease times, and the replication process of the monitored agents. Consequently, the approach seems economical only for networks with cheap link establishment, or where cost is not a factor as in ad-hoc networks. Expensive links as in cell-phone networks should be avoided.

Reconsider failure (3) of the introductory example, where the contracting machine-agent can not deliver its goods within the stipulated time. Assuming that the good to produce is just a piece of information rather than of a physical nature, a replicate machine-agent may be able to deliver on time if not hindered by the same obstacle that already prevented the success of the original agent.

6.4.2 Recovery via Transactional Conversations

Figure 5 shows the central role that error recovery assumes in fault tolerance. Error recovery substitutes an error-free state for the erroneous state. In particular, backward error recovery brings the system back to a state prior to the error becoming effective.

A well-known behavioral abstraction that includes recovery is the transaction. In its purest form the transaction has the ACID properties[1]: It is atomic, i.e., is executed completely or not at all, hence in the latter case, assumes backward recovery; it is consistent, i.e., if executed to completion it performs a legitimate state transition; it is isolated, i.e., remains unaffected by any parallel transactions; and it is durable, i.e., the state reached can only explicitly be changed. Transaction systems are mechanistic systems that guarantee these properties even in the presence of failures, and do so without any knowledge of the algorithms underlying the transactions. Consequently, recovery is a layer L2 technique. To provide the guarantees, transaction systems rely on data redundancy and process histories.

Conversations involve several parties. Therefore, the transactional abstraction of a conversation is the distributed transaction [NiLo2004]. Recovery is then implemented via a 2-Phase-Commit (2PC) protocol, with a single coordinator as the initiator and any number of clients [WeVo2002]. Hence, conversations spawn local transactions in the participating agents, that are coordinated by the initiating agent. Each agent must include a resource manager that locally enforces the ACID-properties and manages access to the data items, and a transaction manager that guarantees, via the 2PC, atomicity for distributed transactions. The data items – the state of the agents and the environment – are kept in local databases. The initiator is chosen as the agent that started the conversation.

Take again the job-shop example Figure 1 with its Contract Net Protocol [Smit1980]. The initiating agent negotiates with the machine agents to

---

[1]   ACID: Atomicity, Durability, Isolation and Consistency, see Weikum and Vossen (2002).

reserve a time slot. During the conversation a machine agent changes its databases according to the machine schedule, and perhaps restores it if it fails to gain the contract. Likewise, the initiator will adjust its database according to the final outcome of the conversation. At the end, the initiating agent's transaction manager decides whether the distributed transaction was successful or not, and accordingly initiates global commit or rollback.

Distributed transactions benefit from a standardized architecture that determines the basic workflow and the interfaces (see, e.g., the X/Open DTP Reference Model [Open1996]) and, hence, can be implemented by commercial products. They also stand a good chance of being incorporated into a dependable FIPA-compliant [PoCh2001] agent development framework. Figure 8 and the description below illustrate how distributed transactions can be integrated into the agent development framework FIPA-OS [PoBH2000] while making use of the commercial products Oracle 9i RDBMS[2] for Resource Manager and ORBacus OTS[3] for Transaction Manager (for technical details see [Vogt2001]).

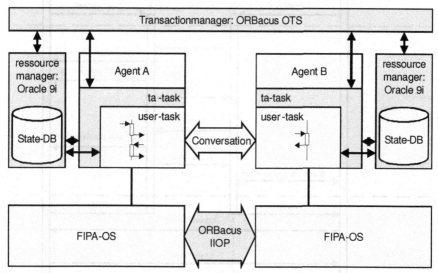

Figure 8. Integration of transactional conversations in FIPA-OS: system architecture

In FIPA-OS the different kinds of functionality of an agent are accomplished by so-called *tasks*. Roughly speaking, an agent has a special task to handle the protocol execution for each conversation type it participates in.

---

[2] Oracle Corporation: http://www.oracle.com/database.
[3] IONA Technologies: ORBacus Object Request Broker:
    http://www.orbacus.com.

To allow for a structured agent design, FIPA-OS provides the ability to split the functionality of a task into so-called *child-tasks*. A *parent-task* initiates its child-tasks, can track their execution, and is informed when a child-task has finished its work. In Figure 1 the order-agent and the two machine-agents would be separate tasks.

Nearly all effort that is necessary to execute the distributed transactions, in particular the interaction with the Transaction Manager and the Resource Managers, are handled transparently by generic transactional tasks (*ta-tasks*). The ta-tasks are parent-tasks of the so-called *user-tasks* that carry out the actual conversations.

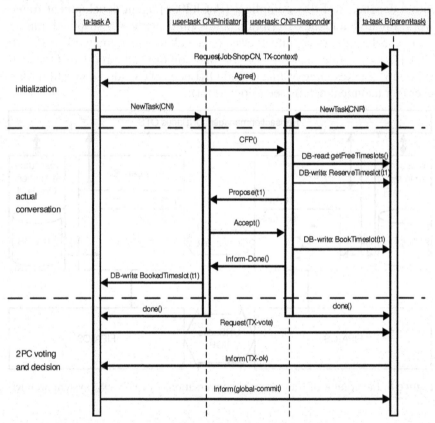

Figure 9. Integration of transactional conversations in FIPA-OS: action sequence

To illustrate the transactional conversations, take the sequence diagram Figure 1 as translated into a distributed transaction according to Figure 9. In the initialization phase when an agent wishes to start a transactional conversation, its *ta-task* generates a transaction context and sends it to the *ta-task* of the peer agents together with an identifier for the requested type of conversation. The local and the remote *ta-task* then initiate the required *user-tasks* to carry out the actual conversation.

In the second phase the user-tasks follow the normal conversation protocol. The *ta-tasks* observe the execution and the occurrence of local state changes. To allow for the developer to have a certain degree of control, he can distinguish between state changes that take part in the distributed transaction and, hence, are globally transactional, and state changes that are of a purely local nature and remain locally transactional. The *user-tasks* have to indicate to the *ta-tasks* their global data items. For these a database connection is established that is under control of the Transaction Manager, whereas the local items use a separate database connection with ACID semantics. In case of a distributed transaction rollback, global state changes are undone, whereas local state changes persist.

The decision of whether to rollback or to commit the distributed transaction takes place in the third phase. The changes in the states of the communicating agents and the environment now are synchronized via the success or failure of the overall distributed transaction. Therefore, the ta-tasks of the communicating agents first vote and then distribute the decision according to the 2-Phase-Commit Protocol, in which the ta-task initiating the conversation has the role of the coordinator node.

Take the lost message (1) of the introductory example. The detection of the message loss leads to a rollback that resets the states of the order-agent and of the involved machine-agents to their original states. In particular, the reserved time-slot of machine-agent A is released. It can be offered again if layer 4 would attempt a retry of the Contract Net Protocol.

Transactional conversations clearly are a technique for fault containment. They give the developer guarantees on consistent agent states, while he may still use the framework he is accustomed to. He only has to annotate the agent and environment states that he wishes to have under global transaction control with a few additional lines of code. Nonetheless, dependability based on 2PC also has its (well-known) price: In case of serious delays or node failures altogether all other agents are held up. Hence, 2PC has a negative effect on agent autonomy.

6.4.3 Mitigation via Transactional Queues

Distributed transactions are less than ideal because they require a fairly tight coupling of agents within a conversation – just the opposite from what we expect from multiagent systems. If we practice looser coupling, though, recovery can no longer be fully coordinated either. For example, we could instead limit backward recovery to each individual agent. The conversation as a whole is no longer protected, that is, left in a state where consistency across the agent society can no longer be guaranteed. Nonetheless, if we can additionally guarantee that communication can be recovered as well we know at least that each part of the conversation individually is in the old or new state. Such a fault mitigation technique could then form the basis for compensation on some higher layer.

The heart of conversations is (asynchronous) message passing that guarantees loose coupling (see IV.3). Fault mitigation as described above can then be achieved by queued transactions [WeVo2002]. They consist of three transactions. The ones at each participating agent are determined by the agent's action but must additionally include the queuing and dequeuing operations (Figure 10). The third transaction covers the queue manager (persistent, recoverable message queues) and, in particular, guards against message loss. Consequently, a persistent queue manager seems to be an absolute necessity for a multiagent system.

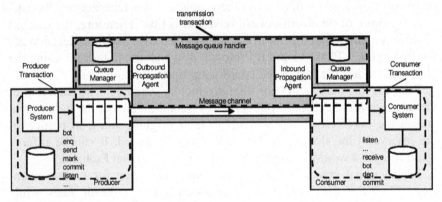

Figure 10. Transactional message queues

6.5 Layer L3/L4 Techniques: Uncertainty Management

Layers L3 and L4, or more precisely the agents incorporating these layers, are cognizant of their goals and intentions, the reasons for communicating with other agents, and have the necessary domain knowledge. Consequently, these layers are the ones that know how to compensate for the states passed up from below by fault containment or mitigation. We discuss below one technique that seems particularly suited to agents.

6.5.1 Compensation via Uncertain Agents

Agents are made to cope with the non-determinism of their environment. The non-determinism arises from the autonomy of other agents with which an agent collaborates, but also from the limited view an agent has of the surrounding system (see I.1.3). One might say the agent often is *uncertain* of its environment. The multiagent system as a whole will remain uncertain as well because global behavior emerges from uncertain local interactions, and also because collectively the agents will never observe the environment at the same instance in time.

Now then, couldn't one view, e.g., fault mitigation as it results from transactional queues as producing a state that appears uncertain to the participating agents? And wouldn't what Pearl [Pear1994] refers to as *uncertainty management* be a suitable abstraction for the needed compensation? And finally, wouldn't agents be ideally suited for such type of compensation because of their capability to deal with uncertainty?

IV.5.4 seems to answer the question in the positive. It points out that in the BDI framework beliefs stand for the knowledge acquired by the agent, and that this knowledge may be uncertain, fuzzy, incomplete, or incorrect – in short, imperfect. To be a bit more precise, several authors in [MoSm1997] distinguish between:

- *Imprecision*: Information is imprecise when it denotes a set of possible values, and the real value though unknown is one of the elements.
- *Inconsistency*: Several pieces of information are in conflict and irreconcilable so that only incoherent conclusions can be drawn.
- *Uncertainty*: A statement is either true or false, but the agent's knowledge about the world does not allow him to state confidently if that statement is true or false.

Beliefs can be considered a subjective opinion held by an agent at a given time on whether a statement holds, i.e., whether it reflects a state in the real world. In general, as the agent receives new information it may have to adjust its beliefs, a process referred to in IV.5.4.

Now suppose that failures occur in a multiagent system while the world keeps going on. After recovery the most likely outcome is uncertainty, with inconsistency a possible consequence. Therefore, it makes sense to concentrate on uncertainty. If the agent recovers from an error it may choose to keep to its old beliefs and then seek information from its environment to adjust its beliefs. If the agent is failed by other agents it may have to question its old beliefs and adjust them on the basis of the failed response. Consequently, managing one's beliefs involves three issues:

- *When* should the agent solicit information from the environment?

- *From where* should the agent solicit *what* information?
- *How* are old beliefs *transformed* to new beliefs?

6.5.2 Belief Management

We examine the third issue in a bit more detail. True, it still is pretty much a research topic [MoSm1997]. There exist a number of theoretical approaches like [LoLI2002] that describe how BDI-Agents can cope with uncertainty. For this purpose they introduce new concepts like norms and sometimes obligations to restrict the agents' actions, thus constraining their autonomy.

In pursuit of practical solutions, a number of belief models have evolved. Transformations of beliefs vary according to the models. What one would expect from them is that they observe certain postulates for updates (see, e.g., [KaMe1992]). Informally speaking, the transformations should reflect the principle that "when changing beliefs in response to new evidence, you should continue to believe as many of the old beliefs as possible" [Harm1986].

Basically there are three transformations that constitute belief revision:

- Expansion: Suppose an agent makes a new observation. This operator simply adds the observation as a new belief no matter whether it contradicts existing beliefs or not. As a consequence, the database may now contain incompatible information.

Expansion makes sense if we wish to defer resolving contradictions, e.g., until the agent had a chance to communicate with others. More often, though, an agent will not tolerate local contradictions but rather resolve them. Two operators follow a resolution principle:

- Revision: Adds a new proposition. If the information is incompatible with the previous state then older contradictory information is removed. Revision is non-deterministic because there may be more than one way to restore consistency, and it may be unknown which one is chosen.
- Contraction: Removes a proposition that until now has been considered valid. Contraction may trigger further removals until no incompatible proposition can further be derived. Hence, contraction is also non-deterministic.
- Revision and Contraction are also non-monotonic.

Belief models and the ensuing transformations are either qualitative or quantitative. Qualitative models are based on some sort of logic, e.g., first-order logic with special predicates, non-monotonic logic, probabilistic logic, and apply plausible reasoning to infer new beliefs. Quantitative models associate numerical belief functions with beliefs. Probabilistic models estimate the chance that a statement is true in the real world. The best-known, efficient mechanism for propagating probabilistic beliefs are Bayesian Networks. A formal framework for probability assignment from statements made by different witnesses is the Dempster-Shafer Theory [Shaf1976]. Possibilistic models estimate the possibility that a statement is true in the real world. Possibility theory is a special interpretation of fuzzy set theory. Update operators called possibilistic imaging achieve effects similar to expansion and revision.

6.6 Layer L4/L5 Techniques: Distributed Nested Transactions

What has been said at the beginning of Section 6.5, that intelligent error processing must be cognizant of an agent's goals, intentions and domain knowledge, and of the reasons for communicating with other agents, should apply to layer L5 as well, although with more emphasis on agent interaction. This raises the question of whether one could not build compensation directly into the conversations. Several transactional models do indeed incorporate compensation, notably Sagas and nested transactions.

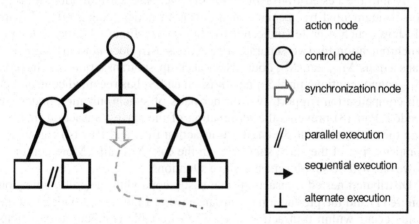

Figure 11. Nested agent transaction

We discuss nested transactions. These seem a natural abstraction to reflect both, the agent behavior that takes the layered architecture into account, and the conversation that ties a group of agents together. In particular, a nested transaction models a behavior where an action may again spawn several related actions that we may consider to be on the next lower level, and so on [Nagi2000] [Nagi2001a]. From the transactional viewpoint, a transaction in a nested transaction model can launch any number of subtransactions, thus forming a transaction tree (Figure 11).

For the individual agent we employ a restricted form of nested transaction: Actions take exclusively place in the leaves, whereas intermediate nodes just control the execution within their subtrees whose subtransactions may execute sequentially, in parallel or alternatively.

Isolation has a tendency to block other transactions from continuing. It thus runs counter to the autonomy and, hence, flexibility of agents. Consequently, we choose the open nested transaction model. In it a subtransaction (or the entire transaction) commits once all its children have terminated, and makes its results available to all other subtransactions. On the other hand, if one of the children fails, the parent transaction has the choice between several actions: abort the subtransaction, backward recover and retry it, or attempt forward recovery by launching a so-called compensating subtransaction. Forward recovery is particularly important because the results of its subtransactions have already become visible.

Next, we need a behavioral abstraction for the conversation. Since compensation is due to the approach of layer L2 where we avoided synchronization by a coordinator in order to maintain autonomy, we cannot re-introduce the coordinator on layer L5. Instead we build the synchronization directly into the nested transactions for the agents. Each individual transaction is augmented by special synchronization nodes [Nagi2001b]. Figure 11 shows such a node (indicated by the arrow). Figure 12 illustrates the synchronization for two separate transactions. M_{11} does not only start subtransactions M_{111} and M_{112} but also wakes up subtransaction S_{11}. In turn, M_{112} cannot continue until S_{11} has finished and S_1 has regained control. For full compensation support, two further pairs of synchronization nodes are needed. Pair (3) prevents the termination of the slave transaction tree before the termination of the master transaction tree, and Pair (4) causes the compensation of the slave subtree S_1 in the case M_{11} fails. More common, however, will be simpler master-slave situations.

Distributed nested transactions can easily cope with the communication failure (1) and the production disturbance (3) of Figure 1, provided that the faults occur within transaction trees where suitable compensation actions are defined.

Distributed nested transactions are a very powerful approach. Alternative compensations can be designed into a tree, and compensations may even be added while the transaction executes. The price is that there is no longer a clear separation between agent behavior and conversation so that conversations are difficult to extract and adapt, and a specific conversation can only be initiated from a specific agent which was prepared beforehand for the task.

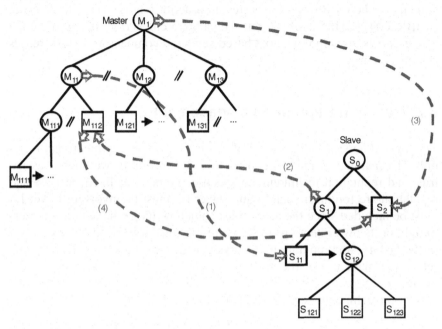

Figure 12. Two synchronized agent transactions

A compromise well worth to investigate could be sagas. Sagas [GaSa 1987] have a fairly rigid transaction model that directly incorporates compensation. A Saga consists of two sets of flat ACID subtransactions. The first set $(T_1, ..., T_n)$ defines the intended behavior with a predefined order of execution. Isolation is relaxed in that other transactions may see the effects of partially executed sagas. The second set of subtransactions $(CT_1, ..., CT_{n-1})$ defines the corresponding compensating actions, where each CT_i can semantically undo the effects of its T_i. A Saga commits if all its subtransactions T_i commit (resulting in the subtransaction sequence $T_1 ... T_n$), and it aborts if one T_i aborts. In the latter case the compensating subtransactions corresponding to the already committed subtransactions are executed in the reverse order $(T_1 ... T_{i-1}CT_{i-1} ... CT_1)$.

Garcia-Molina et al. (in [Gar+1991]) introduce nested sagas that extend the model by a second layer of sagas, and mechanisms for transaction communication that could be used to reflect conversations. Sagas seem particularly attractive because they have been incorporated in current business process modeling languages (e.g., BPEL4WS, WSCI) and workflow systems (e.g., BizTalk Server, WebSphere MQ Workflow) [GFJK2003].

Another approach for compensation-based recovery on layers L4 and L5 similar to Nagi's distributed nested transactions is due to Unruh et al. [UnBR2004] [UHBR2005]. It relies on a hierarchical decomposition of the agents' goals and employs goal-based semantic compensation, task retries and checkpointing.

6.7 Trust and Reputation Management

The layered dependability model of Section 6.3 covers unintentional faults only. To maintain a unified approach to dependability we should assign trust and reputation techniques to specific layers as well. Since trust and reputation are foremost social issues layer L5 must be involved. Layer L4 must be included since the agent must somehow judge the actions of peers in light of its own intentions (see Figure 7). Since trust needs to keep track of the history, and reputation employs communication protocols, trust and reputation make use of the services on layers L1 and L2. In this chapter, though, we concentrate on the higher layers. For overviews on trust and reputation techniques see [RKZF2000] and [RaJe2005].

6.7.1 Trusted Third Parties

If a centralized approach is feasible, one can install a trusted third party (a specialized agent) that maintains trust values for each agent. While it had to be aware of *any* relationships between the agents, it would be easy for an agent to issue queries concerning other agents. A further advantage is the central authentication by assigning immutable identities to the users, and the capability to identify and expel misbehaving participants. On the negative side, centralized reputation systems are always suspected of acting on their own behalf and not in the interest of the users, and can easily become an object of censorship. Also they constitute a single point of failure that can endanger the agent system as a whole.

To avoid these dangers, or whenever a centralized approach is no alternative, one must resort to truly distributed solutions. We discuss some of these in the remainder of Section 6.7.

6.7.2 Individual-Level Trust: A Model

In a distributed approach the trust of one agent into another can only be based on own observations. A suitable reference model is the *iterated prisoners' dilemma,* which is a well-known and well-understood problem in game-theory [Axel1984]. In the prisoners dilemma each of two players tries to maximize its own advantage without any concern for the other. Each player can decide to defect or to cooperate, and both of the players have to decide simultaneously. Individually, a player obtains the maximal payoff if it defects and the other one cooperates, and the minimal payoff if it cooperates and the other one defects. Globally, the optimal payoff is obtained if both of the players cooperate.

Suppose a player uses the strategy with the optimal payoff. Unfortunately, the strategies of the peers are unknown. But it is possible to deduce the strategy of the peers from their behavior in the past. Thus, a cornerstone of these systems is a *private history.* Each agent manages its own history of past transactions, and fills it with its own observations on the outcome of transactions with other peers.

The iterated prisoners dilemma tells us that one of the best deterministic strategies is Tit-for-Tat [Axel1984]. An agent using this strategy first cooperates, and then imitates its opponent, i.e., if the other agent defects, the agent defects as well, and likewise in case of cooperation. However, game-theoretical strategies depend on some assumptions which do not hold in reality, in particular that the agents have to interact many times instead of one-shot interactions, the payoff does not change from transaction to transaction, and there are only two possible actions for each transaction (defect and cooperate). In addition, in multiagent systems the agents can select their transaction partners among a set of agents offering comparable services (disclosed prisoners dilemma). Therefore, trust systems based on local observations provide a more or less complicated *trust measure* that is intended to cope with these challenges.

The model is only of theoretical value. A reliable trust measure depends on a sufficiently large number of observations on a given agent and, consequently, fails in open multiagent systems where agents join and leave at high rates, or in systems where many agents do not interact twice, be it because of unpleasant experiences or because of the limited range of services a single agent offers.

6.7.3 Individual-Level Trust: The Bayesian Approach

A recent approach regarding trust management is the Bayesian network-based trust model [WaVa2003]. The approach is based on *Bayesian learning* in a multiagent system. A Bayesian network is a relationship network using statistical methods to represent probability relationships between the agents, i.e., the agents are the nodes and the probabilities are the weights in a graph.

Each agent maintains a simple Bayesian network for each peer it has interacted with. The network has a root node which can have the values T=0 ("unsatisfying") and T=1 ("satisfying"). The probability $p(T=1)$ = *(number of satisfying interactions/number of all interactions)* = *$1-p(T=0)$* represents the overall amount of trust in the peer.

A leaf node represents a specific capability of the peer in the form of a conditional probability table. For example, in a Bayesian network rating a bakery one node could refer to products with a table of *p("bread"|T=1)*, *p("crackers"|T=1)*, where each term denotes the conditional probability ("weight") that an interaction which involved, say, crackers was satisfying. Another node could refer to the quality with *p("fresh"|T=1)*, *p("aged"|T=1)*, *p("outdated"|T=1)*. Figure 13 shows the Bayesian network for one particular agent. After each transaction the agent updates the weights of the corresponding network. For example, when an agent buys a new bread it may increase the weights for *p("bread"|T=1)* and *p("fresh"|T=1)*.

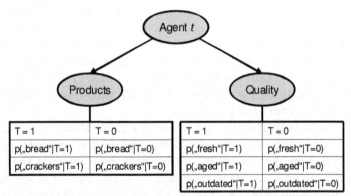

Figure 13. The Bayesian approach

Based on the Bayesian network the agent can compute the probability that the corresponding peer is trustworthy under various conditions. To validate its own observations or to determine the trustworthiness of unknown peers, an agent can issue *recommendation requests*, e.g,

$p(T=1|N_1="bread",N_2="fresh")$, to other agents and combine their trust probabilities with its own observations. Responses from untrusted sources can be discarded at once. The agent may also assign weights to the obtained trust coefficients that indicate its preference for statements coming from trusted and unknown agents.

The Bayesian approach enables the agents to determine the trustworthiness of its partners in a very flexible way, and to share trust coefficients between agents. There are shortcomings though. The approach is not suitable for very large multiagent systems where the majority of agents do not repeatedly interact with each other. Flooding the system with recommendation requests seriously limits its scalability. The division into strangers, trusted and untrusted peers is too static because the assignment of a peer may depend on the issue at hand. Thus, other approaches use more sophisticated trust dissemination protocols and model complex relationships between the agents.

6.7.4 Reputation: The Collaborative Filtering Approach

To share reputation information the participants must agree on a common set of measures and domains that describe the behavior of the agents and the quality of their services. Collaborative filtering is a method to detect common preferences among the opinions of a set of different users. Based on a set of observations, collaborative filtering then makes recommendations to users with similar preferences. For instance, collaborative filtering is used at www.amazon.com.

[ZaMM1999] show that collaborative filtering can be applied to reputation management. In the approach, each agent is assigned a reputation value. The agent system is modeled as a directed graph. Each interaction between two agents form a new edge between the nodes, while the edges are weighted with the rating of the outcomes of the action. If an agent rates the same agent again, the new edge supersedes the old one.

When an agent A queries the reputation value for agent B, the system uses *Breadth First Search* in order to find all directed paths connecting A and B with a length less than n. The trust value of B is now computed as follows: For each path from B to A, the weights of the edges are used to determine an auxiliary trust value, and the values of all of the paths are aggregated to the trust value of B.

The strengths of the approach are the personalized computation of reputation values and the fine-granular representation of relationships between the agents. However, the approach lacks a sophisticated model for different domains of services offered by the agents. Furthermore, it depends on a highly connected graph of relationships between the agents. If there are no short paths between two nodes, Breadth First Search is expensive in distributed applications.

6.7.5 Reputation in Loosely Connected Communities

Finding agents that have relevant information about the behavior of a given agent is one of the most serious challenges in distributed reputation management systems. Solutions like *flooding* (sending each request to all agents) or *random walk* (taking a random way from agent to agent) construct a quorum of statistical significance, but are insufficient with agents that have very few ratings in a system consisting of many participants.

A feasible distributed solution comes from *Distributed Hash Tables (DHT)*, a variant of Peer-to-Peer Overlay Networks. A DHT is a data structure that is distributed among all participants in the system. The DHT allows to store and retrieve (key,value)-pairs very efficiently without involving a trusted third party. [KaSG2003] describe a reputation management system where so-called *score managers* compute the trust values. The score manager for a given agent is hash computed from the agent's IP address. If an agent is aware of the IP address of the agent in question, the DHT is able to locate its score manager.

Trust values are secure because when an agent forwards a request in the approximate 'direction' of the score manager only the score manager IP is known to the intermediate nodes that pass on the request. Further, an agent cannot become its own score manager and manipulate its own score because it cannot compute the manager's IP address.

Using a DHT provides an efficient way to provide global reputation values in loosely connected communities of agents. Each reputation request involves only a small number of hosts, and the only ex-ante knowledge is the distributed hash function. But running a DHT beneath the multiagent system itself increases the complexity of the system as a whole. In addition, global data structures are (even in the distributed case of a peer-to-peer system) vulnerable against attacks.

6.8 Conclusions

These days dependability is considered a major issue by system vendors and researchers. With the ever growing complexity of IT systems much of the more recent efforts go into the direction of self-organizing systems – witness programs such as "autonomic computing" or "organic computing".

Since multiagent systems can be considered a prime example of self-organizing systems one would expect them to benefit from these efforts. So far,
however, dependability still seems to be a neglected issue in the agent literature. This chapter attempted to outline a number of approaches to dependable MAS that range all the way from the application of classical approaches to information systems dependability (Sections 6.3, 6.4 and 6.6)
to approaches that are more in the vein of self-organization (Sections 6.5
and 6.7). Where the authors also see a major contribution is to relate the
dependability issue to the reference architecture of IV.4 and, hence, to provide an organizational framework within which to solve the dependability
issues.

One may argue that a discussion of dependability is incomplete unless
accompanied by a discussion of privacy and security. However, the latter
raises such a large number of intricate issues that it would warrant a separate chapter. Also, our tacit understanding in this chapter is that agents remain stationary. Including mobile agents as well would add further complications such as the trustworthiness of current agent executors.

Further Reading

[Hals1996]   Halsall, F.: Data Communications, Computer Networks and
              Open Systems. Addison-Wesley, Harlow, 1996.
[MoSm1997]   Motro, A.; Smets, P. (Eds): Uncertainty Management in Infor-
              mation Systems – From Needs to Solutions. Kluwer Academic
              Publishers, Boston, 1997.
[WeVo2002]   Weikum, G.; Vossen, G.: Transactional Information Systems:
              Theory, Algorithms, and the Practice of Concurrency Control
              and Recovery. Morgan Kaufmann Publishers, San Francisco,
              2002.

References

[AnLe1981]   Anderson, T.; Lee, P. A.: Fault Tolerance: Principles and Prac-
              tice. Pearson Prentice Hall, Upper Saddle River, 1981.
[Axel1984]   Axelrod, R.: The Evolution of Cooperation. Basic Books, New
              York, 1984.
[BBCP2005]   Bellifemine, F.; Bergenti, F.; Caire, G.; Poggi, A.: JADE – A Ja-
              va Agent Development Framework. In: Bordini, R.; Dastani, M.;
              Dix, J.; El Fallah-Seghrouchni, A. (Eds.): Mutli-Agent Program-
              ming. Kluwer, Dordrecht, 2005.

[GaBa1999]   Galan, A.; Baker, A.: Multi-agent communication in jafmas. In: Working Notes of the Workshop on Specifying and Implementing Conversation Policies. 1999, pp. 67-70.

[Garc1982]   Garcia-Molina, H.: Elections in a Distributed Computing System. In: IEEE Transactions on Computers C-31(1982)1, pp. 48-59.

[GaSa1987]   Garcia-Molina, H.; Salem, K.: SAGAS. In: Dayal, U.; Traiger, I. (Eds.): Proceedings of the SIGMod 1987 Annual Conference. ACM Press, New York, 1987, pp. 249-259.

[Gar+1991]   Garcia-Molina, H.; Gawlick, D.; Klein, J.; Kleissner, K.; Salem, K.: Modeling long-running activities as nested sagas. In: IEEE Data Engineering 14(1991)1, pp. 14-18.

[GFJK2003]   Greenfield, P.; Fekete, A.; Jang, J.; Kuo, D.: Compensation is not enough. In: Proceedings of the 7th IEEE International Enterprise Distributed Object Computing Conference. IEEE Press, New York, 2003, pp. 232-239.

[Hals1996]   Halsall, F.: Data Communications, Computer Networks and Open Systems. Addison-Wesley, Harlow, 1996.

[Hann2002]   Hannebauer, M.: Modeling and verifying agent interaction protocols with algebraic petri nets. In: Proceedings of the Sixth International Conference on Integrated Design and Process Technology (IDPT-2002). 2002.

[Harm1986]   Harman, G. H.: Change in View: Principles of Reasoning. MIT Press, Cambridge, 1986.

[KaSG2003]   Kamvar, S. D.; Schlosser, M. T.; Garcia-Molina, H.: The Eigen-Trust Algorithm for Reputation Management in P2P Networks. In: Hencsey, G.; White, B.; Chen, Y. F. R.; Kovács, L.; Lawrence, S. (Eds.): Proceedings of the Twelfth International World Wide Web Conference (WWW2003). ACM Press, New York, 2003, pp. 640-651.

[KaMe1992]   Katsuno, H.; Mendelzon, A.: On the difference between updating a knowledge base and revising it. In: Gärdenfors, P. (Ed.): Belief Revision. Cambridge University Press, Cambridge, 1992, pp. 183-203.

[KuCo2000]   Kumar, S.; Cohen, P. R.: Towards a fault-tolerant multi-agent system architecture. In: Sierra, C.; Maria, G.; Rosenschein, J. S. (Eds.): Proceedings of the 4th International Conference on Autonomous Agents (Agents 2000). ACM Press, New York, 2000, pp. 459-466.

[Lapr1985]   Laprie, J. C.: Dependable computing and fault tolerance: concepts and terminology. In: Proceedings of the 15th IEEE Symposium on Fault Tolerant Computing Systems (FTCS-15). IEEE Press, New York, 1985, pp. 2-11.

[Lapr1992]   Laprie, J. C. (Ed.): Dependable computing and fault tolerant systems – vol. 5: Dependability: basic concepts and terminology: in

English, French, German, Italian and Japanese. Springer Verlag, Heidelberg, 1992.

[LoLI2002]   Lopez y Lopez, F.; Luck, M.; d'Inverno, M.: Constraining autonomy through norms. In: Gini, M.; Ishida, T.; Castelfranchi, C.; Johnson, W. L. (Eds.): Proceedings of the first international joint conference on autonomous agents and multiagent systems: part 2 (AAMAS 2002). ACM Press, New York, 2002, pp. 674-681.

[Mars1994]   Marsh, S.: Formalizing Trust as a Computational Concept. Ph.D. thesis. Department of Computing Science and Mathematics, University of Stirling, 1994.

[MeIG2000]   Mena, E.; Illarramendi, A.; Goni, A.: Automatic ontology construction for a multiagent-based software gathering service. In: Klusch, M.; Kerschberg, L. (Eds.): Proceedings of the Fourth International ICMAS'2000 Workshop on Cooperative Information Agents (CIA'2000). Springer Verlag, Heidelberg, 2000, pp. 232-243.

[MoSm1997]   Motro, A.; Smets, P. (Eds.): Uncertainty Management in Information Systems – From Needs to Solutions. Kluwer Academic Publishers, Boston, 1997.

[Nagi2000]   Nagi, K.: Scalability of a transactional infrastructure for multiagent systems. In: Wagner, T.; Rana, O. F. (Eds.): Proceedings of the First International Workshop on Infrastructure for Scalable Multi-Agent Systems. Springer-Verlag, Heidelberg, 2000, pp. 266-278.

[Nagi2001a]   Nagi, K.: Transactional Agents: Towards a Robust Multi-Agent System. Lecture Notes in Computer Science 2249. Springer-Verlag, Heidelberg, 2001.

[Nagi2001b]   Nagi, K.: Modeling and simulation of cooperative multi-agents in transactional database environments. In: Wagner, T.; Rana, O. F. (Eds.): Proceedings of the Second International Workshop on Infrastructure for Scalable Multi-Agent Systems. 2001.

[NiLo2004]   Nimis, J.; Lockemann, P. C.: Robust Multi-Agent Systems: The Transactional Conversation Approach. In: Proceedings of the First International Workshop on Safety and Security in Multiagent Systems (SASEMAS 2004). 2004, pp. 73-84.

[NoUn1999]   Nodine, M. H.; Unruh, A.: Constructing robust conversation policies in dynamic agent communities. In: Dignum, F.; Greaves, M. (Eds.): Issues in Agent Communication. Springer Verlag, Heidelberg, 1999, pp. 205-219.

[Open1996]   The Open Group: X/Open Distributed TP: Reference Model. Version 3, 1996. http://www.opengroup.org/products/ publications/catalog/g504.htm, accessed on 2005-12-03.

[PaCJ2003]   Paurobally, S.; Cunningham, J.; Jennings, N. R.: Ensuring consistency in the joint beliefs of interacting agents. In: Rosenschein, S.; Wooldridge, M. J.; Sandholm, T.; Yokoo, M. (Eds.): Proceedings of the second international joint conference on Autonomous agents and multiagent systems (AAMAS 2003). ACM Press, New York, 2003, pp. 662-669.

[Pear1994]   Pearl, J.: Belief Networks Revisited. In: Bobrow, D. G. (Ed.): Artificial intelligence in Perspective. MIT Press, Cambridge, 1994, pp. 49-56.

[PlSc2004]   Pleisch, S.; Schiper, A.: Approaches to Fault-Tolerant and Transactional Mobile Agent Execution – An Algorithmic View. ACM Computing Surveys 36(2004)3, pp. 219-262.

[PoBH2000]   Poslad, S.; Buckle, P.; Hadingham, R.: FIPA-OS: the FIPA agent Platform available as Open Source. In: Bradshaw, J.; Arnold, G. (Eds.): Proceedings of the 5th International Conference on the Practical Application of Intelligent Agents and Multi-Agent Technology (PAAM 2000). 2000, pp. 355-368.

[PoCh2001]   Poslad, S.; Charlton, P.: Standardizing agent interoperability: The FIPA approach. In: Luck, M.; Maík, V.; Stpánková, O.; Trappl, R. (Eds.): Proceedings of Agent Link's Third European Agent Systems Summer School (EASSS 2001). Springer Verlag, Heidelberg, 2001, pp. 98-117.

[RaJe2005]   Ramchurn, S. D.; Jennings, N. R.: Trust in agent-based software. In: Mansell, R.; Collins, B. S. (Eds.): Trust and Crime in Information Societies. Elgar Publishing, Northampton, 2005, pp. 165-204.

[RKZF2000]   Resnick, P.; Kuwabara, K.; Zeckhauser, R.; Friedman, E.: Reputation systems. In: Communications of the ACM 43(2000)12, pp. 45-48.

[Shaf1976]   Shafer, G.: A Mathematical Theory of Evidence. Princeton University Press, Princeton, 1976.

[Smit1980]   Smith, R.: The Contract Net Protocol: High-Level Communication and Control in a Distributed Problem Solver. IEEE Transactions on Computers 29(1980), pp. 1104-1113.

[UnBR2004]   Unruh, A.; Bailey, J.; Ramamohanarao, K.: A Framework for Goal-Based Semantic Compensation in Agent Systems. In: Proceedings of the Second International Workshop on Safety and Security in Multi Agent Systems (SaSeMAS2004). 2004, pp. 125-141.

[UHBR2005]   Unruh, A.; Harjadi, H.; Bailey, J.; Ramamohanarao, K.: Semantic-compensation-based recovery in multi-agent systems. In: Proceedings of the 2nd IEEE Symposium on Multi-Agent Security and Survivability. 2005, pp. 85-94.

[Vogt2001]   Vogt, R.: Embedding a transaction-based robustness-service into a fipa-compliant multi-agent framework (in German). Diploma thesis, Universität Karlsruhe (TH), 2001.

[WaVa2003]   Wang, Y.; Vassileva, J.: Bayesian Network-Based Trust Model. In: Proceedings of the IEEE/WIC International Conference on Web Intelligence (WI 2003). IEEE Press, New York, 2003, pp. 372-378.

[WeVo2002]   Weikum, G.; Vossen, G.: Transactional Information Systems: Theory, Algorithms, and the Practice of Concurrency Control and Recovery. Morgan Kaufmann Publishers, San Francisco, 2002.

[Whit2005]   Whitestein Technologies AG: LS/TS – Living Systems® Technology Suite – Product Flyer. 2005. http://www.whitestein.com/resources/products/whitestein_lsts_flyer.pdf, accessed on 2005-08-24.

[ZaMM1999]   Zacharia, G.; Moukas, A.; Maes, P.: Collaborative Reputation Mechanisms in Electronic Marketplaces. In: Proceedings of the 32nd Annual Hawaii International Conference on System Sciences (HICSS-32). IEEE Press, New York, 1999, p. 8026.

7 Tools and Standards

Lars Braubach, Alexander Pokahr, Winfried Lamersdorf

Universität Hamburg, Fachbereich Informatik, Verteilte Systeme und Informationssysteme, {braubach I pokahr I lamersd}@informatik.uni-hamburg.de

Abstract. In this chapter tools, especially agent platforms, and relevant standards for realizing agent-oriented applications are presented. As there are a plenty of different agent platforms available the objective here is not to present an exhausting platform comparison, but to introduce meaningful platform categories, relate them to existing standards and illustrate them with typical representatives. The categorization helps to understand the existing heterogeneous agent technology landscape and is one integral part of a proposed selection method. This method reflects the fact that different problem domains may demand very different solutions in terms of the used methodology and underlying agent platform. It sketches the important steps that can be used to find a suitable methodology and agent platform fitting to the problem domain at hand.

7.1 Introduction

This chapter discusses how the concepts of the previous chapters can be actually realized as part of a larger agent-based project. Given that most implementation details are to a large extent dependent on the concrete application requirements, this chapter can only provide general considerations regarding the selection of appropriate tools and standards. As the field of Agent Technology matures, tools and standards become an important success factor for the development of agent-based applications, as they allow drawing from the existing experience. Tools, most notably agent platforms, represent reusable implementations of generic technical requirements. Standards capture state-of-the-art knowledge and best practices.

7.2 From the Problem Domain to the Implementation

The reason for selecting agent technology as part of a software project is mostly driven by the characteristics of the application domain at hand. [Weis2002] has identified some domain characteristics that advocate the use of agent technology in general: Agents are a suitable technology and metaphor for the problem domain, when

- There is a dynamic number of components, i.e., the system needs to be open, allowing for new components to be introduced at any time.
- An external control of the entities comprising the system is not possible or not wanted, i.e., the system components have to be autonomous and self-dependent.
- The coordination within the system takes place by using complex communication relationships, i.e., for processes executed by the system complex interactions between the subcomponents of the system are required.

Among others, these characteristics are an important factor influencing the concrete decisions to be taken towards the transition from the requirements to an implemented system. Major decisions that have to be made regard the methodology to be followed (cf. IV.1), and the agent platform to be used as a basis for the implemented system. The methodology guides the development process by proposing different development steps and the modeling artifacts being produced at each step. The agent platform forms the runtime environment for the agents that make up the application.

7.2.1 Criteria for Selecting an Agent Platform and a Methodology

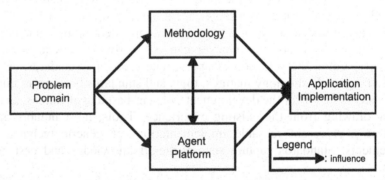

Figure 1. Influence relationships for application realizations

Decisions regarding both the methodology and the platform are influenced by the characteristics of the problem domain. Various catalogs of selection criteria have been proposed for comparing agent platforms (e.g. in [BDDE 2005] [EiMa2002]) and for comparing methodologies (see [SBPL2004]). The following presents some areas of domain dependant criteria considered most important as stated in [PoBL2005b]: *Concepts, Standards, Tools*, and *Applications*.

- Criteria in the area of concepts refer to the agent metaphor (e.g. deliberative entities vs. autonomous processes), and more specifically to details of the agent model (such as which mental attitudes are supported by a deliberative agent architecture).
- Relevant standards may come from two sources; on the one hand some standards are directly relevant to the problem domain (e.g. HL7[1] for health applications), on the other hand approved agent related standards (see Section 7.2.2) facilitate a consistent and interoperable design and implementation.
- Tool support has to address all phases of the development process starting from modeling the domain and elaborating the requirements to the system design and implementation. Implementation level tools can be further subdivided into code-oriented tools such as integrated development environments (IDEs), tools for debugging and testing, and tools for deployment and administration of an implemented system.
- Finally, examples of successful applications provide case studies of how to apply a certain approach and may reveal certain pitfalls.

Evaluation of these criteria is highly interrelated as these criteria apply to methodologies and platforms and to the problem domain as well. Therefore, the choice of an appropriate methodology and agent platform is crucial for the success of a project: The concrete platform determines the means, i.e. the concepts and supported standards that are available for system realization. Hence, it prescribes a certain agent philosophy, which has to be used for system implementation. If this agent philosophy does not reflect the important properties from the problem domain, a mismatch between problem domain and agent platform will complicate the realization. Such interdependencies also exist between the agent platform and the methodology. The methodology has to support the same agent philosophy, otherwise a mismatch between methodology and agent platform occurs, leading to a gap between modeling and implementation [SBPL2004]. Moreover, tool support not only for a methodology or a platform itself but also for mapping methodological design artifacts to a platform-specific implementation (e.g. code generators) further facilitates a smooth transition from design to implementation. Moreover, existing example applications of a methodology or platform allow to draw some conclusions pertinent to the given problem domain, e.g. regarding the context or size of the application.

---

[1]   http://www.hl7.org/

As a result, most of the time a trade-off has to be made regarding concepts and standards. Some of them may match best to the problem domain but there may be insufficient support with respect to existing methodologies or agent platforms (see Figure 1). The availability and quality of tool support, as well as the existence of case studies describing successful (or failed) applications can further support the decision in favor of or against some methodology or agent platform. Finally, there is a number of other selection criteria which can be evaluated independently from the problem domain, such as the performance, availability (free or commercial), or usability of given tools, or the amount and quality of supplied documentation materials.

7.3 Agent Platforms

An agent platform has the purpose to simplify the development of agent applications by providing an infrastructure agents can live in. It consists of the basic management facilities for hosting agents on a uniform infrastructure and, additionally, offers ready-to-use communication means for the agents. Agent platforms are characterized most notably by the internal and social architecture (layer 4 resp. 5 of the reference architecture introduced in IV.4) they employ. The internal architecture determines the internal concepts and mechanisms an agent uses to derive its actions, whereas the social architecture is responsible for coordination between agents and team management. Technically, a platform is characterized by the programming language it provides for realizing agents and the available tools for development, administration, and debugging.

In the remainder of this section an overview of existing agent platforms is given. This overview is not intended as an exhaustive list of all available platforms. For such a list the reader may refer to the "Agent Software" page of AgentLink[2] or (more focused on complete platforms) the agent platform page of the Jadex project[3]. Instead, this section will identify categories of platforms according to the reference architecture, highlight the important properties of these categories with respect to the above mentioned selection criteria, and present some representative platforms for each category. Finally, some general guidelines exemplify how to apply to selection criteria to choose among the available platforms and methodologies.

---

[2] http://www.agentlink.org/
[3] http://vsis-www.informatik.uni-hamburg.de/projects/jadex/links.php

7.3.1 Categorization of Agent Platforms with Respect to the Reference Architecture

Referring to the reference architecture introduced in IV.4 a categorization of agent platforms can be done in accordance to the layers they emphasize (cf. Figure 2).

Considering an agent platform as a *middleware* for agent-based services implies that at least L1-L3 need to be addressed in an adequate manner. *Middleware platforms*, therefore, provide a solid basis for developing open, interoperable agent systems, as they primarily tackle interoperability, agent management, and communication means. Anyhow, not all important aspects of agent development are supported equally well. One important point that is not addressed to a satisfactory degree concerns the agent's reasoning process. Most middleware platforms rely on a simple task-based model that allows for programmatically composing complex behavior out of simpler pieces.

Reasoning platforms focus on L4 and partly on L3 of the general reference architecture and hence employ an internal reasoning architecture for systematically deducing an agent's actions from some internal world knowledge. As the internal reasoning process often is intricate, support for L1-L3 varies greatly for different representatives. Additionally, middleware and reasoning platforms do not conceptually provide means for structuring and programming agent societies.

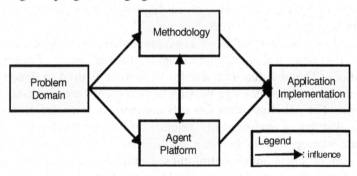

Figure 2. Coverage of layers for different categories of agent platforms

Social platforms address this issue by implementing organizational architectures (L5). An important question considering this kind of platform is, whether the underlying architecture depends on the concepts provided by the internal architecture (L4). In this case, the cooperation and coordination mechanisms of the organizational architecture can be quite elaborated allowing complex structures to be realized. On the other hand, the applicability of such an architecture and platform is restricted to agents conforming to a certain kind of agent type, such as BDI, which is undesirable for open system scenarios.

A common denominator for all the categories is the need for representing knowledge in an adequate manner (L3). At first sight this might be most interesting for reasoning platforms as they use the knowledge for internal deduction processes, but as communication plays a vital role in most multiagent applications the need for exchanging knowledge is a predominant issue.

To capture the semantics of symbolic representations, ontologies can be defined. Ontology descriptions follow standards like RDF[4] and OWL[5] (see IV.1 and IV.2.3). Ontology modeling tools such as Protégé[6] allow creating and editing ontology specifications in various standardized formats. Specialized reasoning engines such as RACER[7] can be used to operate on the represented world knowledge, to derive new facts and possible courses of action.

7.3.1.1 Middleware Platforms

In the field of distributed systems, *middleware* is normally seen as "[...] network-aware system software, layered between an application, the operating system, and the network transport layers, whose purpose is to facilitate some aspect of cooperative processing. Examples of middleware include directory services, message-passing mechanisms, distributed transaction processing (TP) monitors, object request brokers, remote procedure call (RPC) services, and database gateways."[8]

As agent orientation builds on concepts and technology of distributed systems, middleware is equally important for the realization of agent-based applications. Thereby, the term *agent middleware* is used to denote common services such as message passing or persistency management usable for agents. The paradigm shift towards autonomous software components in open, distributed environments requires on the one hand new standards to ensure interoperability between applications. On the other hand new middleware products implementing these standards are needed to facilitate fast development of robust and scalable applications. Agents can be seen as application layer software components using middleware to gain access to standardized services and infrastructure.

---

[4]   http://www.w3.org/RDF/
[5]   http://www.w3.org/2004/OWL/
[6]   http://protege.stanford.edu/
[7]   http://www.racer-systems.com/
[8]   http://iishelp.web.cern.ch/IISHelp/iis/htm/core/iigloss.htm

Before concrete examples of middleware platforms will be described the relevant middleware standards are introduced. Thanks to the FIPA standards the platform architecture has a common ground and interoperability between different middleware platforms could be achieved. Supplementary the MASIF standards define the basic concepts of agent mobility.

FIPA Standards

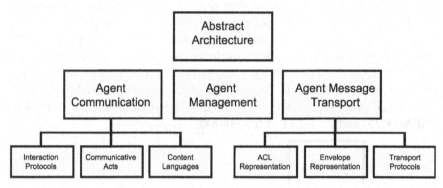

Figure 3. FIPA specification overview (from FIPA website)

An important foundation for the realization of middleware platforms are the specifications of the Foundation for Intelligent Physical Agents (FIPA)[9] (see [PoCh2001]). The work on specifications considered application as well as middleware aspects. Specifications related to applications provide systematically studied example domains with service and ontology descriptions. The middleware-related specifications address in detail all building blocks required for an abstract agent platform architecture (see Figure 3).

The *abstract architecture specification* (FIPA00001) defines at a high level how two agents can find and communicate with each other. For this purpose a set of architectural elements and their relationships are described. Basically, two types of directories, for agents as well as for agent services, are introduced, which can be used by agents to register themselves or search for specific services. The communication between two agents relies on a message transport component, which has the task to send a message following the agent communication language (ACL) format. For agent communication and agent message transport many refining standards are available.

In the area of agent communication, various standards have been defined for diverse interaction protocols, communicative acts, and content

---

[9]   http://www.fipa.org

languages. Interaction protocols set up a context which constrains the possible course of interaction to predefined courses. Examples of interaction protocols include, besides others, Dutch (FIPA00032) and English (FIPA 00031) auctions as well as the contract-net protocol (FIPA00029). The communicative act library specification (FIPA00037) describes the set of allowed performatives, which denote the meaning of a message according to speech act theory [Sear1969]. In addition different content languages can be employed for the representation of the message content. Examples include the FIPA semantic language (FIPA00008) and RDF (FIPA 00011).

On the other hand the message transport has to deal with the representation of ACL messages and their envelopes as well as with the underlying transport protocols. For messages and envelopes different representations such as XML (FIPA00071/85) and a bit-efficient version (FIPA00069/88) have been proposed. Transport protocol specifications exist for IIOP (FIPA00075) and for HTTP (FIPA00084).

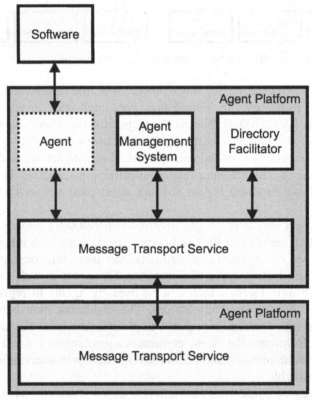

Figure 4. FIPA agent management reference model (from FIPA00023)

Most important for understanding the platform operation according to FIPA is the agent management specification (FIPA00023) (see Figure 4). It defines the necessary building blocks of an agent platform and their relationships, including mechanisms for agent management, as well as infrastructure elements such as directory services and message delivery. In this respect the agent management system (AMS) is responsible for exerting supervisory control over access to and the use of the agent platform. It maintains a directory of all agents living on the platforms. Another important component of an agent platform is the directory facilitator (DF) which provides yellow pages services to other agents. Agents hosted on a platform can access non-agent software and send messages to other agents on the same or another platform using the message transport service.

The FIPA specifications have been implemented in a number of agent platforms and interoperability among those platforms has been shown, for example in the agentcities network [WiCR2002].

MASIF Standards

The Mobile Agent System Interoperability Facility (MASIF) [OMG2000] is a standard for mobile agent systems proposed by the Object Management Group (OMG). The main objective of MASIF is to establish a common ground that allows MASIF compliant agent frameworks to perform agent migration even in heterogeneous environments (assuming a common platform implementation language). It aims to achieve a first level of interoperability for the transportation of agent information where the information format is standardized. This means that once the agent data has been transferred the platform is responsible for interpreting the information. The transmitted data makes explicit the agent profile describing the language, serialization, and further agent requirements on the platform. In this way MASIF enables an agent system to understand the agent's demands.

To achieve this kind of mobile agent interoperability MASIF tackles four different areas in the standard: agent management, agent transfer, agent/platform naming, and agent system type/location syntax. Agent management concerns the life cycle control of agents including agents hosted on remote platforms. The management is addressed by standardized interfaces for agent creation and termination as well as for suspending and resuming agent execution. Agent transfer underpins the main goal of agent mobility and aims at a common infrastructure in which agents can freely move among different platforms. One necessary prerequisite for locating remote agents possibly hosted on another type of platform is the standardization of the syntax and semantics of agent and platform names. In addition, the agent system type is of importance as the agent transfer depends on the fact that the system can support the agent. Finally, the location syntax is standardized to ensure that platforms can find each other (cf. [Mil+1998] for details).

In addition to the functional aspects, MASIF also tackles security issues arising in the context of mobile agents. An agent system has the task to protect its resources from new agents arriving at the platform. For this purpose the platform must be able to identify and verify the authority of an incoming agent. This allows for access control and agent authentication.

One big problem of MASIF is that it is based on CORBA and has therefore never been widely accepted. The MASIF standard has been used mainly for specialized mobile agent platforms such as Aglets [ClPE1997]. Nevertheless, also platforms supporting both FIPA and MASIF have been developed such as Grasshopper [BaMa1999].

JADE

A prominent example of a middleware-oriented agent platform is JADE (Java Agent DEvelopment Framework) [BBCP2005], a Java framework for the development of distributed multiagent applications. It represents an agent middleware providing a set of available and easy-to-use services and several graphical tools for administration and debugging. One main objective of the platform is to support interoperability by strictly adhering to the FIPA specifications concerning the platform architecture as well as the communication infrastructure. Recently, a "Web Services Integration Gateway" added support for agents acting as client or server in a Web Service application. Moreover, JADE is very flexible and can be adapted to be used also on devices with limited resources like PDAs and cell phones. The JADE platform is open source software, distributed by TILAB (Telecom Italia LABoratories). Since May 2003, an international JADE Board has the task of supervising the management of the project. Currently, the JADE Board consists of five members: TILAB, Motorola, Whitestein Technologies AG, Profactor, and France Telecom. Many JADE applications ranging from research prototypes to industrial products have been developed over the last years (see [BBCP2005]). As one example Whitestein has used JADE to construct an agent-based system for decision support in organ transplant centers [CFBB2004].

ADK

The agent development kit (ADK) is a commercial/open-source Java-based agent platform developed by Tryllian Solutions B.V. The main focus of the company is in the application integration area, involving all kinds of legacy system integration. In ADK, agent programming follows a task framework in which behavior is implemented as a set of simple tasks arranged in a workflow-like manner. The platform includes a visual design environment and administrative tools for deployment. The platform is targeted to be used in industrial systems (as opposed to research), and emphasizes mobility and security aspects. To facilitate the integration of legacy systems, interoperability with existing solutions is an important factor for the platform and a number of accepted industry standards are supported: SNMP (Simple Network Management Protocol) allows remote management of the agent platform. JNDI (Java Naming and Directory Interface) can be used for agent naming and lookup. Agents can receive messages sent using JMS (Java Messages Service), FIPA, or the JXTA peer to peer network. Moreover, agents can act as Web Service or interact with existing Web Services using the SOAP/WSDL/UDDI stack. Recently a business rule engine has been added, to support the maintenance of processes directly at the business level. Several production grade applications have been developed such as the "ePosit" system for intelligent Web search, or the "Continuous Auditing" system, which allows monitoring of decentralized organizations and automating routine auditing tasks.

FIPA-OS

FIPA-OS was one of the first open-source, FIPA-compliant software frameworks originating from research at Nortel Networks Harlow Laboratories in the UK. It is implemented in Java and like JADE uses a simple task-based approach as internal agent structure. Although development of FIPA-OS has been discontinued in 2003, the platform is still available for download. In addition FIPA-OS has been released as a reduced version suitable to small and mobile devices (MicroFIPA-OS). Tool support is limited to simple graphical user interfaces for administering and configuring the platform and agents on the platform. Up to now, FIPA-OS has been used mostly in research and beta stage prototype applications. For example, emorphia Ltd. has developed an agent-based intelligent meeting scheduler named Friday based on FIPA-OS.

DIET

DIET Agents is a multiagent platform developed as part of an EU project under the leadership of British Telecom. The DIET (Decentralized Information Ecosystem Technologies) project aimed at developing a lightweight, scalable, and robust agent platform targeted to peer-to-peer (p2p) and/or adaptive, distributed applications. Primary application area of the platform in the course of the project was information retrieval, filtering, mining, and trading. The platform uses bottom-up, nature-inspired techniques from Evolutionary Computation and Artificial Life to provide an open, robust, adaptive, and scalable environment for information processing and management. Tests performed by the project partners showed that the platform supports up to 100000 agents running on a single computer. After the project had finished in 2003, the platform was released as open source and is currently continued to be developed as a generic middleware agent platform. Besides the platform itself, a graphical tool for visualizing and debugging applications has been made available. Existing applications have mostly been developed in the course of the research project as prototypes and proof of concepts, e.g., for a collaborative tool visualizing social networks, self-organizing communities, and p2p content sharing applications.

7.3.1.2 Reasoning Platforms

Reasoning platforms are based on specific internal agent architectures. Such internal agent architectures have been conceived to support the reasoning process of agents and therefore systematize the process of how an agent decides which action it wants to perform in any given situation. According to [WoJe1995] these architectures can be categorized into *reactive*, *deliberative* and *hybrid* architectures.

Reactive architectures abstain from any kind of symbolic knowledge and do not use symbolic reasoning. The most prominent reactive architecture is Brook's subsumption architecture [Broo1986] which assumes that an agent is composed of a hierarchy of task-accomplishing behaviors. Behaviors at a lower level in the hierarchy represent primitive actions and have precedence over higher-level behaviors. Even though the resulting agents are quite simplistic in nature, it could be shown that this kind of architecture is well-suited for certain kinds of applications such as the movement control for robots.

Deliberative architectures require an agent having a symbolic model of the world and using logical (or at least pseudo-logical) reasoning for its decisions. Many deliberative architectures are based on a central planner component which is responsible for deducing reasonable agent actions. Examples of such architectures are IRMA [BrIP1988] and IPEM [AmSt 1988]. Main drawback of most purely deliberative architectures is their inefficiency as symbolic reasoning requires complex computations and thus cannot guarantee responsive agent behavior under all conditions.

To the rescue, many *hybrid architectures* have been proposed, which aim at bringing together the best from both approaches. Hybrid architectures combine reactive and deliberative facets leading to agent behavior that is responsive as well as intelligent. Even though there are no standards for reasoning facets of platforms two predominant architectures exist. Most influential architectures with respect to their practical relevance are the SOAR [LeLR1996] and the BDI [Brat1987] models of agency.

SOAR is based on Newell's psychological theory "Unified Theory of Cognition (UTC)" [Newe1990], which postulates the pursuit for a single set of mechanisms that account for all aspects of cognition such as memory, problem solving, and learning. "A UTC must explain how intelligent organisms flexibly react to stimuli from the environment, how they exhibit goal-directed behavior and acquire goals rationally, how they represent knowledge (or which symbols they use), and learning."[10]

The BDI model was originally conceived by Bratman as a theory of human practical reasoning [Brat1987]. Its success is based on its simplicity reducing the explanation framework for complex human behavior to the *motivational stance* [Denn1987]. Following the motivational stance, causes for actions are only related to desires ignoring other facets of cognition such as emotions. Another advantage of the BDI model is the consistent usage of folk psychological notions that closely correspond to the way people communicate about human behavior [Norl2004]. Starting from Bratman's work, Rao and Georgeff [RaGe1995] conceived a formal BDI theory, which defines beliefs, desires, and intentions as mental attitudes represented as possible world states. The intentions of an agent are subsets of the beliefs and desires, i.e., an agent acts towards some of the world states it desires to be true and believes to be possible. To be computationally tractable Rao and Georgeff also proposed several simplifications to the theory, the most important one being that only beliefs are represented explicitly. Desires are reduced to events that are handled by predefined plan templates, and intentions are represented implicitly by the runtime stack of executed plans. As a multitude of platforms have been developed based on the BDI paradigm, only a small selection is presented here. For a more detailed overview of BDI systems see [MaDA2005].

JACK

The JACK platform is developed as a commercial product by Agent Oriented Software [HRHL2001]. It is based on the BDI architecture and provides its own programming language called JACK agent language (JAL). JAL is a conservative extension of Java introducing BDI concepts and some features of logic languages such as cursors and logical variables. An agent in JACK is composed of a number of different JAL files, mainly rep-

---

[10] http://en.wikipedia.org/wiki/Unified_Theory_of_Cognition

resenting the agent itself as well as its plans, belief base, and events. To execute a JACK agent, its set of JAL files is first precompiled to Java source code and in a second step compiled to executable Java byte code. JACK addresses several weaknesses of traditional BDI systems. Most notably, it introduces the notion of a capability for the modularization of agents [BHRH2000]. Additionally, the SimpleTeams approach (see below) has been conceived to support the cooperation of agents within BDI teams. JACK represents an industry-grade product delivering extensive documentation and supporting tools. Especially, JACK ships with an IDE that supports the detailed design and implementation phase. The IDE supports inter alia the project management, the editing of files by syntax highlighting and the compilation and execution from within the IDE. Additionally, a graphical plan editor allows for creating plans visually and observing their execution at runtime. It has been used in a variety of industrial applications as well as for many research projects. The application areas include Unmanned Aerial Vehicles (UAVs), human-like decision making, and decision support systems (details can be found in [Wini2005]).

Jadex

Jadex [BrPL2005] [PoBL2005] is an open source software framework developed at the University of Hamburg. It allows the creation of goal oriented agents following the belief-desire-intention (BDI) model. The framework is realized as a rational agent layer that sits on top of a middleware agent infrastructure such as JADE [BBCP2005], and supports agent development with well established technologies such as Java and XML. Thereby, Jadex avoids intentionally the introduction of a new programming language and subdivides the agent description into structure and behavior specification. The structure of an agent is described in an XML file following a BDI metamodel defined in XML-schema whereas the behavior is implemented in plans that are ordinary Java files. This has the advantage that any state-of-the art IDE (offering XML and Java support) can be utilized for programming Jadex agents. Jadex introduces the basic concepts beliefs, plans, goals, events for agent programming, and capabilities for modularization purposes. Besides the focus on middleware support, the Jadex reasoning engine addresses traditional limitations of BDI systems by introducing new concepts such as explicit goals and goal deliberation mechanisms (see e.g. [BPML2004] making results from goal oriented analysis and design methods (e.g. KAOS or Tropos) more easily transferable to the implementation layer. Besides the framework, additional tools are included to facilitate administration and debugging of agent applications. Jadex has been used to realize applications in different domains such as simulation, scheduling, and mobile computation. For example, Jadex was used to realize a multiagent application for negotiation of treatment schedules in hospitals (see III.4).

Jason

Jason [BoHV2005] is a platform for programming agents in Agent-Speak(L) [Rao1996], a logic-based agent-oriented programming language that is adequate for the realization of reactive planning systems according to the BDI architecture. In AgentSpeak(L) an agent consists of beliefs represented as ground (first-order) atomic formulae, plans comprising basic actions, and subgoal calls as well as events that represent all kinds of relevant occurrences such as new goals or beliefs. Jason is a relatively slim BDI system strictly adhering to the formal AgentSpeak(L) semantics. This enables Jason to be used for model checking and verification purposes. The platform, which is available as open source, offers means for distributing an MAS over network and comes with a simple IDE for editing and starting agent applications. It has been used so far for several small academic applications.

SOAR

In contrast to the aforementioned reasoning platforms SOAR is not based on BDI, but relies on UTC [Newe1990]. The SOAR architecture at its heart is a typical production system that matches and applies rules on a working memory. It is enhanced with a learning mechanism called chunking [LeLR1996] which infers more abstract rules from observing the rule application process. On top of this production system a goal-driven problem solver following the problem space hypothesis is placed. SOAR utilizes an agent deliberation cycle consisting of the five phases: perceptual input, operator proposal, operator selection, operator application, and output. In the perceptual input phase sensory data from the environment is updated and made available for the system. Next, in the proposal phase, production rules fire to interpret the new data until no new data can be deduced (quiescence), propose operators for the current situation and compare the proposed operators. In the selection phase, the operator to apply is chosen on basis of the proposed set of operators. When no unique operator is preferred, a so called impasse occurs and a new subgoal is created, which has the task to resolve the conflict (a process called *automatic subgoaling hypothesis*). In the application phase the selected operator is executed and, finally, in the output phase output commands are sent to the environment. The SOAR architecture for single agents is supplemented by a social architecture for agent teams (see below). The SOAR platform comes with an extensive tool support, documentation, and example applications. VisualSoar is a simple form of an IDE specifically tailored to support writing SOAR agents and execute them in the runtime environment. In addition a SOAR debugger tool is provided for observing the internal data and behavior of an agent. SOAR has been used in many projects ranging from simple research to complex commercial application scenarios. As an example Soar Technology Inc.[11] uses SOAR agents for building various (e.g., pilot) training applications.

7.3.1.3 Social Platforms

Social agent platforms provide support for expressing group behavior within multiagent systems. These systems build upon different group behavior theories and architectures, which will be discussed next. Fundamentally, teamwork involves the structural as well as behavioral dimension. Nevertheless, current research does not provide integrated theories covering both dimensions at a satisfactory degree within one coherent framework. Hence, in the following both aspects will be discussed separately.

One very simple, but nonetheless influential, structuring mechanism for agent teams is the Agent-Group-Role (AGR) model [Ferb2003]. Basically, an agent is seen as an active, communicating entity playing roles within groups. A group in turn is described as a set of agents sharing some common property. It is used as a context for a pattern of activities and subdivides organizations. Agents are only allowed to communicate, if they belong to the same group. A role is the abstract representation of an agent's functional position in a group. An agent must play a role in a group, but an agent may play arbitrary many roles. One of the basic principles of the AGR model is that at the organizational level no agent description and, therefore, no mental issues should be used. This makes AGR independent of any particular agent model (in L4) and allows simple agents as well as very complex agents, possibly employing the intentional stance, being part of the same organizational structure. There are some approaches to standardize the structural aspects of teamwork; most notably, the role concept and related terms specified as part of the AUML, which has many similarities to the AGR model (see [OdPF2003] for details).

The most influential framework for describing the behavioral aspects of teamwork is the joint intentions theory [CoLe1991]. It formulates the formal principles for describing how agents can pursue a common goal relying on the basic concepts beliefs, goals, and their collective counterparts as

---

[11] http://www.soartech.com/

foundations. The notion of a joint intention is regarded as a joint commitment of some agents to perform a collective action while being in a certain shared mental state. The joint commitment to perform some action is thereby represented as a joint persistent goal shared by all involved agents. One important property of such a joint goal, in contrast to an individual goal, is that the participating agents agree to inform each other about a possibly changing goal state. This means that each individual agent accepts responsibility for the pursuit of the common goal and informs the other if it, e.g., finds out that the goal is unachievable allowing others to share that knowledge. Despite its neatness, the joint intentions theory does not address some important aspects. It is not discussed how agents can establish a joint intention towards some action. Also, the defection of a single agent causes the entire group task to fail. For these reasons, the joint intentions theory was subject to several extensions which tried to expand and enhance the basic model. Examples for such extensions are Jennings' joint responsibility theory [JeMa1992] and Tambe's STEAM model [Tamb 1997].

MadKit

MadKit is a modular and scalable multiagent platform developed by Ferber and colleagues [GuFe2001]. It is built upon the AGR (Agent/Group/Role) organizational model, in which agents are members of groups and play certain roles. As the AGR model is independent from the underlying internal agent model, it allows a high heterogeneity of agent architectures and communication languages to be used. The MadKit platform is realized by following three design principles. Firstly, the system is based on a micro-kernel architecture that provides the basic services for agent resp. group management and message passing. Secondly, most services within MadKit are realized as agents making the system structure very flexible. Thirdly, MadKit provides a component oriented model for displaying agent GUIs within the platform. The tool support for the platform is quite extensive and comprises a graphical administration as well as several monitoring and debugging tools. The platform has been used for the realization of various applications such as TurtleKit, an agent simulation environment, and SEdit, a tool for the design and animation of structured diagrams.

STEAM

STEAM [Tamb1997] is a general model of teamwork conceived to support performing coordinated tasks within some group of agents. It utilizes the formal joint intentions theory as basic building block, but borrows some ideas from the SharedPlans theory as well [GrKr1996]. Moreover, STEAM proposes several improvements regarding practical issues for making the model efficiently implementable. STEAM introduces team operators (team activities) and team beliefs as new concepts. Whenever a team activity needs to be executed, the agents belonging to the relevant team must first establish a joint intention for this team activity. To achieve a joint intention, an "establish commitments" protocol is carried out. After the joint intention has been established, a team operator can only be terminated by modifying the team state (mutual beliefs within this team). Conditions describing success and failure states can be specified for team operators individually. STEAM automatically takes responsibility for updating the team state whenever an important change occurs within a local view of a team belief. In this case the corresponding agent broadcasts this change to all other team members that update their view accordingly. In case of a failure during the team activity STEAM provides also means for replanning the task. For this purpose, the contributions of the team members for a team operator are specified in terms of roles. A role is considered here as the set of activities an individual or subteam undertakes in service of the team's overall task. STEAM allows specific role relationships being specified (and, or, depends on) that are employed to determine the state of a team operator and, possibly, to engage into repair operations, e.g., substitute some critical subteam. STEAM has been implemented for the SOAR agent platform as a set of rules. This implementation has been used for diverse application domains, including RoboCup soccer and simulation environments for training.

JACK SimpleTeams

The JACK SimpleTeams approach [HoRB1999] aims at providing coordinated activities for groups of agents. It is based on the idea that a team is itself an autonomous entity that can exist without its team members and can reason about its behavior. The approach is an extension conceived specifically for BDI agents and adds new team constructs for roles, team plans and team beliefs to the standard BDI concepts. A team is represented as an extended BDI agent that is capable to cope also with these new concepts. The structure of a team is described with roles. More precisely, it is characterized by the roles it performs and the roles it requires others to perform. Thereby, roles are used as abstract placeholders for arbitrary team instances playing that role at runtime. For this reason roles can be seen as a kind of interface for teams. Concretely, a role defines the relationship between teams and subteams in terms of the goal and belief exchanges implied by the relationship. The tasks of a team can be specified via team plans that extend the plan concept of BDI agents and enable coordinated task achievement. A team plan can be used to accomplish some task collaboratively by a (sub-)set of agents belonging to the team. Therefore, a team plan offers possibilities to influence the actual selection of agents working on the task and new means for the distribution of subtasks to the participating members. The distribution of subtasks is done by subgoal delegation to team members. This allows the team members to decide in their own responsibility how to accomplish the goal retaining the full flexibility of multiagent systems. To enable easy information exchange between the team members and the team itself, the concept of team beliefs is introduced. Team beliefs can either distribute data from the team to the subteams or aggregate data from the members back to the team. At runtime, a team runs through different phases. In the initial phase, the team formation is performed. This means that role fillers for all roles within the team are searched. When this formation ends, the team enters the operational phase, in which the actual task processing is done. JACK SimpleTeams is a general purpose teamwork architecture. Nevertheless, it was used primarily for military application scenarios so far.

7.3.2 Platform Summary

Table 1. Platform summary

	Concepts	Standards	Tools	Applications	Availability
JADE	M	FIPA, WS	A, D	Production	Open source
FIPA-OS	M	FIPA	A	Beta	Open source
ADK	M	FIPA, WS, JMS, ...	I, A	Production	Commercial
DIET	M	-	D	Beta	Open source
Jadex	M, R	FIPA, WS, JMS	A, D	Production	Open source
Jason	R	-	I, D	Beta	Open source
JACK +Simple-Teams	R R, S	-	I, D	Production	Commercial
SOAR +STEAM	R R, S	-	I, D	Production	Open source/ Commercial
MadKit	S	-	A, D	Production	Open source

Table 1 shows a summary overview of the presented agent platforms. A first thing to note is that some of the platforms, although historically pertaining to only one of the possible agent metaphors (M=middleware, R=reasoning, S=social) now start to address other areas as well, making them more generic and suitable for a wide range of application domains. JACK and SOAR, which started as pure reasoning platforms, have been extended to support social concepts as well, and the Jadex platform presents an approach to integrate high-level reasoning with existing middleware technology.

Traditionally, only the middleware platforms are directly based on some existing or new standards. Some of them initially focused only on a single set of specifications (e.g. JADE, FIPA-OS), other such as ADK tried to provide support for a wide range of existing standards including FIPA, Web Services (WS), and others. Middleware support is a serious issue, as most newly developed applications have to be integrated with one or more existing systems. Although, nowadays for most standards reusable third party libraries are available, when standards are not supported by the platform directly, the agent programmer has the tedious task of making the application to interoperate with other standards-compliant software.

In the recent years tool support has become more and more an issue for developers of agent platforms, but there is still some way to go until agent technology is supported by development tools of the quality known from object oriented tools. None of the presented platforms provides all kinds of tools desirable for efficient application development (I=integrated development environments, A=administrative tools, D=debugging tools). For platforms supporting agents written in pure Java (here the middleware platforms and MadKit) existing Java-IDEs can still be used, with the advantage of a development environment already familiar to the programmer. In contrast, newly developed IDEs (e.g. for the reasoning platforms) offer the advantage of directly supporting agent-oriented concepts.

Compared to the wide distribution of object oriented application frameworks (e.g. web containers or application servers) real case studies of applications developed with agent platforms are still scarce or at least hard to find. Nevertheless, they do exist for most of the presented platforms, proving that successful agent applications can be built. Given that there is some 10-20 years gap between the first works on object oriented programming and the advent of the agent paradigm, it is reasonable to say that agent technology still has the potential to become as predominant as object oriented technology is at the moment.

Finally, the availability column shows if platforms are distributed as commercial products or open source implementations. Open source platforms are not only free in the sense that one does not have to pay for them, but also that there is the freedom to modify the platform itself, if needed. On the other hand, commercial products offer guaranteed support and should be mature and well tested. Some systems like SOAR are even available in both flavors. Therefore, different options are available for any kind of problem domain, and application developers can usually choose among a set of commercial products and open source implementations.

Although only a small cutout of available agent platforms has been presented, it should now be evident that there exists a large diversity in the different platforms. For example, no platform supports all three agent metaphors (middleware, reasoning, social). Many platforms claim a general applicability, but every platform is based on its own interpretation of the agent paradigm. Therefore, even though it might be somewhat usable in many domains, a platform would perform best in a domain where it offers a fitting agent metaphor, readily available tools, and directly supported standards. Therefore, an agent developer has to choose carefully among the available options. In the following, the authors will try to give some guidelines how this choice can be simplified.

7.4 Guidelines for Choosing among Platforms and Methodologies

One big problem of agent technology nowadays is its strong heterogeneity. This applies to the agent architectures (internal and social), to the methodologies, and to the agent programming languages [PoBL2005b]. To further illustrate this issue one can look closer at the internal agent architecture BDI. Even though a consensus exits with respect to the basic concepts, the concrete interpretations and thus architectures and platforms differ considerably. In the field of agent-oriented software engineering also a great variety of agent methodologies emerged. Some of them claim to be agent architecture independent such as GAIA [WoJK2000] whereas others are specifically tailored for some agent philosophy such as Prometheus [PaWi 2004]. Although it might be tempting to use a generally applicable methodology, it should be clear that such a methodology cannot support agent development with the same concepts as the platform does.

Carrying these considerations to the extreme, it is even contended how agent programming should be done. Some approaches favor new and specialized agent languages (e.g. JACK), whereas others employ existing programming languages such as Java (e.g. Jadex).

Hence, it becomes clear that the choice of the right combination of an agent methodology and a suitable platform is crucial for exploiting the potential of the agent paradigm for a given problem domain. This choice should start with an analysis of the problem domain gathering initial requirements and bringing light to the essential properties of the planned application. From these initial settings, it should be discussed which agent philosophy deems most promising and allows the description of preferably many domain structures and behaviors. Having agreed on a common agent philosophy facilitates the selection of an agent platform and a suitable methodology considerably as it reduces the number of available candidates.

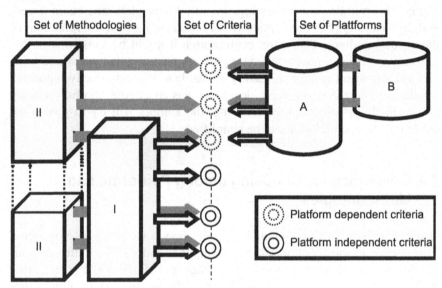

Figure 5. Selection framework

Given that a preselection of platforms and methodologies on basis of the favored agent philosophy has been carried out, the further selection process should not be done in isolation for either of both. Instead, it has to be found a constellation of methodology and platform that fits to each other.

For this process a general framework has been proposed in [SBPL2004]. It is based on a catalog of criteria that should be measured for both, the platform and the methodology candidates (cf. Figure 5). The set of criteria is divided into platform dependent and independent criteria, whereby, the independent criteria can be examined in a feature analysis. Categories for independent criteria include the notation (usability, expressiveness, etc.), the process (coverage of workflows, complexity, etc.), and pragmatic aspects (tool support, documentation, etc.). Independent criteria have been subject of several methodology comparisons that aimed to rank them with respect to the aforementioned factors [ShSt2001].

For platform dependent criteria (e.g. regarding the supported agent concepts), it needs to be determined if and how the methodology as well the platform supports a property. The match between them is analyzed to show their appropriateness. This means that a match with respect to a property exists when either platform and methodology support a considered property in the same (or a very similar) way or when both do not support the property. The shared absence of a property is regarded as a match, because the absence of a concept in both platform and methodology also identifies appropriateness.

To arrive at a final decision, the platform dependent criteria should be weighted according to the demands of the application domain as some agent concepts (e.g. mobility) might be irrelevant for a given domain. For each pair of methodology and platform the overall match quality can be estimated. The platform and methodology pair with the weighted best match should be chosen. This selection process can be simplified, if the preselection phase is rather rigid or if for some external reasons (e.g. company relationships) a certain platform or methodology has to be used.

7.5 Conclusions

This chapter has presented an overview of agent standards and platforms. The agent platforms have been categorized by their main architectural focus leading to three different classes: middleware, reasoning and social platforms. Middleware platforms address primarily layers L1-L3 of the reference architecture focusing on support for interoperability with other FIPA compliant platforms. Secondly, reasoning platforms mainly deal with the agent internal decision process that leads to concrete agent behavior. Thirdly, social platforms highlight organizational structures as well as coordinated (team) behavior. Based on the criteria *Concepts*, *Standards*, *Tools*, and *Applications* typical representatives of the respective categories have been evaluated.

Given that a vast amount of different platforms belonging to one or another category exists, this chapter also sketches a systematical approach for choosing a platform for a specific development project. Roughly speaking, the approach consists of two phases; a domain dependent preselection phase and a subsequent stage for platform/methodology evaluation. In the first stage, a domain analysis is used to set-up a fitting agent metaphor emphasizing the important aspects of the domain. Thereafter, in the second stage, the remaining platforms are evaluated together with possibly fitting methodologies. The basic assumption in this connection is that an agent platform and a concomitant methodology are strongly interrelated and should be chosen together for guaranteeing effective application development. As a result, one obtains estimated quality measurements for platform-methodology pairs. The pair exhibiting the best match and the best criteria coverage should be chosen.

Further Reading

[UnCK2005]   Unland, R.; Calisti, M.; Klusch, M.: Software Agent-Based Applications, Platforms and Development Kits. Birkhäuser, 2005.

[BDDE2005]   Bordini, R.; Dastani, M.; Dix, J.; El Fallah Seghrouchni, A. (Eds.): Programing Multi-Agent Systems. Kluwer Academic Publishers, 2005.

[PoBL2005b]   Pokahr, A.; Braubach, L.; Lamersdorf, W.: Agenten: Technologie für den Mainstream? In: it – Information Technology 5(2005), pp.300-307.

[SBPL2004]   Sudeikat, J.; Braubach, L.; Pokahr, A.; Lamersdorf, W.: Evaluation of Agent-Oriented Software Methodologies – Examination of the Gap Between Modeling and Platform. In: Giorgini, P.; Müller, J.P.; Odell, J. (Eds.): Agent-Oriented Software Engineering V, Fifth International Workshop AOSE 2004. Springer Verlag, 2004, pp. 126-141.

[WeJa2004]   Weiß, G.; Jakob, R.: Agentenorientierte Softwareentwicklung – Methoden und Tools. Xpert.press Reihe, Springer-Verlag, September 2004.

References

[AmSt1988]   Ambros-Ingerson, J.; Steel, S.: Integrating Planning, Execution and Monitoring. In: Proceedings of the Seventh National Conference on Artificial Intelligence (AAAI-88); St. Paul, MN. AAAI Press, Menlo Park, CA, 1988, pp. 83-88.

[BaMa1999]   Baeumer, C.; Magedanz, T.: Grasshopper: A Mobile Agent Platform for Active Telecommunication Networks. In: Proceedings of the 3rd International Workshop on Intelligent Agents for Telecommunication Applications (IATA-99). Springer, Berlin, 1999, pp. 19-32.

[BBCP2005]   Bellifemine, F.; Bergenti, F.; Caire, G.; Poggi, A.: JADE - A Java Agent Development Framework. In: Bordini, R.; Dastani, M.; Dix, J.; El Fallah Seghrouchni, A. (Eds.): Programing Multi-Agent Systems. Kluwer Academic Publishers, 2005.

[BDDE2005]   Bordini, R.; Dastani, M.; Dix, J.; El Fallah Seghrouchni, A. (Eds.): Programing Multi-Agent Systems. Kluwer Academic Publishers, 2005.

[BoHV2005]   Bordini, R.; Hübner, J.; Vieira, R.: Jason and the Golden Fleece of Agent-Oriented Programming. In: Bordini, R.; Dastani, M.; Dix, J.; El Fallah Seghrouchni, A. (Eds.): Programing Multi-Agent Systems. Kluwer Academic Publishers, 2005.

[BPML2004]   Braubach, L.; Pokahr, A.; Moldt, D.; Lamersdorf, W.: Goal Representation for BDI Agent Systems. In: Bordini, R. et al. (Eds.): Proceedings of the 2nd International Workshop on Programming Multiagent Systems, Languages and Tools (PROMAS 2004), 3rd International Joint Conference on Autonomous Agents & Multi-Agent Systems (AAMAS'04), New York, USA. Lecture Notes in Computer Science. Springer-Verlag, Berlin, New York, 2005, pp. 46-67.

[Brat1987]   Bratman, M.: Intention, Plans, and Practical Reason. Harvard University Press, 1987.

[BrIP1988]   Bratman, M.; Israel, D.; Pollack, M.: Plans and Resource-Bounded Practical Reasoning. In: Computational Intelligence 4(1988) 4, pp. 349-355.

[Broo1986]   Brooks, R.: A Robust Layered Control System for a Mobile Robot. In: IEEE Journal of Robotics and Automation 2(1986)1, pp. 24-30.

[BrPL2005]   Braubach, L.; Pokahr, A.; Lamersdorf, W.: Jadex: A BDI Agent System Combining Middleware and Reasoning. In: Unland, R.; Calisti, M.; Klusch, M. (Eds.): Software Agent-Based Applications, Platforms and Development Kits. Birkhäuser, 2005.

[BHRH2000]   Busetta, P.; Howden, N.; Rönnquist, R.; Hodgson, A.: Structuring BDI Agents in Functional Clusters. In: Intelligent Agents VI, Agent Theories, Architectures, and Languages (ATAL'99), LNCS 1757. Springer, 2000, pp. 277-289.

[CFBB2004]   Calisti, M.; Funk, P.; Biellman, S.; Bugnon, T.: A Multi-Agent System for Organ Transplant Management. In: Applications of Software Agent Technology in the Health Care Domain. Springer, Heidelberg, 2004.

[ClPE1997]   Clement, P.; Papaioannou, T.; Edwards, J.: Aglets: Enabling the Virtual Enterprise. In: Proceedings of the International Conference Managing Enterprises – Stakeholders, Engineering, Logistics and Achievement' (ME-SELA '97), 1997.

[CoLe1991]   Cohen, P.; Levesque, H.: Teamwork, SRI International. Technote 504. Menlo Park, CA, 1991.

[Denn1987]   Dennett, D.: The Intentional Stance. Bradford Books, 1987.

[EiMa2002]   Eiter, T.; Mascardi, V.: Comparing Environments for Developing Software Agents. In: AI Communications 15(4), pp. 169-197, 2002.

[Ferb2003]   Ferber, J.: From Agents to Organizations: An Organizational View of Multi-Agent Systems. In: Agent-Oriented Software Engineering IV, 4th International Workshop, AOSE 2003, Melbourne, Australia, July 15, 2003. Revised Papers, 2003, pp. 214-230.

[GrKr1996]   Grosz, B.; Kraus, S.: Collaborative Plans for Complex Group Action. In: Artificial Intelligence 86(1996)2, pp. 269-357.

[GuFe2001]   Gutknecht, O.; Ferber, J.: The MADKIT Agent Platform Architecture. In: Wagner, T.; Rana, O. (Eds.): Revised Papers From the International Workshop on Infrastructure for Multi-Agent Systems: Infrastructure for Agents, Multi-Agent Systems, and Scalable Multi-Agent Systems, June 3-7, 2000. Lecture Notes in Computer Science 1887(2001). Springer-Verlag, London, 2001, pp. 48-55.

[HoRB1999]   Hodgson, A.; Rönnquist, R.; Busetta, P.: Specification of Coordinated Agent Behavior (The SimpleTeam Approach). In: Proceedings of the Workshop on Team Behavior and Plan Recognition at IJCAI-99, Stockholm, Sweden, 1999.

[HRHL2001]   Howden, N.; Rönnquist, R.; Hodgson, A.; Lucas, A.: JACK Intelligent Agents – Summary of an Agent Infrastructure. In: Proceedings of the 5th ACM International Conference on Autonomous Agents. Canada, 2001.

[JeMa1992]   Jennings, N.; Mamdani, E.: Using Joint Responsibility to Coordinate Collaborative Problem Solving in Dynamic Environments. I In Proceedings of 10th National Conf. on Artificial Intelligence (AAAI-92), San Jose, California, USA, pp. 269-275.

[LeLR1996]   Lehman, J.; Laird, J.; Rosenbloom, P.: A gentle introduction to Soar, an architecture for human cognition. In: Invitation to Cognitive Science 4 (1996), MIT Press.

[MaDA2005]   Mascardi, V.; Demergasso, D.; Ancona, D.: Languages for Programming BDI-style Agents: an Overview. In: Corradini, F.; De Paoli, F.; Merelli, E.; Omicini, A. (Eds.): Proceedings of WOA 2005 dagli Oggetti agli Agenti Simulazione e Analisi Formale di Sistemi Complessi Pitagora Editrice Bologna. pp. 9-15.

[Mang2002]   Mangina, E.: Review of Software Products for Multi-Agent Systems. In: AgentLink, software report, 2002.

[Mil+1998]   Milojicic, D.; Breugst, M.; Busse, I.; Campbell, J.; Covaci, S.; Friedman, B.; Kosaka, K.; Lange, D.; Ono, K.; Oshima, M.; Tham, C.; Virdhagriswaran, S.; White, J.: MASIF: The OMG Mobile Agent System Interoperability Facility. In: Proceedings of the International Workshop on Mobile Agents (MA'98), 1998.

[Newe1990]   Newell, A.: Unified Theories of Cognition. Harvard University Press, 1990.

[Norl2004]   Norling, E.: Folk Psychology for Human Modelling: Extending the BDI Paradigm. In: Proceedings of in the Third International

Joint Conference on Autonomous Agents and Multiagent Systems (AAMAS 2004), 2004.

[OdPF2003]   Odell, J.; Parunak, H.; Fleischer, M.: The Role of Roles in Designing Effective Agent Organizations. In: Software Engineering for Large-Scale MAS. Springer, Heidelberg, 2003, pp. 27-38.

[OMG2000]   Object Management Group (OMG): Mobile Agent Facility Specification. http://www.omg.org/cgi-bin/doc?formal/2000-01-02, 2000.

[PaWi2004]   Padgham, L.; Winikoff, M.: Developing Intelligent Agent Systems: A Practical Guide. John Wiley & Sons, New York, 2004.

[PoBL2005a]   Pokahr, A.; Braubach, L.; Lamersdorf, W.: Jadex: A BDI Reasoning Engine. In: Bordini, R.; Dastani, M.; Dix, J.; El Fallah Seghrouchni, A. (Eds.): Programing Multi-Agent Systems. Kluwer Academic Publishers, 2005, pp. 149-174.

[PoBL2005b]   Pokahr, A.; Braubach, L.; Lamersdorf, W.: Agenten: Technologie für den Mainstream? In: it – Information Technology 5(2005), pp.300-307.

[PoCh2001]   Poslad, S.; Charlton, P.: Standardizing Agent Interoperability: The FIPA Approach. In: 9th ECCAI Advanced Course, ACAI 2001 and Agent Links 3rd European Agent Systems Summer School, EASSS 2001, Prague, Czech Republic. Springer, Heidelberg, 2001.

[RaGe1995]   Rao, A.; Georgeff, M.: BDI agents: From theory to practice. In: Proceedings of the 1st International Conference on Multi-Agent Systems (ICMAS-95). San Francisco, CA, USA, 1995, pp. 312-319.

[Rao1996]   Rao, A.: AgentSpeak(L): BDI Agents Speak Out in a Logical Computable Language. In: van der Velde, W.; Perram, J. (Eds.): Agents Breaking Away. Springer, Berlin, Heidelberg, New York, 1996.

[SBPL2004]   Sudeikat, J.; Braubach, L.; Pokahr, A.; Lamersdorf, W.: Evaluation of Agent-Oriented Software Methodologies – Examination of the Gap Between Modeling and Platform. In: Giorgini, P.; Müller, J. P.; Odell, J. (Eds.): Agent-Oriented Software Engineering V, Fifth International Workshop AOSE 2004. Springer Verlag, 2004, pp. 126-141.

[Sear1969]   Searle, J. R.: Speech Acts: an essay in the philosophy of language. Cambridge University Press, 1969.

[ShSt2001]   Shehory, O.; Sturm, A.: Evaluation of modeling techniques for agent-based systems. In: Proceedings of the fifth international conference on Autonomous agents (Agents 2001). ACM, Montreal, Canada, 2001, pp. 624-631.

[Tamb1997]   Tambe, M.: Towards Flexible Teamwork. In: Journal of Artificial Intelligence Research 7(1997), pp. 83-124.

[Weis2002]   Weiß, G.: Agent Orientation in Software Engineering. In: Knowledge Engineering Review 16(2002)4, pp. 349-373.

[WiCR2002]   Willmott, S.; Calisti, M.; Rollon, E.: Challenges in Large-Scale Open Agent Mediated Economies. In: Proceedings of AAMAS '02: Revised Papers from the Workshop on Agent Mediated Electronic Commerce on Agent-Mediated Electronic Commerce IV, Designing Mechanisms and Systems. Springer, Berlin, Heidelberg, New York, 2002.

[Wini2005]   Winikoff, M.: JACK Intelligent Agents: An Industrial Strength Platform. In: Bordini, R.; Dastani, M.; Dix, J.; El Fallah Seghrouchni, A. (Eds.): Programing Multi-Agent Systems. Kluwer Academic Publishers, 2005, pp.175-193.

[WoJe1995]   Wooldridge, M.; Jennings, N.: Intelligent Agents: Theory and Practice. In: The Knowledge Engineering Review 10(1995)2, pp. 115-152.

[WoJK2000]   Wooldridge, M.; Jennings, N.; Kinny, D.: The Gaia Methodology for Agent-Oriented Analysis and Design. In: Autonomous Agents and Multi-Agent Systems 3(2000)3, pp. 285-312.

8 From Testing to Theorem Proving

Ingo J. Timm, Thorsten Scholz
Universität Bremen, Technologie-Zentrum Informatik
{i.timm | scholz}@tzi.de

Hendrik Fürstenau
Universität Hohenheim, Wirtschaftsinformatik II
fuersten@uni-hohenheim.de

Abstract. Verification and validation of software systems are essential aspects in the software development life-cycle. However, verifying AI software is difficult as it suffers from non-determinism. In multiagent systems, this problem is increased by the known problems of verifying concurrent, distributed or object-oriented systems. On the basis of challenges for verification of multiagent systems, approaches for testing, runtime monitoring, static analysis, model checking, and theorem proving are discussed.

8.1 Introduction

Agent technology is often referred to as next generation's paradigm for analyzing, designing, and implementing large scale, adaptive, and intelligent software. Within this book, we are proposing that flexibility is the key benefit of agent technology. The natural distribution of agents as well as their complex interactions (e.g. communication protocols) are used as standard arguments to "prove" the benefit of agent technology. In contrast to these expectations, agent technology has not yet become a standard approach for building large scale, flexible, or intelligent software. Nowadays, major bottlenecks for the application of agent technology are arising from evaluating, validating, or even proving a multiagent system's behavior, mainly because of their nondeterministic characteristics [HuDe2004]. Furthermore, there is no standard for verification and assessing of agent technologies available for ensuring adequate quality of a system. To overcome the gap of a missing quality model for multiagent system a glance towards mainstream software quality looks promising. Thus a sound basis for further considerations about verification methods is set as agent-oriented software engineering can build upon the common state of the art of existing engineering paradigms.

The objective for quality management in software engineering is to reach predefined quality properties. Quality is characterized as the sum of all properties of a (software) product or an activity, which are related to the fulfillment of predefined requirements. Quality properties are those properties that enable the differentiation of entities either in qualitative or quantitative perspective. Software product quality can be defined as follows [Ried1997]:

- *Functionality* is a set of properties with respect to the existence of a set of functions that implement the specified requirements:
  - Adequacy indicates the existence or applicability of the software for the specified tasks,
  - Correctness is used for deciding if the results or effects of a software are correct,
  - Interoperability considers the applicability to interact with predefined systems,
  - Normative adequacy is used for estimation of satisfaction of application specific norms or commitments or juridical rules of the software,
  - Security deals with aspects of unauthorized access to the program or data.
- *Dependability* is the capability of the software to keep a performance portfolio in predefined conditions over a specified time period and is defined by the properties of:
  - Maturity is used for determining the frequency of failures or fault states,
  - Fault tolerance describes the appropriateness with respect to a predefined performance level of a system in situations where either unspecified access to interfaces or software failures occur,
  - Recovery is the possibility of a system to be recovered on a prior performance level including retrieval of data in adequate time.
- *Usability* is the property which is related to the effort required for using the software as well as an individual assessment of using the software by a predefined group of users.
- *Efficiency* is a set of properties which indicates the ratio between the performance level of software and the amount of used resources in predefined conditions.
- *Adaptability* is related to the necessary effort for performing given modifications (corrections, improvements, or adaptations)

Riedemann distinguishes two different types of activities within quality management: constructive and analytic activities [Ried1997]. The constructive quality management covers methods, languages, and tools, which ensure distinct properties of the emergent product, i.e., the constructive approach is pursued within analysis, design, and implementation. In analytic quality management activities are performed in order to diagnose the fulfillment level of the quality properties. They are subdivided into verification, validation and evaluation. Even so [HoMe1993] emphasize that misconceptions arise if terms are used in a different way like formal verification in artificial intelligence. Thus in the remainder we apply the term evaluation to express the determination of how far one or several agreed, prescribed, or expected features of an object are fulfilled in accordance with [HaMS1987]. By this evaluation is one specific type of analytic quality management activities.

In contrast to Riedemann, Menzies and Pecheur differentiate evaluation activities with respect to the required amount of expertise. They identify five approaches differing in strength of proof: testing, run-time monitoring, static analysis, model checking, and theorem proving (cf. Figure 1 following [MePe2004, p. 6]).

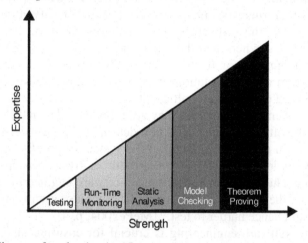

Figure 1. Classes of evaluation in AI

This spectrum of evaluation activities is headed by the most formal approach, theorem proving, which ensures correct system behavior resulting in a formal proof of correctness. Model checking verifies software according to its formal specification on the basis of model satisfaction. In contrast to static analysis, run-time monitoring analyses systems by their run-time behavior with specified input parameters resp. pre-defined conditions. Testing uses special programs that simulate input sequences and analyses the results with respect to the requirements.

In this chapter, we introduce evaluation from software as well as knowledge engineering perspective. Based on the insights gained in these fields, agent oriented software engineering methodologies are discussed with respect to quality assurance. One of the key challenges in the development of agent and multiagent systems lies in ensuring desired flexible behavior. However, flexible behavior is difficult to be proved or evaluated. After identifying the challenges for agent and multiagent evaluation, different approaches are introduced following the five evaluation classes: testing, runtime monitoring, static analysis, model checking, and theorem proving. The main difference to the previously mentioned approaches of evaluation lies in the necessity to specify explicit models for evaluation. Consequently, these approaches are in need of strong expert knowledge.

8.2 Software and Knowledge Engineering

In software engineering, specification and evaluation are crucial for development, maintenance, and extension of non-trivial software systems. The importance of a formal specification, e.g., algebraic specification, grows as the complexity of the software system increases. However, two types of problems may occur here: On the one hand, the specifications may be inconsistent, incomplete, or fuzzy. On the other hand, the implementation may suffer from misinterpretation of the specification as well as from errors. From an AI perspective, multiagent systems are considered as knowledge-based systems and therefore they are more complex and flexible than conventional software. Especially non-deterministic or heuristics algorithms may even prevent evaluation of the system or proof of correctness. However, knowledge-based systems are still software systems and approaches to evaluation from conventional software engineering still apply to them. Yet, "the cost of complexity is that complex systems are harder to understand and hence harder to test." [MePe2004, p. 4].

Testing in software engineering is crucial for ensuring quality of systems [Thal2002]. The main purpose is to identify errors within the algorithms, modules, or software. However, there is no possibility to recognize correctness [Dijk1969]. Testing can be classified with respect to the consideration of system's details as white-box, black-box, and grey-box testing. The traditional approaches to software engineering (e.g., the waterfall model) consider testing after implementation [Royc1970]. In white-box testing, the implementation is analyzed with insight of the source code. Modern software engineering approaches (e.g., RUP [Kruc2001] or extreme programming [BeAn2004]) address testing continuously within the implementation process. Furthermore, developers formulate test cases before or during implementation, and these test cases may be executed automatically on demand. This procedure is also known as "Test-driven Development" [Beck2002]. In test-driven development, part of the system's specification emerges from the collection of formally specified test cases. Unit tests are a realization of white-box tests, where test cases are designed with knowledge of the underlying algorithm [RaSt2005]. These test-cases are typically specified in the programming language used for coding. In black-box approaches, testing analyses the system's behavior on the basis of the input/output behavior only. For these tests, the actual implementation is disregarded, and only the interface specification is taken into account. Black-box testing is usually performed by testers who are not the programmers of the software. The black-box approach is a very general approach and can be applied successfully in any of the three model evaluation steps. The third class of testing, grey-box testing, weakens the assumption that the tester may not have any code insight in such a way that basic concepts of the implementation may be familiar to the tester. This approach is often used in context of agile programming, and may find application within the evaluation of the design and the implementation model.

Run-time monitoring is a procedure to analyze the behavior of a system in run-time. This approach is similar to logfile-profiling and involves more complex analysis methods, e.g., rule-based verification [BGHS2004]. However, commercial tools are available to support this process by knowledge-based systems. For example, Temporal Rover executes inserted code fragments based on complex conditions expressed in temporal logics [Drus2000]. In recent research, there are new approaches to identify problems of concurrency [HaRo2001]. An essential feature is the possibility to store the system's state when errors occur. The benefits of run-time monitoring lie in the efficient usage of system resources, restoring of system states, and scalability. Nevertheless, there is a tendency to analyze standard procedures only, such that exceptional paths stay unconsidered. The limited number of executions yields only uncertain results or even false negatives [MePe2004].

The static analysis concentrates on the structures within the source code without execution of the system. Usually, static analysis is part of the compilation of a system, i.e. compilers are evaluating the syntactical consistency of a system. Objects of the analysis are control flow and data flow. The methods are abstract interpretation, program slicing, and automated analysis of program patterns [NiNH1999]. One of the benefits of the approach is the possibility to find segments of code, which a) are guaranteed to be free from errors, b) are sure to cause errors, c) may cause errors, or d) are unreachable. Moreover, the static analysis can be automated completely, such that even the analysis of huge software systems becomes feasible. However, in these cases understanding, interpretation, and fixing the reported errors, may be troublesome. Additionally, the number of false positives increases with the complexity of the systems, e.g. Brat et al. reported this effect in analyzing the Martian rover software [Bra+2003]. Summarizing, static analysis may be used in early stages of software engineering to notify developers about errors or error potentials and to prevent time-consuming errors at run-time [MePe2004]. In consequence, static analysis is part of most recent integrated development environments.

Clarke and Emerson introduced model checking in the early 80ies for conventional programming paradigms [ClEm1981]. The basic idea of model checking is to verify a property of a system by exploring all of the systems reachable states. In the first applications, model checking was successfully used to analyze communication protocols in concurrent systems since these protocols have finite states [QuSi1981]. However, it devolved as a gold standard for verification of digital hardware. The starting point in model checking is the specification of two models: system model and property model [MePe2004]. In the system model, relevant features of the system are captured as a formal abstraction of the implementation with respect to the properties to be checked while the property model is a formal specification of the requirements the system is supposed to meet. This abstraction is performed by implementing state machines for representing system models. For the representation of system dynamics in the property modal temporal logics, e.g., CTL or LTL, are used [ClGP2000]. Model checking is used for deciding whether or not a system model is valid with respect to the requirements specified in the property model or to identify one counter example. There are two main approaches to model checking: forward state traversal, and backward state traversal. In forward state traversal the evolution of states is computed in a straight forward manner: from a starting state any states which can be computed by a post function are computed until an inconsistency is identified or any possible states have been explored. There is also a differentiation in forward state traversal model checking with respect to the computation of future states. In enumerative model checking any states are actually computed, while in symbolic model checking states are classified with respect to an equivalence relation. In opposite to forward state traversal, symbolic model checking using backward state traversal computes the predecessor states. Hanzinger et al. state that forward state traversal is advantageous over backward state traversal, since successor states are often easier to compute than predecessor states and optimizations to the algorithm, e.g., on-the-fly [GPVW1995] and partial-order [Pele1994] methods, can be incorporated more easily [HeKQ1998].

Theorem proving is used for formal verification of software systems. Here, a mathematical model of a computer program is generated to determine whether it satisfies desired properties. Rushby identifies the achievement of adequate automation as a core challenge to the use of theorem proving to verify parallel systems [Rush2000]. Furthermore, he concludes on the role of human experts in this process: *"Formal deduction by human-guided theorem proving (i.e., interactive proof checking) can, in principle, verify any correct design, but doing so may require unreasonable amounts of effort, time, or skill"* [Rush2000]. The main difference to other approaches is that theorem proving uses symbolic representations of values. In consequence, each operation, procedure, or function within the implementation is computed on a symbolic base. Thus, either the invocation is substituted by a symbolic deduction, or only current symbolic values or parameters are assigned. These are used in the invocation in the course of the calculation as the symbol of the operation, procedure, or function. For solving this problem, a theorem prover is required, which is able to compute any deductions and is proved to be correct. Nevertheless, it is impossible to provide an automatic and complete theorem prover with sufficient expressive power for a programming language [Ried1997]. In recent research, model checking and theorem proving are combined to overcome the shortcoming of these approaches. In proof systems for example, model checkers are used as decision procedures within larger proofs [OwRS1997], while in model checkers proof-based solvers find application in order to prune inaccessible paths in the symbolic state space [PaVi2004] [Mou+2004].

Quality assurance of *large* scale software systems developed in distributed teams of programmers is a challenging task. During development, usually three main models are generated: requirements model, design model, and implementation model. Following Thaller, these models have to be evaluated in order to ensure high quality software [Thal2002]. In most cases, the evaluation process is performed with specific methodologies for each of the models. In Figure 2, the process of the minimal evaluation within software engineering is illustrated.

The evaluation of the models is performed in opposite direction of their construction. In the first step, the implementation is evaluated for example by unit tests during the coding. If the implementation model appears to be correct, modules are integrated and their composite behavior is evaluated. After completion, the software is supposed to satisfy the specification of the design model. However, there may be inconsistencies between the design model and the requirements model. These are identified in the acceptance tests, which are the final stage of evaluation.

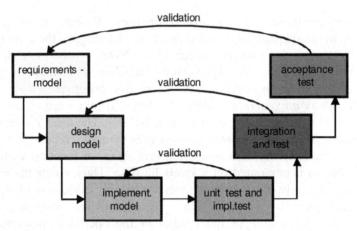

Figure 2. Minimal evaluation in software engineering

8.3 Challenges for Evaluation in Agent Oriented Software Engineering

In software engineering it is crucial to specify requirements formally. This enables the developer or customer to validate or even verify if the software system meets the requirements. In safety or security relevant applications, modern approaches in software engineering propose formal verifications for proving correctness of the system in any possible situation. If formal verification is not necessary or not possible (complexity issues), other evaluation methods are used for assuring software quality, i.e. a software system is tested whether or not it fulfils formal requirements in an explicitly specified range.

As mentioned in IV.5, formal approaches are widely used for agent design. Formal languages are mainly applied as internal or external specification languages. However, the corresponding correctness proofs are at most not terminating or decidable, like multi-modal logics or first-order logic. Although formalization is a key methodology in agent research, formal verification is limited to very specific aspects. In current applications, description logics are widely used for representing communication content such that formal prove of interaction behavior should be feasible.

Evaluation of intelligent agents is far more complex. In contrast to conventional software systems, intelligent agents are acting autonomously (cf. I.1), such that requirements have to be specified primarily as goals or context for agent behavior. Furthermore, intelligent agents should act with respect to the current situation in the environment as well as their internal state. The definition and specification of formal requirements as a basis of evaluation has to include complete state models of the environment and the agent. The main challenge for intelligent agent testing arises from the *individual agent's flexibility.*

However, common agent-oriented methodologies also contain a software engineering process, which in some cases like MaSE [DeWS2001] or Prometheus [PaWi2004] is closely related to object orientation. Similar to AOSE, early object oriented methodologies are not dealing with evaluation explicitly [Booc1994] or even claim for a natural reduction of evaluation efforts [Rum+1991]. However, later studies showed that the actual error rate in object oriented code is even higher than in conventional software [Hatt1998]. The increased modularization is accompanied by increased interdependencies between modules, which are mainly implicit. Methods or classes referring each other may cause procedural coupling or deadlocks [HaWi1994]. The use of objects or classes is not necessarily known at design or implementation time. Therefore, methods have to cope with universal inputs that cannot be predicted and tested sufficiently [SmRo1990]. The properties of an object are determining its state. Conventional testing requires testing in any possible state which is not feasible for complex objects [TuRo1993]. Further problems arise from the concept of information hiding or inheritance (esp. polymorphic inheritance). Summarizing, the coverage of testing of object-oriented code is considerable low in comparison to standard software [SnWi2002]. AOSE testing suffers from similar problems as testing of object oriented software, which can obviously be derived by analyzing the analogous complexity in terms of interaction or distribution of both paradigms.

Another dimension of complexity evolves from the key feature of multi-agent systems, *system flexibility,* realized by emergent effects, emergent properties or emergent organization (cf. I.2, [TTHW2001]). The aspect of emergence is often considered as non-deterministic behavior and increases the testing problem, as for a given input vector the output is unknown, e.g. non-deterministic. Non-determinism arises from runtime behavior leading to flexible solutions (emergent effect), constellation of agents and agent types which determines the properties of the system (emergent property), or interaction within the system which determines the dynamic relationship between agents (emergent organization). The aspects of emergence are not specified explicitly in advance, such that a major challenge for testing multiagent systems may be identified as testing a system with partially implicit specification. The evaluation of a system that contains properties that are not modeled is difficult and may result in an incomplete analysis.

Agents are assumed to be situated in an environment, reflect their internal states with respect to the sensed environment, and act in the environment. Furthermore, in multiagent systems there are multiple agents interacting with each other and the environment. Obviously, this causes concurrency problems. Evaluation of concurrent software is an enormous challenge in conventional software engineering [Ried1997]. However, even if concurrency is handled, non-deterministic environments may cause additional problems. These problems may increase if mobile agents are in question. The challenge for evaluation here is to cope with these difficulties by introducing a new dimension to the evaluation procedure. In concurrent system evaluation, Riedemann proposes explicit control on schedule, time, and invocation of methods [Ried1997].

In the following sections, we will discuss a brief overview on evaluation in current AOSE and possible approaches to meet these challenges, even if there is no gold standard for the problems.

8.4 Evaluation in Agent Oriented Software Engineering

The context of intelligent agents and multiagent system as discussed in the last section is challenging for evaluation. While there are many open problems identified in the agent community, there is still a comparably small amount of approaches dealing with validation and verification in AOSE. Current AOSE methodologies do not integrate evaluation in an adequate way. The state of the art surveys from Weiß & Jakob however emphasize the necessity of verification in real-world applications [WeJa 2005]. In concordance to this, Gómez-Sanz et al. reported that current research is focused on formal verification [GóGW2004]. The state of the art for validation and verification of multiagent systems is discussed in [GóGW2004] in detail. Summarizing, there are multiple approaches to formal verification, which are not integrated in AOSE methodologies. However, the Tropos methodology [MyKC2001] is integrating validation for multiagent systems.

Formal approaches to evaluation suffer from complexity with respect to expertise and computation possibly causing overextended efforts. However we are proposing to apply to AOSE any of the classes of evaluation (cf. IV.8.1): testing, run-time monitoring, static analysis, model checking, and theorem proving, depending on the field of application of the evaluation method. In the following, we are discussing possible approaches to each of these classes.

8.4.1 Testing

In current AOSE, there are no agent-specific approaches for testing. However, in software engineering there are multiple testing methods available which may be applied to the agent engineering process. One of the most prominent testing approaches in SE is the unit test, which finds application during the implementation of functions, methods, interfaces, or classes. The key benefit of the unit test approach is that tests may be applied repeatedly and automatically, i.e. every specified test is automatically performed after changes in the implementation of the unit, even if the changes are not directly connected to the test object. As discussed above, unit tests for object oriented implementation are broadly supported by tools and development environments. In consequence the unit test approach should be applied to the design and implementation of agents, since their structural implementation is carried out usually in an object oriented way.

However, specific aspects of knowledge representation and inference as well as interaction resp. communication in multiagent systems remain unconsidered. There are multiple ways to implement the knowledge base of an agent. In the case of implicit knowledge representation conventional unit test approaches find application as the knowledge is part of the code and architecture. In more sophisticated approaches, explicit knowledge approaches are used based mainly on logics, e.g., description logics (ontologies), or Prolog. These representation approaches should be verified using formal approaches like model checking or theorem proving. These formal approaches can be combined with conventional unit testing, for example to execute a description logic reasoner within object-oriented code.

Testing of interaction is a challenge for AOSE as interaction in multiagent systems is assumed to emerge at run-time. Nevertheless, especially in the design of open multiagent systems, boundaries for the agent behavior are defined for mandatory interactions. These boundaries are usually specified by valid sequences of messages, i.e. interaction protocols. Additionally, propositions on the content of the messages further specify the boundaries. Thus, testing of each agent should include the check of their compliance with these boundaries. In order to test the interaction behavior, it is necessary to establish a controlled test environment for the agent under test. In specialization of unit tests, an agent is considered as a unit. However, the test cases are more complex since they need to include the specifics of the agent environment and consider the variance of the expected results resp. sequence of the interaction. In consequence, testing requires the definition of allowed message sequences; here, we propose to use grammar as syntactical specification of valid sequences. Messages in an interaction are considered as words of a language and sequences as sentences. This allows for application of syntactic checkers like parsers for structural consistency. As mentioned before, in agent interaction the content of a message is also relevant to the behavior of an agent. Different solutions for this problem may be applied. On the one hand, simple approaches are matching content on equivalence, e.g., string comparison. On the other hand, a good compromise between computational complexity and problem adequacy is to use a matching algorithm based on the formal content representation, e.g., subsumption for description logics.

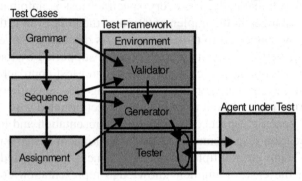

Figure 3. Interaction test framework

An interaction test framework that incorporates these aspects is shown in Figure 3. The controlled environment consists mainly of the tester that utilizes a test case generator for the generation and selection of appropriate test cases. This is done on the basis of a concrete assignment of a message which is evaluated by the validator component using the specified grammar and allowed sequences. This framework enables the test of agent interaction behavior in a controlled way without postponement of the test to the run-time of a multiagent system. The basic approach outlined here is detailed out in [Horm2006]. However, tool-supported approaches are required in order to establish the interaction tests in the AOSE process.

8.4.2 Runtime Monitoring

Analogous to testing, in runtime monitoring the basic idea is to establish a controlled environment and a control structure for running tests under specific configurable conditions. In contrast to testing, not specific units are considered, but the system behavior at run-time. In AOSE the challenge arises from analyzing a distributed and partially non-deterministic system. There are two main testing objectives for runtime monitoring: an agent or a multiagent system. For runtime analysis in AOSE we propose to consider grey- and black-box approaches only, since either in heterogeneous systems, internal structures or details of coding are hidden or the non-deterministic behavior of agent inferences is not suited for simple white-box approaches. In the following we will discuss two pragmatic approaches to runtime monitoring in AOSE: simulation covering both agent and multi-agent runtime monitoring, and certification management only for agent runtime monitoring. Even if there is no domain-independent tool support available for these approaches, the methodologies can be transferred to concrete engineering projects.

In simulation-based runtime monitoring, a controlled environment as well as a control structure are established. Additionally, a specific agent is introduced in the MAS, which is collecting and documenting information about the dynamic system behavior. To cope with the challenge of great variations and unforeseeable states of environment and MAS, a stochastic simulator is introduced that triggers the control unit and establishes varying conditions in a high number of sequential runs. By this, the test procedure becomes a stochastic process and statistical analysis of the system behavior is possible, which is considered as a grey-box test.

In this setting it is possible to evaluate the dynamic and adaptive behavior of the agents and the system. The duration of each simulated run of the system depends on the dynamic characteristics. For example, if the system is supposed to reach a balanced state with respect to the relevant parameters for the test within short time the duration of the simulated run should be short. Relevant parameters for the test procedure may be derived from the set of goals the agents are pursuing respectively the requirements for the MAS behavior.

Statistical analysis is focused on both aspects, the dynamical behavior looking at the parameter development over time (time series analysis) and the summarizing results (reached state at the end of the run or mean values). Special statistical methods fit to these tasks, for example t-test, Kruskal-Wallis-test, ANOVA (analysis of variance).

Timm developed a structured testing environment for runtime analysis of MAS and applied it to different application scenarios and domains [Timm2004a]. Especially interactive behavior of adaptive coordination in electronic market places was tested in the transport logistic domain. In this setting the agents (discourse agents see II.2; IV.5) had to adapt their communication behavior to varying heterogeneous marketplaces. II.2, Figure 8 shows the effect of the induced learning process measured on the evolving profit scale within 10 simulation runs. It is obvious, that the learning process was successful thus meeting the predefined requirement for the system [Timm2004b].

The benefit of a simulation approach for runtime monitoring is, that it is easy to extend the system for benchmarking purposes (cf. II.2, Figure 9. In consequence the monitoring, analysis, and interpretation of multiagent system behavior are enabled, i.e., an accumulation of individual agent's behavior is the basis for interpretation of the key performance indicators resp. quality properties. Algorithms in highly dynamic systems like multiagent systems may be compared and evaluated with respect to required goals as done in [Timm2004a], where more than 2.000 simulation runs consisting of over 1.44 mio. conversations in one scenario and more than 192.000 deliberation cycles in another scenario have been monitored, tested, and interpreted by statistical methods.

The approach discussed above finds practical application when architecture and implementation are known during test specification. However, testing agent behavior during run-time is also necessary, especially in open multiagent systems, where agents may join a society and offer services at any given time. Furthermore, some agents may be provided by third parties. Consequently, there is no knowledge about the internals or architecture available. Third party agents are coupled to the multiagent systems by providing a service description, e.g. following the FIPA standard by means of an entry in the directory facilitator. Certification management as introduced in [ScTS2005] addresses these issues by performing runtime monitoring automatically. The general idea here is to provide a means for the automatic certification of third party agents or web service capabilities.

In this approach a conceptual framework with the objective to support integrated identification, evaluation, and selection of services for reliable behavior of applications using distributed services is provided. On a conceptual level, three main components are mandatory:

- Capability management for the identification of the best-fitting service, i.e. services are identified on basis of their capabilities. The problem here is to match a given task to capabilities; in real-life applications this includes not only direct but also fuzzy mappings [ScTW2004].
- Certification management for the evaluation of the services, i.e. available services need to be evaluated according to the offered capabilities as well as other quality issues resulting in a quality measurement.
- Catalogue management for supporting the service retrieval process, i.e. it integrates capability and certification management for providing a unified service exploration interface for service consumers.

To implement this framework, these components have to be realized and integrated as agents. In Figure 4, the architecture for the agent system realizing an integrated catalogue, capability, and certification management is visualized. The agent for catalogue management is implementing the key-role and is responsible for managing service registration inquiries, invocation of the certification process, and providing an exploration interface to query on registered services. It utilizes the capability management for the match-making between consumer problems and service problem solving capabilities.

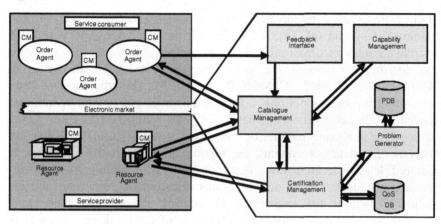

Figure 4. Certification management architecture

The agent for certification management certifies QoS of service providers with regard to provided capabilities using the capability management agent for inference on capabilities. The certification of problem solving capabilities is performed by putting the service to the test with a set of problems and a standard solution. Problems are domain specific, and are either taken from the problem database (PDB) or created dynamically by a problem generator agent. These agents need to be adapted for each domain in order to generate relevant problems for the certification process. The results from this service are evaluated according to a standard solution. On this basis a measure of completeness, which is the QoS for the provided capability, may be derived. The QoS are stored in a database (QoS DB), which is updated in regular intervals with re-certification of the services.

This approach may be easily adapted to domains where services and problems are well understood and formal performance measures exist. In [ScTS2005] the approach has been successfully applied to the search domain and in the IntaPS project (cf. II.2), it is transferred to the manufacturing domain.

The approach of certification management can be generalized to the analysis of multiagent systems. However, as there is no formal specification of services provided by the complete MAS, which differ from the services provided by the agents within the MAS, this generalization seems to be inadequate.

8.4.3 Static Analysis

Static analysis aims to identify structural errors in source code without running the system (cf. IV.8.2). In AOSE, the challenge is to cope with distributed and concurrent processes. *"Especially if it comes to concurrent and distributed processes, e.g., the multiagent systems, the advantages of Petri nets are obvious"* [CaMo2005, pp. 47-48]. The advantage of Petri nets is that it provides not only a formal semantics but also an operational semantics. Consequently, Petri nets have been established as a key methodology for analyzing parallel or concurrent systems [Ried1997]. For the analysis of concurrent systems, the identification of control structures is required, leading to an abstract Petri net model of a system. An early approach introduces control nets as a specialization of Petri nets, and includes a method for translation of control structure to these nets [Herz1976]. Doing so, a worst-case analysis of multitasking processes is established, the respective algorithm runs in polynomial time. This procedure enables the programmer to proof "deadlock-freeness" of a system.

During the last years, Petri nets have been applied successfully to the modeling of agents and multiagent systems. Hanachi et al. used Petri nets for the implementation of agent behavior [HaHS1999]. Here, cooperative nets as a specialization of Petri nets [Sibe1994] are transferred to agents. However, this model does not contain a notion for *multiagent* systems. Further approaches are focused on interaction behavior or multiagent system design. Holvoet addresses the interaction of agents without regard to multiagent systems and he additionally limits the agent's autonomy structurally [Holv1995]. Dealing with multiagent systems and interaction requires more expressiveness in the representation. Thus, Fernandez and Belo research on colored Petri nets to model multiagent system activity. The agents are represented as tokens in this approach [FeBe1998]. Especially Moldt et al. have applied (colored) Petri nets and nets-in-nets to various aspects of agent and multiagent systems [MoWi1997] [MoVa 2000] [MoRo2003]. In [KoMR2001] an integrated approach to modeling of multiagent systems, interaction, and agents is presented. The general approach is based on hierarchical Petri nets, the so called nets-in-nets or reference nets, i.e., nodes which are represented as nets or nets may be represented as nodes. Here, the autonomy of individual agents is preserved. Together with Braubach et al. he introduced a Petri net based modeling approach to goal-based agents [BPLM2004]. However, these approaches do not consider analysis of systems behavior. The formal properties are not completely validated yet; a PhD thesis for formal aspects, e.g., stability, completeness, and correctness is in progress [KoMR2001].

Concluding, Petri nets are especially suited for the analysis of dynamic aspects of interaction in multiagent systems in order to avoid deadlocks. However, the remaining shortcomings discussed in IV.8.2, especially the identification of false positives, are still relevant.

8.4.4 Model Checking

Model checking is a model-based approach that bases on a model of a system and verifies that a temporal logic formula holds for the model [HuDe2004]. Whilst axiomatic approaches are based on syntactic proof, model checking approaches lean onto the specification language's semantics [Wool1998].

Current work concerning the application of model checking approaches in multiagent systems can be divided into two major streams [KaLP2004]: in the first category, standard predicates are used to interpret the various intentional notions of multiagent systems. They are used together with standard model checking techniques based on temporal logics. [WFHP 2002] is a good example for this stream as they build their programming language MABLE for the automatic verification using the model checker SPIN [Holz1997]. In the other stream methods are developed that extend common model checking techniques by adding other operators.

According to [KaLP2004] model checking approaches in the domain of multiagent systems have severe limitations as many of the most interesting properties that have to be checked involve universal formulas which directly lead to a non-finite number of states. In this understanding common approaches are bounded in terms of time and knowledge which was overcome by [KaLP2004] in that they combined the works of unbounded model checking [McMi2002] with agent-relevant issues.

8.4.5 Theorem Proving

Theorem proving is a logic-based proof for checking that a set of formulas satisfies a goal via inferences [HuDe2004]. Therefore both the system and the description of the system's properties have to be available in a formal way. Thus it can only be applied to logic-based multiagent systems. [FiWo 1997] present a temporal belief logics approach to reason about ConcurrentMETATEM systems. Based on security, liveness and fairness-properties of the single agent and the system in total they prove the specification's fulfillment by static and temporal properties of the system to be.

Agent-based systems, in contrast to conventional programs, exhibit intelligent behavior because of their autonomous abilities enabled by their underlying knowledge-bases. As knowledge-bases consist of logical expressions, deriving faults from the verification and validation via theorem proving is a common task in agent-oriented development. [JaAb2001] suggest the analysis of single agent's knowledge-bases by deducing Petrinets from them. Thus they present a theoretical framework for the verification that can be applied to verify any agent-architecture that can be derived to their suggested one, in polynomial time.

On the contrary to the presented agent-based works, [WoCi2000] criticize that one focal problem in the development of agent-based systems concerning the usage of theorem proving has not been solved yet. According to them the problem lies in the connection between the knowledge-bases and the implementation language of the later system. They have to be integrated in a non-logic language which impedes the application of theorem proving methods. Another problem can be found in the formalization of the system's properties due to the fact that the question which properties an agent-based system provides in detail is not answered either.

8.5 Conclusion

Summing up, evaluation is essential for software engineering and due to the huge challenges in AOSE even more crucial. Approaches for evaluation from conventional software engineering however fail to meet the specific requirements and challenges of AOSE. Unfortunately, there is no gold standard to evaluation in MAS; one reason is the multitude and difference of existing MAS-approaches. But on the other hand even current state-of-the-art methodologies fail to integrate a sufficient evaluation philosophy. In consequence, tool support is insufficient. Formal methods introduced in agent research may overextend available resources and efforts. As there is a broad spectrum of domains for agent technology, different evaluation approaches are required taking into account the actual application and domain. Consequently, developers of MAS have to design, execute, and evaluate complex evaluation procedures by themselves.

The classification of evaluation methods (cf. IV.8.2) introduced by Menzies and Pecheur may be used for decision-support in this process to decide on the adequate general evaluation procedure [MePe2004]. On this basis, we discussed different approaches to evaluation with respect to the different classes. Keeping in mind that formal approaches are often of limited use to concrete software projects, we are convinced that especially testing in design time and run-time analysis are crucial to sophisticated development of real-world applications. These approaches have been successfully applied to development of multiagent systems in logistics in our research. However, these approaches are in need of methodology and tool support in order to fit into arbitrary real-world software development.

Further Reading

For further readings on evaluation, please refer to the comprehensive book of Riedemann [Ried1997]. Even, if this book is limited to the validation of conventional software, Riedemann has a strong focus on validation of concurrent and large scale software systems. In [MePe2004], an excellent survey on verification of AI systems is provided. Here, the focus lies mainly on formal verification.

References

[BGHS2004]   Barringer, H.; Goldberg, A.; Havelund, K.; Sen, K.: Rule-based runtime verfication. In: Fifth International Conference on Verfication, Model Checking and Abstract Interpretation (VMCAI 2004). Venice, Italy, 2004.

[Beck2002]   Beck, K.: Test Driven Development by Example. Addison-Wesley Professional, 2002.

[BeAn2004]   Beck, K.; Andres, C.:Extreme Programming Explained. Addison-Wesley Professional, 2004.

[Booc1994]   Booch, G.: Objektorientierte Analyse und Design. Addison-Wesley, Bonn, Paris, 1994.

[Bra+2003]   Brat, G.; Giannakopoulou, D.; Goldberg, A.; Havelund, K.; Lowry, M.; Pasareanu, C.; Venet, A.; Visser, W.: Experimental evaluation of verfication and validation tools on martian rover software. In: CMU/SEI Software Model Checking. Pittsburg, USA, 2003. Extended version to appear in Formal Methods in System Design.

[BPLM2004]   Braubach, L.; Pokahr, A.; Lamersdorf, W.; Moldt, D.: Goal Representation for BDI Agent Systems. In: Bordini, R. H.; Dastani, M.; Dix, J.; Fallah-Seghrouchni, A. E. (Eds.): Proceedings of the Second International Workshop on Programming Multiagent Systems: Languages and Tools. New York, pp. 9-20.

[CaMo2005]   Cabac, L.; Moldt, D.: Formal Semantics for AUML Agent Inter-action Protocols Diagrams. In: Odell, J.; Giorgini, P.; Müller, J. P. (Eds.): Agent-Oriented Software Engineering V. 5th International Workshop (AOSE 2004). Springer, Berlin, Heidelberg, New York, pp. 47-61.

[ClGP2000]   Clarke, E.; Grumberg, O.; Peled, D.: Model Checking. MIT Press, 2000.

[ClEm1981]   Clarke, E.; Emerson, E. M.: Synthesis of Synchronization Skeletons for Branching Time Temporal Logic. In: Logics of Programs, Workshop. Lecture Notes in Computer Science 131. Springer Verlag, New York, 1981.

[DeWS2001]   DeLoach, S. A.; Wood, M. F.; Sparkman, C. H.: Multiagent systems engineering. In: International Journal of Software Engineering and Knowledge Engineering 11(2001)3, pp. 231-258.

[Dijk1969]   Dijkstra, E. W.: The Programming Task Considered as an Intellectual Challenge. Transcription from Dijkstras EW 1969. Transcripted by McCarthy, D. C. Eindhoven, 1969.

[Drus2000]   Drusinky, D.: The Temporal Rover and the ATG Rover. In: SPIN Model Checking and Software Verification. Lecture Notes in Computer Science 1885. Springer, Berlin, Heidelberg, New York, 2000, pp. 323-330.

[EdBr2004]   Edmonds, B.; Bryson, J. J.: The Insufficiency of Formal Design Methods – the necessity of an experimental approach for the understanding and control of complex MAS. In: Proceedings of Autonomous Agents and Multi-Agent Systems (AAMAS 04). The Association for Computing Machinery, Inc., New York, USA, 2004, pp. 936-943.

[FeBe1998]   Fernandes, J.; Bello, O.: Modeling of Multi-agent System Activities through Colored Petri Nets: an Industrial Production System Case Study. In: Proceedings of the16 International Conference on Applied Informatics. Anaheim, CA, 1998, pp. 17-20.

[FiWo1997]   Fisher, M.; Wooldridge, M.: On the formal specification and verification of Multi-Agent Systems. In: International Journal of Cooperative Information Systems 6(1997)1, pp. 37-65.

[GPVW1995]   Gerth, R.; Peled, D.; Vardi, M. Y.; Wolper, P.: Simple on-the-fly automatic verification of linear temporal logic. In: Protocol Specification, Testing, and Verification: Chapman, 1995, pp. 3-18.

[GóGW2004]   Gómez-Sanz, J. J.; Geravis, M.-P.; Weiss, G.: A Survey on Agent-Oriented Software Engineering Research. In: Bergenti, F.; Gleizes, M.-P.; Zambonelli, F. (Eds.): Methodologies and Software Engineering for Agent Systems. Kluwer Academic Publishers, Boston, Dordrecht, London, 2004, pp. 33-64.

[HaWi1994]   Halladay, S.; Wiebel, M.: Object-oriented Software Engineering-Object Verfication. R&D Publications, Lawrence, 1994.

[Hatt1998]   Hatton, L.: Does OO Sync with How We Think? In: IEEE Software 15(1998)3, pp. 46-54.

[HaMS1987]   Hausen, H. L.; Müllerburg, M.; Schmidt, M: Über das Prüfen, Messen und Bewerten von Software (On the Examination, Measurement, and Assessment of Software). In: Informatik Spektrum 10(1987)3, pp. 123-144.

[HaHS1999]   Hanachi, C.; Hameurlain, N.; Sibertin-Blanc, C.: Mobile Agents Behaviours: From Declarative Specifications to Implementation. In: Proceedings of the 3rd Int. Workshop of Cooperative Information Agents (CIA' 99), Uppsala, Sweden. Springer-Verlag, Berlin, 1999, pp. 196-207.

[HaRo2001]   Havelund, K.; Rosu, G.: Monitoring Java programs with Java PathExplorer. In: First Workshop on Runtime Verfication (RV 2001). Electronic Notes in Theoretical Computer Science 55 (2001).

[HeKQ1998]   Henzinger, T. A.; Kupferman, O.; Qadeer, S.: From Pre-historic to Post-modern symbolic model checking. In: Proceedings of the 10th International Conference on Computer Aided Verification. Springer-Verlag, Berlin, 1998.

[Herz1976]   Herzog, O.: Zur Analyse der Kontrollstruktur von parallelen Programmen mit Hilfe von Petri-Netzen. Inform. Dissertation, Universität Dortmund, 1976.

[Holv1995]   Holvoet, T.: Agents and Petri Nets. In: Petri Net Newsletter 49 (1995), pp. 3-8.

[Holz1997]   Holzmann, G.: The Model Checker Spin. In: IEEE Transactions on Software Engineering 23(1995)5, pp. 279-295.

[HoMe1993]   Hoppe, T.; Mesegeur, P.: VVT Terminology: A Proposal. In: IEEE Expert 8(1993)3, pp. 48-55.

[Horm2006]   Hormann, A.: Testbasierte Spezifikation von Agenteninteraktionsverhalten. Diploma Thesis, University of Bremen, 2006.

[HuDe2004]   Huget, M. P.; Demazeau, Y.: Evaluating Multiagent Systems: A Record/Replay Approach. In: Proceedings of the IEEE/WIC/ACM International Conference on Intelligent Agent Technology (IAT04). IEEE Press, 2004.

[JaAb2001]   Jabbar, S.; Abbas, K. Z.: A generalized methodology and framework for the Validation and Verification of Multi-Agent Systems. In: Proceedings of the IEEE International Conference on Systems, Man, and Cybernetics. IEEE, Tucson, 2001.

[KaLP2004]   Kacprzak, M.; Lomuscio, A.; Penczek, W.: Verification of multiagent systems via unbounded model checking. In: Proceedings of the 3rd International Joint Conference on Autonomous Agents and Multiagentsystems (AAMAS 2004). IEEE Computer Society, New York, 2004.

[KoMR2001]   Köhler, M.; Moldt, D.; Rölke, D.: Modelling the Structure and Behaviour of Petri Net Agents. In: Proceedings of the 22nd International Conference on Application and Theory of Petri Nets. Springer-Verlag, London, UK, 2001, pp. 224-241.

[Kruc2001]   Kruchten, P.: The Rational Unified Process – Eine Einführung. 2nd ed., Addison Wesley, 2001.

[McMi2002]   McMillan, K. L.:Applying SAT methods in unbounded symbolic model checking. In: Proceedings of the 14th International Conference on Computer Aided Verification (CAV'02). Lecture Notes in Computer Science 2404. Springer-Verlag, 2002, pp. 250-264.

[MePe2004]   Menzies, T.; Pecheur, C.: Verification and Validation and Artificial Intelligence. In: Advances of Computers 65. Elsevier, 2005.

[MoRo2003]   Moldt, D.; Rölke, H.: Pattern Based Workflow Design Using Reference Nets. In: van der Aalst, W.; Arthur ter Hofstede, A.; Weske, M. (Eds.): Proceedings of International Conference on Business Process Management, Eindhoven, NL. Lecture Notes in Computer Science 2678. Springer-Verlag, Berlin, 2003, pp. 246-260.

[MoVa2000]   Moldt, D.; Valk, R.: Object Oriented Petri Nets in Business Process Modelling. In: Business Process Management, Models, Techniques, and Empirical Studies. Springer-Verlag, London, UK, 2000, pp. 254-273.

[MoWi1997]   Moldt, D.; Wienberg, F.: Multi-Agent-Systems Based on Coloured Petri Nets. In: ICATPN '97: Proceedings of the 18th International Conference on Application and Theory of Petri Nets. Springer-Verlag, London, UK, 1997, pp. 82-101.

[Mou+2004]   Moura, L.; Owre, S.; Ruess, H.; Rushby, J.; Shankar, N.; Sorea, M.; Tiwari, A.: SAL 2. In: Alur, R.; Peled, D. (Eds.): Computer-Aided Verification. Lecture Notes in Computer Science 3114. Springer Verlag, Boston, 2004, pp. 496-500.

[MyKC2001]   Mylopoulos, J.; Kolp, M.; Castro, J.: UML for Agent-Oriented Software Development: The Tropos Proposal. In: Gogolla, M.; Kobryn, C. (Eds.): Proceedings of the 4th International Conference on the Unified Modeling Language, Modeling Languages, Concepts, and Tools. Lecture Notes in Computer Sciences 2185. Springer-Verlag, Berlin, 2001, pp. 422-441.

[NiNH1999]   Nielson, F.; Nielson, H. R.; Hankin, C.: Principles of Program Analysis. Springer, Berlin, Heidelberg, New York, 1999.

[OwRS1997]   Owre, S.; Rushby, J.; Shankar, N.: Analyzing tabular and state-transition requirements specifications in PVS. NASA Contractor Report 201729. SRI International, 1997.

[PaWi2004]   Padgham, L.; Winikoff, M.: Developing intelligent agent systems: A practical guide. Wiley, 2004.

[PaVi2004]   Pasareanu, C. S.; Visser, W.: Verification of Java Programs Using Symbolic Execution and Invariant Generation. In: Graf, S.; Mounier, L. (Eds.): Model Checking Software. Lecture Notes in Computer Science 2989. Springer Verlag, Berlin, 2004.

[Pele1994]   Peled, D.: Combining partial order reductions with on-the-fly model-checking. In: CAV 94: Computer Aided Verification Lecture Notes in Computer Science 818. Springer, 1994, pp. 377-390.

[QuSi1981]   Queille, J. P. M.; Sifakis, J.: Specification and verification of concurrent systems in Cesar. In Proceedings of the 5th International Symposium on Programming. Lecture Notes in Computer Science 137. Springer, 1981, pp. 337-351.

[RaSt2005]   Rainsberger, J. B.; Stirling, S.: JUnit Recipies – Practical Methods for Programmer Testing. Manning Publications Co., 2005.

[Ried1997]   Riedemann, E. H.: Testmethoden für sequentielle und nebenläufige Software-Systeme. B.G. Teubner, Stuttgart, 1997.

[Royc1970]   Royce, W. W.: Managing the Development of Large Software systems. In: Proceedings of the IEEE Wescon, August 1970. TRW, pp. 1-9.

[Rum+1991]   Rumbaugh, J.; Blaha, M.; Premerlani, W.; Eddy, F.; Lorensen, W.: Object-Oriented Modelling and Design. Prentice Hall, Englewood Cliffs, New Jersey, 1991.

[Rush2000]   Rushby, J.: Theorem proving for verification. In: Cassez, F. (Ed.): Modelling and Verification of Parallel Processes: MoVEP 2k, Nantes, France, June 2000. Tutorial presented at MoVEP. Lecture Notes in Artificial Intelligence 2067. Springer, 2000.

[ScTS2005]   Scholz, T.; Timm, I. J.; Spittel, R.: An Agent Architecture for Ensuring Quality by Dynamic Capability Certification. In: Proceedings of the third conference on Multiagent System Technology (MATES 2005). Lecture Notes in Artificial Intelligence (LNAI) 3550. Springer Verlag, Berlin, 2005, pp. 130-140.

[ScTW2004]   Scholz, T.; Timm, I. J.; Woelk, P.-O.: Emerging Capabilities in Intelligent Agents for Flexible Production Control. In: Ueda, K.; Monostri, L.; Markus, A. (Eds.): Proceedings of the 5th International Workshop on Emergent Synthesis (IWES 2004). Budapest, 2004, pp. 99-105.

[Sibe1994]   Sibertin-Blanc, C.: Cooperative Nets. In: Proceedings of the 15th International Conference on Application and Theory of Petri Nets, Zaragoza, Spain. Springer-Verlag, Berlin, 1994, pp. 471-490.

[SmRo1990]   Smith, M.; Robson, D.: Object-Oriented Programming – The Problems of Validation. In: Proceedings of the International Conference on Software Maintenance. IEEE Computer Society Press, San Diego, 1990.

[SnWi2002]   Sneed, H. M.; Winter, M.: Testen objektorientierter Software. Hanser, München, Wien, 2002.

[Thal2002]   Thaller, G. E.: Software-Test – Verifikation und Validation 2. Verlag Heinz Heise GmbH & Co KG, Hannover, 2002.

[Timm2004a]   Timm, I. J: Dynamisches Konfliktmanagement als Verhaltenssteuerung Intelligenter Agenten. DISKI 283. infix, Köln, 2004.

[Timm2004b]   Timm, I. J: Selbstlernprozesse in der Agentenkommunikation. In: Florian, M.; Hillebrandt, F. (Eds.): Adaption und Lernen in und von Organisationen. VS Verlag für Sozialwissenschaften, Wiesbaden, pp. 103-127, to appear.

[TTHW2001]   Timm, I. J.; Tönshoff, H. K.; Herzog, O.; Woelk, P. O.: Synthesis and Adaption of Multiagent Communication Protocols in the Production Engineering Domain. In: Butala, P.; Ueda, K. (Eds.): Proceedings of the 3rd International Workshop on Emergent Synthesis (IWES '01). Bled, Slovenia, March 12-13, 2001, pp. 73-82.

[TuRo1993]   Turner, C.; Robson, D.: State-Based Testing of object-oriented Programs. In: Proceedings of the International Conference on Software Maintenance. IEEE Computer Society Press, Montreal, 1993.

[WeJa2005]   Weiß, G.; Jakob, R.: Agentenorientierte Softwareentwicklung. Springer, Berlin, Heidelberg, New York, 2005.

[Wool1998]   Wooldridge, M. J.: Agents and Software Engineering. In: Journal AI*IA Notizie 11(1998)3, pp. 31-37.

[WoCi2000]   Wooldridge, M. J.; Ciancarini, P.: Agent-Oriented Software Engineering: The State of the Art. In: Ciancarini, P.; Wooldridge, M. (Eds.): Agent-Oriented Software Engineering (AOSE 2000). Lecture Notes in Computer Science 1957. Springer-Verlag, Berlin, 2000.

[WFHP2002]   Wooldridge, M.; Fisher, M.; Huget, M. P.; Parsons, S.: Model checking multiagent systems with mable. In: Proceedings of the First International Conference on Autonomous Agents and Multiagent Systems (AAMAS-02). Bologna, Italy, 2002.

Part V
Evaluation

1 Benchmarking of Multiagent Systems

Anja Zöller, Franz Rothlauf, Torsten O. Paulussen, Armin Heinzl

Universität Mannheim, Lehrstuhl für ABWL und Wirtschaftsinformatik,
{zoeller I rothlauf I paulussen I heinzl}@uni-mannheim.de

Abstract. This chapter introduces benchmarking as a special form of evaluation and addresses problems and demands concerning the benchmarking of multiagent systems. It gives an overview of the evaluation concepts used in the German research program SPP 1083 for intelligent agents and realistic commercial application scenarios as well as examples for evaluation and benchmark studies for multiagent systems. The article provides basics for setting-up evaluation studies, regarding special concerns for the evaluation of multiagent systems. Moreover, the exemplary overview may serve as orientation for further evaluation and benchmarking of multiagent systems in realistic and commercial application scenarios.

1.1 Introduction

Before developers and users may utilize a new technology, such as multiagent systems, several questions need to be answered. For example: Under what circumstances is the use of a multiagent system be appropriate or superior to other systems? And, how can users adapt the system to their needs in the most efficient way? To answer these questions and to be able to make adequate decisions, it is necessary to execute evaluation studies and to provide the relevant information regarding the properties of multiagent systems.

Therefore, the aim of this article is to introduce the purpose of evaluation and the basic concepts for setting up evaluation studies. An important comparative form of evaluation is benchmarking. When setting up evaluation studies, special problems and demands concerning the benchmarking of multiagent systems have to be taken into account. Moreover, the concepts of these studies have to be adjusted to the field of application that is considered. Concerning realistic commercial application scenarios, different evaluation concepts have been developed within the German research program for intelligent agents and realistic commercial application scenarios, which provide an orientation for setting up respective evaluation and benchmark studies.

The chapter is structured as follows: the first part presents different aspects of evaluation and a basic model of evaluation. In the second part benchmarking is discussed in detail, addressing special issues concerning the assessment of multiagent systems. Finally, an overview of the evaluation concepts used in the German research program for intelligent agents and realistic commercial application scenarios is presented.

1.2 Evaluation and Benchmarking

The aim of evaluation is to show the applicability of an approach under certain constraints and to deliver decision support for choosing the best approach for a certain problem. One method to assess these questions is benchmarking, providing a comparative evaluation of different approaches. Depending on the questions under study, any kind of evaluation or benchmarking may have different forms and aspects [MaGr1993], as will be discussed in the next section.

However, regarding the evaluation of information systems in general, all these forms and aspects base on a collective model of evaluation which will be explained in Section 1.2.2.

1.2.1 Important Aspects of Evaluation

1.2.1.1 Point of Reference

Depending on the reference used, evaluation may be descriptive or comparative. Within descriptive evaluation, there is no other concrete system one refers to or compares with. Therefore, relevant performance measures are documented as information that may be used for comparison and evaluation of individual needs for a certain application. Descriptive evaluation is especially important in cases with a lack of adequate reference systems and may serve as reference for future comparative evaluation. Comparative evaluation may also be called benchmarking [HeHR 2004] [RePo1997]. It has a concrete reference system or value to compare with and is especially important when deciding between different approaches or assessing the applicability of two systems. The theoretic background of benchmarking will be discussed in more detail in Section 1.3 of this chapter.

1.2.1.2 Time

Depending on the point of time of the evaluation one can distinguish formative evaluation and summative evaluation [Scri1980]. Formative evaluation is done associated to system development for eliminating problems or enhancing the systems' performance. The information received from evaluation is reused for a redesign of the system. Therefore, evaluation may be used to trigger a feedback-loop until a satisfactory result is gained. In contrary, summative evaluation is done at the end of development to assess the quality of the system developed. This is also the point in time where statements can be given for what kinds of problems multiagent systems are applicable or under which circumstances they are superior to other approaches.

1.2.1.3 Method

Depending on the method of how the results of evaluation are received or measured, one can differentiate between laboratory or real world evaluation [Dix1998]. The advantage of elaborative evaluation is that several parameters may be considered and varied independently. Especially regarding formative evaluation, it may be done where the consequences of real-world tests would be too risky or too costly. Within the research program for multiagent systems in economic applications this is important as the systems directly influence economic performance. Moreover, in the medical domain they influence the treatment process of patients. One way of elaborative evaluation is simulation. As this is an important method within this context, it will be described and discussed in more detail in V.2.

1.2.1.4 Focus

The focus of evaluation distinguishes a micro and macro evaluation, depending on whether only parts of the system are examined, or whether the whole system is under evaluation [MaGr1993].

1.2.2 Model of Evaluation

Evaluating a multiagent system for use in a certain application corresponds to the evaluation of an information system, characterized by interplay of man, task and technology [Hein1993] [GaHa1997]. Men are task managers confronted with a certain task, a certain problem and may use technology, in form of hardware and software to solve the addressed problem.

For these man/task/technology systems a common model of evaluation exists, within each task is represented by its structural organization and the process organization of an institution. This implies that the technology system has to be evaluated within a certain field of application. The input of the evaluation model is a new information technology for which exists the need of evaluation. The output of the model is information to support decisions concerning the adoption of a new technology. The evaluation results may also influence changes of the technology system already in use as well as changes in the application-specific organization of man/task. The evaluation process is determined by a target system and a method of evaluation. The evaluation method determines not only the method but also techniques and tools for the process of evaluation. For example, laboratory studies simulating the task managers and the process organization for the fulfillment of an operational task may be executed. Finally within the evaluation process, the concrete values are measured according to the evaluation criteria of the target system (compare Figure 1).

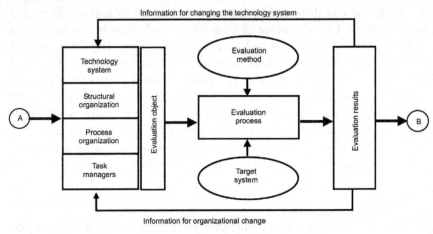

Figure 1. Evaluation model[1]

To evaluate how well a multiagent system is appropriate for a certain economic application by the use of benchmarking, it is necessary to compare procedures and processes and to take into account different methods and information systems for application support. The benchmark objects to be evaluated are different solution approaches or optimization methods and their transformation into agent software. In order to determine target val-

---

[1]   See [GaHa1997].

ues, economic as well as technical metrics may be of interest. As a benchmark an approach may be chosen that is either known to be optimal for the problem or an existing standard procedure. Depending on the benchmark design chosen, the applicability of a technique may be measured by how well it performs in comparison to the best known solution or how much it exceeds an existing standard.

To achieve this aim, simulation is important as it can generate measurements for evaluating the interaction of task and technology. However, the interaction of the system with human task managers can only be assessed in real-world tests as there too many parameters that may be partly hidden, and thus can not be considered in a simulation model.

1.3 Benchmarking of Multiagent Systems

As described in Section 1.2.1, benchmarking is a comparative method of evaluation. It identifies the applicability of certain evaluation objects for a specific task and performs a performance comparison [HeHR2004] [RePo1997]. Instead of normative or prognostic values, benchmarking uses comparative values as target values that serve as a point of reference for evaluating the applicability of an approach. Often, the comparison to the "best practices" or "best in class" is used [BeSc2004]. During the 1980s, the notion of benchmarking was formed by the benchmark study of the copier manufacturer Xerox in 1979 and the publications of Robert Camp [Camp1989] [Camp1995].

Benchmarking uses a systematic procedure for evaluation and contains the phases (1) planning of the measurement, (2) execution of the measurement and (3) interpretation of the measured results [HeHR2004]. Within the planning of the measurement, the objects that have to be evaluated are determined as well as relevant performance criteria. Benchmarks are either developed individually or standard benchmarks are used. During the execution of the measurement corresponding data is gathered or benchmark routines will be processed. In this case, subjective measurement techniques (e.g. interrogation, behavior analysis) and/or objective measurement techniques (e.g. management ratios) may be applied [HeMe 1998]. To interpret the measured results, these are combined in an application value and ranked. Within quantitative benchmarking, a positioning of the own performance towards an objective benchmark or a derived target value is done. In addition, a qualitative benchmarking should give design recommendations and enable the adoption of approaches, concepts or practices [Legn1999]. In addition to formerly reached values, benchmarks provide indices as to whether further improvements are necessary.

Benchmarking can be done in different fields with different aspects of evaluation (see Table 1).

Table 1. Benchmarking for business process management and for measurement of computer performance

	Business process management	Measurement of computer performance
Benchmark object	Business processes	Computer systems
Benchmark criteria	Operational target values: time, costs, quality	Throughput times
Benchmark method	Process analysis	Execution of benchmark routines
Benchmark (reference)	Qualitative	Quantitative

For example, in business process management economic target values such as time, cost and quality should be improved by process analysis. Based on guideline values or reference values of leading enterprises – so called benchmarks - it is the aim of benchmarking to gain a lasting improvement of their own efficiency. Therefore, the focus is not only on how good other enterprises are but also, on how they manage to generate this efficiency [TeRK2000] [ToMa1997]. Another example is the measurement of computer performance. Often throughput times are used as target values for a quantitative benchmarking. Benchmark routines are designed such that they represent a certain workload, or synthetic jobs are constructed that equal a forecasted workload [Hein2002] [HeHR2004].

The following subsections will discuss in more detail the design of benchmark studies. First, the general structure of adequate designs will be shown and subsequently, specific aspects concerning test scenarios as well as possible performance metrics and exemplary studies will be reviewed.

1.3.1 Study Design

The design of evaluation and benchmarking studies basically includes – even if varying terms are used – three elements or dimensions: (1) the problem scenarios to be tested on, (2) the target values or performance metrics of interest and (3) the solution methods to be benchmarked or evaluated. Similarly, Howe and Dahlman [HoDa2002] state that for comparative evaluation and benchmarking for obvious practical reasons it is necessary to run a subset of planners on a subset of problems.

Durfee [Durf2001], for example, gives a more detailed sample on relevant dimensions for evaluating multiagent systems. He considers the agent population that represents the parameters of the solution method, the task environment that represents the parameters of possible problem instances and the solution that represents different dimensions on target or performance values. The agent population may vary in quantity, heterogeneity and complexity. The task environment properties define the degree of interaction, of dynamics, and of distributivity. Finally, the solution properties may focus quality, robustness, overhead limitations, or combined dimensions.

Rardin and Uzsoy [RaUz2001] address the problem of how to develop evaluation designs for heuristic optimization methods. They notice that most evaluation designs of algorithms are designed for exact optimization methods. However, within heuristic optimization the quality of a solution often must be evaluated when there is no exact solution or even a credible estimate of one available. Therefore, they suggest some guidelines that should be addressed when evaluating or benchmarking heuristic optimization methods. To generate benchmarks, different problem instances (varying in problem size or number and nature of constraints) have to be tested with different approaches for discovering how changing problem characteristics affect performance. As significant questions they discuss the trade off between time needed for solution and quality of solution. They give advice on how to generate fair and meaningful benchmark studies when using different solution methods. Concerning performance measurement, they also give an overview on possible methods of how to generate reference values for evaluating the quality of a solution. Regarding small problem instances, exact solutions are available. In other cases, bounds or statistical estimations on optimal values as well as best known solutions may be applicable.

1.3.2 Test Scenarios

In order to perform a fair comparison of different planning approaches, the same problem scenarios and benchmark tests have to be used. There are two possibilities of choosing the benchmark tests, either by applying already existing standard problem scenarios, or developing new application-specific ones.

In the first case, one recalls testbeds documented in the literature and processes them with the mechanism that should be evaluated. Subsequently, the obtained results are compared with those given in the literature. For shop scheduling, for example, such benchmark scenarios can be found in [Tail1992] [DeMU1998] or concerning the traveling salesman problem in [BiRe1990]. The advantage of this approach is that there is a comparison to the current state of research and to the efficiency of approaches from other areas of research. However, the disadvantage of this method is the restriction to the existing standard benchmarks in the literature. A comparison is only possible for previously defined test scenarios and reported target values and performance criteria.

Furthermore, such scenarios do not necessarily represent the problems a multiagent system is designed and suitable for. Especially with respect to flexibility and multidimensional aspects, the existing scenarios are not dynamic enough or focus on a too restrictive and one-sided view of target values. For example, regarding shop scheduling problems, hardly any of the standard benchmarks include uncertainties and stochastic effects in their planning environments. Moreover, there is often one dominant target value for performance measurement such as makespan for shop scheduling problems.

Besides the use of existing benchmark instances it is possible to develop new and more adequate test scenarios. They are set up with characteristics that consider the properties of the system that should be evaluated. The advantage of this approach is the ability to construct benchmarks such that specific questions can be addressed, for example flexibility aspects when choosing problem scenarios with an adequate dynamic environment. However, the disadvantage of defining new benchmark instances is that no standard comparison values exist and benchmarks (in the sense of corresponding guides or comparison values) have to be derived separately. This means that other solution methods or heuristics have to be adapted to and tested on the new problem scenario, or performance data from real-world applications has to be collected as point of reference.

The problem of selecting and defining test scenarios has also been discussed by Howe and Dahlman [HoDa2002]. Regarding systematic evaluation and benchmarking, a lot of combinations of test scenarios and planners exist that might be examined. However, not all possible combinations can be executed and nor would it be meaningful if they were. Therefore, the question is which test problems, planners, and performance metrics shall be chosen. To enable an informed decision, it is necessary to know how variations within these three aspects influence the results. Therefore, Howe and Dahlman [HoDa2002] examine questions like: "May a general purpose planner be biased by a particular selection of problems? What is the effect of parameter settings? Are time cut-offs unfair?" and give guidelines based on tests of several assumptions. They show that the selection of the problem set influences the results of evaluation and state that the problem sets should be constructed to highlight the designers' expectations regarding superior performance for their planners or select the problem set randomly from the benchmark domain if the performance on a "general" problem should be evaluated.

Likewise, Hanks et al. [HaPC1993] state a trend towards controlled experimentation as evaluation method where researchers vary features of a system or features of an environment and measure the effect of these variations on aspects of system performance by using benchmarks (precisely defined standard tasks) and testbeds (challenging environments). They see the danger that scientific progress may focus only on the ability to better solve these abstract standard benchmarks instead of bringing progress for real problems. As benchmarks and testbeds are simplified scenarios to check certain characteristics the results or lessons learned may not be easily applicable to real problems. However, without simplifications it is not possible to carry out systematic experiments. In their paper, they discuss in detail this dilemma against the background of classical planning and agent architectures. As classical planning assumes a completely static planning environment with fully known information, they call for planning testbeds for agent architectures to consider exogenous events, complexity of the world, quality and cost of sensing and effecting, more relative measures of plan quality, multiple agents as well as a clean definition of the interface to the world, a well-defined model of time and support facilitating experimentation. However, the problem of choosing adequate test scenarios still remains and arises especially when deciding between a more real-world domain-dependent scenario and a simplified but generalizable scenario as well as between an easily parameterizable scenario and a more complex scenario.

1.3.3 Performance Metrics

After having defined the test scenarios under study, the next step is to determine performance metrics that represent relevant criteria for the evaluation of the systems' performance and the solution quality reached. These metrics have to be chosen depending on the questions and the target values under research.

Helsinger et al. [HLWZ2003] focus on the evaluation of large distributed multiagent systems and adequate tools and techniques for performance measurement. They distinguish the uses of performance measurement data by who is using it, by the information it imparts, and by the method used for its propagation. Moreover, they separate three abstraction levels for performance measurement: Firstly, the computer system level that measures the effect of a multiagent system on the computer system e.g. by CPU utilization, network throughput, memory consumption. Secondly, there are generic agent system level metrics, e.g. message traffic, task counts. Finally, on the highest level, there are application-specific measurements concerning data structures up to functional performance relative to the applications' requirements. These third level metrics are used to determine the overall system success.

The work of Brennan and O [BrO2000] gives an example for an evaluation study of a job shop scheduling problem experiencing the need for adaptability and flexibility when considering disturbances such as machine failures or uncertain processing times. They model a manufacturing system with job-agents, machine-agents, station-agents and a mediator agent. As benchmark scenario they use a shop floor layout problem taken out of [Cav+1999] that is proposed to serve as a benchmark platform for comparing multiagent system control systems. With this setup, four different coordination strategies, based on the contract-net protocol and on auction-based bidding are tested. The change in solution quality is evaluated while raising the number of jobs to be scheduled in situations with and without machine failure.

Korba and Song [KoSo2002] evaluate the scalability of security services in multiagent systems. They scale the system along the following four dimensions: number of agents on a given platform, number of agents across multiple platforms, size of data on which the agents are operating and diversity of agents. As performance metrics, they use CPU usage and memory requirement, number of searches per second, interaction time, and response time to a request. Based on their tests, they present results on how different designs affect performance and scalability and give advice which system should be used in security services for multiagent systems.

1.4 Benchmarking of Multiagent Systems in Realistic Commercial Application Scenarios

In the research program on intelligent agents and realistic commercial application scenarios of the German research community (DFG), a variety of different multiagent systems have been evaluated and benchmarked for different application scenarios.

The following section gives a summary of the evaluation concepts for multiagent systems in this research program. Based on the theoretical background of evaluation and benchmarking, we structure the overview of the different evaluation concepts using the following four criteria:

- evaluation objects,
- evaluation criteria,
- evaluation method, and
- evaluation reference.

1.4.1 Evaluation Objects

The evaluation objects concerning commercial applications are taken from the fields of manufacturing logistics (see Part II) and hospital logistics (see Part III). For each field, different objects are examined. For example, in manufacturing logistics, stock keeping processes (see II.3), shop floor control processes (see II.2), or supply chain management processes are focused on (see II.5). The field of hospital logistics monitors hospital patient scheduling (see III.4), the control of clinical processes (see III.5), or the trading of work plans according to the detection of the personnels' preference structures (see III.2).

Each evaluation object is examined regarding application scenarios that contain challenges like high dynamics, stochastic effects, or process disruptions. In the field of manufacturing logistics, for example, machine failures and changing customer orders are included. In hospital logistics, highly variable treatment times arise and changes in the amount of patient arrivals including most urgent emergency cases must be considered.

Concerning multiagent systems from a technological point of view, relevant evaluation objects are system properties, software engineering processes, multiagent system skills and agent communication properties. Other evaluation objects are the algorithmic proceeding, the robustness of services, multiagent simulations or software development methods.

1.4.2 Evaluation Criteria

Regarding the evaluation criteria of commercial applications in manufacturing logistics, aspects such as cost and time values are of interest in supply chain management processes, shop floor control, as well as in stock keeping processes (see II.2, II.3 and II.5). Throughput or cycle times are collective criteria in all of these applications. Moreover, many studies measure the costs of disturbances, monitoring costs (see II.5), resource utilization, delivery reliability, capital lockup, production costs (see II.2), adherence to delivery dates, and traceability of the control (see II.3).

In the domain of hospital logistics, the evaluation criteria for hospital patient scheduling, control of clinical processes, and the trading of work plans require a specific quality or efficiency of planning. Amongst others, corresponding criteria are average patient waiting times (see III.4), the reduction of stay time (see III.5), or utility based welfare criteria (see III.2). Further criteria are data security, user satisfaction, or flexibility aspects.

To assess the properties of the developed multiagent systems, the technological view of the systems focuses on evaluation criteria exemplary specifying the response time and reaction time of a multiagent system, the resource or memory consumption, the system availability, the scalability, or the correctness of algorithms. Concerning software development and engineering processes, the time of development or the quality of the resulting system and the development process (for example effectiveness, affordability,or use in practice) are measured.

1.4.3 Evaluation Method

In both application domains (manufacturing logistics and hospital logistics) simulation studies have been performed as evaluation methods (see Tables 2 and 3). The scenarios chosen were implemented as near as possible to a real-world situation, including the dynamic and stochastic effects associated with the evaluation objects. Analytic examinations or user studies are further methods that were used for evaluation. Moreover, empirical tests were used, especially for software development processes.

1.4.4 Evaluation Reference

In the commercial applications, the benchmarks are derived from alternative logistic planning systems or heuristics common to the respective field of application. Examples are analytic comparison values or actual values reached by the status quo of the planning (see Tables 2 and 3). A benchmark system for stock keeping processes was the PP/DS module of the SAP APO system. Other heuristics, for example, were priority rule-based approaches. The status quo of the planning could be represented by data collection from real-world organizations and applications.

Especially concerning technological evaluation, alternative algorithms, multiagent system platforms, simulation systems, or process models for software development were used as benchmark references.

Nevertheless, descriptive evaluation was important for assessing the developed multiagent systems. Often benchmark values on the real-world scenarios under study were not available and mostly had to be derived separately. Furthermore, there were certain questions to be investigated, that should give an insight into the properties of the developed approach. Questions concerning the performance of the system under scaling problem parameters (such as scaling size, disruptions, or stochastic effects) were assessed by descriptive evaluation.

1.4.5 Overview of Evaluation Concepts

This section gives a structured overview of the evaluation concepts explained in the previous sections (see Tables 2 and 3). For each project important application (top of line) and technological aspects (bottom of line) are listed.

Table 2. Overview of the evaluation concepts for manufacturing logistics

Proj.	Object	Criteria	Method	Reference
A4	SCM-processes Event-management	Costs (disruptions, monitoring) Times (throughput times)	Theoretic analysis model, simulation, industrial showcase	Existing monitoring systems
	System properties Use of semantic	1. E.g., response-time, resource-usage. 2. Effort (e.g. for integration)	Simulation, Qualitative evaluation methods	Descriptive evaluation
IntaPS	Shop floor control	Ratio systems (e.g. lead time, resource performance)	Simulation	Analytic comparison values; Existing systems (SAP/R3)
	Agent control, communication, black box testing, capability management	Correctness of problem solutions and algorithms	Simulation, statistic evaluation, unit-tests	Alternative algorithms
KRASH	Stock keeping in job shop manufacturing	Throughput time, adherence to delivery dates	Simulation	PP/DS module of the SAP APO
	Robustness services	QoS: throughput, response time, frequency of conflicts	Simulation	Standard MAS platforms without robustness services
ControMAS	Rule- and norm-based control	1. Throughput time, adherence to delivery dates, 2. Traceability	1. Simulation 2. User study	1. PP/DS module of the SAP APO 2. Descriptive evaluation
	1. Rule- and norm based agent architecture 2. Integration approach	1. a. Response time b. Traceability 2. Throughput	1. a. Simulation b. User study 2. Simulation	1. a. Imperative agent architectures 1. b., 2. Descriptive evaluation

Table 3. Overview of the evaluation concepts for hospital logistics

Proj.	Object	Criteria	Method	Reference
ADAPT II	Clinical processes	Planning quality, utilization, stay-time	Simulation	Current situation
	1. MAS-simulation 2. Process models 3. MAS-assistance system	1. Modeling time, number of agents 2. Development time, quality 3. Re-/planning quality	1. Development projects 2. Analytical/empirical comparisons 3. Simulation	1. Competing systems 2. Alternative models 3. Situation without assistance system
MedPAge	Hospital patient scheduling	Planning quality, flexibility	Practical simulation	"Status quo" and "state-of-the-art" planning
	Software engineering processes	1. SE-tasks 2. Platform properties	1. SE-projects 2. Measurements of test applications	Alternative platforms
	1. Detection of preference structures 2. Negotiation of working plans	1. Contentment, analysis accuracy, learning module 2. Technologic, economic efficiency; overall welfare	1. Use in practice, interviews, simulation 2. Simulation	1. Use in practice (SPSS, TiCon) 2. Different algorithms
Policy Agents	1. Preference structure 2. OP-planning 3. Team building 4. Schedules 5. Heuristics	1./2. User interface, 3. Constraint-/Preference satisfaction, 4. Quality, 5. Complexity	1./2. Use in practice, 2./4. Simulation, 5. Complexity analysis, simulation	1./2. Adaptivity, usability, 3. Overall weights, 4. Performance ratios, 5. Running time

1.5 Conclusion

Experimental evaluation and benchmarking are meaningful instruments to assess multiagent systems and help to make research progress understandable and clear. The article has provided a foundation for setting up evaluation studies, has introduced different aspects of evaluation, and presented a generic model of evaluation.

Benchmarking has been discussed separately as a special form of evaluation. Furthermore, certain problems and demands concerning the benchmarking of multiagent systems have been addressed. When determining evaluation objects and selecting adequate test scenarios, there is a trade off between standard benchmarks and individual benchmarks. Standardized simplified benchmark scenarios allow generalizable conclusions providing common comparison values from different research areas. However, they are less informative for making conclusions on real application problems. Individual benchmarks may include more realistic assumptions on stochastic and dynamic environments thus providing more meaningful conclusions to the applicability of multiagent systems in real-world problems. Yet, these scenarios generate results that are more difficult to generalize and they are only directly comparable with individual and separately derived benchmarks.

Regarding the evaluation of multiagent systems in realistic fields of application, the work of the German research program for intelligent agents and realistic commercial application scenarios was presented. The different evaluation concepts that have been developed were discussed and structured. In common, these concepts had the aim of assessing the applicability of a multiagent system when considering influences from stochastic effects and dynamic environments. The overview of the respective evaluation concepts may serve as a direction for setting up further evaluation and benchmarking studies for multiagent systems in corresponding fields of applications.

References

[BeSc2004]   Becker, J.; Schütte, R.: Handels-Informationssysteme. 2. Auflage, Frankfurt am Main, 2004.
[BiRe1990]   Bixby, B.; Reinelt, G.: TSPLIB, Softwarelibrary. Rice University, Houston, Texas, 1990.
[BrO2000]   Brennan, R. W.; O, W.: A simulation test-bed to evaluate multiagent control of manufacturing systems. In: Joines, J. A.; Bar-

ton, R. R.; Kang, K.; Fishwick, P. A. (Eds.): Proceedings of the 2000 Winter Simulation Conference, 2000.

[Camp1989]   Camp, R. C.: Benchmarking – The Search for Industry Best Practices that Lead to Superior Performance. Quality Press, Milwaukee, 1989.

[Camp1995]   Camp, R. C.: Business Process Benchmarking. ASQC Press, Milwaukee, 1995.

[Cav+1999]   Cavalieri, S.; Bongaerts, L.; Taisch, M.; Macchi, M.; Wyns, J.: A benchmark framework for manufacturing control. In: Proceedings of the Second International Workshop on Intelligent Manufacturing Systems. Leuven, 1999, pp. 22-24.

[DeMU1998]   Demirkol, E.; Mehta, S.; Uzsoy, R.: Benchmarks for shop scheduling problems. European Journal of Operational Research 109(1998), pp. 137-141.

[Dix1998]   Dix, A. J.: Human-computer interaction. 2nd ed., Prentice Hall, Paramus, 1998.

[Durf2001]   Durfee, E. H.: Scaling Up Agent Coordination Strategies. In: Computer 34(2001)7, pp. 39-46.

[GaHa1997]   Gappmair, M.; Häntschel, I.: Die Evaluierung von Workflow-Management-Systemen in Laborstudien. In: Grün, O.; Heinrich, L. J.: Wirtschaftsinformatik – Ergebnisse Empirischer Forschung. Berlin et al., 1997, pp. 63-77.

[HaPC1993]   Hanks, S.; Pollack, M. E.; Cohen, P. R.: Benchmarks, testbeds, controlled experimentation, and the design of agent architectures. In: AI Magazine 14(1993)4, pp. 17-42.

[HeHR2004]   Heinrich, L. J.; Heinzl, A.; Roithmayr, F.: Wirtschaftsinformatik-Lexikon. München, Wien, 2004.

[Hein1993]   Heinrich, L. J.: Wirtschaftsinformatik – Einführung und Grundlegung. München, Wien, 1993.

[Hein2002]   Heinrich, L. J.: Informationsmanagement. 7. Auflage, München, Wien, 2002.

[HeMe1998]   Herzwurm, G.; Mellis, W.: Benchmarking der Kundenorientierung in Softwareunternehmen. In: BFuP – Betriebswirtschaftliche Forschung und Praxis 4(1998), pp. 438-450.

[HLWZ2003]   Helsinger, A.; Lazarus, R.; Wright, W.; Zinky, J.: Tools and techniques for performance measurement of large distributed multiagent systems. In: Proceedings of the second international joint conference on Autonomous agents and multiagent systems. Melbourne, Australia, 2003, pp. 843-850.

[HoDa2002]   Howe, A. E.; Dahlman, E.: A Critical Assessment of Benchmark Comparison in Planning. In: Journal of Artificial Intelligence Research 17(2002), pp. 1-33.

[KoSo2002]   Korba, L.; Song, R.: The Scalability of a Multi-Agent System in Security Services. In: NRC/ERB-1098, NRC 44952, 2002.

[Legn1999]   Legner, C.: Benchmarking informationssystem-gestützter Geschäftsprozesse: Methode und Anwendung. Wiesbaden, 1999.

[LNNW1998]   Lee, L. C.; Nwana, H. S.; Ndumu, D. T.; De Wilde, P.: The Stability, Scalability and Performance of Multi-agent systems. In: BT Technology Journal 16(1998)3, pp 94-103.

[MaGr1993]   Marc, M. A.; Greer, J. E.: Evaluation methodologies for intelligent tutoring systems. In: Journal of Artificial Intelligence in Education 4(1993)3.

[RaUz2001]   Rardin, R. L.; Uzsoy, R.: Experimental evaluation of heuristic optimization algorithms: A tutorial. In: Journal of Heuristics 7 (2001)3, pp. 261-304.

[RePo1997]   Rechenberg, P.; Pomberger, G.: Informatik-Handbuch. München, Wien, 1997.

[Scri1980]   Scriven, M.: The Logic of Evaluation. California, 1980.

[Tail1992]   Taillard, E.: Benchmarks for basic scheduling problems. In: European Journal of Operations Research 64(1992), pp 278-285.

[TeRK2000]   Teubner, A.; Rentmeister, J.; Klein, S.: IT-Fitness für das 21. Jahrhundert – Konzeption eines Evaluationsinstruments. In: Heinrich, L. J.; Häntschel, I. (Eds.): Evaluation und Evaluationsforschung in der Wirtschaftsinformatik. München, Wien, 2000.

[ToMa1997]   Töpfer, A.; Mann, A.: Benchmarking: Lernen von den Besten. In: Töpfer, A. (Ed.): Benchmarking – Der Weg zur Best Practice. Springer, Belin et al., 1997, pp. 31-75.

2 Simulation

Rainer Herrler, Franziska Klügl

Universität Würzburg, Lehrstuhl für Künstliche Intelligenz und Angewandte Informatik, {herrler | kluegl}@informatik.uni-wuerzburg.de

Abstract. Multiagent simulation applies the concepts of multiagent systems to simulation. It is a perfect means to represent and examine emergent effects in distributed systems. Multiagent simulation models may be used to gain insights into system interdependencies, to make predictions and also for testing software systems. This chapter introduces the basic concepts and tools for agent based simulation and shows the possibilities of agent based simulation by means of the particular tool SeSAm. Extensions are presented that allow using multi agent simulation as an evaluation testbed for agent based application systems.

2.1 Introduction

The development of agent-based software is a quite complex task as it involves difficulties like for example dealing with sophisticated software architectures, thinking about control and synchronization of concurrent and interrelated processes, handling distributed control and data and dealing with the unpredictability of interaction patterns [Jenn2000]. Formal, automatic verification and validation of distributed software is a big issue in research, but it's yet far from practical relevance. Therefore, extensive testing and evaluation is very crucial to ensure software quality.

Very often, software tests cannot be performed in the actual deployment environment for various reasons. One reason might be security issues. In a life-critical environment it is too risky to apply immature and uncertified software. Even if we could apply it, we would probably not be able to test it under extreme conditions. Costs are also an important issue: Testing in the real environment can be very expensive and time-consuming. Especially multiagent applications require big and distributed testing environments involving many people and physical devices. Sometimes the application environment and hardware might not even exist at the time the software is developed. Consider for example the introduction of highway toll in different European countries. Usually it is not feasible to wait until the final environment is available. Tests have to be performed as early as possible.

In software projects like characterized above, using simulation for generating a virtual environment can be a suitable means for testing and evaluation. Simulation provides the following options:

- Simulation and especially multiagent simulation helps understanding multiagent systems in the context of a specific environment. Thus, one learns about appropriate architectures on the agent and agent system level and properties of protocols. These things can be examined in a particular environmental setting. The knowledge gained can be used when designing and implementing the software agents.
- Simulation studies can prove the applicability and potential success of a particular approach before much effort is spent in realizing the actual system. The simulation can show how different environmental parameters the system. Simulation studies often are a convincing proof of concept.
- Moreover, agent based simulation models can be used as testbeds for the actual multiagent system or application. In this case a simulated environment is connected to an agent based application. A realistic stream of external events is provided by the simulation environment to test the correctness of the software agents. Additionally, dynamic effects and interdependencies between actors and software agents can be examined.

As shown, simulation is very useful for understanding, designing and especially testing software. It can be applied in different phases of the software engineering process. Regarding the development of multiagent systems especially agent-based simulation seems appropriate, because both techniques are based on the same paradigm. This chapter starts with an introduction to the principles of simulation (Section 2.2) and agent based simulation (Section 2.3). Following a general overview on agent based simulation tools is given (Section 2.4) and one particular system for modeling and simulation is presented in detail (Section 2.5). Whereas these tools are not especially dedicated to test software, Section 2.6 presents extensions, which support the usage of the simulation tool as a software testbed. Finally a summary on the possibilities of agent based simulation is given in Section 2.7.

2.2 Simulation – Theory, Approaches and Definitions

Reviewing the relevant literature, quite a bunch of paradigms and techniques for simulation and modeling can be found: Queuing nets, Petri-nets, discrete event (based) simulation, object oriented simulation, simulation based on cellular automata, macro and micro-simulation, distributed simulation, etc. Agent based simulation, agent-oriented simulation, even agent-directed simulation are nowadays added to this by no way complete list.

Computer simulation in general means "the execution of experiments with a model of a dynamic system". This model is usually simpler than the original system but has to capture the essential characteristics. During simulation the behavior of the model can be observed in the course of time and resulting output variables are evaluated to make statements about the original system. E.g. it might be examined how the system behaves when configured with a particular set of input values [Zeig1984] [Fish1995]. In this case we talk about prediction models. Another aim of simulation models – especially interesting in scientific application domains – is to prove hypotheses and to gain insight into interdependencies of a system, which is not completely known by now. Such models are called explanation models.

A simulation model typically consists of simulation entities and transition rules. Depending on the simulation paradigm entities might be variables, objects, cells or agents. Transformation rules describe how the entities and thus the system are changing over time. The set of model entities and transition rules might be described by a lot of different representations. The most suitable representation is depending on the aim of the simulation study and the necessary level of granularity: Queuing nets are useful to describe and simulate performance of queuing processes. More general process descriptions can be executed by process simulation tools (like eM-Plant). Macro models typically consist of differential equations that connect the variables of the model. The rules of a cellular automaton describe how cell states change over time. Finally a convenient representation of agent behavior consists of activity graphs or rule sets.

Another basic criterion of simulation is the time advance and the way the virtual simulation time is treated. Basically, there are the following options: Simulation time might be *continuous*, discrete *time-stepped* or discrete *event driven* [MoDa2000] [GiTr1999]. In continuous simulation the state of variables can change with arbitrary small time steps. The mathematical base of these continuous models are (nonlinear) systems of differential equations, which can be solved by numeric integration. Discrete simulation on the other hand allows discrete time advance as well as just discrete changes of state variables. Discrete simulation can be either time-stepped or event driven. In time-stepped simulations the simulated time advances with an a priori fixed time advance interval. The constant time advance is advantageous for on-line observation. Modeling is quite intuitive, but simulation time might be wasted if many simulation entities are inactive during a long period of time. In contrast event driven simulation allows a flexible time advance based on the occurrence of events. Entities are only active when they receive an event; after the agent has finished (re-)acting, the current time value is set to the time of the next event. The major drawbacks are that modeling also comprises the intricate handling of an event queue and that on-line observation is rather difficult as time may "jump". In practice event based simulation can be found more in engineering applications, whereas time-stepped simulation is more common in the simulation of biological or physical systems.

Another classification of simulations is based on the distinction between macro simulation and micro simulation. Macro simulation treats the modeled system as one entity with several variables describing its properties. Micro simulation models consist of a set of active objects with distinct local behavior, which act together to produce the overall behavior. Macro models in general are more abstract and allow observations just on the global system level. Thus, they are not appropriate for several simulation purposes, e.g. for the analysis of self-organization or emergence. A famous example of microscopic simulation and demonstration of emergent behavior is the flocking model [Reyn1987]. A good application domain for demonstrating the differences between macroscopic and microscopic simulation is traffic simulation. Macro simulations compute numbers of entities in the network (or in parts of the network) and update these numbers during simulation, micro simulations actually are based on the local route decisions or movement of the entities. Agent-based approaches are highly developed in this domain [KlBO2005].

Besides the model design and execution, a very essential part of the overall simulation study is making experiments and analyzing the results. Simulation models provide input variables for the configuration of the initial scenario, runtime or status variables and output variables (evaluation parameters). An experiment determines input and evaluation parameter of a model and comprises several simulation runs with different initial configuration. Another important term in this context is the "experimental frame" [Zeig1984]. Regarding a certain input variable there may be just a certain interval that produces valid results in the overall model. This set of useful values is called the "experimental frame".

Models may contain stochastic and interactive elements; modeling based on probability distributions is favorably if the distribution is known and modeling detailed cause and effect-relations is too complicated. Interactive elements might be user interfaces to control parameters or agents. If stochastic or interactive elements are used, simulation runs are not deterministic. Therefore it is advisable in this case to make several simulation runs to get meaningful results. During a simulation run evaluation parameters can be recorded and the results can be visualized in different ways. Whereas series chart are useful to show parameter values in the course of time, block charts show cumulated results (e.g. average values) at the end of the simulation. A simulation *experiment* usually involves several simulation runs with different initial values.

2.3 Agent Based Simulation

Agent based simulation or multiagent simulation applies the concept of multi agent systems to simulation. A respective model consists of simulated agents and a simulated environment. Simulated agents might represent concrete individuals or abstract active entities of an original system. The agents act and interact with their environment according to their behavior and emergent phenomena and dynamic interdependencies of agents can be examined. Agents are typically defined by state and attributes and a set of behavior rules, which determines how they change their state and the environment [Klue2001] [KOPD2002].

The agent based simulation paradigm is very similar to other simulation paradigms like object oriented simulation, individual based simulation or cellular automata. The most relevant differentiation criterion from object oriented simulation is that simulation entities are active autonomous components, which is not necessarily the case in object oriented simulation. Thus from the modelers point of view simulated agents are on a higher abstraction level than simulated objects. In pure object oriented simulations there are central transition rules or programs that change the (passive) simulation objects (like e.g. in Netlogo and Starlogo). In some cases we also find distributed behavioral rules but the autonomy of the agents is restricted. Thus, an exact classification is often difficult and there is a continuous transition from object-oriented to agent-based simulation.

Compared with the concept of individual based simulations - agent based simulations do not limit their scope to individuals. They may deal with abstract entities like groups or other organizational units as well. Sometimes, heterogeneity as related to agents is mentioned as a core characteristic of individual based simulation. However, typical agent-based simulations are based on concepts of Artificial Intelligence, like rules or planning, whereas individual-based simulation are based on mathematical formalisms like Logit models or formalisms of Rational Choice, etc [Bier1998]. These formalisms are usually not suitable for agents, because they are not able to represent the locally restricted perception of agents. But there are extensions of these formalisms (e.g. Bounded Rational Choice) that may also be used for agent modeling. Summarized, agent-based simulation can be seen as a more general version of individual-based simulation.

Cellular automata are a very restricted kind of micro simulation. They are based on a special kind of spatial representation (a grid) and contain very homogeneous entities (the cells). The uniform transition rules of an automaton cell are very restricted. A cell may just change its own state in dependence of the state of its neighbors. There is no environment or other model entities beyond the cells. Cellular automata can be realized as simple agent based models as well.

According to the criteria given in Section 2.2 we can characterize multi-agent simulation as follows: The entities in agent-based Simulation are active autonomous entities called agents. Transition rules can be derived from the behavior descriptions of these agents. Time advance in computer based multi agent simulations is necessarily discrete as interaction happens in distinct points of time, but both alternatives are common – event based as well as time driven simulations. Typically agent based simulations are micro simulations with a lot of single agents and emergent effects. Therefore, agent models have to be validated carefully. If properly used, they can provide valuable insight to complex systems.

Besides knowing about the different forms of simulation paradigms it is also important to have criteria to select the appropriate simulation method for the purposes of his modeling effort. The following domain properties argue for agent based simulation:

- *Distributed environment*: Spatially or organizationally distributed entities with local perception and action are subject to the simulation.
- *Active entities*: The simulated entities are actively changing their state and their environment. Autonomy of agents is relevant within the simulated system.
- *Process Interdependency*: Processes and behaviors of agents influence each other. Isolated process simulation is not possible. This argument is even more compelling when there are flexible interaction with a priori unknown partners.
- *Individual properties of the agents*: The heterogeneous properties of the individual agent are of importance. Dynamic interdependencies can not just be explained by using average attribute values. Feedback loops can not be computed in advance.
- *Micro model knowledge*: Detailed knowledge about the behavior and configuration of the model entities is available.

For these reasons multiagent simulation became very popular in artificial life science and biology [KPRT1998], sociology [MaFT2002] or traffic science [KlBO2005].

2.4 Tools for Agent Based Simulation

Creating simulation models from scratch is very effortful, gathering and analyzing simulation data them as well. Thus, tool support for the process of implementing executable models and performing simulation runs is nearly inevitable. A couple of very different tools for multiagent simulation have been developed over the last years. In a short review some popular tools for agent based simulation are presented in this section.

AgentSheets (http://www.agentsheets.com) has already a long tradition (since 1989). It is a completely visual development kit for multi agent simulations and addresses developers with little knowledge about programming. It allows realizing parallel and interactive agent based models. Agents are objects that can be programmed by the user. He can visually construct rules and actions that determine the behavior of the agent, especially in interaction with users. For example, agents can react on mouse and keyboard events, they can move and change their look, play music or videos, talk, send E-mails or calculate functions. Many examples of interactive games have been implemented. However, the program obviously aims on the educational sector as it is very well elaborated in the visual aspects (modeling, animation, language) but contains only basic features for experimenting with multi agent models (experiment scripts, complex analysis features, simulation without animation, …).

MadKit [GuFe2000] is a quite novel toolkit, which is based on a generic, highly customizable and scaleable agent platform. The Java-based platform consists of a micro kernel and various extension libraries. The micro kernel provides agent life cycle management, message passing and control of local groups and roles. A special extension called the "synchronous engine" provides a basic simulation infrastructure. Simulations are basically created by extending java interface classes for agents. Also GUI classes for animation are provided. In contrast to AgentSheets, there is no explicit model representation, but programming knowledge and framework knowledge is required to realize simulations. Summarizing, MadKit is a very flexible framework for building agent based simulations but there is still a lot of work to do to actually implement a simulation.

Swarm [MBLA1996] is the most popular toolkit for agent based simulation. Like MadKit it is a programming framework, but from its beginning it was dedicated to simulation of artificial life (swarm) experiments. Swarm software comprises a set of code libraries for Objective C. They provide a basic programming framework facilitating the creation of agent based models. The basic Swarm system does not provide any declarative behavior description but there are extensions that provide declarative model representations for behavior description like MAML [GuKF1999] or tools for special application domains, like EcoSwarm. The Swarm community is quite active and therefore a lot of useful extensions are available like simulation control, data collection and visualization as well as analysis. Presumed one is a good programmer, Swarm is very powerful and might be a good choice for the intended projects.

Repast (http://repast.sourceforge.net/) is another open source toolkit for agent based simulation developed at the University of Chicago. Newer than Swarm it borrows many concepts of its predecessor. In contrast to Swarm there are implementations in several programming languages like Python, Java or .NET. Additionally it provides built-in adaptive features such as genetic algorithms and regression. Repast is intended to be used for flexible models of living social agents. Therefore the extension to access common GIS-formats are useful for realizing enhanced spatial environments. Like in Swarm programming competence is required to implement simulation models.

Jadex (see IV.7) was developed within the MedPAge Project. It is basically a FIPA-compliant BDI agent system, which allows the development of goal based software agents. In comparison to most other frameworks it has a declarative behavior description. Although originally designed for developing agent applications, several additional tools support the creation of agent based simulations as well. Three components help managing the peculiarities of simulation. An *event service* - realized as an agent - stores upcoming events and controls time advance for the event based simulation. Several groups of service agents can register at the event service for processing the generated event streams. Another component called *ASCML* allows the definition and distributed starting of initial agent scenarios. Finally, a *logger agent* allows debugging and observation of the simulation.

SeSAm – a development at the University of Wuerzburg – was first applied in 1995 for the simulation of social insects. Over the years it grew to a more and more flexible, integrated simulation toolkit. Like AgentSheets, it provides visual agent modeling based on a high-level declarative language with several language concepts for supporting complex models. Also, it offers features for creating systematic experiments and result analysis. SeSAm will be described in more detail in the next section.

Table 1. Overview on agent based simulation toolkits

	First year/ last update	Time advance	Modeling language	Google-links1	Experiments/ analysis
Swarm	1996/2005	Event	Code	327 k	X/X
RePast	2000/2005	Event	Code	69 k	X/X
MadKit	2000/2005	Event/Time	Code	4 k	-/-
MASON	2003/2005	Event	Code	163 k	-/-
Ascape	1998/2000	Time	Code	1 k	-/X
SeSAm	1996/2005	Time	Visual	26 k	X/X
JadeX	2002/2005	Event	Textual/ Code	1 k	-/-
XRaptor	2000/2003	Time	Code	0.2 k	-/-
AgentSheets	1991/2003	Time	Visual	4 k	-/-
Anylogic	1992/2005	Event/Time	Visual	1.3k (+Agent)	X/X
MATLAB	1994/2005			147k (+Agent)	X/X

Several other – historic and recent – toolkits for agent based simulation like MASON [Luk+2003], XRaptor [MPSU1995] or Ascape [Park2001], can be found in the literature. Also several commercial tools, like MAT-LAB (http://www.mathworks.com) [Thor2000] or Anylogic (http://www.xjtek.com) have started to offer extensions for agent-based simulation or can be used to implement agent based models. It would be too much to describe them here in detail. Table 1 gives some insight about actuality, popularity and abilities of some often cited agent simulation tools. In the current stage of development the toolkits are to different make a general statement about the optimal simulation tool. The choice usually depends on the requirements of the projects and the abilities of the modelers. Some projects might be realized more efficiently in an event based manner using some low level simulation programming language. In other cases, the modelers might be domain experts without knowledge of programming languages. These users would probably prefer visual modeling. The availability of different domain specific extensions is another important crite-

---

[1]   The given number represents the number of hits, when searching for the term "agent" in combination with the name of the framework or toolkit. All results where derived at the 26. May 2005.

rion to identify the ideal simulation tool. Detailed comparisons of simulation tools can be found in [ToHo2003] [Oech2004] [Fedr2005].

2.5 The Shell for Simulated Agent Systems Toolkit

At least one of the tools shortly introduced in the previous section shall be described in more detail. SeSAm (ShEll for Simulated Agent systeMs) is a general purpose simulation tool. It provides the following key features, which will be illustrated on the next pages.

Visual agent modeling

Simulation models in SeSAm are constructed completely by visual programming based on a quite intuitive representation for the agent architecture and behavior representation. Thus, agent modelers can start quickly and do not have to learn the syntactic notations of a programming language. Due to the activity-based behavior description, the implemented models are very intuitive. The visual representation can be used for documentation and even if you are not familiar with the system, it gives you an impression on how the simulation works. Graphical editors are available for all model elements like the agents' properties and behavior, the situation or analysis definitions. Visual modeling per se facilitates model implementation as only appropriate input possibilities are offered. However, several aspects provide enhanced usability: different views on complex information, hierarchical views, uniform interaction design, or documentation facilities (like proposed in [GrPe1996]). Additionally, SeSAm was inspired by modern programming environments and also offers code completion, refactoring- and debugging tools. Therefore SeSAm is not only a valuable system for modeling beginners, but also for implementation experts. All user groups can realize complex simulations in a quite comfortable way.

Specifying an agent starts with defining his properties. Agent attributes are characterized by their name, type and accessibility. They may be declared as public attributes, which can be accessed by other agents and represent commonly observable attributes of the agent. The other possibility are private attributes, which can just be accessed and manipulated by the agent himself and represent his internal mental state. The agent's behavior is specified and implemented using an extension of UML activity diagrams [Oech2004]. Basically, these activity diagrams consist of activities and transition rules. The activities represent states containing a series of actions. These actions are executed until an exiting rule condition is evaluated as true and the next activity will be selected. Special activity nodes mark the start and end of the agent behavior. An example of an activity graph can be seen in the left window shown in Figure 1. The simulated environment (also called "world") can be modeled like an agent, also incorporating attributes and behavior for global information and dynamic changes. Additionally, the environment may optionally have one of different forms of spatial extension (2D map, 3D-Map, GIS-Map, etc.).

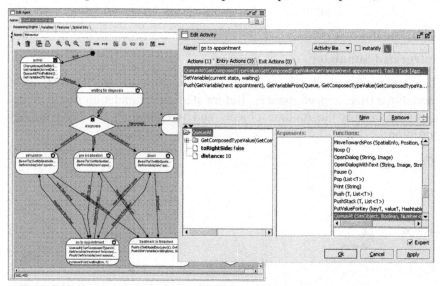

Figure 1. Example of visual behavior modeling in SeSAm[2]

SeSAm is not completely declarative, like e.g. SMDL (http://sdml.cfpm. org). The declaration is based on so called "primitives" – basic primitive functions and actions provided by SeSAm (e.g. Move, SetVariable, GetAllObjectsOnPosition, +). The semantics of these primitives is defined in Java and also documented with text. Primitives are atomic language elements that can be composed to hierarchical function calls and user functions. Basic primitives are put together to define high level primitives in a treelike structure (e.g. MoveToNearestCustomer). During simulation these primitives are executed by agents for perceiving and manipulating the environment. Using the primitives and complex user functions the modeler is able to define the agents' behavior (see Figure 1; right window). In the same way he can also visually define analysis functions or experiment

---

[2]   The left window shows an UML activity graph describing the behaviour of an agent. The right dialog shows the definition of an activity; a series of actions can be defined to specify, what the agent is doing, while he is in this activity.

scripts. For special purposes it is also possible to extend the large set of existing basic primitives with the provided plug-in-mechanism (e.g. including primitives for accessing databases).

After the necessary agent classes are defined, the agents (individual instances of them) are placed into an initial situation. Default settings for attribute values of agents and the world can be overwritten by individual start settings for each instance. A spatial map of configurable size can be used for spatial arrangement, if spatial aspects are of importance for the model.

Integrated Simulator

The integrated simulator interprets and executes the declarative agent model in a time stepped manner. Before starting a simulation run, a model compiler creates the runtime objects and is compiling the behavior description.

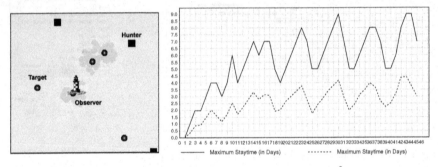

Figure 2. Online animation of the simulated model (left picture)[3]

To improve simulation performance, this compilation includes optimization steps like constant folding, inlining and lazy evaluation of list iterators. These techniques are inspired from compiler design and intended to reduce simulation time. An interactive control panel allows starting, stopping and resuming the simulation at any time. If the model has a spatial component, the agents can be observed on an animated map during the simulation. Each simulation run is started within his own processor thread. At every time step (tick) all agents sequentially get the chance to reason and act. The execution sequence is randomly shuffled every tick. This fact forces modelers to be careful about synchronization. They have to explicitly take care about synchronization of the "virtual parallel actions" of dif-

---

[3] Here, the agents are displayed on a two-dimensional map. To analyze the results different chart views (right picture) can be defined to record important evaluation parameter of the model.

ferent agents instead of making assumptions on a given succession of agents.

Experimentation support

To derive results from the simulation runs, SeSAm provides integrated components for model instrumentation, data preprocessing and systematic experimentation. A model probe collection, a so called "analysis", describes a set of output values which should be recorded together during a simulation run. The modeler also specifies in which time intervals these measurements should be taken. E.g. a particular probe could record the total number of agents every 100th tick. An analysis could comprise probes for all types of agents. Four different possibilities are given for dealing with the values generated by an analysis:

- *Series Chart*: This analysis can be used for online-observation. It shows the recent development of the observed values.
- *Block Chart*: This is an alternative form of presenting values for online observation. The observed values are shown as blocks of different size. This analysis is inappropriate to show parameter evolutions as only the situation at one time step is visible, but it can pinpoint relations between parameters.
- *Table*: This analysis is the numeric form of the "Block chart" analysis. Instead of depicting them as a block charts, the exact values are shown in a table. This form of online visualization is advisable when there are quite different values coming from a probe and these differences would not allow to distinct between lower values.
- *CSV-File*: This analysis writes all recorded data into a comma-separated list. This data can be analyzed off-line with spreadsheet- or statistical programmes. If you use this analysis type and you turn off the on-line animation of the simulation run, computation time is saved, yet no relevant data is lost.

In many cases, simulation runs have to be repeated, either to validate results of stochastic simulation or to examine effects of with different initial conditions. SeSAm provides a generic mechanism to define and execute simulation experiments, i.e. collections of different simulation runs. Since simulation runs can take a lot of time, distributing experiments within the local network is supported. To use this option, a SeSAm client service has to be installed on every machine that may be used for experiments. The service is waiting and simulating in the background and therefore allows to continue working with this machine. If an experiment defining a queue of simulation runs is started, each simulation run will be handed over to one client machine and the results are returned after a simulation run is finished.

Interactive simulation

In the typical case of a simulation experiment, there is no user interaction after start. For some applications and domains interactive simulation is very interesting. This form of simulation is also called "participatory simulation" and currently becomes quite fashionable in the area of agent-based simulation [ReIZ2000] [Sem+2005] [GuDL2005]. The user becomes part of the simulation and may change values, direct agents or induce events. He might e.g. trigger or clear machine malfunction in a factory simulation. Interaction allows testing the simulation model manually, helps to understand the relations between model parts and also allows creating more complex models, where humans are "playing" agents whose behavior is difficult to model.

In recent versions of SeSAm interface designers were provided for creating interaction elements for agents and resources. These interaction elements may be arranged into a user and model specific graphical interface with buttons, sliders and input fields. These graphical components are bound to model parameter and can be used to observe the simulation run, but also to manipulate agents and the world during the simulation run. Thus, several interfaces for different user types (modeler, end user) may be created. This is especially useful for simulation beyond pure science and engineering, in training and educational settings, for marketing and other purposes.

Extensibility

Third party developers can use the flexible plugin mechanism to create extensions and to include additional application- and domain-specific functionality. There are interfaces to the SeSAm core and user interface. They make extensions nearly on every level of model elements possible. The user may define additional primitive functions, new data types, persistence handlers, menu entries, GUI-panels and context menu actions. An example plug-in, which is very often used and therefore part of the standard version, is the 2d-spatial map representation. This plug-in provides a position type, behavior primitives for movement and spatial perception and finally GUI-panels for the animated map. Optionally this plug-in can be replaced by a 3d-representation or a sophisticated representation like it is used in geographical information systems. Recently a plugin to use GIS-maps has been developed. Using this extension simulated vehicles are able to move across some street network [ScHK2004]. Another available extension is able to import data structures from ontologies into the model and therefore prior work can be reused. The database plugin provides primitives for accessing and modifying data in SQL databases. Many plugins like these are already available and prepare SeSAm for future needs.

Summarizing, SeSAm is a very flexible tool for modeling and simulating agents. The main advantage of SeSAm is that it is a very short way from the model idea to simulation implementation and you get results quickly. Visual programming allows even inexperienced modelers to realize their models. It supports model formalization for all users that start with coarse model concepts instead of an elaborated specification. This would be necessary when using standard programming languages. Nevertheless, the declarative agent behavior representation is turing-complete in the sense of computability theory. Advanced developers esteem many features like auto completion, refactoring and debugging support. Thus, even complex models can be handled and the comprehensive environment supports all steps from modeling to analysis of results.

For these reasons SeSAm has already been successfully applied in various domains. In the health care domain, SeSAm was used to find optimizations for hospital patient scheduling (see III.5). In biological simulations hypotheses about ant and bee behavior were examined; e.g. for understanding the process of energy efficient heating of the bee hive brood nest. Psychological experiments using interactive simulation showed how people use strategic knowledge to solve problems; test persons had to intervene into the simulation and to formalize strategies for directing fire fighting units to bring a fire under control. Traffic simulations were implemented to show how traffic jams are emerging on busy streets. The next question was how information about these congestions is influencing route choices of simulated car drivers and in consequence the emergence of jams [KlBa2004]. Quite another intention was pursued by the developers of a high-rack storage simulation. This model served as a testbed for the storage control software [Tri+2005].

These examples show the board applicability of multi agent simulation in general and the tool SeSAm in particular.

2.6 Simulation Testbeds for Agent Based Software

Basically agent based simulation and agent based software development are used with different intentions. Whereas simulation is used for prediction, training or proving hypotheses about an existing or planned system, agent based software is intended to solve actual problems. Nevertheless there are many similarities and analogies according techniques, frameworks and basic theories for the agent system itself.

Software agents are designed to be applied to solve problems in a distributed way. Mostly, this is necessary due to the distributed environment of the software agents. They interact with the real world and legacy systems. In most cases a software agent is part of a multi agent system (= the application software). Due to their autonomy and their interdependent, mostly parallel processes, testing and evaluation of such systems is difficult. Isolated tests of single agents are usually not meaningful as problems often occur due to the interplay between the agents and the environment. On the other hand, comprehensive tests in the real environment would be too costly. Using multiagent simulation to produce environmental inputs and to evaluate agent based software is a logical solution to this dilemma [KlHo2003].

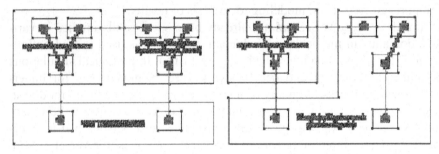

Figure 3. Sketch of a possible scenario where the left diagram describes the original situation and right diagram represents the simulated environment

Figure 3 illustrates how an example agent based application can be embedded to either a real environment (left side) or a simulated environment (right side). A new agent based application (ABA) is planned to work in an environment consisting of additional information systems and users. These users do not have direct access to the ABA or to the information system, but to individual user interface agents, which transmit their inputs, hold some individual preferences but do not perform any major reasoning. This separation is advantageous as the user interface can be adapted to individual users and ABA or information systems can be easily replaced. It is also useful for completely integrating the ABA into a simulated application environment. If the communication protocols between the three systems are standardized, user interface agents and existing systems can be replaced by an agent based simulation (right diagram) that interacts with the agents of the ABA using the same protocols (ontology and message syntax). The real world consisting of user agents and information systems are represented by the simulation model. This testbed can simulate realistic, but also extreme environmental conditions. The environmental dynamics can be reproduced as simulation includes the handling of virtual time. Simulation time may be lots faster than real time leading to stress tests for the ABA system. Such tests usually cannot be done in the real world for technical reasons as well as of cost or security.

A desirable characteristic for the testbed would be that the ABA has not to be adapted to it. It should not make any difference for the ABA agents whether they interact with real user and information agents or with the simulation environment. Therefore standardized communication between the simulated agents and the software agents is of importance. The FIPA standards (see IV.4.6) and a shared, defined ontology may be one solution. Another possible approach is to connect application and simulation by a shared database with well defined structure.

Implementing simulation testbeds raises different difficulties depending on the used tool. In tools like Jadex or Madkit which were designed for interoperability in the first, there is no explicit technical distinction between environmental and application agents. As a consequence integrating the agents does not require additional interfaces, but the developers have to carefully design the overall system. Therefore, replacing parts of the complete system by e.g. simulated user agents or agents that only use a virtual information source is quite hard as there is no separation between them and the application agents themselves. Additionally, there is no basic simulation framework that handles the proceeding of the virtual time.

On the other side, basing the testbed on a simulation environment like e.g. SeSAm, requires that the complete simulation model or parts of it are able to interact with non-virtual agents outside of the simulation run and outside of the regime of the virtual time. For supporting such kind of functionality, SeSAm provides the following plug-in extensions:

- *FIPA-Extension*: This extension allows simulated agents to be addressed and interact with external FIPA-compliant agents. The plugin provides behavior primitives for searching service agents and sending/receiving messages.
- *Ontology Plugin*: In addition to message transport a common ontology is a basic prerequisite for mutual understanding between agents. The ontology plugin allows importing and using ontologies developed with the popular ontology modeling tool Protégé. The ontological information is directly used for generating data structures that can be used in message construction and parsing.
- *Database Plugin*: Real world systems often manage their data in databases. This plugin allows SeSAm agents to access and modify informa-

tion stored in external databases. Behavior primitives allow the agents to perform SQL-Queries and Statements.

Two recent projects shall illustrate the use of multi agent simulation as a testbed in very different domains:

A first example for a multi agent simulation testbed is the integrated health care scenario Agent.Hospital (see III.1). In Agent.Hospital various agent based health care systems offer their services on FIPA compliant platforms, like e.g. patient scheduling, storing medical records or allocation of surgery teams. These multi agent systems have been linked together and also integrated into the worldwide network of agent platforms, named Agentcities. A joint directory facilitator allows finding and addressing certain services within a "virtual hospital".

For testing and presentation an integrated simulation scenario based on a SeSAm model was created. An exemplified patient process was chosen that required interaction with every participating agent system. The simulated patients were modeled by the domain experts and the interaction with the agent applications were specified by the system developers. One prerequisite for interoperability of the SeSAm simulation and the different agent applications was the development of a hospital ontology (see III.1). During the simulation the availability of external services is checked by simulated agents. Requests regarding these services are directed to the according external system and answers were received and processed by the simulated agents. Thus, an integrated system consisting of simulated environment and all agent applications was realized.

There were two benefits of this integration: First the simulation runs illustrated how the many multiagent systems can work together. Secondly the appropriateness of the interaction can be shown. New applications may be easily integrated into the simulated environment as far as the implemented standardized interfaces are supported. This first experiment of connecting agent based applications via a simulated agent-based environment was very encouraging and showed that it is possible and comparatively easy to create simulated environments as testbeds for software agents.

Meanwhile, analogous concepts for testing complex control software are already used in industry. Within a collaboration project between the University of Wuerzburg and industrial partners, agent based simulation models of high bay storages were developed using SeSAm [Tri+2005]. The models were designed for testing the control software of an automatic warehouse containing high rack storages. Although this control software is not agent-based, it has to handle several concurrent and interrelated processes. Therefore the multi agent paradigm seemed very appropriate for implementing a simulation model and due to the graphical user interfaces of SeSAm the simulations were also useful for customer presentations. A high bay warehouse contains active elements like human operators, transport units (conveyer belts, elevators) or scanners as well as passive elements like pallets, bins or boxes. Different factors like the warehouse layout, the amount of orders and error probabilities of scanners have significant effects on the flow of the goods and the transport control. The control software manages complex routing decisions and triggers the conveyers. The simulation model provides interfaces, such that it can be accessed and behaves like the real physical hardware. Interaction basically happens via a common database. Using this approach, the developers are able to test their software before the actual warehouse is build up. Different errors could be found in the early stages of development and costly subsequent changes could be avoided sparing significant costs for each warehouse project.

2.7 Summary

Agent based simulation has shown to be very useful for many purposes like making predictions based on models, understanding complex effects, training users in simulated environments or testing and evaluating software. Especially in distributed environments with dynamic process interdependencies, agent based simulation has advantages compared to other simulation techniques.

Several tools for developing agent simulations can be found in the literature. Some of the available tools have already a very long and continuous tradition, but most of them are still academic. The tools ease the work for modeling and implementation and also provide support for making experiments and analysis.

The simulation tool SeSAm was presented in more detail. Its strength is the usage of a declarative behavior description and the possibility for visual modeling. Influences from modern software engineering make the visual modeling process even more effective. Simulations projects can be accomplished very fast and even by inexperienced modelers.

Finally the approach of testing agent based applications with agent based simulation was presented. In contrast to the traditional applications of agent based simulation in biology and sociology this is quite novel field of research. Nevertheless two examples of this chapter showed that this is a very promising approach and even commercial success can be observed.

References

[Bier1998]   Bierlaire, M.: Discrete choice models. In: Labbé, M.;, Laporte, G.; Tanczos, K.; Toint, P. (Eds.): Operations Research and Decision Aid Methodologies in Traffic and Transportation Management. Vol. 166 of NATO ASI Series, Series F: Computer and Systems Sciences. Springer Verlag, 1998, pp. 203-227.

[Fedr2005]   Fedrizzi, A.: Evaluation of Tools for Agent-Based Simulation. Diploma Thesis, Technische Universität München, 2005.

[Fish1995]   Fishwick, P. A.; Simulation Model Design and Execution: Building Digital Worlds. Pearson Education, Prentice Hall, 1995.

[GiTr1999]   Gilbert, N.; Trotzsch, K. G.: Simulation for the Social Scientist. Open University Press, London, 1999.

[GrPe1996]   Green, T. R. G.; Petre, M.: Usability analysis of visual programming environments: a cognitive dimensions framework. In: Journal of Visual Languages and Computing 7, 1996.

[GuDL2005]   Guyot, P.; Drogoul, A.; Lemaitre, C.: Using emergence in participatory simulations to design multi-agent systems. In: Dignum, F. et al. (Eds): International Joint Conference on Autonomous Agents and Multiagent Systems (AAMAS-05), 2005.

[GuFe2000]   Gutknecht, O.; Ferber, J.: The Madkit agent platform architecture. In: Agents Workshop on Infrastructure for Multi-Agent Systems. Lecture Notes of Computer Science. Springer, 2000, pp. 48-55.

[GuKF1999]   Gulyás, L.;, Kozsik, T.; Fazekas, S.: The Multi-Agent Modeling Language. In: Proceedings of the 4th International Conference on Applied Informatics (ICAI). Eger-Noszvaj, Hungary, 1999, pp. 43-50.

[Jenn2000]   Jennings, N. R.: On agent-based software engineering. In: Artificial Intelligence 177(2000)2, pp. 277-296.

[KlBa2004]   Klügl, F.; Bazzan, A.: Route decision behaviour in a commuting scenario: Simple heuristics adaptation and effect of traffic forecast. In: Journal of Artificial Societies and Social Simulation – JASSS 4(2004)1.

[KlBO2005]   Klügl, F.; Bazzan, A.; Ossowski, S. (Eds.): Agents in Traffic and Transportation. Birkhäuser Verlag, Basel, 2005.

[KlHO2003]   Klügl, F.; Herrler, R.; Oechslein, C.: From simulated to real environments: How to use SeSAm for software development. In: Schillo, M. (Ed.): Multiagent System Technologies – 1st German Conferences MATES. Lecture Notes in Artificial Intelligence 2831, 2003, pp. 13-24.

[Klue2001]   Klügl, F.: Multi-Agent Simulation – Concept, Tools, Applications. Addison-Wesley Verlag, 2001.

[KOPD2002]   Klügl, F.; Oechslein, C.; Puppe, F.; Dornhaus, A.: Multi-agent modelling in comparison to standard modelling. In: Glambiasi, N.; Barros, F. J. (Eds.): AIS'2002 (Artificial Intelligence, Simulation and Planning in High Autonomy Systems), pp. 105-110, 2002.

[KPRT1998]   Klügl, F.; Puppe, F.; Raub, U.; Tautz, J.: Simulating multiple emergent behaviors – exemplified in an ant colony. In: Adami, C.; Belew, R.; Kitano, H.; Taylor, C. (Eds.): Proceedings of Artificial Life VI, Los Angeles. MIT Press, 1998.

[Luk+2003]   Luke, S.; Balan, G. C.; Panait, L.; Cioffi-Revilla, C.; Paus, S.: Mason: A java multi-agent simulation library. In: Proceedings of the Agent 2003 Conference, 2003.

[MaFT2002]   Madey, G.; Freeh, V.; Tynan, R.: Agent-based modeling of open source using swarm. In: Proceedings of the 8th Americas Conference on Information Systems (AMCIS 2002), 2002.

[MBLA1996]   Minar, N.; Burkhart, R.; Langton, C.; Askenazi, M.: The swarm simulation system, a toolkit for building multi-agent simulations. Technical Report 96-04-2, Santa Fe Institute, Santa Fe, 1996.

[MoDa2000]   Moss, S.; Davidsson, P.: Multi-Agent-Based Simulation, Second International Workshop. In: Lecture Notes in Computer Science 1979. Springer Verlag, Boston, MA, USA, 2000.

[MPSU1995]   Mössinger, P.; Polani, D.; Spalt, R.; Uthmann, T.: Xraptor – a synthetic multi-agent environment for evaluation of adaptive control mechanisms. In: Proceedings of the EUROSIM'95 Conference. Elsevier, 1995.

[Oech2004]   Oechslein, C.: Methodology for multi agent simulations with integrated specification- and implementation language. Dissertation, Universität Würzburg, 2004.

[Park2001]   Parker, M. T.: What is Ascape and why should you care? In: Journal of Artificial Societies and Social Simulation – JASSS 4(2001)1.

[ReIZ2000]   Repenning, A.; Ioannidou, A.; Zola, J.: AgentSheets: End-User Programmable Simulations. In: Journal of Artificial Societies and Social Simulation – JASSS 3(2000)3.

[Reyn1987]   Reynolds, C. W.: Flocks, herds, and schools: A distributed behavioral model. In: Computer Graphics 21(1987)4 (SIGGRAPH'87 Conference Proceedings), pp. 25-34, 1987.

[Sem+2005]   Sempe, F.; Nguyen-Duc, M.; Boissau, S.; Boucher, A.; Drogoul, A.: An artificial maieutic approach for eliciting experts knowledge in multi-agent simulations. Proceedings of the Conference on Multi-Agent-Based Simulation, MABS 2005.

[ShHK2004]   Schüle, M.; Herrler, R.; Klügl, F.: Coupling GIS and multi-agent simulation – towards infrastructure for realistic simulation. In: MATES 2004 Conference Proceedings, pp. 228-242, 2004.

[Thor2000]   Thorngate, W.: Teaching social simulation with MATLAB. In: Journal of Artificial Societies and Social Simulation – JASSS 3(2000)1.

[ToHo2003]   Tobias, R.; Hofmann, C.: Evaluation of free java-libraries for so-cial-scientific agent based simulation. In: Journal of Artificial Societies and Social Simulation – JASSS 7(2003)1.

[Tri+2005]   Triebig, C.; Credner, T.; Klügl, F.; Fischer, P.; Leskien, T.; Dep-pisch, A.; Landvogt, S.: Agent-based simulation for testing control software of high bay warehouses. In: CEEMAS 2005, 4th International Central and Eastern European Conference on Multi-Agent Systems, Budapest, Hungary, Lecture Notes in Computer Science 3690, Springer 2005.

[Zeig1984]   Zeigler, B. P.: Theory of Modelling and Simulation. Krieger Publishing Co, Melbourne, FL, USA, 1984.

3 Legal Consequences of Agent Deployment

Tanja Nitschke

Universität Karlsruhe (TH), Institut für Informationsrecht, Zentrum für angewandte Rechtswissenschaft, nitschke@ira.uni-karlsruhe.de

Abstract. The following chapter discusses various legal aspects concerning the
implementation and usage of (software) agents. The underlying question if and
how agents can issue legally effective declarations of intention is paramount in order to enable any reasonable usage of agents and, therefore, evaluated in greater
detail in Section 3.2. Furthermore, the issue of how to deal with potential errors in
agents' declarations (Section 3.3), the requirements of agents' signatures (Section
3.4) as well as liability (Section 3.5) and consumer protection issues (Section 3.6)
are discussed. Finally, data protection issues and their implications on the usage of
agents (Section 3.7) are scrutinized.

3.1 Introduction

The objective of this chapter is the critical discussion and evaluation of the
importance of legal aspects in connection with (the usage of) software
agents. As Parts II and III illustrated, there is a wide scope of potential
fields for the application of agents. In many of them, agents execute declarations for their principals, and those declarations are meant to be legally
binding, otherwise the principal's major benefit from using agents –
mainly a reduction of transaction costs – could be neglected. This applies,
e.g., for agents deployed in enterprise resource planning systems or on
virtual market places as well as agents deployed in hospital scenarios as
described by Paulussen et al. in Chapter III.1.

Apart from the legal bindingness and effectiveness of agents' behavior,
various other legal aspects are interesting in connection with agents. Concerning business transactions performed by agents, consumer protection
and data protection issues as well as electronic signatures, amongst others,
are of great relevance. And, what is more, one also has to consider the
various legal consequences of agents' misconduct: Contractual consequences on the one hand (i.e., the question whether a contract can be retracted) and liability issues on the other hand.

Legislation specifically concerning electronic agents is very rare so far.
Moreover, existing legal instruments reach their limits when being applied

to agents. It is therefore yet not quite clear how to handle most of the above mentioned aspects. In the following chapter possible solutions for these problems in order to legally facilitate a more widespread usage of agents will be outlined.

This chapter mainly refers to the German legal system. References to the legal situation in other countries or to European legislation are made where appropriate.

3.2 Legally Effective Declarations by Agents

Many conceivable fields of application for electronic agents – such as enterprise resource planning, production control, electronic procurement, virtual market places – aim at a situation which is considered binding for both (or all) parties involved in a transaction. The legal instrument to reach such bindingness is the conclusion of a contract. Hence, the primarily interesting question concerning legal aspects of MAS is whether and how contracts can be concluded through agents. And, what is even more important: How can a contract be concluded in a way that is legally binding and enforceable? The question behind this is whether agents have to be regarded as independent persons in this connection, or whether they are things, i.e. mere tools for the conclusion of contracts.

3.2.1 Can Agents Execute Declarations of Intention on Their Own?

The notion of an agent as a person acting as an other person's representative as well as the agent's autonomy – both described by Lockemann in I.1 – suggest that an agent is some kind of personality. This, from a mere philosophical point of view, seems to be one of the most fascinating questions concerning artificial intelligence (see e.g. [Beie2003]). However, the question also has a juridical implication: As an independent personality, an agent could execute declarations and conclude contracts on its own and would have to be considered as its principal's representative not only in a metaphoric sense, but also in a legal one.

The following scenario may help to identify and discuss the underlying legal problems:

A buyer charges his software agent with buying a certain good for him. The agent gathers information from various sellers' websites, picks the most promising, negotiates with the seller (or his agent) about the price and further conditions in accordance to its principal's preferences (which the agent might have learned from earlier transactions), and finally orders the good. The buyer only observes the result of this transaction.

It is quite clear that, in this scenario, not the agent itself becomes a party to the contract. De facto, the agent acts as its principal's representative. But does the law recognize the agent as a representative as well? §§ 164–181 of the German Civil Code [BGB] do not expressly state that a representative needs to be a natural person (i.e. a human), but presume this (which is unquestionable, because the historic legislator of the BGB did not foresee the technical development). Agents are clearly artifacts, not human beings. But is that the final answer to our question or can agents form some kind of legal personality and thus be representatives in a legal sense?

There are basically two ways how agents could be recognized as legal personalities: On the one hand, agents could be legal entities, as e.g. incorporated associations or limited liability companies are. This however requires a statutory act that constitutes an agent's quality as a legal entity. Neither in Germany nor in any other country such legislation exists.

On the other hand, the similarity of agents and humans could be close enough to justify treating agents as (or similar to) natural persons. Reasoning by analogy generally has two prerequisites: An unintended lack of regulation for a situation with comparable interests to an already regulated situation (cf. [Hein2005, preamble § 1 introduction, note 48]). Obviously, there is a lack of regulation for agents, and, this lack does not seem to be intended by legislators as they surely were unable to foresee the technical development towards computer systems with human-like qualities. But can these situations really be compared? If agents' qualities came close to human qualities relevant for the conclusion of contracts, i.e. legal and contractual capacity, or more precisely, the capabilities addressed by these two terms, this would unconditionally be the case.

Legal capacity

In general, legal capacity is understood as the ability to hold rights and obligations (cf. [Schm2001, § 1 note 6]). This implies the ability to hold patrimony and it requires an own identity. As shown above, under existing law agents have not explicitly been conferred legal personality. However, some authors try to enable agents to hold patrimony. Sartor, e.g., proposes that agents could be transferred a certain amount of (electronic) money to be used for transactions and to serve as a warranty for the counter parties involved in contracts with the agent (cf. [Sart2002, pp. 6-8]). Although this and similar concepts may sound promising, currently we have to stick to the finding that agents do not possess legal capacity.

Contractual capacity

Contractual capacity is defined as the ability to independently conclude valid legal transactions (cf. [Hein2005, introduction § 104 note 2]). This requires the ability of free decision-making, backed by (a minimum of) conscious and moral thinking (cf. [NiSe2004, p. 549]). Agents may possess a certain intelligence and autonomy, however, they are incapable of free decision-making as yet.

Conclusion

In summary, agents lack legal as well as contractual capacity and, therefore, are unable to execute their own declarations of intention or rather enter their own contracts. Thus, they are also unable to act as representatives in a legal sense. Even if a special legal subject, such as an "*electronic person*" suggested by some authors, would be created, it can be doubted that this would solve all juridical problems. Being "electronic persons", agents would have to act as representatives for their principals in a legal sense. Although this comes closer to their factual function, it evokes further problems, e.g., how to handle situations where an agent exceeds his principal's will. A human representative would be liable according to § 179 BGB, i.e., he would become party to the contract himself instead of the principal. Agents however currently cannot be subjects of liability or parties to contracts. Questions like this have to be considered when creating a legal framework for electronic agents.

3.2.2 How Can an Agent's Declaration Be Ascribed to Its Principal?

The finding that an agent is incapable of executing its own declarations of intention and, therefore, cannot act as its principal's representative, leads to a further question: Can the declarations of intention issued by an agent be ascribed to its principal? Only if it can is the agent's action legally binding for the principal.

Under German law, it is generally accepted that declarations of intention, which were automatically generated by a computer system on the basis of given parameters, but without any involvement of a human immediately before the declaration is executed – so called *computer declarations* – are declarations of the user of the respective computer system (cf. [Corn2002, p. 354]).

However, the situation is different if autonomous agents instead of automated computer systems are involved in the conclusion of a contract:

Much of the decision-making is shifted from the user to the agent due to the agent's intelligence and autonomy. Consequently, the user lacks the control which would be needed as a link between the user and the final declaration generated by the computer.

A declaration of intention generated by an agent can nevertheless be attributed to the agent's user. The situation equals the one typical for so called *blank declarations*, i.e. declarations that were signed, but deliberately left incomplete and completed by a third person. The original issuer has only very little influence on the final content of the declaration, however, this kind of declaration has long been accepted as a valid declaration of intention (cf. [LaWo2003, § 48 note 34]). If this applies to humans acting completely independent of the principal, it also should be applied to electronic agents, because here, the principal has at least some control through specifying the parameters for the agent's behavior.

To conclude, declarations of intention generated by agents can be attributed to their respective principal and are therefore legally binding.

3.2.3 Execution and Reception of Declarations by Agents

The finding that a declaration of intention generated by an agent is basically attributable to its principal does not automatically imply the legal effectiveness of such a declaration. The declaration needs to be executed by the issuer and (according to § 130 sec. 1 BGB) received by its addressee.

Execution of declarations

Executing a declaration of intention is defined as voluntarily putting it into circulation in a way that is undoubtedly definite (cf. [Hein2005, § 130 note 4]). To provide an example, in case of an e-mail this means voluntarily clicking the "send"-button. Yet, it is certainly more difficult to determine when an agent's declaration was executed. One might be tempted to consider the activation of the agent as a voluntary act by the user, however, this cannot be regarded as execution of a declaration as the agent still needs to concretize the content of the declaration before finally posting it. Hence, the declaration is executed when the respective agent posts it to the recipient (cf. [NiSe2004, p. 551]).

Reception of declarations

The reception of a declaration of intention requires that the declaration reached the addressee's sphere of influence in a way that enables him to take note of it under normal circumstances. An agent certainly belongs to its user's sphere of influence, no matter how autonomously it is able to act. But does the user have the possibility to take note of the declaration as soon as it was stored by the agent? This obviously depends on the capacity and configuration of the agent and, furthermore, on the kind of data the declaration consists of. If the declaration is not interpretable by the agent it simply functions like a mailbox, so that the user is able to take notice of the declaration as soon as it was stored by his agent.

Admittedly, the situation could be judged differently if the content of a declaration is standardized and therefore interpretable for agents and the agent is sufficiently intelligent to comprehend it. One then might assume that the comprehension of the declaration by the agent will suffice as reception, and the user's possibility to take note of it is no longer relevant. This again reflects the agent's factual function as a representative of its user, however, as long as agents are incapable of being representatives in a legal sense, they are (legally) limited to the above-described mailbox function. Consequently, declarations can only be deemed as received by the user when stored by his agent.

3.2.4 Agents' Declarations in Other Legal Systems

As the above written only referred to the German legal system, a brief overview of the legal situation in other countries, especially concerning the conclusion of contracts by agents will be given in this subsection To put it short, no existing legal system grants legal personality to agents. Usually, either legal and/or contractual capacity are prerequisites for conferring legal personality to an entity, or – as in British and American law – some kind of positive justification is needed. The justification can be based on moral entitlement, social reality or legal convenience (cf. [AlWi1996, p. 35]). In the end, the same reasoning as under German law applies: Computer systems lack self-consciousness, they are incapable of conscious, morally backed decision-making and do not possess social capacity for autonomous actions (cf. [Kerr1999, pp. 18-20] and [AlWi1996, pp. 35-37]).

For that reason, agents have to be viewed as auxiliary means used by the principal to facilitate transactions. However, the theoretic constructions for ascribing declarations executed by an agent to its principal differ in various legal systems.

The first attempt to initiate legislation that explicitly regulates contracts concluded by information systems was undertaken by the United Nations Commission on International Trade Law by presenting a model law on Electronic Commerce [UNCITRAL], which was aimed to simplify global electronic commerce. In its Art. 13 the model law regards data messages sent by information systems as equivalent to those sent by individuals. As a consequence, contractual declarations executed by electronic agents are ascribed to the agents' respective principal and therefore regarded as legally valid (cf. [Weit2001, pp. 24-25] and [Kerr1999, pp. 30-32]). However, the UNCITRAL model law is not binding for any state, it is a mere proposition.

Canada and the US were the first two states to adopt explicit legislation concerning contracts concluded with the help of software agents. According to sec. 14 of the US Uniform Electronic Transactions Act [UETA], contracts concluded by electronic agents acting on behalf of both contractual parties or by an electronic agent and an individual acting on its own behalf are legally binding. Additionally, sec. 202 and 213 a) of the Uniform Computer Information Transactions Act [UCITA] make clear that contracts can be formed through electronic agents and that the behavior of electronic agents leading to a contract legally binds their principals. In its sec. 21 the Canadian Uniform Electronic Commerce Act [UECA] also explicitly states that contracts can be formed by the interaction of humans and/or electronic agents.

Concerning the *EU member states*, the Electronic Commerce Directive [EU2000a], or more precisely its Art. 9, gives a strong hint that contracts concluded by means of agents should generally be considered as valid: Art. 9 does not explicitly mention electronic agents, but the European Commission made clear that the deployment of intelligent software modules must not be hindered by the member states' implementation of the directive (cf. [Euro2002, p. 22]). This leads to the conclusion that under the EU Electronic Commerce Directive all member states have to accept contracts concluded by electronic agents as legally valid and binding for their respective principals. Amongst others, [Schw2001] as well as [AlWi1996] illustrate the legal situations in other countries such as Austria or Great Britain.

At large, we can draw the conclusion that – although the preconditions for this differ – under most (at least western) legal systems, agents are capable of executing declarations and concluding contracts that are legally binding for their human principals. Agents are basically regarded as some kind of tool in this connection, not as entities acting independently in a legal sense. With their intelligence and autonomy (in a technical sense) increasing, this might change in the future – and, most probably, will make an adaptation of legal regulations inevitable.

3.3 Handling of Errors in Agents' Declarations

The previous section ascertained that agents are basically capable of acting in a way that legally binds their principals. This evokes a further question: What happens if an agent for some reason acts in a way that does not correspond to its principal's will? Or, more precisely: What are the consequences if the agent concludes a contract its principal would never have entered in such a way? The crucial question is whether the principal is bound by the agent's declaration or whether he can retract such a declaration.

3.3.1 Potential Errors

There are different types of conceivable situations leading to a contract which does not correspond to the principal's will. Thus, some kind of legal error handling is necessary. These situations correspond with the classification of potential failures undertaken by Nimis et al. in IV.6, implying that the question of legal error handling only arises when an error became effective and lead to an unwanted outcome. The dependability model introduced in IV.6 can, therefore, be extended to cover declarations by adding a sixth, legal, layer on top of layer 5. Thus, internal and external faults propagating to the legal layer need to be examined.

First of all, among the *internal faults*, the principal might have faultily instructed his agent by accident, e.g. he mistyped the financial limit or other parameters, and the agent negotiated on that basis.

Secondly, though the principal instructed the agent according to his will, the agent might exceed the limits given by its principal due to miscalculation or design errors or misinterpretation of its scope of discretion, e.g., by prioritizing the principal's preferences in a way that in fact does not meet the principal's will.

Thirdly and as an *external fault*, though the agent was instructed correctly and its decision-making process took place without any errors, the resulting declaration that finally reaches the other contracting party might differ from the one originally sent by the agent because of data loss (*infrastructure failure*) or manipulations by third parties during transmission (*peer failure*).

3.3.2 Legal Solutions

From a legal point of view, these three situations have to be judged differently.

Concerning the first type of errors, a faulty declaration executed by the principal could be retracted by him according to § 119 sec. 1 BGB, if the reason for the faultiness of this declaration is simply misspelling the price or other relevant aspects for the contract. As the source of faultiness is undoubtedly the same, the retraction should apply as well if the principal accidentally instructs his agent wrongfully, so that the agent negotiates on a wrong basis. As shown in Section 3.2.4, the agent is a mere tool the principal uses for generating and executing his declarations of intention. Observing this, it is clearly the principal who causes the error, not the agent, and the error is still persistent in the final declaration received by the other contracting party. Thus, the principal should have the right to retract his declaration of intention according to § 119 sec. 1 BGB.

However, the principal does not have the right to retract his declaration, if the error does not directly affect the declaration executed by the agent but simply consists in the programming or configuration of the agent. Thus, the error is latent and does not need to be treated – just like the latent technical errors described above by Nimis et al.

This is different for errors of the second type. The discrepancy between the principal's will and the content of the actual declaration of intention issued by the agent is not the principal's fault. It rather is the agent's miscalculation that lead to the faulty declaration. Although the reasoning process of an agent is much more complex than that of an inventory control system, the circumstances are similar: In both cases, the user delegated the decision-making to some piece of software. He can only influence this process through setting certain parameters in advance (although in the case of an inventory control system these parameters are quite detailed, i.e., the user can explicitly define business processes), but has no control over the actual result of the decision-making, which normally is directly posted to the other contracting party.

Under German law, errors in the decision-making process do not justify the retraction of a declaration of intention (cf. [Hein2005, § 119 notes 29 and 18]). The German Federal Supreme Court recently clarified this for declarations automatically executed by means of an inventory control system (cf. [Bund2005, p. 178]). This surely cannot be judged differently if the calculating error has been made by an agent – otherwise the use of agents would be privileged in comparison to other technical means. This result seems fair as the principal, who on the one hand has to carry the risk of being bound to a declaration he would not have executed in such a way himself, on the other hand gains economic advantages by the usage of an agent.

Errors of the third type actually comprise two different constellations: On the one hand, data, in our case: a declaration of intention, can get (partially) lost during transmission after the principal or his agent sent the declaration. In such cases, § 120 BGB entitles the principal to retract his declaration as far as the error really occurred outside the principal's sphere (which, in practice, is a question of provableness). On the other hand, the declaration might have other content than intended by the principal due to manipulation by a third party. In this case, the principal also enjoys a right of retraction granted by § 123 sec. 1 BGB.

3.3.3 Consequences

With the capability of agents growing steadily, especially the errors of the second type may increase: The more intelligent agents become and the more autonomously they reach decisions, the more probable does it become that their decisions will differ from the principal's will. This can – at least partly – be compensated through an improvement of the agent's reasoning process. Other technical measures can reduce the risk of errors as well, e.g., secure communication protocols to prevent the manipulation of data during transmission or dependability enhancement to prevent or treat unintended errors (cf. Nimis et al., supra IV.6).

In some situations of course, technical means are incapable of preventing errors in agents' declarations that lead to contracts unwanted by the principal. At least for some of them, there is a legal possibility to revoke these declarations. For one of the possible sources of error however, the agent's reasoning process, there is unfortunately no right of retraction so far. This might pose an impediment to the mass deployment of agents for contractual purposes. However, up to now it seems fairest to impose the risk of being bound to a contract based on a faulty declaration executed by an agent on the agent's user, not on his contractual partner.

3.4 Signatures by Agents and Formal Requirements

An important, yet often underestimated aspect in connection with contracts concluded via electronic networks – especially the internet – is how to produce evidence of the conclusion of such a contract in a legal dispute. After all, it is quite well known that electronic documents can easily be manipulated by third parties. A large number of recently finished or pending law suits concerning online auctions, where vendors or buyers claim not to have made a certain declaration leading to the conclusion of a contract, illustrates this.

An electronic declaration of intention needs to be authentic, integer and authorized in order to have any probative value in a law suit. This applies for e-mails or other electronic documents sent by humans as well as for declarations executed by agents. As a growing number of acknowledgements of orders, invoices, certificates, time stamps and inquiries is generated and signed automatically, the problem already has a huge practical relevance.

Authenticity in this connection means that a declaration was really issued by the person that claims to be the issuer. *Integrity* means that a document has not been altered during the transmission from its issuer to the recipient. *Authorization* means that the transmission of a document was really intended by its issuer.

There is a broad consensus – not only in Germany – that simple e-mails are insufficient to prove the authenticity, integrity and authorization of a declaration of intention as soon as they are contested by one party in a law suit. The situation is different if a declaration is encrypted and/or digitally signed: Contesting the authenticity, integrity or authorization becomes much more difficult, depending on the complexity of the security mechanisms applied.

3.4.1 European and German Signature Regulation

A legal framework for such mechanisms, especially electronic signatures, is provided by the EU signature directive [EU2000b], which is implemented by the German signature code [SigG]. According to the German signature code (and similar to other EU member states legislation), there are three different types of electronic signatures:

- *Simple electronic signatures* merely consist of the name of a person, typed under an electronic declaration, or of a handwritten signature that has been scanned and pasted into the document.
- *Advanced electronic signatures* require a cryptographic key that facilitates the identification of the signatory and that is under his sole control; moreover, the signature has to be uniquely linked to the signed document, so that later changes of the data can be detected. PGP for example meets these conditions.
- *Qualified electronic signatures* additionally require a valid qualified certificate and have to be generated by a secure signature-creation device. According to the EU signature directive and its implementation in the

German BGB, qualified electronic signatures have the force of documents in written form.

Whereas agents can undoubtedly generate *simple electronic signatures* by adding their respective user's name to a declaration, one may wonder if they are able to meet the requirements of the two other types of signatures.

Concerning *advanced electronic signatures*, one of the prerequisites is especially problematic: It is argued that advanced signatures require a secure signature-creation device, which is under the user's sole control. However, [BeNS2005, pp. 215-216] demonstrate that software solutions are sufficient for validly generating advanced electronic signatures. Thus, agents can, in principle, generate signatures of this type.

The situation is even more problematic with regard to *qualified electronic signatures*. Here, using a secure signature-creation device (i.e., smart card and PIN-pad) is compulsory. In order to meet this precondition, users could identify themselves in the required way and then legitimize their respective agent to accomplish one or several business transactions. It could be argued that this procedure would allow presentation problems to occur (i.e. other data than indicated is actually signed) and, what is more, the user possibly would not even notice that his agent generates signatures on his behalf. This consideration of course should be left to the respective user in the light of the economic advantages he gains through the autonomous signature process. Furthermore, the SigG does not explicitly require signatures to be generated by natural persons. Thus, agents are basically capable of creating qualified electronic signatures as well. This is in line with the notion of agent, especially with agents' autonomy. However, it can only be considered as an intermediary result as there are various legal consequences linked with qualified electronic signatures.

3.4.2 Probative Value of Electronically Signed Documents

Whereas simple electronic signatures do not provide any gain in probative value (– the name or scanned signature can as easily be manipulated as the rest of the document –), advanced electronic signatures improve the situation of the party bearing the burden of proof. But still, the evaluation of the authenticity, integrity and authorization underlies the discretion of the court (cf. § 286 German Civil Procedure Code [ZPO], which refers to this as free evaluation of evidence).

With regard to qualified electronic signatures, § 371a ZPO stipulates a prima facie evidence, which makes it easier to furnish evidence of the authenticity, integrity and authorization of an electronic document: They are presumed as long as the other party does not prove the contrary (although jurists still argue about the details of this counter-evidence).

In our view it does not make any difference for the probative value of an electronic declaration whether it was digitally signed with a qualified electronic signature by an agent or by a human.

3.4.3 Agent Signatures and Formal Requirements

However, it does in fact make a difference whether an electronic declaration was signed by an agent or by a human in connection with formal requirements. Qualified electronic signatures have the same force as handwritten signatures according to § 126b BGB in most cases, so that statutory formal requirements can be met by both types of signatures.

Legal requirements of writing usually aim to caution against overhasty contract conclusion (cf. [Hein2005, § 125 Rn. 2]). This warning function, however, cannot work if the user is not personally involved in the signing process, because his agents performs the signature for him. As a consequence, agent and human signatures are not equal in this respect. Thus, statutory writing requirements cannot be met by agent signatures (cf. [BeNS2005, pp. 217-218]).

3.5 Liability

One of the more important legal aspects – also highly relevant in practice – is the question of liability for agent's behavior. As shown in Subsection 3.2.2 of this chapter, users basically are legally bound by contracts entered into by faultily programmed agents. Thus, the possibility to sue the programmer of the agent might be of high interest to the user.

It is quite obvious – under German law as well as under that of other states – that the programmer of an agent is liable for errors of his "product". This comprises as well the liability for misbehavior of the agent as far as this is clearly based on incorrect programming. Of course, it is the user, not the programmer, who is liable for his agent's behavior if it is due to wrongful configuration.

Hence, the problem is actually not a legal but a factual one: It is fairly hard to find out and even harder to prove from whose sphere the error originates.

Quite surprisingly, there is some clarifying regulation which is applicable to a very special field of application: *Mobile agents*. According to § 9 sec. 1 of the German Tele Services Act [TDG], the operator of a server is not liable for the mere transfer or caching of data. As (mobile) agents, in the end, merely are data, the same has to apply for operators transferring mobile agents through their networks. As a consequence, operators cannot be made liable for the behavior of mobile agents who merely migrate through their network or who are cached on their servers.

3.6 Consumer Protection

If agents are applied on virtual market places involving business-to-consumer constellations, another problem arises: Many states, especially those who are members of the European Union, have more or less strict consumer protection regulations, which on the one hand entitle consumers to terminate contracts and on the other hand impose a number of information duties on vendors. The objective of these regulations is to compensate for the information asymmetries typically existing in business transactions. In general, consumers are considered to be less experienced and shall therefore be protected from precipitately concluding disadvantageous contracts (cf. [Jana2003, pp. 1-3]).

For the European Union, the Electronic Commerce Directive stipulates fairly detailed information duties, which were implemented almost literally in most of the member states. The Electronic Commerce Directive has been transposed into German law by §§ 312a–312d BGB. § 312c BGB stipulates various information duties and is only applicable to distance selling contracts. These are defined as contracts about the delivery of goods or the supply of services between a consumer and a vendor, which are exclusively concluded by use of telecommunication means. Therefore, distance selling contracts also encompass the ordering of goods via the internet. As software agents are merely tools in concluding contracts, it is the users whose consumer characteristics are relevant. Additionally, § 312e BGB, which implements the EU Distance Selling Directive [EU1997], stipulates some further information duties for contracts concluded via the internet.

If the aforementioned information duties are not properly and entirely fulfilled by the vendor, the consumer retains the right to terminate the contract without being bound to the relatively short period for revocation (§ 312d sec. 2 BGB). Hence, failure to fulfill the information duties also risks the economic success of the transaction.

3.6.1 Information Duties

§ 312c BGB requires the vendor to inform the consumer about the commercial purpose of the contract, the identity and address of the supplier, the price, fundamental characteristics of the respective good or service and, the existence of a right to terminate the contract. This information has to be provided prior to the conclusion of the contract and in a clear and comprehensible way. Additionally, this information also has to be made lastingly available (cf. § 126b BGB) and provided until the fulfillment of the contract at the latest. Until then, the consumer also has to be notified about how to exercise his right to terminate the contract and the resulting legal consequences, the warranty provisions as well as contact details for potential complaints and objections.

Similar to § 312c BGB, § 312e BGB requires vendors to furnish information and auxiliaries for customers in order to detect and correct errors in their orders, to explain the technical way to the conclusion of a contract, to download the general terms and conditions. Furthermore, the receipt of an order has to be immediately acknowledged.

3.6.2 Performance of Compulsory Information

The fulfillment of the information duties is fairly easily achievable when only humans are involved in a business transaction. However, if electronic agents take part in such a transaction the fulfillment is incomparably more demanding. On the one hand, one has to differentiate between information duties prior and subsequent to the conclusion of the contract. On the other hand, one has to consider whether the fulfillment of information duties is sensible and technically feasible when agents are involved. Hereby, a conflict arises between the objective of the consumer protection regulations, i.e., the comprehensive and personal information of the consumer, and the economic and technical purpose of agents, i.e., information processing for their users in order to relieve them.

Antecedent and subsequent information duties

Information duties subsequent to the conclusion of the contract can quite easily be performed. § 126b BGB requires that users can print or digitally save the information permanently. Hence, vendors either can hand the respective information directly to the agent or notify the agent from where it can gather the information. In the end, it is of little relevance how the information is transferred to the consumer, i.e., if it is directly posted to him via e-mail or if it is sent to his agent. In both cases, the user is put in a position to take note of the respective information.

With respect to antecedent information duties, the case is more difficult. Informing the user prior to the conclusion of a contract is practically impossible because he deploys the agent exactly in order to avoid taking note of any larger amount of information, no matter whether it is based on legal obligations or not.

Usefulness of providing information to agents

A more detailed look at the compulsory information reveals that some of the information does not seem to make sense if an agent acts on behalf of the customer, e.g., the duty to explain the technical steps necessary to conclude a contract (§ 312e sec. 1 s. 1 No. 1 BGB and § 3 No. 1 of the regulation on information duties according to civil law, [BGB-InfoV]) or the duty to explain how to detect and correct errors before posting the order (§ 312e sec. 1 s. 1 No. 1 BGB and § 3 No. 3 BGB-InfoV). This information is completely unnecessary for the agent because it "knows" the technical process of the contract conclusion (as the standards for this need to be defined beforehand) and was assigned by its user in order to avoid mistakes of the type aimed at by the law (i.e., primarily mistyping). For the user the information is useless as he is not involved in the process of concluding the contract.

One might presume that the vendor should be exempted from the duty to provide such "useless" information. However, this presumption is premature: First of all, the vendor cannot necessarily distinguish whether an agent is involved or a person. Furthermore, statutory information duties are mandatory, i.e., they can not be waived by contracting parties and apply no matter if an individual needs the information in a particular case or not (cf. [NiSe2004, p. 553]).

Information that still makes sense when agents are involved in a transaction clearly has to be provided. This requires standardized representation of the respective information in order to make it comprehensible to the agent. Although some attempts to formalize legal norms and terms have already been undertaken, e.g., in the field of data protection (P3P), there are no comprehensive XML schemes, ontologies or negotiation protocols that contain all issues relevant to electronic commerce so far – and, due to the complexity of the task, this might take a while.

But could information duties for that reason be omitted as far as electronic agents are involved in transactions? Gitter and Rossnagel indeed argue that it is the consumer who makes the fulfillment of information duties impossible for the vendor by deploying an agent. According to them it therefore seems unfair to impose the risk of permanent revocability of the contract on the vendor. It could be deemed contradictory behavior if a consumer were able to refer to the lack of certain information in this situation (cf. [GiRo2003, p. 69]).

However, the pitfall of this approach lies in the fact that the argument of contradictory behavior is an exceptional provision under German law, which is only applicable to prevent inequitable results in particular cases (cf. [Hein2005, § 242 note 13]) where no regulation exists. In contrast to that, consumer protection law explicitly regulates the cogent character of information duties. Hence, consumers cannot be deemed to have renounced their rights, less than ever implicitly by deploying an agent. One has to bear in mind that it is the vendor who designs the business models facilitating the use of electronic agents and who not only economically benefits from them, but also knows the limits of the agents' capabilities as well as the mandatory character of consumer protection law (cf. [NiSe2004, p. 554]). As a consequence, the vendor has to technically allow for the statutory information duties.

3.6.3 Related Problems

Similar problems arise in practically any area where statutory information duties are imposed. An example is § 6 of the German Tele Services Act [TDG], which requires suppliers of information or telecommunication services to inform their customers about their name, address, phone and fax numbers, e-mail address, public registers, tax identification number and others.

Again, the question arises if it is sufficient to furnish the user's agent with the required information. And again, it is unclear how to cope with the fact that it is technically impossible to fulfill information duties when agents are involved due to a lack of standardization. Furthermore, the answers to these questions are also similar: As the possibility to gather the respective information from a prominent place on the website of a supplier is normally sufficient to fulfill the requirements of § 6 TDG, it consequently should also suffice to post the (possibly standardized) information to an agent, from whom its user is capable to retrieve the substance of the information. And here as well, the supplier has to technically allow for the statutory information duties.

3.7 Data Protection

Apart from data security, i.e., the technical protection of data against access by third parties, which should go as a matter of course, data protection law plays an important role for business transactions by agents. In connection with electronic commerce as well as with other applications for multi-agent systems such as the ones for the medical sector described in Part III, a large amount of personal data is captured, processed and transmitted. According to German data protection law – which is based on the EU Data Protection Directive [EU2002] – this is generally forbidden, except where permitted by law (which occurs relatively rarely in practice) or consented to by the person concerned. Due to the principle of informed consent (cf. [Simi2003, § 4a notes 23-26]) prevailing in (German) data protection law, two questions arise: What information does the person concerned have to be furnished with and what are the prerequisites for a valid consent?

3.7.1 Compulsory Information Concerning Data Protection

§ 4 sec. 1 of the German Tele Service Data Protection Act [TDDSG] – together with § 4 sec. 3 of the Federal Data Protection Act [BDSG] – stipulates that a person who offers information services has to provide information about the manner, extent and purpose of the capturing and processing of personal data as well as the responsible organization and the eventual transmission of the data to an organization outside the EU (cf. [Zsch2005, p. 725]). This again leads to a question parallel to the one described in Subsection 3.2.3 in connection with consumer protection: Is it sufficient to provide the requested information to the agent or does the principal have to receive it personally, and how can the information be provided?

The second part of the question is relatively easy to answer. As already mentioned, information needs to be provided in a standardized way in order to be interpretable by agents. The P3P initiative (http://www.w3.org/P3P/) already undertook steps in this direction. Thus, either agents or their respective users are, in principle, capable of retrieving the required information.

The first part of the question, however, is more problematic. Basically, as in consumer protection law, furnishing the agent with the relevant information seems sufficient, because the principal has at least the possibility to take note of the information his agent received. Furthermore, one has to keep in mind that the principal deliberately deployed the agent to relieve him from taking note of a huge amount of information, comprising information based on statutory duties as well. With the help of his agent, it is still possible for the user to execute a declaration based on informed consent; the purpose of the information duties is thereby not thwarted. In the end, it should therefore be viewed as sufficient if the information is provided to the agent.

3.7.2 Consent to Capturing and Processing of Personal Data Through Agents

As stated by the law, consent is required explicitly and in written form or alternatively with a qualified electronic signature (cf. § 4a sec. 1 BDSG; § 126 sec. 3 BGB; § 2 SigG). However, under certain circumstances it can be declared electronically according to § 4 sec. 2 together with § 3 sec. 3 TDDSG. This requires that the consent is based on an unequivocal and deliberate act by the person concerned – which underlines the importance of the information duties. What is more, the declaration of consent has to be recorded. Finally, § 4 sec. 3 TDDSG stipulates that consent can be revoked by the person concerned at any time.

As a result, individuals can validly consent to the processing of their personal data via electronic networks. But can agents do the same on behalf of their principals? The BDSG does not explicitly require consent to be declared strictly personally. However, academics heavily debate whether a representative is capable to consent for an individual (cf. [Zsch2005, p. 725]). Critics argue that it is insufficient to only inform the representative, but not the principal because of the highly personal character of the consent. The same could also apply to agents.

However, if we find that agents – no matter how large their autonomy is – are mere tools from a legal point of view, one could as well argue that the loss of control the principal experiences by charging his agent is much smaller compared to charging a human representative. Therefore, it seems acceptable that a tool is executing one's consent despite the highly personal character of this declaration. The deliberate act required by § 4 sec. 2 TDDSG is then represented by the user's charging and instructing of his agent. Consequently, agents are capable of consenting to the processing of personal data on behalf of their users. As this again forms a declaration of intention, the same principles as explained in Subsection 3.2.2 unconditionally apply to the execution of this kind of declaration.

3.8 Conclusion

As the previous sections showed, a number of new legal questions arise in connection with agents deployed in electronic markets as well as in other fields of application. For the time being, the existing legal systems (i.e. not only the German legal system to which this chapter mainly refers to) are capable to provide – more or less satisfying – answers to most of these questions. As a result, agents can, from a legal point of view, be deployed in all of the scenarios mentioned in the foregoing chapters of this book, and are also capable of producing legally valid results for their users. Yet, various questions remain, for which legal answers still need to be found, i.e. existing legal instruments have to be refined in order to be fully applicable to agents. Other issues, like the legal capacity of agents, are currently emerging, but will demand solutions as agent technology and AI advance further and further.

References

[AlWi1996]   Allen, T.; Widdison, R.: Can Computers make Contracts? In: Harvard Journal of Law & Technology 9(1996)1, pp. 25-52.

[Beie2003]   Beiersdörfer, K.: Was ist Denken? Gehirn – Computer – Robo-ter. Schöningh, Paderborn, 2003.

[BeNS2005]   Bergfelder, M.; Nitschke, T.; Sorge, C.: Signaturen durch elektronische Agenten – Vertragsschluss, Form und Beweis. In: Informatik Spektrum 2005, pp. 210-219.

[Bund2005]   Bundesgerichtshof: judgment of January 26, 2005, VIII ZR 79/04. In: Kommunikation & Recht 2005, pp. 176-178.

[Corn2002]   Cornelius, K.: Vertragsabschluss durch autonome elektronische Agenten. In: Multimedia und Recht 2002, pp. 353- 358.

[Euro2002]   European Commission: Annex 1 to the Proposal for an Electronic Commerce Directive presented by the Commission, 2002. http://www.beck.de/mmr/Materialien/english.pdf, accessed on 2005-08-04.

[GiRo2003]   Gitter, R.; Rossnagel, A.: Rechtsfragen mobiler Agentensysteme im E-Commerce. In: Kommunikation und Recht 2003, pp. 64-72.

[Hein2005]   Heinrichs, H., in: Palandt, Otto (Ed.): Bürgerliches Gesetzbuch. 64th edition, C.H. Beck, München, 2005.

[Jana2003]   Janal, R. M.: Sanktionen und Rechtsbehelfe bei der Verletzung verbraucherschützender Informations- und Dokumentations-pflichten im elektronischen Geschäftsverkehr. Tenea, Berlin, 2003.

[Kerr1999]	Kerr, I. R.: Providing for Autonomous Electronic Devices in the Uniform Electronic Commerce Act, 1999. http://www.law.ualberta.ca/alri/ulc/current/ekerr.pdf, accessed on 2005-07-12.
[LaWo2003]	Larenz, K.; Wolf, M.: Allgemeiner Teil des Bürgerlichen Rechts. 9th edition, C. H. Beck, München, 2003.
[NiSe2004]	Nitschke, T.; Sester, P.: Softwareagent mit Lizenz zum...? Vertragsschluss und Verbraucherschutz beim Einsatz von Softwareagenten, In: Computer und Recht, 2004, pp. 548- 554.
[Sart2002]	Sartor, G.: Agents in Cyberlaw. In: Sartor, G.; Cevenini, C. (Eds.): Proceedings of the Workshop on the Law of electronic Agents (LEA02). Gedit, Bologna, 2002.
[Schm2001]	Schmitt, J. In: Rebmann, K.; Säcker, F. J.; Rixecker, R. (Eds.): Münchener Kommentar zum Bürgerlichen Gesetzbuch, Vol. 1 §§ 1–240. 4th edition, C. H. Beck, München, 2001.
[Schw2001]	Schwarz, G.: Die rechtsgeschäftliche Vertretung durch Softwareagenten. Wien, 2001.
[Simi2003]	Simitis, S.: Kommentar zum Bundesdatenschutzgesetz. 5th edition, Nomos, Baden-Baden, 2003.
[Weit2001]	Weitzenboeck, E. M.: Electronic Agents and the formation of contracts. Electronic Commerce Legal Issues Platform. Via http://www.folk.uio.no/emilyw/documents/EMILY%20-Version%2019%20August%20&%20source.pdf, accessed on 2006-01-16.
[Zsch2005]	Zscherpe, K.: Anforderungen an die datenschutzrechtliche Einwilligung im Internet. In: Multimedia und Recht 2005, pp. 723-727.

Laws and Decrees

[BDSG]	Bundesdatenschutzgesetz. Revised version. In: Bundesgesetzblatt 2003 I, p. 66 (Federal Data Protection Act).
[BGB]	Bürgerliches Gesetzbuch. Revised version. Bundesgesetzblatt 2002 I, p. 42. English translation available via the German Law Archive, http://www.iuscomp.org/gla/ (German Civil Code).
[BGB-InfoV]	Verordnung über Informations- und Nachweispflichten nach bürgerlichem Recht. Bundesgesetzblatt 2004 I, p. 3102 (Regulation on Information Duties according to Civil Law).
[EU1997]	Directive 1997/7/EC on consumer protection for the conclusion of contracts via the internet. In: Official Journal of the European Communities L 144 of June 4, 1997, p. 19 (Distance Selling Directive).
[EU2000a]	Directive 2000/31/EC on certain legal aspects of services in the information society, especially electronic commerce, in the in-

ternal market. In: Official Journal of the European Communities L 178 of July 17, 2000, p. 8 (E-Commerce Directive).

[EU2000b]   Directive 1999/93/EC on a Community framework for electronic signatures. In: Official Journal of the European Communities L 13 of January 19, 2000, p. 12 (Signature Directive).

[EU2002]   Directive 2002/58/EC on the processing of personal data and on privacy protection in electronic communication. In: Official Journal of the European Communities L 201 of July 31, 2002, p. 37 (Data Protection Directive).

[SigG]   Gesetz über Rahmenbedingungen für elektronische Signaturen und zur Änderung weiterer Vorschriften (SigG). In: Bundesgesetzblatt 2001 I, p. 876. Modified by the 1st Signaturänderungsgesetz (Signature Modification Code), Bundesgesetzblatt 2005 I, p. 2 (German Signature Code).

[TDG]   Gesetz über die Nutzung von Telediensten (TDG). In: Bundesgesetzblatt 1997 I, p. 1870 (German Tele Services Act).

[TDDSG]   Gesetz über den Datenschutz bei Telediensten (TDDSG). In: Bundesgesetzblatt 1997 I, p. 1871. Last modified December 14, 2001, Bundesgesetzblatt 2001 I, p. 3721 (German Tele Services Data Protection Act).

[UCITA]   US Uniform Computer Information Transcations Act. http://www.law.upenn.edu/bll/ulc/ucita/ucita01.htm, accessed on 2006-06-15.

[UETA]   US Uniform Electronic Transactions Act as adopted by the National Conference of Commissioners on Uniform State Laws. http://www.law.upenn.edu/bll/ulc/fnact99/1990s/uet a99.pdf, accessed on 2005-06-15.

[UECA]   Canadian Uniform Electronic Commerce Act. http://www. law.ualberta.ca/alri/ulc/current/euecafin.htm, accessed on 2005-06-15.

[UNCITRAL]   United Nations Commission on International Trade Law model law on Electronic Commerce. UN General Assembly Resolution 51/162 of December 16, 1996, UN publication V.97-22269-May 1997-5,100.

[ZPO]   Zivilprozessordnung, as published on September 12, 1950. In: Bundesgesetzblatt I, p. 533. Last modified August 18, 2005, Bundesgesetzblatt I, p. 2477 (German Civil Procedure Code)

Index